# The Continental Novel:
## A Checklist of Criticism in English
# 1967-1980

Louise S. Fitzgerald
and
Elizabeth I. Kearney

The Scarecrow Press, Inc.
Metuchen, N.J., & London
1983

A continuation of The Continental Novel: A Checklist of Criticism in English 1900-1966. (Scarecrow Press, 1968)

Library of Congress Cataloging in Publication Data

Fitzgerald, Louise S.
   The continental novel.

   1. European fiction--History and criticism--Bibliography.  I. Kearney, Elizabeth I.  II. Title.
Z5916.F57  1983   [PN3451]    016.8093      82-20454
ISBN 0-8108-1598-2

Copyright © 1983 by L. S. Fitzgerald and E. I. Kearney

Manufactured in the United States of America

## PREFACE

This volume extends The Continental Novel: A Checklist of Criticism in English 1900-1966 to include the years 1967-1980. (Items dated before 1967 but not included in the earlier work are marked with an asterisk.)

All of the criticisms listed herein have been read by the compilers; we regret that this policy has caused the omission of some items that could not be located. The page numbers refer to specific major criticism of each cited novel; minor references may appear elsewhere in the same work. Selective judgment was used only in relation to the amount of critical comment, with very brief criticism sometimes included for novels that have few items of reference. The amount of material read in order to compile this checklist made it impossible, except in a few cases, to check duplicate entries that might be condensations, expansions, or reprints of the original criticism. Such items are therefore listed separately.

Works of short fiction, travel fiction, and autobiographical fiction have been included in this checklist if critics have referred to them as novels or novelles. If a novel is one of a series, additional items of criticism will often be found listed under the collective title, e. g., Human Comedy.

We wish to express our appreciation to the library staffs at the University of California at Los Angeles, the University of Southern California, and the Los Angeles Central Library for their willing cooperation in helping to locate materials and to check information.

L. S. F.
E. I. K.

## TABLE OF CONTENTS

| | |
|---|---|
| Preface | iii |
| Periodical Titles with Abbreviations | vii |
| The French Novel | 1 |
| The Spanish and Portuguese Novel | 189 |
| The Italian Novel | 257 |
| The German Novel | 285 |
| The Scandinavian Novel | 400 |
| The Russian and East European Novel | 415 |

# PERIODICAL TITLES WITH ABBREVIATIONS

| | |
|---|---|
| ABnG | Amsterdamer Beiträge zur neueren Germanistik |
| ABR | American Benedictine Review |
| ACer | Anales Cervantinos |
| Adam | |
| AEASH | Acta Ethnographica Academiae Scientiarum Hungaricae |
| AGald | Anales Galdosianos |
| AI | American Imago |
| AJFS | Australian Journal of French Studies |
| American Historical Review | |
| Anglia | |
| AR | Antioch Review |
| Arcadia | |
| Archiv | Archiv für das Studium der Neueren Sprachen und Literaturen |
| Argenis | |
| Art Internat | Art International |
| ASch | American Scholar |
| ASLHM | American Society of Legion of Honor Magazine |
| ASoc | Arts in Society |
| AUMLA | Journal of the Australasian Universities Language and Literature Association |
| | |
| Babel | |
| BCom | Bulletin of the Comediantes |
| BHR | Bibliothèque d'Humanisme et Renaissance |
| BHS | Bulletin of Hispanic Studies |
| BJA | British Journal of Aesthetics |
| Boundary | |
| BRMMLA | Rocky Mountain Review of Language and Literature (formerly, Bull. ... Rocky Mtn. M. L. A.) |
| BSS | Bulletin of Spanish Studies |
| BSUF | Ball State University Forum |
| BUJ | Boston University Journal |
| BuR | Bucknell Review |
| BYUS | Brigham Young University Studies |
| | |
| CalSS | California Slavic Studies |
| CASS | Canadian-American Slavic Studies |

| | |
|---|---|
| CE | College English |
| CEA | CEA Critic |
| Celestinesca | |
| CentR | The Centennial Review |
| CGP | Carleton Germanic Papers |
| ChiR | Chicago Review |
| CimR | Cimarron Review |
| Cithara | |
| CJItS | Canadian Journal of Italian Studies |
| CL | Comparative Literature |
| CLAJ | College Language Association Journal |
| ClioW | Clio |
| CLS | Comparative Literature Studies |
| CMLR | Canadian Modern Language Review |
| CollG | Colloquia Germanica |
| CollL | College Literature |
| ColQ | Colorado Quarterly |
| CompD | Comparative Drama |
| Computers and the Humanities | |
| ConL | Contemporary Literature |
| ConnR | Connecticut Review |
| Conradiana | |
| Contemporary Psychoanalysis | |
| Coranto | |
| Córonica | |
| CQ | The Cambridge Quarterly |
| CR | The Critical Review |
| CRCL | Canadian Review of Comparative Literature |
| Crit | Critique |
| CritI | Critical Inquiry |
| Criticism | |
| CritQ | Critical Quarterly |
| Cross Currents | |
| CSP | Canadian Slavonic Papers |
| CSS | Canadian Slavic Studies |
| Culture | |
| | |
| Daedalus | |
| DHR | Duquesne Hispanic Review |
| DidS | Diderot Studies |
| Dimension | |
| Discourse | |
| DR | Dalhousie Review |
| DramS | Drama Survey |
| DUJ | Durham University Journal |
| DVLG | Deutsche Vierteljahrsschrift für Literaturwissenschaft und Geistesgeschichte |
| | |
| EAS | Essays in Arts and Sciences |
| ECent | The Eighteenth Century |
| ECLife | Eighteenth-Century Life |

| | |
|---|---|
| ECr | L'Esprit Créateur |
| ECS | Eighteenth-Century Studies |
| Edda | |
| EFL | Essays in French Literature |
| EG | Etudes Germaniques |
| EIA | Estudos Ibero-Americanos |
| EIC | Essays in Criticism |
| Eire | |
| EJ | English Journal |
| ELH | Journal of English Literary History |
| ELWIU | Essays in Literature (Western Ill. Univ.) |
| enclitic | |
| EnlE | Enlightenment Essays |
| ER | Etudes Rabelaisiennes |
| ESl | Etudes Slaves et Est-Européennes |
| Essays in Literature (Denver) | |
| Euphorion | |
| Extrapolation | |
| | |
| FAR | The French-American Review |
| FI | Forum Italicum |
| FMLS | Forum for Modern Language Studies |
| ForumH | Forum (Houston) |
| FR | French Review |
| FrF | French Forum |
| Frontiers | |
| FS | French Studies |
| FurmS | Furman Studies |
| FWF | Far-Western Forum |
| | |
| GaR | Georgia Review |
| Genre | |
| GerSR | German Studies Review |
| GL&L | German Life and Letters |
| Glyph | |
| GN | Germanic Notes |
| GQ | German Quarterly |
| GR | Germanic Review |
| GSlav | Germano-Slavica |
| | |
| Hermathena | |
| Hispania | |
| Hispano | Hispanófila |
| HR | Hispanic Review |
| HSL | Hartford Studies in Literature |
| HudR | Hudson Review |
| HUS | Harvard Ukrainian Studies |
| HUSL | Hebrew University Studies in Literature |

| | |
|---|---|
| IDSB | International Dostoevsky Society Bulletin |
| IFR | International Fiction Review |
| IndL | Indian Literature |
| International Journal of Psycho-Analysis | |
| International Record of Medicine | |
| Interpretations | |
| IowaR | Iowa Review |
| IQ | Italian Quarterly |
| IS | Italian Studies |
| The Israel Annals of Psychiatry and Related Disciplines | |
| ISSJ | International Social Science Journal |
| Italica | |
| | |
| JAAC | Journal of Aesthetics and Art Criticism |
| JAF | Journal of American Folklore |
| JBalS | Journal of Baltic Studies |
| JEGP | Journal of English and Germanic Philology |
| JES | Journal of European Studies |
| JFI | Journal of the Folklore Institute |
| JGE | Journal of General Education |
| JHP | Journal of Hispanic Philology |
| JIASRA | Journal of the International Arthur Schnitzler Research Association |
| JIG | Jahrbuch für Internationale Germanistik |
| JJQ | James Joyce Quarterly |
| JML | Journal of Modern Literature |
| JMRS | Journal of Medieval and Renaissance Studies |
| JNT | Journal of Narrative Technique |
| Journal of the American Academy of Psychoanalysis | |
| Journal of the American Psychoanalytic Association | |
| Journal of the American Society for Psychical Research | |
| Journal of Beckett Studies | |
| JRS | Journal of Russian Studies |
| JSSTC | Journal of Spanish Studies: Twentieth Century |
| Judaism | |
| | |
| KFLQ | Kentucky Foreign Language Quarterly |
| KN | Kwartalnik Neofilologiczny |
| KR | Kenyon Review |
| KRQ | Kentucky Romance Quarterly |
| | |
| L&P | Literature and Psychology |
| Lang&S | Language and Style |
| LangQ | Language Quarterly |
| LBR | Luso-Brazilian Review |
| LCrit | Literary Criterion |

| | |
|---|---|
| LeS | Lingua e Stile |
| LFQ | Literature/Film Quarterly |
| LHY | Literary Half-Yearly |
| LiNQ | Literature in North Queensland |
| Lituanus | |
| LJGG | Literaturwissenschaftliches Jahrbuch der Görres-Gesellschaft |
| LOS | Literary Onomastics Studies |
| LY | Lessing Yearbook |
| | |
| MAL | Modern Austrian Literature |
| Maledicta | |
| M&L | Music and Letters |
| McNR | McNeese Review |
| MD | Modern Drama |
| MDAC | Mystery and Detection Annual |
| Meanjin | |
| Mediaevalia | |
| MelbSS | Melbourne Slavonic Studies |
| MFS | Modern Fiction Studies |
| MGS | Michigan Germanic Studies |
| MHRev | Malahat Review |
| MichA | Michigan Academician |
| Midway | |
| MinnR | Minnesota Review |
| Miorita | |
| MissQ | Mississippi Quarterly |
| ML | Modern Languages |
| MLJ | Modern Language Journal |
| MLN | Modern Language Notes |
| MLQ | Modern Language Quarterly |
| MLR | Modern Language Review |
| MLS | Modern Language Studies |
| MMM | Mélanges Malraux Miscellany |
| Monatshefte | |
| Mosaic | |
| MP | Modern Philology |
| MQ | Midwest Quarterly |
| MQR | Michigan Quarterly Review |
| MR | Massachusetts Review |
| MS | Mediaeval Studies |
| | |
| Names | |
| NCF | Nineteenth-Century Fiction |
| NCFS | Nineteenth-Century French Studies |
| Neohelicon | |
| Neophil | Neohelicon |
| NFS | Nottingham French Studies |
| NGC | New German Critique |
| NGS | New German Studies |
| NLH | New Literary History |

| | |
|---|---|
| NM | Neuphilologische Mitteilungen |
| Novel | |
| NZSJ | New Zealand Slavonic Journal |
| | |
| O&C | Oeuvres & Critiques |
| OGS | Oxford German Studies |
| OL | Orbis Litterarum |
| OSP | Oxford Slavonic Papers |
| | |
| PAPS | Proceedings of the American Philosophical Society |
| PBSA | Papers of the Bibliographical Society of America |
| PCL | Perspectives on Contemporary Literature |
| PCP | Pacific Coast Philology |
| PEGS | Publications of the English Goethe Society |
| Person | The Personalist |
| PFSCL | Papers on French Seventeenth Century Literature |
| Philosophy and Literature | |
| PLL | Papers on Language and Literature |
| PMLA | Publications of the Modern Language Association of America |
| Poetics | |
| PolR | Polish Review |
| PQ | Philological Quarterly |
| PR | Partisan Review |
| PsyculR | Psychocultural Review |
| PsyR | Psychoanalytic Review |
| | |
| QQ | Queen's Quarterly |
| Quest | |
| | |
| RBPH | Revue Belge de Philologie et d'Histoire |
| RCEH | Revista Canadiense de Estudios Hispánicos |
| Reflexión 2 | |
| REH | Revista de Estudios Hispánicos |
| Ren&R | Renaissance and Reformation |
| Renascence | |
| RES | Review of English Studies |
| Review of Existential Psychology and Psychiatry | |
| RF | Romanische Forschungen |
| RHM | Revista Hispánica Moderna |
| RLC | Revue de Littérature Comparée |
| RLJ | Russian Language Journal |
| RLSt | Rackham Literary Studies |
| RLT | Russian Literature Triquarterly |
| RLV | Revue des Langues Vivantes |

| | |
|---|---|
| RMS | Renaissance & Modern Studies |
| RomN | Romance Notes |
| RoR | Romanian Review |
| RPac | Revue du Pacifique |
| RPh | Romance Philology |
| RQ | Riverside Quarterly |
| RR | Romanic Review |
| RS | Research Studies |
| RUO | Revue de l'Université d'Ottawa |
| RUS | Rice University Studies |
| RusL | Russian Literature |
| RusR | Russian Review |
| | |
| SAB | South Atlantic Bulletin |
| Salmagundi | |
| SAQ | South Atlantic Quarterly |
| Scan | Scandinavica |
| SEEJ | Slavic and East European Journal |
| SEER | Slavonic and East European Review |
| Seminar | |
| Semiotica | |
| SFr | Studi Francesi |
| SFR | Stanford French Review |
| SFS | Science-Fiction Studies |
| SHR | Southern Humanities Review |
| SIR | Studies in Romanticism |
| Slavica Hierosolymitana | |
| SlavR | Slavic Review |
| SLitI | Studies in the Literary Imagination |
| Slovak Studies | |
| SNNTS | Studies in the Novel |
| SoQ | The Southern Quarterly |
| SoR | Southern Review |
| SoRA | Southern Review: An Australian Journal of Literary Studies |
| Southerly | |
| SovL | Soviet Literature |
| SP | Studies in Philology |
| Sprachkunst | |
| SR | Sewanee Review |
| SS | Scandinavian Studies |
| SSASH | Studia Slavica Academiae Scientiarum Hungaricae |
| SSe | Studi Secenteschi |
| SSF | Studies in Short Fiction |
| SSI | Social Science Information |
| SSl | Scando-Slavica |
| Standpunte | |
| StHum | Studies in the Humanities |
| StTCL | Studies in Twentieth Century Literature |
| Sub-stance | |
| Survey | |

| | |
|---|---|
| SUS | Susquehanna University Studies |
| SVEC | Studies on Voltaire and the Eighteenth Century |
| SWR | Southwest Review |
| Symposium | |

| | |
|---|---|
| TAH | The American Hispanist |
| TCL | Twentieth Century Literature |
| Theoria | |
| Thesaurus | |
| Thomist | |
| Thought | |
| TQ | Texas Quarterly |
| TriQ | Tri-Quarterly |
| Trivium | |
| TSE | Tulane Studies in English |
| TSL | Tennessee Studies in Literature |
| TSLL | Texas Studies in Literature and Language |

| | |
|---|---|
| UDR | University of Dayton Review |
| UES | Unisa English Studies |
| ULR | University of Leeds Review |
| Univ | Universitas |
| UP | Unterrichtspraxis |
| UQ | Ukrainian Quarterly |
| UTQ | University of Toronto Quarterly |

| | |
|---|---|
| Viator | |
| VQR | Virginia Quarterly Review |

| | |
|---|---|
| WascanaR | Wascana Review |
| WF | Western Folklore |
| WHR | Western Humanities Review |
| WLT | World Literature Today |
| WSCL | Wisconsin Studies in Contemporary Literature |
| WSl | Die Welt der Slaven |
| WVUPP | West Virginia University Philological Papers |

| | |
|---|---|
| XUS | Xavier University Studies |

| | |
|---|---|
| YFS | Yale French Studies |
| YItS | Yale Italian Studies |

| | |
|---|---|
| ZFSL | Zeitschrift für Französische Sprache und Literatur |
| ZRP | Zeitschrift für Romanische Philologie |

# THE FRENCH NOVEL

About, Edmond
### GERMAINE
    Thorberg, Raymond. "GERMAINE, James's NOTEBOOKS, and THE WINGS OF THE DOVE." CL 22:254-264. Summer 1970.

Alain-Fournier
### LE GRAND MEAULNES
    Bouraoui, H. A. "A Structural Diptych in LE GRAND MEAULNES." FR 42: 233-247. December 1968.

    Brosman, Catharine Savage. "Alain-Fournier's Domain: A New Look." FR 44: 499-507. February 1971.

    Cranston, Mechthild. "'La Marquise sortit à cinq heures...': Symbol and Structure in Alain-Fournier's LE GRAND MEAULNES." KRQ 26: 377-395. No. 3, 1979.

    De Lutri, Joseph R. "The Adult World and the Romantic Quest in LE GRAND MEAULNES." LangQ 18: 35-38. Fall/Winter 1979.

    _____. "Rimbaud and Fournier: The End of the Quest." RomN 18: 153-156. Winter 1977.

    Gibson, Robert. The Land Without a Name: Alain-Fournier and His World. London: Paul Elek, 1975. 304 pp.

    Goldgar, Harry. "Alain-Fournier and the Initiation Archetype." FR 43: 87-99. Sp. Issue No. 1, Winter 1970.

    Gross, Ruth V. "The Narrator as Demon in Grass and Alain-Fournier." MFS 25: 625-639. Winter 1979-1980.

    Jones, Louisa. "Window Imagery: Inner and Outer Worlds in Alain-Fournier's LE GRAND MEAULNES." Symposium 27: 333-351. Winter 1973.

Jones, Marian Giles. A Critical Commentary on Alain-Fournier's LE GRAND MEAULNES. London: Macmillan, 1968. 80 pp.

Lainey, Y. "LE GRAND MEAULNES as a Romantic Novel." Theoria 29: 33-43. October 1967.

Maclean, Marie. "Structural Narcissism in LE GRAND MEAULNES." AJFS 14: 152-162. May/August 1977.

Sorrell, Martin R. M. "François Seurel's Personal Adventure in LE GRAND MEAULNES." MLR 69: 79-87. January 1974.

——————. "LE GRAND MEAULNES: a Bergsonian View of the 'fête étrange.'" AJFS 11: 182-187. May/August 1974.

Woodcock, George. "Alain-Fournier and the Lost Land." QQ 81: 348-356. Autumn 1974.

Aragon, Louis
LES COMMUNISTES
Adereth, M. Commitment in Modern French Literature: Politics and Society in Péguy, Aragon, and Sartre. New York: Schocken Books, 1968. pp. 95-98.

Becker, Lucille G. Louis Aragon. New York: Twayne, 1971. pp. 68-71.

LA MISE A MORT
Adereth, M. Commitment in Modern French Literature: Politics and Society in Péguy, Aragon, and Sartre. New York: Schocken Books, 1968. pp. 114-118.

Becker, Lucille G. Louis Aragon. New York: Twayne, 1971. pp. 102-108.

Gutermuth, Mary. "Triangular Schizophrenia and the 'Execution' of Aragon." KRQ 14: 379-392. No. 4, 1967.

LE PAYSAN DE PARIS
Avila, Rose M. "The Function of Surrealistic Myths in Louis Aragon's PAYSAN DE PARIS." FrF 3: 232-238. September 1978.

Matthews, J. H. Toward the Poetics of Surrealism. Syracuse: Syracuse University Press, 1976. pp. 37-42.

d'Arnaud, Baculard
LE BAL DE VENISE
Dawson, Robert L. "Baculard d'Arnaud: Life and Prose Fiction." SVEC 141: 134-141. 1976.
EPREUVES DU SENTIMENT
Dawson, Robert L. "Baculard d'Arnaud: Life and

Prose Fiction." SVEC 141: 267-451. 1976.
NOUVELLES HISTORIQUES
    Dawson, Robert L. "Baculard d'Arnaud: Life and Prose Fiction." SVEC 142: 459-547. 1976.
THERESA
    Dawson, Robert L. "Baculard d'Arnaud: Life and Prose Fiction." SVEC 141: 121-134. 1976.

Balzac, Honoré de
BEATRIX
    Hemmings, F.W.J. Balzac: An Interpretation of LA COMEDIE HUMAINE. New York: Random House, 1967. pp. 72-78; 152-155.

    Kanes, Martin. Balzac's Comedy of Words. Princeton: Princeton University Press, 1975. pp. 179-182.

    Prendergast, C.A. "Towards a Re-assessment of BEATRIX." EFL 9:46-62. November 1972.

    Prendergast, Christopher. Balzac: Fiction and Melodrama. London: Arnold, 1978. pp. 118-128.
LE CENTENAIRE
    Kanes, Martin. Balzac's Comedy of Words. Princeton: Princeton University Press, 1975. pp. 50-56.
CESAR BIROTTEAU
    Hemmings, F.W.J. Balzac: An Interpretation of LA COMEDIE HUMAINE. New York: Random House, 1967. pp. 118-123.

    Pugh, Anthony. "The Ambiguity of CESAR BIROTTEAU." NCFS 8: 173-189. Spring/Summer 1980.

    Pugh, Anthony R. "The Genesis of CESAR BIROTTEAU: Questions of Chronology." FS 22: 9-25. January 1968.
LES CHOUANS
    Haggis, D.R. "Scott, Balzac, and the Historical Novel as Social and Political Analysis: WAVERLEY and LES CHOUANS." MLR 68: 51-68. January 1963.

    Hamilton, James F. "The Novelist as Historian: A Contrast between Balzac's LES CHOUANS and Hugo's QUATREVINGT-TREIZE." FR 49: 661-668. April 1976.

    Kuhn, Reinhard. "Collision of Codes: Portentous Levity in Balzac's LES CHOUANS." FR 53: 248-256. December 1980.

    Mehlman, Jeffrey. Revolution and Repetition: Marx/Hugo/Balzac. Berkeley: University of California Press, 1977. pp. 118-124.
CLOTILDE DE LUSIGNAN
    Haggis, D.R. "CLOTILDE DE LUSIGNAN, IVANHOE, and the Development of Scott's Influence on Balzac."

FS 28: 159-168. April 1974.
LE COLONEL CHABERT
    Dale, R. C. "LE COLONEL CHABERT Between Gothicism and Naturalism." ECr 7: 11-16. Spring 1967.

    Fischler, Alexander. "Fortune in LE COLONEL CHABERT." SIR 8: 65-77. Winter 1969.

    Good, Graham. "LE COLONEL CHABERT: A Masquerade with Documents." FR 42: 846-856. May 1969.

LA CONQUETE DE PLASSANS
    Slater, J. A. "Echoes of Balzac's Provincial Scenes in LA CONQUETE DE PLASSANS." ML 60: 156-160. September 1979.

LA COUSINE BETTE
    Haggis, D. R. "Fiction and Historical Change: LA COUSINE BETTE and the Lesson of Walter Scott." FMLS 10: 323-333. October 1974.

    Hemmings, F. W. J. Balzac: An Interpretation of LA COMEDIE HUMAINE. New York: Random House, 1967. pp. 96-104.

    Jameson, Fredric. "LA COUSINE BETTE and Allegorical Realism." PMLA 86: 241-254. March 1971.

    Ortali, Hélène. "Images of Women in Balzac's LA COUSINE BETTE." NCFS 4: 194-205. Spring 1976.

    Prendergast, C. A. "Antithesis and Moral Ambiguity in LA COUSINE BETTE." MLR 68: 315-332. April 1973.

    Prendergast, Christopher. Balzac: Fiction and Melodrama. London: Arnold, 1978. pp. 91-111; 161-176.

LE CURE DE TOURS
    Tintner, Adeline R. "'The Old Things': Balzac's LE CURE DE TOURS and James's THE SPOILS OF POYNTON." NCF 26: 436-455. March 1972.

    Wirtz, Dorothy. "Animalism in Balzac's CURE DE TOURS and PIERRETTE." RomN 11: 61-67. Autumn 1969.

EUGENIE GRANDET
    Beck, William J. "Dandyism and the Dandy in Balzac's EUGENIE GRANDET." LangQ 18: 23-26. Fall/Winter 1979.

    Conroy, William T., Jr. "Imagistic Metamorphosis in Balzac's EUGENIE GRANDET." NCFS 7: 192-201. Spring/Summer 1979.

    Gurkin, Janet. "Romance Elements in EUGENIE GRANDET." ECr 7: 17-24. Spring 1967.

Hemmings, F.W.J. Balzac: An Interpretation of LA
COMEDIE HUMAINE. New York: Random House, 1967.
pp. 87-96.

Wetherill, P. M. "A Reading of EUGENIE GRANDET."
ML 52: 166-175. December 1971.
LA FEMME DE TRENTE ANS
Hemmings, F.W.J. Balzac: An Interpretation of LA
COMEDIE HUMAINE. New York: Random House, 1967.
pp. 48-54.

Kanes, Martin. Balzac's Comedy of Words. Princeton:
Princeton University Press, 1975. pp. 212-214.
UNE FILLE D'EVE
Pugh, Anthony R. "The Autonomy of Balzac's UNE
FILLE D'EVE." RR 69: 186-195. May 1978.
GAMBARA
Hemmings, F.W.J. Balzac: An Interpretation of LA
COMEDIE HUMAINE. New York: Random House, 1967.
pp. 3-7.
GOBSECK
Pasco, Allan H. "Descriptive Narration in Balzac's
GOBSECK." VQR 56: 99-108. Winter 1980.

Pasco, Allan. "'Nouveau ou Ancien Roman': Open
Structures and Balzac's GOBSECK." TSLL 20: 15-35.
Spring 1978.
HONORINE
Hemmings, F.W.J. Balzac: An Interpretation of LA
COMEDIE HUMAINE. New York: Random House, 1967.
pp. 55-60.
HUMAN COMEDY
*Affron, Charles. Patterns of Failure in LA COMEDIE
HUMAINE. New Haven: Yale University Press, 1966.
pp. 1-131.

Antoniadis, Roxandra V. "Faulkner and Balzac: The
Poetic Web." CLS 9: 303-325. September 1972.

Bershtel, Sara. "Fairy Tales and Success in Balzac's
COMEDIE HUMAINE." CL 31: 47-62. Winter 1979.

Besser, Gretchen R. Balzac's Concept of Genius: The
Theme of Superiority in the COMEDIE HUMAINE. Genève: Librairie Droz, 1969. 270 pp.

Carbonneau, Thomas E. "Balzacian Physics and Metaphysics: The Tension Between Industrialized Society and
Moral Values." RomN 20: 327-332. Spring 1980.

Cherry, Adrian. "Balzac's Madame Marneffe: A Character Study of a Courtesan." LangQ 6: 2-12. Fall/
Winter 1967.

Clark, Priscilla P. "Balzac and the Bourgeoisie."
TSL 14: 51-59. 1969.

Frappier-Mazur, Lucienne. "Balzac and the Sex of
Genius." Renascence 27: 23-30. Autumn 1974.

Gerschenkron, Alexander. "Time Horizon in Balzac and
Others." PAPS 122: 79-83. April 24, 1978.

Grossman, Leonid. Balzac and Dostoevsky. Ann Arbor: Ardis, 1973. pp. 31-49.

Hemmings, F.W.J. Balzac: An Interpretation of LA
COMEDIE HUMAINE. New York: Random House, 1967.
179 pp.

Houston, John Porter. Fictional Technique in France,
1802-1927: An Introduction. Baton Rouge: Louisiana
State University Press, 1972. pp. 26-46.

Kanes, Martin. "Balzac and the Problem of Expression." Symposium 23: 284-293. Fall/Winter 1969.

_____. Balzac's Comedy of Words. Princeton:
Princeton University Press, 1975. pp. 101-126; 129-166.

Lowrie, Joyce Oliver. "Balzac and 'le doigt de Dieu.'"
ECr 7: 36-44. Spring 1967.

McVicker, C.D. "Balzac and Otway." RomN 15: 248-254. Winter 1973.

McVicker, Cecil Don. "Narcotics and Excitants in the
COMEDIE HUMAINE." RomN 11: 291-301. Winter 1969.

Mileham, James W. "Balzac's Seven of Probation."
RomN 21: 161-164. Winter 1980.

Moss, Martha Niess. "Balzac's Villains: The Origins
of Destructiveness in LA COMEDIE HUMAINE." NCFS
6: 36-51. Fall/Winter 1977-1978.

_____. "'L'Enigme du couple': Balzac and Marriage." SAB 44: 73-80. January 1979.

_____. "The Masks of Men and Women in Balzac's
COMEDIE HUMAINE." FR 50: 446-453. February 1977.

_____. "The Metamorphosis of Vautrin in Balzac's
COMEDIE HUMAINE." RomN 20: 44-50. Fall 1979.

Nash, Suzanne. "Story-telling and the Loss of Innocence

Balzac, Honoré de

in Balzac's COMEDIE HUMAINE." RR 70: 249-267. May 1979.

Prendergast, Christopher. "Balzac: Chance and Realism in the COMEDIE HUMAINE." FMLS 10: 109-120. April 1974.

*Raser, George B. Guide to Balzac's Paris: An Analytical Subject Index. Choisy-le-Roi: Imprimerie de France, 1964. 186 pp.

──────. The Heart of Balzac's Paris. Choisy-le-Roi: Imprimerie de France, 1970. 103 pp.

Stary, Sonja G. "Providential Justice in Balzac's COMEDIE HUMAINE." RR 68: 254-263. November 1977.

*Wenger, Jared. The Province and the Provinces in the Work of Honoré de Balzac. Princeton: Banta, 1937. 106 pp.

Whitmore, P. J. S. "Rita-Christina: A Reference to a Real Person in the COMEDIE HUMAINE." FS 21: 319-321. October 1967.

JEAN LOUIS
Butler, R. "Balzac's JEAN LOUIS: Some Links Between a 'Roman de Jeunesse' and the COMEDIE HUMAINE." NFS 16: 31-49. October 1977.

JESUS-CHRIST EN FLANDRE
Champagne, Roland A. "The Architectural Pattern of a Literary Artifact: A Lacanian Reading of Balzac's JESUS-CHRIST EN FLANDRE." SSF 15: 49-54. Winter 1978.

THE LILY OF THE VALLEY
Davies, Howard. "The Relationship of Language and Desire in LE LYS DANS LA VALLEE." NFS 16: 50-59. October 1977.

Fleurant, Kenneth J. "Water and Desert in LE LYS DANS LA VALLEE." RomN 12: 78-85. Autumn 1970.

Haig, Stirling. "Note on a Balzacian Character: Monsieur de Mortsauf." RomN 16: 95-98. Autumn 1974.

Heathcote, Owen N. "Balzac and the Personal Pronoun: Aspects of Narrative Technique in LE LYS DANS LA VALLEE." NFS 16: 60-69. October 1977.

──────. "Time and Félix de Vandenesse: Notes on the Opening of LE LYS DANS LA VALLEE." NCFS 8: 47-52. Fall/Winter 1979-1980.

Hemmings, F.W.J.  Balzac: An Interpretation of LA COMEDIE HUMAINE.  New York: Random House, 1967.  pp. 79-83.

Niess, Robert J.  "Sainte-Beuve and Balzac: VOLUPTE and LE LYS DANS LA VALLEE."  KRQ 20: 113-124.  No. 1, 1973.

LOST ILLUSIONS
Hemmings, F.W.J.  Balzac: An Interpretation of LA COMEDIE HUMAINE.  New York: Random House, 1967.  pp. 128-131; 146-147.

Holoch, George.  "A Reading of ILLUSIONS PERDUES."  RR 69: 307-321.  November 1978.

Kanes, Martin.  Balzac's Comedy of Words.  Princeton: Princeton University Press, 1975.  pp. 168-170; 177-180.

*Raitt, A.W.  Life and Letters in France: The Nineteenth Century.  New York: Charles Scribner's Sons, 1965.  pp. 59-65.

LOUIS LAMBERT
Hemmings, F.W.J.  Balzac: An Interpretation of LA COMEDIE HUMAINE.  New York: Random House, 1967.  pp. 13-16.

Holmberg, Arthur Carl.  "Louis Lambert and Maximiliano Rubín: The Inner Vision and the Outer Man."  HR 46: 119-136.  Spring 1978.

Kanes, Martin.  Balzac's Comedy of Words.  Princeton: Princeton University Press, 1975.  pp. 69-70; 113-114; 121-123.

Knapp, Bettina L.  "Louis Lambert: The Legend of the Thinking Man."  NCFS 6: 21-35.  Fall/Winter 1977-1978.

Lock, Peter W.  "Origins, Desire, and Writing: Balzac's Louis Lambert."  SFR 1: 289-311.  Winter 1977.

MASSIMILLA DONI
Luce, Louise Fiber.  "Honoré de Balzac and the 'Voyant': A Recovered Alchemical Discourse."  ECr 18: 15-18.  Summer 1978.

LA MUSE DU DEPARTEMENT
Hemmings, F.W.J.  Balzac: An Interpretation of LA COMEDIE HUMAINE.  New York: Random House, 1967.  pp. 68-72.

LE PERE GORIOT
Allen, Robert.  "A Stylistic Study of the Adjectives of LE PERE GORIOT."  Lang & S 4: 24-56.  Winter 1971.

Berman, Ronald. "Analogies and Realities in PERE GORIOT." Novel 3: 7-16. Fall 1969.

Besser, Gretchen R. "Lear and Goriot: A Re-evaluation." OL 27: 28-36. 1972.

Bourque, Joseph H. "Latent Symbol and Balzac's LE PERE GORIOT." Symposium 32: 277-287. Winter 1978.

Brooks, Peter. "Balzac: Melodrama and Metaphor." HudR 22: 213-228. Summer 1969.

Coe, Richard N. "'Vers la fin du mois de novembre 1819...' Fact, Music and Fiction in LE PERE GORIOT." AJFS 11: 169-181. May/August 1974.

Fischler, Alexander. "Rastignac-Telemaque: The Epic Scale in LE PERE GORIOT." MLR 63: 840-848. October 1968.

Hemmings, F.W.J. Balzac: An Interpretation of LA COMEDIE HUMAINE. New York: Random House, 1967. pp. 104-116.

Kanes, Martin. Balzac's Comedy of Words. Princeton: Princeton University Press, 1975. pp. 138-139.

Prendergast, Christopher. Balzac: Fiction and Melodrama. London: Arnold, 1978. pp. 71-79; 177-189.

Pugh, Anthony R. "The Complexity of LE PERE GORIOT." ECr 7: 25-35. Spring 1967.

Sobel, Margaret. "Balzac's LE PERE GORIOT and Dickens's DOMBEY AND SON: A Comparison." RUS 59: 71-80. Summer 1973.

PIERRETTE
Wirtz, Dorothy. "Animalism in Balzac's CURE DE TOURS and PIERRETTE." RomN 11: 61-67. Autumn 1969.

THE QUEST OF THE ABSOLUTE
Hemmings, F.W.J. Balzac: An Interpretation of LA COMEDIE HUMAINE. New York: Random House, 1967. pp. 19-30.

Majewski, Henry F. "The Function of the Mythic Patterns in Balzac's LA RECHERCHE DE L'ABSOLU." NCFS 7: 10-27. Fall/Winter 1980-1981.

LA RABOUILLEUSE
Jameson, Fredric. "Imaginary and Symbolic in LA RABOUILLEUSE." SSI 16: 59-80. No. 1, 1977.

SARRASINE

Borowitz, Helen O. "Balzac's SARRASINE: The Sculptor as Narcissus." NCFS 5: 171-185. Spring/Summer 1977.

## THE SPLENDORS AND MISERIES OF COURTESANS

Holmberg, Arthur. "Balzac and Galdós: 'Comment aiment les filles?'" CL 29: 109-123. Spring 1977.

Kanes, Martin. Balzac's Comedy of Words. Princeton: Princeton University Press, 1975. pp. 160-162; 167-169; 192-194.

Prendergast, Christopher. Balzac: Fiction and Melodrama. London: Arnold, 1978. pp. 53-60; 80-89.

――――――. "Melodrama and Totality in SPLENDEURS ET MISÈRES DES COURTISANES." Novel 6: 152-162. Winter 1973.

Schilling, Bernard N. The Hero as Failure: Balzac and the Rubempré Cycle. Chicago: University of Chicago Press, 1968. pp. 193-199.

## LE VICAIRE DES ARDENNES

Kanes, Martin. Balzac's Comedy of Words. Princeton: Princeton University Press, 1975. pp. 50-55.

## LA VIEILLE FILLE

Butler, R. "Restoration Perspectives in Balzac's LA VIEILLE FILLE." ML 57: 126-131. September 1976.

Jameson, Fredric. "The Ideology of Form: Partial Systems in LA VIEILLE FILLE." Sub-Stance 15: 29-47. 1976.

## THE WILD ASS'S SKIN

Araujo, Norman. "Time and Rhythm in Balzac's LA PEAU DE CHAGRIN." FR 44: 59-68. Sp. Issue No. 2, Winter 1971.

Austin, Karen O. "A Note on the Double Nature of Man in Balzac's LA PEAU DE CHAGRIN." SoQ 10: 275-281. April 1972.

Haig, Stirling. "Dualistic Patterns in LA PEAU DE CHAGRIN." NCFS 1: 211-218. September 1973.

Hemmings, F.W.J. Balzac: An Interpretation of LA COMEDIE HUMAINE. New York: Random House, 1967. pp. 168-177.

Kanes, Martin. Balzac's Comedy of Words. Princeton: Princeton University Press, 1975. pp. 65-100; 110-112.

Luce, Louise Fiber. "Honoré de Balzac and the 'Voyant': A Recovered Alchemical Discourse." ECr 18: 18-22. Summer 1978.

Balzac, Honoré de                                                                                          11

Pritchett, V. S. Balzac. New York: Alfred A. Knopf, 1973. pp. 107-110.

Weber, Samuel. Unwrapping Balzac: A Reading of LA PEAU DE CHAGRIN. Toronto: University of Toronto Press, 1979. 167 pp.

Barbey d'Aurevilly, Jules
L'AMOUR IMPOSSIBLE
Chartier, Armand B. Barbey d'Aurevilly. Boston: Twayne, 1977. pp. 47-52.

Rogers, B. G. The Novels and Stories of Barbey d'Aurevilly. Genève: Librairie Droz, 1967. pp. 44-46.
LA BAGUE ANNIBAL
Chartier, Armand B. Barbey d'Aurevilly. Boston: Twayne, 1977. pp. 44-47.
LE CACHET D'ONYX
Rogers, B. G. The Novels and Stories of Barbey d'Aurevilly. Genève: Librairie Droz, 1967. pp. 33-35; 219-222.
CE QUI NE MEURT PAS
Chartier, Armand B. Barbey d'Aurevilly. Boston: Twayne, 1977. pp. 133-143.
LE CHEVALIER DES TOUCHES
Chartier, Armand B. Barbey d'Aurevilly. Boston: Twayne, 1977. pp. 81-91.
L'ENSORCELEE
Chartier, Armand B. Barbey d'Aurevilly. Boston: Twayne, 1977. pp. 70-81.

Rogers, B. G. The Novels and Stories of Barbey d'Aurevilly. Genève: Librairie Droz, 1967. pp. 57-72; 150-154.
UNE HISTOIRE SANS NOM
Chartier, Armand B. Barbey d'Aurevilly. Boston: Twayne, 1977. pp. 128-133.

Rogers, B. G. The Novels and Stories of Barbey d'Aurevilly. Genève: Librairie Droz, 1967. pp. 132-135; 241-242.
UN PRÊTRE MARIE
Chartier, Armand. Barbey d'Aurevilly. Boston: Twayne, 1977. pp. 91-102.

Rogers, B. G. The Novels and Stories of Barbey d'Aurevilly. Genève: Librairie Droz, 1967. pp. 91-105; 161-166.
UNE VIEILLE MAITRESSE
Chartier, Armand B. Barbey d'Aurevilly. Boston: Twayne, 1977. pp. 59-70.

Rogers, B. G. The Novels and Stories of Barbey d'Aurevilly. Genève: Librairie Droz, 1967. pp. 46-54; 146-149.

Barbusse, Henri
LE FEU
King, Jonathan. "Henri Barbusse: LE FEU and the Crisis of Social Realism." The First World War in Fiction: A Collection of Critical Essays. ed. Holger Klein. London: Macmillan, 1976. pp. 43-52.

Barthe, Nicolas-Thomas
LA JOLIE FEMME
Thompsett, Eileen. "The Theme of Seduction in the Eighteenth-Century French Novel: Barthe's LA JOLIE FEMME." FMLS 12: 206-216. July 1976.

Barthes, Roland
SARRASINE
Chambers, Ross. "SARRASINE and the Impact of Art." FrF 5: 218-237. September 1980.
S/Z
Kevelson, Roberta. "A Restructure of Barthes' Readerly Text." Semiotica 18: 253-267. No. 3, 1976.

Bataille, Georges
LE BLEU DU CIEL
Kibler, Louis. "Imagery in Georges Bataille's LE BLEU DU CIEL." FR 47: 208-218. Sp. Issue No. 6, Spring 1974.

Beauvoir, Simone de
ALL MEN ARE MORTAL
Cottrell, Robert D. Simone de Beauvoir. New York: Ungar, 1975. pp. 68-78.
THE BLOOD OF OTHERS
Cottrell, Robert D. Simone de Beauvoir. New York: Ungar, 1975. pp. 50-62.

Leighton, Jean. Simone de Beauvoir on Women. London: Associated University Press, 1975. pp. 125-131; 136-137.
LA FEMME ROMPUE
Keefe, Terry. "Simone de Beauvoir's LA FEMME ROMPUE: Studies in Self-deception." EFL 13: 77-97. November 1976.
L'INVITEE
Cottrell, Robert D. Simone de Beauvoir. New York: Ungar, 1975. pp. 29-42.

Leighton, Jean. Simone de Beauvoir on Women. London: Associated University Press, 1975. pp. 48-74; 132-135; 159-169.
THE MANDARINS

Beauvoir, Simone de

>Cottrell, Robert D. Simone de Beauvoir. New York: Ungar, 1975. pp. 107-121.

>Keefe, Terry. "Psychiatry in the Postwar Fiction of Simone de Beauvoir." L&P 29: 124-127. No. 3, 1979.

>Leighton, Jean. Simone de Beauvoir on Women. London: Associated University Press, 1975. pp. 76-113; 119-125; 169-183.

>Madsen, Axel. Hearts and Minds: The Common Journey of Simone de Beauvoir and Jean-Paul Sartre. New York: William Morrow, 1977. pp. 155-156; 177-184.

THE PRETTY PICTURES
>Keefe, Terry. "Psychiatry in the Postwar Fiction of Simone de Beauvoir." L&P 29: 129-132. No. 3, 1979.

>Pages, Irene M. "Beauvoir's LES BELLES IMAGES: 'Desubstantification' of Reality Through a Narrative." FMLS 11: 133-141. April 1975.

>Waelti-Walters, Jennifer R. "Plus ça change ... (A Study of LES BELLES IMAGES in Relation to LE DEUXIEME SEXE)." PCL 4: 22-30. November 1978.

Beckett, Samuel
 ALL STRANGE AWAY
>Murphy, Peter. "Review Article: ALL STRANGE AWAY by Samuel Beckett." Journal of Beckett Studies 5: 99-113. Autumn 1979.

 DREAM OF FAIR TO MIDDLING WOMEN
>Fletcher, John. The Novels of Samuel Beckett. London: Chatto and Windus, 1970. pp. 14-37.

>Kroll, Jeri L. "Belacqua as Artist and Lover: 'What a Misfortune.'" Journal of Beckett Studies 3:10-39. Summer 1978.

 ENOUGH
>Brater, Enoch. "Why Beckett's ENOUGH Is More or Less Enough." ConL 21:252-266. Spring 1980.

>Murphy, Peter. "The Nature and Art of Love in ENOUGH." Journal of Beckett Studies 4:14-34. Spring 1979.

 HOW IT IS
>Abbott, H. Porter. "Farewell to Incompetence: Beckett's HOW IT IS and IMAGINATION DEAD IMAGINE." ConL 11:37-45. Winter 1970.

>_____. The Fiction of Samuel Beckett: Form and Effect. Berkeley: University of California Press, 1973. pp. 138-149.

Alvarez, A. Samuel Beckett. New York: Viking, 1973. pp. 66-74.

Bair, Deirdre. Samuel Beckett. New York: Harcourt Brace Jovanovich, 1978. pp. 515-516; 520-524.

Barnard, Guy C. Samuel Beckett: A New Approach; A Study of the Novels and Plays. Great Britain: Aldine Press, 1970. pp. 66-74.

Dearlove, Judith. "The Voice and Its Words: How It Is in Beckett's Canon." Journal of Beckett Studies 3:56-75. Summer 1978.

Doherty, Francis. Samuel Beckett. London: Hutchinson, 1971. pp. 119-131.

Elovaara, Raili. The Problem of Identity in Samuel Beckett's Prose: An Approach from Philosophies of Existence. Helsinki: Suomalainen Tiedeakatemia, 1976. pp. 267-275.

Hamilton, Alice and Kenneth. "The Process of Imaginative Creation in Samuel Beckett's HOW IT IS." Mosaic 10:1-12. Summer 1977.

Hamilton, Kenneth and Alice. Condemned to Life: The World of Samuel Beckett. Grand Rapids: Eerdmans, 1976. pp. 178-188.

Hassan, I. The Literature of Silence: Henry Miller and Samuel Beckett. Knopf, 1967. pp. 168-173.

Kenner, Hugh. A Reader's Guide to Samuel Beckett. New York: Farrar, Straus, Giroux, 1973. pp. 136-146.

Kern, Edith. Existential Thought and Fictional Technique: Kierkegaard, Sartre, Beckett. New Haven: Yale University Press, 1970. pp. 233-238.

Knowlson, James and John Pilling. Frescoes of the Skull: The Later Prose and Drama of Samuel Beckett. London: John Calder, 1979. pp. 61-78.

Krance, Charles. "Alienation and Form in Beckett's HOW IT IS." PCL 1:85-99. November 1975.

Levy, Eric P. Beckett and the Voice of Species: A Study of the Prose Fiction. Dublin: Gill and Macmillan, 1980. pp. 83-94.

_____. "The Metaphysics of Ignorance: Time and

Personal Identity in HOW IT IS." Renascence 28:27-37. Autumn 1975.

Pilling, John. Samuel Beckett. London: Routledge & Kegan Paul, 1976. pp. 44-46.

Sage, Victor. "Innovation and Continuity in HOW IT IS." Beckett the Shape Changer. ed. Katharine Worth. London: Routledge & Kegan Paul, 1975. pp. 87-103.

Schwartz, Paul J. "Life and Death in the Mud: A Study of Beckett's COMMENT C'EST." IFR 2:43-48. January 1975.

Shadoian, Jack. "The Achievement of COMMENT C'EST." Crit 12: 5-17. No. 2, 1970.

Van Petten, Carol. "Modulations of Monologue in Beckett's COMMENT C'EST." Symposium 31:243-255. Fall 1977.

Webb, Eugene. Samuel Beckett: A Study of His Novels. Seattle: University of Washington Press. pp. 155-172.

IMAGINATION DEAD IMAGINE
Abbott, H. Porter. "Farewell to Incompetence: Beckett's HOW IT IS and IMAGINATION DEAD IMAGINE." ConL 11:45-47. Winter 1970.

Finney, Brian. "A Reading of Beckett's IMAGINATION DEAD IMAGINE." TCL 17:65-71. April 1971.

KRAPP'S LAST TAPE
Campbell, SueEllen. "KRAPP'S LAST TAPE and Critical Theory." CompD 12: 187-199. Fall 1978.

Gilbert, Sandra M. "'All the Dead Voices': A Study of KRAPP'S LAST TAPE." DramS 6:244-257. Spring 1968.

Gontarski, S. E. "Crapp's First Tapes: Beckett's Manuscript Revisions of KRAPP'S LAST TAPE." JML 6:61-68. February 1977.

Thomas, Lloyd Spencer. "Krapp: Beckett's Aged Narcissus." CEA 39:9-11. January 1977.

LESSNESS
Coetzee, J. M. "Samuel Beckett's LESSNESS: An Exercise in Decomposition." Computers and the Humanities 7:195-198. March 1973.

Solomon, Philip H. "Purgatory Unpurged: Time, Space, and Language in LESSNESS." Journal of Beckett Studies 6:63-72. Autumn 1980.

THE LOST ONES

Brienza, Susan D. "THE LOST ONES: The Reader as Searcher." JML 6:148-168. February 1977.

Federman, Raymond. "The Impossibility of Saying the Same Old Thing the Same Old Way--Samuel Beckett's Fiction Since COMMENT C'EST." ECr 11:39-43. Fall 1971.

Leventhal, A. J. "Samuel Beckett: About Him and About." Hermathena 114:17-22. Winter 1972.

Levy, Eric P. Beckett and the Voice of Species: A Study of the Prose Fiction. Dublin: Gill and Macmillan, 1980. pp. 95-105.

## MALONE DIES

Abbott, H. Porter. The Fiction of Samuel Beckett: Form and Effect. Berkeley: University of California Press, 1973. pp. 110-123.

Alvarez, A. Samuel Beckett. New York: Viking, 1973. pp. 52-57.

Bair, Deirdre. Samuel Beckett. New York: Harcourt Brace Jovanovich, 1978. pp. 374-377.

Barnard, Guy C. Samuel Beckett: A New Approach; A Study of the Novels and Plays. Great Britain: Aldine Press, 1970. pp. 45-56.

Cohn, Ruby. Back to Beckett. Princeton: Princeton University Press, 1973. pp. 91-100.

Conely, James. "ARCANA; MOLLOY, MALONE DIES, THE UNNAMABLE: A Brief Comparison of Forms." HSL 4:187-195. No. 3, 1972.

Doherty, Francis. Samuel Beckett. London: Hutchinson, 1971. pp. 49-85.

Elovaara, Raili. The Problem of Identity in Samuel Beckett's Prose: An Approach from Philosophies of Existence. Helsinki: Suomalainen Tiedeakatemia, 1976. pp. 166-185.

Fletcher, John. "Malone's 'Given Birth to Into Death.'" Twentieth Century Interpretations of MOLLOY, MALONE DIES, THE UNNAMABLE. ed. J. D. O'Hara. Englewood Cliffs: Prentice-Hall, 1970. pp. 58-61.

_____. The Novels of Samuel Beckett. London: Chatto and Windus, 1970. pp. 151-176.

Gluck, Barbara Reich. Beckett and Joyce: Friendship

and Fiction. Lewisburg: Bucknell University Press, 1979. pp. 112-115; 126-140.

Hamilton, Kenneth and Alice. Condemned to Life: The World of Samuel Beckett. Grand Rapids: Eerdmans, 1976. pp. 147-151.

Hassan, I. The Literature of Silence: Henry Miller and Samuel Beckett. New York: Alfred A. Knopf, 1967. pp. 151-152; 158-162.

Hesla, David H. The Shapes of Chaos: An Interpretation of the Art of Samuel Beckett. Minneapolis: University of Minnesota Press, 1971. pp. 86-128; 178-183; 190-192; 219-221.

Hill, Leslie. "Fiction, Myth, and Identity in Samuel Beckett's Novel Trilogy." FMLS 13:230-239. July 1977.

Hoffman, Frederick J. "The Elusive Ego: Beckett's M's." Samuel Beckett Now. ed. Melvin J. Friedman. Chicago: University of Chicago Press, 1970. pp. 50-54.

Kenner, Hugh. A Reader's Guide to Samuel Beckett. New York: Farrar, Straus, Giroux, 1973. pp. 92-115.

Kern, Edith. Existential Thought and Fictional Technique: Kierkegaard, Sartre, Beckett. New Haven: Yale University Press, 1970. pp. 208-221.

Levy, Eric P. Beckett and the Voice of Species: A Study of the Prose Fiction. Dublin: Gill and Macmillan, 1980. pp. 54-71.

_____. "Voice of Species: The Narrator and Beckettian Man in THREE NOVELS." ELH 45:343-357. Summer 1978.

O'Hara, J. D. "About Structure in MALONE DIES." Twentieth Century Interpretations of MOLLOY, MALONE DIES, THE UNNAMABLE. ed. J. D. O'Hara. Englewood Cliffs: Prentice Hall, 1970. pp. 58-70.

Pearce, Richard. Stages of the Clown: Perspectives on Modern Fiction from Dostoyevsky to Beckett. Carbondale: Southern Illinois University Press, 1970. pp. 128-135.

Robinson, Michael. The Long Sonata of the Dead: A Study of Samuel Beckett. London: Rupert Hart-Davis, 1969. pp. 140-148; 170-190.

Sachner, Mark J. "The Artist as Fiction: An Aesthetics of Failure in Samuel Beckett's Trilogy." MQ 18:144-155. January 1977.

Silver, Sally Thrun. "Satire in Beckett: A Study of MOLLOY, MALONE DIES and THE UNNAMABLE." EFL 10:82-99. November 1973.

Solomon, Philip H. The Life After Birth: Imagery in Samuel Beckett's Trilogy. University: Romance Monographs, 1975. 151pp.

MERCIER ET CAMIER

Abbott, H. Porter. The Fiction of Samuel Beckett: Form and Effect. Berkeley: University of California Press, 1973. pp. 75-91.

Levy, Eric P. Beckett and the Voice of Species: A Study of the Prose Fiction. Dublin: Gill and Macmillan, 1980. pp. 39-53.

MOLLOY

Abbott, H. Porter. The Fiction of Samuel Beckett: Form and Effect. Berkeley: University of California Press, 1973. pp. 9-11; 92-115.

Alvarez, A. Samuel Beckett. New York: Viking, 1973. pp. 46-52.

Bair, Deirdre. Samuel Beckett. New York: Harcourt Brace Jovanovich, 1978. pp. 366-372.

Barnard, Guy C. Samuel Beckett: A New Approach; A Study of the Novels and Plays. Great Britain: Aldine Press, 1970. pp. 32-44.

Bové, Paul A. "The Image of the Creator in Beckett's Postmodern Writing." Philosophy and Literature 4:47-65. Spring 1980.

Cohn, Ruby. Back to Beckett. Princeton: Princeton University Press, 1973. pp. 79-90.

Conely, James. "ARCANA; MOLLOY, MALONE DIES, THE UNNAMABLE: A Brief Comparison of Forms." HSL 4:187-195. No. 3, 1972.

Doherty, Francis. Samuel Beckett. London: Hutchinson, 1971. pp. 49-85.

Elovaara, Raili. The Problem of Identity in Samuel Beckett's Prose: An Approach from Philosophies of Existence. Helsinki: Suomalainen Tiedeakatemia, 1976. pp. 80-165.

Fletcher, John. "Interpreting MOLLOY." Samuel Beckett Now. ed. Melvin J. Friedman. Chicago: University of Chicago Press, 1970. pp. 157-170.

_____. The Novels of Samuel Beckett. London: Chatto and Windus, 1970. pp. 119-150.

Friedman, Melvin J. "Molloy's 'Sacred' Stones." RomN 9:8-11. Autumn 1967.

Gebhardt, Richard C. "Technique of Alienation in MOLLOY." PCL 1:74-82. November 1975.

Gluck, Barbara Reich. Beckett and Joyce: Friendship and Fiction. Lewisburg: Bucknell University Press, 1979. pp. 126-140.

Hamilton, Kenneth and Alice. Condemned to Life: The World of Samuel Beckett. Grand Rapids: Eerdmans, 1976. pp. 141-147.

Hassan, I. The Literature of Silence: Henry Miller and Samuel Beckett. New York: Alfred A. Knopf, 1967. pp. 151-158.

Hayman, David. "MOLLOY or the Quest for Meaninglessness: A Global Interpretation." Samuel Beckett Now. ed. Melvin J. Friedman. Chicago: University of Chicago Press, 1970. pp. 129-156.

Hesla, David H. The Shapes of Chaos: An Interpretation of the Art of Samuel Beckett. Minneapolis: University of Minnesota Press, 1971. pp. 86-128.

Hill, Leslie. "Fiction, Myth, and Identity in Samuel Beckett's Novel Trilogy." FMLS 13:230-239. July 1977.

Hoffman, Frederick J. "The Elusive Ego: Beckett's M's." Samuel Beckett Now. ed. Melvin J. Friedman. Chicago: University of Chicago Press, 1970. pp. 44-50.

Honoré, Lionel P. "Metaphysical Anguish and Futility in MOLLOY." KRQ 27:435-444. No. 4, 1980.

Janvier, Ludovic. "MOLLOY." Twentieth Century Interpretations of MOLLOY, MALONE DIES, THE UNNAMABLE. ed. J.D. O'Hara. Englewood Cliffs: Prentice-Hall, 1970. pp. 46-57.

Kellman, Steven G. "Beckett's Fatal Dual." RomN 16:268-273. Winter 1975.

Kenner, Hugh. A Reader's Guide to Samuel Beckett. New York: Farrar, Straus, Giroux, 1973. pp. 92-115.

Kern, Edith. Existential Thought and Fictional Technique: Kierkegaard, Sartre, Beckett. New Haven: Yale University Press, 1970. pp. 194-204.

———. "Moran-Molloy: The Hero as Author." Twentieth Century Interpretations of MOLLOY, MALONE DIES, THE UNNAMABLE. ed. J. D. O'Hara. Englewood Cliffs: Prentice-Hall, 1970. pp. 35-45.

Levy, Eric P. Beckett and the Voice of Species: A Study of the Prose Fiction. Dublin: Gill and Macmillan, 1980. pp. 54-71.

———. "Voices of Species: The Narrator and Beckettian Man in THREE NOVELS." ELH 45:343-357. Summer 1978.

Mooney, Michael E. "MOLLOY, Part I: Beckett's 'Discourse on Method.'" Journal of Beckett Studies 3:40-55. Summer 1978.

Pearce, Richard. Stages of the Clown: Perspectives on Modern Fiction from Dostoyevsky to Beckett. Carbondale: Southern Illinois University Press, 1970. pp. 128-135.

Rabinovitz, Rubin. "MOLLOY and the Archetypal Traveller." Journal of Beckett Studies 5:25-44. Autumn 1979.

Robinson, Michael. The Long Sonata of the Dead: A Study of Samuel Beckett. London: Rupert Hart-Davis, 1969. pp. 140-169.

Rose, Gilbert J. "On the Shores of Self: Samuel Beckett's MOLLOY--Irredentism and the Creative Impulse." PsyR 60:587-603. Winter 1973-1974.

Sachner, Mark J. "The Artist as Fiction: An Aesthetics of Failure in Samuel Beckett's Trilogy." MQ 18:144-155. January 1977.

Solomon, Philip H. The Life After Birth: Imagery in Samuel Beckett's Trilogy. University: Romance Monographs, 1975. 151 pp.

———. "Lousse and Molloy: Beckett's Bower of Bliss." AJFS 6:65-81. January/April 1969.

_____. "Samuel Beckett's MOLLOY: A Dog's Life."
FR 41:84-91. October 1967.

Spraggins, Mary. "Beckett's MOLLOY: As Detective
Novel." Essays in Literature (Denver) 2:11-30. March
1974.

Szanto, George H. Narrative Consciousness: Structure
and Perception in the Fiction of Kafka, Beckett, and
Robbe-Grillet. Austin: University of Texas Press,
1972. pp. 85-90; 116-120.

MORE PRICKS THAN KICKS

Elovaara, Raili. The Problem of Identity in Samuel
Beckett's Prose: An Approach from Philosophies of
Existence. Helsinki: Suomalainen Tiedeakatemia, 1976.
pp. 16-29.

Kroll, Jeri L. "Belacqua as Artist and Lover: 'What
a Misfortune.'" Journal of Beckett Studies 3:10-39.
Summer 1978.

_____. "The Surd as Inadmissible Evidence: The
Case of Attorney-General v. Henry McCabe." Journal
of Beckett Studies 2:47-58. Summer 1977.

Levy, Eric P. Beckett and the Voice of Species: A
Study of the Prose Fiction. Dublin: Gill and Macmillan, 1980. pp. 11-16.

MURPHY

Abbott, H. Porter. The Fiction of Samuel Beckett:
Form and Effect. Berkeley: University of California
Press, 1973. pp. 36-60.

Acheson, James. "Murphy's Metaphysics." Journal of
Beckett Studies 5:9-23. Autumn 1979.

Alvarez, A. Samuel Beckett. New York: Viking, 1973.
pp. 25-32.

Bair, Deirdre. Samuel Beckett. New York: Harcourt
Brace Jovanovich, 1978. pp. 205-237.

Barnard, Guy C. Samuel Beckett: A New Approach; A
Study of the Novels and Plays. Great Britain: Aldine
Press, 1970. pp. 9-15.

Coetzee, J. M. "The Comedy of Point of View in Beckett's MURPHY." Crit 12:19-27. No. 2, 1970.

Culik, Hugh. "Mindful of the Body: Medical Allusions
in Beckett's MURPHY." Eire 14:84-101. Spring 1979.

Doherty, Francis. Samuel Beckett. London: Hutchinson, 1971. pp. 25-34.

Elovaara, Raili. The Problem of Identity in Samuel Beckett's Prose: An Approach from Philosophies of Existence. Helsinki: Suomalainen Tiedeakatemia, 1976. pp. 29-48.

Erickson, John D. "Alienation in Samuel Beckett: The Protagonist as Eiron." PCL 1:65-72. November 1975.

Fletcher, John. The Novels of Samuel Beckett. London: Chatto and Windus, 1970. pp. 38-55.

Gluck, Barbara Reich. Beckett and Joyce: Friendship and Fiction. Lewisburg: Bucknell University Press, 1979. pp. 71-86.

Hamilton, Kenneth and Alice. Condemned to Life: The World of Samuel Beckett. Grand Rapids: Eerdmans, 1976. pp. 70-75; 123-128.

Harrison, Robert. Samuel Beckett's MURPHY: A Critical Excursion. Athens: University of Georgia Press, 1968. 99 pp.

Hassan, I. The Literature of Silence: Henry Miller and Samuel Beckett. New York: Alfred A. Knopf, 1967. pp. 140-145.

Hesla, David H. The Shapes of Chaos: An Interpretation of the Art of Samuel Beckett. Minneapolis: University of Minnesota Press, 1971. pp. 30-58; 86-128.

Hoffman, Frederick J. "The Elusive Ego: Beckett's M's." Samuel Beckett Now. ed. Melvin J. Friedman. Chicago: University of Chicago Press, 1970. pp. 31-38.

Jones, Anthony. "The French Murphy: From 'rare bird' to 'cancre.'" Journal of Beckett Studies 6:36-50. Autumn 1980.

Kennedy, Sighle. Murphy's Bed. Lewisburg: Bucknell University Press, 1971. pp. 1-299.

Kenner, Hugh. A Reader's Guide to Samuel Beckett. New York: Farrar, Straus, Giroux, 1973. pp. 57-71.

Levy, Eric P. Beckett and the Voice of Species: A Study of the Prose Fiction. Dublin: Gill and Macmillan, 1980. pp. 16-26.

Park, Eric. "Fundamental Sounds: Music in Samuel Beckett's MURPHY and WATT." MFS 21:157-171. Summer 1975.

Robinson, Michael. The Long Sonata of the Dead: A Study of Samuel Beckett. London: Rupert Hart-Davis, 1969. pp. 82-99; 190-207.

Steinberg, S. C. "The External and Internal in MURPHY." TCL 18:93-110. April 1972.

THE UNNAMABLE
Abbott, H. Porter. The Fiction of Samuel Beckett: Form and Effect. Berkeley: University of California Press, 1973. pp. 124-137.

_____. "A Grammar for Being Elsewhere." JML 6:39-46. February 1977.

Alvarez, A. Samuel Beckett. New York: Viking, 1973. pp. 57-65.

Barnard, Guy C. Samuel Beckett: A New Approach; A Study of the Novels and Plays. Great Britain: Aldine Press, 1970. pp. 57-66.

Bruns, Gerald L. "The Storyteller and the Problem of Language in Samuel Beckett's Fiction." MLQ 30:274-278. June 1969.

Champigny, Robert. "Adventures of the First Person." Samuel Beckett Now. ed. Melvin J. Friedman. Chicago: University of Chicago Press, 1970. pp. 119-128.

Cohn, Ruby. Back to Beckett. Princeton: Princeton University Press, 1973. pp. 100-112.

Conely, James. "ARCANA; MOLLOY, MALONE DIES, THE UNNAMABLE: A Brief Comparison of Forms." HSL 4:187-195. No. 3, 1972.

Doherty, Francis. Samuel Beckett. London: Hutchinson, 1971. pp. 71-85.

Elovaara, Raili. The Problem of Identity in Samuel Beckett's Prose: An Approach from Philosophies of Existence. Helsinki: Suomalainen Tiedeakatemia, 1976. pp. 186-256.

Fanizza, Franko. "The Word and Silence in Samuel Beckett's UNNAMABLE." Twentieth Century Interpretations of MOLLOY, MALONE DIES, THE UNNAMABLE. ed. J. D. O'Hara. Englewood Cliffs: Prentice-Hall, 1970. pp. 71-81.

Fletcher, John. The Novels of Samuel Beckett. London: Chatto and Windus, 1970. pp. 179-194.

Garzilli, Enrico. Circles Without Center: Paths to the Discovery and Creation of Self in Modern Literature. Cambridge: Harvard University Press, 1972. pp. 47-52.

Hassan, I. The Literature of Silence: Henry Miller and Samuel Beckett. New York: Alfred A. Knopf, 1967. pp. 162-168.

Hesla, David H. The Shapes of Chaos: An Interpretation of the Art of Samuel Beckett. Minneapolis: University of Minnesota Press, 1971. pp. 86-128.

Hill, Leslie. "Fiction, Myth, and Identity in Samuel Beckett's Novel Trilogy." FMLS 13:230-239. July 1977.

Hoffman, Frederick J. "The Elusive Ego: Beckett's M's." Samuel Beckett Now. ed. Melvin J. Friedman. Chicago: University of Chicago Press, 1970. pp. 54-58.

Kenner, Hugh. A Reader's Guide to Samuel Beckett. New York: Farrar, Straus, Giroux, 1973. pp. 92-115.

Kern, Edith. Existential Thought and Fictional Technique: Kierkegaard, Sartre, Beckett. New Haven: Yale University Press, 1970. pp. 221-232.

Levy, Eric P. Beckett and the Voice of Species: A Study of the Prose Fiction. Dublin: Gill and Macmillan, 1980. pp. 54-71.

_____. "Existence Searching Essence: The Plight of the Unnamable." Mosaic 10:103-113. Fall 1976.

_____. "Voice of Species: The Narrator and Beckettian Man in THREE NOVELS." ELH 45:343-357. Summer 1978.

Pearce, Richard. Stages of the Clown: Perspectives on Modern Fiction from Dostoyevsky to Beckett. Carbondale: Southern Illinois University Press, 1970. pp. 128-135.

Sachner, Mark J. "The Artist as Fiction: An Aesthetics of Failure in Samuel Beckett's Trilogy." MQ 18:144-155. January 1977.

Silver, Sally Thrun. "Satire in Beckett: A Study of MOLLOY, MALONE DIES and THE UNNAMABLE." EFL 10:82-99. November 1973.

Solomon, Philip H. The Life After Birth: Imagery in Samuel Beckett's Trilogy. University: Romance Monographs, 1975. 151 pp.

———. "Samuel Beckett's L'INNOMMABLE: The Space of Fiction." FMLS 7:83-91. January 1971.

Webb, Eugene. Samuel Beckett: A Study of His Novels. Seattle: University of Washington Press. pp. 123-128.

## WATT

Abbott, H. Porter. The Fiction of Samuel Beckett: Form and Effect. Berkeley: University of California Press, 1973. pp. 55-74.

Alvarez, A. Samuel Beckett. New York: Viking, 1973. pp. 32-39.

Barnard, Guy C. Samuel Beckett: A New Approach; A Study of the Novels and Plays. Great Britain: Aldine Press, 1970. pp. 16-27.

Bruns, Gerald L. "The Storyteller and the Problem of Language in Samuel Beckett's Fiction." MLQ 30:267-272. June 1969.

Chalker, John. "The Satiric Shape of WATT." Beckett the Shape Changer, ed. Katharine Worth. London: Routledge & Kegan Paul, 1975. pp. 21-37.

Coetzee, J. M. "The Manuscript Revisions of Beckett's WATT." JML 2:472-480. November 1972.

Cousineau, Thomas J. "WATT: Language as Interdiction and Consolation." Journal of Beckett Studies 4:1-13. Spring 1979.

Doherty, Francis. Samuel Beckett. London: Hutchinson, 1971. pp. 34-48.

Elovaara, Raili. The Problem of Identity in Samuel Beckett's Prose: An Approach from Philosophies of Existence. Helsinki: Suomalainen Tiedeakatemia, 1976. pp. 48-73.

Fletcher, John. The Novels of Samuel Beckett. London: Chatto and Windus, 1970. pp. 59-89.

Hamilton, Kenneth and Alice. Condemned to Life: The World of Samuel Beckett. Grand Rapids: Eerdmans, 1976. pp. 128-135.

Hassan, I. The Literature of Silence: Henry Miller

and Samuel Beckett. New York: Alfred A. Knopf, 1967. pp. 145-151.

Henkels, Robert M., Jr. "Novel Quarters for an Odd Couple: Apollo and Dionysis [sic] in Beckett's WATT and Pinget's THE INQUISITORY." StTCL 2:142-150. Spring 1978.

Hesla, David H. The Shapes of Chaos: An Interpretation of the Art of Samuel Beckett. Minneapolis: University of Minnesota Press, 1971. pp. 59-85.

Hoffman, Frederick J. "The Elusive Ego: Beckett's M's." Samuel Beckett Now. ed. Melvin J. Friedman. Chicago: University of Chicago Press, 1970. pp. 39-43.

Kenner, Hugh. A Reader's Guide to Samuel Beckett. New York: Farrar, Straus, Giroux, 1973. pp. 72-82.

Kern, Edith. Existential Thought and Fictional Technique: Kierkegaard, Sartre, Beckett. New Haven: Yale University Press, 1970. pp. 177-194.

Levy, Eric P. Beckett and the Voice of Species: A Study of the Prose Fiction. Dublin: Gill and Macmillan, 1980. pp. 27-38.

Lorich, Bruce. "The Accommodating Form of Samuel Beckett." SWR 55:354-369. Autumn 1970.

Mood, John J. "'The Personal System'--Samuel Beckett's WATT." PMLA 86:255-265. March 1971.

Moorjani, Angela B. "Narrative Game Strategies in Beckett's WATT." ECr 17:235-244. Fall 1977.

Murphy, Vincent J. "La Peinture de l'empêchement--Samuel Beckett's WATT." Criticism 18:353-366. Fall 1976.

Park, Eric. "Fundamental Sounds: Music in Samuel Beckett's MURPHY and WATT." MFS 21:157-171. Summer 1975.

Posnock, Ross. "Beckett, Valery and WATT." Journal of Beckett Studies 6:51-62. Autumn 1980.

Rabinovitz, Rubin. "WATT from Descartes to Schopenhauer." Modern Irish Literature: Essays in Honor of William York Tindall. ed. Raymond J. Porter and James D. Brophy. New York: Twayne, 1972. pp. 261-287.

Robinson, Michael. The Long Sonata of the Dead: A Study of Samuel Beckett. London: Rupert Hart-Davis, 1969. pp. 100-131.

Skerl, Jennie. "Fritz Mauthner's 'Critique of Language' in Samuel Beckett's WATT." ConL 15:474-487. Autumn 1974.

Smith, Frederik N. "The Epistemology of Fictional Failure: Swift's TALE OF A TUB and Beckett's WATT." TSLL 15:649-672. Winter 1974.

Solomon, Philip Howard. "A Ladder Image in WATT: Samuel Beckett and Fritz Mauthner." PLL 7:422-427. Fall 1971.

Swanson, Eleanor. "Samuel Beckett's WATT: A Coming and a Going." MFS 17:264-268. Summer 1971.

Szanto, George H. Narrative Consciousness: Structure and Perception in the Fiction of Kafka, Beckett, and Robbe-Grillet. Austin: University of Texas Press, 1972. pp. 81-85.

Trivisonno, Ann M. "Meaning and Function of the Quest in Beckett's WATT." Crit 12:28-38. No. 2, 1970.

Winston, Mathew. "WATT's First Footnote." JML 6:69-82. February 1977.

de Bergerac, Savinien Cyrano
L'AUTRE MONDE
Van Baelen, Jacqueline. "Reality and Illusion in L'AUTRE MONDE: The Narrative Voyage." YFS 49: 178-184. 1973.

Bernanos, Georges
A CRIME
Bush, William. Georges Bernanos. New York: Twayne, 1969. pp. 84-94.

Speaight, Robert. Georges Bernanos: A Study of the Man and the Writer. New York: Liveright, 1974. pp. 135-138.
DIALOGUES DES CARMELITES
Falk, Eugene H. "The Leap to Faith: Two Paths to the Scaffold." Symposium 21:250-254. Fall 1967.
DIARY OF A COUNTRY PRIEST
Bouraoui, H. A. "The Face in the Mirror: Bernanos' Hero as Artist in JOURNAL D'UN CURE DE CAMPAGNE." MFS 17:181-192. Summer 1971.

Bush, William. Georges Bernanos. New York: Twayne, 1969. pp. 95-104.

Cor, Laurence W. "Mystical Perception in JOURNAL D'UN CURE DE CAMPAGNE." RomN 12:244-250. Spring 1971.

Flower, John. "The 'Comtesse' Episode in the JOURNAL D'UN CURE DE CAMPAGNE." FR 42:673-682. April 1969.

Gerlach, John. "THE DIARY OF A COUNTRY PRIEST: A Total Conversion." LFQ 4:39-45. Winter 1976.

Karnath, David. "Bernanos, Greene, and the Novel Convention." ConL 19:429-445. Autumn 1978.

Lye, John. "THE DIARY OF A COUNTRY PRIEST and the Christian Novel." Renascence 30:19-30. Fall 1978.

Sayre, Robert. Solitude in Society. Cambridge: Harvard University Press, 1978. pp. 137-154.

Sister Marie Céleste. "Bernanos and Graham Greene or the Role of the Priest in THE DIARY OF A COUNTRY PRIEST and THE POWER AND THE GLORY." Culture 30:287-298. December 1969.

Speaight, Robert. Georges Bernanos: A Study of the Man and the Writer. New York: Liveright, 1974. pp. 146-155.

Vineberg, Elsa. "JOURNAL D'UN CURE DE CAMPAGNE: A Psychoanalytic Reading." MLN 92:825-829. May 1977.

L'IMPOSTURE
Bush, William. Georges Bernanos. New York: Twayne, 1969. pp. 78-83.

Speaight, Robert. Georges Bernanos: A Study of the Man and the Writer. New York: Liveright, 1974. pp. 91-97.

JOY
Bush, William. Georges Bernanos. New York: Twayne, 1969. pp. 78-83.

Speaight, Robert. Georges Bernanos: A Study of the Man and the Writer. New York: Liveright, 1974. pp. 97-99.

MONSIEUR OUINE
Bush, William. Georges Bernanos. New York: Twayne, 1969. pp. 105-115.

Field, Frank. Three Great Writers and the Great
War. Cambridge: Cambridge University Press, 1975.
pp. 156-158; 186-187.

Speaight, Robert. Georges Bernanos: A Study of the
Man and the Writer. New York: Liveright, 1974. pp.
215-226.

Weinstein, Arnold L. "Bernanos' MONSIEUR OUINE
and the Esthetic of Chaos." Symposium 25:392-407.
Winter 1971.
MOUCHETTE
 Bush, William. Georges Bernanos. New York: Twayne,
 1969. pp. 95-104.
NIGHT IS DARKEST
 Bush, William. Georges Bernanos. New York: Twayne,
 1969. pp. 84-94.
UNDER THE SUN OF SATAN
 Bush, William. Georges Bernanos. New York: Twayne,
 1969. pp. 69-77.

*Sonnenfeld, Albert. "The Art of Georges Bernanos: The
Prologue to SOUS LE SOLEIL DE SATAN." OL 21:133-
153. No. 2/4, 1966.

Speaight, Robert. Georges Bernanos: A Study of the
Man and the Writer. New York: Liveright, 1974. pp.
68-75.

Blanchot, Maurice
 AMINADAB
  Smock, Ann. "'Où est la loi?': Law and Sovereignty
  in AMINADAB and LE TRES-HAUT." Sub-Stance 14:99-
  115. 1976.
 L'ARRÊT DE MORT
  Laporte, Roger. "White Night." Sub-Stance 14: 59-65.
  1976.
 AU MOMENT VOULU
  Prince, Gerald. "The Point of Narrative: Blanchot's
  AU MOMENT VOULU." Sub-Stance 14:93-98. 1976.
 LE TRES-HAUT
  Smock, Ann. "'Où est la loi?': Law and Sovereignty
  in AMINADAB and LE TRES-HAUT." Sub-Stance 14:99-
  115. 1976.

Borel, Pétrus
 MADAME PUTIPHAR
  Brombert, Victor. "Pétrus Borel, Prison Horrors, and
  the Gothic Tradition." Novel 2: 143-152. Winter 1969.

Bosco, Henri
 MALICROIX
  Prince, John. "New Light on the Origins and Symbolism

of MALICROIX by Henri Bosco." FR 47:773-782. March 1974.

Boudjedra, Rachid
TOPOLOGIE IDEALE POUR UNE AGRESSION CARACTERISEE
Harrow, Kenneth. "A Journey Through the Labyrinth: Rachid Boudjedra's TOPOLOGIE IDEALE POUR UNE AGRESSION CARACTERISEE." IFR 6:63-66. Winter 1979.

Bourget, Paul
THE DISCIPLE
Goetz, T. H. "Paul Bourget's LE DISCIPLE and the Text-Reader Relationship." FR 52:56-61. October 1978.

Singer, Armand. Paul Bourget. Boston: Twayne, 1976. pp. 65-67; 75-76; 120-121.
L'ETAPE
Singer, Armand. Paul Bourget. Boston: Twayne, 1976. pp. 79-82; 135-136.

Breton, André
L'AMOUR FOU
Balakian, Anna. André Breton: Magus of Surrealism. New York: Oxford University Press, 1971. pp. 102-124.

Matthews, J. H. André Breton. New York: Columbia University Press, 1967. pp. 15-19.
NADJA
Balakian, Anna. André Breton: Magus of Surrealism. New York: Oxford University Press, 1971. pp. 102-124.

Hubert, Renée Riese. "The Coherence of Breton's NADJA." ConL 10:241-252. Spring 1969.

Kritzman, Lawrence D. "For a Structural Analysis of NADJA: A Scientific Experiment." RLSt 3:9-23. Spring 1973.

Matthews, J. H. André Breton. New York: Columbia University Press, 1967. pp. 8-12.

Tremaine, Louis. "Breton's NADJA: A Spiritual Ethnography." StTCL 1:91-117. Fall 1976.

Wylie, Harold. "Breton, Schizophrenia and NADJA." FR 43:100-106. Sp. Issue No. 1, Winter 1970.
LES VASES COMMUNICANTS
Balakian, Anna. André Breton: Magus of Surrealism.

New York: Oxford University Press, 1971. pp. 102-124.

Matthews, J. H. André Breton. New York: Columbia University Press, 1967. pp. 12-15.

Butor, Michel
A CHANGE OF HEART
Britton, Celia. "The Status of Representation in Michel Butor's L'EMPLOI DU TEMPS and LA MODIFICATION." Journal of Beckett Studies 3:76-84. Summer 1978.

Grieve, James. "'Rencontre ou piège': A Footnote to LA MODIFICATION." AJFS 8:314-319. September/December 1971.

Larson, Jeffry. "The Sibyl and the Iron Floor Heater in Michel Butor's LA MODIFICATION." PLL 10:403-414. Fall 1974.

Lydon, Mary. "Sibylline Imagery in Butor's LA MODIFICATION." MLR 67:300-308. April 1972.

McWilliams, Dean. The Narratives of Michel Butor: The Writer as Janus. Columbus: Ohio University Press, 1978. pp. 32-44.

Mercier, Vivian. The New Novel from Queneau to Pinget. New York: Farrar, Straus, Giroux, 1971. pp. 215-226.

Passias, Katherine. "Deep and Surface Structure of the Narrative Pronoun 'Vous' in Butor's LA MODIFICATION and Its Relationship to Free Indirect Style." Lang & S 9:197-211. Summer 1976.

Patai, Daphne. "Temporal Structure as a Fictional Category in Michel Butor's LA MODIFICATION." FR 46:1117-1128. May 1973.

Roudiez, Leon S. "Problems of Point of View in the Early Fiction of Michel Butor." KRQ 18:153-155. No. 2, 1971.

Spencer, Michael. Michel Butor. New York: Twayne, 1974. pp. 64-81.

Warme, Lars. "Reflection and Revelation in Michel Butor's LA MODIFICATION." IFR 1:88-95. July 1974.

DEGREES
McWilliams, Dean. The Narratives of Michel Butor: The Writer as Janus. Columbus: Ohio University Press, 1978. pp. 45-56.

Mercier, Vivian. The New Novel from Queneau to Pinget. New York: Farrar, Straus, Giroux, 1971. pp. 250-264.

Roudiez, Leon S. "Problems of Point of View in the Early Fiction of Michel Butor." KRQ 18:155-159. No. 2, 1971.

Spencer, Michael. Michel Butor. New York: Twayne, 1974. pp. 82-95.

Sturrock, John. The French New Novel: Claude Simon, Michel Butor, Alain Robbe-Grillet. London: Oxford University Press, 1969. pp. 130-139.

Waelti-Walters, Jennifer. Michel Butor: A Study of His View of the World and a Panorama of His Work 1954-1974. Victoria: Sono Nis Press, 1977. pp. 96-108.

Walters, Jennifer R. "Butor's Use of Literary Texts in DEGRES." PMLA 88:311-320. March 1973.

DESCRIPTION DE SAN MARCO

Waelti-Walters, Jennifer. "The Architectural and Musical Influences on the Structure of Michel Butor's DESCRIPTION DE SAN MARCO." RLC 53:65-75. January/March, 1979.

PASSAGE DE MILAN

Field, Trevor. "Imagery of Shafts and Tubes in Butor's PASSAGE DE MILAN." MLR 70:760-763. October 1975.

Mason, Barbara. "The Symbolic Function of Birds, Names, Numbers, and Playing Cards in Michel Butor's PASSAGE DE MILAN." IFR 7:99-105. Summer 1980.

McWilliams, Dean. The Narratives of Michel Butor: The Writer as Janus. Columbus: Ohio University Press, 1978. pp. 12-21.

Mercier, Vivian. The New Novel from Queneau to Pinget. New York: Farrar, Straus & Giroux, 1971. pp. 226-239.

Roudiez, Leon S. "Problems of Point of View in the Early Fiction of Michel Butor." KRQ 18:147-152. No. 2, 1971.

Spencer, Michael. Michel Butor. New York: Twayne, 1974. pp. 33-46.

Sturrock, John. The French New Novel: Claude Simon, Michel Butor, Alain Robbe-Grillet. London: Oxford University Press, 1969. pp. 110-116.

Walters, Jennifer R. "Symbolism in PASSAGE DE MILAN." FR 42:223-232. December 1968.

PASSING TIME

Baguley, David. "The Reign of Chronos: (More) on Alchemy in Butor's L'EMPLOI DU TEMPS." FMLS 16:281-292. July 1980.

Britton, Celia. "The Status of Representation in Michel Butor's L'EMPLOI DU TEMPS and LA MODIFICATION." Journal of Beckett Studies 3:76-84. Summer 1978.

Davies, J. C. "Butor and the Power of Art: The Quest of Jacques Revel." AJFS 16:105-115. January/April 1979.

Faris, Wendy B. "Butor and Barth in the Labyrinth." FAR 3:23-29. Winter/Spring 1978-1979.

Howitt, J. B. "Michael Butor and Manchester." NFS 12:79-81. October 1973.

Kubinyi, Laura R. "Defense of a Dialogue: Michel Butor's PASSING TIME." Boundary 4:885-903. Spring 1976.

McWilliams, Dean. The Narratives of Michel Butor: The Writer as Janus. Columbus: Ohio University Press, 1978. pp. 22-31.

_____. "The Novelist as Archaeologist: Butor's L'EMPLOI DU TEMPS." ECr 15:367-376. Fall 1975.

Meakin, D. and E. Dand. "Alchemy and Optimism in Butor's L'EMPLOI DU TEMPS." FMLS 15:264-277. July 1979.

Mercier, Vivian. The New Novel from Queneau to Pinget. New York: Farrar, Straus & Giroux, 1971. pp. 239-249.

Minogue, Valerie. "Distortion and Creativity in the Subjective Viewpoint: Robbe-Grillet, Butor and Nathalie Sarraute." FMLS 12:42-45. January 1976.

O'Donnell, Thomas D. "Michel Butor's PASSING TIME and the Detective Hero." MDAC:211-220. 1973.

O'Neill, Kathleen. "On PASSING TIME." Mosaic 8:29-37. Fall 1974.

Roudiez, Leon S. "Problems of Point of View in the Early Fiction of Michel Butor." KRQ 18:152-153. No. 2, 1971.

Spencer, Michael. Michel Butor. New York: Twayne, 1974. pp. 47-63.

Spencer, M. C. "The Unfinished Cathedral: Michel Butor's L'EMPLOI DU TEMPS." EFL 6:81-99. November 1969.

Sturrock, John. The French New Novel: Claude Simon, Michel Butor, Alain Robbe-Grillet. London: Oxford University Press, 1969. pp. 116-125; 162-167.

Viswanathan, Jacqueline. "The Innocent Bystander: The Narrator's Position in Poe's 'The Fall of the House of Usher,' James's 'The Turn of the Screw' and Butor's L'EMPLOI DU TEMPS." HUSL 4:38-47. Spring 1976.

Waelti-Walters, Jennifer. Michel Butor: A Study of His View of the World and a Panorama of His Work 1954-1974. Victoria: Sono Nis Press, 1977. pp. 44-48.

Weinstein, Arnold. "Order and Excess in Butor's L'EMPLOI DU TEMPS." MFS 16:41-55. Spring 1970.

Witt, Susan C. "The Equivocal Truth." Mosaic 8:39-50. Fall 1974.

PORTRAIT DE L'ARTISTE EN JEUNE SINGE
    Dand, Eleanor and David Meakin. "A Problematic Initiation: Michel Butor's Alchemy Revisited." AJFS 14:313-329. September/December 1977.

Stary, Sonja G. "The Artist and the Monkey in Butor's PORTRAIT DE L'ARTISTE EN JEUNE SINGE." Symposium 34:68-81. Spring 1980.

Camus, Albert
    THE FALL
        Barchilon, Jose. "THE FALL by Albert Camus: A Psychoanalytic Study." International Journal of Psycho-Analysis 49:386-389. Parts 2 & 3, 1968.

_____. "A Study of Camus' Mythopoeic Tale THE FALL with Some Comments about the Origin of Esthetic Feelings." Journal of the American Psychoanalytic Association 19:193-239. April 1971.

Berets, Ralph. "Van Eyck's 'The Just Judges' in Camus' THE FALL." RS 42:112-122. June 1974.

Curtis, Jerry L. "Camus' Hero of Many Faces." SNNTS 6:88-97. Spring 1974.

Davison, Ray. "Clamence and Marmeladov: A Parallel." RomN 14:226-229. Winter 1972.

De Rycke, Robert M. "LA CHUTE: The Sterility of Guilt." RomN 10:197-203. Spring 1969.

Gifford, P. "Socrates in Amsterdam: The Uses of Irony in LA CHUTE." MLR 73:499-512. July 1978.

Hewitt, Nicholas. "LA CHUTE and LES TEMPS MODERNES." EFL 10:64-81. November 1973.

Johnson, Robert B. "Camus' LA CHUTE, or Montherlant s'éloigne." FR 44:1026-1032. May 1971.

Jones, Rosemarie. "Modes of Discourse in LA CHUTE." NFS 15:27-35. November 1976.

Keefe, Terry. "Camus's LA CHUTE: Some Outstanding Problems of Interpretation Concerning Clamence's Past." MLR 69:541-555. July 1974.

_____. "Clamence and Women in Albert Camus' LA CHUTE." MFS 25:646-651. Winter 1979-1980.

_____. "More on Clamence's Interlocutor in Albert Camus' LA CHUTE." RomN 16:552-558. Spring 1975.

Kirk, Irina. Dostoevskij and Camus: The Themes of Consciousness, Isolation, Freedom and Love. München: Fink, 1974. 144 pp.

_____. "Dramatization of Consciousness in Camus and Dostoevsky." BuR 16:96-104. March 1968.

_____. "Polemics and Art in Dostoevsky and Camus." NZSJ 8:62-71. Summer 1971.

Lakich, John J. "Tragedy and Satanism in Camus's LA CHUTE." Symposium 24:262-276. Fall 1970.

Lazere, Donald. The Unique Creation of Albert Camus. New Haven: Yale University Press, 1973. pp. 183-198.

Locke, F.W. "The Metamorphoses of Jean-Baptiste Clamence." Symposium 21:306-315. Winter 1967.

Madden, David. "Ambiguity in Albert Camus' THE FALL." MFS 12:461-472. Winter 1966-1967.

Masters, Brian. Camus: A Study. London: Heinemann, 1974. pp. 117-127.

*Moore, Harry T. Twentieth-Century French Literature Since World War II. Carbondale: Southern Illinois University Press, 1966. pp. 68-72.

O'Brien, Conor Cruise.  Albert Camus of Europe and Africa.  New York:  Viking Press, 1970.  pp. 61-106.

Onimus, Jean.  Albert Camus and Christianity.  University:  University of Alabama Press, 1970.  pp. 91-101.

Petersen, Carol.  Albert Camus.  New York:  Ungar, 1969.  pp. 99-102.

Petrey, Sandy.  "The Function of Christian Imagery in LA CHUTE."  TSLL 11:1445-1454.  Winter 1970.

Quilliot, Roger.  The Sea and Prisons:  A Commentary on the Life and Thought of Albert Camus.  University:  University of Alabama Press, 1970.  pp. 239-251.

Rhein, Phillip H.  Albert Camus.  New York:  Twayne, 1969.  pp. 104-115.

Rysten, Felix S. A.  False Prophets in the Fiction of Camus, Dostoevsky, Melville, and Others.  Coral Gables:  University of Miami Press, 1972.  pp. 52-70.

Sayre, Robert.  Solitude in Society:  A Sociological Study in French Literature.  Cambridge:  Harvard University Press, 1978.  pp. 166-175.

Snipes, Katherine.  "Intellectual Villains in Dostoyevsky, Chaucer and Albert Camus."  Discourse 13:240-250.  Spring 1970.

Sperber, Michael A.  "Camus' THE FALL:  The Icarus Complex."  AI 26:269-280.  Fall 1969.

_____.  "Symptoms and Structure of Borderline Personality Organization:  Camus' THE FALL and Dostoevsky's NOTES FROM UNDERGROUND."  L & P 23:103-108.  No. 3, 1973.

Whartenby, H. Allen.  "The Interlocutor in LA CHUTE:  A Key to Its Meaning."  PMLA 83:1326-1333.  October 1968.

THE PLAGUE

Batchelor, R.  "Unity of Tone in Albert Camus' LA PESTE."  FMLS 11:234-251.  July 1975.

Bernard, Mme Jacqueline.  "The Background of THE PLAGUE:  Albert Camus' Experience in the French Resistance."  KRQ 14:165-173.  No. 2, 1967.

Greene, Robert W.  "Fluency, Muteness and Commitment in Camus's LA PESTE."  FS 34:422-433.  October 1980.

Grobe, Edwin P. "Camus and the Parable of the Perfect Sentence." Symposium 24:254-261. Fall 1970.

Guers-Villate, Yvonne. "A Few Notes Concerning Rambert in THE PLAGUE." Renascence 22:218-222. Summer 1970.

Henninger, Francis J. "Plot-Theme Fusion in THE PLAGUE." MFS 19:216-221. Summer 1973.

Herlan, James J. "A Note on Father Paneloux." MLN 84:675-676. May 1969.

Hollahan, Eugene. "The Orpheus Allusion in EVELINA (1778) and LA PESTE." CLS 16:113-119. June 1979.

———. "The Path of Sympathy: Abstraction and Imagination in Camus' LA PESTE." SNNTS 8:377-393. Winter 1976.

Kellman, Steven G. "Singular Third Person: Camus's LA PESTE." KRQ 25:499-507. No. 4, 1978.

Kellogg, Jean. Dark Prophets of Hope: Dostoevsky, Sartre, Camus, Faulkner. Chicago: Loyola University Press, 1975. pp. 103-113.

Lazere, Donald. The Unique Creation of Albert Camus. New Haven: Yale University Press, 1973. pp. 173-182.

Lewis, Valerie H. "The Healer of the Plague." Standpunte 95:6-11. June 1971.

Masters, Brian. Camus: A Study. London: Heinemann, 1974. pp. 60-97.

McDaniel, Thomas R. "Bureaupathology in THE PLAGUE: On Learning About Administration from the Novel." SoQ 15:97-103. October 1976.

Moses, Edwin. "Functional Complexity: The Narrative Techniques of THE PLAGUE." MFS 20:419-429. Autumn 1974.

O'Brien, Conor Cruise. Albert Camus of Europe and Africa. New York: Viking Press, 1970. pp. 35-60.

O'Hanlon, Redmond. "The Rite of Friendship: An Analysis of the Bathing Scene in LA PESTE." ML 61:120-125. September 1980.

Palmer, R. Barton. "Counting Peas in Camus's LA PESTE." IFR 5:35-39. January 1978.

Petersen, Carol. Albert Camus. New York: Ungar, 1969. pp. 69-76.

Quilliot, Roger. The Sea and Prisons: A Commentary on the Life and Thought of Albert Camus. University: University of Alabama Press, 1970. pp. 136-157.

Rees, Garnet. Baudelaire, Sartre and Camus. Cardiff: University of Wales Press, 1976. pp. 52-73.

Rhein, Phillip H. Albert Camus. New York: Twayne, 1969. pp. 51-66.

Rocks, James E. "Camus Reads Defoe: A JOURNAL OF THE PLAGUE YEAR as a Source of THE PLAGUE." TSE 15:81-87. 1967.

Thomas, P. Aloysius. "Ideal Involvement: The Camusian Hero." LangQ 16:14-16; 20. Fall/Winter 1977.

THE STRANGER

Amash, Paul J. "The Choice of an Arab in L'ETRANGER." RomN 9:6-7. Autumn 1967.

Atkins, Anselm. "Fate and Freedom: Camus' THE STRANGER." Renascence 21:64-75; 110. Winter 1969.

Bersani, Leo. "The Stranger's Secrets." Novel 3:212-224. Spring 1970.

Brady, Patrick. "Manifestations of Eros and Thanatos in L'ETRANGER." TCL 20:183-188. July 1974.

Brady-Papadopoulou, Valentini. "Camus' Meursault: A 'Nocturnal' Being in a 'Diurnal' World." OL 35:74-82. No. 1, 1980.

Bree, Germaine. Camus and Sartre. New York: Delacorte, 1972. pp. 141-147.

Champigny, Robert J. A Pagan Hero: An Interpretation of Meursault in Camus' THE STRANGER. Philadelphia: University of Pennsylvania Press, 1969. 116 pp.

Curtis, Jerry L. "Camus' Outsider: Or, the Games People Play." SSF 9:379-386. Fall 1972.

_____. "Meursault or the Leap of Death." RUS 57:41-47. Spring 1971.

Elbrecht, Joyce. "THE STRANGER and Camus' Transcendental Existentialism." HSL 4:59-80. No. 1, 1972.

Falk, Eugene K. Types of Thematic Structure. Chicago: University of Chicago Press, 1967. pp. 52-116.

Fletcher, Dennis. "Camus Between Yes and No: A Fresh Look at the Murder in L'ETRANGER." Neophil 61:523-532. October 1977.

Fletcher, John. "Interpreting L'ETRANGER." FR 43: 158-167. Sp. Issue No. 1, Winter 1970.

──────. "Meursault's Rhetoric." CritQ 13:125-136. Summer 1971.

Fody, Michael, III. "LA FAMILIA DE PASCUAL DUARTE and L'ETRANGER: A Contrast." WVUPP 24:68-73. November 1977.

Forde, Marianna C. "Condemnation and Imprisonment in L'ETRANGER and LE DERNIER JOUR D'UN CONDAMNE." RomN 13:211-216. Winter 1971.

Gale, John E. "Does America Know THE STRANGER? A Reappraisal of a Translation." MFS 20:139-147. Summer 1974.

──────. "Meursault's Telegram." RomN 16:29-32. Autumn 1974.

Hackel, Sergei. "Raskolnikov Through the Looking-Glass: Dostoevsky and Camus's L'ETRANGER." ConL 9:189-209. Spring 1968.

Hanly, Jeri. "Bridging the Great Gap: L'ETRANGER and the High School Class." FR 49:476-482. March 1976.

Henry, Patrick. "Meursault as Antithesis of 'Homo Ludens' from J. Huizinga to Eric Berne." KRQ 21:365-374. No. 3, 1974.

──────. "Routine and Reflection in L'ETRANGER." EAS 4:1-7. May 1975.

──────. "Voltaire and Camus: The Limits of Reason and the Awareness of Absurdity." SVEC 138:117-175. 1975.

Hewitt, Nicholas. "LA CHUTE and LES TEMPS MODERNES." EFL 10:64-81. November 1973.

Hurley, C. Harold. "Is Joyce's 'A Painful Case' a Source for Camus' L'ETRANGER?" RomN 20:157-162. Winter 1979-1980.

Johnson, Patricia J. "Bergson's LE RIRE: Game Plan for Camus' L'ETRANGER?" FR 47:46-56. October 1973.

_____. "A Further Source for Camus' L'ETRANGER." RomN 11:465-468. Spring 1970.

_____. "Quote, Unquote: Direct Quotation as Anti-Literary Device in L'ETRANGER." RS 47:45-48. March 1979.

Johnson, Roger, Jr. "A Note on Camus's THE STRANGER." SoQ 10:41-42. October 1971.

Kellogg, Jean. Dark Prophets of Hope: Dostoevsky, Sartre, Camus, Faulkner. Chicago: Loyola University Press, 1975. pp. 92-96.

Lazere, Donald. The Unique Creation of Albert Camus. New Haven: Yale University Press, 1973. pp. 151-172.

Lehan, Richard. A Dangerous Crossing: French Literary Existentialism and the Modern American Novel. Carbondale: Southern Illinois University Press, 1973. pp. 56-68.

Leov, Nola M. "L'ETRANGER: The Case for the Defence." EFL 15:82-116. November 1978.

Madden, David. "Camus' THE STRANGER: An Achievement in Simultaneity." Renascence 20:186-197. Summer 1968.

_____. "James M. Cain's THE POSTMAN ALWAYS RINGS TWICE and Albert Camus's L'ETRANGER." PLL 6:407-419. Fall 1970.

*Marson, Eric. "Justice and the Obsessed Character in MICHAEL KOHLHAAS, DER PROZESS and L'ETRANGER." Seminar 2: 21-33. Fall 1966.

Massey, Irving. The Uncreating Word: Romanticism and the Object. Bloomington: Indiana University Press, 1970. 108 pp.

Masters, Brian. Camus: A Study. London: Heinemann, 1974. pp. 19-34.

Matthews, J. H. "From Naturalism to the Absurd: Edmond de Goncourt and Albert Camus." Symposium 22:241-255. Fall 1968.

O'Brien, Conor Cruise. Albert Camus of Europe and Africa. New York: Viking Press, 1970. pp. 1-34.

Onimus, Jean. Albert Camus and Christianity. University: University of Alabama Press, 1970. pp. 66-70.

Otten, Terry. "'Mamam' in Camus' THE STRANGER." CollL 2:105-111. Spring 1975.

Palmer, R. Barton. "THE MYTH OF SISYPHUS and THE STRANGER: Two Portraits of the Young Camus." IFR 7:123-125. Summer 1980.

Panter, James. "Remarks on a Phrase in Camus' L'ETRANGER." RomN 16:25-28. Autumn 1974.

Petersen, Carol. Albert Camus. New York: Ungar, 1969. pp. 44-50.

Pickens, Rupert T., and James D. Tedder. "Liberation in Suicide: Meursault in the Light of Dante." FR 41:524-531. February 1968.

Pratt, Bruce. "Epicureanism in L'ETRANGER." EFL 11:74-82. November 1974.

Purdy, Strother B. "AN AMERICAN TRAGEDY and L'ETRANGER." CL 19:252-268. Summer 1967.

Quilliot, Roger. The Sea and Prisons: A Commentary on the Life and Thought of Albert Camus. University: University of Alabama Press, 1970. pp. 69-83.

Redfern, W. D. "The Prisoners of Stendhal and Camus." FR 41:649-659. April 1968.

Rhein, Phillip H. Albert Camus. New York: Twayne, 1969. pp. 33-41.

Saint-Amour, David. "Underground with Meursault: Myth and Archetype in Camus's L'ETRANGER." IFR 4:110-118. July 1977.

St. Aubyn, F. C. "A Note on Nietzsche and Camus." CL 20:110-115. Spring 1968.

Savage, Catharine. "Tragic Values in THE STRANGER of Camus." LangQ 7:11-16. Fall/Winter 1968.

Sebba, Helen. "Stuart Gilbert's Meursault: A Strange 'Stranger.'" ConL 13:334-340. Summer 1972.

Sellin, Eric. "Meursault and Myshkin on Executions: A Parallel." RomN 10:11-14. Autumn 1968.

Shahbaz, Caterina. "Diversity and Unity in the Naming Technique of Camus' L'ETRANGER." LOS 7:177-187. 1980.

Slochower, Harry. "Camus' THE STRANGER: The Silent Society and the Ecstasy of Rage." AI 26:291-294. Fall 1969.

Smith, Albert B. "Eden as Symbol in Camus' L'ETRANGER." RomN 9:1-5. Autumn 1967.

Solomon, Robert C. "L'ETRANGER and the Truth." Philosophy and Literature 2:141-159. Fall 1978.

Somers, Paul P., Jr. "Camus 'Sí,' Sartre 'No.'" FR 42:693-700. April 1969.

Speer, David G. "Meursault's Newsclipping." MFS 14:225-229. Summer 1968.

Stamm, Julian L. "Camus' Stranger: His Act of Violence." AI 26:281-290. Fall 1969.

Sugden, Leonard W. "Meursault, an Oriental Sage." FR 47:197-207. Sp. Issue No. 6, Spring 1974.

Sutherland, Stewart R. "Imagination in Literature and Philosophy: A Viewpoint on Camus's L'ETRANGER." BJA 10:261-273. July 1970.

Thody, Philip. "Camus's L'ETRANGER Revisited." CritQ 21:61-69. Summer 1979.

Thomas, P. Aloysius. "The Positive Aspect of Violence in L'ETRANGER, Part II." LangQ 16:15-18. Spring/Summer 1978.

Wagner, C. Roland. "The Silence of THE STRANGER." MFS 16:27-40. Spring 1970.

Wagner, Monique. "Physical Malaise and Subconscious Death-Wish in L'ETRANGER." MichA 11:331-341. Winter 1979.

Warde, William B., Jr. "Contrapuntal Images in Camus' THE STRANGER." BSUF 20:60-67. Summer 1979.

Weitz, Morris. "The Coinage of Man: KING LEAR and Camus's L'ETRANGER." MLR 66:31-39. January 1971.

del Castillo, Michel
 TANGUY
  *Moore, Harry T. Twentieth-Century French Literature Since World War II. Carbondale: Southern Illinois University Press, 1966. pp. 78-90.

Cazotte, Jacques
  LE DIABLE AMOUREUX
    O'Reilly, Robert F. "Cazotte's LE DIABLE AMOUREUX
    and the Structure of Romance." Symposium 31:231-241.
    Fall 1977.

    Porter, Laurence M. "The Seductive Satan of Cazotte's
    LE DIABLE AMOUREUX." ECr 18:3-12. Summer
    1978.

Céard, Henry
  UNE BELLE JOURNEE
    Thomas, William W. "Henry Céard's UNE BELLE
    JOURNEE: Reduction and the Novel." NCFS 5:328-340.
    Spring/Summer 1977.

Céline, Louis-Ferdinand
  CASSE-PIPE
    Matthews, J. H. The Inner Dream: Céline as Novelist.
    Syracuse: Syracuse University Press, 1978. pp. 85-103.

    Thomas, Merlin. Louis-Ferdinand Céline. London:
    Faber & Faber, 1979. pp. 196-201.
  CASTLE TO CASTLE
    Bosmajian, Hamida. "Céline's CASTLE TO CASTLE:
    Everyman on a Roundtrip." Crit 14:49-62. No. 1,
    1972.

    Knapp, Bettina. Céline: Man of Hate. University:
    University of Alabama Press, 1974. pp. 181-200.

    Matthews, J. H. The Inner Dream: Céline as Novelist.
    Syracuse: Syracuse University Press, 1978. pp. 156-173.

    Thiher, Allen. Céline: The Novel as Delirium. New
    Brunswick: Rutgers University Press, 1972. pp. 175-183.

    Thomas, Merlin. Louis-Ferdinand Céline. London:
    Faber & Faber, 1979. pp. 209-220.
  DEATH ON THE INSTALLMENT PLAN
    Fraser, John. "The Darkest Journey: Céline's DEATH
    ON THE INSTALLMENT PLAN." WSCL 8:96-110.
    Winter 1967.

    Hayman, David. "The Broken Cranium--Headwounds in
    Zola, Rilke, Céline: A Study in Contrasting Modes."
    CLS 9:222-230. June 1972.

    _____. "Céline." IowaR 3:74-81. Spring 1972.

Hewitt, Nicholas. "Narration and Desolidarisation in Céline's MORT A CREDIT." EFL 12:59-69. November 1975.

Knapp, Bettina. Céline: Man of Hate. University: University of Alabama Press, 1974. pp. 61-85.

Matthews, J. H. The Inner Dream: Céline as Novelist. Syracuse: Syracuse University Press, 1978. pp. 5-7; 55-81; 103-105; 177-180.

O'Brien, Justin. The French Literary Horizon. New Brunswick: Rutgers University Press, 1967. pp. 259-262.

O'Connell, David. Louis-Ferdinand Céline. Boston: Twayne, 1976. pp. 26-27; 38-40; 80-91.

Reck, Rima Drell. "Céline and Wolfe: Toward a Theory of the Autobiographical Novel." MissQ 22:19-27. Winter 1968-1969.

Thiher, Allen. Céline: The Novel as Delirium. New Brunswick: Rutgers University Press, 1972. pp. 45-77.

Thomas, Merlin. Louis-Ferdinand Céline. London: Faber & Faber, 1979. pp. 63-78.

FAIRY TALE FOR ANOTHER TIME
Knapp, Bettina. Céline: Man of Hate. University: University of Alabama Press, 1974. pp. 147-156; 160-163.

Matthews, J. H. The Inner Dream: Céline as Novelist. Syracuse: Syracuse University Press, 1978. pp. 129-155; 177-179; 186-187.

O'Connell, David. Louis-Ferdinand Céline. Boston: Twayne, 1976. pp. 126-129.

Thiher, Allen. Céline: The Novel as Delirium. New Brunswick: Rutgers University Press, 1972. pp. 138-153.

GUIGNOL'S BAND
Knapp, Bettina. Céline: Man of Hate. University: University of Alabama Press, 1974. pp. 133-146; 172-175.

Matthews, J. H. The Inner Dream: Céline as Novelist. Syracuse: Syracuse University Press, 1978. pp. 104-129.

Nettelbeck, C. W. "The Antisemite and the Artist: Céline's Pamphlets and GUIGNOL'S BAND." AJFS 9: 180-189. May/August 1972.

O'Connell, David. Louis-Ferdinand Céline. Boston: Twayne, 1976. pp. 118-121.

Thiher, Allen. Céline: The Novel as Delirium. New Brunswick: Rutgers University Press, 1972. pp. 78-117.

_____. "The Yet To Be Salvaged Céline: GUIGNOL'S BAND." MFS 16:67-75. Spring 1970.

Thomas, Merlin. Louis-Ferdinand Céline. London: Faber & Faber, 1979. pp. 184-195.

JOURNEY TO THE END OF NIGHT
Fortier, Paul A. "Marxist Criticism of Céline's VOYAGE AU BOUT DE LA NUIT." MFS 17:268-272. Summer 1971.

Knapp, Bettina. Céline: Man of Hate. University: University of Alabama Press, 1974. pp. 22-51.

Matthews, J. H. The Inner Dream: Céline as Novelist. Syracuse: Syracuse University Press, 1978. pp. 28-54.

Mitterand, Henri. "Colonial Discourse in THE JOURNEY TO THE END OF THE NIGHT." Sub-Stance 15:21-28. 1976.

Nettelbeck, C. W. "From Inside Destitution: Céline's Bardamu and Ellison's Invisible Man." SoRA 7:246-253. No. 3, 1974.

O'Connell, David. Louis-Ferdinand Céline. Boston: Twayne, 1976. pp. 38-73.

Owen, Carys T. "Networks of Symbol in VOYAGE AU BOUT DE LA NUIT." FMLS 11:46-58. January 1975.

Solomon, Philip H. "The View from a Rump: America as Journey and Landscape of Desire in Céline's VOYAGE AU BOUT DE LA NUIT." YFS 57:5-22. 1979.

Thiher, Allen. "Céline and Sartre." PQ 50:292-305. April 1971.

_____. Céline: The Novel as Delirium. New Brunswick: Rutgers University Press, 1972. pp. 7-47.

Thomas, Merlin. Louis-Ferdinand Céline. London: Faber & Faber, 1979. pp. 43-62.

Widmer, Kingsley. "The Way Down to Wisdom of Louis-Ferdinand Céline." MinnR 8:85-91. No. 1, 1968.

NORTH
>Knapp, Bettina. Céline: Man of Hate. University: University of Alabama Press, 1974. pp. 201-221.

>Matthews, J. H. The Inner Dream: Céline as Novelist. Syracuse: Syracuse University Press, 1978. pp. 177-194.

>Thomas, Merlin. Louis-Ferdinand Céline. London: Faber & Faber, 1979. pp. 220-223.

RIGODON
>Knapp, Bettina. Céline: Man of Hate. University: University of Alabama Press, 1974. pp. 222-232.

>Matthews, J. H. The Inner Dream: Céline as Novelist. Syracuse: Syracuse University Press, 1978. pp. 195-210.

>Thiher, Allen. Céline: The Novel as Delirium. New Brunswick: Rutgers University Press, 1972. pp. 175-180; 186-190.

>Thomas, Merlin. Louis-Ferdinand Céline. London: Faber & Faber, 1979. pp. 223-234.

Challe, Robert
LES ILLUSTRES FRANÇOISES
>Forno, Lawrence J. "Challe's Portrayal of Women." FR 47:865-873. April 1974.

>————. "The Fictional Letter in the Memoir Novel: Robert Challe's ILLUSTRES FRANÇOISES." SVEC 81: 149-161. 1971.

>————. "The Rebirth of a Novelist: Robert Challe in 1973." FR 46:1138-1147. May 1973.

>————. Robert Challe: Intimations of the Enlightenment. Rutherford: Fairleigh Dickinson University Press, 1972. pp. 70-170.

>Root, Tamara Goldstein. "Epicurean Philosophy and the Realism of LES ILLUSTRES FRANÇOISES." FR 47: 31-37. Sp. Issue No. 6, Spring 1974.

>————. "The Notion of the Heroine in Robert Challe's LES ILLUSTRES FRANÇOISES." PFSCL 8:164-179. Winter 1977-1978.

>Showalter, English, Jr. "Did Robert Challe Write a Sequel to DON QUIXOTE?" RR 62:270-282. December 1971.

Challe, Robert

   . "Robert Challe and DON QUIXOTE." FR
  45:1136-1144. May 1972.

Chamson, André
 LES HOMMES DE LA ROUTE
  Rolfe, L. H. "André Chamson: LES HOMMES DE LA
  ROUTE." ML 49:32-35. March 1968.

Chateaubriand, François
 ATALA
  Beeker, Jon. "Archetype and Myth in Chateaubriand's
  ATALA." Symposium 31:93-106. Summer 1977.

  Lowrie, Joyce O. "Motifs of Kingdom and Exile in
  ATALA." FR 43:755-764. April 1970.

  Scanlan, Margaret. "'Le Vide Intérieur': Self and
  Consciousness in RENE, ATALA, and ADOLPHE."
  NCFS 8:30-36. Fall/Winter 1979-1980.

  Spininger, Dennis J. "The Paradise Setting of Chateaubriand's ATALA." PMLA 89:530-536. May 1974.

  Switzer, Richard. Chateaubriand. New York: Twayne,
  1971. pp. 42-48; 55-56.

  Ugrinsky, Alexej. "Chateaubriand and Pushkin: French
  and Russian Variations Upon a Theme by Guillaume
  Thomas Raynol." CLS 17:469-475. December 1980.
 LES AVENTURES DU DERNIER ABENCERAGE
  Street, Jack D. "A Statistical Study of the Vocabulary
  of Chateaubriand's LES AVENTURES DU DERNIER
  ABENCERAGE." FR 43:42-45. October 1969.
 THE GENIUS OF CHRISTIANITY
  Switzer, Richard. Chateaubriand. New York: Twayne,
  1971. pp. 58-75.
 THE MARTYRS
  Switzer, Richard. Chateaubriand. New York: Twayne,
  1971. pp. 76-80; 81-83; 87-88.
 THE NATCHEZ
  Painter, George D. Chateaubriand: A Biography. New
  York: Alfred A. Knopf, 1978. pp. 135-138; 203-205.

  Switzer, Richard. Chateaubriand. New York: Twayne,
  1971. pp. 76-81; 84-88.
 RENE
  Charlton, D. G. "The Ambiguity of Chateaubriand's
  RENE." FS 23:229-243. July 1969.

  Kuhn, Reinhard. The Demon of Noontide: Ennui in
  Western Literature. Princeton: Princeton University
  Press, 1976. pp. 199-213.

Scanlan, Margaret. "'Le Vide Intérieur': Self and Consciousness in RENE, ATALA, and ADOLPHE." NCFS 8:30-36. Fall/Winter 1979-1980.

Switzer, Richard. Chateaubriand. New York: Twayne, 1971. pp. 48-52.

Le Clézio, J. M. G.
THE FLOOD
Salij, H. Jathar. "J. M. G. Le Clézio's LE DELUGE and American Criticism." O&C 2:117-123. No. 2, 1978.

Coccioli, Carlo
MANUEL LE MEXICAIN
Ziolkowski, Theodore. Fictional Transfigurations of Jesus. Princeton: Princeton University Press, 1972. pp. 161-170.

Cocteau, Jean
LES ENFANTS TERRIBLES
Kaplan, Jane P. "Complexity of Character and the Overlapping of a Single Personality in Cocteau's LES ENFANTS TERRIBLES." AJFS 12:89-104. January/April 1975.

Maclean, Mary. "The Artificial Paradise and the Lost Paradise: Baudelairian Themes in Cocteau's LES ENFANTS TERRIBLES." AJFS 12:57-88. January/April 1975.

McNab, James P. "Mythical Space in LES ENFANTS TERRIBLES." FR 47:162-170. Sp. Issue No. 6, Spring 1972.

Roudiez, Leon S. "Cocteau's LES ENFANTS TERRIBLES as a Blind Text." Mosaic 5:159-166. Spring 1972.
THOMAS THE IMPOSTER
*Bancroft, David. "The Poetic Wonderland of Cocteau's THOMAS L'IMPOSTEUR." AJFS 3:36-50. January/April 1966.

Colette
LE BLE EN HERBE
Fischler, Alexander. "Unity in Colette's LE BLE EN HERBE." MLQ 30:248-264. June 1969.
CHERI
Stewart, Joan Hinde. "Colette and the Hallowing of Age." RomN 20:172-177. Winter 1979-1980.
DUO
Stewart, Joan Hinde. "Colette's Gynaeceum: Regression and Renewal." FR 53:662-669. April 1980.

LA FIN DE CHERI
    Stewart, Joan Hinde. "Colette and the Hallowing of Age." RomN 20:172-177. Winter 1979-1980.
LA LUNE DE PLUIE
    Norell, Donna. "Belief and Disbelief: Structure as Meaning in Colette's LA LUNE DE PLUIE." ECr 18: 62-75. Summer 1978.
MITSOU
    Stewart, Joan Hinde. "Colette: The Mirror Image." FrF 3:195-204. September 1978.
LE TOUTOUNIER
    Stewart, Joan Hinde. "Colette's Gynaeceum: Regression and Renewal." FR 53:662-669. April 1980.
LA VAGABONDE
    Stewart, Joan Hinde. "Colette: The Mirror Image." FrF 3:195-204. September 1978.

Constant, Benjamin
ADOLPHE
    Baguley, David. "The Role of Letters in Constant's ADOLPHE." FMLS 11:29-35. January 1975.

    Booker, John T. "The Implied 'Narrataire' in ADOLPHE." FR 51:666-673. April 1978.

    Callen, A. "L'IMMORALISTE as a Modern ADOLPHE." MLQ 31:450-460. December 1970.

    Fairlie, Alison. "The Art of Constant's ADOLPHE: The Stylization of Experience." MLR 62:31-47. January 1967.

    _____. "Framework as a Suggestive Art in Constant's ADOLPHE (with remarks on its relation to Chateaubriand's RENE)." AJFS 16:6-16. January/April 1979.

    Hemmings, F. W. J. "Constant's ADOLPHE: Internal and External Chronology." NCFS 7:153-164. Spring/Summer 1979.

    Hobson, Marian. "Theme and Structure in Adolphe." MLR 66:306-314. April 1971.

    Hoisington, Sona S. "EUGENE ONEGIN: Product of or Challenge to ADOLPHE?" CLS 14:205-213. September 1977.

    Hyslop, Lois Boe. "ADOLPHE: 'Aimer' or 'Etre aimé'?" FR 50:572-578. March 1977.

    Jones, Grahame C. "The Devaluation of Action in Constant's ADOLPHE." AJFS 16: 17-26. January/April 1979.

Mercken-Spaas, Godelieve. "'Ecriture' in Constant's ADOLPHE." FR 47:57-62. Sp. Issue No. 6, Spring 1974.

―――――. "From 'amour de soi' to 'amour passion': Rousseau's Conceptual Categories Exemplified in Constant's ADOLPHE." RR 66:93-99. March 1975.

―――――. "The Gaze and Threat of Death in Constant's ADOLPHE." Neophil 59:352-356. July 1975.

―――――. "The Metaphor of Space in Constant's ADOLPHE." NCFS 5:186-195. Spring/Summer 1977.

Morrison, Ian R. "Emotional Involvement and the Failure of Analysis in ADOLPHE." Neophil 60:334-341. July 1976.

Scanlan, Margaret. "'Le Vide Intérieur': Self and Consciousness in RENE, ATALA, and ADOLPHE." NCFS 8:30-36. Fall/Winter 1979-1980.

Scott, Malcolm. "The Romanticism of ADOLPHE." NFS 6:58-66. October 1967.

Sutton, Howard. "Two 'Confessions': ADOLPHE and DOMINIQUE." ASLHM 40:85-98. 1969.

Thomas, Ruth P. "The Ambiguous Narrator of ADOLPHE." RomN 14:486-495. Spring 1973.

Todorov, Tzvetan. "The Discovery of Language: LES LIAISONS DANGEREUSES and ADOLPHE." YFS 45:113-126. 1970.

DOMINIQUE
Sutton, Howard. "Two 'Confessions': ADOLPHE and DOMINIQUE." ASLHM 40:85-98. 1969.

De Couvray, Louvet
LES AMOURS DU CHEVALIER DE FAUBLAS
Davies, S. F. "Louvet as Social Critic: LES AMOURS DU CHEVALIER DE FAUBLAS." SVEC 183:223-237. 1980.

Crébillon, Claude de
ATHENIAN LETTERS
*Cherpack, Clifton. An Essay on Crébillon fils. Durham: Duke University Press, 1962. pp. 136-148.
LES EGAREMENTS DU COEUR ET DE L'ESPRIT
*Cherpack, Clifton. An Essay on Crébillon fils. Durham: Duke University Press, 1962. pp. 81-93.

Conroy, Peter V., Jr. "Crébillon fils: Techniques of the Novel." SVEC 99:75-141. 1972.

Crébillon, Claude de

> Free, Lloyd Raymond. "Crébillon fils, Laclos, and the Code of the Libertine." EC Life 1:36-40. December 1974.
>
> Jones, James F., Jr. "Visual Communication in LES EGAREMENTS DU COEUR ET DE L'ESPRIT." SVEC 120:319-328. 1974.
>
> Smith, Peter Lester. "Duplicity and Narrative Technique in the 'Roman Libertin.'" KRQ 25:72-74. No. 1, 1978.
>
> LES HEUREUX ORPHELINS
> > Kent, John P. "Crébillon fils, Mrs. Eliza Haywood and LES HEUREUX ORPHELINS: A Problem of Authorship." RomN 11:326-332. Winter 1969.
>
> LETTRES DE LA DUCHESSE DE * * * AU DUC DE * * *
> > *Cherpack, Clifton. An Essay on Crébillon fils. Durham: Duke University Press, 1962. pp. 123-136.
>
> LETTRES DE LA MARQUISE DE M. AU COMTE DE R.
> > *Cherpack, Clifton. An Essay on Crébillon fils. Durham: Duke University Press, 1962. pp. 112-123.
>
> > Conroy, Peter V., Jr. "Crébillon fils: Techniques of the Novel." SVEC 99:16-74. 1972.
>
> LE SOPHA, CONTE MORAL
> > Conroy, Peter V., Jr. "Crébillon fils: Techniques of the Novel." SVEC 99:143-224. 1972.
> >
> > Palmer, Benjamin W. "The Two Introductions to LE SOPHA of Crébillon fils." Lang Q 13:5-6. Fall/Winter 1974.

Cyrano de Bergerac, Savinien see de Bergerac, Savinien Cyrano

Darien, George
> BIRIBI
> > Redfern, W. D. "Exile and Exaggeration: George Darien's BIRIBI." Mosaic 8:161-175. Spring 1975.

Daudet, Alphonse
> L'EVANGELISTE
> > Roche, Alphonse. Alphonse Daudet. Boston: Twayne, 1976. pp. 71-74; 157-158.
>
> FROMONT JEUNE ET RISLER AINE
> > Haig, Stirling. "The Blue Illusion of FROMONT JEUNE ET RISLER AINE." NCFS 6:111-117. Fall/Winter 1977-1978.
> >
> > Roche, Alphonse. Alphonse Daudet. Boston: Twayne, 1976. pp. 51-54.
>
> L'IMMORTEL
> > Roche, Alphonse. Alphonse Daudet. Boston: Twayne, 1976. pp. 88-92.
>
> KINGS IN EXILE

Roche, Alphonse. *Alphonse Daudet.* Boston: Twayne, 1976. pp. 53-54; 63-66.
THE NABAB
    Roche, Alphonse. *Alphonse Daudet.* Boston: Twayne, 1976. pp. 57-63; 143-145.
NUMA ROUMESTAN
    Roche, Alphonse. *Alphonse Daudet.* Boston: Twayne, 1976. pp. 66-71; 142-144; 147-153.
LA PETITE PAROISSE
    Roche, Alphonse. *Alphonse Daudet.* Boston: Twayne, 1976. pp. 17-21; 111-114.
PORT TARASCON
    Roche, Alphonse. *Alphonse Daudet.* Boston: Twayne, 1976. pp. 94-100.
SAPHO
    Roche, Alphonse. *Alphonse Daudet.* Boston: Twayne, 1976. pp. 75-82.
TARTARIN OVER THE ALPS
    Roche, Alphonse. *Alphonse Daudet.* Boston: Twayne, 1976. pp. 46-50; 80-84; 147-150.
LE TRESOR D'ARLATAN
    Grant, Richard B. "Alphonse Daudet's LE TRESOR D'ARLATAN and the Quest for Self-Understanding." *FR* 53:651-661. April 1980.

Denon, Vivant
    POINT DE LENDEMAIN
        Free, Lloyd R. "Point of View and Narrative Space in Vivant Denon's POINT DE LENDEMAIN." *SVEC* 163:89-115. 1976.

        Nowinski, Judith. *Baron Dominique Vivant Denon (1747-1825): Hedonist and Scholar in a Period of Transition.* Rutherford: Fairleigh Dickinson University Press, 1970. pp. 115-207.

Derrida, Jacques
    GLAS
        Hartman, Geoffrey H. "Monsieur Texte: On Jacques Derrida, His GLAS." *GaR* 29:759-793. Winter 1975.

Desnos, Robert
    DEVIL POUR DEVIL
        Caws, Mary Ann. "Techniques of Alienation in the Early Novels of Robert Desnos." *MLQ* 28:473-477. December 1967.
    LA LIBERTE OU L'AMOUR
        Caws, Mary Ann. "Techniques of Alienation in the Early Novels of Robert Desnos." *MLQ* 28:473-477. December 1967.

Diderot, Denis
    LES BIJOUX INDISCRETS
        Adams, David. "Experiment and Experience in LES BIJOUX INDISCRETS." *SVEC* 182:303-317. 1979.

Berry, David. "The Technique of Literary Digression in the Fiction of Diderot." SVEC 118:183-194. 1974.

Creech, James. "Language and Desire in LES BIJOUX INDISCRETS." E Cent 20:182-198. Spring 1979.

Fellows, Otis. Diderot. Boston: Twayne, 1977. pp. 43-47.

──────. "Metaphysics and the BIJOUX INDISCRETS: Diderot's Debt to Prior." SVEC 56:509-540. 1967.

Greenberg, Irwin L. "Narrative Technique and Literary Intent in Diderot's LES BIJOUX INDISCRETS and JACQUES LE FATALISTE." SVEC 79:93-101. 1971.

──────. "The SUPPLEMENT AU VOYAGE DE BOUGAINVILLE and Chapter XVIII of the BIJOUX INDISCRETS." KRQ 15:231-236. No. 3, 1968.

McFadden, Judith. "LES BIJOUX INDISCRETS: A Deterministic Interpretation." SVEC 116:109-135. 1973.

Smith, Peter Lester. "Duplicity and Narrative Technique in the 'Roman Libertin.'" KRQ 25:70-72. No. 1, 1978.

Thomas, Ruth P. "LES BIJOUX INDISCRETS as a Laboratory for Diderot's Later Novels." SVEC 135:199-211. 1975.

JACQUES LE FATALISTE

Adams, D. J. "Style and Social Ideas in JACQUES LE FATALISTE." SVEC 124:231-248. 1974.

Berry, David. "The Technique of Literary Digression in the Fiction of Diderot." SVEC 118:223-257. 1974.

Bonneville, Douglas A. "Two Examples of Time-Technique in JACQUES LE FATALISTE." RomN 8:217-220. Spring 1967.

Brogyanyi, Gabriel John. "The Functions of Narration in Diderot's JACQUES LE FATALISTE." MLN 89:550-559. May 1974.

Cherpack, Clifton. "JACQUES LE FATALISTE and LE COMPERE MATHIEU." SVEC 73:165-191. 1970.

Fellows, Otis. Diderot. Boston: Twayne, 1977. pp. 130-142.

──────. "JACQUES LE FATALISTE Revisited." ECr 8:42-52. Spring 1968.

Greenberg, Irwin L. "Destination in JACQUES LE FATALISTE." SVEC 120:223-226. 1974.

―――. "Manipulation in Diderot's JACQUES LE FATALISTE ET SON MAITRE." RomN 16:605-610. Spring 1975.

―――. "Narrative Technique and Literary Intent in Diderot's LES BIJOUX INDISCRETS and JACQUES LE FATALISTE." SVEC 79:93-101. 1971.

Kavanagh, Thomas M. "The Vacant Mirror: A Study of Mimesis Through Diderot's JACQUES LE FATALISTE." SVEC 104:11-179. 1973.

Mautner, Stephen. "The Story of the Compromised Author: Parabasis in Friedrich Schlegel and Denis Diderot." CLS 16:28-31. March 1979.

O'Gorman, Donal. "Hypotheses for a New Reading of JACQUES LE FATALISTE." DidS 19:129-143. 1978.

Thomas, Ruth P. "JACQUES LE FATALISTE, LES LIAISONS DANGEREUSES and the Autonomy of the Novel." SVEC 117:239-249. 1974.

―――. "LE ROMAN COMIQUE and JACQUES LE FATALISTE: Some Parallels." FR 47:13-24. October 1973.

Werner, Stephen. "Diderot's Great Scroll: Narrative Art in JACQUES LE FATALISTE." SVEC 128:13-148. 1975.

RAMEAU'S NEPHEW

Barzun, Jacques. "The Mystery in RAMEAU'S NEPHEW." DidS 17:109-116. 1973.

Berry, David. "The Technique of Literary Digression in the Fiction of Diderot." SVEC 118:207-221. 1974.

Brady, Patrick. "Structure and Sub-structure of LE NEVEU DE RAMEAU." ECr 8:34-41. Spring 1968.

Bremner, Geoffrey. "Contradictions in Diderot's Scientific Philosophy and LE NEVEU DE RAMEAU." FS 34:153-167. April 1980.

Creech, James. "LE NEVEU DE RAMEAU: The 'Diary' of a Reading." MLN 95:995-1004. May 1980.

Fellows, Otis. Diderot. Boston: Twayne, 1977. pp. 88-95.

Freud, Hilde H. "Palissot and 'Les Philosophes.'"
DidS 9:189-217. 1967.

Hill, Emita B. "The Role of 'le monstre' in Diderot's
Thought." SVEC 97:223-241. 1972.

Josephs, Herbert. Diderot's Dialogue of Language and
Gesture: LE NEVEU DE RAMEAU. Columbus: Ohio
State University Press, 1969. 201 pp.

Kaplan, James M. "Notes on LE NEVEU DE RAMEAU." RomN 20:68-74. Fall 1979.

Kouidis, Apostolos P. "THE PRAISE OF FOLLY:
Diderot's Model for LE NEVEU DE RAMEAU." SVEC
185:237-266. 1980.

Mall, James. "LE NEVEU DE RAMEAU and the Idea
of Genius." ECS 11:26-39. Fall 1977.

Marsland, Amy L. "Identity and Theme in LE NEVEU
DE RAMEAU." RR 60:34-46. February 1969.

O'Gorman, Donal. "Myth and Metaphor in RAMEAU'S
NEPHEW." DidS 17:117-130. 1973.

Perkins, M. L. "Motivation and Behavior in the NEVEU
DE RAMEAU." SVEC 140:85-106. 1975.

Plotkin, Frederick. "Diderot's Nephew and the Mimics
of Enlightenment." CentR 13:409-423. Fall 1969.

_____. "Mime as Pander: Diderot's NEVEU DE
RAMEAU." SVEC 70:27-41. 1970.

Sherman, Carol. "The NEVEU DE RAMEAU and the
Grotesque." RomN 16:103-108. Autumn 1974.

Siegel, June Sigler. "Lovelace and Rameau's Nephew:
Roots of Poetic Amoralism." DidS 19:163-174. 1978.

Slusser, George Edgar. "LE NEVEU DE RAMEAU and
Hoffmann's Johannes Kreisler: Affinities and Influences."
CL 27:327-343. Fall 1975.

Wachs, Morris. "The Identity of the 'renêgat d'Avignon'
in the NEVEU DE RAMEAU." SVEC 90:1747-1756. 1972.

*Wilson, W. D. "A Hidden Parable in the NEVEU DE
RAMEAU?" RF 78:115-118. No. 1, 1966.

LA RELIGIEUSE

Anderson, David L. "The Stigma of Illegitimacy Resolved, or Suzanne Starved to Life." KRQ 23:495-501.
No. 4, 1976.

Berry, David. "The Technique of Literary Digression in the Fiction of Diderot." SVEC 118:195-205. 1974.

Block, C. Joel. "The 'Unnatural' versus the 'Natural' in LA RELIGIEUSE and LE SUPPLEMENT AU VOYAGE DE BOUGAINVILLE." SVEC 124:249-252. 1974.

Edmiston, William F. "Sacrifice and Innocence in LA RELIGIEUSE." DidS 19:67-84. 1978.

Josephs, Herbert. "Diderot's LA RELIGIEUSE: Libertinism and the Dark Cave of the Soul." MLN 91:734-755. May 1976.

Stewart, Philip. "A Note on Chronology in LA RELIGIEUSE." RomN 12:149-156. Autumn 1970.

Thomas, Ruth P. "Montesquieu's Harem and Diderot's Convent: The Woman as Prisoner." FR 52:36-45. October 1978.

SUPPLEMENT AU VOYAGE DE BOUGAINVILLE
McDonald, Christie V. "The Reading and Writing of Utopia in Denis Diderot's SUPPLEMENT AU VOYAGE DE BOUGAINVILLE." SFS 3:248-253. November 1976.

Perkins, M. L. "Community Planning in Diderot's SUPPLEMENT AU VOYAGE DE BOUGAINVILLE." KRQ 21:399-417. No. 4, 1974.

Whatley, Janet S. "'Un Retour secret vers la forêt': The Problem of Privacy and Order in Diderot's Tahiti." KRQ 24:199-208. No. 2, 1977.

Drieu La Rochelle, Pierre
LE FEU FOLLET
Thiher, Allen. "LE FEU FOLLET: The Drug Addict as a Tragic Hero." PMLA 88:34-40. January 1973.

Duhamel, Georges
THE PASQUIER CHRONICLES
Knapp, Bettina. Georges Duhamel. New York: Twayne, 1972. pp. 104-127.
SALAVIN'S JOURNAL
Knapp, Bettina. Georges Duhamel. New York: Twayne, 1972. pp. 72-75.

Dujardin, Edouard
LES LAURIERS SONT COUPES
Alexander, Theodor W. and Beatrice W. "Schnitzler's LEUTNANT GUSTL and Dujardin's LES LAURIERS SONT COUPES." MAL 2:7-15. Summer 1969.

Dumas père
COUNT OF MONTE CRISTO

Hemmings, F. W. J. Alexandre Dumas: The King of
Romance. New York: Charles Scribner's Sons, 1979.
pp. 125-130.

Marinetti, Amelita. "Death, Resurrection, and Fall in
Dumas' COMTE DE MONTE-CRISTO." FR 50:260-269.
December 1976.

Stowe, Richard S. Alexandre Dumas père. Boston:
Twayne, 1976. pp. 116-126.
L'ORFEVRE DU ROI
  Switzer, Richard. "Cellini, Berlioz, Dumas and the
  Foundry." NCFS 8:252-257. Spring/Summer 1980.
LA REINE MARGOT
  Stowe, Richard S. Alexandre Dumas père. Boston:
  Twayne, 1976. pp. 85-92.
THE THREE MUSKETEERS
  Stowe, Richard S. Alexandre Dumas père. Boston:
  Twayne, 1976. pp. 66-75.
TWENTY YEARS AFTER
  Stowe, Richard S. Alexandre Dumas père. Boston:
  Twayne, 1976. pp. 75-81.

Duras, Marguerite
L'APRES-MIDI DE MONSIEUR ANDESMAS
  Cismaru, Alfred. Marguerite Duras. New York:
  Twayne, 1971. pp. 100-108.

  Savage, Catharine. "A Stylistic Analysis of L'APRES-
  MIDI DE MONSIEUR ANDESMAS by Marguerite Duras."
  Lang & S 2:51-62. Winter 1969.
UN BARRAGE CONTRE LA PACIFIQUE
  Cismaru, Alfred. Marguerite Duras. New York:
  Twayne, 1971. pp. 34-46.
DESTROY, SHE SAID
  McWilliams, Dean. "The Novelist as Filmmaker:
  Marguerite Duras' DESTROY, SHE SAID." LFQ 3:264-
  269. Summer 1975.
DIX HEURES ET DEMIE DU SOIR EN ETE
  Cagnon, Maurice. "Marguerite Duras: Willed Imagina-
  tion as Release and Obstacle." NFS 16:55-64. May
  1977.

  Cismaru, Alfred. "DIX HEURES ET DEMIE DU SOIR
  EN ETE." CimR 17:27-32. October 1971.

  _____. Marguerite Duras. New York: Twayne,
  1971. pp. 95-100.

  Heck, Francis S. "DIX HEURES ET DEMIE DU SOIR
  EN ETE: The Heroine as Artist, a New Dimension."
  RomN 16:249-253. Winter 1975.

Murphy, Carol J. "Thematic and Textual Violence in Duras' DIX HEURES ET DEMIE DU SOIR EN ETE." ECr 19:75-84. Summer 1979.
LE MARIN DE GIBRALTER
Cismaru, Alfred. Marguerite Duras. New York: Twayne, 1971. pp. 46-53.
MODERATO CANTABILE
Bassoff, Bruce. "Death and Desire in Marguerite Duras' MODERATO CANTABILE." MLN 94:720-729. May 1979.

Bishop, Lloyd. "The Banquet Scene in MODERATO CANTABILE: A Stylistic Analysis." RR 69:222-235. May 1979.

———. "Classical Structure and Style in MODERATO CANTABILE." FR 47:219-234. Sp. Issue No. 6, Spring 1974.

Champagne, Roland A. "An Incantation of the Sirens: The Structure of MODERATO CANTABILE." FR 48:981-989. May 1975.

Cismaru, Alfred. Marguerite Duras. New York: Twayne, 1971. pp. 88-95.

Weiss, Victoria L. "Form and Meaning in Marguerite Duras' MODERATO CANTABILE." Crit 16:79-87. No. 1, 1974.

Zepp, Evelyn H. "Language as Ritual in Marguerite Duras's MODERATO CANTABILE." Symposium 30:236-259. Fall 1976.
OURIKA
O'Connell, David. "OURIKA: Black Face, White Mask." FR 47:47-56. Sp. Issue No. 6, Spring 1974.

Switzer, Richard. "Mme de Staël, Mme de Duras and the Question of Race." KRQ 20:303-316. No. 3, 1973.
LES PETITS CHEVAUX DE TARQUINIA
Cismaru, Alfred. Marguerite Duras. New York: Twayne, 1971. pp. 55-63.
THE RAVISHING OF LOL V. STEIN
Andermatt, Verena. "Rodomontages of LE RAVISSEMENT DE LOL V. STEIN." YFS 57:23-35. 1979.

Cismaru, Alfred. Marguerite Duras. New York: Twayne, 1971. pp. 108-112.

Enright-Clark Shoukri, Doris. "The Nature of Being in Woolf and Duras." ConL 12:323-328. Summer 1971.
LE SQUARE
Cismaru, Alfred. Marguerite Duras. New York: Twayne, 1971. pp. 82-88.

Duras, Marguerite

LE VICE-CONSUL
Block, C. Joel. "Narrative and Point of View in LE VICE-CONSUL of Marguerite Duras." HUSL 4:114-123. Spring 1976.

Cismaru, Alfred. Marguerite Duras. New York: Twayne, 1971. pp. 112-116.

LA VIE TRANQUILLE
Cismaru, Alfred. Marguerite Duras. New York: Twayne, 1971. pp. 28-34.

Ernst, Max
UNE SEMAINE DE BONTE
Hubert, Renee Riese. "The Fabulous Fiction of Two Surrealist Artists: Giorgio de Chirico and Max Ernst." NLH 4:158-166. Autumn 1972.

Etiemble, René
BLASON D'UN CORPS
Peschel, Enid Rhodes. "Etiemble: The Novelist as Healer." LangQ 12:39-42. Fall/Winter 1973.
L'ENFANT DE CHOEUR
Peschel, Enid Rhodes. "Etiemble: The Novelist as Healer." LangQ 12:35-37. Fall/Winter 1973.
PEAUX DE COULEUVRE
Peschel, Enid Rhodes. "Etiemble: The Novelist as Healer." LangQ 12:37-39. Fall/Winter 1973.

Fénelon, François de
LES AVENTURES DE TELEMAQUE
Davis, James Herbert, Jr. Fénelon. Boston: Twayne, 1979. pp. 90-111.

Gilroy, James P. "Peace and the Pursuit of Happiness in the French Utopian Novel: Fénelon's TELEMAQUE and Prévost's CLEVELAND." SVEC 176:169-187. 1979.

Scaldini, Richard J. "LES AVENTURES DE TELEMAQUE, or Alienated in Ogygia." YFS 57:164-179. 1979.

Whatley, Janet. "Coherent Worlds: Fénelon's TELEMAQUE and Marivaux's TELEMAQUE TRAVESTI." SVEC 171:85-113. 1977.

Finas, Lucette
DONNE
Brée, Germaine. "Lucette Finas: An Introduction." ConL 19:300-319. Summer 1978.

Flaubert, Gustave
BOUVARD AND PECUCHET
Bart, Benjamin F. Flaubert. Syracuse: Syracuse University Press, 1967. pp. 587-620.

Bernheimer, Charles. "Linguistic Realism in Flaubert's BOUVARD ET PECUCHET." Novel 7:143-158. Winter 1974.

*Brombert, Victor. The Novels of Flaubert: A Study of Themes and Techniques. Princeton: Princeton University Press, 1966. pp. 258-281.

Cross, Richard K. Flaubert and Joyce: The Rite of Fiction. Princeton: Princeton University Press, 1971. pp. 153-173.

Gaillard, Françoise. "An Unspeakable (Hi)story." YFS 59:137-154. 1980.

Hill, Leslie. "Flaubert and the Rhetoric of Stupidity." CritI 3:336-344. Winter 1976.

Huss, Roger. "Nature, Final Causality and Anthropocentrism in Flaubert." FS 33:288-304. July 1979.

*Jackson, Ernest. The Critical Reception of Gustave Flaubert in the United States. The Hague: Mouton, 1966. pp. 90-105.

Martin, George. "Friendship--Basic Theme of BOUVARD ET PECUCHET and EN ATTENDANT GODOT." LangQ 14:43-46. Spring/Summer 1976.

Nadeau, Maurice. The Greatness of Flaubert. New York: The Library Press, 1972. pp. 261-279.

Redfern, Walter D. "People and Things in Flaubert." FR 44:83-88. Winter 1971.

Starkie, Enid. Flaubert: The Master. New York: Atheneum, 1971. pp. 307-335.
HERODIAS
Bart, Benjamin F. Flaubert. Syracuse: Syracuse University Press, 1967. pp. 698-704.

*Brombert, Victor. The Novels of Flaubert: A Study of Themes and Techniques. Princeton: Princeton University Press, 1966. pp. 246-257.

Duncan, Phillip A. "The Equation of Theme and Spatial Form in Flaubert's HERODIAS." SSF 14:129-136. Spring 1977.

O'Connor, John R. "Flaubert: TROIS CONTES and the Figure of the Double Cone." PMLA 95:822-824. October 1980.

Wake, C. H. "Symbolism in Flaubert's HERODIAS: An Interpretation." FMLS 4:322-329. October 1968.

Zants, Emily. "TROIS CONTES: A New Dimension in Flaubert." NFS 18:37-44. May 1979.

THE LEGEND OF SAINT JULIAN

Bancroft, W. Jane. "Flaubert's LEGENDE DE SAINT JULIEN: The Duality of the Artist-Saint." ECr 10:75-84. Spring 1970.

Bart, Benjamin F. Flaubert. Syracuse: Syracuse University Press, 1967. pp. 670-686.

_____. "Flaubert and Hunting: LA LEGENDE DE ST-JULIEN L'HOSPITALIER." NCFS 4:31-52. Fall/Winter 1975-1976.

_____. "Psyche into Myth: Humanity and Animality in Flaubert's SAINT-JULIEN." KRQ 20:317-341. No. 3, 1973.

Bart, Benjamin F. and Robert Francis Cook. The Legendary Sources of Flaubert's SAINT JULIEN. Toronto: University of Toronto Press, 1977. 177 pp.

Bart, Heidi Culbertson and Benjamin F. Bart. "Space, Time, and Reality in Flaubert's SAINT JULIEN." RR 59:30-39. February 1968.

*Brombert, Victor. The Novels of Flaubert: A Study of Themes and Techniques. Princeton: Princeton University Press, 1966. pp. 217-232.

Duckworth, Colin. "Flaubert and the Legend of St Julian: A Non-exclusive View of Sources." FS 22:107-113. April 1968.

Gervais, David. Flaubert and Henry James. London: Macmillan, 1978. pp. 143-146.

McCrady, James Waring. "The Saint Julien Window at Rouen as a Source for Flaubert's LEGENDE DE SAINT JULIEN L'HOSPITALIER." RomN 10:268-276. Spring 1969.

O'Connor, John R. "Flaubert: TROIS CONTES and the Figure of the Double Cone." PMLA 95:817-822. October 1980.

Pilkington, A. E. "Point of View in Flaubert's LA LEGENDE DE SAINT JULIEN." FS 29:266-279. July 1975.

Sherzer, Dina. "Narrative Figures in LA LEGENDE DE SAINT JULIEN L'HOSPITALIER." Genre 7:54-66. March 1974.

Zants, Emily. "TROIS CONTES: A New Dimension in Flaubert." NFS 18:37-44. May 1979.

MADAME BOVARY

Barber, Raymond E. "Capernaum and the Lame and the Blind: A Complex Metaphor." IFR 5:124-128. July 1978.

Bart, Benjamin F. Flaubert. Syracuse: Syracuse University Press, 1967. pp. 315-366.

Bersani, Leo. "The Anxious Imagination." PR 35:57-66. Winter 1968.

_____. "Flaubert and Emma Bovary: The Hazards of Literary Fusion." Novel 8:16-28. Fall 1974.

_____. "Flaubert: The Politics of Mystical Realism." MR 11:35-47. Winter 1970.

*Brombert, Victor. The Novels of Flaubert: A Study of Themes and Techniques. Princeton: Princeton University Press, 1966. pp. 37-91.

Brown, James W. "A Note on Kitchens in MADAME BOVARY." LangQ 17:55-56. Fall/Winter 1978.

Church, Margaret. "A Triad of Images: Nature in MADAME BOVARY." Mosaic 5:203-213. Spring 1972.

Cross, Richard K. Flaubert and Joyce: The Rite of Fiction. Princeton: Princeton University Press, 1971. pp. 71-121.

Culler, Jonathan. Flaubert: The Uses of Uncertainty. London: Paul Elek, 1974. pp. 138-147; 187-198.

Daniels, Graham. "Emma Bovary's Opera--Flaubert, Scott and Donizetti." FS 32:285-303. July 1978.

Duncan, Phillip A. "Charles 'Bovaryste': Romantic Prefiguration in MADAME BOVARY." SAB 44:11-19. November 1979.

Evans, William M. "The Question of Emma's Eyes." RomN 16:274-277. Winter 1975.

Furst, Lilian R. "The Role of Food in MADAME BOVARY." OL 34:53-65. No. 1, 1979.

Gale, John E. "Sainte-Beuve and Baudelaire on MADAME BOVARY." FR 41:30-37. October 1967.

Garrett, Peter K. Scene and Symbol from George Eliot to James Joyce. New Haven: Yale University Press, 1969. pp. 68-74.

Gervais, David. Flaubert and Henry James. London: Macmillan, 1978. pp. 32-117.

──────. "James's Reading of MADAME BOVARY." CQ 7:1-26. 1976.

Gill, Richard. "The Soundtrack of MADAME BOVARY: Flaubert's Orchestration of Aural Imagery." LFQ 1:206-217. Summer 1973.

Goodhand, Robert. "Emma Bovary, the Baker's Paramour." RUS 59:37-41. Summer 1973.

Goodheart, Eugene. "Flaubert and the Powerlessness of Art." CentR 19:157-166. Summer 1975.

Gray, Eugene F. "Emma by Twilight: Flawed Perception in MADAME BOVARY." NCFS 6:231-240. Spring/Summer 1978.

Greene, Robert W. "Clichés, Moral Censure, and Heroism in Flaubert's MADAME BOVARY." Symposium 32:289-302. Winter 1978.

Hagan, John. "Une Ruse de Style: A Pattern of Allusion in MADAME BOVARY." SNNTS 1:6-16. Spring 1969.

Haig, Stirling. "The MADAME BOVARY Blues." RR 61:27-34. February 1970.

Hamilton, James F. "The Anti-Rousseauism of MADAME BOVARY." RomN 21:68-72. Fall 1980.

Hemmings, F. W. J. "Emma and the 'Maw of Wifedom.'" ECr 10:13-23. Spring 1970.

Hollahan, Eugene. "Irruption of Nothingness: Sleep and Freedom in MADAME BOVARY." SP 70:92-107. January 1973.

Hyslop, Lois Boe. "Baudelaire: 'Madame Bovary, C'est moi'?" KRQ 20:343-358. No. 3, 1973.

*Jackson, Ernest. The Critical Reception of Gustave

Flaubert in the United States. The Hague: Mouton and Co., 1966. pp. 51-82.

Kirton, W. J. S. "Flaubert's Use of Sound in MADAME BOVARY." FMLS 11:36-45. January 1975.

Lowe, A. M. "Emma Bovary, a Modern Arachne." FS 26:30-41. January 1972.

Mall, Rita S. "The Dream-Merchants: Musicians in MADAME BOVARY." HSL 11:185-195. No. 3, 1979.

Martin, Catherine Matthews. "Looking for Lestiboudois." RomN 17:152-155. Winter 1976.

McConnell, Frank D. "Félicité, Passion, Ivresse: The Lexicography of MADAME BOVARY." Novel 3:153-166. Winter 1970.

Mein, Margaret. A Foretaste of Proust: A Study of Proust and His Precursors. Westmead: Saxon House, 1974. pp. 162-176.

Nadeau, Maurice. The Greatness of Flaubert. New York: The Library Press, 1972. pp. 107-143.

Niess, Robert J. "On Listening to Homais." FR 51: 22-28. October 1977.

Peterson, Carla L. "Reading and Imagining in MADAME BOVARY." KRQ 27:163-178. No. 2, 1980.

Porter, Dennis. "Gustave Flaubert's Middle-Class Tragedy." FMLS 13:61-68. January 1977.

Redfern, Walter D. "People and Things in Flaubert." FR 44:79-88. Winter 1971.

Sachs, Murray. "The Role of the Blind Beggar in MADAME BOVARY." Symposium 22:72-80. Spring 1968.

St. Aubyn, F. C. "Madame Bovary Outside the Window." NCFS 1:105-111. Winter 1973.

Schor, Naomi. "Details and Decadence: End-Troping in MADAME BOVARY." Sub-stance 26:27-35. 1980.

Sherrington, R. J. Three Novels by Flaubert: A Study of Techniques. Oxford: Clarendon Press, 1970. pp. 79-152.

Shriver, M. "MADAME BOVARY versus THE WOMAN OF ROME." NCFS 1:197-209. Summer 1973.

Shukis, David T. "The Dusty World of MADAME BOVARY." NCFS 7:213-219. Spring/Summer 1979.

Smalley, Barbara. George Eliot and Flaubert: Pioneers of the Modern Novel. Athens: Ohio University Press, 1974. pp. 1-10; 51-123.

Spiegel, Alan. "Flaubert to Joyce: Evolution of a Cinematographic Form." Novel 6:230-233. Spring 1973.

Stephens, Doris. "A Focus on Fingernails in MADAME BOVARY." RomN 12:74-77. Autumn 1970.

Terdiman, Richard. The Dialectics of Isolation: Self and Society in the French Novel from the Realists to Proust. New Haven: Yale University Press, 1976. pp. 65-68.

Thornton, Lawrence. "The Fairest of Them All: Modes of Vision in MADAME BOVARY." PMLA 93:982-991. October 1978.

Topazio, Virgil W. "Emma vs Madame Bovary." RUS 57:103-112. Spring 1971.

Turner, Alison M. "Why Emma? Subtlety and Subtitle in MADAME BOVARY." RomN 20:51-57. Fall 1979.

Virtanen, Reino. "A Possible Source for a Passage of MADAME BOVARY." RomN 11:302-304. Winter 1969.

Weinberg, Henry H. "The Function of Italics in MADAME BOVARY." NCFS 3:97-111. Fall/Winter 1974-1975.

_____. "The 'style direct libre': a Variant of the 'style indirect libre' in MADAME BOVARY." RPac 4:23-29. Spring 1978.

Wetherill, P. M. "MADAME BOVARY's Blind Man: Symbolism in Flaubert." RR 61:35-42. February 1970.

Wiedner, Elsie M. "Emma Bovary and Hedda Gabler: A Comparative Study." MLS 8:56-64. Fall 1978.

Williams, D. A. "Generalizations in MADAME BOVARY." Neophil 62:492-502. October 1978.

_____. Psychological Determinism in MADAME BOVARY. Hull: University of Hull, 1973. 81 pp.

_____. "The Role of Binet in MADAME BOVARY." RR 71:149-166. March 1980.

_____. "Water Imagery in MADAME BOVARY."
FMLS 13:70-84. January 1977.

Williams, John R. "Flaubert and the Religion of Art."
FR 41:38-47. October 1967.
NOVEMBRE
Bart, Benjamin F. Flaubert. Syracuse: Syracuse University Press, 1967. pp. 75-77.

Diamond, Marie J. Flaubert: The Problem of Aesthetic Discontinuity. Port Washington: Kennikat Press, 1975. pp. 47-75.

Starkie, Enid. Flaubert: The Making of the Master. New York: Atheneum, 1967. pp. 73-89.
SALAMMBO
Bart, Benjamin F. Flaubert. Syracuse: Syracuse University Press, 1967. pp. 393-436.

_____. "Louis Bouilhet and the Redaction of SALAMMBO." Symposium 27:197-213. Fall 1973.

Brady, Patrick. "Archetypes and the Historical Novel: The Case of SALAMMBO." SFR 1:313-324. Winter 1977.

*Brombert, Victor. The Novels of Flaubert: A Study of Themes and Techniques. Princeton: Princeton University Press, 1966. pp. 92-124.

Culler, Jonathan. Flaubert: The Uses of Uncertainty. London: Paul Elek, 1974. pp. 212-227.

Dugan, J.R. "Flaubert's SALAMMBO, a Study in Immobility." ZFSL 79:193-206. September 1969.

Forrest-Thomson, Veronica. "The Ritual of Reading SALAMMBO." MLR 67:787-798. October 1972.

Godfrey, Sima. "The Fabrication of SALAMMBO: The Surface of the Veil." MLN 95:1005-1016. May 1980.

Green, Anne. "Salammbô and the Myth of Pasiphaë."
FS 32:170-178. April 1978.

*Jackson, Ernest. The Critical Reception of Gustave Flaubert in the United States. The Hague: Mouton, 1966. pp. 83-89.

Jay, Bruce Louis. "Anti-History and the Method of SALAMMBO." RR 63:20-33. February 1972.

Kennard, Lindsay C. "The Idology of Violence in Flaubert's SALAMMBO." Trivium 13:53-61. May 1978.

Koelb, Clayton and Reena Spicehandler. "The Influence of Flaubert's SALAMMBO on Mann's JOSEPH UND SEINE BRÜDER." CLS 13:315-322. December 1976.

Leal, R. B. "SALAMMBO: An Aspect of Structure." FS 27:16-29. January 1973.

Nadeau, Maurice. The Greatness of Flaubert. New York: The Library Press, 1972. pp. 159-174.

Porter, Dennis. "Aestheticism versus the Novel: The Example of SALAMMBO." Novel 4:101-106. Winter 1971.

_____. "Critical Exchange--SALAMMBO: A Rebuttal." Novel 6:70-72. Fall 1972.

Rose, Marilyn Gaddis. "Critical Exchange--SALAMMBO: A Meaningful Novel." Novel 6:66-69. Fall 1972.

_____. "Decadent Prose: The Example of SALAMMBO." NCFS 3:213-223. Spring/Summer 1975.

Sherrington, R. J. Three Novels by Flaubert: A Study of Techniques. Oxford: Clarendon Press, 1970. pp. 153-231.

Shroder, Maurice Z. "On Reading SALAMMBO." ECr 10:24-35. Spring 1970.

Starkie, Enid. Flaubert: The Master. New York: Atheneum, 1971. pp. 55-85.

Strong, Isabelle. "Deciphering the SALAMMBO Dossier: Appendix 4 of the 'Club de l'Honnête Homme' Edition." MLR 72:538-554. July 1977.

A SENTIMENTAL EDUCATION

Bart, Benjamin F. Flaubert. Syracuse: Syracuse University Press, 1967. pp. 474-540.

Bersani, Leo. "Flaubert: The Politics of Mystical Realism." MR 11:47-50. Winter 1970.

Brombert, Victor. "Flaubert and the Impossible Artist-Hero." SoR 5:976-986. October 1969.

* _____. The Novels of Flaubert: A Study of Themes and Techniques. Princeton: Princeton University Press, 1966. pp. 125-185.

Coates, Carrol F. "Daumier and Flaubert: Examples of Graphic and Literary Caricature." NCFS 4:303-311. Spring 1976.

Cortland, Peter. "Homecoming: The Fate of the Flaubertian Hero." BSUF 9:10-18. Spring 1968.

Culler, Jonathan. Flaubert: The Uses of Uncertainty. London: Paul Elek, 1974. pp. 94-107; 147-156.

Danahy, Michael. "Chronoscapes in L'EDUCATION SENTIMENTALE." AJFS 15:253-265. September/December 1978.

_____. "The Esthetics of Documentation: The Case of L'EDUCATION SENTIMENTALE." RomN 14:61-65. Autumn 1972.

_____. "Flaubert Describes." KRQ 26:359-374. No. 3, 1979.

_____. "Narrative Timing and the Structures of L'EDUCATION SENTIMENTALE." RR 66:32-46. January 1975.

Demorest, Jean-Jacques. "Flaubert's First SENTIMENTAL EDUCATION." ASLHM 38:97-110. 1967.

Denommé, Robert T. "Flaubert's Portrayal of Mood and Temperament in L'EDUCATION SENTIMENTALE." NCFS 7:59-75. Fall/Winter 1978-1979.

_____. "The Theme of Disintegration in Flaubert's EDUCATION SENTIMENTALE." KRQ 20:163-171. No. 2, 1973.

Diamond, Marie J. Flaubert: The Problem of Aesthetic Discontinuity. Port Washington: Kennikat Press, 1975. pp. 76-104.

Diaz, Nancy Gray. "Imagery and the Theme of Perception: L'EDUCATION SENTIMENTALE and NIEBLA." CLS 17:429-437. December 1980.

Engelberg, Edward. "Hemingway's 'True Penelope': Flaubert's L'EDUCATION SENTIMENTALE and A FAREWELL TO ARMS." CLS 16:189-206. September 1979.

Fairlie, Alison. "Some Patterns of Suggestion in L'EDUCATION SENTIMENTALE." AJFS 6:266-293. May/December 1969.

Gans, Eric. "EDUCATION SENTIMENTALE: The Hero as Storyteller." MLN 89:614-625. May 1974.

Gerhardi, Gerhard C. "Romantic Love and the Prosti-

tution of Politics: On the Structural Unity in L'EDU-
CATION SENTIMENTALE." SNNTS 4:402-415. Fall
1972.

Gervais, David. Flaubert and Henry James. London:
Macmillan, 1978. pp. 198-223.

Grover, P.R. "Two Modes of Possessing: THE
PRINCESS OF CASAMASSIMA and L'EDUCATION
SENTIMENTALE." MLR 66:760-771. October 1971.

*Jackson, Ernest. The Critical Reception of Gustave
Flaubert in the United States. The Hague: Mouton,
1966. pp. 90-105.

Lebowitz, Naomi. Humanism and the Absurd in the
Modern Novel. Evanston: Northwestern University
Press, 1971. pp. 23-44.

Miller, Marcia K. "A Note on Structure and Theme in
L'EDUCATION SENTIMENTALE." SIR 10:130-136.
Spring 1971.

Nadeau, Maurice. The Greatness of Flaubert. New
York: The Library Press, 1972. pp. 49-61; 175-195.

*Raitt, A.W. Life and Letters in France: The Nine-
teenth Century. New York: Charles Scribner's Sons,
1965. pp. 75-83.

Redfern, Walter D. "People and Things in Flaubert."
FR 44:82-88. Winter 1971.

Seaton, Beverly. "Mirror Imagery and Related Concepts
in L'EDUCATION SENTIMENTALE." RomN 11:46-50.
Autumn 1969.

Sherrington, R.J. "Louise Roque and L'EDUCATION
SENTIMENTALE." FS 25:427-435. October 1971.

_____. Three Novels by Flaubert: A Study of Tech-
niques. Oxford: Clarendon Press, 1970. pp. 232-335.

Smalley, Barbara. George Eliot and Flaubert: Pioneers
of the Modern Novel. Athens: Ohio University Press,
1974. pp. 108-114.

Starkie, Enid. Flaubert: The Making of the Master.
New York: Atheneum, 1967. pp. 103-119.

_____. Flaubert: The Master. New York: Athen-
eum, 1971. pp. 140-178.

Thiher, Roberta Joyce. "Dehumanization Through Style." RomN 10:265-267. Spring 1969.

Unwin, Timothy A. "The Significance of the Encounter with the Dog in Flaubert's First EDUCATION SENTIMENTALE." FrF 4:232-237. September 1979.

Williams, D. A. "Determinism in the First EDUCATION SENTIMENTALE." FMLS 7:101-108. April 1971.

_____. "Sacred and Profane in L'EDUCATION SENTIMENTALE." MLR 73:786-798. October 1978.

A SIMPLE HEART

Bart, Benjamin F. Flaubert. Syracuse: Syracuse University Press, 1967. pp. 686-697.

Beck, William J. "Félicité and the Bull in Flaubert's UN COEUR SIMPLE." XUS 10:17-26. Spring 1971.

_____. "Flaubert's UN COEUR SIMPLE: The Path to Sainthood?" XUS 7:59-67. July 1968.

*Brombert, Victor. The Novels of Flaubert: A Study of Themes and Techniques. Princeton: Princeton University Press, 1966. pp. 233-245.

Denommé, Robert T. "Félicité's View of Reality and the Nature of Flaubert's Irony in UN COEUR SIMPLE." SSF 7:573-581. Fall 1970.

de Dobay-Rifelj, Carol. "Doors, Walls, and Barriers in Flaubert's UN COEUR SIMPLE." SSF 11:291-295. Summer 1974.

Gervais, David. Flaubert and Henry James. London: Macmillan, 1978. pp. 138-142.

Kuhn, Reinhard. The Demon of Noontide: Ennui in Western Literature. Princeton: Princeton University Press, 1976. pp. 264-269.

Mall, James P. "Flaubert's UN COEUR SIMPLE, Myth and the Genealogy of Religion." AUMLA 47:39-47. May 1977.

O'Connor, John R. "Flaubert: TROIS CONTES and the Figure of the Double Cone." PMLA 95:813-817. October 1980.

Smalley, Barbara. George Eliot and Flaubert: Pioneers of the Modern Novel. Athens: Ohio University Press, 1974. pp. 115-123.

Uitti, Karl D. "Figures and Fiction: Linguistic Deformation and the Novel." KRQ 17:160-169. No. 2, 1970.

Wake, C. H. "Flaubert's Search for an Identity: Some Reflections on UN COEUR SIMPLE." FR 44:89-96. Sp. Issue No. 2, Winter 1971.

Willenbrink, George A. The Dossier of Flaubert's UN COEUR SIMPLE. Amsterdam: Rodopi, 1976. 247 pp.

Winner, Anthony. "Flaubert's Félicité." Mosaic 10:57-68. Fall 1976.

Zants, Emily. "TROIS CONTES: A New Dimension in Flaubert." NFS 18:37-44. May 1979.

THE TEMPTATION OF ST. ANTHONY

Bernheimer, Charles. "'Etre la matière': Origin and Difference in Flaubert's LA TENTATION DE SAINT ANTOINE." Novel 10:65-78. Fall 1976.

*Brombert, Victor. The Novels of Flaubert: A Study of Themes and Techniques. Princeton: Princeton University Press, 1966. pp. 186-216.

Cross, Richard K. Flaubert and Joyce: The Rite of Fiction. Princeton: Princeton University Press, 1971. pp. 125-149.

Culler, Jonathan. Flaubert: The Uses of Uncertainty. London: Paul Elek, 1974. pp. 180-184.

Diamond, Marie J. Flaubert: The Problem of Aesthetic Discontinuity. Port Washington: Kennikat Press, 1975. pp. 105-131.

*Jackson, Ernest. The Critical Reception of Gustave Flaubert in the United States. The Hague: Mouton, 1966. pp. 83-89.

Nadeau, Maurice. The Greatness of Flaubert. New York: The Library Press, 1972. pp. 62-74.

Porter, Laurence M. "The Devil as Double in Nineteenth-Century Literature: Goethe, Dostoevsky, and Flaubert." CLS 15:325-329. September 1978.

_____. "A Fourth Version of Flaubert's TENTATION DE SAINT ANTOINE (1869)." NCFS 4:53-66. Fall/Winter 1975-1976.

Starkie, Enid. Flaubert: The Making of the Master. New York: Atheneum, 1967. pp. 159-166.

_____. Flaubert: The Master. New York: Atheneum, 1971. pp. 213-228.

Zants, Emily. "Flaubert's TENTATION: An Escape from Power Over Others." FR 52:604-610. March 1979.

TROIS CONTES
Beck, William J. "Flaubert's Tripartite Concept of History and TROIS CONTES." CLAJ 21:74-78. September 1977.

Cross, Richard K. Flaubert and Joyce: The Rite of Fiction. Princeton: Princeton University Press, 1971. pp. 17-34.

Sachs, Murray. "Flaubert's TROIS CONTES: The Reconquest of Art." ECr 10:62-74. Spring 1970.

Starkie, Enid. Flaubert: The Master. New York: Atheneum, 1971. pp. 244-274.

des Forêts, Louis-René
LE BAVARD
Ungar, Steven. "Rules of the Game: First-Person Singular in des Forêts' LE BAVARD." ECr 20:66-77. Fall 1980.

Fougeret de Monbron, Jean-Louis
MARGOT LA RAVAUDEUSE
Pizzorusso, Arnaldo. "Situations and Environment in MARGOT LA RAVAUDEUSE." YFS 40:142-155. 1968.

Fouqué, Baron de la Motte
UNDINE
Lillyman, W. J. "Fouqué's UNDINE." SIR 10:94-104. Spring 1971.

McHaney, Thomas L. "Fouqué's UNDINE and Edith Wharton's CUSTOM OF THE COUNTRY." RLC 45:180-186. April/June 1971.

France, Anatole
THE AMETHYST RING
*Raitt, A. W. Life and Letters in France: The Nineteenth Century. New York: Charles Scribner's Sons, 1965. pp. 162-169.

Virtanen, Reino. Anatole France. New York: Twayne, 1968. pp. 109-112.
BOOK OF MY FRIEND
Virtanen, Reino. Anatole France. New York: Twayne, 1968. pp. 13-24.
THE CRIME OF SYLVESTER BONNARD

France, Anatole

Virtanen, Reino. Anatole France. New York: Twayne, 1968. pp. 47-51.
DESIRES OF JEAN SERVIEN
Virtanen, Reino. Anatole France. New York: Twayne, 1968. pp. 51-54.
ELM ON THE MALL
Virtanen, Reino. Anatole France. New York: Twayne, 1968. pp. 105-108.
THE GODS ARE ATHIRST
Tylden-Wright, David. Anatole France. New York: Walker & Company, 1967. pp. 277-281.

Virtanen, Reino. Anatole France. New York: Twayne, 1968. pp. 135-150.
M. BERGERET IN PARIS
Virtanen, Reino. Anatole France. New York: Twayne, 1968. pp. 111-115.
PENGUIN ISLAND
Virtanen, Reino. Anatole France. New York: Twayne, 1968. pp. 128-134.
THE REVOLT OF THE ANGELS
Virtanen, Reino. Anatole France. New York: Twayne, 1968. pp. 150-156.
LES SEPT FEMMES DE LA BARBE-BLEUE
Levy, Diane Wolfe. Techniques of Irony in Anatole France: Essay on LES SEPT FEMMES DE LA BARBE-BLEUE. Chapel Hill: University of North Carolina Press, 1978. 144 pp.
THAÏS
Booth, Wayne C. "Irony and Pity Once Again: THAÏS Revisited." CritI 2:327-344. Winter 1975.

*Hartley, Kelver. "A Spanish Source for Anatole France's THAÏS." AJFS 3:105-109. January/April 1966.

Virtanen, Reino. Anatole France. New York: Twayne, 1968. pp. 54-60.

Franconi, Gabriel-Tristan
UNTEL DE L'ARMEE FRANÇAISE
Klein, Holger. "Projections of Everyman: The Common Soldier in Franconi, Wiechert and Williamson." The First World War in Fiction: A Collection of Critical Essays. ed. Holger Klein. London: Macmillan, 1976. pp. 84-100.

Fromentin, Eugene
DOMINIQUE
Armstrong, Judith. The Novel of Adultery. London: Macmillan, 1976. pp. 88-92.

Bremner, Geoffrey. "Ambivalence in DOMINIQUE." FMLS 5:323-330. October 1969.

Grant, Richard B. and Nelly H. Severin. "Weaving Imagery in Fromentin's DOMINIQUE." NCFS 1:155-161. May 1973.

Hubert, Renée Riese. "Fromentin's DOMINIQUE: The Confession of a Man Who Judges Himself." PMLA 82: 634-639. December 1967.

Latiolais, F. M. "'Not Quite a Masterpiece'--Fromentin's DOMINIQUE Reconsidered." Mosaic 4:35-48. Fall 1970.

Magowan, Robin. "DOMINIQUE: The Genesis of a Pastoral." ECr 13:340-350. Winter 1973.

Mein, Margaret. A Foretaste of Proust: A Study of Proust and His Precursors. Westmead: Saxon House, 1974. pp. 143-160.

_____. "Fromentin, a Precursor of Proust." FMLS 7:221-236. July 1971.

Furetière, Antoine
ROMAN BOURGEOIS
  Thiher, Roberta J. "The Depersonalized World of the ROMAN BOURGEOIS." RomN 11:127-129. Autumn 1969.

  Wine, Kathleen. "Furetière's ROMAN BOURGEOIS: The Triumph of Process." ECr 19:50-63. Spring 1979.

Gautier, Théophile
ARRIA MARCELLA
  Smith, Albert B. "The Changing Ideal in Two of Gautier's Fictional Narratives." RR 60:168-173. October 1969.
LE CAPITAINE FRACASSE
  Grant, Richard B. Théophile Gautier. Boston: Twayne, 1975. pp. 146-157.

  Rossiter, Andrew. "Metamorphosis and the Second Self in Gautier's LE CAPITAINE FRACASSE." FMLS 11:213-226. July 1975.
MADEMOISELLE DE MAUPIN
  Brians, Paul. "Sexuality and the Opposite Sex: Variations on a Theme by Théophile Gautier and Anaïs Nin." ELWIU 4:122-136. Spring 1977.

  Grant, Richard B. Théophile Gautier. Boston: Twayne, 1975. pp. 34-42; 47-49.

  Smith, Albert B. "Gautier's MADEMOISELLE DE MAUPIN: The Quest for Happiness." MLQ 32:168-174. June 1971.

Gautier, Théophile
"MADEMOISELLE DE MAUPIN, Chapter XI: Plot, Character, Literary Theory." KRQ 25:245-256. No. 3, 1978.

Tennant, P. E. Théophile Gautier. London: The Athlone Press, 1975. pp. 59-60; 87-89; 117-118.

LA MORTE AMOUREUSE
Smith, Albert B. "The Changing Ideal in Two of Gautier's Fictional Narratives." RR 60:168-173. October 1969.

SPIRITE
Lowin, Joseph G. "Two 'Inédits' of Théophile Gautier: Letters to Carlotta Grisi à Propos of His Novel SPIRITE." RomN 16:54-56. Autumn 1974.

Genevoix, Maurice
RABOLIOT
Walling, J. J. "RABOLIOT: A Major French Regional Novel." ML 55:182-188. December 1974.

Gennari, Genevieve
LA FUGUE IRLANDAISE
Robinson, Jean Hardy. "Poetic and Philosophic Counterpoint in Gennari's LA FUGUE IRLANDAISE." ECr 19: 85-94. Summer 1979.

Gide, André
THE CAVES OF THE VATICAN
Atkinson, John Keith. "LES CAVES DU VATICAN and Bergson's LE RIRE." PMLA 84:328-335. March 1969.

Bell, W. M. L. "Convention and Plausibility in LES CAVES DU VATICAN." AJFS 7:76-92. January/August 1970.

Bettinson, C. D. "Gide and Religious Conversion: The Case of LES CAVES DU VATICAN." FMLS 12:105-117. April 1976.

Bettinson, Christopher. Gide: A Study. London: Heinemann, 1977. pp. 35-52.

Bettinson, C. D. "Gide's Use of Technical Vocabulary-- A Note on the Disability of Anthime Armand-Dubois." ML 53:112-115. September 1972.

Bettinson, C. D. and L. J. Newton. "Gide, Zola and the Legacy of Naturalism in LES CAVES DU VATICAN." Neophil 60:200-204. April 1976.

Green, Mary Jean. "The Legacy of LES CAVES DU VATICAN." KRQ 26:113-121. No. 1, 1979.

\*Grieve, James A. "Lafcadio: A Reappraisal." AJFS 3:22-35. January/April 1966.

Guerard, Albert J. André Gide. Cambridge: Harvard University Press, 1969. pp. 82-84; 128-138; 195-197.

Ireland, G. W. André Gide: A Study of His Creative Writings. Oxford: Clarendon Press, 1970. pp. 249-273.

Kloss, Robert J. "The Gratuitous Act: Gide's Lafcadio Reconsidered." PsyR 64:111-134. Spring 1977.

McClelland, John. "The Lexicon of LES CAVES DU VATICAN." PMLA 89:256-267. March 1974.

Peters, Arthur King. Jean Cocteau and André Gide: An Abrasive Friendship. New Brunswick: Rutgers University Press, 1973. pp. 194-195; 198-201.

Steel, D. A. "'Lafcadio Ludens': Ideas of Play and Levity in LES CAVES DU VATICAN." MLR 66:554-564. July 1971.

Strauss, George. "The Original Juste-Agénor: An Unpublished Fragment of LES CAVES DU VATICAN." AJFS 7:9-15. January/August 1970.

\*Watson, Graeme. "Protos." AJFS 3:16-21. January/April 1966.

CORYDON

Ireland, G. W. André Gide: A Study of His Creative Writings. Oxford: Clarendon Press, 1970. pp. 309-325.

O'Brien, Justin. The French Literary Horizon. New Brunswick: Rutgers University Press, 1967. pp. 73-74.

Stoltzfus, Ben. Gide's Eagles. London: Fiffer and Simons, 1969. pp. 15-16.

THE COUNTERFEITERS

Barry, Catherine A. "Some Transpositions of Dostoevsky in LES FAUX-MONNAYEURS." FR 45:580-587. February 1972.

Bettinson, Christopher. Gide: A Study. London: Heinemann, 1977. pp. 67-86.

Bouraoui, H. A. "Gide's LES FAUX-MONNAYEURS: Hidden Metaphor and the Pure Novel." AJFS 8:15-35. January/April 1971.

Bree, Germaine. "THE COUNTERFEITERS." Gide:

A Collection of Critical Essays. ed. David Littlejohn. Englewood Cliffs: Prentice-Hall, 1970. pp. 112-128.

Brosman, Catharine Savage. "The Novelist as Natural Historian in LES FAUX-MONNAYEURS." EFL 14:48-59. November 1977.

_____. "The Relativization of Character in LES FAUX-MONNAYEURS." MLR 69:770-778. October 1974.

Davies, J. C. "Sincerity and Self-delusion in LES FAUX-MONNAYEURS." AJFS 7:123-141. January/August 1970.

Derome, R. F. "Some Reflections on Gide's LES FAUX-MONNAYEURS. An Attempt at a 'Mise au Point.'" ML 56:185-188. December 1975.

Fletcher, D. J. "The Epic Strain in LES FAUX-MONNAYEURS." MLR 72:53-61. January 1977.

Garzilli, Enrico. Circles Without Center: Paths to the Discovery and Creation of Self in Modern Literature. Cambridge: Harvard University Press, 1972. pp. 118-127.

Grieve, James. "A Footnote to LES FAUX-MONNAYEURS." AJFS 7:142-148. January/August 1970.

* _____. "Love in the Work of André Gide." AJFS 3:162-179. May/August 1966.

Guerard, Albert J. André Gide. Cambridge: Harvard University Press, 1969. pp. 148-174.

Haberstich, David. "Gide and the Fantasts: The Nature of Reality and Freedom." Criticism 11:140-150. Spring 1969.

Ireland, G. W. André Gide: A Study of His Creative Writings. Oxford: Clarendon Press, 1970. pp. 340-376.

Kadish, Doris Y. "Structures of Criminality in Gide's LES FAUX-MONNAYEURS." KRQ 25:95-107. No. 1, 1978.

Landy, Marcia. "Gide's Pastoralism and Critics of the New Novel." FR 47:356-359. December 1973.

O'Brien, Justin. The French Literary Horizon. New Brunswick: Rutgers University Press, 1967. pp. 103-108.

Painter, George D.  André Gide:  A Critical Biography.
London:  Weidenfeld and Nicolson, 1968.  pp. 88-98.

Peters, Arthur King.  Jean Cocteau and André Gide:
An Abrasive Friendship.  New Brunswick:  Rutgers University Press, 1973.  pp. 298-303.

Rieder, Dolly S.  "LES FAUX-MONNAYEURS:  Gide's Essay on Bad Faith."  RR 62:87-98.  April 1971.

Ringler, Susan J.  "Gide's LES FAUX-MONNAYEURS: Demons and Present Tense Verbs."  RomN 20:29-34. Fall 1979.

Rossi, Vinio.  André Gide:  The Evolution of an Aesthetic.  New Brunswick:  Rutgers University Press, 1967.  pp. 157-159.

Shepard, Leslie A.  "The Development of Gide's Concept of Personality."  BuR 17:55-66.  May 1969.

Tilby, Michael.  "'Self-conscious' Narration and 'Self-Reflexivity' in Gide's LES FAUX-MONNAYEURS."  EFL 15:56-81.  November 1978.

Tolton, C. D. E.  "André Gide and Christopher Isherwood: Two Worlds of Counterfeiters."  CRCL 5:193-200. Spring 1978.

Watson, Graeme.  "Gide and the Devil."  AJFS 4:86-96. January/April 1967.

Watson-Williams, Helen.  "The Principle of Duality in Gide's LES FAUX-MONNAYEURS."  AJFS 7:234-253. January/August 1970.

THE FRUITS OF THE EARTH

Faletti, Heidi E.  "An Aesthetic Perspective of Gide and Nietzsche:  The Problem of Decadence for Creative Effort."  RLC 52:46-51.  January/March 1978.

Lindsay, Marshall.  "Time in Gide's Early Fiction." Symposium 26:47-56.  Spring 1972.

Shackleton, M.  "The Dichotomy of Art and Life in André Gide."  AJFS 7:207-219.  January/August 1970.

Walker, David H.  "The Dual Composition of LES NOURRITURES TERRESTRES: Autour du 'Récit de Ménalque.'" FS 29:421-433.  October 1975.

GENEVIÈVE

Guerard, Albert J.  André Gide.  Cambridge:  Harvard University Press, 1969.  pp. 144-148.

Ireland, G.W. André Gide: A Study of His Creative Writings. Oxford: Clarendon Press, 1970. pp. 377-392.

THE IMMORALIST
Bettinson, Christopher. Gide: A Study. London: Heinemann, 1977. pp. 15-25.

Booker, John T. "THE IMMORALIST and the Rhetoric of First-Person Narration." StTCL 2:5-22. Fall 1977.

Brennan, Joseph Gerard. "Three Novels of 'Dépaysment.'" CL 22:223-236. Summer 1970.

Brown, Frieda S. "L'IMMORALISTE: Prelude to the Gidian Problem of the Individual and Society." FR 43: 65-76. Sp. Issue No. 1, Winter 1970.

Callen, A. "L'IMMORALISTE as a Modern ADOLPHE." MLQ 31:450-460. December 1970.

Faletti, Heidi E. "An Aesthetic Perspective of Gide and Nietzsche: The Problem of Decadence for Creative Effort." RLC 52:51-58. January/March 1978.

Goodhand, Robert. "Locale as Thematic Expression in L'IMMORALISTE." FR 43:77-86. Sp. Issue No. 1, Winter 1970.

Guerard, Albert J. André Gide. Cambridge: Harvard University Press, 1969. pp. 99-118; 179-182.

Ireland, G.W. André Gide: A Study of His Creative Writings. Oxford: Clarendon Press, 1970. pp. 178-198.

Kusch, Manfred. "The Gardens of L'IMMORALISTE." FFr 4:206-218. September 1979.

Landy, Marcia. "Gide's Pastoralism and Critics of the New Novel." FR 47:351-356. December 1973.

Mistacco, Vicki. "Narcissus and the Image: Symbol and Meaning in L'IMMORALISTE." KRQ 23:247-258. No. 2, 1976.

Nelson, Roy Jay. "Gidean Causality: L'IMMORALISTE and LA PORTE ETROITE." Symposium 31:43-58. Spring 1977.

O'Reilly, Robert F. "Ritual, Myth, and Symbol in Gide's L'IMMORALISTE." Symposium 28:346-355. Winter 1974.

Pasco, Allan H. "Irony and Art in Gide's L'IMMORAL-ISTE." RR 64:184-203. May 1973.

Perry, Kenneth I. The Religious Symbolism of André Gide. The Hague: Mouton, 1969. pp. 77-97.

Porter, Laurence M. "Autobiography Versus Confessional Novel: Gide's L'IMMORALISTE and SI LE GRAIN NE MEURT." Symposium 30:144-159. Summer 1976.

──────. "The Generativity Crisis of Gide's IMMORAL-ISTE." FrF 2:58-68. January 1977.

Rossi, Vinio. André Gide: The Evolution of an Aesthetic. New Brunswick: Rutgers University Press, 1967. pp. 117-119; 153-157.

Savage, Catharine H. "L'IMMORALISTE: Psychology and Rhetoric." XUS 6:43-62. February 1967.

Sonnenfeld, Albert. "On Readers and Reading in LA PORTE ETROITE and L'IMMORALISTE." RR 67:172-186. May 1976.

Wing, Nathaniel. "The Disruptions of Irony in Gide's L'IMMORALISTE." Sub-stance 26:76-85. 1980.

ISABELLE

Guerard, Albert J. André Gide. Cambridge: Harvard University Press, 1969. pp. 124-128.

Horn, Pierre. "ISABELLE: A Detective Novel by André Gide." RomN 18:54-61. Fall 1977.

Ireland, G. W. André Gide: A Study of His Creative Writings. Oxford: Clarendon Press, 1970. pp. 237-248.

Martin, Anne L. "ISABELLE, or André Gide at the Crossroads." EFL 14:34-47. November 1977.

Peters, Arthur King. Jean Cocteau and André Gide: An Abrasive Friendship. New Brunswick: Rutgers University Press, 1973. pp. 196-198.

MARSHLANDS

Bulgin, Kathleen. "Swamp Imagery and the Moral-Esthetic Problem in Gide's Early Works." FR 45:813-818. March 1972.

Rinsler, N. S. "Gide and Symbolism: The Evidence of PALUDES." EFL 13:62-76. November 1976.

Spininger, Dennis J. "The Complex Generic Mode of André Gide's PALUDES." Twentieth Century French

Fiction: Essays for Germaine Brée. ed. George Stambolian. New Brunswick: Rutgers University Press, 1975. pp. 3-25.
THE NOTEBOOKS OF ANDRE WALTER
Franklin, Ursula. "Mallarméan Affinities in Gide's CAHIERS D'ANDRE WALTER." RomN 17:1-6. Fall 1976.

Guerard, Albert J. André Gide. Cambridge: Harvard University Press, 1969. pp. 54-58.

Ireland, G. W. André Gide: A Study of His Creative Writings. Oxford: Clarendon Press, 1970. pp. 24-48.

Painter, George D. André Gide: A Critical Biography. London: Weidenfeld and Nicolson, 1968. pp. 9-17.

Perry, Kenneth I. The Religious Symbolism of André Gide. The Hague: Mouton, 1969. pp. 26-35.

Rossi, Vinio. André Gide: The Evolution of an Aesthetic. New Brunswick: Rutgers University Press, 1967. pp. 17-37.

Stoltzfus, Ben. Gide and Hemingway: Rebels Against God. Port Washington: Kennikat Press, 1978. pp. 21-28.

Storzer, Gerald H. "LES CAHIERS D'ANDRE WALTER: Idea, Emotion, and Dream in the Gidian Novel." PQ 54:647-662. Summer 1975.

Watson-Williams, Helen. André Gide and the Greek Myth. Oxford: Clarendon Press, 1967. pp. 7-8.
THE PASTORAL SYMPHONY
Babcock, Arthur E. "LA SYMPHONIE PASTORALE as Self-Conscious Fiction." FrF 3:65-71. January 1978.

Bettinson, Christopher. Gide: A Study. London: Heinemann, 1977. pp. 53-66.

Cardinal, John P. "Musical Blindness: A Study of Gide's LA SYMPHONIE PASTORALE." ML 60:19-23. March 1979.

Falk, Eugene K. Types of Thematic Structure: The Nature and Function of Motifs in Gide, Camus, and Sartre. Chicago: University of Chicago Press, 1967. pp. 30-51.

Grobe, Edwin P. "Estrangement as Verbal Aspect in LA SYMPHONIE PASTORALE." FR 43:56-64. Sp. Issue No. 1, Winter 1970.

Guerard, Albert J. André Gide. Cambridge: Harvard University Press, 1969. pp. 139-144.

Ireland, G. W. André Gide: A Study of His Creative Writings. Oxford: Clarendon Press, 1970. pp. 283-308.

Perry, Kenneth I. The Religious Symbolism of André Gide. The Hague: Mouton, 1969. pp. 117-127.

Ralston, Zachary T. Synesthesia in Gide's LA SYMPHONIE PASTORALE. Charleston: The Citadel, 1976. 7 pp.

Stoltzfus, Ben. Gide and Hemingway: Rebels Against God. Port Washington: Kennikat Press, 1978. pp. 38-50.

PROMETHEUS UNBOUND

Guerard, Albert J. André Gide. Cambridge: Harvard University Press, 1969. pp. 76-78.

Ireland, G. W. André Gide: A Study of His Creative Writings. Oxford: Clarendon Press, 1970. pp. 249-273.

Rossi, Vinio. André Gide: The Evolution of an Aesthetic. New Brunswick: Rutgers University Press, 1967. pp. 146-150.

Watson-Williams, Helen. André Gide and the Greek Myth. Oxford: Clarendon Press, 1967. pp. 42-57.

Weinberg, Kurt. On Gide's PROMETHEE: Private Myth and Public Mystification. Princeton: Princeton University Press, 1972. 138 pp.

RETURN OF THE PRODIGAL

Guerard, Albert J. André Gide. Cambridge: Harvard University Press, 1969. pp. 80-82.

Perry, Kenneth I. The Religious Symbolism of André Gide. The Hague: Mouton, 1979. pp. 98-116.

Turner, Alison M. "An Interpretation of André Gide's LE RETOUR DE L'ENFANT PRODIGUE in the Light of Its Dual Inspiration." KRQ 21:183-194. No. 2, 1974.

ROBERT

Guerard, Albert J. André Gide. Cambridge: Harvard University Press, 1969. pp. 144-146.

Ireland, G. W. André Gide: A Study of His Creative Writings. Oxford: Clarendon Press, 1970. pp. 377-392.

SCHOOL FOR WIVES

Guerard, Albert J.  André Gide.  Cambridge:  Harvard University Press, 1969.  pp. 144-146.

Ireland, G. W.  André Gide: A Study of His Creative Writings.  Oxford:  Clarendon Press, 1970.  pp. 377-392.

Stoltzfus, Ben.  Gide's Eagles.  London:  Fiffer and Simons, 1969.  pp. 132-136.

STRAIT IS THE GATE
Bettinson, Christopher.  Gide: A Study.  London: Heinemann, 1977.  pp. 25-34.

Brown, Frieda S.  "Montaigne and Gide's LA PORTE ETROITE."  PMLA 82:136-141.  March 1967.

Defaux, Gerard.  "Gide, Virgil, and La Porte Etroite."  ASLHM 46:155-173.  1975.

Eisinger, Erica M.  "The Hidden Eye:  Clandestine Observation in Gide's LA PORTE ETROITE."  KRQ 24:221-229.  No. 2, 1977.

Guerard, Albert J.  André Gide.  Cambridge:  Harvard University Press, 1969.  pp. 118-124.

Hooks, Z. and M. C. Vos.  "Who Caused Alissa's Death?  Gide's STRAIGHT [sic] IS THE GATE Reconsidered."  LangQ 11:48-50.  Spring/Summer 1973.

Hunt, Tony.  "Alissa-Eloissa."  OL 33:183-190.  1978.

Ireland, G. W.  André Gide: A Study of His Creative Writings.  Oxford:  Clarendon Press, 1970.  pp. 199-221.

Knecht, Loring D.  "A New Reading of Gide's LA PORTE ETROITE."  PMLA 82:640-648.  December 1967.  Reprinted in Gide: A Collection of Critical Essays.  ed.  David Littlejohn.  Englewood Cliffs:  Prentice-Hall, 1970.  pp. 93-111.

Nelson, Roy Jay.  "Gidean Causality: L'IMMORALISTE and LA PORTE ETROITE."  Symposium 31:43-58.  Spring 1977.

Perry, Kenneth I.  The Religious Symbolism of André Gide.  The Hague:  Mouton, 1969.  pp. 77-97.

Rossi, Vinio.  André Gide: The Evolution of an Aesthetic.  New Brunswick:  Rutgers University Press, 1967.  pp. 153-156.

Sonnenfeld, Albert. "On Readers and Reading in LA PORTE ETROITE and L'IMMORALISTE." RR 67:172-186. May 1976.

———. "STRAIT IS THE GATE: Byroads in Gide's Labyrinth." Novel 1:118-132. Winter 1968.

Stoltzfus, Ben. Gide's Eagles. London: Fiffer and Simons, 1969. pp. 24-37.

## LA TENTATIVE AMOUREUSE

Ireland, G. W. André Gide: A Study of His Creative Writings. Oxford: Clarendon Press, 1970. pp. 70-77.

Perry, Kenneth I. The Religious Symbolism of André Gide. The Hague: Mouton, 1969. pp. 36-53.

Rossi, Vinio. André Gide: The Evolution of an Aesthetic. New Brunswick: Rutgers University Press, 1967. pp. 82-88; 100-101.

## THESEUS

Guerard, Albert J. André Gide. Cambridge: Harvard University Press, 1969. pp. 90-92.

Ireland, G. W. André Gide: A Study of His Creative Writings. Oxford: Clarendon Press, 1970. pp. 408-422.

Pollard, Patrick. "Gide's THESEE: The Diary of a Moralist." FS 26:166-177. April 1972.

———. "The Sources of André Gide's THESEE." MLR 65:290-297. April 1970.

Watson-Williams, Helen. André Gide and the Greek Myth. Oxford: Clarendon Press, 1967. pp. 125-175; 188-192.

## LE TRAITE DU NARCISSE

Bulgin, Kathleen. "Swamp Imagery and the Moral-Esthetic Problem in Gide's Early Works." FR 45:813-818. March 1972.

Pollard, P. "LE TRAITE DU NARCISSE: A Point of Contact Between Gide and Schopenhauer." NFS 16:51-54. May 1977.

Rossi, Vinio. André Gide: The Evolution of an Aesthetic. New Brunswick: Rutgers University Press, 1967. pp. 52-63.

Watson-Williams, Helen. André Gide and the Greek Myth. Oxford: Clarendon Press, 1967. pp. 30-40.

## URIEN'S VOYAGE

Bulgin, Kathleen. "Swamp Imagery and the Moral-

Gide, André

Esthetic Problem in Gide's Early Works." FR 45:813-818. March 1972.

Franklin, Ursula. "Urien's Anti-quest: Gide's Parting Statement to Symbolism." NCFS 7:258-271. Spring/Summer 1979.

Guerard, Albert J. André Gide. Cambridge: Harvard University Press, 1969. pp. 58-69.

────── . "LE VOYAGE D'URIEN." Gide: A Collection of Critical Essays. ed. David Littlejohn. Englewood Cliffs: Prentice-Hall, 1970. pp. 63-72.

Ireland, G. W. André Gide: A Study of His Creative Writings. Oxford: Clarendon Press, 1970. pp. 78-90.

Perry, Kenneth I. The Religious Symbolism of André Gide. The Hague: Mouton, 1969. pp. 36-53.

Rossio, Vinio. André Gide: The Evolution of an Aesthetic. New Brunswick: Rutgers University Press, 1967. pp. 63-81.

Giono, Jean
ANGELO
Lawrence, Derek W. "The Transitional Works of Jean Giono (1937-1946)." FR 43:126-134. Winter 1970.
BATTLES IN THE MOUNTAIN
Goodrich, Norma L. Giono: Master of Fictional Modes. Princeton: Princeton University Press, 1973. pp. 139-162.

Redfern, W. D. The Private World of Jean Giono. Oxford: Basil Blackwell, 1967. pp. 110-118.
BLUE BOY
Goodrich, Norma L. Giono: Master of Fictional Modes. Princeton: Princeton University Press, 1973. pp. 251-271.
COLLINE
Clayton, Alan J. "Giono's COLLINE: Pantheism or Humanism?" FMLS 7:109-120. April 1971.

Redfern, W. D. The Private World of Jean Giono. Oxford: Basil Blackwell, 1967. pp. 20-28.
DEUX CAVALIERS DE L'ORAGE
Goodrich, Norma L. Giono: Master of Fictional Modes. Princeton: Princeton University Press, 1973. pp. 162-182.

Lawrence, Derek W. "The Transitional Works of Jean Giono (1937-1946)." FR 43:132-134. Winter 1970.
LE GRAND TROUPEAU

Goodrich, Norma L. Giono: Master of Fictional Modes. Princeton: Princeton University Press, 1973. pp. 25-39.

Redfern, W. D. "Against Nature: Jean Giono and LE GRAND TROUPEAU." The First World War in Fiction: A Collection of Critical Essays. ed. Holger Klein. London: Macmillan, 1976. pp. 73-83.

──────. The Private World of Jean Giono. Oxford: Basil Blackwell, 1967. pp. 63-70.

LES GRANDS CHEMINS
Goodrich, Norma Lorre. "Bachelors in Fiction, Through John Steinbeck and Jean Giono." KRQ 14:374-378. No. 4, 1967.

──────. Giono: Master of Fictional Modes. Princeton: Princeton University Press, 1973. pp. 95-111.

THE HORSEMAN ON THE ROOF
Goodrich, Norma L. "Further Investigation Concerning Jean Giono's HUSSARD SUR LE TOIT." RR 59:267-277. December 1968.

──────. Giono: Master of Fictional Modes. Princeton: Princeton University Press, 1973. pp. 111-138.

Lawrence, Derek W. "The Transitional Works of Jean Giono (1937-1946)." FR 43:126-134. Winter 1970.

MORT D'UN PERSONNAGE
Goodrich, Norma L. Giono: Master of Fictional Modes. Princeton: Princeton University Press, 1973. pp. 231-250.

LE MOULIN DE POLOGNE
Goodrich, Norma L. Giono: Master of Fictional Modes. Princeton: Princeton University Press, 1973. pp. 205-230.

──────. "LE MOULIN DE POLOGNE: Modern Novel and Elizabethan Tragedy." RLC 41:88-97. January/March 1967.

LA NAISSANCE DE L'ODYSSEE
Madden, Marilyn I. "Imagery in Giono's Novels, with Special Consideration of LA NAISSANCE DE L'ODYSSEE." FR 46:522-534. February 1973.

Redfern, W. D. The Private World of Jean Giono. Oxford: Basil Blackwell, 1967. pp. 11-19.

Rysten, Felix. "Jean Giono's NAISSANCE DE L'ODYSSEE." FR 45:378-387. December 1971.

POUR SALUER MELVILLE
Lawrence, Derek W. "The Transitional Works of Jean Giono (1937-1946)." FR 43:131-134. Winter 1970.

QUE MA JOIE DEMEURE
    Redfern, W. D. The Private World of Jean Giono. Oxford: Basil Blackwell, 1967. pp. 72-82.
REGAIN
    Redfern, W. D. The Private World of Jean Giono. Oxford: Basil Blackwell, 1967. pp. 33-40.
UN DE BAUMUGNES
    Redfern, W. D. The Private World of Jean Giono. Oxford: Basil Blackwell, 1967. pp. 28-33.
UN ROI SANS DIVERTISSEMENT
    Goodrich, Norma L. Giono: Master of Fictional Modes. Princeton: Princeton University Press, 1973. pp. 183-205.

Giraudoux, Jean
    ADVENTURES OF JEROME BARDINI
        Lemaître, Georges. Jean Giraudoux: The Writer and His Work. New York: Frederick Ungar, 1971. pp. 76-79.

        Lewis, Roy. "Giraudoux's Dark Night of the Soul: A Study of LES AVENTURES DE JEROME BARDINI." FS 28:421-434. October 1974.

        Reilly, John H. Jean Giraudoux. Boston: Twayne, 1978. pp. 70-73.
    BELLA
        Lemaître, Georges. Jean Giraudoux: The Writer and His Work. New York: Frederick Ungar, 1971. pp. 67-72.
    THE CHOSEN ONES
        Lemaître, Georges. Jean Giraudoux: The Writer and His Work. New York: Frederick Ungar, 1971. pp. 84-90.

        Reilly, John H. Jean Giraudoux. Boston: Twayne, 1978. pp. 112-115.
    COMBAT AVEC L'ANGE
        Lemaître, Georges. Jean Giraudoux: The Writer and His Work. New York: Frederick Ungar, 1971. pp. 79-81.
    EGLANTINE
        Reilly, John H. Jean Giraudoux. Boston: Twayne, 1978. pp. 57-59.
    JULIETTE IN THE LAND OF MEN
        Lemaître, Georges. Jean Giraudoux: The Writer and His Work. New York: Frederick Ungar, 1971. pp. 60-61.

        Reilly, John H. Jean Giraudoux. Boston: Twayne, 1978. pp. 51-53.
    LAST DREAM OF EDMOND ABOUT
        Reilly, John H. Jean Giraudoux. Boston: Twayne, 1978. pp. 27-29.

THE LIAR
    Lemaître, Georges. Jean Giraudoux: The Writer and His Work. New York: Frederick Ungar, 1971. pp. 81-84.

    Reilly, John H. Jean Giraudoux. Boston: Twayne, 1978. pp. 102-105.
MY FRIEND FROM LIMOUSIN
    Lemaître, Georges. Jean Giraudoux: The Writer and His Work. New York: Frederick Ungar, 1971. pp. 62-67.

    Reilly, John H. Jean Giraudoux. Boston: Twayne, 1978. pp. 47-51.
SCHOOL FOR THE INDIFFERENT
    Reilly, John H. Jean Giraudoux. Boston: Twayne, 1978. pp. 31-33.
SIMON THE PATHETIC
    Lemaître, Georges. Jean Giraudoux: The Writer and His Work. New York: Frederick Ungar, 1971. pp. 56-57.

    Reilly, John H. Jean Giraudoux. Boston: Twayne, 1978. pp. 37-39.
SUZANNE ET LE PACIFIQUE
    Krance, Charles. "Giraudoux's SUZANNE ET LE PACIFIQUE: Text, Topoi, and Community." AJFS 14:164-173. May/August 1977.

    Lemaître, Georges. Jean Giraudoux: The Writer and His Work. New York: Frederick Ungar, 1971. pp. 58-60.

    Reilly, John H. Jean Giraudoux. Boston: Twayne, 1978. pp. 44-47.

Glissant, Edouard
    LA LEZARDE
        Miller, Elinor S. "The Identity of the Narrator in Edouard Glissant's LA LEZARDE." SAB 43:17-26. May 1978.

Goncourt, Edmond de
    CHERIE
        Grant, Richard. The Goncourt Brothers. New York: Twayne, 1972. pp. 136-139.
    LA FAUSTIN
        Grant, Richard. The Goncourt Brothers. New York: Twayne, 1972. pp. 131-136.
    LA FILLE ELISA
        Grant, Richard. The Goncourt Brothers. New York: Twayne, 1972. pp. 108-118.

        Matthews, J. H. "From Naturalism to the Absurd: Ed-

mond de Goncourt and Albert Camus." Symposium 22: 241-255. Fall 1968.
THE ZEMGANNO BROTHERS
Grant, Richard. The Goncourt Brothers. New York: Twayne, 1972. pp. 119-130.

Goncourt, Edmond and Jules de
CHARLES DEMAILLY
Grant, Richard. The Goncourt Brothers. New York: Twayne, 1972. pp. 33-44.
EN 18
Grant, Richard. The Goncourt Brothers. New York: Twayne, 1972. pp. 18-24; 41-43.
GERMINIE LACERTEUX
Duncan, J. Ann. "Self and Others: The Pattern of Neurosis and Conflict in GERMINIE LACERTEUX." FMLS 13:204-218. July 1977.

Grant, Richard. The Goncourt Brothers. New York: Twayne, 1972. pp. 62-72.

Lee, Philip A., Jr. "Name Symbolism in the Goncourts' GERMINIE LACERTEUX." RomN 20:65-67. Fall 1979.
MADAME GERVAISAIS
Grant, Richard. The Goncourt Brothers. New York: Twayne, 1972. pp. 97-102.
MANETTE SALOMON
Grant, Richard. The Goncourt Brothers. New York: Twayne, 1972. pp. 85-97.
RENEE MAUPERIN
Grant, Richard. The Goncourt Brothers. New York: Twayne, 1972. pp. 55-62.
SOEUR PHILOMENE
Grant, Richard. The Goncourt Brothers. New York: Twayne, 1972. pp. 44-53; 65-67.

Raitt, A. W. Life and Letters in France: The Nineteenth Century. New York: Charles Scribner's Sons, 1965. pp. 118-126.

Gracq, Julien
UN BALCON EN FORÊT
Broome, Peter. "Julien Gracq's Surrealist Hero." FMLS 5:64-67. January 1969.

Dobbs, Annie-Claude. "Reality and Dream in Julien Gracq: A Stylistic Study." Twentieth Century French Fiction: Essays for Germaine Bree. ed. George Stambolian. New Brunswick: Rutgers University Press, 1975. pp. 158-163.

Gaudon, Sheila. "Julien Gracq's UN BALCON EN

FORÊT: The Ambiguities of Initiation." RR 67:132-146. March 1976.
UN BEAU TENEBREUX
    Broome, Peter. "Julien Gracq's Surrealist Hero." FMLS 5:51-55. January 1969.
THE CASTLE OF ARGOL
    Broome, Peter. "Julien Gracq's Surrealist Hero." FMLS 5:51-57. January 1969.

    Dobbs, Annie-Claude. "The Problematics of Space in Julien Gracq: Fiction and Narration in a Chapter of AU CHATEAU D'ARGOL." YFS 57:86-101. 1979.

    *Matthews, J. H. Surrealism and the Novel. Ann Arbor: University of Michigan Press, 1966. pp. 91-106.

    Osgood, Eugenia V. "A Surrealist Synthesis of History: AU CHATEAU D'ARGOL." ECr 15:319-331. Fall 1975.
LE RIVAGE DES SYRTES
    Broome, Peter. "Julien Gracq's Surrealist Hero." FMLS 5:58-64. January 1969.

Green[e], Julian [Julien]
    ADRIENNE MESURAT
        Kostis, Nicholas. The Exorcism of Sex and Death in Julien Green's Novels. The Hague: Mouton, 1973. pp. 26-34.
    L'AUTRE SOMMEIL
        Kostis, Nicholas. The Exorcism of Sex and Death in Julien Green's Novels. The Hague: Mouton, 1973. pp. 50-57.
    AVARICE HOUSE
        Burne, Glenn S. Julian Green. New York: Twayne, 1972. pp. 32-34; 53-58.
    THE CLOSED GARDEN
        Burne, Glenn S. Julian Green. New York: Twayne, 1972. pp. 32-34; 58-65.
    DARK JOURNEY
        Burne, Glenn S. Julian Green. New York: Twayne, 1972. pp. 65-68; 136-138.
    THE DREAMER
        Burne, Glenn S. Julian Green. New York: Twayne, 1972. pp. 81-97.
    EACH IN HIS DARKNESS
        Burne, Glenn S. Julian Green. New York: Twayne, 1972. pp. 130-134
    EPAVES
        Alter, Jean. "Julien Green: Structure of the Catholic Imagination." The Vision Obscured: Perceptions of Some Twentieth-Century Catholic Novelists. ed. Melvin J. Friedman. New York: Fordham University Press, 1970. pp. 151-185.

Green[e], Julian [Julien]

Batchelor, R. "Julien Green's EPAVES." EFL 10:23-39. November 1973.

Field, Trevor. "Reflections of a Novelist: Mirror Imagery in Julien Green's EPAVES." Symposium 29: 103-115. Spring/Summer 1975.

Kostis, Nicholas. The Exorcism of Sex and Death in Julien Green's Novels. The Hague: Mouton, 1973. pp. 58-64.

THE KEYS OF DEATH
Burne, Glenn S. Julian Green. New York: Twayne, 1972. pp. 48-52.

LEVIATHAN
Kostis, Nicholas. The Exorcism of Sex and Death in Julien Green's Novels. The Hague: Mouton, 1973. pp. 43-49.

MIDNIGHT
Burne, Glenn S. Julian Green. New York: Twayne, 1972. pp. 97-103.

Kostis, Nicholas. The Exorcism of Sex and Death in Julien Green's Novels. The Hague: Mouton, 1973. pp. 76-89.

MOÏRA
Burne, Glenn S. Julian Green. New York: Twayne, 1972. pp. 125-130.

Joslin, Mary Coker. "A Nature Lover's View of MOÏRA by Julien Green." RomN 13:8-11. Autumn 1971.

Sheehan, Bernard. "The Creation of Julien Green's MOÏRA: Autobiographical and Psychological Considerations." ABR 24:434-454. December 1973.

MONT-CINERE
Kostis, Nicholas. The Exorcism of Sex and Death in Julien Green's Novels. The Hague: Mouton, 1973. pp. 18-26.

PILGRIM OF THE EARTH
Burne, Glenn S. Julian Green. New York: Twayne, 1972. pp. 43-48.

THEN SHALL THE DUST RETURN
Burne, Glenn S. Julian Green. New York: Twayne, 1972. pp. 102-109.

THE TRANSGRESSOR
Burne, Glenn S. Julian Green. New York: Twayne, 1972. pp. 112-117.

LE VISIONNAIRE
Kostis, Nicholas. The Exorcism of Sex and Death in Julien Green's Novels. The Hague: Mouton, 1973. pp. 65-75.

Guilloux, Louis
ANGELINA
> Green, Mary Jean Matthews. Louis Guilloux: An Artisan of Language. York: French Literature Publications, 1980. pp. 37-45.
>
> King, J. H. "Louis Guilloux's Working Class Novels: Some Problems of Social Realism." MLR 68:69-76. January 1973.

LES BATAILLES PERDUES
> Green, Mary Jean Matthews. Louis Guilloux: An Artisan of Language. York: French Literature Publications, 1980. pp. 145-149.

COMPAGNONS
> Green, Mary Jean Matthews. Louis Guilloux: An Artisan of Language. York: French Literature Publications, 1980. pp. 27-32.
>
> King, J. H. "Louis Guilloux's Working Class Novels: Some Problems of Social Realism." MLR 68:69-76. January 1973.

LA CONFRONTATION
> Green, Mary Jean Matthews. Louis Guilloux: An Artisan of Language. York: French Literature Publications, 1980. pp. 149-155.

DOSSIER CONFIDENTIAL
> Green, Mary Jean Matthews. Louis Guilloux: An Artisan of Language. York: French Literature Publications, 1980. pp. 49-63.

HYMENEE
> Green, Mary Jean Matthews. Louis Guilloux: An Artisan of Language. York: French Literature Publications, 1980. pp. 32-36.

LE JEU DE PATIENCE
> Green, Mary Jean Matthews. Louis Guilloux: An Artisan of Language. York: French Literature Publications, 1980. pp. 113-137.
>
> King, J. H. "Louis Guilloux's LE JEU DE PATIENCE: Time and the Novelist." Trivium 8:40-55. May 1973.

LA MAISON DU PEUPLE
> Green, Mary Jean Matthews. Louis Guilloux: An Artisan of Language. York: French Literature Publications, 1980. pp. 20-27.
>
> King, J. H. "Louis Guilloux's Working Class Novels: Some Problems of Social Realism." MLR 68:69-76. January 1973.
>
> Redfern, W. D. "Political Novel and Art of Simplicity: Louis Guilloux." JES 1:115-127. June 1971.

LE PAIN DES REVES
> Green, Mary Jean Matthews. Louis Guilloux: An Arti-

san of Language. York: French Literature Publications, 1980. pp. 99-111.
PARPAGNACCO OU LA CONJURATION
Green, Mary Jean Matthews. Louis Guilloux: An Artisan of Language. York: French Literature Publications, 1980. pp. 139-144.
LE SANG NOIR
Green, Mary Jean Matthews. Louis Guilloux: An Artisan of Language. York: French Literature Publications, 1980. pp. 65-97.

Greene, Francis J. "Louis Guilloux's LE SANG NOIR: A Prefiguration of Sartre's LA NAUSEE." FR 43:205-214. December 1969.

King, J. H. "Louis Guilloux's Ambiguous Epic LE SANG NOIR." FMLS 8:1-14. January 1972.

Hugo, Victor
BUG-JARGAL
Grant, Richard B. The Perilous Quest: Image, Myth, and Prophecy in the Narratives of Victor Hugo. Durham: Duke University Press, 1968. pp. 18-27.

Lafontant, Julien J. "A Tribute to Victor Hugo's BUG-JARGAL." BRMMLA 32:195-210. Autumn 1978.
LE DERNIER JOUR D'UN CONDAMNE
Andrews, Larry R. "Dostoevskij and Hugo's LE DERNIER JOUR D'UN CONDAMNE." CL 29:1-16. Winter 1977.

Forde, Marianna C. "Condemnation and Imprisonment in L'ETRANGER and LE DERNIER JOUR D'UN CONDAMNE." RomN 13:211-216. Winter 1971.
HAN D'ISLANDE
Grant, Richard B. The Perilous Quest: Image, Myth, and Prophecy in the Narratives of Victor Hugo. Durham: Duke University Press, 1968. pp. 3-18.
THE HUNCHBACK OF NOTRE DAME
*Adamson, Donald. The Genesis of LE COUSIN PONS. Oxford: Oxford University Press, 1966. pp. 70-124.

Brown, Nathalie Babel. Hugo and Dostoevsky. Ann Arbor: Ardis, 1978. pp. 13-16.

Grant, Richard B. The Perilous Quest: Image, Myth, and Prophecy in the Narratives of Victor Hugo. Durham: Duke University Press, 1968. pp. 46-72.

Haig, Stirling. "From Cathedral to Book, from Stone to Press: Hugo's Portrait of the Artist in NOTRE-DAME DE PARIS." SFR 3:343-350. Winter 1979.

Holdheim, W. Wolfgang. "The History of Art in Victor Hugo's NOTRE-DAME DE PARIS." NCFS 5:58-70. Fall/Winter 1976-1977.

Houston, John Porter. Victor Hugo. New York: Twayne, 1974. pp. 33-40.

Maxwell, Richard. "City Life and the Novel: Hugo, Ainsworth, Dickens." CL 30:157-171. Spring 1978.

Mehlman, Jeffrey. Revolution and Repetition: Marx/ Hugo/Balzac. Berkeley: University of California Press, 1977. pp. 71-103.

Ward, Patricia A. The Medievalism of Victor Hugo. University Park: Penn. State University Press, 1975. pp. 34-52.

Wildgen, Kathryn E. "Romance and Myth in NOTRE-DAME DE PARIS." FR 49:319-327. February 1976.

THE MAN WHO LAUGHS

Forde, Marianna C. "The Pessimism of an Idealist: Hugo's L'HOMME QUI RIT." FR 41:641-648. April 1968.

Grant, Richard B. The Perilous Quest: Image, Myth, and Prophecy in the Narratives of Victor Hugo. Durham: Duke University Press, 1968. pp. 199-221.

Richardson, Joanna. Victor Hugo. New York: St. Martin's Press, 1976. pp. 203-207.

LES MISERABLES

Brombert, Victor. "Hugo's Waterloo: The Victory of Cambronne." SFR 3:235-242. Fall 1979.

Brown, Nathalie Babel. Hugo and Dostoevsky. Ann Arbor: Ardis, 1978. pp. 13-18; 23-28; 101-106.

Denommé, Robert T. "Lamartine's Criticism of LES MISERABLES." OL 26:211-219. 1971.

Grant, Richard B. The Perilous Quest: Image, Myth, and Prophecy in the Narratives of Victor Hugo. Durham: Duke University Press, 1968. pp. 154-176.

Grossman, Kathryn M. "Jean Valjean and France: Outlaws in Search of Integrity." SFR 2:363-374. Winter 1978.

Houston, John Porter. Victor Hugo. New York: Twayne, 1974. pp. 143-146.

Hyslop, Lois Boe. "Baudelaire on LES MISERABLES." FR 41:23-29. October 1967.

Richardson, Joanna. Victor Hugo. New York: St. Martin's Press, 1976. pp. 163-169.

Welsh, Alexander. "Opening and Closing LES MISERABLES." NCF 33:8-23. June 1978.

QUATREVINGT-TREIZE
Grant, Richard B. The Perilous Quest: Image, Myth, and Prophecy in the Narratives of Victor Hugo. Durham: Duke University Press, 1968. pp. 222-238.

Hamilton, James F. "The Novelist as Historian: A Contrast Between Balzac's LES CHOUANS and Hugo's QUATREVINGT-TREIZE." FR 49:661-668. April 1976.

Mehlman, Jeffrey. Revolution and Repetition: Marx/ Hugo/Balzac. Berkeley: University of California Press, 1977. pp. 45-125.

THE TOILERS OF THE SEA
Grant, Richard B. The Perilous Quest: Image, Myth, and Prophecy in the Narratives of Victor Hugo. Durham: Duke University Press, 1968. pp. 177-198.

Richardson, Joanna. Victor Hugo. New York: St. Martin's Press, 1976. pp. 189-192.

Huysmans, Joris-Karl
AGAINST THE GRAIN
Cevasco, G. A. "A REBOURS and Poe's Reputation in France." RomN 13:255-261. Winter 1971.

_____. "Satirical and Parodical Interpretations of J.-K. Huysmans' A REBOURS." RomN 16:278-282. Winter 1975.

Furst, Lilian R. "The Structure of Romantic Agony." CLS 10:127-137. June 1973.

Halpern, Joseph. "Decadent Narrative: A REBOURS." SFR 2:91-102. Spring 1978.

Matthews, J. H. Toward the Poetics of Surrealism. Syracuse: Syracuse University Press, 1976. pp. 34-36; 97-98.

Mickelsen, David. "A REBOURS: Spatial Form." FrF 3:48-54. January 1978.

Nuccitelli, Angela. "A REBOURS's Symbol of the 'Femme-Fleur': A Key to des Esseintes's Obsession." Symposium 28:336-345. Winter 1974.

Reising, Robert W. "Huysman's [sic] AGAINST NATURE and Eça de Queroz's [sic] THE CITY AND THE MOUN-

TAINS: A Comparative Study." LangQ 9:37-40. Fall/
Winter 1970.

Ridge, George Ross. Joris-Karl Huysmans. New York:
Twayne, 1968. pp. 60-65.

*van Roosbroeck, Gustave L. "Huysmans the Sphinx:
The Riddle of A REBOURS." RR 18:306-328. October/
December 1927.

Taylor, John. "Joris-Karl Huysmans as Impressionist
in Prose." PLL 8:67-75. Fall 1972.

Weinreb, Ruth Plaut. "Structural Techniques in A RE-
BOURS." FR 49:222-233. December 1975.

West, Thomas G. "Schopenhauer, Huysmans and French
Naturalism." JES 1:313-324. December 1971.
UN DILEMME
　　Ridge, George Ross. Joris-Karl Huysmans. New York:
　　Twayne, 1968. pp. 69-72.
DOWNSTREAM
　　Ridge, George Ross. Joris-Karl Huysmans. New York:
　　Twayne, 1968. pp. 57-59.

Shenton, C. G. "A VAU-L'EAU: A Naturalist 'Sotie.'"
MLR 72:300-309. April 1977.

Winner, Anthony. "The Indigestible Reality: J.-K.
Huysmans' DOWN STREAM." VQR 50:39-50. Winter
1974.
EN MENAGE
　　Ridge, George Ross. Joris-Karl Huysmans. New York:
　　Twayne, 1968. pp. 52-57.
EN RADE
　　*Matthews, J. H. Surrealism and the Novel. Ann Arbor:
　　University of Michigan Press, 1966. pp. 30-40.

Wade, Claire. "The Contributions of Color and Light to
Differing Levels of Reality in the Novels of Joris-Karl
Huysmans." Symposium 28:371-376. Winter 1974.
EN ROUTE
　　Ridge, George Ross. Joris-Karl Huysmans. New York:
　　Twayne, 1968. pp. 81-86.

Wade, Claire. "The Contributions of Color and Light to
Differing Levels of Reality in the Novels of Joris-Karl
Huysmans." Symposium 28:376-379. Winter 1974.
LA-BAS
　　Erickson, John D. "Huysmans' LA-BAS: A Metaphor of
　　Search." FR 43:418-425. February 1970.

Taylor, John. "Joris-Karl Huysmans as Impressionist in
Prose." PLL 8:75-78. Fall 1972.

MARTHE
    Ridge, George Ross. Joris-Karl Huysmans. New York:
    Twayne, 1968. pp. 41-45.

    Wade, Claire. "The Contributions of Color and Light to
    Differing Levels of Reality in the Novels of Joris-Karl
    Huysmans." Symposium 28:366-370. Winter 1974.
THE OBLATE
    Ridge, George Ross. Joris-Karl Huysmans. New York:
    Twayne, 1968. pp. 95-98.
LES SOEURS VATARD
    Ridge, George Ross. Joris-Karl Huysmans. New York:
    Twayne, 1968. pp. 45-48.

Janin, Jules
    L'ANE MORT ET LA FEMME GUILLOTINEE
    Clark, Roger J. B. "Parody and Revolt: A Reading of
    Janin's L'ANE MORT ET LA FEMME GUILLOTINEE."
    OL 31:243-262. 1976.

Janvier, Ludovic
    LA BAIGNEUSE
    Lustig, Bette H. "Ludovic Janvier: A Newer Novelist."
    Sub-stance 15:187-198. 1976.
    FACE
    Lustig, Bette H. "Ludovic Janvier: A Newer Novelist."
    Sub-stance 15:198-207. 1976.

Jarry, Alfred
    GESTES ET OPINIONS DU DOCTEUR FAUSTROLL
    Stillman, Linda Klieger. "Physics and Pataphysics:
    The Sources of FAUSTROLL." KRQ 26:81-91. No. 1,
    1979.

de Krüdener, M.
    VALERIE
    Lacy, K. Wesley, Jr. "A Forgotten Best-Seller:
    Madame de Krüdener's VALERIE." RomN 18:362-367.
    Spring 1978.

Laclos, Pierre de
    LES LIAISONS DANGEREUSES
    Alstad, Dianne. "LES LIAISONS DANGEREUSES:
    Hustlers and Hypocrites." YFS 40:156-167. 1968.

    Blum, Carol. "A Hint from the Author of LES LIAISONS
    DANGEREUSES?" MLN 84:662-667. May 1969.

    _____. "Styles of Cognition as Moral Options in LA
    NOUVELLE HELOÏSE and LES LIAISONS DANGEREUSES."
    PMLA 88:289-298. March 1973.

    Champagne, Roland A. "The Spiralling 'Discours':

Todorov's Model for a Narratology in LES LIAISONS DANGEREUSES." ECr 14:342-352. Winter 1974.

Coward, D. A. "Laclos and the 'Dénouement' of the LIAISONS DANGEREUSES." ECS 5:431-449. Spring 1972.

Dunn, Susan. "Education and Seduction in LES LIAISONS DANGEREUSES." Symposium 34:125-137. Summer 1980.

Free, Lloyd Raymond. "Crébillon fils, Laclos, and the Code of the Libertine." EC Life 1:36-40. December 1974.

_____. Laclos: Critical Approaches to LES LIAISONS DANGEREUSES. Madrid: Turanzas, 1978. 296 pp.

_____. "Laclos and the Myth of Courtly Love." SVEC 148:201-223. 1976.

Fries, Thomas. "The Impossible Object: The Feminine, The Narrative (Laclos' LIAISONS DANGEREUSES and Kleist's MARQUISE VON O...)." MLN 91:1304-1315. December 1976.

Greene, Mildred S. "LES LIAISONS DANGEREUSES and THE GOLDEN BOWL: Maggie's 'Loving Reason.'" MFS 19:531-540. Winter 1973.

Gutwirth, Madelyn. "Laclos and 'Le sexe': The Rack of Ambivalence." SVEC 189:247-296. 1980.

Hill, Emita B. "Man and Mask: The Art of the Actor in the LIAISONS DANGEREUSES." RR 63:111-124. April 1972.

Katz, Eve. "Ambiguity in LES LIAISONS DANGEREUSES." FMLS 10:121-129. April 1974.

Lee, Vera. "Decoding Letter 50 in LES LIAISONS DANGEREUSES." RomN 10:305-310. Spring 1969.

Lynch, Lawrence W. "Laclos and Standards in Fiction." KRQ 25:178-182. No. 2, 1978.

*Martin, Angus A. "Choderlos de Laclos: An Unsuccessful Moralist?" AJFS 1:164-173. May/August 1964.

Martindale, Colin. "Structural Balance and the Rules of Narrative in LES LIAISONS DANGEREUSES." Poetics 5:57-72. March 1976.

Laclos, Pierre de

McLaughlin, Blandine. "LES LIAISONS DANGEREUSES --A Quest for Freedom." Adam 41:8-21. 1979.

Minogue, Valerie. "LES LIAISONS DANGEREUSES: A Practical Lesson in the Art of Seduction." MLR 67: 775-786. October 1972.

Palka, Keith A. "The Workings of Chance in LES LIAISONS DANGEREUSES." RLSt 5:47-71. 1974.

Preston, John. "LES LIAISONS DANGEREUSES: Epistolary Narrative and Moral Discovery." FS 24:23-35. January 1970.

Rosbottom, Ronald C. Choderlos de Laclos. Boston: Twayne, 1978. Chaps. II, IV, V.

Rosenberg, Sondra. "Form and Sensibility in LES LIAISONS DANGEREUSES and VANITY FAIR." EnlE 3:18-36. Spring 1972.

Smith, Peter Lester. "Duplicity and Narrative Technique in the 'Roman Libertin.'" KRQ 25:74-77. No. 1, 1978.

Thody, Philip. Laclos: LES LIAISONS DANGEREUSES. London: Edward Arnold, 1970. 63 pp.

_____. "LES LIAISONS DANGEREUSES: Some Problems of Interpretation." MLR 63:832-839. October 1968.

Thody, P. M. W. "MANON LESCAUT and LES LIAISONS DANGEREUSES: The Problems of Morality in Literature." ML 51:61-72. June 1975.

Thomas, Ruth P. "JACQUES LE FATALISTE, LES LIAISONS DANGEREUSES and the Autonomy of the Novel." SVEC 117:239-249. 1974.

Todorov, Tzvetan. "The Categories of Literary Narrative." PLL 16:3-36. Winter 1980.

_____. "The Discovery of Language: LES LIAISONS DANGEREUSES and ADOLPHE." YFS 45:113-126. 1970.

Toplak, Maria. "Homo Ludens et Homo Belligerens." MLQ 28:167-176. June 1967.

Lafayette, Madame de
 LA COMTESSE DE TENDE
  Haig, Stirling. "LA COMTESSE DE TENDE: A Singular Heroine." RomN 10:311-316. Spring 1969.

_____. Madame de Lafayette. New York: Twayne, 1970. pp. 135-140.

Koppisch, Michael. "The Dynamics of Jealousy in the Work of Madame de Lafayette." MLN 94:763-765. May 1979.

LA PRINCESSE DE CLEVES
Allentuch, Harriet Ray. "Pauline and the Princesse de Clèves." MLQ 30:171-182. June 1969.

_____. "The Will to Refuse in the PRINCESSE DE CLEVES." UTQ 44:185-198. Spring 1975.

Betts, C. J. "An Aspect of Mme de Lafayette's Narrative Technique: Correspondences of Physical Details in LA PRINCESSE DE CLEVES." AJFS 10:130-143. May/August 1973.

Bidwell, Jean S. "LA PRINCESSE DE CLEVES and LE ROMAN COMIQUE--Two Different Worlds." LangQ 11:43-47. Spring/Summer 1973.

Brody, Jules. "LA PRINCESSE DE CLEVES and the Myth of Courtly Love." UTQ 38:105-135. January 1969.

Goode, William O. "A Mother's Goals in LA PRINCESSE DE CLEVES: Worldly and Spiritual Distinction." Neophil 56:398-406. October 1972.

Greene, Mildred S. "Isolation and Integrity: Madame de Lafayette's Princesse de Clèves and George Eliot's Dorothea Brooke." RLC 44:145-154. April/June 1970.

_____. "The Victorian Romanticizing of Sex: Changes in English Translations of Madame de Lafayette's LA PRINCESSE DE CLEVES." PBSA 70:501-511. No. 4, 1976.

Grossvogel, David I. Limits of the Novel: Evolutions of a Form from Chaucer to Robbe-Grillet. Ithaca: Cornell University Press, 1968. pp. 100-135.

Haig, Stirling. Madame de Lafayette. New York: Twayne, 1970. pp. 39-48; 105-134.

_____. "LA PRINCESSE DE CLEVES and Saint-Réal's DOM CARLOS." FS 22:201-205. July 1968.

Hunwick, Andrew. "The 'Prudent' Prince de Clèves." EFL 13:1-12. November 1976.

Kaps, Helen Karen. Moral Perspective in LA PRIN-

CESSE DE CLEVES. Eugene: University of Oregon, 1968. 88 pp.

Koppisch, Michael S. "The Dynamics of Jealousy in the Work of Madame de Lafayette." MLN 94:757-772. May 1979.

Kuizenga, Donna. Narrative Strategies in LA PRINCESSE DE CLEVES. Lexington: French Forum, 1976. 146 pp.

Kusch, Manfred. "Narrative Technique and Cognitive Modes in LA PRINCESSE DE CLEVES." Symposium 30:308-324. Winter 1976.

Leov, Nola M. "Sincerity and Order in the PRINCESSE DE CLEVES." AUMLA 30:133-150. November 1968.

Nicolich, Robert N. "The Language of Vision in LA PRINCESSE DE CLEVES: The Baroque Principle of Control and Release." Lang & S 4:279-296. Fall 1971.

Nurse, Peter H. Classical Voices: Studies of Corneille, Racine, Molière. London: George G. Harrap, 1971. pp. 198-223.

Raitt, Janet. Madame de Lafayette and LA PRINCESSE DE CLEVES. London: George G. Harrap, 1971. 187 pp.

Scanlan, Timothy M. "Comic Elements in LA PRINCESSE DE CLEVES." RomN 17:281-285. Spring 1977.

_____. "Maternal Mask and Literary Craft in LA PRINCESSE DE CLEVES." RPac 2:23-32. Spring 1976.

Singerman, Alan J. "History as Metaphor in Mme de Lafayette's LA PRINCESSE DE CLEVES." MLQ 36:261-271. September 1975.

Tiefenbrun, Susan W. "The Art of Repetition in LA PRINCESSE DE CLEVES." MLR 68:40-50. January 1973.

_____. "Big Women." RR 69:34-47. January/March 1978.

_____. "Computational Stylistics and the French Classical Novel." Lang & S 11:94-115. Spring 1978.

Weinberg, Kurt. "The Lady and the Unicorn, or M. de Nemours à Coulommiers: Enigma, Device, Blazon and Emblem in LA PRINCESSE DE CLEVES." Euphorion 71:306-335. No. 4, 1977.

Woshinsky, Barbara R. "The Art of Persuasion in the PRINCESSE DE CLEVES." LangQ 12:34-38; 42. Spring/Summer 1974.

_____. LA PRINCESSE DE CLEVES: The Tension of Elegance. The Hague: Mouton, 1973. 119 pp.

ZAIDE
  Haig, Stirling. Madame de Lafayette. New York: Twayne, 1970. pp. 91-104.

  Koppisch, Michael S. "The Dynamics of Jealousy in the Work of Madame de Lafayette." MLN 94:765-769. May 1979.

de Lannel, Jean
 ROMANT SATYRIQUE
  Cramer, Hazel. "Si on m'a bien entendu: A Study of the Role of the Reader in Jean de Lannel's ROMANT SATYRIQUE." AJFS 16:307-322. May/August 1979.

  Hardee, A. Maynor. Jean de Lannel and the Pre-Classical French Novel. Genève: Librairie Droz, 1967. 143 pp.

Larbaud, Valery
 FERMINA
  Simon, John Kenneth. "Valery Larbaud's FERMINA." MLN 83:543-564. May 1968.

Lartéguy, Jean
 LES CENTURIONS
  O'Connell, David. "Jean Lartéguy: A Popular Phenomenon." FR 45:1087-1097. May 1972.
 LES MERCENAIRES
  O'Connell, David. "Jean Lartéguy: A Popular Phenomenon." FR 45:1088-1091. May 1972.
 LES PRETORIENS
  O'Connell, David. "Jean Lartéguy: A Popular Phenomenon." FR 45:1089-1091. May 1972.

Lautréamont, Comte de (Isidore Ducasse)
 LES CHANTS DE MALDOROR
  Fowlie, Wallace. Lautréamont. New York: Twayne, 1973. pp. 34-76.

  Gasché, Rodolphe. "Onslaught on Filiation: Lautréamont and the Greeks." Genre 11:479-504. Winter 1978.

  de Jonge, Alex. Nightmare Culture: Lautréamont and LES CHANTS DE MALDOROR. London: Secker & Warburg, 1973. pp. 55-120.

Lydenberg, Robin. "Metaphor and Metamorphosis in LES CHANTS DE MALDOROR." ECr 18:3-14. Winter 1978.

_____. "Surviving Lautréamont: The Reader in LES CHANTS DE MALDOROR." ECr 17:211-227. Fall 1977.

Nesselroth, Peter W. Lautréamont's Imagery: A Stylistic Approach. Genève: Librairie Droz, 1969. 123 pp.

Porter, Laurence M. "Modernist Maldoror: The De-Euphemization of Metaphor." ECr 18:25-34. Winter 1978.

Sussman, Henry. "The Anterior Tail: The Code of LES CHANTS DE MALDOROR." MLN 89:957-977. December 1974.

Wade, Claire. "The Importance and Implications of Animal-Human Figures in LES CHANTS DE MALDOROR." ECr 18:47-65. Winter 1978.

Woodard, Kay B. "Celui qui lit: Reader in the Text/Reader of the Text in LES CHANTS DE MALDOROR." FrF 3:159-167. May 1978.

_____. "A Poetics of Violence: Aggression, Reform, and the Reader in LES CHANTS DE MALDOROR." ECr 18:15-24. Winter 1978.

Zweig, Paul. Lautréamont: The Violent Narcissus. Port Washington: Kennikat, 1972. pp. 5-90.

Le Clézio, J. M. G.
  THE BOOK OF FLIGHTS
    Waelti-Walters, Jennifer R. J. M. G. Le Clézio. Boston: Twayne, 1977. pp. 81-93.
  THE FLOOD
    Waelti-Walters, Jennifer R. J. M. G. Le Clézio. Boston: Twayne, 1977. pp. 45-56.
  THE GIANTS
    Waelti-Walters, Jennifer R. J. M. G. Le Clézio. Boston: Twayne, 1977. pp. 118-131.
  THE INTERROGATION
    Waelti-Walters, Jennifer R. J. M. G. Le Clézio. Boston: Twayne, 1977. pp. 16-31.
  JOURNEYS TO THE OTHER SIDE
    Waelti-Walters, Jennifer R. J. M. G. Le Clézio. Boston: Twayne, 1977. pp. 132-146.
  TERRA AMATA
    Waelti-Walters, Jennifer R. J. M. G. Le Clézio. Boston: Twayne, 1977. pp. 69-80.

WAR
 Waelti-Walters, Jennifer R. J. M. G. Le Clézio. Boston: Twayne, 1977. pp. 94-106.

Leduc, Violette
 L'AFFAMEE
  de Courtivron, Isabelle. "Violette Leduc's L'AFFAMEE: The Courage to Displease." ECr 19:95-106. Summer 1979.

Lesage, Alain
 GIL BLAS
  Bjornson, Richard. The Picaresque Hero in European Fiction. Madison: University of Wisconsin Press, 1977. pp. 207-227.

  Carson, Katharine Whitman. "Aspects of Contemporary Society in GIL BLAS." SVEC 110:11-148. 1973.

  Runte, Roseann. "Gil Blas and Roderick Random: Food for Thought." FR 50:698-705. April 1977.

Loti, Pierre
 AU MAROC
  Lerner, Michael. Pierre Loti. New York: Twayne, 1974. pp. 89-92.
 AZIYADE
  Lerner, Michael. Pierre Loti. New York: Twayne, 1974. pp. 35-41.

  Wake, Clive. The Novels of Pierre Loti. The Hague: Mouton, 1974. pp. 49-66.
 THE DISENCHANTED
  Lerner, Michael. Pierre Loti. New York: Twayne, 1974. pp. 119-125.

  Wake, Clive. The Novels of Pierre Loti. The Hague: Mouton, 1974. pp. 173-175.
 FANTOME D'ORIENT
  Lerner, Michael. Pierre Loti. New York: Twayne, 1974. pp. 79-81.
 FLEURS D'ENNUI
  Lerner, Michael. Pierre Loti. New York: Twayne, 1974. pp. 49-52.
 MADAME CHRYSANTHEMUM
  Lerner, Michael. Pierre Loti. New York: Twayne, 1974. pp. 69-72.

  Wake, Clive. The Novels of Pierre Loti. The Hague: Mouton, 1974. pp. 143-146.
 LE MARIAGE DE LOTI
  Lerner, Michael. Pierre Loti. New York: Twayne, 1974. pp. 24-31.

Loti, Pierre

    Wake, Clive. The Novels of Pierre Loti. The Hague:
    Mouton, 1974. pp. 67-78.
MATELOT
    Lerner, Michael. Pierre Loti. New York: Twayne,
    1974. pp. 83-85.

    Wake, Clive. The Novels of Pierre Loti. The Hague:
    Mouton, 1974. pp. 147-160.
MY BROTHER YVES
    Lerner, Michael. Pierre Loti. New York: Twayne,
    1974. pp. 52-57; 62-65.

    Wake, Clive. The Novels of Pierre Loti. The Hague:
    Mouton, 1974. pp. 95-115.
PECHEUR D'ISLANDE
    Lerner, Michael. Pierre Loti. New York: Twayne,
    1974. pp. 58-65.

    Wake, Clive. The Novels of Pierre Loti. The Hague:
    Mouton, 1974. pp. 116-142.
RAMUNTCHO
    Lerner, Michael. Pierre Loti. New York: Twayne,
    1974. pp. 98-102.

    *Raitt, A. W. Life and Letters in France: The Nineteenth Century. New York: Charles Scribner's Sons, 1965. pp. 144-151.

    Wake, Clive. The Novels of Pierre Loti. The Hague:
    Mouton, 1974. pp. 161-172.
LE ROMAN D'UN SPAHI
    Lerner, Michael. Pierre Loti. New York: Twayne,
    1974. pp. 29-34.

    Wake, Clive. The Novels of Pierre Loti. The Hague:
    Mouton, 1974. pp. 79-94.

Mallet-Joris, Françoise
    LE JEU DU SOUTERRAIN
        Soos, Emese. "The Only Motion Is Returning: The Metaphor of Alchemy in Mallet-Joris and Yourcenar." FrF 4:3-15. January 1979.

Malraux, André
    THE CONQUERORS
        Batchelor, R. E. "André Malraux's LES CONQUERANTS and the Art of Focussing." NFS 18:45-57. May 1979.

        Boak, Denis. André Malraux. Oxford: Clarendon Press, 1968. pp. 44-62.

        Britwum, Kwabena. "Garine, the Self and the Tragic Theme in LES CONQUERANTS." MLR 69:779-784. October 1974.

Chua, Cheng Lok. "The International Theme in André Malraux's Asian Novels." MLQ 39:173-175. June 1978.

Greenlee, James W. Malraux's Heroes and History. De Kalb: Northern Illinois University Press, 1975. pp. 33-46.

Hewitt, James Robert. André Malraux. New York: Frederick Ungar, 1978. pp. 26-39.

Horvath, Violet. André Malraux: The Human Adventure. New York: New York University Press, 1969. pp. 163-177.

Jenkins, Cecil. André Malraux. New York: Twayne, 1972. pp. 44-47; 49-59.

Kline, Thomas Jefferson. André Malraux and the Metamorphosis of Death. New York: Columbia University Press, 1973. pp. 11-29.

Lacouture, Jean. André Malraux. New York: Pantheon Books, 1975. pp. 131-135; 217-220.

Madsen, Axel. Hearts and Minds. New York: William Morrow, 1977. pp. 107-111; 121-124.

Payne, Robert. A Portrait of André Malraux. Englewood Cliffs: Prentice-Hall, 1970. pp. 129-139.

Rysten, Felix S. A. False Prophets in the Fiction of Camus, Dostoevsky, Melville, and Others. Coral Gables: University of Miami Press, 1972. pp. 25-30.

Wilkinson, David. Malraux: An Essay in Political Criticism. Cambridge: Harvard University Press, 1967. pp. 36-43.

## DAYS OF WRATH

Boak, Denis. André Malraux. Oxford: Clarendon Press, 1968. pp. 96-105.

Greenlee, James W. Malraux's Heroes and History. De Kalb: Northern Illinois University Press, 1975. pp. 87-99.

Hewitt, James Robert. André Malraux. New York: Frederick Ungar, 1978. pp. 52-63.

Horvath, Violet. André Malraux: The Human Adventure. New York: New York University Press, 1969. pp. 217-227.

Kline, Thomas Jefferson. André Malraux and the Metamorphosis of Death. New York: Columbia University Press, 1973. pp. 84-98.

Lacouture, Jean. André Malraux. New York: Pantheon Books, 1975. pp. 183-185.

Langlois, Walter G. "Autobiographical Aspects of Malraux's Novel LE TEMPS DU MEPRIS." ECr 20:21-37. Fall 1980.

Madsen, Axel. Hearts and Minds. New York: William Morris, 1977. pp. 165-167.

Payne, Robert. A Portrait of André Malraux. Englewood Cliffs: Prentice-Hall, 1970. pp. 220-230.

Wilkinson, David. Malraux: An Essay in Political Criticism. Cambridge: Harvard University Press, 1967. pp. 72-76.

MAN'S FATE

Boak, Denis. André Malraux. Oxford: Clarendon Press, 1968. pp. 63-95.

Brombert, Victor. "Remembering Malraux: On Violence and the Image of Man." Salmagundi 38/39:177-186. Summer/Fall 1977. Reprinted in Dialogues with the Unseen and the Unknown: Essays in Memory of André Malraux. Saratoga Springs: Skidmore College, 1978. pp. 5-14.

Chua, Cheng Lok. "The International Theme in André Malraux's Asian Novels." MLQ 39:176-182. June 1978.

Festa-McCormick, Diana. "Tchen and the Temptation of the Flesh." TCL 24:314-323. Fall 1978.

Friedman, Melvin J. "Some Notes on the Technique of MAN'S FATE." The Shaken Realist. ed. Melvin J. Friedman and John B. Vickery. Baton Rouge: Louisiana State University Press, 1970. pp. 128-143.

Gill, Gillian C. "'Le Jeu de l'amour et du hasard': Tchen Ludens." MMM 12:3-18. Autumn 1980.

Greenlee, James W. Malraux's Heroes and History. De Kalb: Northern Illinois University Press, 1975. pp. 59-85.

Groves, Margaret. "Malraux's Lyricism and the Death of Kyo." MLR 64:53-61. January 1969.

Hewitt, James Robert. André Malraux. New York: Frederick Ungar, 1978. pp. 37-50.

Horvath, Violet. André Malraux: The Human Adventure. New York: New York University Press, 1969. pp. 195-216.

Jenkins, Cecil. André Malraux. New York: Twayne, 1972. pp. 61-77.

Joyaux, Georges J. "Malraux's Search for Man: 'du fanatisme de la différence à la passion de la fraternité.'" CentR 20:324-328. Fall 1976.

Kline, Thomas Jefferson. André Malraux and the Metamorphosis of Death. New York: Columbia University Press, 1973. pp. 59-83.

Lacouture, Jean. André Malraux. New York: Pantheon Books, 1975. pp. 145-149; 218-222.

Madsen, Axel. Hearts and Minds. New York: William Morrow, 1977. pp. 128-137.

McGrath, Susan McLean. "Baron Clappique--Toto--...." MMM 11:28-39. Autumn 1979.

Payne, Robert. A Portrait of André Malraux. Englewood Cliffs: Prentice-Hall, 1970. pp. 165-178.

Roudiez, Leon S. "LA CONDITION HUMAINE: An Awareness of the Other." TCL 24:303-313. Fall 1978.

Sayre, Robert. "Solitude and Solidarity: The Case of André Malraux." Mosaic 9:58-66. Fall 1975.

Villani, Sergio. "Folly's Wisdom: Clappique as Erasmian Fool." MMM 12:30-39. Autumn 1980.

Wilkinson, David. Malraux: An Essay in Political Criticism. Cambridge: Harvard University Press, 1967. pp. 72-80.

MAN'S HOPE

Batchelor, R. "The Role of Manuel in André Malraux's L'ESPOIR." Neophil 59:512-521. October 1975.

Berenguer, Joan. "A Sociological View of Malraux's Novel." Dialogues with the Unseen and the Unknown: Essays in Memory of André Malraux. Saratoga Springs: Skidmore College, 1978. pp. 68-74.

Boak, Denis. André Malraux. Oxford: Clarendon Press, 1968. pp. 106-138.

Chua, C. L. "Nature and Art in the Aesthetics of Malraux's L'ESPOIR." Symposium 26:114-127. Summer 1972.

## Malraux, André

Duchet, Claude. "The Object-Event of the Ram's Charge: An Ideological Reading of an Image." YFS 59:155-174. 1980.

Goldberger, Avriel H. "Transmutation of Roles into Authentic Personae in L'ESPOIR." TCL 24:335-343. Fall 1978.

Greenlee, James W. Malraux's Heroes and History. De Kalb: Northern Illinois University Press, 1975. pp. 101-138.

Hewitt, James Robert. André Malraux. New York: Frederick Ungar, 1978. pp. 65-75.

Horvath, Violet. André Malraux: The Human Adventure. New York: New York University Press, 1969. pp. 229-249.

Jenkins, Cecil. André Malraux. New York: Twayne, 1972. pp. 87-102.

Kline, Thomas Jefferson. André Malraux and the Metamorphosis of Death. New York: Columbia University Press, 1973. pp. 99-120.

Lacouture, Jean. André Malraux. New York: Pantheon Books, 1975. pp. 278-286.

Langlois, Walter G. "Malraux and Medellin." Wascana R 14:37-54. Spring 1979.

_____. "The Novelist Malraux and History." ECr 15:345-366. Fall 1975.

Madsen, Axel. Hearts and Minds. New York: William Morrow, 1977. pp. 200-202.

O'Brien, Justin. The French Literary Horizon. New Brunswick: Rutgers University Press, 1967. pp. 253-256.

Payne, Robert. A Portrait of André Malraux. Englewood Cliffs: Prentice-Hall, 1970. pp. 247-261.

Rowland, Michael L. and Sonja G. Stary. "Mask and Vision in Malraux's L'ESPOIR." FR 47:189-196. Sp. Issue No. 6, Spring 1974.

Thomas, Hugh. "The Lyrical Illusion: Spain 1936." Malraux: Life and Work. ed. Martine de Courcel. New York: Harcourt Brace Jovanovich, 1976. pp. 44-50.

Wilkinson, David. Malraux: An Essay in Political Criticism. Cambridge: Harvard University Press, 1967. pp. 76-104.

PAPER MOONS
Horvath, Violet. André Malraux: The Human Adventure. New York: New York University Press, 1969. pp. 125-134.

Payne, Robert. A Portrait of André Malraux. Englewood Cliffs: Prentice-Hall, 1970. pp. 29-38.

THE ROYAL WAY
Boak, Denis. André Malraux. Oxford: Clarendon Press, 1968. pp. 29-43.

Dale, Jonathan. "Sartre and Malraux: LA NAUSEE and LA VOIE ROYALE." FMLS 4:335-346. October 1968.

Greenlee, James W. Malraux's Heroes and History. De Kalb: Northern Illinois University Press, 1975. pp. 45-58.

Hewitt, James Robert. André Malraux. New York: Frederick Ungar, 1978. pp. 88-95.

Horvath, Violet. André Malraux: The Human Adventure. New York: New York University Press, 1969. pp. 179-193.

Jenkins, Cecil. André Malraux. New York: Twayne, 1972. pp. 47-51.

Kline, Thomas Jefferson. André Malraux and the Metamorphosis of Death. New York: Columbia University Press, 1973. pp. 30-58.

Lacouture, Jean. André Malraux. New York: Pantheon Books, 1975. pp. 58-65.

Madsen, Axel. Hearts and Minds. New York: William Morrow, 1977. pp. 117-121.

Payne, Robert. A Portrait of André Malraux. Englewood Cliffs: Prentice-Hall, 1970. pp. 151-165.

Romeiser, John B. "Portrait of the Artist as a Young Man: Claude in LA VOIE ROYALE." MMM 11:20-27. Autumn 1979.

Rowland, Michael and Sonja G. Stary. "Recollections of Dante's INFERNO in Malraux's LA VOIE ROYALE." Symposium 30:160-169. Summer 1976.

Stary, S. G. and M. L. Rowland. "Cyclic Time in Malraux's LA VOIE ROYALE." Neophil 60:49-55. January 1976.

Swenson, Birgit. "Death and Transfiguration in THE ROYAL WAY." Dialogues with the Unseen and the Unknown: Essays in Memory of André Malraux. Saratoga Springs: Skidmore College, 1978. pp. 63-67.

Tenenbaum, Elizabeth Brody. The Problematic Self: Approaches to Identity in Stendhal, D. H. Lawrence, and Malraux. Cambridge: Harvard University Press, 1977. pp. 122-129.

Wilkinson, David. Malraux: An Essay in Political Criticism. Cambridge: Harvard University Press, 1967. pp. 32-37.

THE TEMPTATION OF THE WEST
Boak, Denis. André Malraux. Oxford: Clarendon Press, 1968. pp. 22-28.

Chua, Cheng Lok. "The International Theme in André Malraux's Asian Novels." MLQ 39:170-173. June 1978.

Greenlee, James W. "Malraux's Erotic Response to the Absurd." MMM 10:17-27. Autumn 1978.

Horvath, Violet. André Malraux: The Human Adventure. New York: New York University Press, 1969. pp. 147-163.

THE WALNUT TREES OF ALTENBURG
Boak, Denis. André Malraux. Oxford: Clarendon Press, 1968. pp. 139-176.

Chua, C. L. "André Malraux's Unfinished Novel, LES NOYERS DE L'ALTENBURG: A Caveat for Critics." Neophil 53:10-13. January 1969.

Greenlee, James W. Malraux's Heroes and History. De Kalb: Northern Illinois University Press, 1975. pp. 141-178.

Hewitt, James Robert. André Malraux. New York: Frederick Ungar, 1978. pp. 79-88.

Horvath, Violet. André Malraux: The Human Adventure. New York: New York University Press, 1969. pp. 249-283.

Jenkins, Cecil. André Malraux. New York: Twayne, 1972. pp. 103-115.

Kline, Thomas Jefferson. André Malraux and the Metamorphosis of Death. New York: Columbia University Press, 1973. pp. 121-156.

Madsen, Axel. Hearts and Minds. New York: William Morrow, 1977. pp. 222-233.

Ortoleva, Madeleine Y. "LES NOYERS DE L'ALTENBURG: An Interpretation." Dialogues with the Unseen and the Unknown: Essays in Memory of André Malraux. Saratoga Springs: Skidmore College, 1978. pp. 57-62.

Payne, Robert. A Portrait of André Malraux. Englewood Cliffs: Prentice-Hall, 1970. pp. 303-315.

Wilkinson, David. Malraux: An Essay in Political Criticism. Cambridge: Harvard University Press, 1967. pp. 102-115.

Marguerite de Navarre
HEPTAMERON
Arrathoon, Leigh A. "The 'Compte en Viel Langaige' Behind HEPTAMERON, LXX." RPh 30:192-199. August 1976.

Baker, M. J. "Didacticism and the HEPTAMERON: The Misinterpretation of the Tenth Tale as an 'Exemplum.'" FR 45:84-90. Sp. Issue No. 3, Fall 1971.

_____. "The Role of the Moral Lesson in HEPTAMERON No. 30." FS 31:18-25. January 1977.

Benson, Edward. "Marriage Ancestral and Conjugal in the HEPTAMERON." JMRS 9:261-275. Fall 1979.

*Gelernt, Jules. World of Many Loves: THE HEPTAMERON of Marguerite de Navarre. Chapel Hill: University of North Carolina Press, 1966. 167 pp.

Heller, H. "Marguerite of Navarre and the Reformers of Meaux." BHR 33:292-300. 1971.

Tetel, Marcel. Marguerite de Navarre's HEPTAMERON: Themes, Language, and Structure. Durham: Duke University Press, 1973. 208 pp.

Marivaux, Pierre de
LE PAYSAN PARVENU
Adams, D. J. "Society and Self in LE PAYSAN PARVENU." FMLS 14:378-386. October 1978.

Fleming, John A. "Textual Autogenesis in Marivaux's PAYSAN PARVENU." SVEC 189:191-203. 1980.

Marivaux, Pierre de

>Haac, Oscar. Marivaux. New York: Twayne, 1973. pp. 83-86.
>
>Hill, Emita B. "Sincerity and Self-Awareness in the PAYSAN PARVENU." SVEC 88:735-748. 1972.
>
>Josephs, Herbert. "LE PAYSAN PARVENU: Satire and the Fiction of Innocence." FrF 5:22-29. January 1980.
>
>Rosbottom, Ronald C. Marivaux's Novels: Theme and Function in Early Eighteenth-Century Narrative. Rutherford: Fairleigh Dickinson University Press, 1974. pp. 171-222.
>
>Sturzer, Felicia. "'Marivaudage' as Self-Representation." FR 49:212-221. December 1975.
>
>Thomas, Ruth P. "The Art of the Portrait in the Novels of Marivaux." FR 42:23-31. October 1968.
>
>_____. "The Critical Narrators of Marivaux's Unfinished Novels." FMLS 9:363-369. October 1973.
>
>_____. "The Role of the Narrator in the Comic Tone of LE PAYSAN PARVENU." RomN 12:134-141. Autumn 1970.
>
>Whatley, Janet. "'L'Age équivoque': Marivaux and the Middle-Aged Woman." UTQ 46:75-80. Fall 1976.

PHARSAMON
>Hartwig, Robert J. "PHARSAMON and JOSEPH ANDREWS." TSLL 14:45-52. Spring 1972.

TELEMAQUE TRAVESTI
>Howells, R.J. "Marivaux and the Heroic." SVEC 171: 115-136. 1977.
>
>Whatley, Janet. "Coherent Worlds: Fénelon's TELEMAQUE and Marivaux's TELEMAQUE TRAVESTI." SVEC 171:85-113. 1977.

LA VIE DE MARIANNE
>Brady, Patrick. "Deceit and Self-deceit in MANON LESCAUT and LA VIE DE MARIANNE: Extrinsic, Rhetorical, and Immanent Perspectives on First-person Narration." MLR 72:50-52. January 1977.
>
>_____. "Other-Portrayal and Self-Betrayal in MANON LESCAUT and LA VIE DE MARIANNE." RR 64:99-110. March 1973.
>
>_____. "Rococo Style in the Novel: LA VIE DE MARIANNE." SFr 19:225-243. May/August 1975.

──────. "Socio-criticism as Genetic Structuralism: Value and Limitations of the Goldmann Method." ECr 14:209-218. Fall 1974.

──────. "Structural Analysis of Prose Fiction: A Re-evaluation." ECr 14:314-332. Winter 1974.

Brooks, Peter. The Novel of Worldliness: Crébillon, Marivaux, Laclos, Stendhal. Princeton: Princeton University Press, 1969. pp. 96-141.

Haac, Oscar. Marivaux. New York: Twayne, 1973. pp. 69-75.

──────. "Violence in Marivaux." KRQ 14:191-199. No. 3, 1967.

Heckman, John. "MARIANNE: The Making of an Author." MLN 86:509-522. May 1971.

Larson, Jeffry. "'La Vie de Marianne Pajot': A Real-life Source of Marivaux's Heroine." MLN 83:598-609. May 1968.

Robbins, Arthur. "Marianne and Moral Expediency." RLV 36:258-265. No. 3, 1970.

Rosbottom, Ronald C. "Marivaux and the Possibilities of the Memoir-Novel." Neophil 56:43-48. January 1972.

──────. Marivaux's Novels: Theme and Function in Early Eighteenth-Century Narrative. Rutherford: Fairleigh Dickinson University Press, 1974. pp. 93-170.

Sturzer, Felicia. "'Marivaudage' as Self-Representation." FR 49:212-221. December 1975.

Thomas, Ruth P. "The Art of the Portrait in the Novels of Marivaux." FR 42:23-31. October 1968.

──────. "The Critical Narrators of Marivaux's Unfinished Novels." FMLS 9:363-369. October 1973.

Trapnell, William H. "Marivaux's Unfinished Narratives." FS 24:242-247. July 1970.

Martin du Gard, Roger
    LA BELLE SAISON
        Savage, Catharine. Roger Martin du Gard. New York: Twayne, 1968. pp. 88-97.
    LE CONSULTATION
        Savage, Catharine. Roger Martin du Gard. New York: Twayne, 1968. pp. 97-104.

Schalk, David L. Roger Martin du Gard: The Novelist and History. Ithaca: Cornell University Press, 1967. pp. 83-88.

DEVENIR!
Savage, Catharine. Roger Martin du Gard. New York: Twayne, 1968. pp. 35-41.

Spurdle, Sonia. "Some Sources of Roger Martin du Gard's Inspiration in DEVENIR!" Neophil 55:261-269. July 1971.

L'ETE 1914
Savage, Catharine. Roger Martin du Gard. New York: Twayne, 1968. pp. 116-141.

Schalk, David L. Roger Martin du Gard: The Novelist and History. Ithaca: Cornell University Press, 1967. pp. 124-156.

JEAN BAROIS
Field, Trevor. "The Internal Chronology of JEAN BAROIS." SFr 50:300-303. 1973.

Savage, Catharine. Roger Martin du Gard. New York: Twayne, 1968. pp. 34-37; 41-64.

Schalk, David L. Roger Martin du Gard: The Novelist and History. Ithaca: Cornell University Press, 1967. pp. 24-27; 34-55; 184-185.

LA MORT DU PERE
Schalk, David L. Roger Martin du Gard: The Novelist and History. Ithaca: Cornell University Press, 1967. pp. 90-96.

LE PENITENCIER
Savage, Catharine. Roger Martin du Gard. New York: Twayne, 1968. pp. 80-87.

LA SORELLINA
Savage, Catharine. Roger Martin du Gard. New York: Twayne, 1968. pp. 103-110.

Schalk, David L. Roger Martin du Gard: The Novelist and History. Ithaca: Cornell University Press, 1967. pp. 88-90.

LES THIBAULT
DeJongh, William F. "Unnatural Death in LES THIBAULT." RomN 9:190-194. Spring 1968.

O'Brien, Justin. The French Literary Horizon. New Brunswick: Rutgers University Press, 1967. pp. 245-250.

Savage, Catharine. Roger Martin du Gard. New York: Twayne, 1968. pp. 65-74.

Schalk, David L. Roger Martin du Gard: The Novelist

and History. Ithaca: Cornell University Press, 1967. pp. 112-117.

Spurdle, Sonia M. "André Gide, Roger Martin du Gard, and Some Characters in LES THIBAULT." Trivium 4: 76-93. May 1969.

──────. "Roger Martin du Gard's Debt to Ibsen in L'UNE DE NOUS ... and LES THIBAULT." MLR 65: 57-64. January 1970.

──────. "Tolstoy and Martin du Gard's LES THIBAULT." CL 23:325-345. Fall 1971.
L'UNE DE NOUS
    Spurdle, Sonia M. "Roger Martin du Gard's Debt to Ibsen in L'UNE DE NOUS ... and LES THIBAULT." MLR 65:54-57. January 1970.

Maupassant, Guy de
    L'AME ETRANGERE
        *Ignotus, Paul. The Paradox of Maupassant. New York: Funk & Wagnalls, 1966. pp. 236-239.
    L'ANGELUS
        *Ignotus, Paul. The Paradox of Maupassant. New York: Funk & Wagnalls, 1966. pp. 236-240.
    BEL-AMI
        Dugan, John Raymond. Illusion and Reality: A Study of Descriptive Techniques in the Works of Guy de Maupassant. The Hague: Mouton, 1973. pp. 38-42.

        Hydak, Michael G. "Door Imagery in Maupassant's BEL-AMI." FR 49:337-341. February 1976.

        ──────. "Mars, Venus and Maupassant's BEL-AMI." RomN 18:178-182. Winter 1977.

        *Ignotus, Paul. The Paradox of Maupassant. New York: Funk & Wagnalls, 1966. pp. 150-154.

        Lerner, Michael G. Maupassant. New York: George Braziller, 1975. pp. 201-206.
    BOULE DE SUIF
        Denommé, Robert T. "Maupassant's Use of Unanimism in BOULE DE SUIF." RUO 37:159-166. January/March 1967.
    FORT COMME LA MORT
        Dugan, John Raymond. Illusion and Reality: A Study of Descriptive Techniques in the Works of Guy de Maupassant. The Hague: Mouton, 1973. pp. 49-54.

        *Ignotus, Paul. The Paradox of Maupassant. New York: Funk & Wagnalls, 1966. pp. 215-222.
    LE HORLA

*Ignotus, Paul. The Paradox of Maupassant. New York: Funk & Wagnalls, 1966. pp. 231-235.
MONT-ORIOL
Dugan, John Raymond. Illusion and Reality: A Study of Descriptive Techniques in the Works of Guy de Maupassant. The Hague: Mouton, 1973. pp. 42-46.

*Ignotus, Paul. The Paradox of Maupassant. New York: Funk & Wagnalls, 1966. pp. 190-193.

Lerner, Michael G. Maupassant. New York: George Braziller, 1975. pp. 221-223.
ONE LIFE
DeCoster, Cyrus C. "Maupassant's UNE VIE and Pardo Bazan's LOS PAZOS DE ULLOA." Hispania 56:587-591. September 1973.

Dugan, John Raymond. Illusion and Reality: A Study of Descriptive Techniques in the Works of Guy de Maupassant. The Hague: Mouton, 1973. pp. 35-41.

*Ignotus, Paul. The Paradox of Maupassant. New York: Funk & Wagnalls, 1966. pp. 50-52.

Lerner, Michael G. Maupassant. New York: George Braziller, 1975. pp. 166-170.
OUR HEART
Dugan, John Raymond. Illusion and Reality: A Study of Descriptive Techniques in the Works of Guy de Maupassant. The Hague: Mouton, 1973. pp. 54-58; 169-174.

*Ignotus, Paul. The Paradox of Maupassant. New York: Funk & Wagnalls, 1966. pp. 215-221.

Lerner, Michael G. Maupassant. New York: George Braziller, 1975. pp. 254-262.
PIERRE ET JEAN
Artinian, Robert Willard. "'Then, Venom, to Thy Work': Pathological Representation in PIERRE ET JEAN." MFS 18:225-229. Summer 1972.

Boak, Denis. "PIERRE ET JEAN: The Banal as Tragic." EFL 15:48-55. November 1978.

Donaldson-Evans, Mary. "The Sea as Symbol: A Key to the Structure of Maupassant's PIERRE ET JEAN." NFS 17:36-43. October 1978.

Dugan, John Raymond. Illusion and Reality: A Study of Descriptive Techniques in the Works of Guy de Maupassant. The Hague: Mouton, 1973. pp. 45-49; 89-91; 153-157.

Lerner, Michael G. Maupassant. New York: George
Braziller, 1975. pp. 235-238.
YVETTE
Alexander, Theodor W. and Beatrice W. "Maupassant's
YVETTE and Schnitzler's FRÄULEIN ELSE." MAL 4:
44-53. Fall 1971.

Mauriac, Claude
L'AGRANDISSEMENT
Boschetto, Sandra M. "Silence as an Element of Dialogue in Claude Mauriac's L'AGRANDISSEMENT." IFR
7:35-38. Winter 1980.
ALL WOMEN ARE FATAL
Mercier, Vivian. The New Novel from Queneau to
Pinget. New York: Farrar, Straus & Giroux, 1971.
pp. 317-327.
THE DINNER PARTY
Mercier, Vivian. The New Novel from Queneau to
Pinget. New York: Farrar, Straus & Giroux, 1971.
pp. 327-336.
THE MARQUISE WENT OUT AT FIVE
Mercier, Vivian. The New Novel from Queneau to
Pinget. New York: Farrar, Straus & Giroux, 1971.
pp. 336-347.

Mauriac, François
UN ADOLESCENT D'AUTREFOIS
Lewis, Valerie H. "François Mauriac--A Self-Critical
Catholic Novelist." Standpunte 86:16-19. December
1969.
THE DARK ANGELS
Flower, J. E. "Form and Unity in Muriac's [sic] THE
BLACK ANGELS." Renascence 19:79-87. Winter 1967.

Smith, Maxwell A. François Mauriac. New York:
Twayne, 1970. pp. 65-70.

Speaight, Robert. François Mauriac: A Study of the
Writer and the Man. London: Chatto and Windus, 1976.
pp. 125-129.
THE DESERT OF LOVE
Caspary, Sister Anita Marie. "The Theme of Isolation
in Mauriac's THE DESERT OF LOVE." François
Mauriac. St. Louis: Herder. pp. 67-77.

Smith, Maxwell A. François Mauriac. New York:
Twayne, 1970. pp. 91-96.

Speaight, Robert. François Mauriac: A Study of the
Writer and the Man. London: Chatto and Windus, 1976.
pp. 82-86.
THE END OF NIGHT
Smith, Maxwell A. François Mauriac. New York:
Twayne, 1970. pp. 104-107.

Speaight, Robert. François Mauriac: A Study of the Writer and the Man. London: Chatto and Windus, 1976. pp. 122-125.

Thornton-Smith, C. B. "Sincerity and Self-Justification: The Repudiated Preface of LA FIN DE LA NUIT." AJFS 5:222-230. May/August 1968.

THE ENEMY
Smith, Maxwell A. François Mauriac. New York: Twayne, 1970. pp. 36-39.

FLESH AND BLOOD
Smith, Maxwell A. François Mauriac. New York: Twayne, 1970. pp. 33-35.

Speaight, Robert. François Mauriac: A Study of the Writer and the Man. London: Chatto and Windus, 1976. pp. 65-69.

THE FRONTENAC MYSTERY
Smith, Maxwell A. François Mauriac. New York: Twayne, 1970. pp. 61-65.

Speaight, Robert. François Mauriac: A Study of the Writer and the Man. London: Chatto and Windus, 1976. pp. 116-119.

GALIGAI
Smith, Maxwell A. François Mauriac. New York: Twayne, 1970. pp. 74-77.

Speaight, Robert. François Mauriac: A Study of the Writer and the Man. London: Chatto and Windus, 1976. pp. 184-186.

GENITRIX
Flower, J. E. Intention and Achievement: An Essay on the Novels of François Mauriac. Oxford: Clarendon Press, 1969. pp. 69-73.

McNab, James P. "The Mother in François Mauriac's GENITRIX." HSL 2:207-213. No. 3, 1970.

Smith, Maxwell A. François Mauriac. New York: Twayne, 1970. pp. 86-91.

Speaight, Robert. François Mauriac: A Study of the Writer and the Man. London: Chatto and Windus, 1976. pp. 78-80.

A KISS FOR THE LEPER
Flower, J. E. Intention and Achievement: An Essay on the Novels of François Mauriac. Oxford: Clarendon Press, 1969. pp. 58-63; 69-71.

Mellard, James M. "The Constructed Reality: Mauriac's A KISS FOR THE LEPER." Renascence 25:24-34. Autumn 1972.

Smith, Maxwell A.  François Mauriac.  New York: Twayne, 1970.  pp. 82-86.

Speaight, Robert.  François Mauriac: A Study of the Writer and the Man.  London: Chatto and Windus, 1976.  pp. 76-79.

THE LAMB

Flower, J. E.  Intention and Achievement: An Essay on the Novels of François Mauriac.  Oxford: Clarendon Press, 1969.  pp. 98-105.

Smith, Maxwell A.  François Mauriac.  New York: Twayne, 1970.  pp. 77-81.

Speaight, Robert.  François Mauriac: A Study of the Writer and the Man.  London: Chatto and Windus, 1976.  pp. 194-197.

THE LINES OF LIFE

Smith, Maxwell A.  François Mauriac.  New York: Twayne, 1970.  pp. 54-59.

A NEST OF VIPERS

Batchelor, R.  "Art and Theology in Mauriac's LE NOEUD DE VIPERES."  NFS 12:33-43.  May 1973.

Fischler, Alexander.  "Thematic Keys in François Mauriac's THERESE DESQUEYROUX and LE NOEUD DE VIPERES."  MLQ 40:383-388.  December 1979.

Flower, J. E.  Intention and Achievement: An Essay on the Novels of François Mauriac.  Oxford: Clarendon Press, 1969.  pp. 74-83.

Morrissette, Laurence.  "The Family as Fantasy System in Mauriac's LE NOEUD DE VIPERES."  BRMMLA 31: 84-93.  Spring 1977.

Smith, Maxwell A.  François Mauriac.  New York: Twayne, 1970.  pp. 108-115.

Speaight, Robert.  François Mauriac: A Study of the Writer and the Man.  London: Chatto and Windus, 1976.  pp. 111-113.

Wentersdorf, Karl P.  "The Chronology of Mauriac's LE NOEUD DE VIPERES."  KFLQ 13:89-100.  Supplement 1967.

THERESE DESQUEYROUX

Brosman, Catharine Savage.  "Point of View and Christian Viewpoint in THERESE DESQUEYROUX."  EFL 11: 69-73.  November 1974.

Farrell, C. Frederick, Jr. and Edith R. Farrell.  "The Animal Imagery of THERESE DESQUEYROUX."  KRQ 21: 429-445.  No. 4, 1974.

Mauriac, François

    ———. "The Multiple Murders of Thérèse Desqueyroux." HSL 2:195-206. No. 3, 1970.

    Farrell, Edith R. and C. Frederick. "Thérèse Desqueyroux: A Complete Suicide." LangQ 14:13-15; 18; 22. Spring/Summer 1976.

    Fischler, Alexander. "Thematic Keys in François Mauriac's THERESE DESQUEYROUX and LE NOEUD DE VIPERES." MLQ 40:378-383. December 1979.

    Flower, J. E. Intention and Achievement: An Essay on the Novels of François Mauriac. Oxford: Clarendon Press, 1969. pp. 72-78.

    Smith, Maxwell A. François Mauriac. New York: Twayne, 1970. pp. 96-104.

    Speaight, Robert. François Mauriac: A Study of the Writer and the Man. London: Chatto and Windus, 1976. pp. 87-89; 121-125; 143-146.

THE UNKNOWN SEA
    Smith, Maxwell A. François Mauriac. New York: Twayne, 1970. pp. 70-73.

    Speaight, Robert. François Mauriac: A Study of the Writer and the Man. London: Chatto and Windus, 1976. pp. 148-150.

THE WEAKLING
    Lewis, Valerie H. "François Mauriac: LE SAGOUIN." Standpunte 118:55-58. April 1975.

WOMAN OF THE PHARISEES
    Smith, Maxwell A. François Mauriac. New York: Twayne, 1970. pp. 115-120.

    Speaight, Robert. François Mauriac: A Study of the Writer and the Man. London: Chatto and Windus, 1976. pp. 159-161.

YOUNG MAN IN CHAINS
    Flower, J. E. Intention and Achievement: An Essay on the Novels of François Mauriac. Oxford: Clarendon Press, 1969. pp. 31-41.

Mérimée, Prosper
  LES AMES DU PURGATOIRE
    Thompson, C. W. "Mérimée and Pictorial Inspiration: The Sources of LES AMES DU PURGATOIRE." MLR 67:62-73. January 1972.
  CARMEN
    Smith, Maxwell. Prosper Mérimée. New York: Twayne, 1972. pp. 143-147.

    Tilby, Michael. "Language and Sexuality in Mérimée's CARMEN." FMLS 15:255-263. July 1979.

COLOMBA
    Raitt, A. W. Prosper Mérimée. New York: Charles Scribner's Sons, 1970. pp. 187-192.

    Smith, Maxwell. Prosper Mérimée. New York: Twayne, 1972. pp. 133-139.

THE DOUBLE MISTAKE
    Lethbridge, Robert and Michael Tilby. "Reading Mérimée's LA DOUBLE MEPRISE." MLR 73:767-785. October 1978.

    Raitt, A. W. Prosper Mérimée. New York: Charles Scribner's Sons, 1970. pp. 172-176.

    Smith, Maxwell. Prosper Mérimée. New York: Twayne, 1972. pp. 117-123.

LE ENLEVEMENT DE LA REDOUTE
    Smith, Maxwell. Prosper Mérimée. New York: Twayne, 1972. pp. 102-105.

MATEO FALCONE
    Raitt, A. W. Prosper Mérimée. New York: Charles Scribner's Sons, 1970. pp. 130-133.

    Smith, Maxwell. Prosper Mérimée. New York: Twayne, 1972. pp. 98-100.

1572. CHRONIQUE DU REGNE DE CHARLES IX
    Cogman, P. W. M. "Historical and Moral Perspective in Mérimée's '1572.'" FMLS 10:313-322. October 1974.

    Mickel, Emanuel J., Jr. "Some Sources for Mérimée's CHARLES IX." MLQ 29: 190-195. June 1968.

LE VASE ETRUSQUE
    Smith, Maxwell. Prosper Mérimée. New York: Twayne, 1972. pp. 128-133.

LA VENUS D'ILLE
    Pilkington, Anthony E. "Narrator and Supernatural in Mérimée's LA VENUS D'ILLE." NCFS 4:24-30. Fall/Winter 1975-1976.

    Raitt, A. W. Prosper Mérimée. New York: Charles Scribner's Sons, 1970. pp. 182-188.

    Smith, Maxwell. Prosper Mérimée. New York: Twayne, 1972. pp. 128-133.

Mirbeau, Octave
    LE JOURNAL D'UNE FEMME DE CHAMBRE
        Halpern, Joseph. "Desire and Mask in LE JOURNAL D'UNE FEMME DE CHAMBRE." KRQ 27:313-326. No. 3, 1980.

Montesquieu
    LETTRES PERSANES

Thomas, Ruth P. "Montesquieu's Harem and Diderot's Convent: The Woman as Prisoner." FR 52:36-45. October 1978.

de Montherlant, Henry
THE BACHELORS
Johnson, Robert B. Henry de Montherlant. New York: Twayne, 1968. pp. 51-55.
CHAOS AND NIGHT
Johnson, Robert B. Henry de Montherlant. New York: Twayne, 1968. pp. 75-80.
DEMON OF GOOD
Johnson, Robert B. Henry de Montherlant. New York: Twayne, 1968. pp. 69-73.
PITY FOR WOMEN
Johnson, Robert B. Henry de Montherlant. New York: Twayne, 1968. pp. 62-69.

O'Brien, Justin. The French Literary Horizon. New Brunswick: Rutgers University Press, 1967. pp. 209-213.
LE SONGE
Arthos, John. "The Montherlant Manner." FR 43:137-139. Winter 1970.
YOUNG GIRLS
Becker, Lucille. Henry de Montherlant: A Critical Biography. Carbondale: Southern Illinois University Press, 1970. pp. 22-27.

Johnson, Robert B. Henry de Montherlant. New York: Twayne, 1968. pp. 55-62.

La Mortière
MOTIFS DE RETRAITE
Grieder, Josephine. "La Mortière's MOTIFS DE RETRAITE: An Eighteenth-Century Metamorphosis of LA PRINCESSE DE CLEVES." FR 51:10-14. October 1977.

de Musset, Alfred
LA CONFESSION D'UN ENFANT DU SIECLE
King, Russell S. "Romanticism and Musset's CONFESSION D'UN ENFANT DU SIECLE." NFS 9:3-13. May 1972.

*Raitt, A.W. Life and Letters in France: The Nineteenth Century. New York: Charles Scribner's Sons, 1965. pp. 19-35.

Rizzuto, Anthony. "Octave in Alfred de Musset's LA CONFESSION D'UN ENFANT DU SIECLE." KRQ 24:83-94. No. 1, 1977.

de Nerval, Gérard
AURELIA

Jones, Robert Emmet. Gérard de Nerval. New York: Twayne, 1974. pp. 122-146.

Knapp, Bettina L. Gérard de Nerval: The Mystic's Dilemma. University, Ala.: University of Alabama Press, 1980. pp. 285-318.

Rinsler, Norma. Gérard de Nerval. London: Athlone Press, 1973. pp. 92-111.

## THE MARQUIS DE FAYOLLE

Knapp, Bettina L. Gérard de Nerval: The Mystic's Dilemma. University, Ala.: University of Alabama Press, 1980. pp. 165-176.

## OCTAVIE

Jones, Robert Emmet. Gérard de Nerval. New York: Twayne, 1974. pp. 110-113.

## ROMAN TRAGIQUE

Zuckerman, Phyllis. "Comedy, Tragedy, and Madness in Nerval's ROMAN TRAGIQUE." MLN 89:600-613. May 1974.

## SYLVIE

Carroll, Robert C. "Gérard de Nerval: Prodigal Son of History." NCFS 4:267-273. Spring 1976.

———. "Romanesque Seduction in Nerval's SYLVIE." NCFS 5:222-235. Spring/Summer 1977.

Jones, Robert Emmet. Gérard de Nerval. New York: Twayne, 1974. pp. 103-110.

Mein, Margaret. A Foretaste of Proust: A Study of Proust and His Precursors. Westmead: Saxon House, 1974. pp. 50-59.

Padgett, Jacqueline Olson. "Spirits and Their Bodies: Images of Woman in Nerval's SYLVIE." KRQ 27:327-333. No. 3, 1980.

Porter, Laurence M. "Nerval's SYLVIE: The Flight from Materiality." NCFS 4:258-262. Spring 1976.

## VOYAGE EN ORIENT

Jones, Robert Emmet. Gérard de Nerval. New York: Twayne, 1974. pp. 79-91.

# Nizan, Paul

## ANTOINE BLOYE

Redfern, W. D. Paul Nizan: Committed Literature in a Conspiratorial World. Princeton: Princeton University Press, 1972. pp. 47-77.

Wasson, Richard. "'The True Possession of Time': Paul Nizan, Marxism, and Modernism." Boundary 5: 397-410. Winter 1977.

Nizan, Paul

LE CHEVAL DE TROIE
Redfern, W. D. Paul Nizan: Committed Literature in a Conspiratorial World. Princeton: Princeton University Press, 1972. pp. 119-150.
LA CONSPIRATION
Redfern, W. D. Paul Nizan: Committed Literature in a Conspiratorial World. Princeton: Princeton University Press, 1972. pp. 151-182.

———. "A Vigorous Corpse: Paul Nizan and LA CONSPIRATION." RR 59:278-295. December 1968.

Nodier, Charles
LA FEE AUX MIETTES
Maples, Robert J. B. "Individuation in Nodier's LA FEE AUX MIETTES." SIR 8:43-64. Autumn 1968.

Nelson, Hilda. Charles Nodier. New York: Twayne, 1972. pp. 81-91.

Porter, Laurence M. "Hoffmannesque and Hamiltonian Sources of Nodier's FEE AUX MIETTES." RomN 19:341-344. Spring 1979.
JEAN SBOGAR
Nelson, Hilda. Charles Nodier. New York: Twayne, 1972. pp. 51-56.
SMARRA
Porter, Laurence M. "The Forbidden City: A Psychoanalytical Interpretation of Nodier's SMARRA." Symposium 26:331-348. Winter 1972.
TRILBY
Nelson, Hilda. Charles Nodier. New York: Twayne, 1972. pp. 69-73.

Porter, Laurence M. "Towards a Prehistory of Depth Psychology in French Romanticism: Temptation and Repression in Nodier's TRILBY." NCFS 2:97-110. Spring/Summer 1974.

Ollier, Claude
LE MAINTIEN DE L'ORDRE
Tixier, Jean-Max. "The Fictional Development in LE MAINTIEN DE L'ORDRE." Sub-stance 13:45-51. 1976.
LA MISE EN SCENE
Lovichi, Jacques. "Ollier in Wonderland, or On the Other Side of the Mirror." Sub-stance 13:68-74. 1976.

Pieyre de Mandiargues, André
LA MOTOCYCLETTE
Lowrie, Joyce O. "The 'Rota Fortunae' in Pieyre de Mandiargues's LA MOTOCYCLETTE." FR 53:378-388. February 1980.

Pinget, Robert
　　BAGA
　　　　Henkels, Robert M., Jr. Robert Pinget: The Novel as Quest. University, Ala.: University of Alabama Press, 1979. pp. 53-62.

　　　　Mercier, Vivian. The New Novel from Queneau to Pinget. New York: Farrar, Straus & Giroux, 1971. pp. 387-391.
　　BETWEEN FANTOINE AND AGAPA
　　　　Henkels, Robert M., Jr. Robert Pinget: The Novel as Quest. University, Ala.: University of Alabama Press, 1979. pp. 13-20.
　　CLOPE TO THE DOSSIER
　　　　Henkels, Robert M., Jr. Robert Pinget: The Novel as Quest. University, Ala.: University of Alabama Press, 1979. pp. 84-97.

　　　　Mercier, Vivian. The New Novel from Queneau to Pinget. New York: Farrar, Straus & Giroux, 1971. pp. 397-402.
　　LE FISTON
　　　　Henkels, Robert M., Jr. Robert Pinget: The Novel as Quest. University, Ala.: University of Alabama Press, 1979. pp. 107-109; 124-127.

　　　　Mercier, Vivian. The New Novel from Queneau to Pinget. New York: Farrar, Straus & Giroux, 1971. pp. 391-397.
　　THE FOX AND THE COMPASS
　　　　Henkels, Robert M., Jr. Robert Pinget: The Novel as Quest. University, Ala.: University of Alabama Press, 1979. pp. 27-35.
　　GRAAL FLIBUSTE
　　　　Henkels, Robert M., Jr. Robert Pinget: The Novel as Quest. University, Ala.: University of Alabama Press, 1979. pp. 36-53.
　　THE INQUISITORY
　　　　Henkels, Robert M., Jr. "Novel Quarters for an Odd Couple: Apollo and Dionysis [sic] in Beckett's WATT and Pinget's THE INQUISITORY." StTCL 2:150-155. Spring 1978.

　　　　_____. Robert Pinget: The Novel as Quest. University, Ala.: University of Alabama Press, 1979. pp. 98-110.

　　　　Mercier, Vivian. The New Novel from Queneau to Pinget. New York: Farrar, Straus & Giroux, 1971. pp. 363-376.
　　MAHU OU LE MATERIAU
　　　　Henkels, Robert M., Jr. Robert Pinget: The Novel as Quest. University, Ala.: University of Alabama Press, 1979. pp. 21-28.

Mercier, Vivian. The New Novel from Queneau to Pinget. New York: Farrar, Straus & Giroux, 1971. pp. 376-379.
PASSACAILLE
    Broome, Peter. "A New Mode of Reading: Pinget's PASSACAILLE." NFS 12:86-99. October 1973.

    _____. "Robert Pinget's PASSACAILLE." IFR 1: 135-138. July 1974.

    Jones, Tobin H. "Toward a More Primitive Reading: Aesthetic Response to Radical Form in the New French Novel." ELWIU 3:272-276. Fall 1976.
QUELQU'UN
    Henkels, Robert M., Jr. Robert Pinget: The Novel as Quest. University, Ala.: University of Alabama Press, 1979. pp. 111-119.

    Kellman, Steven G. "'Quelqu'un' in Robert Pinget's Fiction." Mosaic 5:137-144. Spring 1972.

    Livingston, Beverly. "From A to F and Back: Pinget's Fictive Arena." YFS 57:72-85. 1979.

    Mercier, Vivian. The New Novel from Queneau to Pinget. New York: Farrar, Straus & Giroux, 1971. pp. 403-410.

Pourrat, Henri
    GASPARD DES MONTAGNES
        Sussex, R. T. "Henri Pourrat's GASPARD DES MONTAGNES." AJFS 6:447-453. May/December 1969.

Prévost, Antoine François
    CLEVELAND
        Cherpack, Clifton. "Literature and Belief: The Example of Prévost's CLEVELAND." ECS 6:186-202. Winter 1972-1973.

        Gilroy, James P. "Peace and the Pursuit of Happiness in the French Utopian Novel: Fénelon's TELEMAQUE and Prévost's CLEVELAND." SVEC 176:169-187. 1979.

        Stewart, Philip. "Vox Naturae: A Reading of Prévost." RR 71:141-148. March 1980.
    LE DOYEN DE KILLERINE
        Mead, William. "The Puzzle of Prévost: LE DOYEN DE KILLERINE." ECr 12:82-93. Summer 1972.
    HISTOIRE D'UNE GRECQUE MODERNE
        Hill, Emita B. "Virtue on Trial: A Defense of Prévost's Théophé." SVEC 67:191-209. 1969.

        Holland, Allan. "The Miracle of Prévost's GRECQUE MODERNE." AJFS 16:278-280. January/April 1979.

Singerman, Alan J. "The Abbé Prévost's GRECQUE MODERNE: A Witness for the Defense." FR 46:938-945. April 1973.

HISTOIRE DE MARGUERITE D'ANJOU
Francis, R. A. "The Abbé Prévost's HISTOIRE DE MARGUERITE D'ANJOU: Novel or History?" MLR 71:31-41. January 1976.

MANON LESCAUT
Brady, Patrick. "Deceit and Self-deceit in MANON LESCAUT and LA VIE DE MARIANNE: Extrinsic, Rhetorical, and Immanent Perspectives on First-person Narration." MLR 72:47-50. January 1977.

_____. "MANON LESCAUT: Classical, Romantic, or Rococo?" SVEC 53:339-360. 1967.

_____. "Other-Portrayal and Self-Betrayal in MANON LESCAUT and LA VIE DE MARIANNE." RR 64:99-110. March 1973.

_____. "Socio-criticism as Genetic Structuralism: Value and Limitations of the Goldmann Method." ECr 14:209-218. Fall 1974.

_____. "Structural Analysis of Prose Fiction: A Re-evaluation." ECr 14:314-332. Winter 1974.

Costich, Julia F. "Fortune in MANON LESCAUT." FR 49:522-527. March 1976.

Donohoe, Joseph I., Jr. "The Death of Manon: A Literary Inquest." ECr 12:129-146. Summer 1972.

Fambrough, Preston. "'L'Ame Généreuse' in Prévost's Romantic Hero." RomN 14:112-115. Autumn 1972.

Frautschi, Richard L. (with Diana Apostolides). "Narrative Voice in MANON LESCAUT: Some Quantitative Observations." ECr 12:103-117. Summer 1972.

Gossman, Lionel. "Prévost's MANON: Love in the New World." YFS 40:91-102. 1968.

Greshoff, C. J. "A Note on the Ambiguity of MANON LESCAUT." FMLS 3:166-171. April 1967.

Higgins, I. R. W. "The Ambiguity of MANON LESCAUT: A Reply to C. J. Greshoff." FMLS 4:192-198. April 1968.

Jones, Grahame. "MANON LESCAUT: An Exercise in Literary Persuasion." RR 69:48-59. January/March 1978.

Prévost, Antoine François

    Jones, Grahame C. "MANON LESCAUT: Morality and Style." EFL 9:30-45. November 1972.

    Josephs, Herbert. "MANON LESCAUT: A Rhetoric of Intellectual Evasion." RR 59:185-197. October 1968.

    O'Reilly, Robert F. "New Considerations on Point of View in MANON LESCAUT." RomN 13:107-112. Autumn 1971.

    Singerman, Alan J. "A 'fille de plaisir' and Her 'greluchon': Society and the Perspective of Manon Lescaut." ECr 12:118-128. Summer 1972.

    Tate, Robert S., Jr. "MANON LESCAUT and the Enlightenment." SVEC 70:15-25. 1970.

    Thody, P. M. W. "MANON LESCAUT and LES LIAISONS DANGEREUSES: The Problems of Morality in Literature." ML 51:61-72. June 1975.

MEMOIRES D'UN HOMME DE QUALITE
    Francis, R. A. "The Additional Tales in the 1756 Edition of Prévost's MEMOIRES D'UN HOMME DE QUALITE: Technique and Function." FS 32:408-419. October 1978.

Proust, Marcel
A L'OMBRE DES JEUNES FILLES EN FLEURS
    Fisher, Mark Lawrence. "Albertine Misconstrued: Complicity and Duplicity in Proust." ELWIU 6:117-128. Spring 1979.

    Splitter, Randolph. "Proust, Joyce, and the Theory of Metaphor." L & P 29:4-18. No. 1/2, 1979.

UN AMOUR DE SWANN
    *Brée, Germaine. The World of Marcel Proust. Boston: Houghton Mifflin, 1966. pp. 169-174; 199-203.

    Jones, Louisa. "Swann and the 'Tables Tournantes.'" FR 48:711-721. March 1975.

    Lapp, John C. "The Jealous Window-Watcher in Zola and Proust." FS 29:166-175. April 1975.

    *Linn, John Gaywood. The Theater in the Fiction of Marcel Proust. Athens: Ohio State University Press, 1966. pp. 75-83.

    Zimmermann, Eleonore M. "Proust's Novel in a Novel: UN AMOUR DE SWANN." MLR 68:551-558. July 1973.

THE CAPTIVE
    Sonnenfeld, Albert. "TRISTAN for Pianoforte: Thomas Mann and Marcel Proust." SoR 5:1004-1018. October 1969.

## CITIES OF THE PLAIN

Bryant, Margaret M. "Marcel Proust's Interest in Names." Names 26:20-26. March 1978.

## COMBRAY

Taylor, Rosalie. "The Adult World and Childhood in COMBRAY." FS 22:26-36. January 1968.

Wolitz, Seth. "Food in Proust's COMBRAY." Adam 40:63-73. 1976.

## THE FUGITIVE

*Brée, Germaine. The World of Marcel Proust. Boston: Houghton Mifflin, 1966. pp. 108-110.

Terdiman, Richard. The Dialectics of Isolation: Self and Society in the French Novel from the Realists to Proust. New Haven: Yale University Press, 1976. pp. 203-223.

Weinstein, Philip M. "Caddy 'Disparue': Exploring an Episode Common to Proust and Faulkner." CLS 14:38-52. March 1977.

## JEAN SANTEUIL

Alden, Douglas W. "The Break with Realism." Marcel Proust: A Critical Panorama. ed. Larkin B. Price. Urbana: University of Illinois Press, 1973. pp. 24-47.

*Brée, Germaine. The World of Marcel Proust. Boston: Houghton Mifflin, 1966. pp. 48-63.

Cattaui, Georges. Marcel Proust. London: Merlin, 1967. pp. 24-41.

Finn, Michael R. "JEAN SANTEUIL and A LA RECHERCHE DU TEMPS PERDU: Instinct and Intellect." FMLS 11:122-132. April 1975.

Jephcott, E. F. N. Proust and Rilke: The Literature of Expanded Consciousness. London: Chatto and Windus, 1972. pp. 82-94.

*Linn, John Gaywood. The Theater in the Fiction of Marcel Proust. Athens: Ohio State University Press, 1966. pp. 40-44; 204-214.

Price, Larkin B. "Marcel Proust's 'dieu déguisé': The Artist-Myth in JEAN SANTEUIL." ECr 11:60-73. Spring 1971.

Slater, Maya. "L'INCONNU: A Fragment of JEAN SANTEUIL." MLR 65:778-784. October 1970.

Stambolian, George. Marcel Proust and the Creative Encounter. Chicago: University of Chicago Press, 1972. pp. 235-240.

Ullman, Stephen. Meaning and Style. New York: Barnes and Noble, 1973. pp. 98-121.

Weber, Jean-Paul. "Bergson and Proust." In Search of Marcel Proust. ed. Monique Chefdor. [Los Angeles]: Ritchie, 1973. pp. 55-77.

## LA MORT DE BALDASSARE SILVANDE

Zimmerman, Eugenia N. "Death and Transfiguration in Proust and Tolstoy." Mosaic 6:161-172. Winter 1973.

## PLEASURES AND DAYS

*Brée, Germaine. The World of Marcel Proust. Boston: Houghton Mifflin, 1966. pp. 35-47.

Jephcott, E. F. N. Proust and Rilke: The Literature of Expanded Consciousness. London: Chatto and Windus, 1972. pp. 39-46.

*Linn, John Gaywood. The Theater in the Fiction of Marcel Proust. Athens: Ohio State University Press, 1966. pp. 59-61.

Stambolian, George. Marcel Proust and the Creative Encounter. Chicago: University of Chicago Press, 1972. pp. 24-30.

## REMEMBRANCE OF THINGS PAST

Acheson, James. "Beckett, Proust, and Schopenhauer." ConL 19:165-179. Spring 1978.

Amadou, Anne-Lisa. "The Theme of Water in A LA RECHERCHE DU TEMPS PERDU." MLR 72:310-321. April 1977.

Appignanesi, Lisa. Femininity & the Creative Imagination: A Study of Henry James, Robert Musil & Marcel Proust. New York: Barnes & Noble, 1973. pp. 157-215.

Aynesworth, Donald. "Essence and Apparition in Proust." SNNTS 12:29-45. Spring 1980.

Balakian, Anna. "Proust Fifty Years Later." CLS 10:93-111. June 1973.

Bell, Clive. "Proust." Adam 37:31-62. 1972.

Beznos, Maurice J. "Aspects of Time According to the Theories of Relativity in Marcel Proust's A LA RECHERCHE DU TEMPS PERDU: A Study of the Similitudes in Conceptual Limits." OUR 10:74-102. 1968.

Birn, Randi. "Proust, Claude Simon, and the Art of the Novel." PLL 13:168-186. Spring 1977.

Birn, Randi Marie. "The Theoretical Background for Proust's Personnages 'préparés.'" ECr 11:42-51. Spring 1971.

――――. "The Windows of Imagination in A LA RECHERCHE DU TEMPS PERDU." PCP 5:5-10. April 1970.

Bondanella, Peter E. and J. E. Rivers. "Sacripant and Sacripante: A Note on Proust and Ariosto." RomN 11: 4-7. Autumn 1969.

Bowen, Elizabeth. "Bergotte." Marcel Proust 1871-1922. ed. Peter Quennell. New York: Simon and Schuster, 1971. pp. 59-75.

Brady, Patrick. "Farms, Trees, and Bell-Towers: The 'Hidden Meaning' of Triads in Proust's RECHERCHE." Neophil 61:371-376. July 1977.

*Brée, Germaine. "Marcel Proust: Changing Perspectives." AJFS 1:104-113. January/April 1964.

――――. "Proust's Combray Church: Illiers or Vermeer?" PAPS 112:5-7. February 15, 1968.

――――. "Proust's Dormant Gods." YFS 38:183-194. 1967.

Bucknall, Barbara J. "From Material to Spiritual Food in A LA RECHERCHE DU TEMPS PERDU." ECr 11:52-60. Spring 1971.

――――. The Religion of Art in Proust. Urbana: University of Illinois Press, 1969. 203 pp.

Cattaui, Georges. Marcel Proust. London: Merlin, 1967. 112 pp.

Cocking, J. M. "The Coherence of LE TEMPS RETROUVE." Marcel Proust: A Critical Panorama. ed. Larkin B. Price. Urbana: University of Illinois Press, 1973. pp. 82-101.

――――. "Proust and Music." EFL 4:13-28. November 1967.

Cohn, Robert G. "Proust and Mallarmé." FS 24:262-275. July 1970.

Collins, P. H. "Proust, Time, and Beckett's HAPPY DAYS." FR 47:105-119. Spring 1974.

Conroy, Peter V. "The Hôtel de Balbec as a Church and Theater." Marcel Proust: A Critical Panorama. ed. Larkin B. Price. Urbana: University of Illinois Press, 1973. pp. 206-225.

Crosman, Inge Karalus. "Metaphoric Function in A LA RECHERCHE DU TEMPS PERDU." RR 67:290-299. November 1976.

―――――. Metaphoric Narration: The Structure and Function of Metaphors in A LA RECHERCHE DU TEMPS PERDU. Chapel Hill: University of North Carolina Press, 1978. 218 pp.

De Ley, Herbert. "'L'Hôpital sans style vaut le glorieux portail': Salon Painters in A LA RECHERCHE DU TEMPS PERDU." ECr 11:32-41. Spring 1971.

Doubrovsky, Serge. "The Place of the Madeleine: Writing and Phantasy in Proust." Boundary 4:107-133. Fall 1975.

Duncan, J. Ann. "Imaginary Artists in A LA RECHERCHE DU TEMPS PERDU." MLR 64:555-564. July 1969.

Ellison, David R. "Who Is 'Marcel'?: Proust and the Question of Autobiographical Identity." ECr 20:78-86. Fall 1980.

Erickson, John D. "The Proust-Einstein Relation: A Study in Relative Point of View." Marcel Proust: A Critical Panorama. ed. Larkin B. Price. Urbana: University of Illinois Press, 1973. pp. 247-276.

Festa-McCormick, Diana. "Proust and the Image of Venice." BUJ 25:7-15. No. 3, 1978.

―――――. "Proustian Aesthetics of Ambiguity: Elstir's 'Miss Sacripant.'" IFR 3:92-99. July 1976.

Finn, Michael R. "Proust and Dumas fils: Odette and 'La Dame aux camélias.'" FR 47:528-542. February 1974.

Fisher, Clarice. "Character as a Way of Knowing in A LA RECHERCHE DU TEMPS PERDU: The Baron de Charlus." MFS 20:407-418. Autumn 1974.

Graham, Victor E. "Marcel Proust and the MILLE ET UNE NUITS." CRCL 1:89-96. Winter 1974.

―――――. "Proust's Etymologies." FS 29:300-312. July 1975.

Greshoff, C. J. "Proust as Symbolist Novelist." Standpunte 81:5-15. February 1969.

Grossvogel, David I. Limits of the Novel: Evolutions of a Form from Chaucer to Robbe-Grillet. Ithaca: Cornell University Press, 1968. pp. 189-225.

Grunmann, Minette H. "A LA RECHERCHE DU TEMPS PERDU." LangQ 15:12-14. Spring/Summer 1977.

Hokenson, Jan. "Proust in the Palace of Sheriar." FWF 1:187-198. May 1974.

Holdridge, David. "Suspended Structures in Proust's A LA RECHERCHE DU TEMPS PERDU." ML 52:112-118. September 1971.

Houston, John Porter. Fictional Technique in France, 1802-1927: An Introduction. Baton Rouge: Louisiana State University Press, 1972. pp. 132-151.

_____. "Theme and Structure in A LA RECHERCHE DU TEMPS PERDU." KRQ 17:209-221. No. 3, 1970.

_____. "Thought, Style, and Shape in Proust's Novel." SoR 5:987-1003. October 1969.

Howard, R. G. "The Construction of an Episode in A LA RECHERCHE DU TEMPS PERDU." AJFS 4:74-85. January/April 1967.

Hyde, John K. "Proust's Metaphor of Illness and Infirmity: Approaches to a Higher Reality." PCL 5:10-16. 1979.

Johnson, J. Theodore, Jr. "'La Lanterne magique': Proust's Metaphorical Toy." ECr 11:17-31. Spring 1971.

_____. "Proust and Giotto: Foundations for an Allegorical Interpretation of A LA RECHERCHE DU TEMPS PERDU." Marcel Proust: A Critical Panorama. ed. Larkin B. Price. Urbana: University of Illinois Press, 1973. pp. 168-205.

_____. "Proust's 'Impressionism' Reconsidered in the Light of the Visual Arts of the Twentieth Century." Twentieth Century French Fiction: Essays for Germaine Bree. ed. George Stambolian. New Brunswick: Rutgers University Press, 1975. pp. 27-55.

Johnson, Pamela Hansford. "Triumph over Time." Marcel Proust 1871-1922. ed. Peter Quennell. New York: Simon and Schuster, 1971. pp. 195-205.

Jones, David L. "Proust and Doderer as Historical Novelists." CLS 10:9-16. March 1973.

Jones, Peter. "Knowledge and Illusion in A LA RECHERCHE DU TEMPS PERDU." FMLS 5:303-322. October 1969.

Josipovici, Gabriel. The World and the Book: A Study of Modern Fiction. Stanford: Stanford University Press, 1971. pp. 1-24. Reprinted as "Proust: A Voice in Search of Itself" in CritQ 13:105-123. Summer 1971.

Kamber, Gerald and Richard Macksey. "'Negative Metaphor' and Proust's Rhetoric of Absence." MLN 85:858-883. December 1970.

Kellman, Steven G. "The Mirror and the Magic Lantern in A LA RECHERCHE." Neophil 61:43-47. January 1977.

Kolb, Philip. "The Birth of Elstir and Vinteuil." Marcel Proust: A Critical Panorama. ed. Larkin B. Price. Urbana: University of Illinois Press, 1973. pp. 147-167.

―――. "The Making of a Novel." In Search of Marcel Proust. ed. Monique Chefdor. [Los Angeles]: Ward Ritchie, 1973. pp. 21-39.

―――. "The Making of a Novel." Marcel Proust 1871-1922. ed. Peter Quennell. New York: Simon and Schuster, 1971. pp. 25-37.

Kostis, Nicholas. "Albertine: Characterization Through Image and Symbol." PMLA 84:125-135. January 1969.

Labat, Alvin. "Proust's Mme de Sévigné." ECr 15:271-285. Spring/Summer 1975.

Ladimer, Bethany. "The Narrator as Voyeur in A LA RECHERCHE DU TEMPS PERDU." CritQ 19:5-20. Autumn 1977.

Lapp, John C. "Proust's Windows to Reality." RR 67:38-49. January 1976.

Lynn, Thérèse B. "The Narrator, Not Marcel: Manuscript Proofs." RomN 16:258-261. Winter 1975.

Megay, Joyce N. "Elie Rabier: An Unknown Source of Proust's Psychology." MLQ 39:38-49. March 1978.

Mein, Margaret. A Foretaste of Proust: A Study of

Proust and His Precursors. Westmead: Saxon House, 1974. 192 pp.

———. "'Le Moi Oeuvrant': The Enigma of a Proustian Theme." FMLS 8:215-229. July 1972.

———. "Nerval: A Precursor of Proust." RR 62:99-112. April 1971.

———. "Novalis a Precursor of Proust." CL 23: 217-232. Summer 1971.

———. "Proust and Pascal." ECr 11:74-93. Spring 1971.

Melnick, Daniel. "Proust, Music, and the Reader." MLQ 41:181-192. June 1980.

Meyers, Jeffrey. "Proust and Vermeer." Art Internat. 17:68-71. May 1973.

Murray, Jack. "Melodrama in Proust." ConL 21:572-587. Autumn 1980.

———. "Proust's Views on Perception as a Metaphoric Framework." FR 42:380-394. February 1969.

———. The Proustian Comedy. York: French Literature Publications, 1980. 166 pp.

Nuccitelli, Angela. "Sunrise and the Hero's Awakening in A LA RECHERCHE DU TEMPS PERDU." RR 70:159-171. March 1979.

Pasco, Allan H. "Albertine's Equivocal Eyes." AJFS 5:257-262. September/December 1968.

———. "Blue and the Ideal of A LA RECHERCHE DU TEMPS PERDU." RF 85:119-138. No. 1/2, 1973.

———. The Color-Keys to A LA RECHERCHE DU TEMPS PERDU. Genève: Librairie Droz, 1976. 224 pp.

———. "Marcel, Albertine and Balbec in Proust's Allusive Complex." RR 62:113-126. April 1971.

———. "Proust's Reader and the Voyage of Self-Discovery." ConL 18:20-37. Winter 1977.

Pellón, Gustavo. "Giving the Lie to Liars: A Note on Anacoluthon in A LA RECHERCHE DU TEMPS PERDU." MLN 95:1347-1352. December 1980.

Porter, Agnes R. "Proust's Final Montesquiou Pastiche." Marcel Proust: A Critical Panorama. ed. Larkin B. Price. Urbana: University of Illinois Press, 1973. pp. 124-146.

Price, Larkin B. "Bird Imagery Surrounding Proust's Albertine." Symposium 26:242-260. Fall 1972.

Quennell, J. M. "The World of Fashion." Marcel Proust 1891-1922. ed. Peter Quennell. New York: Simon and Schuster, 1971. pp. 167-183.

Reddick, Bryan. "Proust: The 'La Berma' Passages." FR 42:683-692. April 1969.

Rivers, J. E. "The Myth and Science of Homosexuality in A LA RECHERCHE DU TEMPS PERDU." Homosexualities and French Literature. ed. George Stambolian and Elaine Marks. Ithaca: Cornell University Press, 1979. pp. 262-278.

_____. "Proust and the Aesthetics of Suffering." ConL 18:425-442. Autumn 1977.

_____. Proust & the Art of Love: The Aesthetics of Sexuality in the Life, Times, & Art of Marcel Proust. New York: Columbia University Press, 1980. 271 pp.

Robertson, Jane. "The Organisation of Time in A LA RECHERCHE DU TEMPS PERDU." AJFS 14:278-296. September/December 1977.

_____. "Place-change in Proust." AJFS 12:295-313. September/December 1975.

_____. "The Relationship Between the Hero and Françoise in A LA RECHERCHE DU TEMPS PERDU." FS 25:437-441. October 1971.

Roditi, Edouard. "Proust Recaptured." KR 30:23-39. 1968.

Rowland, Michael. "CONTRE SAINTE-BEUVE and Character-Presentation in A LA RECHERCHE DU TEMPS PERDU." RomN 8:183-187. Spring 1967.

Sankovitch, Tilde. "The Middle Ages as a Normative Element in Proust." OL 33:301-309. 1978.

Scanlan, Margaret. "The Subversion of History: The Dreyfus Affair in A LA RECHERCHE DU TEMPS PERDU." IFR 6:3-10. Winter 1979.

Seiden, Melvin. "Proust's Marcel and Saint-Loup: Inversion Reconsidered." ConL 10:220-240. Spring 1969.

Slater, Maya. "Some Recurrent Comparisons in A LA RECHERCHE DU TEMPS PERDU." MLR 62:629-632. October 1967.

Soucy, Robert. "Bad Readers in the World of Proust." FR 44:677-686. March 1971.

_____. "Proust's Aesthetics of Reading." FR 41: 48-59. October 1967.

Spalding, P. A., comp. Rev. by R. H. Cortie. A Reader's Handbook to Proust: An Index Guide to REMEMBRANCE OF THINGS PAST. New York: Barnes & Noble, 1975. 303 pp.

Splitter, Randolph. "Proust's Myth of Artistic Creation." AI 37:386-398. Winter 1980.

Straus, Bernard. Maladies of Marcel Proust: Doctors and Disease in His Life and Work. New York: Holmes & Meier, 1980. 164 pp.

Strauss, Walter A. "Nonrecognition and Recognition in Proust." NCFS 4:105-123. Fall/Winter 1975-1976.

Suleiman, Susan. "The Parenthetical Function in A LA RECHERCHE DU TEMPS PERDU." PMLA 92:458-470. May 1977.

Sullivan, Dennis G. "On Theatricality in Proust: Desire and the Actress." MLN 86:532-554. May 1971.

_____. "On Vision in Proust: The Icon and the 'Voyeur.'" MLN 84:646-661. May 1969.

Tukey, Ann. "Notes on Involuntary Memory in Proust." FR 42:395-402. February 1969.

Virtanen, Reino. "Differing Essences: Santayana and Proust." Marcel Proust: A Critical Panorama. ed. Larkin B. Price. Urbana: University of Illinois Press, 1973. pp. 277-288.

Weber, Samuel M. "The Madrepore." MLN 87:915-961. December 1972.

Weiner, Marc A. "Zwieback and Madeleine: Creative Recall in Wagner and Proust." MLN 95:679-683. April 1980.

Proust, Marcel

Wilson, Stephen. "Proust's A LA RECHERCHE DU TEMPS PERDU as a Document of Social History." JES 1:213-243. September 1971.

Winton, Alison. "The Developing Role of Money in Proust's A LA RECHERCHE DU TEMPS PERDU." FS 31:164-181. April 1977.

──────. Proust's Additions: The Making of A LA RECHERCHE DU TEMPS PERDU. 2 vols. Cambridge: Cambridge University Press, 1977. 393 pp.; 209 pp.

Wolitz, Seth L. The Proustian Community. New York: New York University Press, 1971. 209 pp.

Zants, Emily. "The Comic Structure of A LA RECHERCHE DU TEMPS PERDU." FR 47:144-150. Sp. Issue No. 6, Spring 1974.

──────. "Proust and the New Novel in France." PMLA 88:25-33. January 1973.

──────. "Proust's Magic Lantern." MFS 19:211-216. Summer 1973.

Zimmerman, Eugenia Noik. "The Metamorphoses of Adam: Names and Things in Sartre and Proust." Twentieth Century French Fiction: Essays for Germaine Brée. ed. George Stambolian. New Brunswick: Rutgers University Press, 1975. pp. 57-69.

SWANN'S WAY

Cunningham, William. "Giorgione Transfigured--A Note on Proust's Method." RomN 9:12-15. Autumn 1967.

Finch (Winton), Alison. "Characterization in the Early DU COTE DE CHEZ SWANN." MLR 74:49-61. January 1979.

──────. "Stylistic Revisions in DU COTE DE CHEZ SWANN." FrF 3:220-229. September 1978.

Husson, Roland. "The Concept of Love in SWANN'S WAY." In Search of Marcel Proust. ed. Monique Chefdor. [Los Angeles]: Ritchie, 1973. pp. 40-54.

Meyers, Jeffrey. "Proust's Aesthetic Analogies: Character and Painting in SWANN'S WAY." JAAC 30:377-388. Spring 1972.

Nitzberg, Howard. "DU COTE DE CHEZ SWANN: The Orpheus and Euridice Theme." LangQ 14:15; 26. Fall/Winter 1975.

O'Brien, Justin. The French Literary Horizon. New Brunswick: Rutgers University Press, 1967. pp. 11-17.

Winton, Alison. "Structural Weaknesses in the Early DU COTE DE CHEZ SWANN." EFL 12:22-36. November 1975.
TIME RECAPTURED
Beynon, Susan E. "Life, Time and Art in Proust's LE TEMPS RETROUVE." NFS 14:86-93. October 1975.

Sayce, R. A. "The Goncourt Pastiche in LE TEMPS RETROUVE." Marcel Proust: A Critical Panorama. ed. Larkin B. Price. Urbana: University of Illinois Press, 1973. pp. 102-123.

Queneau, Raymond
CHENE ET CHIEN
Mercier, Vivian. The New Novel from Queneau to Pinget. New York: Farrar, Straus & Giroux, 1971. pp. 77-81.
LES ENFANTS DU LIMON
Mercier, Vivian. The New Novel from Queneau to Pinget. New York: Farrar, Straus & Giroux, 1971. pp. 81-87.
LES FLEURS BLEUES
Jones, Louisa E. "Event and Invention: History in Queneau's LES FLEURS BLEUES." Symposium 31:322-336. Winter 1977.

Rabelais, François
GARGANTUA AND PANTAGRUEL
Baker, Paul V. "Loup Garou and the Green Knight: A Reassessment of the Deaths of Loup Garou and Epistémon. (PANTAGRUEL XXX)." ER 14:47-57. 1977.

Bakhtin, Mikhail. Rabelais and His World. Cambridge: M. I. T. Press, 1968. pp. 158-179; 326-340.

_____. "The Role of Games in Rabelais." YFS 41: 124-132. 1968. Reprinted from Rabelais and His World.

Benson, Ed. "Rabelais' Developing Historical Consciousness in His Portrayal of the Dipsodean & Picrocholine Wars." ER 13:147-161. 1976.

Berrong, Richard M. "Genealogies and the Search for an Origin in the 'Oeuvres' of Rabelais." SAB 42:75-83. November 1977.

_____. "Note for the Commentary on the CINQUIEME LIVRE: 'un pot aux roses' (Ch. 4)." RomN 19:78-82. Fall 1978.

Berry, Alice Fiola. "Apollo versus Bacchus: The Dynamics of Inspiration (Rabelais's Prologues to GARGANTUA and to the TIERS LIVRE)." PMLA 90:88-95. January 1975.

_____. "'Les Mithologies Pantagruelicques': Introduction to a Study of Rabelais's QUART LIVRE." PMLA 92:471-480. May 1977.

_____. "The Mix, the Mask and the Medical Farce: A Study of the Prologues to Rabelais's QUART LIVRE." RR 71:10-27. January 1980.

_____. "Rabelais: Homo Logos." JMRS 3:51-67. Spring 1973.

Bowen, Barbara. "Rabelais and the Comedy of the Spoken Word." MLR 63:575-580. July 1968.

Bowen, Barbara C. "Rabelais and P.G. Wodehouse: Two Comic Worlds." ECr 16:63-77. Winter 1976.

Brault, Gerard J. "A Neglected Aspect of Rabelaisian Pedagogy: Associating with Men of Letters." RomN 14:151-153. Autumn 1972.

_____. "The Significance of Eudemon's Praise of Gargantua (Rabelais, I, 15)." KRQ 18:307-317. No. 3, 1971.

Brent, Steven T. "Concerning the Resurrection of Epistémon." RomN 12:392-396. Spring 1971.

Brown, Jack Davis. "Hans Carvel's Ring: Elements, Literary Tradition, Rabelais's Source." RomN 13:515-522. Spring 1972.

Cameron, Keith. "Panurge and the Screech-Owl: An Interpretation of Rabelais, LE TIERS LIVRE, Ch. XIV." NM 77:161-165. No. 1, 1976.

Chesney, Elizabeth. "The Theme of Folly in Rabelais and Ariosto." JMRS 7:67-93. Spring 1977.

Cholakian, Rouben C. "Narrative Structure in Rabelais and the Question of the Authenticity of the CINQUIEME LIVRE." FS 33:1-12. January 1979.

_____. "A Re-examination of the Tempest Scene in the QUART LIVRE." FS 21:104-109. April 1967.

Clark, Carol. "'The Onely Languag'd-Men of All the

World'--Rabelais and the Art of the Mountebank." MLR 74:538-552. July 1979.

Coleman, Dorothy. "The Prologues of Rabelais." MLR 62:407-419. July 1967.

──────. Rabelais: A Critical Study in Prose Fiction. Cambridge: Cambridge University Press, 1971. pp. 62-82.

──────. "Rabelais: Two Versions of the 'Storm at Sea' Episode." FS 23:113-130. April 1969.

Cottrell, Robert D. "The Poetic Function of 'io' in Rabelais's QUART LIVRE." RPac 3:93-101. Fall 1977.

de Rocher, Gregory. "The Fusion of Priapus and the Muses: Rabelaisian Metaphors in the Prologue to the QUART LIVRE." KRQ 27:413-420. No. 4, 1980.

Derrett, J. Duncan M. "Rabelaisian Kyrielles and Their Source." ER 7:85-89. 1967.

Downes, Michael. "ARBRE=MAT: Why Pantagruel Does Not Hold the Rudder (QUART LIVRE, XIX)." ER 11:73-80. 1974.

Eldridge, Paul. François Rabelais: The Great Story Teller. South Brunswick: Barnes, 1971. pp. 85-215.

Eskin, Stanley G. "Politics and Imagination in Rabelais." KRQ 14:157-164. No. 2, 1967.

Frame, Donald M. François Rabelais: A Study. New York: Harcourt Brace Jovanovich, 1977. pp. 20-46.

──────. "Interaction of Characters in Rabelais." MLN 87:12-23. November 1972.

Gauna, S. M. "De Genio Pantagruelis: An Examination of Rabelaisian Demonology." BHR 33:557-570. 1971.

Goodrich, N. L. "The Dream of Panurge." ER 7:93-103. 1967.

Greene, Thomas M. Rabelais: A Study in Comic Courage. Englewood Cliffs: Prentice Hall, 1970. pp. 20-58.

Griffin, Robert. "The Devil and Panurge." SFr 47/48: 329-336. 1972.

Groos, Robert S. "The Enigmas of Quaresmeprenant:

Rabelais and Defamiliarization." RR 69:22-33. January/March 1978.

Guerlac, Rita. "Vives and the Education of Gargantua." ER 11:63-72. 1974.

Ianziti, Gary. "Rabelais and Machiavelli." RomN 16: 460-473. Winter 1975.

Josipovici, Gabriel. The World and the Book: A Study of Modern Fiction. Stanford: Stanford University Press, 1971. pp. 100-121.

Keller, Abraham C. "Absurd and Absurdity in Rabelais." KRQ 19:149-157. No. 2, 1972.

_____. "Stage and Theater in Rabelais." FR 41:479-484. February 1968.

Kirstein, Boni H.-J. "Could the Lion-Fox Episode in Chapter XV of PANTAGRUEL Be a Fable?" RomN 12: 180-185. Autumn 1970.

Kittay, Jeffrey S. "From Telling to Talking: A Study of Style and Sequence in Rabelais." ER 14:113-214. 1977.

Kleis, Charlotte Costa. "Structural Parallels and Thematic Unity in Rabelais." MLQ 31:403-423. December 1970.

Kushner, Eva. "Was King Picrochole Free? Rabelais Between Luther and Erasmus." CLS 14:306-320. December 1977.

La Charité, Raymond C. "Chapter Division and Narrative Structure in Rabelais's PANTAGRUEL." FrF 3:263-270. September 1978.

_____. "Devildom and Rabelais's PANTAGRUEL." FR 49:42-50. October 1975.

_____. "The Drum and the Owl: Functional Symbolism in Panurge's Quest." Symposium 28:154-165. Summer 1974.

_____. "Interpenetration in Rabelais's PANTAGRUEL: A Study of the Lion-Fox Episode." KRQ 21:239-264. Supplement No. 2, 1974.

_____. "'Mundus Inversus': The Fictional World of Rabelais's PANTAGRUEL." SFR 1:95-105. Spring 1977.

———. "Panurge's Heartbeat: An Interpretation of 'Mitaine' (TIERS LIVRE, Ch. XI)." RomN 15:479-485. Spring 1974.

———. "The Unity of Rabelais's PANTAGRUEL." FS 26:257-265. July 1972.

Lanius, Edward W. "Sense of Group and Accommodation in Rabelais's Comic Universe." ZRP 89:167-181. 1973.

Losse, Deborah. "Thematic and Structural Unity in the Symposium of Rabelais's TIERS LIVRE." RomN 16:390-405. Winter 1975.

Lydgate, Barry. "Printing, Narrative and the Genesis of the Rabelaisian Novel." RR 71:356-373. November 1980.

Masters, Brian. A Student's Guide to Rabelais. London: Heinemann, 1971. 108 pp.

Masters, G. Mallary. "On 'Learned Ignorance,' or How to Read Rabelais: Part I, Theory." RomN 19:127-132. Fall 1978.

———. "On 'Learned Ignorance,' or How to Read Rabelais: Part II, Application." RomN 19:254-260. Winter 1978.

———. "Panurge at the Crossroads: A Mythopoetic Study of the Pythagorean Y in Rabelais's Satirical Romance (QL/33-34)." RomN 15:134-154. Autumn 1973.

———. "Rabelais and Renaissance Figure Poems." ER 8:53-68. 1969.

———. Rabelaisian Dialectic and the Platonic-Hermetic Tradition. Albany: State University of New York Press, 1969. 97 pp.

Morrison, Ian R. "Ambiguity, Detachment, and Joy in GARGANTUA." MLR 71:513-522. July 1976.

———. "Peace and War in GARGANTUA: A Question of Didacticism." RR 70:219-233. May 1979.

Muir, Lynette R. "The Abbey and the City: Two Aspects of the Christian Community." AJFS 14:32-38. January/April 1977.

Mulhauser, Ruth. "Rabelais and the Fictional World of Alcofribas Nasier." RR 64:175-183. May 1973.

Mustacchi, Marianne M. "The Harangue in Rabelais' GARGANTUA and PANTAGRUEL." KRQ 23:225-230. No. 2, 1976.

Norton, Glyn P. "Rabelais and the Epic of Palpability: 'Enargeia' and History (CINQUIESME LIVRE: 38-40)." Symposium 33:171-185. Summer 1979.

Petrossian, George A. "The Problem of the Authenticity of the CINQUIESME LIVRE DE PANTAGRUEL: A Quantitative Study." ER 13:1-64. 1976.

Price, Robert H. "PANTAGRUEL and LE PETIT PRINCE." Symposium 21:264-270. Fall 1967.

Ragland, Mary E. "A New Look at Panurge." HSL 8:61-76. No. 2, 1976.

_____. Rabelais and Panurge: A Psychological Approach to Literary Character. Amsterdam: Rodopi, 1976. 159 pp.

Rebhorn, Wayne A. "The Burdens and Joys of Freedom: An Interpretation of the Five Books of Rabelais." ER 9:71-90. 1971.

Regosin, Richard L. "The Artist and the 'Abbaye.'" SP 68:121-129. April 1971.

de Rocher, Gregory. Rabelais's Laughers and Joubert's "Traité du Ris." University: University of Alabama Press, 1979. 142 pp.

Russell, Daniel. "A Note on Panurge's 'Pusse en l'Aureille.'" ER 11:83-87. 1974.

_____. "Panurge and His New Clothes." ER 14:89-104. 1977.

_____. "Some Observations on Rabelais's Choice of Names: Nazdecabre." RomN 12:186-188. Autumn 1970.

Screech, M. A. "Eleven-Month Pregnancies: A Legal and Medical Quarrel à Propos of GARGANTUA, Chapter Three, Rabelais, Alciati and Tiraqueau." ER 8:93-106. 1969.

_____. "Lorenzo Spiritu's DU PASSE TEMPS DES DEZ and the TIERS LIVRE DE PANTAGRUEL." ER 13:65-67. 1976.

_____. "Some Further Reflexions on the Dating of GARGANTUA (A) and (B) and on the Possible Meanings of Some of the Episodes." ER 13:79-111. 1976.

―――――. "Some Reflexions on the Abbey of Thelema." ER 8:109-114. 1969.

―――――. "Some Reflexions on the Problem of Dating GARGANTUA, A and B." ER 11:9-56. 1974.

Schwartz, Jerome. "Gargantua's Device and the Abbey of Theleme: A Study in Rabelais' Iconography." YFS 47:232-242. 1972.

―――――. "Panurge's Impact on Pantagruel (PANTA-GRUEL, Chapter IX)." RR 67:1-8. January 1976.

―――――. "Scatology and Eschatology in Gargantua's Androgyne Device." ER 14:265-275. 1977.

Spanos, Margaret. "The Function of the Prologues in the Works of Rabelais." ER 9:29-48. 1971.

Stone, Donald. "A Word About the Prologue to GARGANTUA." RomN 13:511-514. Spring 1972.

Tetel, Marcel. "The Function and Meaning of the Mock Epic Framework in Rabelais." Neophil 59:157-163. April 1975.

―――――. Rabelais. New York: Twayne, 1967. pp. 17-48; 82-89.

Thompson, Paul L. "Thematic Consistency in TIERS LIVRE, Chapter 28." RomN 14:577-582. Spring 1973.

Wasserman, Jerry. "The Word as Object: The Rabelaisian Novel." Novel 8:123-137. Winter 1975.

Weinberg, Florence. "Chess as a Literary Idea in Colonna's HYPNEROTOMACHIA and in Rabelais' CINQUIESME LIVRE." RR 70:321-335. November 1979.

Weinberg, Florence M. "Frère Jean, Evangélique: His Function in the Rabelaisian World." MLR 66: 298-305. April 1971.

―――――. The Wine and the Will: Rabelais's Bacchic Christianity. Detroit: Wayne State University Press, 1972. 175 pp.

Wood, Hadley. "An Interpretation of Rabelais's 'Ancien Prologue.'" FS 32:398-407. October 1978.

Wortley, W. Victor. "From PANTAGRUEL to GARGANTUA: The Development of an Action Scene." RomN 10:129-138. Autumn 1968.

Radiguet, Raymond
LE BAL DU COMTE D'ORGEL
    Crosland, Margaret. Raymond Radiguet. London: Peter Owen, 1976. pp. 133-136.
LE DIABLE AU CORPS
    Bouraoui, H. A. "Radiguet's LE DIABLE AU CORPS: Beneath the Glass Cage of Form." MLQ 34:64-77. March 1973.

    Crosland, Margaret. Raymond Radiguet. London: Peter Owen, 1976. pp. 125-132.

Réage, Pauline
THE STORY OF O
    Gordon, Jan B. "THE STORY OF O and the Strategy of Pornography: Cosmos and Nothingness." WHR 25:27-43. Winter 1971.

    Mickelsen, David. "X-Rated O." WHR 31:165-173. Spring 1977.

Ricardou, Jean
LA PRISE DE CONSTANTINOPLE
    Jones, Tobin H. "In Quest of a Newer New Novel: Ricardou's LA PRISE DE CONSTANTINOPLE." ConL 14:296-309. Summer 1973.

    Rice, Donald B. "The Ex-centricities of Jean Ricardou's LA PRISE/PROSE DE CONSTANTINOPLE." IFR 2:106-112. July 1975.

Robbe-Grillet, Alain
LA BELLE CAPTIVE
    O'Donnell, Thomas. "Robbe-Grillet's Ghost Town." YFS 57:196-207. 1979.
THE GUM ERASERS
    Bassoff, Bruce. "Freedom and Fatality in Robbe-Grillet's LES GOMMES." ConL 20:434-451. Autumn 1979.

    Grossvogel, David I. Limits of the Novel: Evolutions of a Form from Chaucer to Robbe-Grillet. Ithaca: Cornell University Press, 1968. pp. 283-291.

    Heck, Francis S. "Sábato, Robbe-Grillet, and the New Novel." REH 12:41-54. January 1978.

    Mercier, Vivian. The New Novel from Queneau to Pinget. New York: Farrar, Straus & Giroux, 1971. pp. 185-190.

    Minogue, Valerie. "The Workings of Fiction in LES GOMMES." MLR 62:430-442. July 1967.

Morrissette, Bruce. The Novels of Robbe-Grillet.
Ithaca: Cornell University Press, 1971. pp. 38-74.

Sturrock, John. The French New Novel. London:
Oxford University Press, 1969. pp. 172-181.

Tremewan, P. J. "Allusions to Christ in Robbe-Grillet's
LES GOMMES." AUMLA 51:40-48. May 1979.

L'IMMORTELLE

Honeycutt, Benjamin L. "The Structure of Actants in
Robbe-Grillet's L'IMMORTELLE." LangQ 12:26-28.
Spring/Summer 1974.

Sturdza, Paltin. "The Rebirth Archetype in Robbe-
Grillet's L'IMMORTELLE." FR 48:990-995. May 1975.

IN THE LABYRINTH

Mercier, Vivian. The New Novel from Queneau to
Pinget. New York: Farrar, Straus & Giroux, 1971.
pp. 194-198.

Morrissette, Bruce. The Novels of Robbe-Grillet.
Ithaca: Cornell University Press, 1971. pp. 153-184.

Raho, E. T. "Robbe-Grillet's Uses of the Past in
DANS LE LABYRINTHE." MLR 66:76-84. January
1971.

Storey, Robert. "Oedipus in the Labyrinth: A Psychoanalytic Reading of Robbe-Grillet's IN THE LABY-
RINTH." L&P 28:4-16. No. 1, 1978.

JEALOUSY

Bersani, Leo. "Narrative Murder." YR 59:376-390.
Spring 1970.

Carrabino, Victor. "Robbe-Grillet's LA JALOUSIE and
the Phenomenological 'Epochê.'" KRQ 22:159-167. No.
2, 1975.

Deneau, Daniel P. "Crouching Natives in Robbe-
Grillet's JEALOUSY." MFS 20:429-436. Autumn 1974.

D'Haen, Theo. "ROBINSON CRUSOE and LA JALOUSIE."
RLV 44:28-36. No. 1, 1978.

Ellis, Zilpha. "Robbe-Grillet's Use of Pun and Related
Figures in LA JALOUSIE." IFR 2:9-17. January 1975.

Fedkiw, Patricia. "A Letter-al Re-covery." enclitic
2:73-85. Fall 1978.

Lecuyer, Maurice A. "Robbe-Grillet's LA JALOUSIE
and a Parallel in the Graphic Arts." HSL 3:19-38.
No. 1, 1971.

Mercier, Vivian. The New Novel from Queneau to Pinget. New York: Farrar, Straus & Giroux, 1971. pp. 165-184.

Morrissette, Bruce. The Novels of Robbe-Grillet. Ithaca: Cornell University Press, 1971. pp. 112-152.

Ravaux, Françoise. "The Return of the Reader." FR 52:708-713. April 1979.

_____. "Robbe-Grillet's JEALOUSY: A Phenomenological Novel?" PCL 4:21-26. May 1978.

Simonton, Margaret. "Faulkner's Influence on Robbe-Grillet: The Quentin Section of THE SOUND AND THE FURY and LA JALOUSIE." IFR 7:11-19. Winter 1980.
LAST YEAR AT MARIENBAD
Mercier, Vivian. The New Novel from Queneau to Pinget. New York: Farrar, Straus & Giroux, 1971. pp. 167-169; 198-201.

Morrissette, Bruce. The Novels of Robbe-Grillet. Ithaca: Cornell University Press, 1971. pp. 185-212.
LA MAISON DE RENDEZ-VOUS
Clayton, John J. "Alain Robbe-Grillet: The Aesthetics of Sado Masochism." MR 18:106-119. Spring 1977.

Deneau, Daniel P. "Notes on Robbe-Grillet's LA MAISON DE RENDEZ-VOUS." Neophil 63:521-529. October 1979.

Goodstein, Jack. "Pattern and Structure in Robbe-Grillet's LA MAISON DE RENDEZ-VOUS." Crit 14:91-97. No. 1, 1972.

Mercier, Vivian. The New Novel from Queneau to Pinget. New York: Farrar, Straus & Giroux, 1971. pp. 208-214.

Morrissette, Bruce. The Novels of Robbe-Grillet. Ithaca: Cornell University Press, 1971. pp. 237-261.
PROJECT FOR A REVOLUTION IN NEW YORK
Deneau, Daniel P. "Bits and Pieces Concerning One of Robbe-Grillet's Latest Verbal Happenings: The 'Sado-Erotic' PROJECT." TCL 25:37-53. Spring 1979.

Morrissette, Bruce. "Robbe-Grillet's PROJECT FOR A REVOLUTION IN NEW YORK." ASLHM 42:73-88. 1971.

O'Donnell, Thomas D. "Thematic Generation in Robbe-Grillet's PROJET POUR UNE REVOLUTION A NEW YORK." Twentieth Century French Fiction: Essays for Germaine Brée. ed. George Stambolian. New Brunswick: Rutgers University Press, 1975. pp. 184-197.

Pugh, Anthony R. "Robbe-Grillet in New York." IFR 1:120-124. July 1974.

Suleiman, Susan. "Reading Robbe-Grillet: Sadism and Text in PROJET POUR UNE REVOLUTION A NEW YORK." RR 68:43-62. January 1977.

UN REGICIDE
Kafalenos, Emma. "Robbe-Grillet's UN REGICIDE: An Extraordinary First Novel." IFR 6:49-54. Winter 1979.

Stoltzfus, Ben. "UN REGICIDE: A Metaphorical Intrigue." FrF 5:269-282. September 1980.

TOPOLOGIE D'UNE CITE FANTOME
Ellison, David R. "Reappearing Man in Robbe-Grillet's TOPOLOGIE D'UNE CITE FANTOME." SFR 3:97-110. Spring 1979.

Meltzer, Françoise. "Preliminary Excavations of Robbe-Grillet's Phantom City." ChiR 28:41-50. Summer 1976.

Morrissette, Bruce. "Intertextual Assemblage as Fictional Generator: TOPOLOGIE D'UNE CITE FANTOME." IFR 5:1-14. January 1978.

O'Donnell, Thomas. "Robbe-Grillet's Ghost Town." YFS 57:196-207. 1979.

O'Donnell, Thomas D. "Robbe-Grillet's 'métaphoricité fantôme.'" StTCL 2:55-68. Fall 1977.

THE VOYEUR
Connerton, Paul. "Alain Robbe-Grillet: A Question of Self-Deception?" FMLS 4:351-357. October 1968.

Duncan, Alastair B. "Robbe-Grillet's LE VOYEUR: A Reassessment." Symposium 34:107-123. Summer 1980.

Gerhart, Mary Jane. "The Purpose of Meaninglessness in Robbe-Grillet." Renascence 23:83-86. Winter 1971.

Johnson, Patricia J. "Light Phenomena as Erotic Indicators in Robbe-Grillet's LE VOYEUR." RS 39:11-19. March 1971.

_____. "Robbe-Grillet on Robbe-Grillet: A Study in Applied Criticism." RS 40:95-102. June 1972.

Kittay, Jeffrey. "'Alibi': On Handwriting, Rewriting, and Writing Rhythms and LE VOYEUR." RR 71:57-74. January 1980.

Mercier, Vivian. The New Novel from Queneau to Pinget. New York: Farrar, Straus & Giroux, 1971. pp. 189-194.

Minogue, Valerie. "The Creator's Game: Some Reflections on Robbe-Grillet's LE VOYEUR." MLR 72: 815-828. October 1977.

_____. "Distortion and Creativity in the Subjective Viewpoint: Robbe-Grillet, Butor and Nathalie Sarraute." FMLS 12:38-41. January 1976.

*Moore, Harry T. Twentieth-Century French Literature Since World War II. Carbondale: Southern Illinois University Press, 1966. pp. 123-127.

Morrissette, Bruce. The Novels of Robbe-Grillet. Ithaca: Cornell University Press, 1971. pp. 75-111.

Phillips, Kathy J. "The Double Trap of Robbe-Grillet: A Reading of LE VOYEUR." TCL 26:323-331. Fall 1980.

Roche, Maurice
    COMPACT
        Smith, Stephen. "Fragments of Landscape, Scraps of Décor: Maurice Roche's COMPACT." YFS 57:48-57. 1979.

Rolland, Romain
    L'AME ENCHANTEE
        Alden, Douglas W. "Léon Blum as a Source for L'AME ENCHANTEE." KRQ 17:9-18. No. 1, 1970.

        March, Harold. Romain Rolland. New York: Twayne, 1971. pp. 99-107.

        Starr, William Thomas. Romain Rolland: One Against All. The Hague: Mouton, 1971. pp. 185-195.

        _____. "Water Symbols in the Novels of Romain Rolland." Neophil 56:146-159. April 1972.
    JEAN-CHRISTOPHE
        Alden, Douglas W. "Proustian Configuration in JEAN-CHRISTOPHE." FR 41:262-271. November 1967.

        Harris, Frederick John. André Gide and Romain Rolland. New Brunswick: Rutgers University Press, 1973. pp. 44-51.

        March, Harold. Romain Rolland. New York: Twayne, 1971. pp. 56-68.

        Scales, Derek P. "Feeling for Nature in Romain Rolland." AJFS 9:40-54. January/April 1972.

        Sices, David. Music and the Musician in JEAN-

CHRISTOPHE. New Haven: Yale University Press, 1968. 178 pp.

Starr, William Thomas. Romain Rolland: One Against All. The Hague: Mouton, 1971. pp. 124-145.

_____. "Water Symbols in the Novels of Romain Rolland." Neophil 56:146-159. April 1972.

Romains, Jules
  MEN OF GOOD WILL
    Alden, Douglas W. "Quinette, Landru, and Raskolnikoff." FR 43:215-226. December 1969.

    O'Brien, Justin. The French Literary Horizon. New Brunswick: Rutgers University Press, 1967. pp. 221-232.

Rousseau, Jean Jacques
  EMILE
    Bloom, Allan. "The Education of Democratic Man: EMILE." Daedalus 107:135-153. Summer 1978.

    Carroll, Malcolm. "Method and Intention in Rousseau's 'Profession de Foi du Vicaire Savoyard.'" NFS 16:20-30. October 1977.

    Coleman, Patrick. "Characterizing Rousseau's EMILE." MLN 92:761-778. May 1977.

    Dobinson, C. H. Jean-Jacques Rousseau: His Thought and Its Relevance Today. London: Methuen, 1969. pp. 70-127.

    Hamilton, James F. "Stendhal's LE ROUGE ET LE NOIR and Rousseau's L'EMILE: Contrary Experiments." NCFS 6:199-212. Spring/Summer 1978.

    Hammer, Carl, Jr. Goethe and Rousseau. Lexington: University Press of Kentucky, 1973. pp. 122-136; 156-170.

    Jordan, R. J. P. "A New Look at Rousseau as Educator." SVEC 182:59-72. 1979.

    Mercken-Spaas, Godelieve. "The Social Anthropology of Rousseau's EMILE." SVEC 132:137-181. 1975.

    Scanlan, Timothy. "A Biblical Allusion in Rousseau's EMILE." LangQ 14:13-14. Fall/Winter 1975.

    Senior, Nancy. "LES SOLITAIRES as a Test for Emile and Sophie." FR 49:528-535. March 1976.

Rousseau, Jean Jacques

    ———. "Sophie and the State of Nature." FrF 2:134-145. May 1977.

    Sewall, Bronwen. "The Similarity Between Rousseau's EMILE and the Early Poetry of Wordsworth." SVEC 106:157-174. 1973.

    Wexler, Victor G. "'Made for Man's Delight': Rousseau as Antifeminist." The American Historical Review 81:270-275. April 1976.

LA NOUVELLE HELOÏSE
    Anderson, David L. "Aspects of Motif in LA NOUVELLE HELOÏSE." SVEC 94:25-72. 1972.

    Attridge, Anna. "The Reception of LA NOUVELLE HELOÏSE." SVEC 120:227-267. 1974.

    Blum, Carol. "LA NOUVELLE HELOÏSE: An Act in the Life of Jean-Jacques Rousseau." ECr 9:198-206. Fall 1969.

    ———. "Styles of Cognition as Moral Options in LA NOUVELLE HELOÏSE and LES LIAISONS DANGEREUSES." PMLA 88:289-298. March 1973.

    Brady, Patrick. "Structural Affiliations of LA NOUVELLE HELOÏSE." ECr 9:207-218. Fall 1969.

    Carroll, M. G. "Morality and Letters in LA NOUVELLE HELOÏSE." FMLS 13:359-367. October 1977.

    Davis, James Herbert, Jr. "Montherlant, LA NOUVELLE HELOÏSE, and the 'Argument de Renfort.'" RomN 13:397-401. Spring 1972.

    Dobinson, C. H. Jean-Jacques Rousseau: His Thought and Its Relevance Today. London: Methuen, 1969. pp. 50-59.

    Gelley, Alexander. "The Two Julies: Conversion and Imagination in LA NOUVELLE HELOÏSE." MLN 92:749-760. May 1977.

    Hammer, Carl, Jr. Goethe and Rousseau. Lexington: University Press of Kentucky, 1973. pp. 65-80; 107-122.

    Kamuf, Peggy. "Inside Julie's Closet." RR 69:296-306. November 1978.

    Kusch, Manfred. "Landscape and Literary Form: Structural Parallels in LA NOUVELLE HELOÏSE." ECr 17:349-360. Winter 1977.

———. "The River and the Garden: Basic Spatial Models in CANDIDE and LA NOUVELLE HELOÏSE." ECS 12:8-14. Fall 1978.

Scanlan, Timothy M. "The Dynamics of Separation and Communication in Rousseau's JULIE." ECr 17:336-348. Winter 1977.

———. "The Notion of 'Paradis sur la Terre' in Rousseau's LA NOUVELLE HELOÏSE." NFS 13:12-22. May 1974.

———. "LA NOUVELLE HELOÏSE: The Story of a Failure and the Success of a Story." ML 61:71-80. June 1980.

———. "Voltaire and Rousseau: Their Rencontre Fortuite." OL 32:302-309. 1977.

Smith, Louise Z. "Sensibility and Epistolary Form in HELOÏSE and WERTHER." ECr 17:361-368. Winter 1977.

Temmer, Mark J. "Rousseau's LA NOUVELLE HELOÏSE and Goethe's WILHELM MEISTERS LEHRJAHRE." SIR 10:309-339. Fall 1971.

Ulmer, Gregory L. "CLARISSA and LA NOUVELLE HELOÏSE." CL 24:289-308. Fall 1972.

Vance, Christie. "LA NOUVELLE HELOÏSE: The Language of Paris." YFS 45:127-136. 1970.

Vance, Christie McDonald. "The Extravagant Shepherd: A Study of the Pastoral Vision in Rousseau's NOUVELLE HELOÏSE." SVEC 105:13-179. 1973.

Webb, Donald P. "Did Rousseau Bungle the 'nuit d'amour'?" KRQ 17:3-8. No, 1, 1970.

———. "Julie D'Etange and the 'Lac(s) d'amour.'" RomN 12:343-345. 1971.

———. "Wolmar's 'Méthode' and the Function of Identity in LA NOUVELLE HELOÏSE." RR 70:113-118. March 1979.

Weightman, John. "The Conflict of Values in LA NOUVELLE HELOÏSE." FMLS 4:309-321. October 1968.

Wexler, Victor G. "'Made for Man's Delight': Rousseau as Antifeminist." The American Historical Review 81:275-281. April 1976.

Willis, Peter. "Rousseau, Stowe and 'le jardin anglais': Speculations on Visual Sources for LA NOUVELLE HELOÏSE." SVEC 90:1791-1798. 1972.

Sainte-Beuve, Charles
VOLUPTE
   Niess, Robert J. "Sainte-Beuve and Balzac: VOLUPTE and LE LYS DANS LA VALLEE." KRQ 20:113-124. No. 1, 1973.

Saint-Exupéry, Antoine de
COURRIER SUD
   McKeon, Joseph T. "Saint-Exupéry, the Myth of the Pilot." PMLA 89:1084-1089. October 1974.

   Parry, M. "A Symbolic Interpretation of COURRIER SUD." MLR 69:296-307. April 1974.
LE PETIT PRINCE
   Price, Robert H. "PANTAGRUEL and LE PETIT PRINCE." Symposium 21:264-270. Fall 1967.
PILOTE DE GUERRE
   McKeon, Joseph T. "Saint-Exupéry, the Myth of the Pilot." PMLA 89:1084-1089. October 1974.
TERRE DES HOMMES
   McKeon, Joseph T. "Saint-Exupéry, the Myth of the Pilot." PMLA 89:1084-1089. October 1974.
VOL DE NUIT
   McKeon, Joseph T. "Saint-Exupéry, the Myth of the Pilot." PMLA 89:1084-1089. October 1974.

Saint-Pierre, Bernardin de
LA CHAUMIERE INDIENNE
   Runte, Roseann. "LA CHAUMIERE INDIENNE: Counterpart and Complement to PAUL ET VIRGINIE." MLR 75:774-780. October 1980.

   _____. "LA CHAUMIERE INDIENNE: A Study in Satire." FR 53:557-565. March 1980.
PAUL AND VIRGINIA
   Brown, James W. "The Ideological and Aesthetic Functions of Food in PAUL ET VIRGINIE." EC Life 4:61-67. March 1978.

   Cherpack, Clifton. "PAUL ET VIRGINIE and the Myths of Death." PMLA 90:247-255. March 1975.

   Dunkley, John. "PAUL ET VIRGINIE: Aesthetic Appeal and Archetypal Structures." Trivium 13:95-111. May 1978.

   Francis, R. A. "Bernardin de Saint-Pierre's PAUL ET VIRGINIE and the Failure of the Ideal State in the Eighteenth-Century French Novel." NFS 13:51-60. October 1974.

Garson, R. W. "Two Pastoral Romances: Longus' DAPHNIS AND CHLOE and Bernardin de Saint-Pierre's PAUL ET VIRGINIE." Trivium 9:81-87. 1974.

Lowrie, Joyce O. "The Structural Significance of Sensual Imagery in PAUL ET VIRGINIE." RomN 12:351-356. Spring 1971.

Runte, Roseann. "LA CHAUMIERE INDIENNE: Counterpart and Complement to PAUL ET VIRGINIE." MLR 75:774-780. October 1980.

de la Sale, Antoine
LE PETIT JEHAN DE SAINTRE
Cherpack, Clifton. "LE PETIT JEHAN DE SAINTRE: The Archetypal Background." JMRS 5:243-252. Fall 1975.

Cholakian, Patricia Francis. "The Two Narrative Styles of A. de la Sale." RomN 10:362-372. Spring 1969.
RECONFORT DE MME DU FRESNE
Vesce, Thomas E. "Notes on Antoine de la Sale's RECONFORT DE MME DU FRESNE." MS 37:478-493. 1975.

Sand, George
CONSUELO
Thomson, Patricia. George Sand and the Victorians: Her Influence and Reputation in Nineteenth-Century England. New York: Columbia University Press, 1977. pp. 39-50; 164-168.
LA DANIELLE
Barry, Joseph. Infamous Woman: The Life of George Sand. Garden City: Doubleday, 1977. pp. 324-335.
INDIANA
Barry, Joseph. Infamous Woman: The Life of George Sand. Garden City: Doubleday, 1977. pp. 128-136.

Vest, James M. "Dreams and the Romance Tradition in George Sand's INDIANA." FrF 3:35-47. January 1978.

Winegarten, Renee. The Double Life of George Sand: Woman and Writer. New York: Basic Books, 1978. pp. 105-109.
JACQUES
Herrmann, Lesley. "JACQUES in Russia: A Program of Domestic Reform for Husbands." S Lit I 12:61-72. Fall 1979.
LELIA
Barry, Joseph. Infamous Woman: The Life of George Sand. Garden City: Doubleday, 1977. pp. 152-159; 168-171.

Thomson, Patricia. George Sand and the Victorians: Her Influence and Reputation in Nineteenth-Century England. New York: Columbia University Press, 1977. pp. 97-112.

MAUPRAT

Arnold, J. V. "George Sand's MAUPRAT and Emily Brontë's WUTHERING HEIGHTS." RLC 46:209-218. April/June 1972.

Thomson, Patricia. "WUTHERING HEIGHTS and MAUPRAT." RES 24:26-37. February 1973.

STORY OF MY LIFE

Brée, Germaine. "George Sand: The Fictions of Autobiography." NCFS 4:438-449. Summer 1976.

Saporta, Marc

COMPOSITION NO I

Grimm, Reinhold. "Marc Saporta: The Novel as Card Game." ConL 19:280-299. Summer 1978.

Sarraute, Nathalie

BETWEEN LIFE AND DEATH

Jefferson, Ann. "Imagery Versus Description: The Problematics of Representation in the Novels of Nathalie Sarraute." MLR 73:520-522. July 1978.

Mercier, Vivian. The New Novel from Queneau to Pinget. New York: Farrar, Straus & Giroux, 1971. pp. 157-163.

Racevskis, Karlis. "Irony as a Creative and Critical Force in Three Novels of Nathalie Sarraute." FR 51: 37-44. October 1977.

FOOLS SAY

Britton, Celia. "Review Article: FOOLS SAY by Nathalie Sarraute." Journal of Beckett Studies 5:114-118. Autumn 1979.

Racevskis, Karlis. "Irony as a Creative and Critical Force in Three Novels of Nathalie Sarraute." FR 51:37-44. October 1977.

THE GOLDEN FRUITS

Jefferson, Ann. "Imagery Versus Description: The Problematics of Representation in the Novels of Nathalie Sarraute." MLR 73:514-517. July 1978.

Mercier, Vivian. The New Novel from Queneau to Pinget. New York: Farrar, Straus & Giroux, 1971. pp. 148-157.

Racevskis, Karlis. "Irony as a Creative and Critical Force in Three Novels of Nathalie Sarraute." FR 51: 37-44. October 1977.

Whiting, Charles G. "Nathalie Sarraute: 'Moraliste.'"
FR 43:168-174. Winter 1970.
MARTEREAU
Mercier, Vivian. The New Novel from Queneau to
Pinget. New York: Farrar, Straus & Giroux, 1971.
pp. 126-134.

Whiting, Charles G. "Nathalie Sarraute: 'Moraliste.'"
FR 43:168-174. Winter 1970.
THE PLANETARIUM
Mercier, Vivian. The New Novel from Queneau to
Pinget. New York: Farrar, Straus & Giroux, 1971.
pp. 140-148.

Minogue, Valerie. "Nathalie Sarraute's LE PLANE-
TARIUM: The Narrator Narrated." FMLS 9:217-234.
July 1973.

Newman, A. S. "For a New Writing--a New Criticism:
Nathalie Sarraute, LE PLANETARIUM." AJFS 11:118-
128. January/April 1974.

Whiting, Charles G. "Nathalie Sarraute: 'Moraliste.'"
FR 43:168-174. Winter 1970.
PORTRAIT OF A MAN UNKNOWN
Bouraoui, H. A. "Sarraute's Narrative Portraiture:
The Artist in Search of a Voice." Crit 14:77-88. No.
1, 1972.

Mercier, Vivian. The New Novel from Queneau to
Pinget. New York: Farrar, Straus & Giroux, 1971.
pp. 116-127.

Minogue, Valerie. "Distortion and Creativity in the
Subjective Viewpoint: Robbe-Grillet, Butor and Nathalie
Sarraute." FMLS 12:46-49. January 1976.

_____. "The Imagery of Childhood in Nathalie Sar-
raute's PORTRAIT D'UN INCONNU." FS 27:177-186.
April 1973.

St. Aubyn, F. C. "Rilke, Sartre, and Sarraute: The
Role of the Third." RLC 41:275-284. April/June 1967.

Whiting, Charles G. "Nathalie Sarraute: 'Moraliste.'"
FR 43:168-174. Winter 1970.
LE SILENCE SUIVI DE LE MENSONGE
Whiting, Charles G. "Nathalie Sarraute: 'Moraliste.'"
FR 43:168-174. Winter 1970.
TROPISMES
Murch, Anne C. "Eric Berne's GAMES and Nathalie
Sarraute's TROPISMES." AJFS 8:62-83. January/April
1971.

Whiting, Charles G.  "Nathalie Sarraute: 'Moraliste.'"
FR 43:168-174.  Winter 1970.
VOUS LES ENTENDEZ?
Jefferson, Ann. "Imagery Versus Description: The Problematics of Representation in the Novels of Nathalie Sarraute." MLR 73:517-520. July 1978.

Sarrazin, Albertine
L'ASTRAGALE
Cothran, Ann. "Narrative Structure as Expression of the Self in Sarrazin's L'ASTRAGALE." ECr 19:13-22. Summer 1979.

Gelfand, Elissa. "Albertine Sarrazin: The Confined Imagination." ECr 19:51-52. Summer 1979.
LA CAVALE
Gelfand, Elissa. "Albertine Sarrazin: The Confined Imagination." ECr 19: 53-57. Summer 1979.
JOURNAL DE PRISON
Gelfand, Elissa. "Albertine Sarrazin: The Confined Imagination." ECr 19:48-50. Summer 1979.

Sartre, Jean Paul
AGE OF REASON
Halpern, Joseph. "Sartre's Enclosed Space." YFS 57: 58-71. 1979.

Tarbox, Raymond. "Exhaustion Psychology and Sartre's THE AGE OF REASON." AI 30:80-95. Spring 1973.
NAUSEA
Bauer, George Howard. Sartre and the Artist. Chicago: University of Chicago Press, 1969. pp. 17-44.

Brosman, Catharine Savage. "Sartre's Nature: Animal Images in LA NAUSEE." Symposium 31:107-125. Summer 1977.

Dale, Jonathan. "Sartre and Malraux: LA NAUSEE and LA VOIE ROYALE." FMLS 4:335-346. October 1968.

Davis, John F. "LA NAUSEE: Imagery and Use of the Diary Form." NFS 10:33-46. May 1971.

Doubrovsky, Serge. "'The Nine of Hearts': Fragment of a Psycho-Reading of LA NAUSEE." Boundary 5:411-420. Winter 1977.

Edwards, Michael. "LA NAUSEE--A Symbolist Novel." Adam 35:9-21. 1970.

Falk, Eugene K. Types of Thematic Structure: The Nature and Function of Motifs in Gide, Camus, and

Sartre. Chicago: University of Chicago Press, 1967. pp. 117-178.

Fletcher, Dennis J. "Sartre and Barres: Some Notes on LA NAUSEE." FMLS 4:330-334. October 1968.

―――――. "The Use of Colour in LA NAUSEE." MLR 63:370-380. April 1968.

Fletcher, John. "Sartre's NAUSEA: A Modern Classic Revisited." CritQ 18:11-20. Spring 1976.

Goldthorpe, Rhiannon. "The Presentation of Consciousness in Sartre's LA NAUSEE and Its Theoretical Basis: Reflection and Facticity." FS 22:114-132. April 1968.

―――――. "The Presentation of Consciousness in Sartre's LA NAUSEE and Its Theoretical Basis: 2. Transcendence and Intentionality." FS 25:32-46. January 1971.

Greene, Francis J. "Louis Guilloux's LE SANG NOIR: A Prefiguration of Sartre's LA NAUSEE." FR 43:205-214. December 1969.

Johnson, Patricia J. "Empty Gesture: Descriptive Technique in Sartre's LA NAUSEE." RomN 14:421-424. Spring 1973.

Kamber, Richard. "The Creative Solution in NAUSEA." SUS 9:227-241. June 1974.

Keefe, Terry. "The Ending of Sartre's LA NAUSEE." FMLS 12:217-235. July 1976.

Kellman, Steven G. "Sartre's LA NAUSEE as Self-begetting Novel." Symposium 28:303-314. Winter 1974.

Lyon, Laurence Gill. "Related Images in MALTE LAURIDS BRIGGE and LA NAUSEE." CL 30:53-71. Winter 1978.

Marantz, Enid. "The Theme of Alienation in the Literary Works of Jean-Paul Sartre." Mosaic 2:32-34. Fall 1968.

Moravcevich, June. "LA NAUSEE and LES MOTS: Vision and Revision." SP 70:222-232. April 1973.

Porter, Dennis. "Sartre, Robbe-Grillet and the Psychotic Hero." MFS 16:16-22. Spring 1970.

Ruppert, Peter. "The Aesthetic Solution in NAUSEA and MALTE LAURIDS BRIGGE." CL 29:17-34. Winter 1977.

Somers, Paul P., Jr. "Camus 'Sí,' Sartre 'No.'"
FR 42:693-700. April 1969.

Spanos, William V. "The Un-Naming of the Beasts: The Postmodernity of Sartre's LA NAUSEE." Criticism 20:223-280. Summer 1978.

Thiher, Allen. "Céline and Sartre." PQ 50:292-305. April 1971.

Vickery, John B. "The Dilemmas of Language: Sartre's LA NAUSEE and Iris Murdoch's UNDER THE NET." JNT 1:69-76. May 1971.

Zimmerman, Eugenia N. "LA NAUSEE and the Avators of Being." Mosaic 5:151-157. Spring 1972.

Zimmerman, Eugenia Noik. "'Some of These Days': Sartre's 'Petite Phrase.'" ConL 11:375-381. Summer 1970.

THE REPRIEVE
Bauer, George Howard. Sartre and the Artist. Chicago: University of Chicago Press, 1969. pp. 65-91.

ROADS TO FREEDOM
Nichols, Prescott S. "Paris as Subjectivity in Sartre's ROADS TO FREEDOM." MFS 24:3-21. Spring 1978.

Wardman, H.W. "Sartre and the Literature of 'praxis': LES CHEMINS DE LA LIBERTE." EFL 4:44-67. November 1967.

Scarron, Paul
NOUVELLES TRAGICOMIQUES
Wadsworth, Philip A. "Scarron's NOUVELLES TRAGICOMIQUES." RUS 59:93-100. Summer 1973.

LE ROMAN COMIQUE
Bidwell, Jean S. "LA PRINCESSE DE CLEVES and LE ROMAN COMIQUE--Two Different Worlds." LangQ 11:43-47. Spring/Summer 1973.

Carter, Nancy G. "The Theme of Sleep in LE ROMAN COMIQUE." RomN 11:362-367. Winter 1969.

Conroy, Peter V., Jr. "The Narrative Stance in Scarron's ROMAN COMIQUE." FR 47:18-30. Sp. Issue No. 6, Spring 1974.

de Armas, Frederick A. Paul Scarron. New York: Twayne, 1972. pp. 38-100.

De Jean, Joan. "Scarron's ROMAN COMIQUE: The Other Side of Parody." PFSCL 10:51-63. No. 1, 1978-1979.

Thomas, Ruth P. "LE ROMAN COMIQUE and JACQUES LE FATALISTE: Some Parallels." FR 47:13-24. October 1973.

Wine, Kathleen. "Self-Parody in the ROMAN COMIQUE." PFSCL 10:65-77. No. 1, 1978-1979.

de Scudéry, Mlle
CLELIE
Aronson, Nicole. Mademoiselle de Scudéry. Boston: Twayne, 1978. pp. 82-95.

Nunn, Robert R. "Mlle. de Scudéry and the Development of the Literary Portrait: Some Unusual Portraits in CLELIE." RomN 17:180-184. Winter 1976.
LE GRAND CYRUS
Aronson, Nicole. Mademoiselle de Scudéry. Boston: Twayne, 1978. pp. 68-82.
IBRAHIM
Aronson, Nicole. Mademoiselle de Scudéry. Boston: Twayne, 1978. pp. 54-68.

de Ségur, Comtesse
LES PETITES FILLES MODELES
Laden, Richard A. "Terror, Nature, and the Sacrifice in the Comtesse de Ségur's LES PETITES FILLES MODELES." MLN 94:742-756. May 1979.

Semprun, Jorge
LE GRAND VOYAGE
King, J. H. "Jorge Semprun's Long Journey." AJFS 10:223-235. May/August 1973.

Serge, Victor
BIRTH OF OUR POWER
Greeman, Richard. "'The laws are burning'--Literary and Revolutionary Realism in Victor Serge." YFS 39: 146-159. 1967.

Simon, Claude
LA BATAILLE DE PHARSALE
Birn, Randi. "Proust, Claude Simon, and the Art of the Novel." PLL 13:168-186. Spring 1977.

Jimenez-Fajardo, Salvador. Claude Simon. Boston: Twayne, 1975. pp. 120-145.

Jones, Tobin H. "Toward a More Primitive Reading: Aesthetic Response to Radical Form in the New French Novel." ELWIU 3:276-282. Fall 1976.

Loubère, J. A. E. The Novels of Claude Simon. Ithaca: Cornell University Press, 1975. pp. 151-173.

Sykes, S.W. "Ternary Form in Three Novels by Claude Simon." Symposium 32:25-40. Spring 1978.
LES CORPS CONDUCTEURS
Jimenez-Fajardo, Salvador. Claude Simon. Boston: Twayne, 1975. pp. 146-166.

Loubère, J. A. E. The Novels of Claude Simon. Ithaca: Cornell University Press, 1975. pp. 174-196.
THE FLANDERS ROAD
Brosman, Catharine Savage. "Man's Animal Condition in Claude Simon's LA ROUTE DES FLANDRES." Symposium 29:57-68. Spring/Summer 1975.

Fletcher, John. Claude Simon and Fiction Now. London: Calder & Boyars, 1975. pp. 117-134.

Jimenez-Fajardo, Salvador. Claude Simon. Boston: Twayne, 1975. pp. 54-73.

Levitt, Morton P. "Disillusionment and Epiphany: The Novels of Claude Simon." Crit 12:54-59. No. 1, 1970.

Loubère, J. A. E. The Novels of Claude Simon. Ithaca: Cornell University Press, 1975. pp. 86-104.

Mercier, Vivian. The New Novel from Queneau to Pinget. New York: Farrar, Straus & Giroux, 1971. pp. 267-279.

Ricardou, Jean. "Composition Discomposed." CritI 3:79-91. Autumn 1976.

Sims, Robert L. "Myth and Historico-Primordial Memory in Claude Simon's LA ROUTE DES FLANDRES." NFS 17:74-86. October 1978.

Solomon, Philip H. "Claude Simon's LA ROUTE DES FLANDRES: A Horse of a Different Colour?" AJFS 9:190-201. May/August 1972.

Sykes, S.W. "The Novel as Conjuration: ABSALOM, ABSALOM! and LA ROUTE DES FLANDRES." RLC 53:348-357. July/September 1979.

―――. "Ternary Form in Three Novels by Claude Simon." Symposium 32:25-40. Spring 1978.
THE GRASS
Fletcher, John. Claude Simon and Fiction Now. London: Calder & Boyars, 1975. pp. 135-153.

Jimenez-Fajardo, Salvador. Claude Simon. Boston: Twayne, 1975. pp. 35-54.

Leonard, Diane R. "Simon's L'HERBE: Beyond Sound and Fury." FAR 1:13-30. Winter 1976.

Levitt, Morton P. "Disillusionment and Epiphany: The Novels of Claude Simon." Crit 12:50-54. No. 1, 1970.

Loubère, J. A. E. The Novels of Claude Simon. Ithaca: Cornell University Press, 1975. pp. 74-85.

Mercier, Vivian. The New Novel from Queneau to Pinget. New York: Farrar, Straus & Giroux, 1971. pp. 294-300.

HISTOIRE
Fletcher, John. Claude Simon and Fiction Now. London: Calder & Boyars, 1975. pp. 156-173.

Jimenez-Fajardo, Salvador. Claude Simon. Boston: Twayne, 1975. pp. 95-119.

Kelly, Lynda Harper. "Spatial Composition and Formal Harmonies in Claude Simon's HISTOIRE." MLS 9:73-83. Winter 1978-1979.

Levitt, Morton P. "Disillusionment and Epiphany: The Novels of Claude Simon." Crit 12:63-69. No. 1, 1970.

Loubère, J. A. E. The Novels of Claude Simon. Ithaca: Cornell University Press, 1975. pp. 135-150.

LEÇON DE CHOSES
Evans, Michael. "Two Uses of Intertextuality: References to Impressionist Painting and MADAME BOVARY in Claude Simon's LEÇON DE CHOSES." NFS 19:33-45. May 1980.

O'Donnell, Thomas D. "Claude Simon's LEÇON DE CHOSES: Myth and Ritual Displaced." IFR 5:134-142. July 1978.

THE PALACE
Fletcher, John. Claude Simon and Fiction Now. London: Calder & Boyars, 1975. pp. 97-116.

Jimenez-Fajardo, Salvador. Claude Simon. Boston: Twayne, 1975. pp. 73-95.

Kadish, Doris Y. "From the Narration of Crime to the Crime of Narration: Claude Simon's LE PALACE." IFR 4:128-135. July 1977.

Levitt, Morton P. "Disillusionment and Epiphany: The Novels of Claude Simon." Crit 12:59-63. No. 1, 1970.

Loubère, J. A. E. "Claude Simon's LE PALACE: A Paradigm of Otherness." Symposium 27:46-63. Spring 1973.

Simon, Claude

    _____. The Novels of Claude Simon. Ithaca: Cornell University Press, 1975. pp. 105-134.

    Solomon, Philip H. "Flights of Time Lost: Bird Imagery in Claude Simon's LE PALACE. " Twentieth Century French Fiction: Essays for Germaine Brée. ed. George Stambolian. New Brunswick: Rutgers University Press, 1975. pp. 166-182.

TRIPTYQUE
    Jimenez-Fajardo, Salvador. Claude Simon. Boston: Twayne, 1975. pp. 167-190.

    Loubère, J.A.E. The Novels of Claude Simon. Ithaca: Cornell University Press, 1975. pp. 197-226.

    Sykes, S.W. "Ternary Form in Three Novels by Claude Simon." Symposium 32:25-40. Spring 1978.

THE WIND
    Duncan, Alastair B. "Claude Simon and William Faulkner." FMLS 9:238-252. July 1973.

    Jimenez-Fajardo, Salvador. Claude Simon. Boston: Twayne, 1975. pp. 15-36.

    Levitt, Morton P. "Disillusionment and Epiphany: The Novels of Claude Simon." Crit 12:46-50. No. 1, 1970.

    Loubère, J.A.E. The Novels of Claude Simon. Ithaca: Cornell University Press, 1975. pp. 60-73.

    Mercier, Vivian. The New Novel from Queneau to Pinget. New York: Farrar, Straus & Giroux, 1971. pp. 288-294.

Sollers, Philippe
    NOMBRES
        Kafalenos, Emma. "Philippe Sollers' NOMBRES: Structure and Sources." ConL 19:320-335. Summer 1978.

Sorel, Charles
    LE BERGER EXTRAVAGANT (ANTI-ROMAN)
        Kay, Burf. "A Writer Turns Against Literature: Charles Sorel's LE BERGER EXTRAVAGANT." RUO 43:277-291. April/June 1973.

        Tilton, Elizabeth M. "Structural and Linguistic Patterns in the Seventeenth-Century Novel and Anti-Novel." Neophil 62:212-221. April 1978.
    HISTOIRE COMIQUE DE FRANCION
        Griffiths, Michael and Wolfgang Leiner. "Some Thoughts on the Names of the Characters in Charles Sorel's

HISTOIRE COMIQUE DE FRANCION." RomN 15:445-453. Spring 1974.

Guthrie, J. Richard, Jr. "An Analysis of Style and Purpose in the First Episode of the HISTOIRE COMIQUE DE FRANCION." RomN 15:99-103. Autumn 1973.

Ridgely, Beverly S. "The Cosmic Voyage in Charles Sorel's FRANCION." MP 65:1-8. August 1967.

Suozzo, Andrew G., Jr. "Disguise and the Rites of Death and Resurrection in Sorel's FRANCION." FR 53:23-28. October 1979.

———. "Hortensius and Collinet: Gradations and Implications of Madness in the FRANCION." RomN 20:81-86. Fall 1979.

———. "Nays as the Vicarious Heroine: The FRANCION's Book XII." FrF 3:3-9. January 1978.

Tilton, Elizabeth Meier. "Charles Sorel's Alternative Paradise: The Ideal of Unproblematic Love." YFS 58: 165-181. 1979.

L'ORPHIZE DE CHRYSANTE
Verdier, Gabrielle. "Tradition and 'Textuality' in a Baroque Romance: Charles Sorel's L'ORPHIZE DE CHRYSANTE." KRQ 26:491-508. No. 4, 1979.

de Staël, Madame
CORINNE
Daemmrich, Ingrid G. "The Fuction of the Ruins Motif in Madame de Staël's CORINNE." RomN 15:255-258. Winter 1973.

Gutwirth, Madelyn. Madame de Staël, Novelist: The Emergence of the Artist as Woman. Urbana: University of Illinois Press, 1978. pp. 154-258.

Moers, Ellen. "Mme de Staël and the Woman of Genius." ASch 44:225-241. Spring 1975.
DELPHINE
Gutwirth, Madelyn. Madame de Staël, Novelist: The Emergence of the Artist as Woman. Urbana: University of Illinois Press, 1978. pp. 76-153.
MIRZA
Switzer, Richard. "Mme de Staël, Mme de Duras and the Question of Race." KRQ 20:303-316. No. 3, 1973.

Stendhal
ARMANCE
Alter, Robert. A Lion for Love: A Critical Biography

of Stendhal. New York: Basic Books, 1979. pp. 173-180.

Brombert, Victor. Stendhal: Fiction and the Themes of Freedom. New York: Random House, 1968. pp. 27-60.

Brotherson, Lee. "Impotence in ARMANCE: A Medium for Social Criticism." AJFS 16:55-67. January/April 1979.

Comeau, Paul T. "The Love Theme and the Monologue Structure in ARMANCE." NCFS 7:37-58. Fall/Winter 1980-1981.

Fowlie, Wallace. Stendhal. London: Macmillan, 1969. pp. 71-90.

─────. "A Study of Stendhal's ARMANCE." Novel 2:230-240. Spring 1969.

Mickel, Emanuel J., Jr. "Stendahl's [sic] Use of Irony in ARMANCE." SAB 35:11-18. November 1970.

Mouillaud, Geneviève. "The Sociology of Stendhal's Novels: Preliminary Research." ISSJ 19:581-598. No. 4, 1967.

O'Keefe, Charles. "A Function of Narrative Uncertainty in Stendhal's ARMANCE." FR 50:579-585. March 1977.

Place, David. "The Problems of Stendhal's ARMANCE." FS 33:27-37. January 1979.

Talbot, Emile J. "The Impossible Ethic: A Reading of Stendhal's ARMANCE." FrF 3:147-157. May 1978.

Tillett, Margaret. Stendhal: The Background to the Novels. London: Oxford University Press, 1971. pp. 83-96.

Wood, Michael. Stendhal. Ithaca: Cornell University Press, 1971. pp. 52-64.

THE CHARTERHOUSE OF PARMA
Alter, Robert. A Lion for Love: A Critical Biography of Stendhal. New York: Basic Books, 1979. pp. 246-261.

Brombert, Victor. Stendhal: Fiction and the Themes of Freedom. New York: Random House, 1968. pp. 149-176.

Brooks, Peter. The Novel of Worldliness: Crébillon, Marivaux, Laclos, Stendhal. Princeton: Princeton University Press, 1969. pp. 266-278.

Denommé, Robert T. "Changing Perspectives in Stendhal's VIE DE HENRY BRULARD and LA CHARTREUSE DE PARME." RR 67:35-37. January 1976.

Fowlie, Wallace. Stendhal. London: MacMillan, 1969. pp. 159-204.

Gelley, Alexander. "The Landscape of Happiness in LA CHARTREUSE DE PARME." HUSL 1:86-110. Spring 1973.

Goodheart, Eugene. "Aristocrats and Jacobins: 'The Happy Few' in THE CHARTERHOUSE OF PARMA." YR 65:370-391. March 1976.

Gutwirth, Marcel. Stendhal. New York: Twayne, 1971. pp. 35-41; 55-60; 107-111.

Houston, John Porter. Fictional Technique in France, 1802-1927: An Introduction. Baton Rouge: Louisiana State University Press, 1972. pp. 13-25.

Kirton, W. J. S. "Stendhal, Lampedusa and the Limits of Admiration." Trivium 10:101-108. May 1975.

Kogan, Vivian. "Signs and Signals in LA CHARTREUSE DE PARME." NCFS 2:29-38. Fall/Winter 1973-1974.

May, Gita. Stendhal and the Age of Napoleon. New York: Columbia University Press, 1977. pp. 259-271.

Miel, Jan. "Temporal Form in the Novel." MLN 84:926-928. December 1969.

Purdy, Strother B. "Manzoni, Stendhal, and the Murder of Prina: A Counterpoint of Literature and History." SIR 7:140-158. Spring 1968.

Rabine, Leslie. "Ideology and Contradiction in LA CHARTREUSE DE PARME." Sub-stance 21:117-137. 1978.

Talbot, Emile J. "Stendhal, the Artist, and Society." SIR 13:213-223. Summer 1974.

_____. "Style and the Self: Some Notes on LA CHARTREUSE DE PARME." Lang & S 5:299-311. Fall 1972.

Terdiman, Richard. The Dialectics of Isolation: Self and Society in the French Novel from the Realists to Proust. New Haven: Yale University Press, 1976. pp. 21-62.

Tillett, Margaret. Stendhal: The Background to the Novels. London: Oxford University Press, 1971. pp. 124-142.

Vineberg, Elsa. "The Limits of Excavation: A Study of Perception and Memory in Stendhal's LA CHARTREUSE DE PARME." RPac 4:13-22. Spring 1978.

Wood, Michael. Stendhal. Ithaca: Cornell University Press, 1971. pp. 157-188.

## LAMIEL

Alter, Robert. A Lion for Love: A Critical Biography of Stendhal. New York: Basic Books, 1979. pp. 266-270.

May, Gita. Stendhal and the Age of Napoleon. New York: Columbia University Press, 1977. pp. 271-278.

Porter, Dennis. "LAMIEL: The Wild Child and the Ugly Men." Novel 12:21-32. Fall 1978.

## LUCIEN LEUWEN

Alter, Robert. A Lion for Love: A Critical Biography of Stendhal. New York: Basic Books, 1979. pp. 223-233.

Brombert, Victor. Stendhal: Fiction and the Themes of Freedom. New York: Random House, 1968. pp. 101-128.

Brooks, Peter. The Novel of Worldliness: Crébillon, Marivaux, Laclos, Stendhal. Princeton: Princeton University Press, 1969. pp. 229-269.

Fowlie, Wallace. Stendhal. London: Macmillan, 1969. pp. 131-140.

Gutwirth, Marcel. Stendhal. New York: Twayne, 1971. pp. 29-35; 50-55; 70-77; 103-107.

May, Gita. Stendhal and the Age of Napoleon. New York: Columbia University Press, 1977. pp. 238-243.

Place, David. "Stendhal's Rhetoric of Love in LUCIEN LEUWEN." MLR 74:39-48. January 1979.

Strickland, Geoffrey. Stendhal: The Education of a Novelist. Cambridge: Cambridge University Press, 1974. pp. 165-219.

Terdiman, Richard. The Dialectics of Isolation: Self and Society in the French Novel from the Realists to Proust. New Haven: Yale University Press, 1976. pp. 26-31.

Viti, Robert M. "The Dual Role of Enclosed Space in LUCIEN LEUWEN." RomN 20:344-348. Spring 1980.

Wood, Michael. Stendhal. Ithaca: Cornell University Press, 1971. pp. 115-141.

## THE RED AND THE BLACK

Abeel, Erica. "The Multiple Authors in Stendhal's Ironic Interventions." FR 50:21-34. October 1976.

Alter, Robert. A Lion for Love: A Critical Biography of Stendhal. New York: Basic Books, 1979. pp. 186-203.

Bart, B. F. "Hypercreativity in Stendhal and Balzac." NCFS 3:18-31. Fall/Winter 1974-1975.

Borgerhoff, E. B. O. "Hammer, Saw and Wheel in LE ROUGE ET LE NOIR." FR 42:518-523. March 1969.

Brombert, Victor. Stendhal: Fiction and the Themes of Freedom. New York: Random House, 1968. pp. 61-100.

Cameron, J. L. "Sons and Lovers in LE ROUGE ET LE NOIR." AUMLA 36:206-209. November 1971.

Cook, Albert. "Stendhal and the Discovery of Ironic Interplay." Novel 9:40-46. Fall 1975.

DeLutri, Joseph R. "Notes on the Chapter Titles and Content of LE ROUGE ET LE NOIR." RomN 15:64-67. Autumn 1973.

_____. "On an Episode of LE ROUGE ET LE NOIR, 'L'Ennui.'" NCFS 3:192-199. Spring/Summer 1975.

Denommé, Robert T. "Julien Sorel and the Modern Conscience." WHR 21:227-234. Summer 1967.

Diorio, Dorothy M. "LE ROUGE ET LE NOIR: The Enigma of a Title." WVUPP 19:12-19. July 1972.

Feldman, Burton. "Stendhal and Helvétius." Symposium 23:129-136. Summer 1969.

Fowlie, Wallace. Stendhal. London: Macmillan, 1969. pp. 91-130.

Gerhardi, Gerhard C. "Psychological Time and Revolutionary Action in LE ROUGE ET LE NOIR." PMLA 88:1115-1126. October 1973.

Godfrey, Gary M. "Julien Sorel--Soldier in Blue." MLQ 37:339-348. December 1976.

Gutwirth, Marcel. Stendhal. New York: Twayne, 1971. pp. 20-31; 42-50; 66-70; 97-103.

Hamilton, James F. "Stendhal's LE ROUGE ET LE NOIR and Rousseau's L'EMILE: Contrary Experiments." NCFS 6:199-212. Spring/Summer 1978.

Horn, Pierre L. "Reflections on Madame de Rênal's First Name." NCFS 6:52-56. Fall/Winter 1977-1978.

Jameson, Storm. Speaking of Stendhal. London: Victor Gollancz, 1979. pp. 111-120.

Jones, Grahame C. "The Dramatic Tempo of LE ROUGE ET LE NOIR." EFL 6:74-80. November 1969.

May, Gita. Stendhal and the Age of Napoleon. New York: Columbia University Press, 1977. pp. 211-221.

Miel, Jan. "Temporal Form in the Novel." MLN 84:924-926. December 1969.

Mitchell, John. Stendhal: LE ROUGE ET LE NOIR. [London]: Edward Arnold, 1973. 64 pp.

Mossop, D. J. "Julien Sorel, the Vulgar Assassin." FS 23:138-144. April 1969.

Mouillaud, Geneviève. "The Sociology of Stendhal's Novels: Preliminary Research." ISSJ 19:581-598. No. 4, 1967.

Palmer, William J. "Abelard's Fate: Sexual Politics in Stendhal, Faulkner and Camus." Mosaic 7:29-41. Spring 1974.

Paris, Bernard J. A Psychological Approach to Fiction: Studies in Thackeray, Stendhal, George Eliot, Dostoevsky, and Conrad. Bloomington: Indiana University Press, 1974. pp. 133-164.

Ragland-Sullivan, Mary Eloise. "Julien's Quest for 'Self': 'Qui suis-je?'" NCFS 8:1-13. Fall/Winter 1979-1980.

Redfern, W. D. "The Prisoners of Stendhal and Camus." FR 41:649-659. April 1968.

Richardson, Joanna. Stendhal. New York: McCann & Geoghegan, 1974. pp. 223-229.

Rogers, Nancy E. "The Use of Eye Language in Stendhal's LE ROUGE ET LE NOIR." RomN 20:339-343. Spring 1980.

Sands, Steven. "The Narcissism of Stendhal and Julien Sorel." SIR 14:337-363. Fall 1975.

Strickland, Geoffrey. Stendhal: The Education of a Novelist. Cambridge: Cambridge University Press, 1974. pp. 126-164.

Tenenbaum, Elizabeth Brody. The Problematic Self: Approaches to Identity in Stendhal, D.H. Lawrence, and Malraux. Cambridge: Harvard University Press, 1977. pp. 36-64.

Vos, Marianne Cramer. "Love in the Stendhalian Hero." LangQ 15:39-42. Fall/Winter 1976.

Wood, Michael. Stendhal. Ithaca: Cornell University Press, 1971. pp. 65-94.

VIE DE HENRY BRULARD

Coe, Richard N. "Stendhal, Rousseau and the Search for Self." AJFS 16:27-47. January/April 1979.

Denommé, Robert T. "Changing Perspectives in Stendhal's VIE DE HENRY BRULARD and LA CHARTREUSE DE PARME." RR 67:28-35. January 1976.

Porter, Dennis. "Stendhal and the Impossibility of Autobiography." FS 32:158-169. April 1978.

Wood, Michael. Stendhal. Ithaca: Cornell University Press, 1971. pp. 142-156.

Stern, David (Marie D'Agoult)
VALENTIA

Rabine, Leslie. "Feminist Writers in French Romanticism." SIR 16:496-502. Fall 1977.

Sue, Eugène
MATHILDE

Jones, Malcolm V. "An Aspect of Romanticism in Dostoyevsky: NETOCHKA NEZVANOVA and Eugène Sue's MATHILDE." RMS 17:38-61. 1973.

LES MYSTERES DE PARIS

Eco, Umberto. "Rhetoric and Ideology in Sue's LES MYSTERES DE PARIS." ISSJ 19:551-569. No. 4, 1967.

Sue, Eugène

    Luce, Louise Fiber. "The Masked Avenger: Historical Analogue in Eugène Sue's LES MYSTERES DE PARIS." FrF 1:227-236. September 1976.

    Sobkowska-Ashcroft, Irina. "PETERBURSKIE TRUSH-CHOBY: A Russian Version of LES MYSTERES DE PARIS." RLC 53:163-175. April/June 1979.

Triolet, Elsa
  LE CHEVAL BLANC
    DeJean, Joan E. "The Writer as Literary Citation: Remarks on a Device in Seventeenth-Century French Comic Fiction." PFSCL 9:119-134. Summer 1978.

Tristan, Flora
  MEPHIS
    Rabine, Leslie. "Feminist Writers in French Romanticism." SIR 16:504-506. Fall 1977.

Troyat, Henri
  L'ARAIGNE
    George, K.E.M. "The Rôle of the Suffix in Troyat's L'ARAIGNE." ML 50:107-111. September 1969.
  LA NEIGE EN DEUIL
    Harrison, M.J. "The Imagery in Troyat's LA NEIGE EN DEUIL." ML 52:151-156. December 1971.

d'Urfé, Honoré
  L'ASTREE
    Carroll, M.G. "L'ASTREE, or Virtue Corrupted." Trivium 8:27-35. May 1973.

    De Ley, Herbert. "Two Modes of Thought in L'ASTREE." YFS 49:143-153. 1973.

    Jehenson, Yvonne. "Realism in Honoré d'Urfé's L'ASTREE." PFSCL 10:59-73. No. 2, 1978-1979.

    Poirier, Suzanne. "L'ASTREE Revisited: A 17th Century Model for THE MAGUS." CLS 17:269-285. September 1980.

    Tilton, Elizabeth M. "Rhetorical Structure in the Silvanire Debate of L'ASTREE." KRQ 27:299-311. No. 3, 1980.

Vailland, Roger
  325.000 FRANCS
    Flower, J.E. "Roger Vailland: 325.000 FRANCS." ML 53:63-71. June 1972.

Valéry, Paul
  MONSIEUR TESTE

Charney, Hanna. "Monsieur Teste and der Mann ohne Eigenschaften: 'Homo Possibilis' in Fiction." CL 27: 1-7. Winter 1975.

Whiting, Charles. Paul Valéry. London: The Athlone Press, 1978. pp. 56-59.

## Vallès, Jules
### L'ENFANT
Redfern, W.D. "Delinquent Parents: Jules Vallès and L'ENFANT." Mosaic 5:167-177. Spring 1972.
### JACQUES VINGTRAS
Edmonds, Barbara P. "In Search of Jules Vallès." FR 40:636-642. April 1967.

## Verne, Jules
### AROUND THE WORLD IN EIGHTY DAYS
Costello, Peter. Jules Verne: Inventor of Science Fiction. New York: Scribner's, 1978. pp. 118-123.

Jules-Verne, Jean. Jules Verne: A Biography. New York: Taplinger, 1976. pp. 106-109.
### CASTLE IN THE CARPATHIANS
Jules-Verne, Jean. Jules Verne: A Biography. New York: Taplinger, 1976. pp. 171-179.

Rose, Marilyn Gaddis. "Two Misogynist Novels: A Feminist Reading of Villiers and Verne." NCFS 7:117-123. Fall/Winter 1980-1981.
### THE CHILDREN OF CAPTAIN GRANT
Costello, Peter. Jules Verne: Inventor of Science Fiction. New York: Charles Scribner's Sons, 1978. pp. 92-95.

Jules-Verne, Jean. Jules Verne: A Biography. New York: Taplinger, 1976. pp. 77-84.
### JOURNEY TO THE CENTER OF THE EARTH
Jules-Verne, Jean. Jules Verne: A Biography. New York: Taplinger, 1976. pp. 63-69.
### A LIVONIAN TRAGEDY
Cap, Biruta. "A French Observer of the Baltic." J Bal S 3:133-137. Summer 1972.
### TWENTY THOUSAND LEAGUES UNDER THE SEA
Costello, Peter. Jules Verne: Inventor of Science Fiction. New York: Charles Scribner's Sons, 1978. pp. 101-109.
### VOYAGES EXTRAORDINAIRES
Aberger, Peter. "The Portrayal of Blacks in Jules Verne's VOYAGES EXTRAORDINAIRES." FR 53:199-206. December 1979.

Winandy, André. "The Twilight Zone: Imagination and Reality in Jules Verne's STRANGE JOURNEYS." YFS 43:97-110. 1969.

Vian, Boris
 L'ARRACHE-COEUR
  Cismaru, Alfred. Boris Vian. Twayne, 1974. pp. 82-88.

  Lerner, Michael G. "Boris Vian's L'ARRACHE-COEUR: Some Comments on His Style." Neophil 58: 195-198. April 1974.

de Vigny, Alfred
 CINQ MARS
  Doolittle, James. Alfred de Vigny. New York: Twayne, 1967. pp. 47-57.
 SERVITUDE ET GRANDEUR MILITAIRES
  Doolittle, James. Alfred de Vigny. New York: Twayne, 1967. pp. 113-124.

  Haig, Stirling. "Conscience and Antimilitarism in Vigny's SERVITUDE ET GRANDEUR MILITAIRES." PMLA 89:50-56. January 1974.
 STELLO
  Lowrie, Joyce O. "The Structural and Ideological Significance of Vigny's 'Man of Destiny' in STELLO." PMLA 87:278-283. March 1972.

Villiers de l'Isle-Adam
 L'EVE FUTURE
  Conroy, William T., Jr. Villiers de l'Isle-Adam. Boston: Twayne, 1978. pp. 109-115.

  Rose, Marilyn Gaddis. "Two Misogynist Novels: A Feminist Reading of Villiers and Verne." NCFS 7:117-123. Fall/Winter 1980-1981.

Voltaire
 CANDIDE
  Aldridge, A. Owen. Voltaire and the Century of Light. Princeton: Princeton University Press, 1975. pp. 250-260.

  Besterman, Theodore. Voltaire. Oxford: Basil Blackwell, 1969. pp. 429-436.

  Bonneville, Douglas A. "CANDIDE as Symbolic Experience." SVEC 76:7-14. 1970.

  Brady, Patrick. "Is CANDIDE Really 'Rococo'?" ECr 7:234-242. Winter 1967.

  Crocker, Lester G. "Professor Wolper's Interpretation of CANDIDE." ECS 5:145-151. Fall 1971. Reply by Roy S. Wolper, pp. 151-156.

Dalnekoff, Donna Isaacs. "The Meaning of Eldorado: Utopia and Satire in CANDIDE." SVEC 127:41-59. 1974.

Danahy, Michael. "The Nature of Narrative Norms in CANDIDE." SVEC 114:113-140. 1973.

Dieckmann, Herbert. "Philosophy and Literature in Eighteenth-Century France." CLS 8:35-39. March 1971.

Fazziola, Peter. "Candide Among the Bulgares: A Parody of Pascal's 'Pari.'" PQ 53:430-434. Summer 1974.

Fletcher, Dennis. "CANDIDE and the Philosophy of the Garden." Trivium 13:18-29. May 1978.

_____. "CANDIDE and the Theme of the Happy Husbandman." SVEC 161:137-147. 1976.

Grobe, Edwin P. "Aspectual Parody in Voltaire's CANDIDE." Symposium 21:38-49. Spring 1967.

_____. "Discontinuous Aspect in Voltaire's CANDIDE." MLN 82:334-346. May 1967.

Gullace, Giovanni. "Voltaire's Idea of Progress and CANDIDE's Conclusion." Person 48:167-185. Spring 1967.

Havens, George R. "Some Notes on CANDIDE." MLN 88:841-847. May 1973.

Henry, Patrick. "Candide as 'Etranger.'" CLAJ 19: 504-512. June 1976.

_____. "The Metaphysical Puppets of CANDIDE." RomN 17:166-169. Winter 1976.

_____. "On the Theme of Homosexuality in CANDIDE." RomN 19:44-48. Fall 1978.

_____. "Sacred and Profane Gardens in CANDIDE." SVEC 176:133-152. 1979.

_____. "Time in CANDIDE." SSF 14:86-88. Winter 1977.

_____. "Travel in CANDIDE: Moving on but Going Nowhere." PLL 13:193-197. Spring 1977.

_____. "Voltaire and Camus: The Limits of Reason

and the Awareness of Absurdity." SVEC 138:177-247. 1975.

_____. "War as Play in CANDIDE." EAS 5:65-72. May 1976.

_____. "Working in Candide's Garden." SSF 14:183-184. Spring 1977.

Hutton, Patrick H. "Companionship in Voltaire's CANDIDE." EnlE 4:39-45. Spring 1973.

Ilie, Paul. "The Voices in Candide's Garden, 1755-1759: A Methodology for Voltaire's Correspondence." SVEC 148:37-113. 1976.

Jory, D. H. "The Source of a Name in CANDIDE?" RomN 13:113-116. Autumn 1971.

Kivy, Peter. "Voltaire, Hume, and the Problem of Evil." Philosophy and Literature 3:211-224. Fall 1979.

Knowlson, James. "Voltaire, Lucian and CANDIDE." SVEC 161:149-160. 1976.

Korsmeyer, Carolyn. "Is Pangloss Leibniz?" Philosophy and Literature 1:201-208. Spring 1977.

Kusch, Manfred. "The River and the Garden: Basic Spatial Models in CANDIDE and LA NOUVELLE HELOÏSE." ECS 12:5-8. Fall 1978.

Levitt, Jesse. "Onomastic Devices in Voltaire's CANDIDE." LOS 7:55-65. 1980.

Mason, Haydn. Voltaire. London: Hutchinson, 1975. pp. 57-73.

McGregor, Rob Roy. "Heraldic Quarterings and Voltaire's CANDIDE." SVEC 183:83-87. 1980.

McGregor, Rob Roy, Jr. "The Misunderstanding over the Sabbath in CANDIDE." RomN 13:288-291. Winter 1971.

_____. "Pangloss' Final Observation, an Ironic Flaw in Voltaire's CANDIDE." RomN 20:361-365. Spring 1980.

Murray, Geoffrey. "Voltaire's CANDIDE: The Protean Gardener, 1755-1762." SVEC 69:13-384. 1970.

Mylne, Vivienne G. "A Pícara in CANDIDE: Paquette." CollL 6:205-209. Fall 1979.

Richter, Peyton and Ilona Ricardo. Voltaire. Boston: Twayne, 1980. pp. 131-139; 412-419.

Scanlan, Timothy M. "Subliminal Obscenity in CANDIDE." Maledicta 3:29-35. Summer 1979.

_____. "Voltaire and Rousseau: Their Rencontre Fortuite." OL 32:302-309. 1977.

Severin, Nelly H. "Hagiographic Parody in CANDIDE." FR 50:842-849. May 1977.

_____. "A Note on the Name of Voltaire's Cunégonde." RomN 19:212-216. Winter 1978.

Stewart, Philip. "Holding the Mirror Up to Fiction: Generic Parody in CANDIDE." FS 33:411-419. October 1979.

Torrey, Virgil W. Voltaire: A Critical Study. New York: Random House, 1967. pp. 38-46.

Wolper, Roy S. "Candide, Gull in the Garden?" ECS 3:265-277. Winter 1969.

HISTOIRE DE JENNI
 Carr, Thomas M., Jr. "Eloquence in the Defense of Deism: Voltaire's HISTOIRE DE JENNI." KRQ 25:471-480. No. 4, 1978.

L'INGENU
 Aldridge, A. Owen. Voltaire and the Century of Light. Princeton: Princeton University Press, 1975. pp. 349-351.

 Carroll, M.C. "Some Implications of 'vraisemblance' in Voltaire's L'INGENU." SVEC 183:35-44. 1980.

 Havens, George R. "Voltaire's L'INGENU: Composition and Publication." RR 63:261-271. December 1972.

 Highnam, David E. "L'INGENU: Flawed Masterpiece or Masterful Innovation." SVEC 143:71-83. 1975.

 Mason, Haydn. Voltaire. London: Hutchinson, 1975. pp. 73-79.

 Richter, Peyton and Ilona Ricardo. Voltaire. Boston: Twayne, 1980. pp. 139-143.

 Ridgway, R.S. Voltaire and Sensibility. Montreal: McGill-Queen's University Press, 1975. pp. 242-247.

 Torrey, Virgil W. Voltaire: A Critical Study. New York: Random House, 1967. pp. 46-60.

Valis, Noël M. "Paris as a Prison in Voltaire's L'INGENU." LangQ 18:13-14. Fall/Winter 1979.
MICROMEGAS
Havens, George R. "Voltaire's MICROMEGAS (1739-52): Composition and Publication." MLQ 33:113-118. June 1972.

Mason, Haydn. Voltaire. London: Hutchinson, 1975. pp. 48-52.

Richter, Peyton and Ilona Ricardo. Voltaire. Boston: Twayne, 1980. pp. 126-131.

Smith, Peter Lester. "New Light on the Publication of MICROMEGAS." MP 73:77-80. August 1975.

Torrey, Virgil W. Voltaire: A Critical Study. New York: Random House, 1967. pp. 35-38.
LE MONDE COMME IL VA
Wolper, Roy S. "The Final Foolishness of Babouc: The Dark Centre of LE MONDE COMME IL VA." MLR 75:766-773. October 1980.
LA PRINCESSE DE BABYLONE
Mitchell, P.C. "An Underlying Theme in LA PRINCESSE DE BABYLONE." SVEC 137:31-45. 1975.
LE TAUREAU BLANC
O'Meara, Maureen F. "LE TAUREAU BLANC and the Activity of Language." SVEC 148:115-175. 1976.
ZADIG
Aldridge, A. Owen. Voltaire and the Century of Light. Princeton: Princeton University Press, 1975. pp. 155-160.

Gertner, Michael H. "Five Comic Devices in ZADIG." SVEC 117:133-152. 1974.

Greene, E.J.H. "The Destiny of ZADIG." ECr 7:243-251. Winter 1967.

Kra, Pauline. "Note on the Derivation of Names in Voltaire's ZADIG." RomN 16:342-344. Winter 1975.

Mason, Haydn. Voltaire. London: Hutchinson, 1975. pp. 52-57.

Perla, George A. "Zadig, Hero of the Absurd." SVEC 143:49-70. 1975.

Richter, Peyton and Ilona Ricardo. Voltaire. Boston: Twayne, 1980. pp. 121-126.

Senior, Nancy. "The Structure of ZADIG." SVEC 135:135-141. 1975.

Smith, Peter Lester. "A Note on the Publication of ZADIG: Why Voltaire Cried Slander." RomN 16:345-350. Winter 1975.

Torrey, Virgil W. Voltaire: A Critical Study. New York: Random House, 1967. pp. 31-35.

Wolper, Roy S. "ZADIG, a Grim Comedy?" RR 65: 237-248. November 1974.

ZAIRE
    Cherpack, Clifton. "Love and Alienation in Voltaire's ZAIRE." FrF 2:47-56. January 1977.

Wittig, Monique
    LES GUERILLERES
        Durand, Laura G. "Heroic Feminism as Art." Novel 8:71-77. Fall 1974.

        Ostrovsky, Erika. "A Cosomogony of O: Wittig's LES GUERILLERES." Twentieth-Century French Fiction: Essays for Germaine Brée. ed. George Stambolian. New Brunswick: Rutgers University Press, 1975. pp. 241-251.

Yourcenar, Marguerite
    L'OEUVRE AU NOIR
        Soos, Emese. "The Only Motion Is Returning: The Metaphor of Alchemy in Mallet-Joris and Yourcenar." FrF 4:3-15. January 1979.

Zola, Emile
    L'ASSOMMOIR
        Baguley, David. "Event and Structure: The Plot of Zola's L'ASSOMMOIR." PMLA 90:823-833. October 1975.

        Duncan, Phillip A. "Symbols of the Benign and the Malevolent in Zola's L'ASSOMMOIR." FR 54:52-57. October 1980.

        *Grant, Elliott Mansfield. Emile Zola. New York: Twayne, 1966. pp. 83-101.

        Grobe, Edwin P. "Narrative Technique in L'ASSOMMOIR." ECr 11:56-66. Winter 1971.

        King, Graham. Garden of Zola. London: Barrie & Jenkins, 1978. pp. 105-124.

        Niess, Robert J. "Remarks on the 'Style Indirect Libre' in L'ASSOMMOIR." NCFS 3:124-135. Fall/Winter 1974-1975.

_____. "Some Notes on Authenticity: L'ASSOMMOIR." KRQ 26:509-521. No. 4, 1979.

Petrey, Sandy. "Goujet as God and Worker in L'ASSOMMOIR." FrF 1:239-250. September 1976.

Place, David. "Zola and the Working Class: The Meaning of L'ASSOMMOIR." FS 28:39-49. January 1974.

Richardson, Joanna. Zola. New York: St. Martin's Press, 1978. pp. 61-69.

## AU BONHEUR DES DAMES

King, Graham. Garden of Zola. London: Barrie & Jenkins, 1978. pp. 169-175.

Matthews, J. H. Toward the Poetics of Surrealism. Syracuse: Syracuse University Press, 1976. pp. 41-44.

Richardson, Joanna. Zola. New York: St. Martin's Press, 1978. pp. 101-104.

Schor, Naomi. Zola's Crowds. Baltimore: Johns Hopkins University Press, 1978. pp. 153-162.

## LA BETE HUMAINE

*Grant, Elliott Mansfield. Emile Zola. New York: Twayne, 1966. pp. 147-151.

King, Graham. Garden of Zola. London: Barrie & Jenkins, 1978. pp. 277-283.

Richardson, Joanna. Zola. New York: St. Martin's Press, 1978. pp. 133-140.

Schor, Naomi. Zola's Crowds. Baltimore: Johns Hopkins University Press, 1978. pp. 133-136.

## THE CONQUEST OF PLASSANS

King, Graham. Garden of Zola. London: Barrie & Jenkins, 1978. pp. 85-90.

Schor, Naomi. Zola's Crowds. Baltimore: Johns Hopkins University Press, 1978. pp. 37-42; 54-64.

## LA CUREE

King, Graham. Garden of Zola. London: Barrie & Jenkins, 1978. pp. 65-75.

Lethbridge, Robert. "Zola: Decadence and Autobiography in the Genesis of a Fictional Character." NFS 17:39-51. May 1978.

Nelson, Brian. "Speculation and Dissipation: A Reading of Zola's LA CUREE." EFL 14:1-33. November 1977.

_____. "Zola's Metaphoric Language: A Paragraph from LA CUREE." ML 59:61-64. June 1978.

Petrey, Sandy. "Stylistics and Society in LA CUREE." MLN 89:626-640. May 1974.

Richardson, Joanna. Zola. New York: St. Martin's Press, 1978. pp. 43-46.

LA DEBACLE
*Grant, Elliott Mansfield. Emile Zola. New York: Twayne, 1966. pp. 153-162.

King, Graham. Garden of Zola. London: Barrie & Jenkins, 1978. pp. 288-295.

*Raitt, A.W. Life and Letters in France: The Nineteenth Century. New York: Charles Scribner's Sons, 1965. pp. 127-134.

Richardson, Joanna. Zola. New York: St. Martin's Press, 1978. pp. 149-152.

Schor, Naomi. Zola's Crowds. Baltimore: Johns Hopkins University Press, 1978. pp. 103-119.

LE DOCTEUR PASCAL
Farrag, Aida. "Zola, Dickens, and Spontaneous Combustion Again." RomN 19:190-195. Winter 1978.

King, Graham. Garden of Zola. London: Barrie & Jenkins, 1978. pp. 297-303.

Richardson, Joanna. Zola. New York: St. Martin's Press, 1978. pp. 157-159.

Schor, Naomi. Zola's Crowds. Baltimore: Johns Hopkins University Press, 1978. pp. 67-70.

THE EARTH
*Grant, Elliott Mansfield. Emile Zola. New York: Twayne, 1966. pp. 137-145.

Hemmings, F.W.J. The Life and Times of Emile Zola. New York: Charles Scribner's Sons, 1977. pp. 134-138.

King, Graham. Garden of Zola. London: Barrie & Jenkins, 1978. pp. 212-227.

Richardson, Joanna. Zola. New York: St. Martin's Press, 1978. pp. 118-123.

LA FAUTE DE L'ABBE MOURET
King, Graham. Garden of Zola. London: Barrie & Jenkins, 1978. pp. 89-96.

Minogue, Valerie. "Zola's Mythology: That Forbidden Tree." FMLS 14:217-230. July 1978.

Musumeci, Antonino. "Tasso, Zola and the Vicissitudes of Pastoralism." NCFS 4:347-360. Spring 1976.

Ormerod, Beverley. "Zola's Enclosed Gardens." EFL 11:35-46. November 1974..

Pasco, Allan H. "Literary History and Quinet in the Meaning of LA FAUTE DE L'ABBE MOURET." FMLS 14:208-216. July 1978.

──────. "Love à la Michelet in Zola's LA FAUTE DE L'ABBE MOURET." NCFS 7:232-244. Spring/Summer 1979.

Richardson, Joanna. Zola. New York: St. Martin's Press, 1978. pp. 51-55.

FECONDITE

King, Graham. Garden of Zola. London: Barrie & Jenkins, 1978. pp. 323-325; 355-358.

Richardson, Joanna. Zola. New York: St. Martin's Press, 1978. pp. 204-206.

Schor, Naomi. Zola's Crowds. Baltimore: Johns Hopkins University Press, 1978. pp. 119-121; 138-140.

LA FORTUNE DES ROUGON

Chaitin, Gilbert. "The Voices of the Dead: Love, Death and Politics in Zola's FORTUNE DES ROUGON (Part I)." L & P 26:131-144. No. 3, 1976.

──────. "The Voices of the Dead: Love, Death and Politics in Zola's FORTUNE DES ROUGON (Part II)." L & P 26:148-158. No. 4, 1976.

Gerhardi, Gerhard C. "Zola's Biological Vision of Politics: Revolutionary Figures in LA FORTUNE DES ROUGON and LE VENTRE DE PARIS." NCFS 2:164-180. Spring/Summer 1974.

Kanes, Martin. "LA FORTUNE DES ROUGON and the Thirty-Third Cousin." ECr 11:36-44. Winter 1971.

King, Graham. Garden of Zola. London: Barrie & Jenkins, 1978. pp. 54-57.

Richardson, Joanna. Zola. New York: St. Martin's Press, 1978. pp. 40-42.

Schor, Naomi. "Zola: From Window to Window." YFS 42:40-51. 1969.

_____. Zola's Crowds. Baltimore: Johns Hopkins University Press, 1978. pp. 8-21; 136-141.

GERMINAL

Baguley, David. "The Function of Zola's Souvarine." MLR 66:786-797. October 1971.

Bellos, David. "From the Bowels of the Earth: An Essay on GERMINAL." FMLS 15:35-45. January 1979.

Berg, William. "A Note on Imagery as Ideology in Zola's GERMINAL." ClioW 2:43-45. October 1972.

Cirillo, N.R. "Marxism as Myth in Zola's GERMINAL." CLS 14:244-255. September 1977.

Fuller, Carol S. "The Symbolic and Structural Function of Jeanlin." FR 54:58-65. October 1980.

Goldberg, M.A. "Zola and Social Revolution: A Study of GERMINAL." AR 27:491-507. Winter 1967-1968.

Hayman, David. "The Broken Cranium--Headwounds in Zola, Rilke, Céline: A Study in Contrasting Modes." CLS 9:208-215. June 1972.

King, Graham. Garden of Zola. London: Barrie & Jenkins, 1978. pp. 176-196.

Mitterand, Henri. "The Calvary of Catherine Maheu: The Description of a Page in GERMINAL." YFS 42:115-125. 1969.

Newton, Joy. "Zola and Eisenstein." FR 44:106-116. Sp. Issue No. 2, Winter 1971.

Pasco, Allan H. "Myth, Metaphor, and Meaning in GERMINAL." FR 46:739-749. March 1973.

Petrey, D. Sandy. "The Revolutionary Setting of GERMINAL." FR 43:54-63. October 1969.

Richardson, Joanna. Zola. New York: St. Martin's Press, 1978. pp. 108-111.

Rosenberg, Rachelle A. "The Slaying of the Dragon: An Archetypal Study of Zola's GERMINAL." Symposium 26:349-362. Winter 1972.

Schor, Naomi. Zola's Crowds. Baltimore: Johns Hopkins University Press, 1978. pp. 47-53; 74-78; 124-128; 173-178.

Shor, Ira Neil. "The Novel in History: Lukács and Zola." ClioW 2:26-33. October 1972.

Smethurst, Colin. Emile Zola: GERMINAL. Great Britain: Edward Arnold, 1974. 64 pp.

Topazio, Virgil W. "A Study of Motion in GERMINAL." KFLQ 13:60-70. Supplement 1967.

THE JOY OF LIFE

Alcorn, Clayton, Jr. "Zola's Forgotten Spokesman: Véronique in LA JOIE DE VIVRE." FR 49:76-80. October 1975.

King, Graham. Garden of Zola. London: Barrie & Jenkins, 1978. pp. 259-264.

Kuhn, Reinhard. The Demon of Noontide: Ennui in Western Literature. Princeton: Princeton University Press, 1976. pp. 270-276.

NANA

Armstrong, Judith. The Novel of Adultery. London: Macmillan, 1976. pp. 116-119; 156-158.

Conroy, Peter V., Jr. "The Metaphorical Web in Zola's NANA." UTQ 47:239-258. Spring 1978.

Hamilton, James F. "Zola's NANA and Jeanne d'Arc: Contrary Myths and the Creative Process." LangQ 19:7-10. Fall/Winter 1980.

Hemmings, F. W. J. The Life and Times of Emile Zola. New York: Charles Scribner's Sons, 1977. pp. 94-96.

King, Graham. Garden of Zola. London: Barrie & Jenkins, 1978. pp. 125-143.

Kobzina, Norma G. "An Argentine NANA: Gálvez and Zola." REH 10:163-179. May 1976.

Lapp, John C. "The Jealous Window-Watcher in Zola and Proust." FS 29:166-175. April 1975.

Richardson, Joanna. Zola. New York: St. Martin's Press, 1978. pp. 89-92.

Schor, Naomi. Zola's Crowds. Baltimore: Johns Hopkins University Press, 1978. pp. 83-86; 89-105; 116-119; 166-171.

L'OEUVRE

King, Graham. Garden of Zola. London: Barrie & Jenkins, 1978. pp. 199-211.

Knapp, Bettina. "The Creative Impulse--To Paint 'Literarily': Emile Zola and THE MASTERPIECE." RS 48:71-81. June 1980.

Niess, Robert J. Zola, Cézanne, and Manet: A Study

of L'OEUVRE. Ann Arbor: University of Michigan Press, 1968. 249 pp.

Pasco, Allan H. "The Failure of L'OEUVRE." ECr 11:45-55. Winter 1971.

Richardson, Joanna. Zola. New York: St. Martin's Press, 1978. pp. 111-117.

Schor, Naomi. Zola's Crowds. Baltimore: Johns Hopkins University Press, 1978. pp. 83-86; 169-172.

UNE PAGE D'AMOUR
King, Graham. Garden of Zola. London: Barrie & Jenkins, 1978. pp. 255-259.

Nelson, Brian. "Zola and the Ambiguities of Passion: UNE PAGE D'AMOUR." EFL 10:1-22. November 1973.

PARIS
Niess, Robert J. "Zola's PARIS and the Novels of the ROUGON-MACQUART Series." NCFS 4:89-104. Fall/Winter 1975-1976.

Richardson, Joanna. Zola. New York: St. Martin's Press, 1978. pp. 182-184.

POT-BOUILLE
Armstrong, Judith. The Novel of Adultery. London: Macmillan Press, 1976. pp. 66-68.

King, Graham. Garden of Zola. London: Barrie & Jenkins, 1978. pp. 161-169.

Nelson, Brian. "Black Comedy: Notes on Zola's POT-BOUILLE." RomN 17:156-161. Winter 1976.

———. "Zola and the Bourgeoisie: A Reading of POT-BOUILLE." NFS 17:58-70. May 1978.

Richardson, Joanna. Zola. New York: St. Martin's Press, 1978. pp. 98-101.

ROUGON-MACQUART
Alcorn, Clayton R., Jr. "The Child and His Milieu in the ROUGON-MACQUART." YFS 42:105-114. 1969.

Gerschenkron, Alexander. "Time Horizon in Balzac and Others." PAPS 122:84-86. April 24, 1978.

Gingell, E. "The Theme of Fertility in Zola's ROUGON-MACQUART." FMLS 13:350-358. October 1977.

Hemmings, F.W.J. The Life and Times of Emile Zola. New York: Charles Scribner's Sons, 1977. pp. 69-72; 79-82.

Kamm, Lewis. "People and Things in Zola's ROUGON-MACQUART: Reification Re-humanized." PQ 53:100-109. January 1974.

――――. "The Structural and Functional Manifestation of Space in Zola's ROUGON-MACQUART." NCFS 3: 224-236. Spring/Summer 1975.

――――. "Time and Zola's Characters in the ROUGON-MACQUART." RomN 16:83-86. Autumn 1974.

――――. "Zola's Conception of Time in LES ROUGON-MACQUART." FR 47:63-72. Sp. Issue No. 6, Spring 1974.

Knapp, Bettina. Emile Zola. New York: Frederick Ungar, 1980. pp. 27-143.

Lewis, Paula Gilbert. "Zola and Mallarmé: The Search for an Absolute Faith." RomN 18:183-191. Winter 1977.

Niess, Robert J. "Emile Zola: 'Libido dominandi.'" NCFS 7:220-231. Spring/Summer 1979.

――――. "Zola's PARIS and the Novels of the ROUGON-MACQUART Series." NCFS 4:89-104. Fall/Winter 1975-1976.

Petrey, Sandy. "Sociocriticism and LES ROUGON-MACQUART." ECr 14:219-235. Fall 1974.

Schor, Naomi. Zola's Crowds. Baltimore: Johns Hopkins University Press, 1978. pp. 19-21; 129-131.

SON EXCELLENCE EUGENE ROUGON

Richardson, Joanna. Zola. New York: St. Martin's Press, 1978. pp. 63-66.

Schor, Naomi. Zola's Crowds. Baltimore: Johns Hopkins University Press, 1978. pp. 140-154.

THERESE RAQUIN

Furst, Lilian R. "Zola's THERESE RAQUIN: A Re-Evaluation." Mosaic 5:189-202. Spring 1972.

King, Graham. Garden of Zola. London: Barrie & Jenkins, 1978. pp. 34-37; 40-43.

Lethbridge, Robert. "Zola, Manet and THERESE RAQUIN." FS 34:278-299. July 1980.

Richardson, Joanna. Zola. New York: St. Martin's Press, 1978. pp. 24-29.

LE VENTRE DE PARIS

Gerhardi, Gerhard C. "Zola's Biological Vision of Politics: Revolutionary Figures in LA FORTUNE DES ROUGON and LE VENTRE DE PARIS." NCFS 2:164-180. Spring/Summer 1974.

Petrey, Sandy. "Historical Reference and Stylistic Opacity in LE VENTRE DE PARIS." KRQ 24:325-340. No. 3, 1977.

Schor, Naomi. Zola's Crowds. Baltimore: Johns Hopkins University Press, 1978. pp. 21-34.

VERITE

King, Graham. Garden of Zola. London: Barrie & Jenkins, 1978. pp. 327-329.

Ross, Peter. "Emile Zola, the Teachers and the Dreyfus Affair." NFS 14:77-85. October 1975.

Schor, Naomi. Zola's Crowds. Baltimore: Johns Hopkins University Press, 1978. pp. 40-47.

## SPANISH AND PORTUGUESE NOVEL

Alarcón, Pedro Antonio de
EL CAPITAN VENENO
DeCoster, Cyrus. Pedro Antonio De Alarcón. Boston: Twayne, 1979. pp. 118-123.
EL ESCANDALO
DeCoster, Cyrus. Pedro Antonio De Alarcón. Boston: Twayne, 1979. pp. 93-108.

Hafter, Monroe Z. "Alarcón in EL ESCANDALO." MLN 83:212-225. March 1968.

McClendon, Barnett A. "Influences of EL ESCANDALO on the Colombian Novel AYER, NADA MAS." RomN 14:96-104. Autumn 1972.

Powers, Harriet B. "Allegory in EL ESCANDALO." MLN 87:324-329. March 1972.
EL FINAL DE NORMA
DeCoster, Cyrus. Pedro Antonio De Alarcón. Boston: Twayne, 1979. pp. 70-78.
EL NIÑO DE LA BOLA
DeCoster, Cyrus. Pedro Antonio De Alarcón. Boston: Twayne, 1979. pp. 109-117.
LA PRODIGA
DeCoster, Cyrus. Pedro Antonio De Alarcón. Boston: Twayne, 1979. pp. 124-130.
EL SOMBRERO DE TRES PICOS
Armistead, Samuel G. and Joseph H. Silverman. "'El corregidor y la molinera': Some Unnoticed Germanic Antecedents." PQ 51:279-291. January 1972.

DeCoster, Cyrus. Pedro Antonio de Alarcón. Boston: Twayne, 1979. pp. 79-92.

Medina, Jeremy T. "Structural Techniques of Alarcón's EL SOMBRERO DE TRES PICOS." RomN 14:83-85. Autumn 1972.
LA ULTIMA CALAVERADA
Quinn, David. "An Ironic Reading of Pedro de Alarcón's LA ULTIMA CALAVERADA." Symposium 31:346-356. Winter 1977.

Alas, Leopoldo (Clarín)
ANTONIO AZORIN
    Glenn, Kathleen M. The Novelistic Technique of Azorín. Madrid: Playor, 1973. pp. 23-36.
DOÑA BERTA
    Boring, Phyllis Z. "Some Reflections on Clarín's DOÑA BERTA." RomN 11:322-325. Winter 1969.
UNA MEDIANIA
    Valis, Noël M. "A Spanish Decadent Hero: Clarín's Antonio Reyes of UNA MEDIANIA." MLS 9:53-60. Spring 1979.
LA REGENTA
    Ife, Barry W. "Idealism and Materialism in Clarín's LA REGENTA: Two Comparative Studies." RLC 44: 273-295. July/September 1970.

    Jackson, Robert M. "'Cervantismo' in the Creative Process of Clarín's LA REGENTA." MLN 84:208-227. March 1969.

    _____. "LA REGENTA and Contemporary History." REH 11:287-302. May 1977.

    Mazzeo, Guido E. "The Banquet Scene in LA REGENTA, a Case of Sacrilege." RomN 10:68-72. Autumn 1968.

    Nimetz, Michael. "'Eros' and 'Ecclesia' in Clarín's Vetusta." MLN 86:242-253. March 1971.

    Rice, Miriam Wagner. "The Meaning of Metaphor in LA REGENTA." REH 11:141-151. January 1977.

    Rogers, Douglass. "Don Juan, 'Donjuanismo,' and Death in Clarín." Symposium 30:325-342. Winter 1976.

    Rutherford, John. Leopoldo Alas: LA REGENTA. London: Grant & Cutter, 1974. 77 pp.

    Sánchez, Roberto G. "The Presence of the Theater and 'The Consciousness of Theater' in Clarín's LA REGENTA." HR 37:491-509. October 1969.

    Thompson, Clifford R., Jr. "Egoism and Alienation in the Works of Leopoldo Alas." RF 81:198-203. No. 1/2, 1969.

    Valis, Noel M. "The Landscape of the Soul in Clarín and Baudelaire." RLC 54:17-31. January/March 1980.
SU UNICO HIJO
    Ullman, Pierre L. "The Antifeminist Premises of Clarín's SU UNICO HIJO." EIA 1:57-91. No. 1, 1975.
SUPERCHERIA
    Round, Nicholas G. "The Fictional Integrity of Leopoldo Alas' SUPERCHERIA." BHS 47:97-116. April 1970.

Aldecoa, Ignacio
EL FULGOR Y LA SANGRE
Fiddian, Robin. Ignacio Aldecoa. Boston: Twayne, 1979. pp. 44-53.

Pérez Firmat, Gustavo. "The Structure of EL FULGOR Y LA SANGRE." HR 45:1-12. Winter 1977.
GREAT SOLE
Fiddian, Robin. Ignacio Aldecoa. Boston: Twayne, 1979. pp. 65-77.
PARTE DE UNA HISTORIA
Fiddian, Robin. Ignacio Aldecoa. Boston: Twayne, 1979. pp. 78-90.

─────. "Urban Man and the Pastoral Illusion: An Interpretation of Ignacio Aldecoa's PARTE DE UNA HISTORIA." REH 9:371-389. October 1975.
WITH THE EAST WIND
Fiddian, Robin. Ignacio Aldecoa. Boston: Twayne, 1979. pp. 54-64.

Alemán, Mateo
GUZMAN DE ALFARACHE
Arias, Joan. Guzmán de Alfarache: The Unrepentant Narrator. London: Tamesis Books, 1977. 95 pp.

Bjornson, Richard. "GUZMAN DE ALFARACHE: Apologia for a 'Converso.'" RF 85:314-329. No. 3, 1973.

─────. The Picaresque Hero in European Fiction. Madison: University of Wisconsin Press, 1977. pp. 43-71.

Cascardi, Anthony J. "The Rhetoric of Defense in the GUZMAN DE ALFARACHE." Neophil 63:380-387. July 1979.

Davis, Barbara. "The Style of Mateo Alemán's GUZMAN DE ALFARACHE." RR 66:199-213. May 1975.

Dunn, Peter N. The Spanish Picaresque Novel. Boston: Twayne, 1979. pp. 41-63.

Folkenflik, Vivian. "Vision and Truth: Baroque Art Metaphors in GUZMAN DE ALFARACHE." MLN 88:347-355. March 1973.

McGrady, Donald. Mateo Alemán. New York: Twayne, 1968. pp. 44-167.

Norval, M.N. "Original Sin and the 'Conversion' in the GUZMAN DE ALFARACHE." BHS 51:346-364. October 1974.

Pérez, Rosa Perelmuter. "The Rogue as Trickster in GUZMAN DE ALFARACHE." Hispania 59:820-826. December 1976.

Ramirez, Genevieve M. "Guzmán de Alfarache and the Concept of Honor." REH 14:61-75. October 1980.

Ricapito, J. V. "'Comparatistica'--Two Versions of Sin, Moral Transgression and Divine Will: GUZMAN DE ALFARACHE and I PROMESSI SPOSI." KRQ 16: 111-118. No. 2, 1969.

———. "From Boccaccio to Mateo Alemán: An Essay on Literary Sources and Adaptations." RR 60:83-95. April 1969.

———. "Love and Marriage in GUZMAN DE ALFARACHE: An Essay on Literary and Artistic Unity." KRQ 15:123-138. No. 2, 1968.

Smith, Hilary S.D. "The 'Picaro' Turns Preacher: Guzmán de Alfarache's Missed Vocation." FMLS 14: 387-397. October 1978.

Woods, M.J. "The Teasing Opening of GUZMAN DE ALFARACHE." BHS 57:213-218. July 1980.

Alós, Concha
OS HABLA ELECTRA
Ordóñez, Elizabeth J. "The Female Quest Pattern in Concha Alós' OS HABLA ELECTRA." REH 14:51-63. January 1980.

Arbó, Sebastián Juan
MARTIN DE CARETAS
Eustis, Christopher. "MARTIN DE CARETAS: The Picaresque Myth Transformed." RCEH 5:19-35. No. 1, 1980.

Ayala, Francisco
THE BOTTOM OF THE GLASS
Bieder, Maryellen. Narrative Perspective in the Post-Civil War Novels of Francisco Ayala: MUERTES DE PERRO and EL FONDO DEL VASO. Chapel Hill: University of North Carolina Press, 1979. pp. 71-110.

Irizarry, Estelle. Francisco Ayala. Boston: Twayne, 1977. pp. 83-87.
DOG's DEATH
Bieder, Maryellen. Narrative Perspective in the Post-Civil War Novels of Francisco Ayala: MUERTES DE PERRO and EL FONDO DEL VASO. Chapel Hill: University of North Carolina Press, 1979. pp. 38-70.

Ayala, Francisco

    Irizarry, Estelle. Francisco Ayala. Boston: Twayne, 1977. pp. 78-83.
EL RAPTO
    Ellis, Keith. "Cervantes and Ayala's EL RAPTO: The Art of Reworking a Story." PMLA 84:14-19. January 1969.

Azorín, Gabriel
EL CABALLERO INACTUAL
    Joiner, Lawrence D. "Félix Vargas, Azorín's Proustian Protagonist." RomN 19:177-182. Winter 1978.

    _____. "The Portrayal of the Artist in Proust and Azorín." REH 10:184-188. May 1976.

    *Lott, Robert E. The Structure and Style of Azorín's EL CABALLERO INACTUAL. Athens: University of Georgia Press, 1963. 100 pp.
DOÑA INES
    Glenn, Kathleen M. The Novelistic Technique of Azorín. Madrid: Playor, 1973. pp. 72-94.

    Palley, Julian. "Images of Time in DOÑA INES." Hispania 54:250-255. May 1971.

    Wilson, S.R. "The Colours of DOÑA INES." BHS 56: 117-121. April 1979.
SALVADORA DE OLBENA
    Glenn, Kathleen M. "Azorín's SALVADORA DE OLBENA: Reality and the Artist." Hispano 56:53-62. 1976.

    _____. The Novelistic Technique of Azorín. Madrid: Playor, 1973. pp. 105-118.

    Joiner, Lawrence D. and Joseph W. Zdenek. "SALVADORA DE OLBENA: A 'Summa' of Azorín's Artistic Credo." RS 44:111-118. June 1976.
TOMAS RUEDA
    Glenn, Kathleen M. "The Narrator's Changing Perspective in Azorín's TOMAS RUEDA." REH 9:343-357. October 1975.

    _____. The Novelistic Technique of Azorín. Madrid: Playor, 1973. pp. 39-54.
LA VOLUNTAD
    Fiddian, R.W. "Cyclical Time and the Structure of Azorín's LA VOLUNTAD." FMLS 12:163-175. April 1976.

Baroja, Pío
AGONIAS DE NUESTRO TIEMPO
    Patt, Beatrice. Pío Baroja. New York: Twayne, 1971. pp. 147-151.

AVENTURAS, INVENTOS Y MIXTIFICACIONES DE SILVESTRE PARADOX
    Patt, Beatrice. Pío Baroja. New York: Twayne, 1971. pp. 84-88.
CAESAR OR NOTHING
    Longhurst, C.A. "Ironic Distance in Baroja: CESAR O NADA." BHS 57:129-142. April 1980.

    Patt, Beatrice. Pío Baroja. New York: Twayne, 1971. pp. 106-110.
EL ESCUADRON DEL BRIGANTE
    Lovett, Gabriel H. "Two Views of Guerrilla Warfare: Galdós' JUAN MARTIN EL EMPECINADO and Baroja's EL ESCUADRON DEL BRIGANTE." REH 6:335-344. October 1972.
EL GRAN TORBELLINO DEL MUNDO
    Patt, Beatrice. Pío Baroja. New York: Twayne, 1971. pp. 147-151.
MEMORIAS DE UN HOMBRE DE ACCION
    Ciplijauskaite, Birute. "Anti-Heroic Vision in MEMORIAS DE UN HOMBRE DE ACCION." PCP 7:29-34. April 1972.

    Longhurst, C.A. "Pío Baroja and Aviraneta: Some Sources of the MEMORIAS DE UN HOMBRE DE ACCION." BHS 48:328-345. October 1971.
THE TREE OF KNOWLEDGE
    Eller, Kenneth. "The Autobiographical Sources of Baroja's EL ARBOL DE LA CIENCIA." REH 12:323-335. October 1978.

    Millner, Curtis. "Structural Consistency and Artistic Economy in EL ARBOL DE LA CIENCIA." REH 9:99-105. January 1975.

    Patt, Beatrice. Pío Baroja. New York: Twayne, 1971. pp. 112-122.
THE WAY TO PERFECTION
    Olstad, Charles. "Symbolic Structure in Baroja's CAMINO DE PERFECCION." KRQ 23:451-465. No. 4, 1976.

    Patt, Beatrice. Pío Baroja. New York: Twayne, 1971. pp. 88-94.

Blasco Ibáñez, Vicente
    LA ARAÑA NEGRA
        Dendle, Brian J. "Blasco Ibáñez and Coloma's PEQUEÑECES." RomN 8:200-203. Spring 1967.
    LA BARRACA
        Rogers, Douglass. "The Descriptive Simile in Galdós and Blasco Ibáñez: A Study in Contrasts." Hispania 53:864-869. December 1970.

Blasco Ibáñez, Vicente

CAÑAS Y BARRO
Medina, Jeremy T. "The Artistry of Blasco Ibáñez's CAÑAS Y BARRO." Hispania 60:275-284. May 1977.
FLOR DE MAYO
Smith, Paul. "On Blasco Ibáñez's FLOR DE MAYO." Symposium 24:55-66. Spring 1970.

Caballero, Fernán
CLEMENCIA
Klibbe, Lawrence. Fernán Caballero. New York: Twayne, 1973. pp. 112-118.
THE FAMILY OF ALVAREDA
Klibbe, Lawrence. Fernán Caballero. New York: Twayne, 1973. pp. 82-111.
LAGRIMAS
Klibbe, Lawrence. Fernán Caballero. New York: Twayne, 1973. pp. 118-127.
THE SEA GULL
Klibbe, Lawrence. Fernán Caballero. New York: Twayne, 1973. pp. 46-81.

Carranque de Ríos, Andrés
CINEMATOGRAFO
Henn, David. "Social and Artistic Criticism in the Novels of Andrés Carranque de Ríos." Hispano 54:26-29. 1975.
UNO
Henn, David. "Social and Artistic Criticism in the Novels of Andrés Carranque de Ríos." Hispano 54:18-22. 1975.
LA VIDA DIFICIL
Henn, David. "Social and Artistic Criticism in the Novels of Andrés Carranque de Ríos." Hispano 54:22-26. 1975.

Cela, Camilo José
LA CATIRA
Foster, David W. Forms of the Novel in the Work of Camilo José Cela. Columbia: University of Missouri Press, 1967. pp. 100-118.

McPheeters, D. W. Camilo José Cela. New York: Twayne, 1969. pp. 114-121.
LA COLMENA
Foster, David W. Forms of the Novel in the Work of Camilo José Cela. Columbia: University of Missouri Press, 1967. pp. 61-81.

Henn, David. "Cela's Portrayal of Martin Marco in LA COLMENA." Neophil 55:142-148. April 1971.

_____. "LA COLMENA--An Oversight on the Part of Cela." RomN 13:414-418. Spring 1972.

_____. "Theme and Structure in LA COLMENA." FMLS 8:304-319. October 1972.

McPheeters, D.W. Camilo José Cela. New York: Twayne, 1969. pp. 84-101.

Spires, Robert C. "Cela's LA COLMENA: The Creative Process as Message." Hispania 55:873-880. December 1972.

THE FAMILY OF PASCUAL DUARTE
Bernstein, J.S. "Pascual Duarte and Orestes." Symposium 22:301-318. Winter 1968.

Busette, Cedric. "LA FAMILIA DE PASCUAL DUARTE and the Prominence of Fate." REH 8:61-67. January 1974.

Fody, Michael III. "LA FAMILIA DE PASCUAL DUARTE and L'ETRANGER: A Contrast." WVUPP 24:68-73. November 1977.

Foster, David W. Forms of the Novel in the Work of Camilo José Cela. Columbia: University of Missouri Press, 1967. pp. 16-33.

_____. "Social Criticism, Existentialism, and 'Tremendismo' in Cela's LA FAMILIA DE PASCUAL DUARTE." KFLQ 13:25-33. Supplement 1967.

Hutman, Norma Louise. "Disproportionate Doom: Tragic Irony in the Spanish Post Civil War Novel." MFS 18:199-206. Summer 1972.

McPheeters, D.W. Camilo José Cela. New York: Twayne, 1969. pp. 31-51.

Spires, Robert C. "Systematic Doubt: The Moral Art of LA FAMILIA DE PASCUAL DUARTE." HR 40:283-302. Summer 1972.

Thomas, Michael D. "Narrative Tension and Structural Unity in Cela's LA FAMILIA DE PASCUAL DUARTE." Symposium 31:165-178. Summer 1977.

Tinnell, Roger D. "Carl Jung, Pascual Duarte, Secret Stones, and the Individuation Process." PLL 14:91-94. Winter 1978.

_____. "Role Playing and Motherhood in LA FAMILIA DE PASCUAL DUARTE." IFR 3:160-162. July 1976.

Wicks, Ulrich. "Onlyman." Mosaic 8:33-40. Spring 1975.

Cela, Camilo José

MRS. CALDWELL HABLA CON SU HIJO
Foster, David W. Forms of the Novel in the Work of Camilo José Cela. Columbia: University of Missouri Press, 1967. pp. 82-99.

McPheeters, D. W. Camilo José Cela. New York: Twayne, 1969. pp. 102-113.
NUEVAS ANDANZAS Y DESVENTURAS DE LAZARILLO DE TORMES
Foster, David W. Forms of the Novel in the Work of Camilo José Cela. Columbia: University of Missouri Press, 1967. pp. 49-60.

McPheeters, D. W. Camilo José Cela. New York: Twayne, 1969. pp. 62-71.
PABELLON DE REPOSO
Foster, David W. Forms of the Novel in the Work of Camilo José Cela. Columbia: University of Missouri Press, 1967. pp. 34-48.

McPheeters, D. W. Camilo José Cela. New York: Twayne, 1969. pp. 52-61.
SAN CAMILO
Bernstein, J. S. "Confession and Inaction in SAN CAMILO." Hispano 51:47-63. 1974.
TOBOGGAN OF HUNGRY PEOPLE
Foster, David W. Forms of the Novel in the Work of Camilo José Cela. Columbia: University of Missouri Press, 1967. pp. 120-136.

McPheeters, D. W. Camilo José Cela. New York: Twayne, 1969. pp. 141-146.

LA CELESTINA
Abrams, Fred. "The Name 'Celestina': Why Did Fernando de Rojas Choose It?" RomN 14:165-167. Autumn 1972.

de Armas, F. A. "LA CELESTINA: An Example of Love Melancholy." RR 66:288-295. November 1975.

_____. "The Demoniacal in LA CELESTINA." SAB 36:10-13. November 1971.

Austin, Karen O. "A Possible Resolution for Some of the Ambiguities and Contradictions in LA CELESTINA." SoQ 12:335-351. 1974.

Baldwin, Spurgeon W., Jr. "'En tan pocas palabras' (LA CELESTINA, Auto IV)." RomN 9:120-125. Autumn 1967.

Barbera, Raymond E. "Medieval Iconography in the CELESTINA." RR 61:5-13. February 1970.

Brault, Gerard J. "Textual Filiation of the Early Editions of the CELESTINA and the First French Translation (1527)." HR 36:95-109. April 1968.

Burke, James F. "Calisto's Imagination and His Grandmother's Ape." Corónica 5:84-90. Spring 1977.

──────. "Metamorphosis and the Imagery of Alchemy in LA CELESTINA." RCEH 1:129-152. Winter 1977.

Clarke, Dorothy Clotelle. Allegory, Decalogue, and Deadly Sins in LA CELESTINA. Berkeley: University of California Press, 1968. 117 pp.

Deyermond, Alan. "Hilado-Cordón-Cadena: Symbolic Equivalence in LA CELESTINA." Celestinesca 1:6-12. No. 1, 1977.

──────. The Middle Ages. New York: Barnes and Noble, 1971. pp. 167-170.

──────. "Symbolic Equivalence in LA CELESTINA: A Postscript." Celestinesca 2:25-30. No. 1, 1978.

Dial, Eleanore Maxwell. "Notes on Adapting and Interpreting LA CELESTINA: The Art of Alvaro Custodio and Amparo Villegas." Celestinesca 1:13-17. No. 1, 1977.

Drysdall, D. L. "Two Notes on LA CELESTINA." RomN 14:589-592. Spring 1973.

Dunn, Peter N. Fernando de Rojas. Boston: Twayne, 1975. pp. 32-42.

──────. "Pleberio's World." PMLA 91:406-419. May 1976.

Faulhaber, Charles B. "The Hawk in Melibea's Garden." HR 45:435-450. Autumn 1977.

*Fraker, Charles F. "The Importance of Pleberio's Soliloquy." RF 78:515-529. No. 4, 1966.

Gerli, E. Michael. "CELESTINA, Act I, Reconsidered: Cota, Mena ... or Alfonso Martinez de Toledo?" KRQ 23:29-46. No. 1, 1976.

──────. "Pleberio's Lament and Two Literary 'Topoi': 'Expositor' and 'Planctus.'" RF 88:67-74. No. 1, 1976.

Gilman, Stephen. "A Generation of 'Conversos.'" RPh 33:87-101. August 1979.

_____. The Spain of Fernando de Rojas. Princeton: Princeton University Press, 1972. 488 pp.

Griffin, Clive. "Four Rare Editions of LA CELESTINA." MLR 75:561-574. July 1980.

Gulstad, Daniel E. "Melibea's Demise: The Death of Courtly Love." Corónica 7:71-80. Spring 1979.

Hanrahan, Thomas, S. J. "Sin, the CELESTINA and Iñigo López de Loyola." RomN 11:385-391. Winter 1969.

Herriott, J. Homer. "Notes on Selectivity of Language in the CELESTINA." HR 37:77-101. January 1969.

Hook, David. "'¿Para quien edifique torres?': A Footnote to Pleberio's Lament." FMLS 14:25-31. January 1978.

Johnson, Carroll B. "Cervantes as a Reader of LA CELESTINA." FWF 1:233-247. May 1974.

Kassier, Theodore L. "'Cancionero' Poetry and the CELESTINA: From Metaphor to Reality." Hispano 56: 1-28. 1976.

Kish, Kathleen. "The Wages of Sin Is Life--For a Sixteenth-Century Best Seller or the Anatomy of a Classic." Theoria 47:23-32. October 1976.

Kotzmanidou, Maria. "The Spanish and Arabic Characterization of the Go-Between in the Light of Popular Performance." HR 48:95-106. Winter 1980.

Mancing, Howard. "Fernando de Rojas, LA CELESTINA, and LAZARILLO DE TORMES." KRQ 23:47-61. No. 1, 1976.

Mandel, Adrienne Schizzano. LA CELESTINA Studies: A Thematic Survey and Bibliography 1824-1970. Metuchen: Scarecrow, 1971. 261 pp.

*Martí-Ibáñez, Félix. "The Medico-pharmaceutical Arts of LA CELESTINA: A Study of a Fifteenth Century Spanish Sorceress and 'Dealer in Love.'" International Record of Medicine 169:233-249. April 1956.

Martin, June Hall. Love's Fools: Aucassin, Troilus, Calisto and the Parody of the Courtly Lover. London: Tamesis, 1972. pp. 71-134.

Mendeloff, Henry. "Pleberio in Contemporary CELESTINA Criticism." RomN 13:369-373. Winter 1971.

_____. "'Sharing' in LA CELESTINA." Thesaurus 32:173-177. No. 1, 1977.

Morgan, Erica. "Rhetorical Technique in the Persuasion of Melibea." Celestinesca 3:7-18. No. 2, 1979.

Nepaulsingh, Colbert. "The Rhetorical Structure of the Prologues to the LIBRO DE BUEN AMOR and the CELESTINA." BHS 51:330-334. October 1974.

Phillips, Katharine Kaiper. "Ironic Foreshadowing in LA CELESTINA." KRQ 21:469-482. No. 4, 1974.

Purcell, H.D. "The CELESTINA and the INTERLUDE OF CALISTO AND MELIBEA." BHS 44:1-15. January 1967.

Rank, Jerry. "Awareness and Reaction: The Underlying Elements of Characterization in the Servants of the CELESTINA." KRQ 19:223-236. No. 2, 1972.

_____. "The Significance of Leon Amarita's 1822 Edition of LA CELESTINA." PBSA 69:243-255. No. 2, 1975.

_____. "The Uses of 'Dios' and the Concept of God in LA CELESTINA." RCEH 5:75-91. No. 1, 1980.

Read, Malcolm K. "LA CELESTINA and the Renaissance Philosophy of Language." PQ 55:166-177. Spring 1976.

_____. "Fernando de Rojas's Vision of the Birth and Death of Language." MLN 93:163-175. March 1978.

Ruggerio, M.J. "LA CELESTINA: Didacticism Once More." RF 82:56-64. No. 1/2, 1970.

Sánchez, Elizabeth. "Magic in LA CELESTINA." HR 46:481-494. Autumn 1978.

Severin, Dorothy S. "Cota, His Imitator, and LA CELESTINA: The Evidence Re-Examined." Celestinesca 4:3-8. August 1980.

_____. "Humour in LA CELESTINA." RPh 32:274-291. February 1979.

_____. Memory in LA CELESTINA. London: Tamesis Books, 1970. 70 pp.

Shipley, George A. "Concerting Through Conceit: Unconventional Uses of Conventional Sickness Images in LA CELESTINA." MLR 70:324-332. April 1975.

_____. "'Non erat hic locus'; The Disconcerted Reader in Melibea's Garden." RPh 27:286-303. February 1974.

_____. "'Qual dolor puede ser tal...?': A Rhetorical Strategy for Containing Pain in LA CELESTINA." MLN 90:143-153. March 1975.

Snow, Joseph T. "An Additional Attestation to the Popularity of Rojas' Character Creations from an Early Seventeenth-Century Manuscript." HR 48:479-486. Autumn 1980.

Stamm, James R. A Short History of Spanish Literature. Garden City: Doubleday, 1967. pp. 97-102.

Thompson, B. Bussell. "Misogyny and Misprint in LA CELESTINA, Act I." Celestinesca 1:21-28. No. 2, 1977.

Truesdell, William D. "The 'Hortus Conclusus' Tradition, and the Implications of Its Absence, in the CELESTINA." KRQ 20:257-277. No. 3, 1973.

Weinberg, F.M. "Aspects of Symbolism in LA CELESTINA." MLN 86:136-153. March 1971.

Weiner, Jack. "Adam and Eve Imagery in LA CELESTINA." PLL 5:389-396. Fall 1969.

West, Geoffrey. "The Unseemliness of Calisto's Toothache." Celestinesca 3:3-10. No. 1, 1979.

Whinnom, Keith. "'El plebérico corazón' and the Authorship of Act I of CELESTINA." HR 45:195-199. Spring 1977.

*_____. "The Relationship of the Early Editions of the CELESTINA." ZRP 82:22-40. 1966.

Wilhite, John F. "Fernando de Rojas' Pármeno: The Making of a Pícaro." SAB 41:137-144. May 1976.

Cervantes, Miguel de
EL AMANTE LIBERAL
El Saffar, Ruth S. Novel to Romance: A Study of Cervantes's NOVELAS EJEMPLARES. Baltimore: Johns Hopkins University Press, 1974. pp. 139-149.

Lowe, Jennifer. "A Note on Cervantes' EL AMANTE LIBERAL." RomN 12:400-403. Spring 1971.
EL CASAMIENTO ENGAÑOSO
El Saffar, Ruth. "Montesinos' Cave and the CASAMI-

ENTO ENGANOSO in the Development of Cervantes' Prose Fiction." KRQ 20:451-467. No. 4, 1973.

──────. Novel to Romance: A Study of Cervantes's NOVELAS EJEMPLARES. Baltimore: Johns Hopkins University Press, 1974. pp. 62-82.

EL CELOSO EXTREMEÑO
El Saffar, Ruth S. Novel to Romance: A Study of Cervantes's NOVELAS EJEMPLARES. Baltimore: Johns Hopkins University Press, 1974. pp. 40-50.

Lambert, A. F. "The Two Versions of Cervantes' EL CELOSO EXTREMEÑO: Ideology and Criticism." BHS 57:219-231. July 1980.

EL COLOQUIO DE LOS PERROS
Dunn, Peter N. The Spanish Picaresque Novel. Boston: Twayne, 1979. pp. 85-91.

El Saffar, Ruth. "Montesinos' Cave and the CASAMIENTO ENGANOSO in the Development of Cervantes' Prose Fiction." KRQ 20:451-467. No. 4, 1973.

──────. Novel to Romance: A Study of Cervantes's NOVELAS EJEMPLARES. Baltimore: Johns Hopkins University Press, 1974. pp. 62-82.

Hart, Thomas R. "Cervantes' Sententious Dogs." MLN 94:377-386. March 1979.

Riley, E. C. "Cervantes and the Cynics (EL LICENCIADO VIDRIERA and EL COLOQUIO DE LOS PERROS)." BHS 53:195-198. July 1976.

Vranich, S. B. "Sigmund Freud and 'The Case History of Berganza': Freud's Psychoanalytic Beginnings." PsyR 63:73-81. Spring 1976.

EL CURIOSO IMPERTINENTE
Sieber, Harry. "On Juan Huarte de San Juan and Anselmo's 'locura' in EL CURIOSO IMPERTINENTE." RHM 36:1-8. No. 1/2, 1970-1971.

DON QUIXOTE
*Abrams, Fred. "Aliaga, Avellaneda, and a Curious Passage in the QUIJOTE (II, 61)." RomN 8:86-90. Autumn 1966.

──────. "Avellaneda and Tirso de Molina in Cervantes' Second Prologue to the QUIJOTE." RomN 11: 137-143. Autumn 1969.

──────. "Pedro Noriz and Tirso de Molina in the Enchanted Head Episode of the QUIJOTE." RomN 10: 122-128. Autumn 1968.

Cervantes, Miguel de

──────. "'Tirso de Molina Alias Sancho Panza and a New Cervantine Etymology for 'Barataria.'" RomN 9:281-286. Spring 1968.

Agheana, Ion T. "La cueva de Montesinos: Don Quijote's Humanistic Triumph." ACer 16:85-95. 1977.

Allen, John J. Don Quixote: Hero or Fool? A Study in Narrative Technique. Gainesville: University of Florida Press, 1969. 90 pp.

──────. "The Governorship of Sancho and Don Quijote's Chivalric Career." RHM 38:141-152. No. 4, 1974-1975.

──────. "Melisendra's Mishap in Maese Pedro's Puppet Show." MLN 88:330-335. March 1973.

──────. "The Narrators, the Reader and Don Quijote." MLN 91:201-212. March 1976.

Alvarez-Altman, Grace. "Cervantes' Expertise in Nominology: Technique in Synecdochism and Polyanthroponism--Book I, Chapter I of DON QUIJOTE." LOS 7:285-294. 1980.

Auden, W.H. "The Ironic Hero: Some Reflections on Don Quixote." Cervantes: A Collection of Critical Essays. ed. Lowry Nelson, Jr. Englewood Cliffs: Prentice-Hall, 1969. pp. 73-81.

Auerbach, Erich. "The Enchanted Dulcinea." Cervantes: A Collection of Critical Essays. ed. Lowry Nelson, Jr. Englewood Cliffs: Prentice-Hall, 1969. pp. 98-122.

Baker, Armand F. "A New Look at the Structure of DON QUIJOTE." REH 7:3-21. January 1973.

Bandera, Cesáreo. "Cervantes' QUIJOTE and the Critical Illusion." MLN 94:702-718. May 1979.

Barr, Alan P. "Cervantes' Probing of Reality and Psychological Realism in DON QUIXOTE." L&P 18:111-122. No. 2/3, 1968.

Barrett, Betty P. "The Cave of Montesinos: Cervantes and the Collective Unconscious." ELWIU 7:101-114. Spring 1980.

Barrick, Mac E. "The Form and Function of Folktales in DON QUIJOTE." JMRS 6:101-138. Spring 1976.

Bell, Michael. "The Structure of DON QUIXOTE." EIC 18:241-257. July 1968.

Brantley, Franklin O. "Sancho's Ascent into the Spheres." Hispania 53:37-44. May 1970.

Brenan, Gerald. "Cervantes." Cervantes: A Collection of Critical Essays. ed. Lowry Nelson, Jr. Englewood Cliffs: Prentice-Hall, 1969. pp. 13-33.

Brody, Robert. "Don Quijote's Emotive Adventures: Fulling Hammers and Lions." Neophil 59:372-381. July 1975.

Byron, William. Cervantes: A Biography. Garden City: Doubleday, 1978. pp. 422-442.

Chamberlin, Vernon A. and Jack Weiner. "Color Symbolism: A Key to a Possible New Interpretation of Cervantes' 'Caballero del Verde Gabán.'" RomN 10:342-347. Spring 1969.

Chambers, Leland H. "Irony in the Final Chapter of the QUIJOTE." RR 61:14-22. February 1970.

_____. "Structure and the Search for Truth in the QUIJOTE: Notes Toward a Comprehensive View." HR 35:309-326. October 1967.

Church, Margaret. Don Quixote: The Knight of La Mancha. New York: New York University Press, 1971. 172 pp.

Close, A. J. "DON QUIXOTE and the 'Intentionalist Fallacy.'" BJA 12:19-39. Winter 1972.

_____. "Don Quixote as a Burlesque Hero: A Re-Constructed Eighteenth-Century View." FMLS 10:365-378. October 1974.

_____. "Don Quixote's Love for Dulcinea: A Study of Cervantine Irony." BHS 50:237-255. July 1973.

_____. "Don Quixote's Sophistry and Wisdom." BHS 55:103-114. April 1978.

_____. The Romantic Approach to DON QUIXOTE. Cambridge: Cambridge University Press, 1978. 252 pp.

_____. "Sancho Panza: Wise Fool." MLR 68:344-357. April 1973.

Cervantes, Miguel de

Dimler, G. Richard. "Alienation in DON QUIXOTE and SIMPLICIUS SIMPLICISSIMUS." Thought 49:72-80. March 1974.

Doody, Terrence. "DON QUIXOTE, ULYSSES, and the Idea of Realism." Novel 12:197-214. Spring 1979.

Dudley, Edward. "Don Quijote as Magus: The Rhetoric of Interpolation." BHS 49:355-368. October 1972.

Dunn, Peter N. "Two Classical Myths in DON QUIJOTE." Ren & R 9:2-10. No. 1, 1972.

Duran, Manuel. Cervantes. New York: Twayne, 1974. pp. 88-146.

Efron, Arthur. DON QUIXOTE and the Dulcineated World. Austin: University of Texas Press, 1971. 144 pp.

_____. "Perspectivism and the Nature of Fiction: DON QUIXOTE and Borges." Thought 50:148-175. June 1975.

Eisenberg, Daniel. "DON QUIJOTE and the Romances of Chivalry: The Need for a Reexamination." HR 41:511-523. Summer 1973.

_____. "Pero Perez the Priest and His Comment on 'Tirant lo Blanch.'" MLN 88:321-330. March 1973.

El Saffar, Ruth. "Apropos of DON QUIXOTE: HERO OR FOOL?" MLN 85:269-273. March 1970.

_____. Distance and Control in DON QUIXOTE: A Study in Narrative Technique. Chapel Hill: North Carolina Studies in Romance Languages and Literature, 1975. 139 pp.

_____. "The Function of the Fictional Narrator in DON QUIJOTE." MLN 83:164-177. March 1968.

_____. "Montesinos' Cave and the CASAMIENTO ENGANOSO in the Development of Cervantes' Prose Fiction." KRQ 20:451-467. No. 4, 1973.

_____. Novel to Romance: A Study of Cervantes's NOVELAS EJEMPLARES. Baltimore: Johns Hopkins University Press, 1974. pp. 1-29.

Flores, R.M. "Cervantes at Work: The Writing of DON QUIXOTE, Part I." JHP 3:135-160. Winter 1979.

_____. "The Loss and Recovery of Sancho's Ass in DON QUIXOTE, Part I." MLR 75:301-310. April 1980.

_____. "Sancho's Fabrications: A Mirror of the Development of His Imagination." HR 38:174-182. April 1970.

Forcione, Alban K. "Cervantes and the Freedom of the Artist." RR 61:243-255. December 1970.

_____. Cervantes, Aristotle, and the PERSILES. Princeton: Princeton University Press, 1970. pp. 91-166.

Gale, Steven H. "The Relationship Between Beaumont's THE KNIGHT OF THE BURNING PESTLE and Cervantes' DON QUIXOTE." ACer 11:87-96. 1972.

Galligan, Edward L. "True Comedians and False: DON QUIXOTE and HUCKLEBERRY FINN." SR 86:66-83. Winter 1978.

Grossvogel, David I. Limits of the Novel: Evolutions of a Form from Chaucer to Robbe-Grillet. Ithaca: Cornell University Press, 1968. pp. 74-107.

Hahn, Juergen. "'El Capitán Cautivo': The Soldier's Truth and Literary Precept in DON QUIJOTE, Part I." JHP 3:269-303. Spring 1979.

_____. "EL CURIOSO IMPERTINENTE and Don Quijote's Symbolic Struggle Against 'Curiositas.'" BHS 49:128-140. April 1972.

Hart, Thomas R. and Steven Rendall. "Rhetoric and Persuasion in Marcela's Address to the Shepherds." HR 46:287-298. Summer 1978.

Hatzfeld, Helmut A. "Why Is DON QUIJOTE Baroque?" PQ 51:158-176. January 1972.

Herrero, Javier. "Arcadia's Inferno: Cervantes' Attack on Pastoral." BHS 55:289-299. October 1978.

_____. "The Beheading of the Giant: An Obscene Metaphor in DON QUIJOTE." RHM 39:141-149. No. 4, 1977.

Holmes, Theodore. "Don Quixote and Modern Man." SR 78:40-59. January/March 1970.

Hughes, Gethin. "The Cave of Montesinos: Don Quixote's Interpretation and Dulcinea's Disenchantment." BHS 54:107-113. April 1977.

Iventosch, Herman. "Cervantes and Courtly Love: The Grisóstomo-Marcela Episode of DON QUIXOTE." PMLA 89:64-76. January 1974.

Johnson, Carroll B. "Cervantes as a Reader of LA CELESTINA." FWF 1:233-247. May 1974.

_____. "A Second Look at Dulcinea's Ass: DON QUIJOTE, II. 10." HR 43:191-198. Spring 1975.

Jones, Joseph R. "Historical Materials for the Study of the 'Cabeza Encantada' Episode in DON QUIJOTE II. 62." HR 47:87-103. Winter 1979.

Lavin, James Duncan. "Cervantes' Ramón de Hoces el Sevillano." RomN 18:124-128. Fall 1977.

Levin, Harry. "The Example of Cervantes." Cervantes: A Collection of Critical Essays. ed. Lowry Nelson, Jr. Englewood Cliffs: Prentice-Hall, 1969. pp. 34-48.

Locke, F. W. "El Sabio Encantador: The Author of DON QUIXOTE." Symposium 23:46-61. Spring 1969.

Maccurdy, Raymond R. and Alfred Rodriguez. "An Archetypal Factor in the Enchantment of Dulcinea." REH 14:73-80. May 1980.

Mackey, Mary. "Rhetoric and Characterization in DON QUIJOTE." HR 42:51-66. Winter 1974.

Maelsaeke, D. Van. "The Paradox of Humour: A Comparative Study of DON QUIXOTE." Theoria 28:24-41. May 1967.

Mancing, Howard. "Cervantes and the Tradition of Chivalric Parody." FMLS 11:177-187. April 1975.

_____. "The Comic Function of Chivalric Names in DON QUIJOTE." Names 21:220-235. December 1973.

_____. "Dulcinea's Ass: A Note on DON QUIJOTE, Part II, Chapter 10." HR 40:73-77. Winter 1972.

Mann, Thomas. "Voyage with Don Quixote." Cervantes: A Collection of Critical Essays. ed. Lowry Nelson, Jr. Englewood Cliffs: Prentice-Hall, 1969. pp. 49-72.

McGaha, Michael D. "Cervantes and Virgil: A New Look at an Old Problem." CLS 16:96-109. June 1979.

_____. "The Influence of Macrobius on Cervantes." RLC 53:462-469. October/December 1979.

———. "Oaths in DON QUIXOTE." RomN 14:561-569. Spring 1973.

———. "The Sources and Meaning of the Grisóstomo-Marcela Episode in the 1605 QUIJOTE." ACer 16:33-69. 1977.

McGrady, Donald. "The 'Sospiros' of Sancho's Donkey." MLN 88:335-337. March 1973.

McKendrick, Melveena. Cervantes. Boston: Little, Brown, 1980. pp. 210-230.

McQueen, Marian. "Narrative Structure and Reader Response in SIMPLICISSIMUS and DON QUIXOTE: A Contrastive Study." Argenis 1:229-256. 1977.

Mendeloff, Henry. "The Maritornes Episode (DQ:I, 16): A Cervantine Bedroom Farce." RomN 16:753-759. Spring 1975.

———. "The Pejorative Epithet in DON QUIJOTE." Hispano 55:47-55. 1975.

Moore, John A. "The Pastoral in the QUIXOTE or Nuestro gozo en el pozo." RomN 13:531-534. Spring 1972.

Murillo, L. A. "The Summer of Myth: DON QUIJOTE DE LA MANCHA and AMADIS DE GAULA." PQ 51:145-157. January 1972.

Nepaulsingh, Colbert I. "Cervantes, DON QUIJOTE: The Unity of the Action." RCEH 2:239-255. Spring 1978.

Newberry, Wilma. The Pirandellian Mode in Spanish Literature from Cervantes to Sastre. Albany: State University of New York Press, 1973. pp. 3-12.

Palomo, Dolores. "Chaucer, Cervantes, and the Birth of the Novel." Mosaic 8:61-72. Summer 1975.

Pérez, Louis C. "Wilder and Cervantes: In the Spirit of the Tapestry." Symposium 25:249-259. Fall 1971.

Piper, Anson C. "A Possible Source of the Clawing-Cat Episode in DON QUIJOTE (Part Two)." REH 14:3-10. October 1980.

Predmore, Richard L. The World of Don Quixote. Cambridge: Harvard University Press, 1967. 127 pp.

Rey, Arsenio. "Onomastic Perspectivism of DON QUIX-OTE." LOS 7:257-266. 1980.

Riley, E. C. "Literature and Life in DON QUIXOTE." Cervantes: A Collection of Critical Essays. ed. Lowry Nelson, Jr. Englewood Cliffs: Prentice-Hall, 1969. pp. 123-136.

──────. "Symbolism in DON QUIXOTE, Part II, Chapter 73." JHP 3:161-174. Winter 1979.

──────. "Three Versions of Don Quixote." MLR 68:807-819. October 1973.

Rivers, Elias L. "Talking and Writing in DON QUIXOTE." Thought 51:296-305. September 1976.

Robert, Marthe. The Old and the New: From Don Quixote to Kafka. Berkeley: University of California Press, 1977. pp. 11-168.

Russell, P. E. "DON QUIXOTE as a Funny Book." MLR 64:312-326. April 1969.

Saldívar, Ramón. "Don Quijote's Metaphors and the Grammar of Proper Language." MLN 95:252-278. March 1980.

Selig, Karl-Ludwig. "The Battle of the Sheep (DON QUIXOTE, I, xviii)." RHM 38:64-71. No. 1/2, 1974-1975.

──────. "Cervantes: 'En un lugar de....'" MLN 86:266-268. March 1971.

──────. "The Ricote Episode in DON QUIXOTE: Observations on Literary Refractions." RHM 38:73-77. No. 3, 1974-1975.

Serrano-Plaja, Arturo. "Magic" Realism in Cervantes: DON QUIXOTE as Seen Through TOM SAWYER and THE IDIOT. Berkeley: University of California Press, 1970. 213 pp.

Siciliano, Ernest A. "The Absent Hermit of the QUIJOTE." RomN 12:404-406. Spring 1971.

──────. "Don Quijote's Housekeeper--'Algebrista'?" JAF 86:387-390. 1973.

──────. "The Use of Conscience in the QUIJOTE." RomN 11:607-610. Spring 1970.

Sieber, Harry. "Literary Time in the 'Cueva de Montesinos.'" MLN 86:268-273. March 1971.

Sinnigen, John. "Themes and Structures in the 'Bodas de Camacho.'" MLN 84:157-170. March 1969.

Snodgrass, W. D. "Glorying in Failure: Cervantes and Don Quixote." MHRev 28:17-45. October 1973.

Sobré, J. M. "Don Quixote, the Hero Upside-Down." HR 44:127-141. Spring 1976.

Spitzer, Leo. "On the Significance of DON QUIJOTE." Cervantes: A Collection of Critical Essays. ed. Lowry Nelson, Jr. Englewood Cliffs: Prentice-Hall, 1969. pp. 82-97.

Steele, Charles W. "Functions of the Grisóstomo-Marcela Episode in DON QUIJOTE: Symbolism, Drama, Parody." REH 14:3-16. January 1980.

Thorburn, David. "Fiction and Imagination in DON QUIXOTE." PR 42:431-443. No. 3, 1975.

Ullman, Pierre L. "The Heading of Chapter X in the 1605 QUIJOTE." FMLS 7:43-51. January 1971.

de Unamuno, Miguel. "On the Reading and Interpretation of DON QUIXOTE." MHRev 2:35-49. April 1967.

Valdes, M. J. "The Reader's Cervantes in DON QUIXOTE." IFR 4:46-55. January 1977.

Walker, Roger M. "Did Cervantes Know the CAVALLERO ZIFAR?" BHS 49:120-127. April 1972.

Wardropper, Bruce W. "'Duelos y quebrantos,' Once Again." RomN 20:413-416. Spring 1980.

Willey, Frederick. "DON QUIXOTE and the Theatre of Life and Art." GaR 31:907-930. Winter 1977.

Willis, Raymond S. "Sancho Panza: Prototype for the Modern Novel." HR 37:207-227. January 1969.

Wilson, Rawdon. "Drawing New Lessons from Old Masters: The Concept of 'Character' in the QUIJOTE." MP 78:117-138. November 1980.

Wiltrout, Ann E. "Ginés de Pasamonte: The 'Pícaro' and His Art." ACer 17:11-17. 1978.

Ziomek, Henryk. "Parallel Ingredients in DON QUIXOTE

and DOM CASMURRO." REH 2:228-240. November 1968.
LAS DOS DONCELLAS
El Saffar, Ruth S. Novel to Romance: A Study of Cervantes's NOVELAS EJEMPLARES. Baltimore: Johns Hopkins University Press, 1974. pp. 109-118.

Pabon, Thomas. "Secular Resurrection Through Marriage in Cervantes' LA SEÑORA CORNELIA, LAS DOS DONCELLAS and LA FUERZA DE LA SANGRE." ACer 16:114-119. 1977.
LA ESPAÑOLA INGLESA
Cluff, David. "The Structure and Theme of LA ESPAÑOLA INGLESA: A Reconsideration." REH 10:261-281. May 1976.

da Costa Fontes, Manuel. "Love as an Equalizer in LA ESPAÑOLA INGLESA." RomN 16:742-748. Spring 1975.

El Saffar, Ruth S. Novel to Romance: A Study of Cervantes's NOVELAS EJEMPLARES. Baltimore: Johns Hopkins University Press, 1974. pp. 150-162.

Hanrahan, Thomas. "History in the ESPAÑOLA INGLESA." MLN 83:267-271. March 1968.

Lowe, Jennifer. "The Structure of Cervantes' LA ESPAÑOLA INGLESA." RomN 9:287-290. Spring 1968.

Pabón, Thomas A. "The Symbolic Significance of Marriage in Cervantes' LA ESPAÑOLA INGLESA." Hispano 63:59-66. 1978.
LA FUERZA DE LA SANGRE
Allen, John J. "EL CRISTO DE LA VEGA and LA FUERZA DE LA SANGRE." MLN 83:271-275. March 1968.

El Saffar, Ruth S. Novel to Romance: A Study of Cervantes's NOVELAS EJEMPLARES. Baltimore: Johns Hopkins University Press, 1974. pp. 128-138.

Pabon, Thomas. "Secular Resurrection Through Marriage in Cervantes' LA SEÑORA CORNELIA, LAS DOS DONCELLAS and LA FUERZA DE LA SANGRE." ACer 16:119-124. 1977.

Selig, Karl-Ludwig. "Some Observations on LA FUERZA DE LA SANGRE." MLN 87:121-125. November 1972.
GALATEA
Allen, Kenneth P. "Cervantes' GALATEA and the 'Discorso intorno al comporre dei romanzi' of Giraldi Cinthio." RHM 39:52-68. No. 1/2, 1976-1977.

Duran, Manuel. Cervantes. New York: Twayne, 1974. pp. 77-87.

Johnson, Leslie Deutsch. "Three Who Made a Revolution: Cervantes, Galatea and Caliope." Hispano 57:23-33. 1976.

Keightley, R. G. "Narrative Perspectives in Spanish Pastoral Fiction." AUMLA 44:197-217. November 1975.

Mujica, Barbara. "Antiutopian Elements in the Spanish Pastoral Novel." KRQ 26:275-279. No. 3, 1979.

LA GITANILLA

El Saffar, Ruth S. Novel to Romance: A Study of Cervantes's NOVELAS EJEMPLARES. Baltimore: Johns Hopkins University Press, 1974. pp. 86-108.

Pierce, Frank. "LA GITANILLA: A Tale of High Romance." BHS 54:283-295. October 1977.

LA ILUSTRE FREGONA

El Saffar, Ruth S. Novel to Romance: A Study of Cervantes's NOVELAS EJEMPLARES. Baltimore: Johns Hopkins University Press, 1974. pp. 86-108.

Weber, Alison. "LA ILUSTRE FREGONA and the Barriers of Caste." PLL 15:73-81. Winter 1979.

EL LICENCIADO VIDRIERA

Edwards, Gwynne. "Cervantes's EL LICENCIADO VIDRIERA: Meaning and Structure." MLR 68:559-568. July 1973.

El Saffar, Ruth S. Novel to Romance: A Study of Cervantes's NOVELAS EJEMPLARES. Baltimore: Johns Hopkins University Press, 1974. pp. 50-61.

Friedman, Edward H. "Conceptual Proportion in Cervantes' EL LICENCIADO VIDRIERA." SAB 39:51-59. November 1974.

Messick, Alan R. "Tomás Rodaja: A Clinical Case?" RomN 11:623-628. Spring 1970.

Riley, E. C. "Cervantes and the Cynics (EL LICENCIADO VIDRIERA and EL COLOQUIO DE LOS PERROS)." BHS 53:189-195. July 1976.

PERSILES AND SIGISMUNDA

Allen, Kenneth P. "Aspects of Time in LOS TRABAJOS DE PERSILES Y SIGISMUNDA." RHM 36:77-101. No. 3, 1970-1971.

Beringer, Arthur A. "PERSILES and the Time Labyrinth." Hispano 41:1-11. 1971.

Cervantes, Miguel de

Duran, Manuel. Cervantes. New York: Twayne, 1974. pp. 147-171.

El Saffar, Ruth S. Novel to Romance: A Study of Cervantes's NOVELAS EJEMPLARES. Baltimore: Johns Hopkins University Press, 1974. pp. 1-29.

──────. "Periandro: Exemplary Character--Exemplary Narrator." Hispano 69:9-16. May 1980.

Forcione, Alban K. Cervantes, Aristotle, and the PERSILES. Princeton: Princeton University Press, 1970. pp. 169-301.

Lowe, Jennifer. "Themes and Structure in Cervantes' PERSILES Y SIGISMUNDA." FMLS 3:334-351. October 1967.

Pope, Randolph D. "The Autobiographical Form in the PERSILES." ACer 13/14:93-106. 1974-1975.

Selig, Karl-Ludwig. "PERSILES Y SIGISMUNDA: Notes on Pictures, Portraits, and Portraiture." HR 41:305-312. Special Issue 1973.

Weiger, John G. The Individuated Self: Cervantes and the Emergence of the Individual. Athens: Ohio University Press, 1979. pp. 81-87.

RINCONETE AND CORTADILLO
Dunn, Peter N. The Spanish Picaresque Novel. Boston: Twayne, 1979. pp. 79-85.

El Saffar, Ruth S. Novel to Romance: A Study of Cervantes's NOVELAS EJEMPLARES. Baltimore: Johns Hopkins University Press, 1974. pp. 30-40.

LA SEÑORA CORNELIA
El Saffar, Ruth S. Novel to Romance: A Study of Cervantes's NOVELAS EJEMPLARES. Baltimore: Johns Hopkins University Press, 1974. pp. 118-128.

Pabon, Thomas. "Secular Resurrection Through Marriage in Cervantes' LA SEÑORA CORNELIA, LAS DOS DONCELLAS and LA FUERZA DE LA SANGRE." ACer 16:110-114. 1977.

EL VIEJO CELOSO
Kenworthy, Patricia. "The Character of Lorenza and the Moral of Cervantes' EL VIEJO CELOSO." BCom 31:103-107. Fall 1979.

Cortes de Tolosa, Juan
LAZARILLO DE MANZANARES
Rudder, Robert S. "LAZARILLO DE MANZANARES: A Reconsideration." KRQ 24:141-150. No. 2, 1977.

Cunqueiro, Alvaro
    UN HOMBRE QUE SE PARECIA A ORESTES
        Thomas, Michael D. "Cunqueiro's UN HOMBRE QUE
        SE PARECIA A ORESTES: A Humorous Revitalization
        of an Ancient Myth." Hispania 61:35-45. March 1978.
    CURIAL E GÜELFA
        Waley, Pamela. "In Search of an Author for CURIAL
        E GÜELFA: The French Clues." BHS 53:117-126.
        April 1976.

Delibes, Miguel
    EL CAMINO
        Diaz, Janet. Miguel Delibes. New York: Twayne,
        1971. pp. 51-58.
    DIARY OF A HUNTER
        Diaz, Janet. Miguel Delibes. New York: Twayne,
        1971. pp. 86-93.
    FIVE HOURS WITH MARIO
        Boring, Phyllis Zatlin. "Delibes' Two Views of the
        Spanish Mother." Hispano 63:79-87. 1978.

        Diaz, Janet. Miguel Delibes. New York: Twayne,
        1971. pp. 140-148.
    LAS GUERRAS DE NUESTROS ANTEPASADOS
        Diaz, Janet W. and Ricardo Landeira. "Structural and
        Thematic Reiteration in Delibes's Recent Fiction."
        Hispania 63:674-683. December 1980.
    LONG IS THE CYPRESS' SHADOW
        Diaz, Janet. Miguel Delibes. New York: Twayne,
        1971. pp. 38-44.
    MY ADORED SON, SISI
        Diaz, Janet. Miguel Delibes. New York: Twayne,
        1971. pp. 59-64.
    PARABLE OF THE DROWNING MAN
        Boudreau, H. L. "Miguel Delibes' PARABOLA DEL
        NAUFRAGO: Utopia Redreamed." StTCL 1:27-46.
        Fall 1976.

        Diaz, Janet. Miguel Delibes. New York: Twayne,
        1971. pp. 150-158.

        Herzberger, David K. "Automatization and Defamiliarization in Delibes' PARABOLA DEL NAUFRAGO." MLN
        95:357-375. March 1980.

        Quance, Roberta A. "Language Manipulation and Social
        Order in Delibes' PARABOLA DEL NAUFRAGO."
        ELWIU 3:119-130. Spring 1976.
    EL PRINCIPE DESTRONADO
        Boring, Phyllis Zatlin. "Delibes' Two Views of the
        Spanish Mother." Hispano 63:79-87. 1978.

        Diaz, Janet W. and Ricardo Landeira. "Structural and

Delibes, Miguel

  Thematic Reiteration in Delibes's Recent Fiction."
  Hispania 63:674-683. December 1980.
LAS RATAS
  Diaz, Janet. Miguel Delibes. New York: Twayne,
  1971. pp. 132-139.

  Ewing, Dorothy. "The Religious Significance of Miguel
  Delibes' LAS RATAS." RomN 11:492-497. Spring 1970.
STILL IT IS DAY
  Diaz, Janet. Miguel Delibes. New York: Twayne,
  1971. pp. 44-51.

Delicado, Francisco
 LA LOZANA ANDALUZA
  Damiani, Bruno M. "Delicado and Aretino: Aspects of
  a Literary Profile." KRQ 17:309-324. No. 4, 1970.

  ————. Francisco Delicado. New York: Twayne,
  1974. pp. 18-102.

Espina, Concha
 THE GIRL FROM LUZMELA
  Bretz, Mary Lee. Concha Espina. Boston: Twayne,
  1980. pp. 27-32.

  Moore, Roger. "The Role of the 'nétigua' in LA NIÑA
  DE LUZMELA." IFR 7:24-28. Winter 1980.
 HIGH ALTAR
  Bretz, Mary Lee. Concha Espina. Boston: Twayne,
  1980. pp. 88-91.
 MARIFLOR
  Bretz, Mary Lee. Concha Espina. Boston: Twayne,
  1980. pp. 45-53.
 THE METAL OF THE DEAD
  Bretz, Mary Lee. Concha Espina. Boston: Twayne,
  1980. pp. 64-71.
 A NOVEL OF LOVE
  Bretz, Mary Lee. Concha Espina. Boston: Twayne,
  1980. pp. 141-144.
 THE PRUDENT VIRGIN
  Bretz, Mary Lee. Concha Espina. Boston: Twayne,
  1980. pp. 95-99.
 THE RED BEACON
  Bretz, Mary Lee. Concha Espina. Boston: Twayne,
  1980. pp. 74-78.
 THE RED CHALICE
  Bretz, Mary Lee. Concha Espina. Boston: Twayne,
  1980. pp. 82-85.
 RETAGUARDIA
  Bretz, Mary Lee. Concha Espina. Boston: Twayne,
  1980. pp. 108-111.
 ROSE OF THE WINDS
  Bretz, Mary Lee. Concha Espina. Boston: Twayne,
  1980. pp. 53-58.

THE STRONGEST ONE
 Bretz, Mary Lee. Concha Espina. Boston: Twayne, 1980. pp. 130-134.
TO WAKE UP AND DIE
 Bretz, Mary Lee. Concha Espina. Boston: Twayne, 1980. pp. 33-38.
A VALLEY IN THE SEA
 Bretz, Mary Lee. Concha Espina. Boston: Twayne, 1980. pp. 134-139.
VICTORIA IN AMERICA
 Bretz, Mary Lee. Concha Espina. Boston: Twayne, 1980. pp. 125-129.
THE WOMAN AND THE SEA
 Bretz, Mary Lee. Concha Espina. Boston: Twayne, 1980. pp. 39-45.
YESTERDAY'S FLOWER
 Bretz, Mary Lee. Concha Espina. Boston: Twayne, 1980. pp. 103-106.

Espinel, Vicente
 MARCOS DE OBREGON
  Bjornson, Richard. "Social Conformity and Justice in MARCOS DE OBREGON." REH 9:285-307. May 1975.

  Dunn, Peter N. The Spanish Picaresque Novel. Boston: Twayne, 1979. pp. 92-112.

  Heathcote, A. Antony. Vicente Espinel. Boston: Twayne, 1977. pp. 61-143.

Ferreira de Castro, José
 A LÃ E A NEVE
  Megenney, William W. "Descriptive Sensationalism in Ferreira de Castro." RomN 13:61-66. Autumn 1971.

Ferres, Antonio
 CON LAS MANOS VACIAS
  Feeny, Thomas. "Suspense and Understatement in Antonio Ferres' CON LAS MANOS VACIAS." SAB 43:58-66. January 1978.

de Flores, Juan
 GRIMALTE Y GRADISSA
  Baker, M. J. "The Unpopularity of the DEPLOURABLE FIN DE FLAMETE." RomN 14:570-576. Spring 1973.

  Waley, Pamela. "Fiammetta and Panfilo Continued." IS 24:15-31. 1969.
 GRISEL Y MIRABELLA
  Waley, Pamela. "CARCEL DE AMOR and GRISEL Y MIRABELLA: A Question of Priority." BHS 50:340-356. October 1973.

Flórez, Wenceslao
  EL HOMBRE QUE COMPRO UN AUTOMOVIL
    Zaetta, Robert. "Wenceslao Fernández Flórez: The Evolution of His Technique in His Novels." KRQ 17: 133-136. No. 2, 1970.
  EL SISTEMA PELEGRIN
    Zaetta, Robert. "Wenceslao Fernández Flórez' Comic Technique in EL SISTEMA PELEGRIN." RomN 15:234-237. Winter 1973.

García, Carlos
  LA DESORDENADA CODICIA DE LOS BIENES AJENOS
    Thacker, M.J. "LA DESORDENADA CODICIA DE LOS BIENES AJENOS--a 'caso límite' of the Picaresque?" BHS 55:33-41. January 1978.

Gil Polo, Gaspar
  DIANA ENAMORADA
    Keightley, R.G. "Narrative Perspectives in Spanish Pastoral Fiction." AUMLA 44:197-217. November 1975.

    Mujica, Barbara. "Antiutopian Elements in the Spanish Pastoral Novel." KRQ 26:271-275. No. 3, 1979.

Gironella, José María
  LOS CIPRESES CREEN EN DIOS
    Ilie, Paul. "Fictive History in Gironella." JSSTC 2:77-94. Fall 1974.

    Schwartz, Ronald. José María Gironella. New York: Twayne, 1972. pp. 51-69.
  UN MILLON DE MUERTOS
    Ilie, Paul. "Fictive History in Gironella." JSSTC 2:77-94. Fall 1974.

    Schwartz, Ronald. José María Gironella. New York: Twayne, 1972. pp. 70-85.
  THE PEACE HAS BROKEN OUT
    Schwartz, Ronald. José María Gironella. New York: Twayne, 1972. pp. 150-156.

Goytisolo, Juan
  THE CIRCUS
    Schwartz, Kessel. Juan Goytisolo. New York: Twayne, 1970. pp. 60-66.
  COUNT JULIAN
    Anderson, Reed. "Luis Martin-Santos and Juan Goytisolo: Irony and Satire in the Contemporary Spanish Novel." OL 33:366-373. 1978.

    Pérez, Genaro J. "Some Leitmotifs and Bridges in the

Sonata Form Structure of Juan Goytisolo's REIVINDICA-
CION DEL CONDE DON JULIAN." Hispano 66:41-51.
May 1979.

Ugarte, Michael. "Juan Goytisolo's Mirrors: Intertextuality and Self-Reflection in REIVINDICACION DEL CONDE DON JULIAN and JUAN SIN TIERRA." MFS 26:616-619. Winter 1980-1981.

FIESTAS
Busette, Cedric. "Goytisolo's FIESTA: A Search for Meaning." RomN 12:270-273. Spring 1971.

Peden, Margaret Sayers. "Juan Goytisolo's FIESTAS, an Analysis and Commentary." Hispania 50:461-466. September 1967.

Schwartz, Kessel. Juan Goytisolo. New York: Twayne, 1970. pp. 67-73.

FIN DE FIESTA
Newberry, Wilma. "The Baptist Betrayed: Juan Goytisolo's LA RESACA and FIN DE FIESTA." REH 9:57-63. January 1975.

Schwartz, Kessel. Juan Goytisolo. New York: Twayne, 1970. pp. 92-95.

THE ISLAND
Schwartz, Kessel. Juan Goytisolo. New York: Twayne, 1970. pp. 86-91.

JUAN THE LANDLESS
Díaz-Migoyo, Gonzalo. "JUAN THE LANDLESS." BUJ 26:71-75. No. 2, 1978.

Levine, Susan F. "The Lesson of the QUIJOTE in the Works of Carlos Fuentes and Juan Goytisolo." JSSTC 7:179-182. Fall 1979.

Pérez, Genaro J. "Form in Juan Goytisolo's JUAN SIN TIERRA." JSSTC 5:137-159. Fall 1977.

Schwartz, Kessel. "Juan Goytisolo, JUAN SIN TIERRA, and the Anal Aesthetic." Hispania 62:9-19. March 1979.

Spires, Robert C. "Latrines, Whirlpools, and Voids: The Metafictional Mode of JUAN SIN TIERRA." HR 48:151-169. Spring 1980.

Ugarte, Michael. "Juan Goytisolo's Mirrors: Intertextuality and Self-Reflection in REIVINDICACION DEL CONDE DON JULIAN and JUAN SIN TIERRA." MFS 26:619-623. Winter 1980-1981.

MARKS OF IDENTITY
Anderson, Reed. "SEÑAS DE IDENTIDAD: Chronicle of Rebellion." JSSTC 2:3-19. Spring 1974.

Goytisolo, Juan

> Bieder, Maryellen. "A Case of Altered Identity: Two Editions of Juan Goytisolo's SEÑAS DE IDENTIDAD." MLN 89:298-310. March 1974.
>
> Schwartz, Kessel. Juan Goytisolo. New York: Twayne, 1970. pp. 95-107.
> SLEIGHT OF HAND
> Giles, Mary E. "Juan Goytisolo's JUEGOS DE MANOS: An Archetypal Interpretation." Hispania 56:1021-1029. December 1973.
>
> Schwartz, Kessel. Juan Goytisolo. New York: Twayne, 1970. pp. 38-48.
> SORROW AT PARADISE HOUSE
> Boring, Phyllis Zatlin. "Adolescent Friendship in Two Contemporary Spanish Novels." Hispano 60:53-57. 1977.
>
> Schwartz, Kessel. Juan Goytisolo. New York: Twayne, 1970. pp. 49-59.
> THE UNDERTOW
> Newberry, Wilma. "The Baptist Betrayed: Juan Goytisolo's LA RESACA and FIN DE FIESTA." REH 9:47-56. January 1975.
>
> Schwartz, Kessel. Juan Goytisolo. New York: Twayne, 1970. pp. 77-85.

Gracián, Baltasar
> EL CRITICON
> Darst, David H. "Andrenio's Perception of Reality and the Structure of EL CRITICON." Hispania 60:907-915. December 1977.
>
> Foster, Virginia Ramos. Baltasar Gracián. Boston: Twayne, 1975. pp. 68-117.
>
> *Hafter, Monroe Z. Gracián and Perfection. Cambridge: Harvard University Press, 1966. pp. 107-120.
>
> Jones, Joseph R. "From Abraham to Andrenio: Observations on the Evolution of the Abraham Legend, Its Diffusion in Spain, and Its Relation to the Theme of the Self-Taught Philosopher." CLS 6:85-92. March 1969.
>
> Kassier, Theodore L. The Truth Disguised: Allegorical Structure and Technique in Gracián's CRITICON. London: Tamesis Books, 1976. 142 pp.
>
> Welles, Marcia L. Style and Structure in Gracián's EL CRITICON. Chapel Hill: University of North Carolina Press, 1976. 197 pp.

Jarnés, Benjamín
    THE MADNESS AND DEATH OF NOBODY
        Bernstein, J.S. Benjamín Jarnés. New York: Twayne, 1972. pp. 78-82.
    THE PAPER GUEST
        Bernstein, J.S. Benjamín Jarnés. New York: Twayne, 1972. pp. 65-72.
    PAULA AND PAULITA
        Bernstein, J.S. Benjamín Jarnés. New York: Twayne, 1972. pp. 72-78.
    THE RED AND THE BLUE
        Bernstein, J.S. Benjamín Jarnés. New York: Twayne, 1972. pp. 91-96.
    SCENES ON THE BRINK OF DEATH
        Bernstein, J.S. Benjamín Jarnés. New York: Twayne, 1972. pp. 88-91.
    SUMMER SALON
        Bernstein, J.S. Benjamín Jarnés. New York: Twayne, 1972. pp. 96-100.
    THEORY OF THE TOP-STRING
        Bernstein, J.S. Benjamín Jarnés. New York: Twayne, 1972. pp. 82-88.
    THE USELESS PROFESSOR
        Bernstein, J.S. Benjamín Jarnés. New York: Twayne, 1972. pp. 57-65.
    THE WIND'S SWEETHEART
        Bernstein, J.S. Benjamín Jarnés. New York: Twayne, 1972. pp. 100-105.

Laforet, Carmen
    LA ISLA Y LOS DEMONIOS
        Ullman, Pierre L. "The Moral Structure of Carmen Laforet's Novels." The Vision Obscured: Perceptions of Some Twentieth-Century Catholic Novelists. ed. Melvin J. Friedman. New York: Fordham University Press, 1970. pp. 205-210.
    NADA
        El Saffar, Ruth. "Structural and Thematic Tactics of Suppression in Carmen Laforet's NADA." Symposium 28:119-129. Summer 1974.

        Galerstein, Carolyn L. "Carmen Laforet and the Spanish Spinster." REH 11:311-315. May 1977.

        Glenn, Kathleen M. "Animal Imagery in NADA." REH 11:381-394. October 1977.

        Newberry, Wilma. "The Solstitial Holidays in Carmen Laforet's NADA: Christmas and Midsummer." RomN 17:76-81. Fall 1976.
    UN NOVIAZGO
        Galerstein, Carolyn L. "Carmen Laforet and the Spanish Spinster." REH 11:304-311. May 1977.

## LAZARILLO DE TORMES

Abrams, Fred. "Hurtado de Mendoza's Concealed Signatures in the LAZARILLO DE TORMES." RomN 15:341-345. Winter 1973.

_____. "A Note on the Mercedarian Friar in the LAZARILLO DE TORMES." RomN 11:444-446. Winter 1969.

_____. "To Whom Was the Anonymous LAZARILLO DE TORMES Dedicated?" RomN 8:273-277. Spring 1967.

Bell, A. "The Rhetoric of Self-Defence of 'Lázaro de Tormes.'" MLR 68:84-93. January 1973.

Bjornson, Richard. "Lazarillo 'arrimándose a los buenos.'" RomN 19:67-71. Fall 1978.

_____. The Picaresque Hero in European Fiction. Madison: University of Wisconsin Press, 1977. pp. 21-42.

Carey, Douglas M. "Asides and Interiority in LAZARILLO DE TORMES: A Study in Psychological Realism." SP 66:119-134. April 1969.

_____. "LAZARILLO DE TORMES and the Quest for Authority." PMLA 94:36-46. January 1979.

Cervigni, Dino S. "LAZARILLO DE TORMES and the VITA of Benvenuto Cellini: An Inquiry into Prose Narrative and Genre." KRQ 27: 373-389. No. 4, 1980.

Collard, Andree. "The Unity of LAZARILLO DE TORMES." MLN 83:262-267. March 1968.

Cortina Gómez, Rodolfo. "On Dating the LAZARILLO." HR 45:61-66. Winter 1977.

Davey, E.R. "The Concept of Man in LAZARILLO DE TORMES." MLR 72:597-604. July 1977.

Dunn, Peter N. The Spanish Picaresque Novel. Boston: Twayne, 1979. pp. 17-40.

Durand, Frank. "The Author and Lázaro: Levels of Comic Meaning." BHS 45:89-101. April 1968.

Herrero, Javier. "The Ending of LAZARILLO: The 'Wine' Against the 'Water.'" MLN 93:313-319. March 1978.

———. "Renaissance Poverty and Lazarillo's Family: The Birth of the Picaresque Genre." PMLA 94: 876-886. October 1979.

Hesse, Everett W. "The LAZARILLO DE TORMES and the Playing of a Role." KRQ 22:61-76. No. 1, 1975.

———. "The LAZARILLO DE TORMES and the Way of the World." REH 11:163-180. May 1977.

Hitchcock, Richard. "Lazarillo and 'Vuestra Merced.'" MLN 86:264-266. March 1971.

Holzinger, Walter. "The Breadly Paradise Revisited: LAZARILLO DE TORMES, Segundo Tratado." RHM 37:229-236. No. 4, 1972-1973.

Hughes, Gethin. "LAZARILLO DE TORMES: The Fifth 'Tratado.'" Hispano 61:1-9. 1977.

Mancing, Howard. "The Deceptiveness of LAZARILLO DE TORMES." PMLA 90:426-432. May 1975.

———. "Fernando de Rojas, LA CELESTINA, and LAZARILLO DE TORMES." KRQ 23:47-61. No. 1, 1976.

McGrady, Donald. "Social Irony in LAZARILLO DE TORMES and Its Implications for Authorship." RPh 23:557-567. May 1970.

Nepaulsingh, Colbert I. "Lázaro's Fortune." RomN 20:417-423. Spring 1980.

Perry, T. Anthony. "Biblical Symbolism in the LAZARILLO DE TORMES." SP 67:139-146. April 1970.

Piper, Anson C. "Lazarillo's 'Arcaz' and Rosalía de Bringas' 'Cajoncillo.'" RHM 39:119-122. No. 3, 1976-1977.

Ricapito, Joseph V. "LAZARILLO DE TORMES and Machiavelli: Two Facets of Renaissance Perspective." RF 83:151-172. No. 2/3, 1971.

———. "LAZARILLO DE TORMES (Chap. V) and Masuccio's Fourth NOVELLA." RPh 23:305-311. February 1970.

Schwartz, Kessel. "A Statistical Note on the Authorship of LAZARILLO DE TORMES." RomN 9:118-119. Autumn 1967.

Sieber, Harry. Language and Society in LA VIDA DE LAZARILLO DE TORMES. Baltimore: Johns Hopkins University Press, 1978. 97 pp.

Spivakovsky, Erika. "New Arguments in Favor of Mendoza's Authorship of the LAZARILLO DE TORMES." Symposium 24:67-80. Spring 1970.

Truman, R.W. "LAZARILLO DE TORMES, Petrarch's DE REMEDIIS ADVERSAE FORTUNAE, and Erasmus's PRAISE OF FOLLY." BHS 52:33-53. January 1975.

──────. "Lázaro de Tormes and the 'Homo Novus' Tradition." MLR 64:62-67. January 1969.

──────. "Parody and Irony in the Self-Portrayal of Lázaro de Tormes." MLR 63:600-605. July 1968.

Wardropper, Bruce W. "The Strange Case of Lázaro Gonzales Pérez." MLN 92:202-212. March 1977.

Wiltrout, Ann. "The LAZARILLO DE TORMES and Erasmus' 'Opulentia Sordida.'" RF 81:550-564. No. 4, 1969.

Woods, M.J. "Pitfalls for the Moralizer in LAZARILLO DE TORMES." MLR 74:580-598. July 1979.

## EL LIBRO DEL CAVALLERO CIFAR

Burke, James F. "The LIBRO DEL CAVALLERO ZIFAR and the Medieval Sermon." Viator 1:207-221. 1970.

──────. "The Meaning of the 'Islas Dotadas' Episode in the LIBRO DEL CAVALLERO CIFAR." HR 38:56-68. January 1970.

──────. "Names and the Significance of Etymology in the LIBRO DEL CAVALLERO CIFAR." RR 59:161-173. October 1968.

──────. "Symbolic Allegory in the Portus Salutaris Episode in the LIBRO DEL CAVALLERO CIFAR." KRQ 15:69-84. No. 1, 1968.

Hernández, Francisco J. "EL LIBRO DEL CAVALLERO ZIFAR: Meaning and Structure." RCEH 2:89-121. Winter 1978.

Keightley, Ronald G. "Models and Meanings for the LIBRO DEL CAVALLERO ZIFAR." Mosaic 12:55-73. Winter 1979.

_____. "The Story of Zifar and the Structure of the LIBRO DEL CAVALLERO ZIFAR." MLR 73:308-327. April 1978.

Mullen, Edward J. "The Role of the Supernatural in EL LIBRO DEL CAVALLERO ZIFAR." REH 5:257-268. May 1971.

Walker, Roger M. "Did Cervantes Know the CAVALLERO ZIFAR?" BHS 49:120-127. April 1972.

_____. "The Genesis of EL LIBRO DEL CAVALLERO ZIFAR." MLR 62:60-69. January 1967.

Lopez de Ubeda, Francisco
   THE ROGUE JUSTINA
      Damiani, Bruno M. Francisco Lopez de Ubeda. Boston: Twayne, 1977. pp. 19-149.

      Dunn, Peter N. The Spanish Picaresque Novel. Boston: Twayne, 1979. pp. 113-133.

Lopez Pacheco, Jesus
   CENTRAL ELECTRICA
      Jimenez-Fajardo, Salvador. "Lopez Pacheco's CENTRAL ELECTRICA." Crit 14:5-15. No. 1, 1972.

Marsé, Juan
   SI TE DICEN QUE CAI
      Garvey, Diane I. "Juan Marsé's SI TE DICEN QUE CAI: The Self-reflexive Text and the Question of Referentiality." MLN 95:376-387. March 1980.
   ULTIMAS TARDES CON TERESA
      Nichols, Geraldine Cleary. "Dialectical Realism and Beyond: ULTIMAS TARDES CON TERESA." JSSTC 3:163-173. Winter 1975.

Martín Gaite, Carmen
   EL BALNEARIO
      Brown, Joan Lipman. "EL BALNEARIO by Carmen Martín Gaite: Conceptual Aesthetics and 'l'étrange pur.'" JSSTC 6:163-174. Winter 1978.
   RETAHILAS
      Glenn, Kathleen M. "Communication in the Works of Carmen Martín Gaite." RomN 19:277-283. Spring 1979.

      Ordóñez, Elizabeth. "The Decoding and Encoding of Sex Roles in Carmen Martín Gaite's RETAHILAS." KRQ 27:237-244. No. 2, 1980.
   RITMO LENTO
      Boring, Phyllis Zatlin. "Carmen Martín Gaite and the Generation of 1898." RomN 20:293-297. Spring 1980.

Martin-Santos, Luis
TIEMPO DE SILENCIO
Anderson, Reed. "Luis Martin-Santos and Juan Goytisolo: Irony and Satire in the Contemporary Spanish Novel." OL 33:360-366. 1978.

Anderson, Robert K. "Self-Estrangement in TIEMPO DE SILENCIO." REH 13:299-317. May 1979.

Caviglia, John. "A Simple Question of Symmetry: Psyche as Structure in TIEMPO DE SILENCIO." Hispania 60:452-460. September 1977.

Craige, Betty Jean. "TIEMPO DE SILENCIO: 'Le Grand Bouc' and the Maestro." REH 13:99-113. January 1979.

Diaz, Janet Winecoff. "Luis Martin Santos and the Contemporary Spanish Novel." Hispania 51:232-238. May 1968.

Holzinger, Walter. "TIEMPO DE SILENCIO: An Analysis." RHM 37:73-90. No. 1/2, 1972-1973.

Lyon, J.E. "Don Pedro's Complicity: An Existential Dimension of TIEMPO DE SILENCIO." MLR 74:69-78. January 1979.

Palley, Julian. "The Periplus of Don Pedro: TIEMPO DE SILENCIO." BHS 48:239-254. July 1971.

Seale, Mary L. "Hangman and Victim: An Analysis of Martin-Santos' TIEMPO DE SILENCIO." Hispano 44:45-52. 1972.

Waller, Myriam. "The Ethics of Existentialism in TIEMPO DE SILENCIO." Reflexión 2 3/4:174-180. 1974-1975.

Martorell, Joannot
TIRANT LO BLANC
Llosa, Mario Vargas. "A Challenge on Behalf of TIRANT LO BLANC." RS 37:1-16. March 1969.

Matute, Ana María
EN ESTA TIERRA
Diaz, Janet. Ana María Matute. New York: Twayne, 1971. pp. 62-70.

Shelby, J. Townsend. "Retrospection as a Technique in Matute's LOS HIJOS MUERTOS and EN ESTA TIERRA." REH 14:81-92. May 1980.

FIESTA AL NOROESTE
  Boring, Phyllis Zatlin. "Adolescent Friendship in Two
  Contemporary Spanish Novels." Hispano 60:53-57.
  1977.

  Diaz, Janet. Ana María Matute. New York: Twayne,
  1971. pp. 102-108.

  Jones, Margaret W. "Antipathetic Fallacy: The Hostile World of Ana María Matute's Novels." KFLQ
  13:7-9. Supplement 1967.
LOS HIJOS MUERTOS
  Diaz, Janet. Ana María Matute. New York: Twayne,
  1971. pp. 122-129.

  Jones, Margaret W. "Antipathetic Fallacy: The Hostile
  World of Ana María Matute's Novels." KFLQ 13:9-12.
  Supplement 1967.

  Shelby, J. Townsend. "Retrospection as a Technique in
  Matute's LOS HIJOS MUERTOS and EN ESTA TIERRA."
  REH 14:81-92. May 1980.
LITTLE THEATER
  Diaz, Janet. Ana María Matute. New York: Twayne,
  1971. pp. 54-61.
THE MERCHANTS
  Diaz, Janet. Ana María Matute. New York: Twayne,
  1971. pp. 132-143.
PRIMERA MEMORIA
  Jones, Margaret W. "Antipathetic Fallacy: The Hostile
  World of Ana María Matute's Novels." KFLQ 13:12-15.
  Supplement 1967.

  Stevens, James R. "Myth and Memory: Ana María
  Matute's PRIMERA MEMORIA." Symposium 25:198-203.
  Summer 1971.

  Thomas, Michael D. "The Rite of Initiation in Matute's
  PRIMERA MEMORIA." KRQ 25:153-164. No. 2, 1978.
LA TRAMPA
  Ordóñez, Elizabeth. "Forms of Alienation in Matute's
  LA TRAMPA." JSSTC 4:179-189. Winter 1976.

Medio, Dolores
  BIBIANA
    Jones, Margaret E.W. Dolores Medio. New York:
    Twayne, 1974. pp. 109-124.
  DIARY OF A SCHOOLTEACHER
    Jones, Margaret E.W. Dolores Medio. New York:
    Twayne, 1974. pp. 94-108.

    Penuel, Arnold M. "The Influence of Galdós' EL
    AMIGO MANSO on Dolores Medio's EL DIARIO DE UNA
    MAESTRA." REH 7:91-96. January 1973.

THE FISH STAYS AFLOAT
   Jones, Margaret E.W.  Dolores Medio.  New York: Twayne, 1974.  pp. 82-94.
PUBLIC SERVANT
   Hutman, Norma Louise.  "Disproportionate Doom: Tragic Irony in the Spanish Post Civil War Novel." MFS 18:199-206.  Summer 1972.

   Jones, Margaret E.W.  Dolores Medio.  New York: Twayne, 1974.  pp. 65-82.
WE RIVEROS
   Jones, Margaret E.W.  Dolores Medio.  New York: Twayne, 1974.  pp. 43-64.

Miguéis, José Rodrigues
   UMA AVENTURA INQUIETANTE
      Kerr, John Austin, Jr.  "Precision, Concentricity and Wave-Form in UMA AVENTURA INQUIETANTE: Notes on Its Temporal and Locational Referents." EIA 2:261-266.  No. 2, 1976.
   A ESCOLA DO PARAISO
      Kerr, John Austin.  "On Time and Place in A ESCOLA DO PARAISO." LangQ 15:35-38.  Fall/Winter 1976.

      Kerr, John Austin, Jr.  "A Paradise That Never Was: A ESCOLA DO PARAISO." KRQ 25:225-241.  No. 2, 1978.
   LODO
      Kerr, John A.  "Thematic Consistency in a New Manner in José Rodrigues Miguéis' LODO." RF 88:79-83.  No. 1, 1976.

      Kerr, John A., Jr.  "Thematic Consistency in a New Manner in José Rodrigues Miguéis' LODO." LBR 11:231-235.  Winter 1974.
   PASCOA FELIZ
      Sousa, Ronald W.  "The Father-figure Motif in the Worlds of PEDRO PARAMO and PASCOA FELIZ." BHS 54:33-38.  January 1977.
   SAUDADES PARA A DONA GENCIANA
      Kerr, John Austin, Jr.  "Notes on the Significance of SAUDADES PARA A DONA GENCIANA in Miguéis's Prose Fiction." Hispania 63:25-30.  March 1980.

Miró, Gabriel
   DENTRO DEL CERCADO
      Norden, Ernest E.  "Celestial Imagery in Gabriel Miró's DENTRO DEL CERCADO." JSSTC 7:73-86.  Spring 1979.
   NUESTRO PADRE SAN DANIEL
      Brown, G.G.  "The Biblical Allusions in Gabriel Miró's Oleza Novels." MLR 70:786-794.  October 1975.

EL OBISPO LEPROSO
    Brown, G. G. "The Biblical Allusions in Gabriel Miró's Oleza Novels." MLR 70:786-794. October 1975.

    Johnson, Roberta. "Miró's EL OBISPO LEPROSO: Echoes of Pauline Theology in Alicante." Hispania 59: 239-245. May 1976.

Montalvo, Garci
  AMADIS DE GAULA
    O'Connor, John J. AMADIS DE GAULE and Its Influence on Elizabethan Literature. New Brunswick: Rutgers University Press, 1970. 248 pp.

    Pierce, Frank. AMADIS DE GAULA. Boston: Twayne, 1976. 160 pp.

    Place, Edwin B. "Montalvo's Outrageous Recantation." HR 37:192-198. January 1969.

Montemayor, Jorge
  DIANA
    El Saffar, Ruth. "Structural and Thematic Discontinuity in Montemayor's DIANA." MLN 86:182-198. March 1971.

    Hoffmeister, Gerhart. "Courtly Decorum: Kuffstein and the Spanish DIANA." CLS 8:214-223. September 1971.

    Johnson, Carroll B. "Montemayor's DIANA: A Novel Pastoral." BHS 48:20-35. January 1971.

    Jones, Joseph R. "'Human Time' in LA DIANA." RomN 10:139-146. Autumn 1968.

    Keightley, R. G. "Narrative Perspectives in Spanish Pastoral Fiction." AUMLA 44:197-217. November 1975.

    Mujica, Barbara. "Antiutopian Elements in the Spanish Pastoral Novel." KRQ 26:266-271. No. 3, 1979.

    Perry, T. Anthony. "Ideal Love and Human Reality in Montemayor's LA DIANA." PMLA 84:227-234. March 1969.

    Reynolds, John J. "Alanio or Montano: A Note on Montemayor's DIANA." MLN 87:315-317. March 1972.

Oller, Narcís
  LA FEBRE D'OR

Yates, Alan. "The Creation of Narcís Oller's LA
FEBRE D'OR." BHS 52:55-77. January 1975.

Palacio Valdés, Armando
LA NOVELA DE UN NOVELISTA
Jones, R. J. "The Setting of LA NOVELA DE UN
NOVELISTA." CMLR 24:35-46. January 1968.
EL SEÑORITO OCTAVIO
Valis, Noël M. "Palacio Valdés' First Novel." RomN
20:317-321. Spring 1980.

Pardo Bazán, Emilia
ADAM AND EVE
Pattison, Walter T. Emilia Pardo Bazán. New York:
Twayne, 1971. pp. 71-74.
A CHRISTIAN WOMAN
Pattison, Walter T. Emilia Pardo Bazán. New York:
Twayne, 1971. pp. 67-71.
DULCE DUEÑO
Bradford, Carole A. "Alienation and the Dual Personality in the Last Three Novels of Emilia Pardo Bazán."
REH 12:399-417. October 1978.
INSOLACION
DeCoster, Cyrus C. "Pardo Bazán's INSOLACION: A
Naturalistic Novel?" RomN 13:87-91. Autumn 1971.

Giles, Mary E. "Feminism and the Feminine in Emilia
Pardo Bazán's Novels." Hispania 63:356-360. May
1980.

Pattison, Walter T. Emilia Pardo Bazán. New York:
Twayne, 1971. pp. 59-62.

Schmidt, Ruth A. "Woman's Place in the Sun: Feminism in INSOLACION." REH 8:68-81. January 1974.
LA MADRE NATURALEZA
Kirby, Harry L., Jr. "Pardo Bazán's Use of the 'Cantar de los cantares' in LA MADRE NATURALEZA."
Hispania 61:905-911. December 1978.
MEMORIAS DE UN SOLTERON
Bieder, Maryellen. "Capitulation: Marriage, Not Freedom--A Study of Emilia Pardo Bazán's MEMORIAS DE
UN SOLTERON and Galdós' TRISTANA." Symposium
30:93-109. Summer 1976.
PASCUAL LOPEZ
Pattison, Walter T. Emilia Pardo Bazán. New York:
Twayne, 1971. pp. 51-57.
LOS PAZOS DE ULLOA
DeCoster, Cyrus C. "Maupassant's UNE VIE and Pardo
Bazán's LOS PAZOS DE ULLOA." Hispania 56:587-591.
September 1973.

Gerli, E. Michael. "Apropos of Naturalism and Regionalism in LOS PAZOS DE ULLOA." SAB 42:55-60. May 1977.

Lott, Robert E. "Observations on the Narrative Method, the Psychology, and the Style of LOS PAZOS DE ULLOA." Hispania 52:3-11. March 1969.

Pattison, Walter T. Emilia Pardo Bazán. New York: Twayne, 1971. pp. 51-57.

Rodriguez, Alfred and Newell Morgan. "A Calderonian Resonance in LOS PAZOS DE ULLOA." RomN 19:33-37. Fall 1978.

Thompson, Currie Kerr. "The Use and Function of Dreaming in Four Novels by Emilia Pardo Bazán." Hispania 59:856-858. December 1976.

LA QUIMERA
Bradford, Carole A. "Alienation and the Dual Personality in the Last Three Novels of Emilia Pardo Bazán." REH 12:399-417. October 1978.

Pattison, Walter T. Emilia Pardo Bazán. New York: Twayne, 1971. pp. 85-88.

LA SIRENA NEGRA
Bradford, Carole A. "Alienation and the Dual Personality in the Last Three Novels of Emilia Pardo Bazán." REH 12:399-417. October 1978.

———. "The Treatment of Death and Rebirth in LA SIRENA NEGRA." RHM 39:175-182. No. 4, 1976-1977.

Giles, Mary E. "Symbolic Imagery in LA SIRENA NEGRA." PLL 4:182-191. Spring 1968.

Hemingway, M. J. D. "The Religious Content of Pardo Bazán's LA SIRENA NEGRA." BHS 49:369-382. October 1972.

Pereda, José María de
   EL BUEY SUELTO
      Klibbe, Lawrence H. José María de Pereda. Boston: Twayne, 1975. pp. 66-69.
   DE TAL PALO, TAL ASTILLA
      Klibbe, Lawrence H. José María de Pereda. Boston: Twayne, 1975. pp. 75-89.
   DON GONZALO GONZALEZ DE LA GONZALERA
      Klibbe, Lawrence H. José María de Pereda. Boston: Twayne, 1975. pp. 68-76.
   PEDRO SANCHEZ
      Klibbe, Lawrence H. José María de Pereda. Boston: Twayne, 1975. pp. 93-105.
   PENAS ARRIBA

Klibbe, Lawrence H. José María de Pereda. Boston: Twayne, 1975. pp. 130-144.
LA PUCHERA
Klibbe, Lawrence H. José María de Pereda. Boston: Twayne, 1975. pp. 146-149.
EL SABOR DE LA TIERRUCA
Klibbe, Lawrence H. José María de Pereda. Boston: Twayne, 1975. pp. 86-94.
SOTILEZA
Klibbe, Lawrence H. José María de Pereda. Boston: Twayne, 1975. pp. 104-133.

Pérez de Ayala, Ramón
A. M. D. G.
Rand, Marguerite. Ramón Pérez de Ayala. New York: Twayne, 1971. pp. 65-69.
BAJO EL SIGNO DE ARTEMISA
Feeny, Thomas P. "'El Hombre de Acción' as Hero in Pérez de Ayala's BAJO EL SIGNO DE ARTEMISA." REH 9:231-240. May 1975.
BELARMINO Y APOLONIO
Newberry, Wilma. "Ramón Pérez de Ayala's Concept of the 'Doppelgänger' in BELARMINO Y APOLONIO." Symposium 34:56-67. Spring 1980.

Rand, Marguerite. Ramón Pérez de Ayala. New York: Twayne, 1971. pp. 95-108.

Read, M. K. "BELARMINO Y APOLONIO and the Modern Linguistic Tradition." BHS 55:329-335. October 1978.
LA CAIDA DE LOS LIMONES
Rand, Marguerite. Ramón Pérez de Ayala. New York: Twayne, 1971. pp. 87-91.
EL CURANDERO DE SU HONRA
Macklin, J. J. "Myth and Mimesis: The Artistic Integrity of Pérez de Ayala's TIGRE JUAN and EL CURANDERO DE SU HONRA." HR 48:15-36. Winter 1980.

Newberry, Wilma. "Three Examples of the Midsummer Theme in Modern Spanish Literature: GLORIA, LA DAMA DEL ALBA, and EL CURANDERO DE SU HONRA." KRQ 21:248-259. No. 2, 1974.

Rand, Marguerite. Ramón Pérez de Ayala. New York: Twayne, 1971. pp. 118-125.
LUNA DE MIEL, LUNA DE HIEL
Rand, Marguerite. Ramón Pérez de Ayala. New York: Twayne, 1971. pp. 108-112.
LA PATA DE LA RAPOSA
Macklin, J. J. "Literature and Experience: The Problem of Distance in Pérez de Ayala's LA PATA DE LA RAPOSA." BHS 55:129-141. April 1978.

Rand, Marguerite. Ramón Pérez de Ayala. New York: Twayne, 1971. pp. 69-74.
TIGRE JUAN
Cargill, Maruxa Salgués and Julián Palley. "Myth and Anti-Myth in TIGRE JUAN." REH 7:399-416. October 1973.

Macklin, J. J. "Myth and Mimesis: The Artistic Integrity of Pérez de Ayala's TIGRE JUAN and EL CURANDERO DE SU HONRA." HR 48:15-36. Winter 1980.
TINIEBLAS EN LAS CUMBRES
Rand, Marguerite. Ramón Pérez de Ayala. New York: Twayne, 1971. pp. 61-65.
LOS TRABAJOS DE URBANO Y SIMONA
Rand, Marguerite. Ramón Pérez de Ayala. New York: Twayne, 1971. pp. 112-116.

Pérez Galdós, Benito
EL ABUELO
Colin, Vera. "A Note on Tolstoy and Galdós." AGald 2:164-167. 1967.

Pattison, Walter T. Benito Pérez Galdós. Boston: Twayne, 1975. pp. 137-139.
AITA TETTAUEN
Cohen, Sara E. "Christians, Jews, and Moors: Galdós' Search for Values in AITA TETTAUEN and CARLOS VI, EN LA RAPITA." Symposium 29:84-102. Spring/Summer 1975.

Colin, Vera. "Tolstoy and Galdós' Santiuste: Their Ideology on War and Their Spiritual Conversion." Hispania 53:836-841. December 1970.
EL AMIGO MANSO
Engler, Kay. The Structure of Realism: The NOVELAS CONTEMPORANEAS of Benito Pérez Galdós. Chapel Hill: North Carolina Studies in Romance Languages and Literature, 1977. pp. 141-143.

Kronik, John W. "EL AMIGO MANSO and the Game of Fictive Autonomy." AGald 12:71-94. 1977.

Newton, Nancy A. "EL AMIGO MANSO and the Relativity of Reality." REH 7:113-125. January 1973.

Nimetz, Michael. Humor in Galdós: A Study of the NOVELAS CONTEMPORANEAS. New Haven: Yale University Press, 1968. pp. 44-46.

Pattison, Walter T. Benito Pérez Galdós. Boston: Twayne, 1975. pp. 67-69.

Penuel, Arnold M. Charity in the Novels of Galdós. Athens: University of Georgia Press, 1972. pp. 36-39.

_____. "Some Aesthetic Implications of Galdós' EL AMIGO MANSO." AGald 9:145-148. 1974.

Price, R. M. "The Five 'Padrotes' in Pérez Galdós' EL AMIGO MANSO." PQ 48:234-246. April 1969.

ANGEL GUERRA
Colin, Vera. "Tolstoy and ANGEL GUERRA." Galdós Studies. ed. J. E. Varey. London: Tamesis, 1970. pp. 114-135.

Fedorchek, Robert M. "The Ideal of Christian Poverty in Galdós' Novels." RomN 11:76-78. Autumn 1969.

Hafter, Monroe Z. "'Bálsamo contra bálsamo' in ANGEL GUERRA." AGald 4:39-48. 1969.

Lowe, Jennifer. "Structural and Linguistic Presentation in Galdós' ANGEL GUERRA." AGald 10:45-53. 1975.

Pattison, Walter T. Benito Pérez Galdós. Boston: Twayne, 1975. pp. 117-124.

Penuel, Arnold M. Charity in the Novels of Galdós. Athens: University of Georgia Press, 1972. pp. 65-67.

Scanlon, Geraldine M. "Religion and Art in ANGEL GUERRA." AGald 8:99-105. 1973.

Sinnigen, John H. "The Problem of Individual and Social Redemption in ANGEL GUERRA." AGald 12:129-140. 1977.

EL CABALLERO ENCANTADO
Bly, Peter A. "Sex, Egotism and Social Regeneration in Galdós' EL CABALLERO ENCANTADO." Hispania 62:20-29. March 1979.

Hoar, Leo J., Jr. "Benito Pérez Galdós and the Spirit of 1808 at Its Centenary." REH 10:203-216. May 1976.

CARLOS VI, EN LA RAPITA
Cohen, Sara E. "Christians, Jews, and Moors: Galdós' Search for Values in AITA TETTAUEN and CARLOS VI, EN LA RAPITA." Symposium 29:84-102. Spring/Summer 1975.

LOS CIEN MIL HIJOS DE SAN LUIS
Letemendía, Emily. "Galdós and Chateaubriand: LOS CIEN MIL HIJOS DE SAN LUIS." BHS 57:309-318. October 1980.

LA DE BRINGAS
Bly, Peter A. "From Disorder to Order: The Pattern of 'Arreglar' References in Galdós' TORMENTO and LA DE BRINGAS." Neophil 62:396-400. July 1978.

_____. "The Use of Distance in Galdós's LA DE BRINGAS." MLR 69:88-97. January 1974.

Fedorchek, Robert M. "Rosalía and the Rhetoric of Dialogue in Galdós' TORMENTO and LA DE BRINGAS." REH 12:208-216. May 1978.

Lowe, Jennifer. "Galdós' Presentation of Rosalía in LA DE BRINGAS." Hispano 50:49-65. January 1974.

Nimetz, Michael. Humor in Galdós: A Study of the NOVELAS CONTEMPORANEAS. New Haven: Yale University Press, 1968. pp. 80-84.

Pattison, Walter T. Benito Pérez Galdós. Boston: Twayne, 1975. pp. 78-81.

Piper, Anson C. "Lazarillo's 'Arcaz' and Rosalía de Bringas' 'Cajoncillo.'" RHM 39:119-122. No. 3, 1976-1977.

Ramirez, Arthur. "The Heraldic Emblematic Image in Galdós' LA DE BRINGAS." REH 14:65-74. January 1980.

Round, Nicholas G. "Rosalía Bringas' Children." AGald 6:43-49. 1971.

Sánchez, Roberto G. "The Function of Dates and Deadlines in Galdós' LA DE BRINGAS." HR 46:299-311. Summer 1978.

Wright, Chad C. "Imagery of Light and Darkness in LA DE BRINGAS." AGald 13:5-12. 1978.

LA DESHEREDADA

Durand, Frank. "The Reality of Illusion: LA DESHEREDADA." MLN 89:191-201. March 1974.

Engler, Kay. "Linguistic Determination of Point of View: LA DESHEREDADA." AGald 5:67-73. 1970.

Fedorchek, Robert M. "Social Reprehension in LA DESHEREDADA." REH 8:43-59. January 1974.

Gordon, M. "'Lo que le falta a un enfermo le sobra a otro': Galdós' Conception of Humanity in LA DESHEREDADA." AGald 12:29-37. 1977.

_____. "The Medical Background to Galdós' LA DESHEREDADA." AGald 7:67-76. 1972.

Hoddie, James H. "The Genesis of LA DESHEREDADA: Beethoven, the Picaresque and Plato." AGald 14:27-50. 1979.

Krow-Lucal, Martha G. "The Evolution of Encarnación Guillén in LA DESHEREDADA." AGald 12:21-27. 1977.

Labanyi, J.M. "The Political Significance of LA DESHEREDADA." AGald 14:51-58. 1979.

Nimetz, Michael. Humor in Galdós: A Study of the NOVELAS CONTEMPORANEAS. New Haven: Yale University Press, 1968. pp. 111-114.

Pattison, Walter T. Benito Pérez Galdós. Boston: Twayne, 1975. pp. 65-67.

Penuel, Arnold M. Charity in the Novels of Galdós. Athens: University of Georgia Press, 1972. pp. 40-46.

Rodgers, Eamonn. "Galdós' LA DESHEREDADA and Naturalism." BHS 45:285-298. October 1968.

Wright, Chad C. "The Representational Qualities of Isidora Rufete's House and Her Son Riquin in Benito Pérez Galdós' Novel LA DESHEREDADA." RF 83:230-245. No. 2/3, 1971.

EL DOCTOR CENTENO
Pattison, Walter T. Benito Pérez Galdós. Boston: Twayne, 1975. pp. 71-74.

Scanlon, Geraldine M. "EL DOCTOR CENTENO: A Study in Obsolescent Values." BHS 55:245-253. July 1978.

DOÑA PERFECTA
Alfaro, Gustavo A. "Religious Symbolism in Galdós' DOÑA PERFECTA: Pepe Rey's Passion." REH 14:75-82. January 1980.

Cardwell, Richard A. "Galdós' DOÑA PERFECTA: Art or Argument?" AGald 7:29-47. 1972.

Chamberlin, Vernon A. and Jack Weiner. "Galdós' DOÑA PERFECTA and Turgenev's FATHERS AND SONS: Two Interpretations of the Conflict Between Generations." PMLA 86:19-24. January 1971.

Fontanella, Lee. "DOÑA PERFECTA as Historiographic Lesson." AGald 11:59-69. 1976.

Gilman, Stephen. "Novel and Society: DOÑA PERFECTA." AGald 11:15-27. 1976.

Hall, J.B. "Galdós's Use of the Christ-Symbol in DOÑA PERFECTA." AGald 8:95-98. 1973.

Lowe, Jennifer. "Theme, Imagery and Dramatic Irony in DOÑA PERFECTA." AGald 4:49-53. 1969.

Pattison, Walter T. Benito Pérez Galdós. Boston: Twayne, 1975. pp. 53-55.

Penuel, Arnold M. "Narcissism in Galdós' DOÑA PERFECTA." Hispania 62:282-288. May/September 1979.

———. "The Problem of Ambiguity in Galdós' DOÑA PERFECTA." AGald 11:71-88. 1976.

Sánchez, Roberto G. "DOÑA PERFECTA and the Histrionic Projection of Character." REH 3:175-190. November 1969.

Standish, Peter. "Theatricality and Humour: Galdós' Technique in DOÑA PERFECTA." BHS 54:223-231. July 1977.

Tsurinov, K. V. "Benito Pérez Galdós and His Novel DOÑA PERFECTA." AGald 10:64-80. 1975.

Zahareas, Anthony N. "Galdós' DOÑA PERFECTA: Fiction, History and Ideology." AGald 11:29-58. 1976.

EPISODIOS NACIONALES

Glendinning, Nigel. "Psychology and Politics in the First Series of the EPISODIOS NACIONALES." Galdos Studies. ed. J. E. Varey. London: Tamesis, 1970. pp. 36-61.

Lovett, Gabriel H. "Galdós' Alleged Francophobia in the EPISODIOS NACIONALES." REH 13:115-134. January 1979.

Pattison, Walter T. Benito Pérez Galdós. Boston: Twayne, 1975. pp. 46-52.

ESPAÑA TRÁGICA

Dendle, Brian J. "Galdós and the Death of Prim." AGald 4:63-71. 1969.

LA FAMILIA DE LEON ROCH

Pattison, Walter T. Benito Pérez Galdós. Boston: Twayne, 1975. pp. 58-61.

Penuel, Arnold M. Charity in the Novels of Galdós. Athens: University of Georgia Press, 1972. pp. 58-62.

Seybolt, Richard A. "The Function of Imagery in LA FAMILIA DE LEON ROCH." REH 14:79-92. October 1980.

LA FONTANA DE ORO

Flint, Noma and Weston. "More on Galdós' LA FONTANA DE ORO." RomN 17:146-151. Winter 1976.

Pattison, Walter T. Benito Pérez Galdós. Twayne, 1975. pp. 37-40.

Wellington, Marie A. "The Awakening of Galdós' Lázaro." Hispania 55:463-470. September 1972.

Wright, Chad C. "Artifacts and Effigies: The Porreño Household Revisited." AGald 14:13-26. 1979.

Zlotchew, Clark M. "Galdós and Mass Psychology." AGald 12:5-17. 1977.

FORTUNATA Y JACINTA
Blanco-Aguinaga, Carlos. "On 'The Birth of Fortunata.'" AGald 3:13-22. 1968.

Bly, Peter A. "Fortunata and No. 11, Cava de San Miguel." Hispano 59:31-48. 1977.

Boring, Phyllis Zatlin. "The Streets of Madrid as a Structuring Device in FORTUNATA Y JACINTA." AGald 13:13-22. 1978.

Braun, Lucille V. "Galdós' Re-creation of Ernestina Manuel de Villena as Guillermina Pacheco." HR 38:32-55. January 1970.

_____. "The Novelistic Function of Mauricia la Dura in Galdós' FORTUNATA Y JACINTA." Symposium 31:277-289. Winter 1977.

Chamberlin, Vernon A. Galdós and Beethoven: FORTUNATA Y JACINTA, A Symphonic Novel. London: Tamesis, 1977. 119 pp.

Engler, Kay. "Notes on the Narrative Structure of FORTUNATA Y JACINTA." Symposium 24:111-127. Summer 1970.

Gilman, Stephen. "The Consciousness of Fortunata." AGald 5:55-65. 1970.

Gullón, Agnes Moncy. "The Bird Motif and the Introductory Motif: Structure in FORTUNATA Y JACINTA." AGald 9:51-74. 1974.

Hoddie, James H. "FORTUNATA Y JACINTA and the 'Eroica.'" AGald 14:133-139. 1979.

Holmberg, Arthur. "Balzac and Galdós: 'Comment aiment les filles?'" CL 29:109-123. Spring 1977.

Holmberg, Arthur Carl. "Louis Lambert and Maximiliano Rubín: The Inner Vision and the Outer Man." HR 46:119-136. Spring 1978.

Nimetz, Michael. Humor in Galdós: A Study of the

NOVELAS CONTEMPORANEAS. New Haven: Yale University Press, 1968. pp. 186-208.

Pattison, Walter T. Benito Pérez Galdós. Boston: Twayne, 1975. pp. 90-106.

Penuel, Arnold M. Charity in the Novels of Galdós. Athens: University of Georgia Press, 1972. pp. 95-105.

Randolph, E. Dale A. "A Source for Maxi Rubin in FORTUNATA Y JACINTA." Hispania 51:49-55. March 1968.

Ribbans, Geoffrey. "Contemporary History in the Structure and Characterization of FORTUNATA Y JACINTA." Galdos Studies. ed. J. E. Varey. London: Tamesis, 1970. pp. 90-113.

_____. Pérez Galdós: FORTUNATA Y JACINTA. London: Grant & Cutler, 1977. 122 pp.

Rogers, Douglass. "The Descriptive Simile in Galdós and Blasco Ibáñez: A Study in Contrasts." Hispania 53:864-869. December 1970.

Ullman, Joan Connelly and George H. Allison. "Galdós as Psychiatrist in FORTUNATA Y JACINTA." AGald 9:7-36. 1974.

Whiston, James. "Determinism and Freedom in FORTUNATA Y JACINTA." BHS 57:113-127. April 1980.

_____. "Language and Situation in Part I of FORTUNATA Y JACINTA." AGald 7:79-91. 1972.

_____. "The Materialism of Life: Religion in FORTUNATA Y JACINTA." AGald 14:65-80. 1979.

GLORIA

Hoddie, James H. "Some Observations on the Sources of Galdós' GLORIA." REH 14:85-91. January 1980.

Lewis, Thomas E. "Galdós' GLORIA as Ideological 'Dispositio.'" MLN 94:258-282. March 1979.

Newberry, Wilma. "Three Examples of the Midsummer Theme in Modern Spanish Literature: GLORIA, LA DAMA DEL ALBA, and EL CURANDERO DE SU HONRA." KRQ 21:242-244. No. 2, 1974.

Pattison, Walter T. Benito Pérez Galdós. Boston: Twayne, 1975. pp. 55-57.

_____. "The Manuscript of GLORIA." AGald 4:55-61. 1969.

Penuel, Arnold M. Charity in the Novels of Galdós. Athens: University of Georgia Press, 1972. pp. 54-58.

Schyfter, Sara E. "The Judaism of Galdós' Daniel Morton." Hispania 59:24-32. March 1976.

Shoemaker, W. H. "A Note on Galdós' Religion in GLORIA." AGald 11:109-118. 1976.

Zlotchew, Clark M. "Galdós's GLORIA: A New Annunciation." Hispania 62:655-661. December 1979.

HALMA
Minter, G. G. "HALMA and the Writings of St. Augustine." AGald 13:73-97. 1978.

Pattison, Walter T. Benito Pérez Galdós. Boston: Twayne, 1975. pp. 131-134.

Penuel, Arnold M. Charity in the Novels of Galdós. Athens: University of Georgia Press, 1972. pp. 10-14.

Sinnigen, J. "The Search for a New Totality in NAZARIN, HALMA, MISERICORDIA." MLN 93:238-242. March 1978.

Varey, J. E. "Man and Nature in Galdós' HALMA." AGald 13:59-71. 1978.

LA INCOGNITA
Pattison, Walter T. Benito Pérez Galdós. Boston: Twayne, 1975. pp. 111-115.

Penuel, Arnold M. "The Ambiguity of Orozco's Virtue in Galdós' LA INCOGNITA and REALIDAD." Hispania 53:411-418. September 1970.

JUAN MARTIN EL EMPECINADO
Lovett, Gabriel H. "Some Observations on Galdós' JUAN MARTIN EL EMPECINADO." MLN 84:196-207. March 1969.

_____. "Two Views of Guerrilla Warfare: Galdós' JUAN MARTIN EL EMPECINADO and Baroja's EL ESCUADRON DEL BRIGANTE." REH 6:335-344. October 1972.

MARIANELA
Bly, Peter A. "Egotism and Charity in MARIANELA." AGald 7:49-66. 1972.

Dendle, Brian J. "Shipwreck and Discovery: A Study

of Imagery in MARIANELA." NM 74:326-332. No. 2, 1973.

Green, Otis H. "Two Deaths: Don Quijote and Marianela." AGald 2:131-133. 1967.

MIAU

Bretz, Mary Lee. "The Ironic Vision in MIAU." TAH 4:16-19. October 1978.

Miller, Stephen. "Villaamil's Suicide: Action, Character and Motivation in MIAU." AGald 14:83-96. 1979.

Nimetz, Michael. Humor in Galdós: A Study of the NOVELAS CONTEMPORANEAS. New Haven: Yale University Press, 1968. pp. 123-127.

Parker, Alexander A. "Villaamil--Tragic Victim or Comic Failure?" AGald 4:13-23. 1969.

Pattison, Walter T. Benito Pérez Galdós. Boston: Twayne, 1975. pp. 106-110.

Penuel, Arnold M. "Yet Another View of Galdós' MIAU." REH 12:3-14. January 1978.

Ramsden, Herbert. "The Question of Responsibility in Galdós' MIAU." AGald 6:63-77. 1971.

Rodgers, Eamonn. Pérez Galdós: MIAU. London: Grant and Cutler, 1978. 72 pp.

Sackett, Theodore A. "The Meaning of MIAU." AGald 4:25-38. 1969.

Scanlon, Geraldine M. and R.O. Jones. "MIAU: Prelude to a Reassessment." AGald 6:53-61. 1971.

MISERICORDIA

Chamberlin, Vernon A. "The Importance of Rodrigo Soriano's MOROS Y CRISTIANOS in the Creation of MISERICORDIA." AGald 13:105-109. 1978.

Cohen, Sara E. "Almudena and the Jewish Theme in MISERICORDIA." AGald 8:51-61. 1973.

Penuel, Arnold M. Charity in the Novels of Galdós. Athens: University of Georgia Press, 1972. pp. 78-87.

———. "Galdós, Freud, and Humanistic Psychology." Hispania 55:69-74. March 1972.

Russell, Robert H. "The Christ Figure in MISERICORDIA." AGald 2:103-129. 1967. Reprinted in The Christ Figure in the Novels of Perez Galdós. ed. R.

Cardona and A. N. Zahareas. New York: Las Americas, 1967. pp. 51-78.

Sinnigen, J. "The Search for a New Totality in NAZARIN, HALMA, MISERICORDIA." MLN 93:242-251. March 1978.

Varey, J. E. "Charity in MISERICORDIA." Galdós Studies. ed. J. E. Varey. London: Tamesis, 1970. pp. 164-194.

NAZARIN
Colin, Vera. "A Note on Tolstoy and Galdós." AGald 2:157-164. 1967. Reprinted in The Christ Figure in the Novels of Pérez Galdós. ed. R. Cardona and A. N. Zahareas. New York: Las Americas, 1967. pp. 81-88.

Dendle, Brian J. "Point of View in NAZARIN: An Appendix to Goldman." AGald 9:113-121. 1974.

Fedorchek, Robert M. "The Ideal of Christian Poverty in Galdós' Novels." RomN 11:78-81. Autumn 1969.

Goldman, Peter B. "Galdós and the Aesthetic of Ambiguity: Notes on the Thematic Structure of NAZARIN." AGald 9:99-112. 1974.

Nimetz, Michael. Humor in Galdós: A Study of the NOVELAS CONTEMPORANEAS. New Haven: Yale University Press, 1968. pp. 95-97.

Parker, Alexander A. "NAZARIN, or the Passion of Our Lord Jesus Christ According to Galdós." AGald 2: 83-99. 1967. Reprinted in The Christ Figure in the Novels of Perez Galdós. ed. R. Cardona and A. N. Zahareas. New York: Las Americas, 1967. pp. 31-49.

Pattison, Walter T. Benito Pérez Galdós. Boston: Twayne, 1975. pp. 130-132.

Penuel, Arnold M. Charity in the Novels of Galdós. Athens: University of Georgia Press, 1972. pp. 67-70.

Sinnigen, J. "The Search for a New Totality in NAZARIN, HALMA, MISERICORDIA." MLN 93:235-238. March 1978.

Ziolkowski, Theodore. Fictional Transfigurations of Jesus. Princeton: Princeton University Press, 1972. pp. 69-78.

LO PROHIBIDO
Engler, Kay. The Structure of Realism: The NOVELAS

CONTEMPORANEAS of Benito Pérez Galdós. Chapel Hill: University of North Carolina Press, 1977. pp. 160-182.

Munsen, Morris D., Jr. "Galdós' Use of the 'Nabucodonosor' Parallel in LO PROHIBIDO--Punishment or Redemption?" Hispano 57:65-70. 1976.

O'Neil, Mary Anne. "The Hall of Mirrors in Galdós' LO PROHIBIDO." AGald 14:59-64. 1979.

Pattison, Walter T. Benito Pérez Galdós. Boston: Twayne, 1975. pp. 81-87.

Terry, Arthur. "LO PROHIBIDO: Unreliable Narrator and Untruthful Narrative." Galdós Studies. ed. J. E. Varey. London: Tamesis, 1970. pp. 62-89.

REALIDAD

Chorpenning, Joseph F. "Ilusion [sic], Reality and REALIDAD." AGald 12:39-44. 1977.

Pattison, Walter T. Benito Pérez Galdós. Boston: Twayne, 1975. pp. 111-115.

Penuel, Arnold M. "The Ambiguity of Orozco's Virtue in Galdós' LA INCOGNITA and REALIDAD." Hispania 53:411-418. September 1970.

_____. Charity in the Novels of Galdós. Athens: University of Georgia Press, 1972. pp. 71-76.

LA SOMBRA

Pattison, Walter T. Benito Pérez Galdós. Boston: Twayne, 1975. pp. 34-37.

Turner, Harriet S. "Rhetoric in LA SOMBRA: The Author and His Story." AGald 6:5-19. 1971.

TORMENTO

Bly, Peter A. "From Disorder to Order: The Pattern of 'Arreglar' References in Galdós' TORMENTO and LA DE BRINGAS." Neophil 62:392-396. July 1978.

Cluff, David. "The Structure and Meaning of Galdós' TORMENTO." Reflexión 2 3/4:159-167. 1974-1975.

Deutsch, Lou Charnon. "Inhabited Space in Galdós' TORMENTO." AGald 10:35-43. 1975.

Fedorchek, Robert M. "Rosalía and the Rhetoric of Dialogue in Galdós' TORMENTO and LA DE BRINGAS." REH 12:200-208. May 1978.

Nimetz, Michael. Humor in Galdós: A Study of the NOVELAS CONTEMPORANEAS. New Haven: Yale University Press, 1968. pp. 70-72.

Pattison, Walter T. Benito Pérez Galdós. Boston: Twayne, 1975. pp. 74-78.

Rodgers, Eamonn. "The Appearance-Reality Contrast in Galdós' TORMENTO." FMLS 6:382-398. October 1970.
TORQUEMADA
Bly, Peter A. "The Mysterious Disappearance of Torquemada's 'Rosquilla.'" RomN 18:80-87. Fall 1977.

Folley, Terence T. "Some Considerations of the Religious Allusions in Pérez Galdós' TORQUEMADA Novels." AGald 13:41-47. 1978.

Hall, H. B. "Torquemada: The Man and His Language." Galdós Studies. ed. J. E. Varey. London: Tamesis, 1970. pp. 136-163.

Scanlon, Geraldine M. "Torquemada: 'Becerro de oro.'" MLN 91:264-276. March 1976.

Sherzer, Wm. M. "Death and Succession in the TORQUEMADA Series." AGald 13:33-38. 1978.
TORQUEMADA EN LA HOGUERA
Bly, Peter A. "Sallies and Encounters in TORQUEMADA EN LA HOGUERA: Patterns of Significance." AGald 13:23-31. 1978.

Nimetz, Michael. Humor in Galdós: A Study of the NOVELAS CONTEMPORANEAS. New Haven: Yale University Press, 1968. pp. 160-173.

Zeidner Bäuml, B. J. "The Mundane Demon: The Bourgeois Grotesque in Galdós' TORQUEMADA EN LA HOGUERA." Symposium 24:158-165. Summer 1970.
TORQUEMADA Y SAN PEDRO
Weber, Robert J. "Galdós' Preliminary Sketches for TORQUEMADA Y SAN PEDRO." BHS 44:16-27. January 1967.
TRISTANA
Bieder, Maryellen. "Capitulation: Marriage, Not Freedom--A Study of Emilia Pardo-Bazán's MEMORIAS DE UN SOLTERON and Galdós' TRISTANA." Symposium 30: 93-109. Summer 1976.

Engler, Kay. "The Ghostly Lover: The Portrayal of the Animus in TRISTANA." AGald 12:95-108. 1977.

Livingstone, Leon. "The Law of Nature and Women's Liberation in TRISTANA." AGald 7:93-99. 1972.

Nimetz, Michael. Humor in Galdós: A Study of the

NOVELAS CONTEMPORANEAS. New Haven: Yale University Press, 1968. pp. 89-91.

Pattison, Walter T. Benito Pérez Galdós. Boston: Twayne, 1975. pp. 124-126.

Sackett, Theodore A. "Creation and Destruction of Personality in TRISTANA: Galdós and Buñuel." AGald 13:71-88. 1978.

Sánchez, Roberto G. "Galdós' TRISTANA, Anatomy of a 'Disappointment.'" AGald 12:111-125. 1977.

Schmidt, Ruth A. "TRISTANA and the Importance of Opportunity." AGald 9:135-144. 1974.

Sinnigen, John H. "Resistance and Rebellion in TRISTANA." MLN 91:277-291. March 1976.

de Queirós, Eça
    ALVES E CIA
        Brown, Timothy, Jr. "ALVES E CIA as Comedy." KRQ 16:135-141. No. 2, 1969.

        Fedorchek, Robert M. "Presentation of Prontagonist [sic] in ALVES & Cª." KRQ 25:109-116. No. 1, 1978.
    THE CITY AND THE MOUNTAINS
        Coleman, Alexander. Eça de Queirós and European Realism. New York: New York University Press, 1980. pp. 268-282.

        de Costa, René. "The Mythic Quest Theme in A CIDADE E AS SERRAS." LBR 5:71-79. Winter 1968.

        Reising, Robert W. "Huysman's [sic] AGAINST NATURE and Eça de Queroz's [sic] THE CITY AND THE MOUNTAINS: A Comparative Study." LangQ 9:37-40. Fall/Winter 1970.
    COUSIN BAZILIO
        Coleman, Alexander. Eça de Queirós and European Realism. New York: New York University Press, 1980. pp. 113-131.
    O CRIME DO PADRE AMARO
        Coleman, Alexander. Eça de Queirós and European Realism. New York: New York University Press, 1980. pp. 82-113; 132-143.

        Fedorchek, Robert M. "On Character Portrayal in O CRIME DO PADRE AMARO." Hispania 59:34-40. March 1976.

        Freeland, Alan. "Degrees of Determinism: The Three Versions of O CRIME DO PADRE AMARO." BHS 57: 321-337. October 1980.

de Queirós, Eça 245

    Whitmore, Don. "Music in O CRIME DO PADRE AMARO." LBR 10:247-255. Winter 1973.
A ILUSTRE CASA DE RAMIRES
    Brown, Timothy, Jr. "The Individual and Society: An Interpretation of A ILUSTRE CASA DE RAMIRES." REH 8:381-392. October 1974.

    _____. "The Love Triangle in A ILUSTRE CASA DE RAMIRES." RomN 12:312-317. Spring 1971.

    Coleman, Alexander. Eça de Queirós and European Realism. New York: New York University Press, 1980. pp. 257-268.
THE MANDARIN
    Coleman, Alexander. Eça de Queirós and European Realism. New York: New York University Press, 1980. pp. 151-162.
O PRIMO BASILIO
    Fedorchek, Robert M. "Luísa's Dream Worlds in O PRIMO BASILIO." RomN 15:532-535. Spring 1974.
THE RELIC
    Coleman, Alexander. Eça de Queirós and European Realism. New York: New York University Press, 1980. pp. 162-181.

Quevedo, Francisco de
EL BUSCON
    Bagby, Albert I., Jr. "The Conventional Golden Age 'Pícaro' and Quevedo's Criminal 'Picaro.'" KRQ 14:311-319. No. 4, 1967.

    Bjornson, Richard. "Moral Blindness in Quevedo's EL BUSCON." RR 67:50-59. January 1976.

    _____. The Picaresque Hero in European Fiction. Madison: University of Wisconsin Press, 1977. pp. 106-126.

    Bleznick, Donald. Quevedo. New York: Twayne, 1972. pp. 79-92.

    Boyce, Elizabeth S. "Evidence of Moral Values Implicit in Quevedo's BUSCON." FMLS 12:336-353. October 1976.

    Chorpenning, Joseph F. "Classical Satire and LA VIDA DEL BUSCON." Neophil 61:212-219. April 1977.

    Clamurro, William H. "The Destabilized Sign: Word and Form in Quevedo's BUSCON." MLN 95:295-311. March 1980.

    Dunn, Peter N. The Spanish Picaresque Novel. Boston: Twayne, 1979. pp. 64-75.

Hesse, Everett W. "The Protean Changes in Quevedo's BUSCON." KRQ 16:243-259. No. 3, 1969.

May, T. E. "A Narrative Conceit in LA VIDA DEL BUSCON." MLR 64:327-333. April 1969.

Neumann, Dwight K. "Excremental Fantasies and Shame in Quevedo's BUSCON." L&P 28:186-191. No. 3/4, 1978.

Price, R. M. "On Religious Parody in the BUSCON." MLN 86:273-279. March 1971.

Sieber, Harry. "Apostrophes in the BUSCON: An Approach to Quevedo's Narrative Technique." MLN 83: 178-211. March 1968.

Williamson, Edwin. "The Conflict Between Author and Protagonist in Quevedo's BUSCON." JHP 2:45-60. Autumn 1977.

LA HORA DE TODOS
 Kent, Conrad. "Politics in LA HORA DE TODOS." JHP 1:99-119. Winter 1977.

 Price, R. M. "Fiction and False Testimony in LA HORA DE TODOS." RR 66:113-122. March 1975.

Quiroga, Elena
 BLOOD
  Boring, Phyllis Zatlin. Elena Quiroga. Boston: Twayne, 1977. pp. 39-45.
 BUS ONE
  Boring, Phyllis Zatlin. Elena Quiroga. Boston: Twayne, 1977. pp. 46-50.
 I WRITE YOUR NAME
  Boring, Phyllis Zatlin. Elena Quiroga. Boston: Twayne, 1977. pp. 96-104.
 THE MASK
  Boring, Phyllis Zatlin. Elena Quiroga. Boston: Twayne, 1977. pp. 73-87.
 NORTHWIND
  Boring, Phyllis Zatlin. Elena Quiroga. Boston: Twayne, 1977. pp. 32-39.
 THE OTHER CITY
  Boring, Phyllis Zatlin. Elena Quiroga. Boston: Twayne, 1977. pp. 50-53.
 PROFOUND PRESENT
  Boring, Phyllis Zatlin. Elena Quiroga. Boston: Twayne, 1977. pp. 106-115.
 SADNESS
  Boring, Phyllis Zatlin. Elena Quiroga. Boston: Twayne, 1977. pp. 89-95.
 THE SICK WOMAN

Quiroga, Elena

 Boring, Phyllis Zatlin. Elena Quiroga. Boston:
 Twayne, 1977. pp. 64-73.
 SOMETHING'S HAPPENING IN THE STREET
  Boring, Phyllis Zatlin. Elena Quiroga. Boston:
  Twayne, 1977. pp. 57-64.
 SONOROUS SOLITUDE
  Boring, Phyllis Zatlin. Elena Quiroga. Boston:
  Twayne, 1977. pp. 27-31.
 THE YOUNG PLACIDA
  Boring, Phyllis Zatlin. Elena Quiroga. Boston:
  Twayne, 1977. pp. 53-56.

Rodríguez del Padrón, Juan
 SIERVO LIBRE DE AMOR
  Andrachuk, Gregory Peter. "On the Missing Third Part of SIERVO LIBRE DE AMOR." HR 45:171-180. Spring 1977.

  Dudley, Edward. "Court and Country: The Fusion of Two Images of Love in Juan Rodríguez's EL SIERVO LIBRE DE AMOR." PMLA 82:117-120. March 1967.

Romero, Luis
 THE CURRENT
  Gonzalez-del-Valle, Luis. Luis Romero. Boston:
  Twayne, 1979. pp. 63-69.
 LETTER FROM THE PAST
  Gonzalez-del-Valle, Luis. Luis Romero. Boston:
  Twayne, 1979. pp. 43-48.
 THE OLD VOICES
  Gonzalez-del-Valle, Luis. Luis Romero. Boston:
  Twayne, 1979. pp. 49-55.
 THE OTHERS
  Gonzalez-del-Valle, Luis. Luis Romero. Boston:
  Twayne, 1979. pp. 57-63.
 THE TREADMILL
  Gonzalez-del-Valle, Luis. Luis Romero. Boston:
  Twayne, 1979. pp. 26-42; 116-122.

de Salas Barbadillo, Alonso
 THE CORRECTION OF VICES
  Peyton, Myron A. Alonso Jeronimo de Salas Barbadillo.
  New York: Twayne, 1973. pp. 80-89.
 THE CURIOUS AND WISE ALEXANDER
  Peyton, Myron A. Alonso Jeronimo de Salas Barbadillo.
  New York: Twayne, 1973. pp. 117-122.
 THE DAUGHTER OF CELESTINA
  Peyton, Myron A. Alonso Jeronimo de Salas Barbadillo.
  New York: Twayne, 1973. pp. 55-60.
 THE DISCOURTEOUS COURTIER
  Peyton, Myron A. Alonso Jeronimo de Salas Barbadillo.
  New York: Twayne, 1973. pp. 127-131.
 DON DIEGO, NOCTURNAL ADVENTURER

Peyton, Myron A. Alonso Jeronimo de Salas Barbadillo.
New York: Twayne, 1973. pp. 99-115.
FLORA, CLEVER AND TOO CLEVER
Peyton, Myron A. Alonso Jeronimo de Salas Barbadillo.
New York: Twayne, 1973. pp. 131-135.
THE FORTUNATE FOOL
Peyton, Myron A. Alonso Jeronimo de Salas Barbadillo.
New York: Twayne, 1973. pp. 73-79.
THE HOUSE OF VIRTUOUS PLEASURE
Peyton, Myron A. Alonso Jeronimo de Salas Barbadillo.
New York: Twayne, 1973. pp. 89-99.
THE POST OFFICE OF THE GOD MOMUS
Peyton, Myron A. Alonso Jeronimo de Salas Barbadillo.
New York: Twayne, 1973. pp. 115-117.
THE PROPER GENTLEMAN
Peyton, Myron A. Alonso Jeronimo de Salas Barbadillo.
New York: Twayne, 1973. pp. 60-73.

San Pedro, Diego de
ARNALTE AND LUCENDA
Whinnom, Keith. Diego de San Pedro. New York:
Twayne, 1974. pp. 62-87.
CARCEL DE AMOR
Chorpenning, Joseph F. "Rhetoric and Feminism in the
CARCEL DE AMOR." BHS 54:1-8. January 1977.

Severin, Dorothy Sherman. "Structure and Thematic
Repetitions in Diego de San Pedro's CARCEL DE AMOR
and ARNALTE Y LUCENDA." HR 45:165-169. Spring
1977.

Waley, Pamela. "CARCEL DE AMOR and GRISEL Y
MIRABELLA: A Question of Priority." BHS 50:340-
356. October 1973.

Sánchez Ferlosio, Rafael
ALFANHUI
Reynolds, Harold. "Archetypal Perception in Rafael
Sánchez Ferlosio's ALFANHUI." BHS 53:215-224.
July 1976.

Sender, Ramón
LAS CRIATURAS SATURNIANAS
King, Charles L. Ramón J. Sender. New York:
Twayne, 1974. pp. 145-147.
CRONICA DEL ALBA
Jones, Margaret E.W. "Saints, Heroes, and Poets:
Social and Archetypal Considerations in CRONICA DEL
ALBA." HR 45:385-396. Autumn 1977.

King, Charles L. Ramón J. Sender. New York:
Twayne, 1974. pp. 133-135.
EPITALAMIO DEL PRIETO TRINIDAD

Jones, Margaret E.W. "'A Positive Geometry': Structural Patterns and Symbols in Sender's EPITALAMIO DEL PRIETO TRINIDAD." Symposium 29:117-130. Spring/Summer 1975.

King, Charles L. Ramón J. Sender. New York: Twayne, 1974. pp. 123-126.

### EL FUGITIVO

O'Brien, Mary Eide. "Fantasy in EL FUGITIVO." JSSTC 2:95-107. Fall 1974.

### IMAN

King, Charles L. Ramón J. Sender. New York: Twayne, 1974. pp. 45-52.

Olstad, Charles. "Sender's IMAN and Remarque's ALL QUIET ON THE WESTERN FRONT." REH 11:133-140. January 1977.

### LOS LAURELES DE ANSELMO

Richards, Donnie D. "Sender's LOS LAURELES DE ANSELMO: A Dialectical Confrontation." SAB 44:41-51. January 1979.

### EL LUGAR DE UN HOMBRE

King, Charles L. Ramón J. Sender. New York: Twayne, 1974. pp. 68-71.

### MOSEN MILLAN

Busette, Cedric. "Religious Symbolism in Sender's MOSEN MILLAN." RomN 11:482-486. Spring 1970.

### MR. WITT AMONG THE REBELS

King, Charles L. Ramón J. Sender. New York: Twayne, 1974. pp. 59-62.

### REQUIEM POR UN CAMPESINO ESPAÑOL

Bly, Peter A. "A Confused Reality and Its Presentation: Ramón Sender's REQUIEM POR UN CAMPESINO ESPAÑOL." IFR 5:96-102. July 1978.

Henn, David. "The Priest in Sender's REQUIEM POR UN CAMPESINO ESPAÑOL." IFR 1:106-111. July 1974.

### EL REY Y LA REINA

King, Charles L. Ramón J. Sender. New York: Twayne, 1974. pp. 107-122.

_____. "Surrealism in Two Novels by Sender." Hispania 51:244-250. May 1968.

### THE SPHERE

King, Charles L. Ramón J. Sender. New York: Twayne, 1974. pp. 81-106.

_____. "Surrealism in Two Novels by Sender." Hispania 51:244-250. May 1968.

Palley, Julian. "THE SPHERE Revisited." Symposium 25:171-179. Summer 1971.

Unamuno, Miguel de
ABEL SANCHEZ
  Dobson, A. "Unamuno's ABEL SANCHEZ: An Interpretation." ML 54:62-67. June 1973.

  Foster, David William. Unamuno and the Novel as Expressionistic Conceit. Hato Rey, Puerto Rico: Inter American University Press, 1973. pp. 34-43.

  Horowitz, Renee B. "Cain and Abel as Existentialist Symbols for Unamuno and Hesse." PLL 16:174-183. Spring 1980.

  Jiménez-Fajardo, Salvador. "Unamuno's ABEL SANCHEZ: Envy as a Work of Art." JSSTC 4:89-103. Fall 1976.

  Lee, Dorothy H. "Joaquín Monegro in Unamuno's ABEL SANCHEZ Thrice Exile--Cain/Esau/Satan." JSSTC 7:63-70. Spring 1979.

  Nozick, Martin. Miguel de Unamuno. New York: Twayne, 1971. pp. 150-152.

  Palley, Julián. "Unamuno: The Critique of Progress." REH 10:250-254. May 1976.

  Richards, Katharine C. "Unamuno and 'The Other.'" KRQ 23:442-448. No. 4, 1976.

  Round, Nicholas G. Unamuno: ABEL SANCHEZ. London: Grant & Cutler, 1974. 97 pp.

  Slade, Carole. "Unamuno's ABEL SANCHEZ: 'l'ombre dolenti nelle ghiaccia' (Inf. XXXII, 35)." Symposium 28:356-365. Winter 1974.

  Turner, David G. Unamuno's Webs of Fatality. London: Tamesis Books, 1974. pp. 63-77.
LA AGONIA DEL CRISTIANISMO
  Mermall, Thomas. "Unamuno and Dostoevsky's Grand Inquisitor." Hispania 61:851-858. December 1978.
AMOR Y PEDAGOGIA
  Franz, Thomas R. "Ancient Rites and the Structure of Unamuno's AMOR Y PEDAGOGIA." RomN 13:217-220. Winter 1971.

  _____. "Parenthood, Authorship, and Immortality in Unamuno's Narratives." Hispania 63:647-657. December 1980.

  _____. "The Philosophical Bases of Fulgencio Entrambosmares in Unamuno's AMOR Y PEDAGOGIA." Hispania 60:443-451. September 1977.

Unamuno, Miguel de

    Olson, Paul R. "The Novelistic Logos in Unamuno's AMOR Y PEDAGOGIA. " MLN 84:248-268. March 1969.

    Palley, Julián. "Unamuno: The Critique of Progress. " REH 10:244-246. May 1976.
COMO SE HACE UNA NOVELA
    Olson, Paul R. "Unamuno's Lacquered Boxes: COMO SE HACE UNA NOVELA and the Ontology of Writing. " RHM 36:186-199. No. 4, 1970-1971.

    Turner, David G. Unamuno's Webs of Fatality. London: Tamesis Books, 1974. pp. 107-121.
NADA MENOS QUE TODO UN HOMBRE
    Abrams, Fred. "Alejandro's Carbajedo Estate in Unamuno's NADA MENOS QUE TODO UN HOMBRE. " REH 10:405-407. October 1976.

    Durand, Frank. "Search for Reality in NADA MENOS QUE TODO UN HOMBRE. " MLN 84:239-247. March 1969.

    Johnson, Carroll B. "Unamuno and His Spanish Past: NADA MENOS QUE TODO UN HOMBRE. " KRQ 15:319-340. No. 4, 1968.

    Palley, Julián. "Unamuno: The Critique of Progress. " REH 10:254-256. May 1976.
NIEBLA
    Abrams, Fred. "Unamuno's Menéndez Pelayo Cryptogram in NIEBLA. " PLL 11:203-205. Spring 1975.

    Batchelor, R. "Form and Content in Unamuno's NIEBLA. " FMLS 8:197-214. July 1972.

    Berns, Gabriel. "Another Look Through Unamuno's NIEBLA: Augusto Pérez, 'Agonista-Lector.'" RomN 11:26-29. Autumn 1969.

    Diaz, Nancy Gray. "Imagery and the Theme of Perception: L'EDUCATION SENTIMENTALE and NIEBLA. " CLS 17:429-437. December 1980.

    Foster, David William. Unamuno and the Novel as Expressionistic Conceit. Hato Rey, Puerto Rico: Inter American University Press, 1973. pp. 18-34.

    Franz, Thomas R. "Menéndez Pelayo as Antolín S. Paparrigópulos of Unamuno's NIEBLA. " PLL 9:84-88. Winter 1973.

    Gunn, James Dayton. "The Creation of the Self: The Influence of Don Quixote on Unamuno's NIEBLA. " RomN 21:54-57. Fall 1980.

Livingstone, Leon. "The Novel as Self-Creation." Unamuno: Creator and Creation. ed. José Rubia Barcia and M.A. Zeitlin. Berkeley: University of California Press, 1967. pp. 92-113.

Olson, Paul R. "Unamuno's NIEBLA: The Question of the Novel." GaR 29:652-672. Fall 1975.

Palley, Julián. "Unamuno: The Critique of Progress." REH 10:246-249. May 1976.

Parker, Alexander A. "On the Interpretation of NIEBLA." Unamuno: Creator and Creation. ed. José Rubia Barcia and M.A. Zeitlin. Berkeley: University of California Press, 1967. pp. 116-138.

Turner, David G. Unamuno's Webs of Fatality. London: Tamesis Books, 1974. pp. 44-62.

Weber, Frances W. "Unamuno's NIEBLA: From Novel to Dream." PMLA 88:209-218. March 1973.

LA NOVELA DE DON SANDALIO, JUGADOR DE AJEDREZ

Nozick, Martin. Miguel de Unamuno. New York: Twayne, 1971. pp. 159-170.

Shaw, D.L. "Concerning Unamuno's LA NOVELA DE DON SANDALIO, JUGADOR DE AJEDREZ." BHS 54:115-123. April 1977.

Stevens, James R. "Unamuno's DON SANDALIO: Two Opposed Concepts of Fiction." RomN 11:266-271. Winter 1969.

Turner, David G. Unamuno's Webs of Fatality. London: Tamesis Books, 1974. pp. 129-137.

PAZ EN LA GUERRA

Palley, Julián. "Unamuno: The Critique of Progress." REH 10:242-244. May 1976.

Turner, David G. Unamuno's Webs of Fatality. London: Tamesis Books, 1974. pp. 9-26.

SAN MANUEL BUENO, MARTIR

Anderson, Reed. "The Narrative Voice in Unamuno's SAN MANUEL BUENO, MARTIR." Hispano 50:67-76. 1974.

Carey, Douglas M. and Phillip G. Williams. "Religious Confession as Perspective and Mediation in Unamuno's SAN MANUEL BUENO, MARTIR." MLN 91:292-310. March 1976.

Crone, Anna Lisa. "Unamuno and Dostoevsky: Some Thoughts on Atheistic Humanitarianism." Hispano 64:43-59. 1978.

Unamuno, Miguel de

Lathrop, Thomas A. "Greek Origin Names in SAN MANUEL BUENO, MARTIR." RomN 11:505-506. Spring 1970.

Mermall, Thomas. "Unamuno and Dostoevsky's Grand Inquisitor." Hispania 61:851-858. December 1978.

Molina, Ida. "Truth Versus Myth in EN LA ARDIENTE OSCURIDAD and in SAN MANUEL BUENO [,] MARTIR." Hispano 52:45-49. 1974.

Natella, Arthur A., Jr. "Saint Theresa and Unamuno's SAN MANUEL BUENO, MARTIR." PLL 5:458-464. Fall 1969.

Palley, Julián. "Unamuno: The Critique of Progress." REH 10:256-260. May 1976.

Predmore, Susan. "SAN MANUEL BUENO, MARTIR: A Jungian Perspective." Hispano 64:15-28. 1978.

Stohl, Johan H. "Unamuno and the 'Imitatio Christi.'" MichA 6:263-272. Winter 1974.

Turner, David G. Unamuno's Webs of Fatality. London: Tamesis Books, 1974. pp. 122-128.

Valdés, Mario J. "Archetype and Re-creation: A Comparative Study of William Blake and Miguel de Unamuno." UTQ 40:62-69. Fall 1970.

Wyers, Frances. Miguel de Unamuno: The Contrary Self. London: Tamesis, 1976. pp. 104-116.

LA TIA TULA
Kaatz, Gerda R. "The Theme of Motherhood in YERMA and LA TIA TULA." LangQ 15:15-18. Spring/Summer 1977.

Nozick, Martin. Miguel de Unamuno. New York: Twayne, 1971. pp. 154-157.

Turner, David G. Unamuno's Webs of Fatality. London: Tamesis Books, 1974. pp. 92-106.

Valera, Juan
COMMANDER MENDOZA
De Coster, Cyrus. Juan Valera. New York: Twayne, 1974. pp. 113-119.
DON BRAULIO
De Coster, Cyrus. Juan Valera. New York: Twayne, 1974. pp. 120-124.
DOÑA LUZ
Bacigalupo, Mario Ford. "Discretion in Valera's DOÑA LUZ." KRQ 26:293-303. No. 3, 1979.

De Coster, Cyrus. Juan Valera. New York: Twayne, 1974. pp. 125-131.
FORMIDABLE JUANITA
De Coster, Cyrus. Juan Valera. New York: Twayne, 1974. pp. 132-140.

Marcus, Roxanne B. "An Application of Jungian Theory to the Interpretation of Doña Inés in Valera's JUANITA LA LARGA." RCEH 3:259-274. Spring 1979.
THE ILLUSIONS OF DOCTOR FAUSTINO
De Coster, Cyrus. Juan Valera. New York: Twayne, 1974. pp. 104-112.
MORSAMOR
De Coster, Cyrus. Juan Valera. New York: Twayne, 1974. pp. 150-156.
PEPITA JIMENEZ
De Coster, Cyrus. Juan Valera. New York: Twayne, 1974. pp. 95-103.

Knowlton, John F. "The Hippolytus Myth in PEPITA JIMENEZ." RomN 11:73-75. Autumn 1969.

Lott, Robert E. Language and Psychology in PEPITA JIMENEZ. Urbana: University of Illinois Press, 1970. 270 pp.

Madland, Helga Stipa. "Time in PEPITA JIMENEZ." RomN 21:169-173. Winter 1980.
RAFAELA
De Coster, Cyrus. Juan Valera. New York: Twayne, 1974. pp. 141-147.

Valle-Inclán, Ramón del
BAZA DE ESPADAS
Sinclair, Alison. "Nineteenth-Century Popular Literature as a Source of Linguistic Enrichment in Valle-Inclán's RUEDO IBERICO." MLR 70:84-96. January 1975.

Smith, Verity. Ramón del Valle-Inclán. New York: Twayne, 1973. pp. 140-145.
LA CARA DE DIOS
García-Sabell, Domingo. "LA CARA DE DIOS." Ramón del Valle-Inclán: An Appraisal of His Life and Works. ed. Anthony N. Zahareas. New York: Las Americas, 1968. pp. 813-818.
LA CORTE DE LOS MILAGROS
Sinclair, Alison. "Nineteenth-Century Popular Literature as a Source of Linguistic Enrichment in Valle-Inclán's RUEDO IBERICO." MLR 70:84-96. January 1975.

Smith, Verity. Ramón del Valle-Inclán. New York: Twayne, 1973. pp. 136-138.

JARDIN UMBRIO
    Rehder, Ernest C. "Concentric Patterns in Valle-Inclan's JARDIN UMBRIO." RomN 18:62-65. Fall 1977.
LUCES DE BOHEMIA
    Weber, Frances Wyers. "LUCES DE BOHEMIA and the Impossibility of Art." MLN 82:575-589. December 1967.
ROSARITO
    Gillespie, Gerald and A. N. Zahareas. "ROSARITO and the Novella Tradition." Ramón del Valle-Inclán: An Appraisal of His Life and Works. ed. Anthony N. Zahareas. New York: Las Americas, 1968. pp. 281-287.
RUEDO IBERICO
    Boudreau, Harold L. "Banditry and Valle-Inclán's RUEDO IBERICO." HR 35:85-92. January 1967.

    _____. "The Circular Structure of Valle-Inclán's RUEDO IBERICO." PMLA 82:128-135. March 1967.

    _____. "Continuity in the RUEDO IBERICO." Ramón del Valle-Inclán: An Appraisal of His Life and Works. ed. Anthony N. Zahareas. New York: Las Americas, 1968. pp. 777-790.

    _____. "The Metamorphosis of the RUEDO IBERICO." Ramón del Valle-Inclán: An Appraisal of His Life and Works. ed. Anthony N. Zahareas. New York: Las Americas, 1968. pp. 758-774.

    _____. "The Moral Comment of the RUEDO IBERICO." Ramón del Valle-Inclán: An Appraisal of His Life and Works. ed. Anthony N. Zahareas. New York: Las Americas, 1968. pp. 792-802.

    Sinclair, Alison. "The First Fragment of EL RUEDO IBERICO?" BHS 49:165-174. April 1972.

    _____. Valle-Inclán's RUEDO IBERICO: A Popular View of Revolution. London: Tamesis, 1977. 121 pp.
SONATA DE PRIMAVERA
    Greenfield, Sumner M. "Bradomín and the Ironies of Evil: A Reconsideration of SONATA DE PRIMAVERA." StTCL 2:23-32. Fall 1977.
TIRANO BANDERAS
    Dougherty, Dru. "The Question of Revolution in TIRANO BANDERAS." BHS 53:207-213. July 1976.

    Smith, Verity. Ramón del Valle-Inclán. New York: Twayne, 1973. pp. 127-134.
VIVA MI DUEÑO
    Sinclair, Alison. "Nineteenth-Century Popular Literature as a Source of Linguistic Enrichment in Valle-

Inclán's RUEDO IBERICO." MLR 70:84-96. January 1975.

Smith, Verity. Ramón del Valle-Inclán. New York: Twayne, 1973. pp. 138-140.

Vélez de Guevara, Luis
EL DIABLO COJUELO
Bjornson, Richard. "Thematic Structure in EL DIABLO COJUELO." Hispano 60:13-19. 1977.

Ventura Agudiez, Juan
LAS TARDES DE THEREZE LAMARCK
Clarke, Dorothy Clotelle. "An Hispanic Variation on a French Theme: Mme. de Staël, Butor, Agudiez." Symposium 22:208-214. Fall 1968.

LA VIDA Y HECHOS DE ESTEBANILLO GONZALEZ
Bjornson, Richard. The Picaresque Hero in European Fiction. Madison: University of Wisconsin Press, 1977. pp. 132-137.

Spadaccini, Nicholas. "ESTEBANILLO GONZALEZ and the Nature of Picaresque 'Lives.'" CL 30:209-222. Summer 1978.

_____. "History and Fiction: The Thirty Years' War in ESTEBANILLO GONZALEZ." KRQ 24:373-387. No. 4, 1977.

de Zayas, María
EL CASTIGO DE LA MISERIA
Foa, Sandra M. "Humor and Suicide in Zayas and Cervantes." ACer 16:71-83. 1977.

Zunzunegui, Juan Antonio de
ESTA OSCURA DESBANDADA
Fulk, Randal C. "The False Rhetoric of Juan Antonio de Zunzunegui's ESTA OSCURA DESBANDADA." REH 13:323-337. October 1979.

THE ITALIAN NOVEL

Aleramo, Sibilla
A WOMAN AT BAY
  Pacifici, Sergio. The Modern Italian Novel from Capu-
    ana to Tozzi. Carbondale: Southern Illinois University
    Press, 1973. pp. 63-67.

Alvaro, Corrado
  GENTE IN ASPROMONTE
    Pacifici, Sergio. The Modern Italian Novel from Pea to
      Moravia. Carbondale: Southern Illinois University
      Press, 1979. pp. 50-56.
  L'UOMO NEL LABIRINTO
    Terrizzi, Anthony R. "Another Look at Corrado Alvaro's
      L'UOMO NEL LABIRINTO." FI 7:23-29. March 1973.

d'Annunzio, Gabriele
  THE CHILD OF PLEASURE
    *Gullace, Giovanni. Gabriele D'Annunzio in France: A
      Study in Cultural Relations. Syracuse: Syracuse Univer-
      sity Press, 1966. pp. 11-15.

    Pacifici, Sergio. The Modern Italian Novel from Capuana
      to Tozzi. Carbondale: Southern Illinois University
      Press, 1973. pp. 39-44.
  FORSE CHE SI FORSE CHE NO
    *Gullace, Giovanni. Gabriele D'Annunzio in France: A
      Study in Cultural Relations. Syracuse: Syracuse Univer-
      sity Press, 1966. pp. 36-40.
  IL FUOCO
    *Gullace, Giovanni. Gabriele D'Annunzio in France: A
      Study in Cultural Relations. Syracuse: Syracuse Univer-
      sity Press, 1966. pp. 31-36.

    Lucente, Gregory L. "D'Annunzio's IL FUOCO and
      Joyce's PORTRAIT OF THE ARTIST: From Allegory to
      Irony." Italica 57:19-33. Spring 1980.
  L'INTRUS
    *Gullace, Giovanni. Gabriele D'Annunzio in France: A
      Study in Cultural Relations. Syracuse: Syracuse Univer-
      sity Press, 1966. pp. 1-8.
  LE VERGINI DELLE ROCCE

*Gullace, Giovanni. Gabriele D'Annunzio in France: A Study in Cultural Relations. Syracuse: Syracuse University Press, 1966. pp. 25-30.

Bassani, Giorgio
THE GARDEN OF THE FINZI-CONTINIS
Eskin, Stanley G. "THE GARDEN OF THE FINZI-CONTINIS." LFQ 1:171-175. Spring 1973.

Radcliff-Umstead, Douglas. "Transformation in Bassani's Garden." MFS 21:521-533. Winter 1975-1976.

Schneider, Marilyn. "Mythical Dimensions of Micòl Finzi-Contini." Italica 51:43-67. Spring 1974.

Bernari, Carlo
UN FORO NEL PARABREZZA
Capozzi, Rocco. "The Narrator-Protagonist and the Creative Process in Carlo Bernari's UN FORO NEL PARABREZZA." RomN 17:230-235. Spring 1977.
LE RADIOSE GIORNATE
Capozzi, Rocco. "Time and Aesthetic Distance in Carlo Bernari's LE RADIOSE GIORNATE." IFR 2:153-156. July 1975.

Boccaccio, Giovanni
ANDREUCCIO DA PERUGIA
Lucente, Greg. "The Fortunate Fall of Andreuccio da Perugia." FI 10:323-344. December 1976.
CORBACCIO
Barricelli, Gian Piero. "Satire of Satire: Boccaccio's CORBACCIO." IQ 18:95-111. Spring 1975.

Cassell, Anthony K. "IL CORBACCIO and the Secundus Tradition." CL 25:352-360. Fall 1973.

Hollander, Robert. Boccaccio's Two Venuses. New York: Columbia University Press, 1977. pp. 20-30; 139-148.
DECAMERON
Allen, Shirley S. "The Griselda Tale and the Portrayal of Women in the DECAMERON." PQ 56:1-13. Winter 1977.

Almansi, Guido. The Writer as Liar: Narrative Technique in the DECAMERON. London: Routledge & Kegan Paul, 1975. 112 pp.

Auerbach, Erich. "Frate Alberto." Critical Perspectives on the DECAMERON. ed. Robert S. Dombrowski. London: Hodder and Stroughton, 1976. pp. 69-81.

Bonadeo, A. "Some Aspects of Love and Nobility in the

Society of the DECAMERON." PQ 47:513-525. October 1968.

Branca, Vittore. Boccaccio: The Man and His Works. New York: New York University Press, 1976. pp. 197-331.

―――――. "The Epic of the Italian Merchant." Critical Perspectives on the DECAMERON. ed. Robert S. Dombrowski. London: Hodder and Stroughton, 1976. pp. 38-47.

Brown, Marshall. "In the Valley of the Ladies." IQ 18:33-52. Spring 1975.

Brown, Peter. "Aims and Methods of the Second 'Rassettatura' of the DECAMERON." SSe 8:3-40. 1967.

Clark, Susan L. "DECAMERON 2.4: The Journey of the Hero." Mediaevalia 1:1-16. Fall 1975.

Cole, Howard C. "Dramatic Interplay in the DECAMERON: Boccaccio, Neifile and Giletta di Nerbona." MLN 90:38-57. January 1975.

Cottino-Jones, Marga. An Anatomy of Boccaccio's Style. Napoli: Cymba, 1968. pp. 9-96; 121-147.

―――――. "Magic and Superstition in Boccaccio's DECAMERON." IQ 18:5-32. Spring 1975.

―――――. "The Mode and Structure of Tragedy in Boccaccio's DECAMERON (LV, 9)." IQ 11:63-88. Winter 1967.

―――――. "Observations on the Structure of the DECAMERON Novella." RomN 15:378-387. Winter 1973.

Cuilleanáin, Cormac O. "Man and Beast in the DECAMERON." MLR 75:86-93. January 1980.

Deligiorgis, Stavros. "Boccaccio and the Greek Romances." CL 19:97-113. Spring 1967.

―――――. Narrative Intellection in the DECAMERON. Iowa City: University of Iowa Press, 1975. 233 pp.

De Sanctis, Francesco. "Boccaccio's Human Comedy." Critical Perspectives on the DECAMERON. ed. Robert S. Dombrowski. London: Hodder and Stroughton, 1976. pp. 26-37.

Ferrante, Joan M. "Narrative Patterns in the DECAMERON." RPh 31:585-604. May 1978.

Fido, Franco. "Rhetoric and Semantics in the DECAMERON: Tropes and Signs in a Narrative Function." YItS 2:1-12. Winter 1978.

Gibaldi, Joseph. "The DECAMERON Cornice and the Responses to the Disintegration of Civilization." KRQ 24:349-355. No. 3, 1977.

Greene, Thomas M. "Forms of Accommodation in the DECAMERON." Italica 45:297-313. September 1968. Abridged in Critical Perspectives on the DECAMERON. ed. Robert S. Dombrowski. London: Hodder and Stroughton, 1976. pp. 113-128.

Hasting, R. Nature and Reason in the DECAMERON. Manchester [Eng.] University Press, 1975. 108 pp.

Hesse, Hermann. "Giovanni Boccaccio's Comments on Giovanni Boccaccio as Author of the DECAMERON." My Belief: Essays on Life and Art. New York: Farrar, Straus and Giroux, 1974. pp. 294-304.

Hollander, Robert. Boccaccio's Two Venuses. New York: Columbia University Press, 1977. pp. 95-102; 105-109.

Holloway, John. "Supposition and Supersession: A Model of Analysis for Narrative Structure." CritI 3:39-52. Autumn 1976.

Janssens, Marcel. "The Internal Reception of the Stories Within the DECAMERON." Boccaccio in Europe. ed. Gilbert Tournoy. Leuven: Leuven University Press, 1977. pp. 135-148.

Layman, B. J. "Boccaccio's Paradigm of the Artist and His Art." IQ 13:19-36. Winter 1970.

_____. "Eloquence of Pattern in Boccaccio's Tale of the Falcon." Italica 46:3-16. Spring 1969.

Marcus, Millicent. "The Accommodating Frate Alberto: A Gloss on DECAMERON 1V, 2." Italica 56:3-18. Spring 1979.

_____. "Faith's Fiction: A Gloss on the Tale of Melchisedech (DECAMERON I, 3)." CJIS 2:40-55. Fall/Winter 1978-1979.

_____. "Seduction by Silence: A Gloss on the Tales of Masetto (DECAMERON III, 1) and Alatiel (DECAMERON II, 7)." PQ 58:1-15. Winter 1979.

## Boccaccio, Giovanni

———. "The Sweet New Style Reconsidered: A Gloss on the Tale of Cimone (DECAMERON V, 1)." IQ 21:5-15. Summer 1980.

Mazzotta, Giuseppe. "The DECAMERON: The Literal and the Allegorical." IQ 18:53-73. Spring 1975.

———. "The DECAMERON: The Marginality of Literature." UTQ 42:64-80. Fall 1972. Abridged in Critical Perspectives on the DECAMERON. ed. Robert S. Dombrowski. London: Hodder and Stroughton, 1976. pp. 129-143.

———. "Games of Laughter in the DECAMERON." RR 69:115-131. January/March 1978.

Moore, Cassandra. "The Favola of the 'Papere' in Boccaccio: A Study of Two Sources and an Analysis." RLSt 3:9-22. 1972.

Mulryan, John. "The Three Images of Venus: Boccaccio's Theory of Love in the GENEALOGY OF THE GODS and His Aesthetic Vision of Love in the DECAMERON." RomN 19:388-394. Spring 1979.

de' Negri, Enrico. "The Legendary Style of the DECAMERON." Critical Perspectives on the DECAMERON. ed. Robert S. Dombrowski. London: Hodder and Stroughton, 1976. pp. 82-98.

Petronio, Giuseppe. "The Place of the DECAMERON." Critical Perspectives on the DECAMERON. ed. Robert S. Dombrowski. London: Hodder and Stroughton, 1976. pp. 48-60.

Radcliff-Umstead, Douglas. "Boccaccio's Adaptation of Some Latin Sources for the DECAMERON." Italica 45: 171-194. June 1968.

Richardson, Brian. "The 'Ghibelline' Narrator in the DECAMERON." IS 33:20-28. 1978.

Scaglione, Aldo. "Giovanni Boccaccio, or the Narrative Vocation." Boccacio: Secoli di vita. ed. Marga Cottino-Jones and Edward F. Tuttle. Ravenna: Longo Editore, 1975. pp. 81-104.

Shklovskif, Victor. "Some Reflections on the DECAMERON." Critical Perspectives on the DECAMERON. ed. Robert S. Dombrowski. London: Hodder and Stroughton, 1976. pp. 61-68.

Wheelock, James T. S. "The Rhetoric of Polarity in DECAMERON III, 3." LeS 9:257-274. No. 2, 1974.

FIAMMETTA
- Griffin, Robert. "Boccaccio's FIAMMETTA: Pictures at an Exhibition." IQ 18:75-94. Spring 1975.

FILOCOLO
- Hollander, Robert. Boccaccio's Two Venuses. New York: Columbia University Press, 1977. pp. 31-40; 149-158.

- Smarr, Janet Levarie. "Boccaccio's FILOCOLO: Romance, Epic, and Religious Allegory." FI 12:26-41. Spring 1978.

Buzzati, Dino
A LOVE AFFAIR
- Atchity, Kenneth. "Time in Two Novels of Dino Buzzati." Italica 55:3-19. Spring 1978.

- Schneider, Marilyn. "Beyond the Eroticism of Dino Buzzati's UN AMORE." Italica 46:292-299. Autumn 1969.

THE TARTAR STEPPE
- Atchity, Kenneth. "Time in Two Novels of Dino Buzzati." Italica 55:3-19. Spring 1978.

- Pacifici, Sergio. The Modern Italian Novel from Pea to Moravia. Carbondale: Southern Illinois University Press, 1979. pp. 84-89.

Calvino, Italo
IL BARONE RAMPANTE
- Cannon, Joann. "Literary Signification: An Analysis of Calvino's Trilogy." Symposium 34:3-12. Spring 1980.

THE CASTLE OF CROSSED DESTINIES
- Cannon, JoAnn. "Literature as Combinatory Game: Italo Calvino's THE CASTLE OF CROSSED DESTINIES." Crit 21:83-91. No. 1, 1979.

- Schneider, Marilyn. "Calvino at a Crossroads: IL CASTELLO DEI DESTINI INCROCIATI." PMLA 95:73-90. January 1980.

IL CAVALIERE INESISTENTE
- Cannon, Joann. "Literary Signification: An Analysis of Calvino's Trilogy." Symposium 34:3-12. Spring 1980.

LE CITTA INVISIBILI
- Cannon, Joann. "Storyteller and Critic in LE CITTA INVISIBILI." FI 12:274-282. Summer 1978.

- Jeannet, Angela M. "Italo Calvino's Invisible City." PCL 3:38-47. May 1977.

- de Lauretis, Teresa. "Semiotic Models, INVISIBLE CITIES." YItS 2:13-37. Winter 1978.

COSMICOMICS

Calvino, Italo

    Fontana, Ernest L. "Metamorphoses of Proteus: Calvino's COSMICOMICS." PCL 5:147-154. 1979.
MARCOVALDO
    Cannon, JoAnn. "The Image of the City in the Novels of Italo Calvino." MFS 24:83-87. Spring 1978.
I NORTRI ANTENATI
    Woodhouse, J. R. Italo Calvino: A Reappraisal and an Appreciation of the Trilogy. Hull: University of Hull, 1968. 90 pp.
IL SENTIERO DEI NIDI DI RAGNO
    DeMara, Nicholas A. "Pathway to Calvino: Fantasy and Reality in IL SENTIERO DEI NIDI DI RAGNO." IQ 14:25-49. Winter 1971.

    Woodhouse, J. R. "Italo Calvino and the Rediscovery of a Genre." IQ 12:50-61. Summer 1968.
SMOG
    Cannon, JoAnn. "The Image of the City in the Novels of Italo Calvino." MFS 24:87-90. Spring 1978.
IL VISCONTE DIMEZZATO
    Cannon, Joann. "Literary Signification: An Analysis of Calvino's Trilogy." Symposium 34:3-12. Spring 1980.

Canetti, Elias
    AUTO DA FE
        Sacharoff, Mark. "Grotesque Comedy in Canetti's AUTO DA FE." Crit 14:99-112. No. 1, 1972.

Capuana, Luigi
    GIACINTA
        Traversa, Vincenzo Paolo. Luigi Capuana: Critic and Novelist. The Hague: Mouton, 1968. pp. 72-89.
    IL MARCHESE DI ROCCAVERDINA
        Traversa, Vincenzo Paolo. Luigi Capuana: Critic and Novelist. The Hague: Mouton, 1968. pp. 101-120.
    PROFUMO
        Traversa, Vincenzo Paolo. Luigi Capuana: Critic and Novelist. The Hague: Mouton, 1968. pp. 89-100.
    RASSEGNAZIONE
        Traversa, Vincenzo Paolo. Luigi Capuana: Critic and Novelist. The Hague: Mouton, 1968. pp. 121-129.

Cassola, Carlo
    LA RAGAZZA DI BUBE
        Pedroni, Peter N. "Carlo Cassola's LA RAGAZZA DI BUBE." FI 11:47-64. March 1977.

Coccioli, Carlo
    THE STRINGS OF THE HARP
        Fonda, Carlo. "Narcissus' Complex: A Critico-psychological Interpretation of Carlo Coccioli's THE STRINGS OF THE HARP." IQ 15:17-57. Fall/Winter 1971.

Delicado, Francisco
   LA LOZANA ANDALUZA
      Damiani, Bruno M. "Delicado and Aretino: Aspects of a Literary Profile." KRQ 17:309-324. No. 4, 1970.

      Pike, Ruth. "The 'Conversos' in LA LOZANA ANDALUZA." MLN 84:304-308. March 1969.

De Roberto, Federico
   I VICERE
      O'Neill, Tom. "Lampedusa and De Roberto." Italica 47:170-182. Summer 1970.

      Pacifici, Sergio. The Modern Italian Novel from Manzoni to Svevo. Carbondale: Southern Illinois University Press, 1967. pp. 85-97.

Fogazzaro, Antonio
   DANIELE CORTIS
      Hall, Robert A., Jr. Antonio Fogazzaro. Boston: Twayne, 1978. pp. 36-47.
   LEILA
      Hall, Robert A., Jr. Antonio Fogazzaro. Boston: Twayne, 1978. pp. 84-94.
   LITTLE WORLD OF NOWADAYS
      Hall, Robert A., Jr. Antonio Fogazzaro. Boston: Twayne, 1978. pp. 68-76.
   LITTLE WORLD OF THE PAST
      Hall, Robert A., Jr. Antonio Fogazzaro. Boston: Twayne, 1978. pp. 59-71.

      Pacifici, Sergio. The Modern Italian Novel from Manzoni to Svevo. Carbondale: Southern Illinois University Press, 1967. pp. 144-148.
   MALOMBRA
      Hall, Robert A., Jr. Antonio Fogazzaro. Boston: Twayne, 1978. pp. 26-36.
   MIRANDA
      Hall, Robert A., Jr. Antonio Fogazzaro. Boston: Twayne, 1978. pp. 20-26.
   THE MYSTERY OF THE POET
      Hall, Robert A., Jr. Antonio Fogazzaro. Boston: Twayne, 1978. pp. 49-58.
   THE SAINT
      Ziolkowski, Theodore. Fictional Transfigurations of Jesus. Princeton: Princeton University Press, 1972. pp. 85-93.

Foscolo, Ugo
   LAST LETTERS OF JACOPO ORTIS
      Cambon, Glauco. Ugo Foscolo: Poet of Exile. Princeton: Princeton University Press, 1980. pp. 27-116.

Foscolo, Ugo

> Radcliff-Umstead, Douglas. Ugo Foscolo. New York: Twayne, 1970. pp. 12-21; 44-76.

Gadda, Carlo Emilio
ACQUAINTED WITH GRIEF
> Biasin, Gian-Paolo. "Literary Diseases: From Pathology to Ontology." MLN 82:97-101. January 1967.

> ———. Literary Diseases: Theme and Metaphor in the Italian Novel. Austin: University of Texas Press, 1975. pp. 136-155.

> Pacifici, Sergio. The Modern Italian Novel from Pea to Moravia. Carbondale: Southern Illinois University Press, 1979. pp. 111-117.

> Pucci, Pietro. "The Obscure Sickness." IQ 11:43-62. Fall 1967.

THAT AWFUL MESS ON VIA MERULANA
> Bongiorno, Robert. "Prose Texture as Content in QUER PASTICCIACCIO BRUTTO DE VIA MERULANA." RomN 14:49-56. Autumn 1972.

> Cannon, JoAnn. "The Reader as Detective: Notes on Gadda's PASTICCIACCIO." MLS 10:41-48. Fall 1980.

> Dombroski, Robert S. "Some Observations on the Revision of QUER PASTICCIACCIO." MLN 86:61-72. January 1971.

> Pacifici, Sergio. The Modern Italian Novel from Pea to Moravia. Carbondale: Southern Illinois University Press, 1979. pp. 105-111.

Garibaldi
CANTONI IL VOLONTARIO
> Griffiths, C. E. J. "The Novels of Garibaldi." IS 30:86-98. 1975.

I MILLE
> Griffiths, C. E. J. "The Novels of Garibaldi." IS 30:86-98. 1975.

THE RULE OF THE MONK
> Griffiths, C. E. J. "The Novels of Garibaldi." IS 30:86-98. 1975.

Guerrazzi, F. D.
PASQUALE PAOLI
> Constable, M. V. "F. D. Guerrazzi's Corsican Novel PASQUALE PAOLI: A Contribution to the Regional Novel of the 'Verismo' Period." FI 5:187-202. June 1971.

IL SECOLO CHE MUORE
> Roy, Marilyn Piccini. "Social Inquiry in F. D. Guer-

razzi's IL SECOLO CHE MUORE." FI 7/8:56-68. December 1973/March 1974.

Invernizio, Carolina
STORIA D'UNA SARTINA
Lepschy, A. L. "Carolina Invernizio's IJ DELIT D'NA BELA FIA and STORIA D'UNA SARTINA." IS 34:93-104. 1979.

Jovine, Francesco
SIGNORA AVA
Moloney, Brian. "The Novels of Francesco Jovine." IS 23:143-146. 1968.
LE TERRE DEL SACRAMENTO
Moloney, Brian. "The Novels of Francesco Jovine." IS 23:146-155. 1968.

Lampedusa, Giuseppe Tomasi di
THE LEOPARD
Kirton, W. J. S. "Stendhal, Lampedusa and the Limits of Admiration." Trivium 10:101-108. May 1975.

Kuhns, Richard F. "Modernity and Death: THE LEOPARD by Giuseppe di Lampedusa." Contemporary Psychoanalysis 5:95-119. Spring 1969.

Lansing, Richard H. "The Structure of Meaning in Lampedusa's IL GATTOPARDO." PMLA 93:409-422. May 1978.

Lucente, Gregory L. "Lampedusa's IL GATTOPARDO: Figure and Temporality in an Historical Novel." MLN 93:82-108. January 1978.

McSweeney, Kerry. "Lampedusa and the Hour of Death." SHR 12:213-220. Summer 1978.

Meyers, Jeffrey. "Greuze and Lampedusa's IL GATTOPARDO." MLR 69:308-315. April 1974.

_____. "The Influence of LA CHARTREUSE DE PARME on IL GATTOPARDO." Italica 44:314-325. September 1967.

O'Neill, Tom. "Lampedusa and De Roberto." Italica 47:170-182. Summer 1970.

Pacifici, Sergio. The Modern Italian Novel from Pea to Moravia. Carbondale: Southern Illinois University Press, 1979. pp. 68-78.

Ragusa, Olga. "Stendhal, Tomasi di Lampedusa, and the Novel." CLS 10:195-228. September 1973.

Lampedusa, Giuseppe Tomasi di

Van Eerde, John. "The Function of Synesthesia in IL GATTOPARDO." IFR 3:157-159. July 1976.

Levi, Carlo
THE WATCH
Pacifici, Sergio. The Modern Italian Novel from Pea to Moravia. Carbondale: Southern Illinois University Press, 1979. pp. 92-98.

Loredano, Giovanni Francesco
LA DIANEA
Dünnhaupt, Gerhard. "Giovanni Francesco Loredano's Novel LA DIANEA: Its Structure and Didactic Aims." SSe 16:43-52. 1975.

Malerba, Luigi
IL PATAFFIO
Schneider, Marilyn. "IL PATAFFIO, or How to Feed on Laughter." ConL 20:471-483. Autumn 1979.
THE SERPENT
Schneider, Marilyn. "To Know Is to Eat: A Reading of IL SERPENTE." YItS 2:71-83. Winter 1978.

Manzoni, Alessandro
THE BETROTHED
Ambrose, Mary. "Error and the Abuse of Language in the PROMESSI SPOSI." MLR 72:62-72. January 1977.

Barricelli, Gian Piero. Alessandro Manzoni. Boston: Twayne, 1976. pp. 111-163.

Barricelli, Jean-Pierre. "Structure and Symbol in Manzoni's I PROMESSI SPOSI." PMLA 87:499-507. May 1972. Reprinted in IQ 17:79-102. Fall/Winter (Special Issue) 1973.

Caserta, Ernesto G. Manzoni's Christian Realism. Firenze: Olschki, 1977. pp. 131-219.

Chandler, S. B. Alessandro Manzoni: The Story of a Spiritual Quest. Edinburgh: Edinburgh University Press, 1974. pp. 86-115.

Dombroski, Robert S. "The Seicento as Strategy: 'Providence' and the 'Bourgeois' in I PROMESSI SPOSI." MLN 91:80-100. January 1976.

Jones, Ann Rosalind. "Manzoni's PROMESSI SPOSI and Lukács' THEORIE DES ROMANS." Arcadia 11:126-138. 1976.

Lansing, Richard H. "Stylistic and Structural Duality in Manzoni's I PROMESSI SPOSI." Italica 53:347-361. Autumn 1976.

Lanyi, Gabriel. "Plot-time and Rhythm in Manzoni's
I PROMESSI SPOSI." MLN 93:36-51. January 1978.

Pacifici, Sergio. The Modern Italian Novel from Manzoni to Svevo. Carbondale: Southern Illinois University Press, 1967. pp. 32-56.

Pallotta, Augustus. "British and American Translations of I PROMESSI SPOSI." Italica 50:483-523. Winter 1973.

Purdy, Strother B. "Manzoni, Stendhal, and the Murder of Prina: A Counterpoint of Literature and History." SIR 7:140-158. Spring 1968.

Ricapito, J. V. "'Comparatistica'--Two Versions of Sin, Moral Transgression and Divine Will: GUZMAN DE ALFARACHE and I PROMESSI SPOSI." KRQ 16:111-118. No. 2, 1969.

White, D. M. "Manzoni and the Novel." ULR 14:128-150. May 1971.

Montale, Eugenio
FARFALLA DI DINARD
Huffman, Claire L. "FARFALLA DI DINARD of Eugenio Montale." FI 3:232-250. June 1969.

Moravia, Alberto
THE CONFORMIST
Cottrell, Jane E. Alberto Moravia. New York: Frederick Ungar, 1974. pp. 87-91.

Culbertson, Diana and John A. Valley. "Alberto Moravia's Melancholy Murderer: The Conformist as Personality Type." L&P 25:79-85. No. 2, 1975.

Heiney, Donald. Three Italian Novelists: Moravia, Pavese, Vittorini. Ann Arbor: University of Michigan Press, 1968. pp. 46-51.
CONJUGAL LOVE
Cottrell, Jane E. Alberto Moravia. New York: Frederick Ungar, 1974. pp. 80-83.

Ross, Joan and Donald Freed. The Existentialism of Alberto Moravia. Carbondale: Southern Illinois University Press, 1972. pp. 108-115.
THE EMPTY CANVAS
Cottrell, Jane E. Alberto Moravia. New York: Frederick Ungar, 1974. pp. 94-101.

Heiney, Donald. Three Italian Novelists: Moravia, Pavese, Vittorini. Ann Arbor: University of Michigan Press, 1968. pp. 65-73.

Pacifici, Sergio. The Modern Italian Novel from Pea to Moravia. Carbondale: Southern Illinois University Press, 1979. pp. 226-229.
THE FANCY DRESS PARTY
Cottrell, Jane E. Alberto Moravia. New York: Frederick Ungar, 1974. pp. 48-51.

Heiney, Donald. Three Italian Novelists: Moravia, Pavese, Vittorini. Ann Arbor: University of Michigan Press, 1968. pp. 32-36.
A GHOST AT NOON
Cottrell, Jane E. Alberto Moravia. New York: Frederick Ungar, 1974. pp. 83-87.

Heiney, Donald. Three Italian Novelists: Moravia, Pavese, Vittorini. Ann Arbor: University of Michigan Press, 1968. pp. 51-58.
THE INDIFFERENT
Cottrell, Jane E. Alberto Moravia. New York: Frederick Ungar, 1974. pp. 36-47.

Heiney, Donald. Three Italian Novelists: Moravia, Pavese, Vittorini. Ann Arbor: University of Michigan Press, 1968. pp. 23-29.

Kibler, Louis. "Imagery as Expression: Moravia's GLI INDIFFERENTI." Italica 49:315-334. Autumn 1972.

Pacifici, Sergio. The Modern Italian Novel from Pea to Moravia. Carbondale: Southern Illinois University Press, 1979. pp. 205-210.

Radcliff-Umstead, Douglas. "Moravia's Indifferent Puppets." Symposium 24:44-53. Spring 1970.
THE LIE
Baldanza, Frank. "Mature Moravia." ConL 9:514-520. Autumn 1968.

Cottrell, Jane E. Alberto Moravia. New York: Frederick Ungar, 1974. pp. 101-105.

Heiney, Donald. Three Italian Novelists: Moravia, Pavese, Vittorini. Ann Arbor: University of Michigan Press, 1968. pp. 73-82.

Pacifici, Sergio. The Modern Italian Novel from Pea to Moravia. Carbondale: Southern Illinois University Press, 1979. pp. 230-235.
MISTAKEN AMBITIONS
Cottrell, Jane E. Alberto Moravia. New York: Frederick Ungar, 1974. pp. 44-48.

Heiney, Donald. Three Italian Novelists: Moravia,

Pavese, Vittorini. Ann Arbor: University of Michigan Press, 1968. pp. 29-32.
TWO: A PHALLIC NOVEL
Becker, Gustave H. "A Note on Creative Vitality in Hermann Hesse's NARZISS UND GOLDMUND and Alberto Moravia's TWO: A PHALLIC NOVEL." FurmS 21:49-54. June 1974.

Pacifici, Sergio. The Modern Italian Novel from Pea to Moravia. Carbondale: Southern Illinois University Press, 1979. pp. 236-238.
TWO ADOLESCENTS
Cerreta, Florindo. "Moravia's Luca Mansi and His Dreams of Transcendence." Italica 53:8-28. Spring 1976.

Rimanelli, Giose. "Moravia and the Philosophy of Personal Existence." IQ 11:44-54. Summer 1967.
TWO WOMEN
Cerreta, Florindo V. "Structure and Meaning in Moravia's LA CIOCIARA." FI 12:324-338. Fall 1978.

Cottrell, Jane E. Alberto Moravia. New York: Frederick Ungar, 1974. pp. 72-77.

Heiney, Donald. Three Italian Novelists: Moravia, Pavese, Vittorini. Ann Arbor: University of Michigan Press, 1968. pp. 58-65.
THE WOMAN OF ROME
Cottrell, Jane E. Alberto Moravia. New York: Frederick Ungar, 1974. pp. 66-72.

Heiney, Donald. Three Italian Novelists: Moravia, Pavese, Vittorini. Ann Arbor: University of Michigan Press, 1968. pp. 37-46.

Nievo, Ippolito
CONFESSIONS OF AN ITALIAN
Pacifici, Sergio. The Modern Italian Novel from Manzoni to Svevo. Carbondale: Southern Illinois University Press, 1967. pp. 58-72.

Pierce, Wilbur F. "LE CONFESSIONI DI UN ITALIANO: The Family Grammar." FI 12:175-205. Summer 1978.

Oriani, Alfredo
VORTICE
Dombroski, Robert S. "Oriani's VORTICE as a Political Metaphor." FI 6:488-496. December 1972.

Palazzeschi, Aldo
THE SISTERS MATERASSI
Pacifici, Sergio. The Modern Italian Novel from Pea to

Palazzeschi, Aldo

Moravia. Carbondale: Southern Illinois University Press, 1979. pp. 41-46.

Singh, G. "Aldo Palazzeschi: A Survey." From "Verismo" to Experimentalism: Essays on the Modern Italian Novel. ed. Sergio Pacifici. Bloomington: Indiana University Press, 1969. pp. 90-100.

Panzini, Alfredo
LA MADONNA DI MAMA
Pacifici, Sergio. The Modern Italian Novel from Capuana to Tozzi. Carbondale: Southern Illinois University Press, 1973. pp. 74-77.

Pavese, Cesare
AMONG WOMEN ONLY
Biasin, Gian-Paolo. The Smile of the Gods: A Thematic Study of Cesare Pavese's Works. Ithaca: Cornell University Press, 1968. pp. 153-162.

Heiney, Donald. Three Italian Novelists: Moravia, Pavese, Vittorini. Ann Arbor: University of Michigan Press, 1968. pp. 109-118.

Pacifici, Sergio. The Modern Italian Novel from Pea to Moravia. Carbondale: Southern Illinois University Press, 1979. pp. 152-154.
THE BEACH
Biasin, Gian-Paolo. The Smile of the Gods: A Thematic Study of Cesare Pavese's Works. Ithaca: Cornell University Press, 1968. pp. 133-138.

Heiney, Donald. Three Italian Novelists: Moravia, Pavese, Vittorini. Ann Arbor: University of Michigan Press, 1968. pp. 118-123.

Pacifici, Sergio. The Modern Italian Novel from Pea to Moravia. Carbondale: Southern Illinois University Press, 1979. pp. 142-144.
THE BEAUTIFUL SUMMER
Biasin, Gian-Paolo. The Smile of the Gods: A Thematic Study of Cesare Pavese's Works. Ithaca: Cornell University Press, 1968. pp. 87-99.

Heiney, Donald. Three Italian Novelists: Moravia, Pavese, Vittorini. Ann Arbor: University of Michigan Press, 1968. pp. 109-118.

Pacifici, Sergio. The Modern Italian Novel from Pea to Moravia. Carbondale: Southern Illinois University Press, 1979. pp. 139-142.
THE COMRADE
Biasin, Gian-Paolo. The Smile of the Gods: A The-

matic Study of Cesare Pavese's Works. Ithaca: Cornell University Press, 1968. pp. 165-173.

Heiney, Donald. Three Italian Novelists: Moravia, Pavese, Vittorini. Ann Arbor: University of Michigan Press, 1968. pp. 129-131.

Pacifici, Sergio. The Modern Italian Novel from Pea to Moravia. Carbondale: Southern Illinois University Press, 1979. pp. 144-146.

THE DEVIL IN THE HILLS
Biasin, Gian-Paolo. The Smile of the Gods: A Thematic Study of Cesare Pavese's Works. Ithaca: Cornell University Press, 1968. pp. 138-153.

Heiney, Donald. Three Italian Novelists: Moravia, Pavese, Vittorini. Ann Arbor: University of Michigan Press, 1968. pp. 123-128.

Montano, Rocco. "The Wrong Religious Search: Pavese as Poli." IQ 18:63-69. Fall 1974.

Pacifici, Sergio. The Modern Italian Novel from Pea to Moravia. Carbondale: Southern Illinois University Press, 1979. pp. 150-152.

Schneider, Franz K. "Quest, Romance and Myth in Pavese's THE DEVIL IN THE HILLS." Italica 49:393-425. Winter 1972.

THE HARVESTERS
Biasin, Gian-Paolo. The Smile of the Gods: A Thematic Study of Cesare Pavese's Works. Ithaca: Cornell University Press, 1968. pp. 62-77.

Heiney, Donald. "Pavese: The Geography of the Moon." ConL 9:522-537. Autumn 1968.

_____. Three Italian Novelists: Moravia, Pavese, Vittorini. Ann Arbor: University of Michigan Press, 1968. pp. 101-109.

Pacifici, Sergio. The Modern Italian Novel from Pea to Moravia. Carbondale: Southern Illinois University Press, 1979. pp. 135-139.

THE HOUSE ON THE HILL
Biasin, Gian-Paolo. The Smile of the Gods: A Thematic Study of Cesare Pavese's Works. Ithaca: Cornell University Press, 1968. pp. 178-188.

Heiney, Donald. Three Italian Novelists: Moravia, Pavese, Vittorini. Ann Arbor: University of Michigan Press, 1968. pp. 131-136.

Pacifici, Sergio. The Modern Italian Novel from Pea to Moravia. Carbondale: Southern Illinois University Press, 1979. pp. 146-150.

THE MOON AND THE BONFIRES
Biasin, Gian-Paolo. "Myth and Death in Cesare Pavese's THE MOON AND THE BONFIRES." From "Verismo" to Experimentalism: Essays on the Modern Italian Novel. ed. Sergio Pacifici. Bloomington: Indiana University Press, 1969. pp. 184-211.

──────. The Smile of the Gods: A Thematic Study of Cesare Pavese's Works. Ithaca: Cornell University Press, 1968. pp. 215-252.

Biernaczky, Szilárd. "Cesare Pavese's Folklorism." AEASH 25:287-294. No. 3/4, 1976.

Heiney, Donald. "Pavese: The Geography of the Moon." ConL 9:522-537. Autumn 1968.

──────. Three Italian Novelists: Moravia, Pavese, Vittorini. Ann Arbor: University of Michigan Press, 1968. pp. 136-146.

Kibler, Louis. "Patterns of Time in Pavese's LA LUNA E I FALO." FI 12:339-350. Fall 1978.

Merry, Bruce. "Artifice and Structure in LA LUNA E I FALO." FI 5:351-358. September 1971.

Musumeci, Antonino. "Pavese: Stylistics of a Mythology." Symposium 34:265-268. Fall 1980.

Pacifici, Sergio. The Modern Italian Novel from Pea to Moravia. Carbondale: Southern Illinois University Press, 1979. pp. 155-159.

Thompson, A. D. "'Slow Rotation Suggesting Permanence': History, Symbol and Myth in Pavese's Last Novel." IS 34:105-121. 1979.

THE POLITICAL PRISONER
Heiney, Donald. Three Italian Novelists: Moravia, Pavese, Vittorini. Ann Arbor: University of Michigan Press, 1968. pp. 96-101.

Pacifici, Sergio. The Modern Italian Novel from Pea to Moravia. Carbondale: Southern Illinois University Press, 1979. pp. 132-135.

Roopnaraine, R. Rupert. "Structures of Self and Art in Pavese's IL CARCERE." IQ 17:25-46. Fall/Winter 1973.

Pea, Enrico
    MOSCARDINO
        Pacifici, Sergio. The Modern Italian Novel from Pea to
        Moravia. Carbondale: Southern Illinois University
        Press, 1979. pp. 21-23.

Pirandello, Luigi
    I VECCHI E I GIOVANI
        Radcliff-Umstead, Douglas. The Mirror of Our Anguish:
        A Study of Luigi Pirandello's Narrative Writings. Rutherford: Fairleigh Dickinson University Press, 1978.
        pp. 198-234.
    THE LATE MATTIA PASCAL
        de Castris, A. L. "The Experimental Novelist." Pirandello: A Collection of Critical Essays. ed. Glauco
        Cambon. Englewood Cliffs: Prentice-Hall, 1967. pp.
        91-95.

        Pacifici, Sergio. The Modern Italian Novel from Capuana to Tozzi. Carbondale: Southern Illinois University
        Press, 1973. pp. 122-128.

        Radcliff-Umstead, Douglas. The Mirror of Our Anguish:
        A Study of Luigi Pirandello's Narrative Writings. Rutherford: Fairleigh Dickinson University Press, 1978.
        pp. 162-197.

        Ragusa, Olga. Luigi Pirandello. New York: Columbia
        University Press, 1968. pp. 14-19.
    ONE, NONE AND A HUNDRED THOUSAND
        Biasin, Gian-Paolo. Literary Diseases: Theme and
        Metaphor in the Italian Novel. Austin: University of
        Texas Press, 1975. pp. 100-126.

        Pacifici, Sergio. The Modern Italian Novel from Capuana to Tozzi. Carbondale: Southern Illinois University
        Press, 1973. pp. 128-133.

        Radcliff-Umstead, Douglas. The Mirror of Our Anguish:
        A Study of Luigi Pirandello's Narrative Writings. Rutherford: Fairleigh Dickinson University Press, 1978.
        pp. 269-293.
    THE OUTCAST
        Pacifici, Sergio. The Modern Italian Novel from Capuana to Tozzi. Carbondale: Southern Illinois University
        Press, 1973. pp. 119-122.

        Radcliff-Umstead, Douglas. The Mirror of Our Anguish:
        A Study of Luigi Pirandello's Narrative Writings. Rutherford: Fairleigh Dickinson University Press, 1978.
        pp. 128-140.
    SI GIRA
        de Castris, A. L. "The Experimental Novelist." Piran-

Pirandello, Luigi

dello: A Collection of Critical Essays. ed. Glauco Cambon. Englewood Cliffs: Prentice-Hall, 1967. pp. 95-102.

Radcliff-Umstead, Douglas. The Mirror of Our Anguish: A Study of Luigi Pirandello's Narrative Writings. Rutherford: Fairleigh Dickinson University Press, 1978. pp. 249-268.
SUO MARITO
Radcliff-Umstead, Douglas. The Mirror of Our Anguish: A Study of Luigi Pirandello's Narrative Writings. Rutherford: Fairleigh Dickinson University Press, 1978. pp. 235-249.
THE TURN
Radcliff-Umstead, Douglas. The Mirror of Our Anguish: A Study of Luigi Pirandello's Narrative Writings. Rutherford: Fairleigh Dickinson University Press, 1978. pp. 149-161.

Pratolini, Vasco
CRONACHE DI POVERI AMANTI
Kozma, Janice M. "Metaphor in Pratolini's Novels: IL QUARTIERE and CRONACHE DI POVERI AMANTI." RomN 20:298-303. Spring 1980.
IL QUARTIERE
Kozma, Janice M. "Metaphor in Pratolini's Novels: IL QUARTIERE and CRONACHE DI POVERI AMANTI." RomN 20:298-303. Spring 1980.

Samonà, Carmelo
BROTHERS
Biasin, Gian-Paolo. "Disease as Language: The Case of the Writer and the Madman." IQ 21:77-81. Winter 1980.

Serao, Matilde
LA CONQUISTA DI ROMA
Gisolfi, Anthony M. The Essential Matilde Serao. New York: Las Americas, 1968. pp. 64-72.
CUORE INFERMO
Gisolfi, Anthony M. The Essential Matilde Serao. New York: Las Americas, 1968. pp. 35-45.
FANTASIA
Gisolfi, Anthony M. The Essential Matilde Serao. New York: Las Americas, 1968. pp. 44-54.
IL PAESE DI CUCCAGNA
Gisolfi, Anthony M. The Essential Matilde Serao. New York: Las Americas, 1968. pp. 92-98.
VITA E AVVENTURE DI RICCARDO JOANNA
Gisolfi, Anthony M. The Essential Matilde Serao. New York: Las Americas, 1968. pp. 72-79.

Silone, Ignazio
L'AVVENTURA DI UN POVERO CRISTIANO

Whyte, Jean. "The Evolution of Silone's Central Theme." IS 25:58-62. 1970.
BREAD AND WINE
Howe, Irving. "Ignazio Silone: Politics and the Novel." From "Verismo" to Experimentalism: Essays on the Modern Italian Novel. ed. Sergio Pacifici. Bloomington: Indiana University Press, 1969. pp. 126-130.

Radcliff-Umstead, Douglas. "Animal Symbolism in Silone's VINO E PANE." Italica 49:18-29. Spring 1972.

Rühle, Jürgen. Literature and Revolution: A Critical Study of the Writer and Communism in the Twentieth Century. New York: Frederick A. Praeger, 1969. pp. 368-371.

Schneider, Franz. "Scriptural Symbolism in Silone's BREAD AND WINE." Italica 44:387-399. December 1967.

Ziolkowski, Theodore. Fictional Transfigurations of Jesus. Princeton: Princeton University Press, 1972. pp. 197-206.

Svevo, Italo
AS A MAN GROWS OLDER
Biasin, Gian-Paolo. "Literary Diseases: From Pathology to Ontology." MLN 82:81-85. January 1967.

*Furbank, P. N. Italo Svevo: The Man and the Writer. Berkeley: University of California Press, 1966. pp. 162-173.

Lebowitz, Naomi. Italo Svevo. New Brunswick: Rutgers University Press, 1978. pp. 95-110.

Marampon, Lucio. "In Defense of the Title SENILITA." IQ 17:27-38. Summer 1973.

Moloney, Brian. Italo Svevo: A Critical Introduction. Edinburgh: Edinburgh University Press, 1974. pp. 39-55.

Pacifici, Sergio. The Modern Italian Novel from Manzoni to Svevo. Carbondale: Southern Illinois University Press, 1967. pp. 166-174.

Robison, Paula. "SENILITA: The Secret of Svevo's Weeping Madonna." IQ 14:61-84. Winter 1971.

Russell, Charles C. Italo Svevo: The Writer from Trieste. Ravenna: Longo, 1978. pp. 132-161.
THE CONFESSIONS OF ZENO

Biasin, Gian-Paolo. "Literary Diseases: From Pathology to Ontology." MLN 82:85-97. January 1967.

_____. Literary Diseases: Theme and Metaphor in the Italian Novel. Austin: University of Texas Press, 1975. pp. 63-99.

_____. "Zeno's Last Bomb." MFS 18:17-32. Spring 1972.

Bini, Daniela. "'Kairos' and 'Chronos' in Svevo's CONFESSIONS OF ZENO." CJIS 3:102-107. Winter 1980.

Bondy, François. "Italo Svevo and Ripe Old Age." HudR 20:575-598. Winter 1967-1968.

Davis, Barbara A. "Zeno's Ontological Confessions." TCL 18:45-56. January 1972.

de Lauretis, Teresa. "Discourse and the Conquest of Desire in Svevo's Fiction." MFS 18:100-109. Spring 1972.

_____. "Dreams as Metalanguage in Svevo's CONFESSIONS OF ZENO." Lang & S 4:208-220. Summer 1971.

Fifer, Elizabeth. "The Confessions of Italo Svevo." ConL 14:320-329. Summer 1973.

Freccero, John. "Italo Svevo: Zeno's Last Cigarette." From "Verismo" to Experimentalism: Essays on the Modern Italian Novel. ed. Sergio Pacifici. Bloomington: Indiana University Press, 1969. pp. 35-60.

*Furbank, P. N. Italo Svevo: The Man and the Writer. Berkeley: University of California Press, 1966. pp. 174-209.

Furst, Lilian R. "Italo Svevo's LA COSCIENZA DI ZENO and Thomas Mann's DER ZAUBERBERG." ConL 9:492-506. Autumn 1968.

Gatt-Rutter, John. "Non-commitment in Italo Svevo." JES 3:123-146. June 1973.

Godt, Clareece. "Svevo and Coincidence." MLN 89:84-92. January 1974.

Jacobs, Lee. "Zeno's Sickness Unto Death." IQ 11:51-66. Spring 1968.

Lebowitz, Naomi. Humanism and the Absurd in the Modern Novel. Evanston: Northwestern University Press, 1971. pp. 110-117.

──────. Italo Svevo. New Brunswick: Rutgers University Press, 1978. pp. 10-28; 108-131.

Machala, Susan Perschetz. "The Late Svevo and the 'Literaturization' of Life." Italica 55:433-448. Winter 1978.

Marampon, Lucio. "The Insight to Necessity of Zeno." IQ 18:23-38. Winter 1975.

Meyer, Mark. "Zeno: His Fictions and His Problems." Sub-Stance 3:121-124. 1972.

Moloney, Brian. Italo Svevo: A Critical Introduction. Edinburgh: Edinburgh University Press, 1974. pp. 67-88.

──────. "Psychoanalysis and Irony in LA COSCIENZA DI ZENO." MLR 67:309-318. April 1972.

──────. "Svevo as a Jewish Writer." IS 28:60-63. 1973.

Pacifici, Sergio. The Modern Italian Novel from Manzoni to Svevo. Carbondale: Southern Illinois University Press, 1967. pp. 174-183.

Robison, Paula. "Svevo: Secrets of the Confessional." L&P 20:101-114. No. 3, 1970.

Russell, Charles C. Italo Svevo: The Writer from Trieste. Ravenna: Longo, 1978. pp. 198-238.

Salvatori, Mariolina. "The Conscience's Voice and Its Temporal Realm in LA COSCIENZA DI ZENO." FI 13:169-185. Summer 1979.

Treitel, Renata Minerbi. "Schopenhauer's Philosophy in Italo Svevo's LA COSCIENZA DI ZENO." MFS 18:53-64. Spring 1972.

──────. "Zeno Cosini: The Meaning Behind the Name." Italica 48:234-245. Summer 1971.

Wagner, C. Roland. "Italo Svevo: The Vocations of Old Age." HSL 2:218-228. No. 3, 1970.

Wilden, Anthony. "Death, Desire, and Repetition in Svevo's ZENO." MLN 84:98-119. January 1969.

A LIFE
*Furbank, P. N. Italo Svevo: The Man and the Writer. Berkeley: University of California Press, 1966. pp. 158-162.

Lebowitz, Naomi. Italo Svevo. New Brunswick: Rutgers University Press, 1978. pp. 75-95.

Moloney, Brian. Italo Svevo: A Critical Introduction. Edinburgh: Edinburgh University Press, 1974. pp. 31-38.

Pacifici, Sergio. The Modern Italian Novel from Manzoni to Svevo. Carbondale: Southern Illinois University Press, 1967. pp. 160-166.

Robison, Paula. "UNA VITA and the Family Romance." MFS 18:33-44. Spring 1972.

Russell, Charles C. Italo Svevo: The Writer from Trieste. Ravenna: Longo, 1978. pp. 84-109.

Terruggi, Ugo
LUISA E IL PRESIDENTE
Gatt-Rutter, John. "An Unread Novel: Ugo Terruggi's LUISA E IL PRESIDENTE." MFS 23:167-170. Summer 1977.

Tozzi, Federigo
CON GLI OCCHI CHIUSI
Pacifici, Sergio. The Modern Italian Novel from Capuana to Tozzi. Carbondale: Southern Illinois University Press, 1973. pp. 147-151.
THE FARM
Pacifici, Sergio. The Modern Italian Novel from Capuana to Tozzi. Carbondale: Southern Illinois University Press, 1973. pp. 151-156.
JOURNAL OF A CLERK
Pacifici, Sergio. The Modern Italian Novel from Capuana to Tozzi. Carbondale: Southern Illinois University Press, 1973. pp. 144-146.
THREE CROSSES
Pacifici, Sergio. The Modern Italian Novel from Capuana to Tozzi. Carbondale: Southern Illinois University Press, 1973. pp. 156-162.

Verga, Giovanni
LA DUCHESSA DI LEYRA
Cecchetti, Giovanni. Giovanni Verga. Boston: Twayne, 1978. pp. 145-147.
EROS
Cecchetti, Giovanni. "EROS." FI 5:169-178. June 1971.

Patruno, Nicholas. Language in Giovanni Verga's Early Novels. Chapel Hill: University of North Carolina Press, 1977. 122 pp.

## EVA

Patruno, Nicholas. "An Interpretation of Verga's EVA." RomN 17:57-65. Fall 1976.

⎯⎯⎯. Language in Giovanni Verga's Early Novels. Chapel Hill: University of North Carolina Press, 1977. 122 pp.

## THE HOUSE BY THE MEDLAR TREE

Cecchetti, Giovanni. Giovanni Verga. Boston: Twayne, 1978. pp. 68-97.

Chandler, S. B. "The Primitive World of Giovanni Verga." Mosaic 5:117-128. Spring 1972.

Ginsburg, Michal Peled. "I MALAVOGLIA and Verga's 'Progress.'" MLN 95:82-103. January 1980.

Hatzantonis, Emmanuel and John H. Dye. "The Dimensions of Tragedy in Verga's I MALAVOGLIA." Neophil 62:555-566. October 1978.

Pacifici, Sergio. The Modern Italian Novel from Manzoni to Svevo. Carbondale: Southern Illinois University Press, 1967. pp. 108-122.

⎯⎯⎯. "The Tragic World of Verga's Primitives." From "Verismo" to Experimentalism: Essays on the Modern Italian Novel. ed. Sergio Pacifici. Bloomington: Indiana University Press, 1969. pp. 16-28.

Woolf, D. The Art of Verga: A Study in Objectivity. Sydney: Sydney University Press, 1977. pp. 53-73.

## LA LUPA

Lucente, Gregory L. "The Ideology of Form in Verga's LA LUPA: Realism, Myth, and the Passion of Control." MLN 95:104-138. January 1980.

## IL MARITO DI ELENA

Cecchetti, Giovanni. Giovanni Verga. Boston: Twayne, 1978. pp. 98-103.

## MASTRO-DON GESUALDO

Pacifici, Sergio. The Modern Italian Novel from Manzoni to Svevo. Carbondale: Southern Illinois University Press, 1967. pp. 123-128.

⎯⎯⎯. "The Tragic World of Verga's Primitives." From "Verismo" to Experimentalism: Essays on the Modern Italian Novel. ed. Sergio Pacifici. Bloomington: Indiana University Press, 1969. pp. 28-34.

Woolf, D. The Art of Verga: A Study in Objectivity. Sydney: Sydney University Press, 1977. pp. 74-95.

Verga, Giovanni

NOVELLE RUSTICANE
Lepschy, Anna Laura. "Aspects of Verga's Narrative Technique in VITA DEI CAMPI and NOVELLE RUSTICANE: Pointers Forward and Flashbacks." FI 13:454-463. Winter 1979.

Woolf, D. The Art of Verga: A Study in Objectivity. Sydney: Sydney University Press, 1977. pp. 30-52.

──────. "Three Stories from the NOVELLE RUSTICANE." Italica 52:238-257. Summer 1975.

STORIA DI UNA CAPINERA
Patruno, Nicholas. Language in Giovanni Verga's Early Novels. Chapel Hill: University of North Carolina Press, 1977. 122 pp.

Wilkin, Andrew. "Giovanni Verga's STORIA DI UNA CAPINERA--100 Years On." ML 52:177-181. December 1971.

LE STORIE DEL CASTELLO DI TREZZA
Jones, James F., Jr. "Narrative Technique in Verga's LE STORIE DEL CASTELLO DI TREZZA." Italica 52: 221-234. Summer 1975.

TIGRE REALE
Patruno, Nicholas. Language in Giovanni Verga's Early Novels. Chapel Hill: University of North Carolina Press, 1977. 122 pp.

UNA PECCATRICE
Biasin, Gian-Paolo. Literary Diseases: Theme and Metaphor in the Italian Novel. Austin: University of Texas Press, 1975. pp. 36-62.

Patruno, Nicholas. Language in Giovanni Verga's Early Novels. Chapel Hill: University of North Carolina Press, 1977. 122 pp.

VITA DEI CAMPI
Lepschy, Anna Laura. "Aspects of Verga's Narrative Technique in VITA DEI CAMPI and NOVELLE RUSTICANE: Pointers Forward and Flashbacks." FI 13:454-463. Winter 1979.

Woolf, D. The Art of Verga: A Study in Objectivity. Sydney: Sydney University Press, 1977. pp. 3-29.

Viganò, Renata
L'AGNESE VA A MORIRE
Klopp, Charles D. "Nature and Human Nature in Renata Viganò's L'AGNESE VA A MORIRE." IQ 19:35-52. Summer/Fall 1975.

Vittorini, Elio
CITTA DEL MONDO
Potter, Joy Hambuechen. Elio Vittorini. Boston: Twayne, 1979. pp. 118-123.

CONVERSATION IN SICILY
Evans, Annette. "Allusion as Structure: Vittorini and Dante." Symposium 34:13-28. Spring 1980.

Hanne, Michael. "Significant Allusions in Vittorini's CONVERSAZIONE IN SICILIA." MLR 70:75-83. January 1975.

Heiney, Donald. "Elio Vittorini: The Operatic Novel." From "Verismo" to Experimentalism: Essays on the Modern Italian Novel. ed. Sergio Pacifici. Bloomington: Indiana University Press, 1969. pp. 168-182.

_____. Three Italian Novelists: Moravia, Pavese, Vittorini. Ann Arbor: University of Michigan Press, 1968. pp. 177-189.

Merry, Bruce. "Four Versions for a Reading of Vittorini's CONVERSAZIONE IN SICILIA." LCrit 10:35-43. Winter 1971.

_____. "Vittorini's Multiple Resources of Style: CONVERSAZIONE IN SICILIA." Mosaic 5:107-116. Spring 1972.

Pacifici, Sergio. The Modern Italian Novel from Pea to Moravia. Carbondale: Southern Illinois University Press, 1979. pp. 172-181.

Potter, Joy Hambuechen. Elio Vittorini. Boston: Twayne, 1979. pp. 67-80.

_____. "An Ideological Substructure in CONVERSAZIONE IN SICILIA." Italica 52:50-69. Spring 1975.

_____. "Patterns of Meaning in CONVERSAZIONE IN SICILIA." FI 9:60-72. March 1975.

Schneider, Marilyn. "Circularity as Mode and Meaning in CONVERSAZIONE IN SICILIA." MLN 90:93-108. January 1975.

Shapiro, Marianne. "The 'Gran Lombardo': Vittorini and Dante." Italica 52:70-77. Spring 1975.

ERICA
Heiney, Donald. Three Italian Novelists: Moravia, Pavese, Vittorini. Ann Arbor: University of Michigan Press, 1968. pp. 169-175.

Pacifici, Sergio. The Modern Italian Novel from Pea to Moravia. Carbondale: Southern Illinois University Press, 1979. pp. 168-171.

Potter, Joy Hambuechen. Elio Vittorini. Boston: Twayne, 1979. pp. 59-66.

────────. "The Poetic and Symbolic Function of Fable in ERICA." Italica 48:51-70. Spring 1971.
LA GARIBALDINA
Heiney, Donald. Three Italian Novelists: Moravia, Pavese, Vittorini. Ann Arbor: University of Michigan Press, 1968. pp. 207-212.

Pacifici, Sergio. The Modern Italian Novel from Pea to Moravia. Carbondale: Southern Illinois University Press, 1979. pp. 195-198.
MEN AND NON-MEN
Heiney, Donald. Three Italian Novelists: Moravia, Pavese, Vittorini. Ann Arbor: University of Michigan Press, 1968. pp. 190-194.

Pacifici, Sergio. The Modern Italian Novel from Pea to Moravia. Carbondale: Southern Illinois University Press, 1979. pp. 181-184.

Potter, Joy Hambuechen. Elio Vittorini. Boston: Twayne, 1979. pp. 81-91.

Vittorini, Edwina. "Vittorini's UOMINI E NO: An Epic of the Resistance?" DUJ 62:65-80. March 1970.
THE RED CARNATION
Heiney, Donald. Three Italian Novelists: Moravia, Pavese, Vittorini. Ann Arbor: University of Michigan Press, 1968. pp. 163-169.

Pacifici, Sergio. The Modern Italian Novel from Pea to Moravia. Carbondale: Southern Illinois University Press, 1979. pp. 165-168.

Potter, Joy Hambuechen. Elio Vittorini. Boston: Twayne, 1979. pp. 51-59.
THE TWILIGHT OF THE ELEPHANT
Heiney, Donald. Three Italian Novelists: Moravia, Pavese, Vittorini. Ann Arbor: University of Michigan Press, 1968. pp. 194-200.

Pacifici, Sergio. The Modern Italian Novel from Pea to Moravia. Carbondale: Southern Illinois University Press, 1979. pp. 168-172.

Potter, Joy Hambuechen. Elio Vittorini. Boston: Twayne, 1979. pp. 91-97.
THE WOMAN OF ROME
Potter, Joy Hambuechen. Elio Vittorini. Boston: Twayne, 1979. pp. 98-111.
THE WOMEN OF MESSINA

Heiney, Donald. Three Italian Novelists: Moravia, Pavese, Vittorini. Ann Arbor: University of Michigan Press, 1968. pp. 200-206.

Pacifici, Sergio. The Modern Italian Novel from Pea to Moravia. Carbondale: Southern Illinois University Press, 1979. pp. 188-195.

Volponi, Paolo
   CORPORALE
      Capozzi, Rocco. "The Narrator-Protagonist and the Divided Self in Volponi's CORPORALE." FI 10:203-216. September 1976.

# THE GERMAN NOVEL

Andersch, Alfred
 DIE ROTE
  Bance, A. F. "DER TOD IN ROM and DIE ROTE: Two Italian Episodes." FMLS 3:126-134. April 1967.

Arnim, Achim von
 DIE KRONENWÄCHTER
  Holt, R. F. "Achim von Arnim and Sir Walter Scott." GL&L 26:142-160. January 1973.

  Riley, Helene M. "Scientist, Sorcerer, or Servant of Humanity: The Many Faces of Faust in the Work of Achim von Arnim." Seminar 13:4-8. February 1977.
 DIE MAJORATSHERREN
  Casey, Paul F. "Images of Birds in Arnim's MAJORATSHERREN." GL&L 33:190-198. April 1980.
 OWEN TUDOR
  Stopp, Elisabeth. "Arnim's OWEN TUDOR and Its Background." GL&L 29:155-165. October 1975.
 SELTSAMES BEGEGNEN UND WIEDERSEHEN
  Duncan, Bruce. "Fate and Coincidence in Arnim's SELTSAMES BEGEGNEN UND WIEDERSEHEN." Seminar 15:181-189. September 1979.
 DER TOLLE INVALIDE
  Butler, Colin. "Psychology and Faith in Arnim's DER TOLLE INVALIDE." SIR 17:149-162. Spring 1978.

  Lösel, F. "Psychology, Religion and Myth in Arnim's DER TOLLE INVALIDE AUF DEM FORT RATONNEAU." NGS 5:75-90. Summer 1977.

Bachmann, Ingeborg
 MALINA
  Reinhardt, George W. "Form as Consolation: Thematic Development in Ingeborg Bachmann's MALINA." Symposium 33:41-63. Spring 1979.

Bachstrom, Johann Friedrich
 DAS LAND DER INQUIRANER
  *Lamport, F. J. "Utopia and 'Robinsonade': Schnabel's INSEL FELSENBURG and Bachstrom's LAND DER INQUIRANER." OGS 1:10-30. 1966.

Ball, Hugo
    FLAMETTI
        Last, Rex W. German Dadaist Literature: Kurt Schwitters, Hugo Ball, Hans Arp. New York: Twayne, 1973. pp. 106-113.

        Steinke, Gerhardt Edward. The Life and Work of Hugo Ball, Founder of Dadaism. The Hague: Mouton, 1967. pp. 190-204.
    TENDERENDA THE DREAMER
        Hohendahl, Peter Uwe. "A Surrealistic Novel." Dimension 1:456-463. No. 3, 1968.

        Last, Rex W. German Dadaist Literature: Kurt Schwitters, Hugo Ball, Hans Arp. New York: Twayne, 1973. pp. 101-106.

Bergengruen, Werner
    AM HIMMEL WIE AUF ERDEN
        Waidson, H. M. "Prose Fiction: Some Outstanding German Novels." Twentieth Century German Literature. ed. August Closs. New York: Barnes and Noble, 1969. pp. 141-145.
    JUNGFRAULICHKEIT
        Alexander, Mary. "Virgo-Virago? Werner Bergengruen's Novelle JUNGFRÄULICHKEIT." GL&L 23:206-216. April 1970.
    A MATTER OF CONSCIENCE
        Eickhorst, William. "Werner Bergengruen's A MATTER OF CONSCIENCE (DER GROSSTYRANN UND DAS GERICHT): The Summit and Substance of Literary Crime Fiction." BSUF 9:13-16. Winter 1968.
    DIE WUNDERBARE SCHREIBMASCHINE
        Bedwell, Carol B. "The Disappointing Miracle in Werner Bergengruen's DIE WUNDERBARE SCHREIBMASCHINE." SSF 5:18-23. Fall 1967.

Bernhard, Thomas
    DAS KALKWERK
        Craig, D. A. "The Novels of Thomas Bernhard--A Report." GL&L 25:343-353. July 1972.

Bieler, Manfred
    BONIFAZ ODER DER MATROSE IN DER FLASCHE
        Andrews, R. C. "A Comic Novel from East Germany: Manfred Bieler, BONIFAZ ODER DER MATROSE IN DER FLASCHE." GL&L 20:101-106. January 1967.

Bienek, Horst
    DIE ZELLE
        White, J. J. "Horst Bienek's DIE ZELLE--Novel and Film." GL&L 32:229-245. April 1979.

Bleibtreu, Carl
DIE VIELZUVIELEN
    Humble, M. E. "Zarathustra's Return: Two Novels by Michael Georg Conrad and Carl Bleibtreu and the Contemporary Reception of Nietzsche." GL&L 33:214-218. April 1980.

Bobrowski, Johannes
LEVINS MÜHLE
    Barnouw, Dagmar. "Bobrowski and Socialist Realism." GR 48:288-314. November 1973.

    Scrase, David A. "Point Counterpoint: Variations on the 'Fest' Theme in Johannes Bobrowski's LEVINS MÜHLE." GL&L 32:177-184. January 1979.

    Waidson, H. M. "Bobrowski's LEVINS MÜHLE." Essays in German Language, Culture and Society. ed. Siegbert S. Prawer et al. London: Maney, 1969. pp. 149-159.
LITAUISCHE CLAVIERE
    Barnouw, Dagmar. "Bobrowski and Socialist Realism." GR 48:288-314. November 1973.

Böll, Heinrich
ANSICHTEN EINES CLOWNS
    Conard, Robert C. "Two Novels About Outsiders: The Kinship of J. D. Salinger's THE CATCHER IN THE RYE with Heinrich Böll's ANSICHTEN EINES CLOWNS." UDR 5:23-26. Winter 1968.

    Duroche, Leonard L. "Böll's ANSICHTEN EINES CLOWNS in Existentialist Perspective." Symposium 25:347-358. Winter 1971.

    Nicolai, Ralf R. "Böll's Attitude Toward Religion in THE CLOWN and GROUP PORTRAIT WITH LADY." KN 25:487-498. No. 4, 1978.

    Paslick, Robert H. "A Defense of Existence: Böll's ANSICHTEN EINES CLOWNS." GQ 41:698-710. November 1968.

    Pickar, Gertrud B. "The Impact of Narrative Perspective on Character Portrayal in Three Novels of Heinrich Böll: BILLARD UM HALBZEHN, ANSICHTEN EINES CLOWNS, and GRUPPENBILD MIT DAME." UDR 11:28-31. Winter 1974.

    Thomas, R. Hinton and Wilfried van der Will. The German Novel and the Affluent Society. Manchester: Manchester University Press, 1968. pp. 55-65.
BILLIARDS AT HALF PAST NINE

Baker, Donna. "Nazism and the Petit Bourgeois Protagonist: The Novels of Grass, Böll, and Mann." NGC 5:94-100. Spring 1975.

Boa, Elizabeth and J. H. Reid. Critical Strategies: German Fiction in the Twentieth Century. London: Edward Arnold, 1972. pp. 97-102.

Pickar, Gertrud B. "The Impact of Narrative Perspective on Character Portrayal in Three Novels of Heinrich Böll: BILLARD UM HALBZEHN, ANSICHTEN EINES CLOWNS, and GRUPPENBILD MIT DAME." UDR 11:25-28. Winter 1974.

Thomas, R. Hinton and Wilfried van der Will. The German Novel and the Affluent Society. Manchester: Manchester University Press, 1968. pp. 44-55.

Waidson, H. M. "Prose Fiction: Some Outstanding German Novels." Twentieth Century German Literature. ed. August Closs. New York: Barnes and Noble, 1969. pp. 155-158.

DAS BROT DER FRÜHEN JAHRE
Hanson, W. P. "Heinrich Böll: DAS BROT DER FRÜHEN JAHRE." ML 48:148-151. December 1967.

GROUP PORTRAIT WITH LADY
Deschner, Margareta. "Böll's 'Lady': A New Eve." UDR 11:11-22. Winter 1974.

Ghurye, Charlotte W. The Writer and Society: Studies in the Fiction of Günter Grass and Heinrich Böll. Bern: Lang, 1976. pp. 37-62.

Ley, Ralph. "Compassion, Catholicism, and Communism: Reflections on Böll's GRUPPENBILD MIT DAME." UDR 10:25-38. Fall 1973.

Meyers, David. "Heinrich Böll's GRUPPENBILD MIT DAME: Aesthetic Play and Ethical Seriousness." Seminar 13:189-198. September 1977.

Nicolai, Ralf R. "Böll's Attitude Toward Religion in THE CLOWN and GROUP PORTRAIT WITH LADY." KN 25:487-498. No. 4, 1978.

Pickar, Gertrud B. "The Impact of Narrative Perspective on Character Portrayal in Three Novels of Heinrich Böll: BILLARD UM HALBZEHN, ANSICHTEN EINES CLOWNS, and GRUPPENBILD MIT DAME." UDR 11:31-35. Winter 1974.

Reid, James Henderson. Heinrich Böll: Withdrawal and Re-emergence. London: Wolff, 1973. pp. 69-79.

Waidson, H. M. "Heroine and Narrator in Heinrich Böll's GRUPPENBILD MIT DAME." FMLS 9:123-131. April 1973.

THE LOST HONOUR OF KATHARINA BLUM
Franklin, J. C. "Alienation and the Retention of the Self: The Heroines of DER GUTE MENSCH VON SEZUAN, ABSCHIED VON GESTERN, and DIE VERLORENE EHRE DER KATHARINA BLUM." Mosaic 12:87-98. Summer 1979.

Ghuyre, Charlotte W. The Writer and Society: Studies in the Fiction of Günter Grass and Heinrich Böll. Bern: Lang, 1976. pp. 63-76.

Payne, Philip. "Heinrich Böll Versus Axel Springer: Some Observations on DIE VERLORENE EHRE DER KATHARINA BLUM." NGS 6:45-57. Spring 1978.

Williams, Rhys W. "Heinrich Böll and the KATHARINA BLUM Debate." CritQ 21:49-58. Autumn 1979.

Zipes, Jack. "The Political Dimensions of THE LOST HONOR OF KATHARINA BLUM." NGC 12:75-84. Fall 1977.

UND SAGTE KEIN EINZIGES WORT
Whitcomb, Richard O. "Heinrich Böll and the Mirror-Image Technique." UDR 10:41-46. Fall 1973.

DIE WAAGE DER BALEKS
Fetzer, John. "The Scales of Injustice: Comments on Heinrich Böll's DIE WAAGE DER BALEKS." GQ 45:472-479. May 1972.

WO WARST DU, ADAM?
Ghurye, Charlotte W. The Writer and Society: Studies in the Fiction of Günter Grass and Heinrich Böll. Bern: Lang, 1976. pp. 21-36.

Bonaventura
NACHTWACHEN
Finger, Ellis. "Bonaventura Through Kreuzgang: NACHTWACHEN as Autobiography." GQ 54:282-297. May 1980.

Gillespie, Gerald. "Bonaventura's Romantic Agony: Prevision of an Art of Existential Despair." MLN 85: 697-726. October 1970.

Hunter, Rosemarie. "NACHTWACHEN VON BONAVENTURA and TRISTRAM SHANDY." CRCL 1:218-234. Fall 1974.

Pribić, Rado. "Alienation in NACHTWACHEN by Bonaventura and Dostoevskij's NOTES FROM THE UNDERGROUND." GSlav 5:19-27. Spring 1975.

_____. Bonaventura's NACHTWACHEN and Dostoevsky's NOTES FROM THE UNDERGROUND: A Comparison in Nihilism. München: Verlag Otto Sagner, 1974. 149 pp.

*Sammons, Jeffrey L. The NACHTWACHEN VON BONAVENTURA: A Structural Interpretation. The Hague: Mouton, 1965. 120 pp.

Braun, Volker
  UNVOLLENDETE GESCHICHTE
    Bodi, Leslie. "The Art of Paradox: Volker Braun's UNVOLLENDETE GESCHICHTE." AUMLA 48:268-281. November 1977.

Brecht, Bertolt
  THE BUSINESS DEALS OF MR. JULIUS CAESAR
    Dickson, Keith. Towards Utopia: A Study of Brecht. Oxford: Clarendon Press, 1978. pp. 64-79; 268-273.
  THE THREEPENNY NOVEL
    Benjamin, Walter. Understanding Brecht. London: N. L. B., 1973. pp. 75-84.

    Dickson, Keith. Towards Utopia: A Study of Brecht. Oxford: Clarendon Press, 1978. pp. 255-268.

    Ewen, Frederic. Bertolt Brecht: His Life, His Art, and His Times. New York: Citadel Press, 1967. pp. 304-307.

Brentano, Clemens
  DIE GESCHICHTE VOM BRAVEN KASPERL UND DEM SCHÖNEN ANNERL
    Swales, Martin. "Narrative Sleight-of-Hand: Some Notes on Two German Romantic Tales." NGS 6:1-4. Spring 1978.
  GODWI
    Fetzer, John. "Clemens Brentano's GODWI: Variations on the Melos-Eros Theme." GR 42:108-123. March 1967.

    _____. Romantic Orpheus: Profiles of Clemens Brentano. Berkeley: University of California Press, 1974. pp. 81-96.
  DAS MÄRCHEN VON GOCKEL UND HINKEL
    Frye, Lawrence O. "The Art of Narrating a Rooster Hero in Brentano's DAS MÄRCHEN VON GOCKEL UND HINKEL." Euphorion 72:400-420. No. 4, 1978.
  DIE SCHACHTEL MIT DER FRIEDENSPUPPE
    Ziegler, Vickie L. "Justice in Brentano's DIE SCHACHTEL MIT DER FRIEDENSPUPPE." GR 53:174-179. Fall 1978.

Broch, Hermann
  THE DEATH OF VIRGIL
    Baumann, Walter. "Ezra Pound and Hermann Broch: A Comparison." Seminar 4:100-112. Fall 1968.

    ———. "The Idea of Fate in Hermann Broch's TOD DES VERGIL." MLQ 29:196-206. June 1968.

    Cohn, Dorrit. "Laughter at the Nadir: On a Theme in Hermann Broch's Novels." Monatshefte 61:113-121. Summer 1969.

    Lipman-Wulf, Peter. "Remarks on My Graphic Interpretation of THE DEATH OF VERGIL." MAL 13:51-58. No. 4, 1980.

    Peters, George F. "THE DEATH OF VIRGIL: 'Ein Englisches Gedicht?'" MAL 10:43-53. No. 1, 1977.

    Schlant, Ernestine. Hermann Broch. Boston: Twayne, 1978. pp. 97-124.

    ———. "Hermann Broch's Theory of Symbols Exemplified in a Scene from DER TOD DES VERGIL." Neophil 54:53-63. January 1970.

    Strelka, Joseph. "Hermann Broch: Comparatist and Humanist." CLS 12:67-79. March 1975.

    Ziolkowski, Theodore. "Broch's Image of Vergil and Its Context." MAL 13:1-30. No. 4, 1980.
  THE GUILTLESS
    Schlant, Ernestine. Hermann Broch. Boston: Twayne, 1978. pp. 125-141.
  THE MOUNTAIN NOVEL
    Schlant, Ernestine. Hermann Broch. Boston: Twayne, 1978. pp. 76-86.
  THE SLEEPWALKERS
    Bernheim, Mark. "Style: Abstraction and Empathy in Hermann Broch's DIE SCHLAFWANDLER." MAL 13:59-76. No. 4, 1980.

    Cohn, Dorrit. "Laughter at the Nadir: On a Theme in Hermann Broch's Novels." Monatshefte 61:113-121. Summer 1969.

    *———. THE SLEEPWALKERS: Elucidations of Hermann Broch's Trilogy. The Hague: Mouton, 1966. 167 pp.

    Herd, Eric W. "Essay and Novel: Hermann Broch's DIE SCHLAFWANDLER." JIG 8:47-67. No. 1, 1976.

Kurz, Paul Konrad, S.J. On Modern German Literature. Vol. I. University, Ala.: The University of Alabama Press, 1967. pp. 105-130.

Osterle, Heinz D. "Hermann Broch, DIE SCHLAFWANDLER: Revolution and Apocalypse." PMLA 86:946-958. October 1971.

Schlant, Ernestine. Hermann Broch. Boston: Twayne, 1978. pp. 40-67.

──────. "Hermann Broch's SLEEPWALKERS: Dialectical Structure and Epistemological Unity." GR 43: 201-214. May 1968.

Waidson, H. M. "Prose Fiction: Some Outstanding German Novels." Twentieth Century German Literature. ed. August Closs. New York: Barnes and Noble, 1969. pp. 132-136.

White, J.J. "The Identity and Function of Bertrand in Hermann Broch's DIE SCHLAFWANDLER." GL&L 24: 135-144. January 1971.

Ziolkowski, Theodore. Dimensions of the Modern Novel: German Texts and European Contexts. Princeton: Princeton University Press, 1969. pp. 138-180.

──────. "Hermann Broch and Relativity in Fiction." WSCL 8:371-376. Summer 1967.

DIE UNBEKANNTE GRÖSSE
Hanson, W. P. "Hermann Broch's 'Unknown Quantity.'" NGS 2:157-170. Autumn 1974.

Watt, Roderick H. "Hermann Broch's DIE UNBEKANNTE GRÖSSE: The Central Symbol of 'Sterne im Wasser.'" MLN 89:840-848. October 1974.

DER VERSUCHER
Boa, Elizabeth and J. H. Reid. Critical Strategies: German Fiction in the Twentieth Century. London: Edward Arnold, 1972. pp. 119-122.

Casey, Timothy J. "Questioning Broch's DER VERSUCHER." DVLG 47:467-507. No. 3, 1973.

Hardin, James. "Hermann Broch's Theories on Mass Psychology and DER VERSUCHER." GQ 47:24-33. January 1974.

Lauckner, Nancy A. "The Surrogate Jew in the Postwar German Novel." Monatshefte 66:136-140. Summer 1974.

Bruyn, Günter de
PREISVERLEIHUNG
    Frank, Ted E. "Günter de Bruyn's PREISVERLEIHUNG: A GDR Novel with a Mission." UDR 13:83-89. Winter 1978.

Büchner, Georg
LENZ
    Bell, Gerda E. "Windows: A Study of a Symbol in Georg Büchner's Work." GR 47:103-105. March 1972.

    Benn, Maurice B. The Drama of Revolt: A Critical Study of Georg Büchner. Cambridge: Cambridge University Press, 1976. pp. 186-216.

    Cowen, Roy C. "Identity and Conscience in Büchner's Works." GR 43:258-266. November 1968.

    Hauser, Ronald. Georg Büchner. New York: Twayne, 1974. pp. 49-71.

    Jansen, Peter K. "The Structural Function of the 'Kunstgesprach' in Büchner's LENZ." Monatshefte 67:145-156. Summer 1975.

    King, Janet K. "Lenz Viewed Sane." GR 49:146-153. March 1974.

    Knight, A. H. J. Georg Büchner. London: Methuen, 1974. pp. 143-157.

    Parker, John J. "Some Reflections on Georg Büchner's LENZ and Its Principal Source, the Oberlin Record." GL&L 21:103-111. January 1968.

    Pascal, Roy. "Büchner's LENZ--Style and Message." OGS 9:68-83. 1978.

    Reeve, William C. Georg Büchner. New York: Frederick Ungar, 1979. pp. 25-46.

    Struc, Roman S. "Madness as Existence: An Essay on a Literary Theme." RS 38:80-84. June 1970.

Büchner, Luise
EIN DICHTER
    Joeres, Ruth-Ellen Boetcher. "EIN DICHTER: An Introduction to the World of Luise Büchner." GQ 52:32-49. January 1979.

Canetti, Elias
DIE BLENDUNG
    Boa, Elizabeth and J. H. Reid. Critical Strategies: Ger-

man Fiction in the Twentieth Century. London: Edward Arnold, 1972. pp. 83-85.

  Russell, Peter. "The Vision of Man in Elias Canetti's DIE BLENDUNG." GL&L 28:24-35. October 1974.

  Sacharoff, Mark. "Grotesque Comedy in Canetti's AUTO DA FE." Crit 14:99-112. No. 1, 1972.

  Thomson, Edward A. "Elias Canetti's DIE BLENDUNG and the Changing Image of Madness." GL&L 26:38-47. October 1972.

Carossa, Hans
 EIN TAG IM SPÄTSOMMER 1947
  Kahn, Robert L. "Carossa's EIN TAG IM SPÄTSOMMER 1947: Healing the Wounds of War." RUS 53:1-12. Fall 1967.

Chamisso, Adalbert von
 PETER SCHLEMIHL
  Butler, Colin. "Hobson's Choice: A Note on PETER SCHLEMIHL." Monatshefte 69:5-15. Spring 1977.

  Flores, Ralph. "The Lost Shadow of Peter Schlemihl." GQ 47:567-584. November 1974.

  Neumarkt, Paul. "Chamisso's PETER SCHLEMIHL (A Literary Approach in Terms of Analytical Psychology)." L&P 17:120-127. No. 2/3, 1967.

Conrad, Michael Georg
 IN PURPURNER FINSTERNISS
  Humble, M. E. "Zarathustra's Return: Two Novels by Michael Georg Conrad and Carl Bleibtreu and the Contemporary Reception of Nietzsche." GL&L 33:210-214. April 1980.

Delblanc, Sven
 HOMUNCULUS
  Sjoberg, Leif. "Delblanc's HOMUNCULUS: Some Magic Elements." GR 49:105-124. January 1974.

Döblin, Alfred
 THE AMAZON
  Kort, Wolfgang. Alfred Döblin. New York: Twayne, 1974. pp. 119-127.
 BABYLONISCHE WANDRUNG
  Kort, Wolfgang. Alfred Döblin. New York: Twayne, 1974. pp. 111-116.
 BERGE MEERE UND GIGANTEN
  Kort, Wolfgang. Alfred Döblin. New York: Twayne, 1974. pp. 78-90.

## Döblin, Alfred

### BERLIN ALEXANDERPLATZ

Boa, Elizabeth and J. H. Reid. Critical Strategies: German Fiction in the Twentieth Century. London: Edward Arnold, 1972. pp. 38-40; 133-135.

Dollenmayer, David B. "An Urban Montage and Its Significance in Döblin's BERLIN ALEXANDERPLATZ." GQ 54:317-336. May 1980.

Fries, Marilyn Sibley. "The City as Metaphor for the Human Condition: Alfred Döblin's BERLIN ALEXANDERPLATZ (1929)." MFS 24:41-64. Spring 1978.

Kort, Wolfgang. Alfred Döblin. New York: Twayne, 1974. pp. 99-109.

McLean, Andrew M. "Joyce's ULYSSES and Döblin's ALEXANDERPLATZ BERLIN." CL 25:97-113. Spring 1973.

Mitchell, Breon. "Joyce and Döblin: At the Crossroads of BERLIN ALEXANDERPLATZ." ConL 12:173-187. Spring 1971.

Reid, James H. "BERLIN ALEXANDERPLATZ: A Political Novel." GL&L 21:214-223. April 1968.

Schoonover, Henrietta S. The Humorous and Grotesque Elements in Döblin's BERLIN ALEXANDERPLATZ. Berne: Peter Lang, 1977. 255 pp.

Titche, Leon L., Jr. "Döblin and Dos Passos: Aspects of the City Novel." MFS 17:125-135. Spring 1971.

Zimmermann, Ulf. "Benjamin and BERLIN ALEXANDERPLATZ: Some Notes Towards a View of Literature and the City." CollG 12:256-268. No. 2, 1979.

Ziolkowski, Theodore. Dimensions of the Modern Novel: German Texts and European Contexts. Princeton: Princeton University Press, 1969. pp. 99-137.

### HAMLET OR THE LONG NIGHT COMES TO AN END

Riley, Anthony W. "Jaufré Rudel in Alfred Döblin's Last Novel, HAMLET." Mosaic 10:130-145. Winter 1977.

### NOVEMBER 1918

Kort, Wolfgang. Alfred Döblin. New York: Twayne, 1974. pp. 127-135.

### PARDON WILL NOT BE GRANTED

Kort, Wolfgang. Alfred Döblin. New York: Twayne, 1974. pp. 115-119.

O'Neill, Patrick. "The Anatomy of Crisis: Alfred Döblin's Novel PARDON WIRD NICHT GEGEBEN." Seminar 14:195-213. September 1978.
WALLENSTEIN
Kort, Wolfgang. Alfred Döblin. New York: Twayne, 1974. pp. 70-78.

Doderer, Heimito von
DIE DÄMONEN
Barthofer, Alfred. "Leonhard Kakabsa: Success or Failure? Marginalia to a Key Character in Doderer's Novel DIE DÄMONEN." FMLS 14:304-315. October 1978.

Jones, David L. "Proust and Doderer as Historical Novelists." CLS 10:16-23. March 1973.

Williams, C. E. "Down a Steep Place ... A Study of Heimito von Doderer's DIE DÄMONEN." FMLS 7:76-82. January 1971.
DIE POSAUNEN VON JERICHO
Shaw, Michael. "Doderer's POSAUNEN VON JERICHO." Symposium 21:141-154. Summer 1967.
DIE STRUDELHOFSTIEGE
Guenther, Paul F. "Heimito von Doderer's TANGENTEN and the Genesis of DIE STRUDELHOFSTIEGE." PLL 11:177-185. Spring 1975.
ZWEI LÜGEN
Knust, Von Herbert. "Camus' LE MALENTENDU and Doderer's ZWEI LÜGEN." Archiv 208:23-34. June 1971.

Droste-Hülshoff, Annette von
DIE JUDENBUCHE
Belchamber, N. P. "A Case of Identity: A New Look at DIE JUDENBUCHE by Annette von Droste-Hülshoff." ML 55:80-82. June 1974.

Brown, Jane K. "The Real Mystery in Droste-Hülshoff's DIE JUDENBUCHE." MLR 73:835-846. October 1978.

Chick, Edson. "Voices in Discord: Some Observations on DIE JUDENBUCHE." GQ 42:147-157. March 1969.

Cottrell, Alan P. "The Significance of the Name 'Johannes' in DIE JUDENBUCHE." Seminar 6:207-215. October 1970.

King, Janet K. "Conscience and Conviction in DIE JUDENBUCHE." Monatshefte 64:349-355. Winter 1972.

*Mare, Margaret. Annette von Droste-Hülshoff. Lincoln: University of Nebraska Press, 1965. pp. 253-266.

Wells, Larry D. "Annette von Droste-Hülshoff's Johannes Niemond: Much Ado About Nobody." GR 52:109-121. March 1977.

———. "Indeterminacy as Provocation: The Reader's Role in Annette von Droste-Hülshoff's DIE JUDENBUCHE." MLN 94:475-492. April 1979.

Whitinger, Raleigh. "From Confusion to Clarity: Further Reflections on the Revelatory Function of Narrative Technique and Symbolism in Annette von Droste-Hülshoff's DIE JUDENBUCHE." DVLG 54:259-283. No. 2, 1980.

Dürrenmatt, Friedrich
A DANGEROUS GAME
Tiusanen, Timo. Dürrenmatt: A Study in Plays, Prose, Theory. Princeton: Princeton University Press, 1977. pp. 149-165.
THE JUDGE AND HIS HANGMAN
Arnold, Armin. Friedrich Dürrenmatt. New York: Frederick Ungar, 1972. pp. 48-51.

Benham, G. F. "'Escape into Inquietude.' DER RICHTER UND SEIN HANKER." RLV 42:147-154. No. 2, 1976.

Tiusanen, Timo. Dürrenmatt: A Study in Plays, Prose, Theory. Princeton: Princeton University Press, 1977. pp. 128-137.
ONCE A GREEK...
Tiusanen, Timo. Dürrenmatt: A Study in Plays, Prose, Theory. Princeton: Princeton University Press, 1977. pp. 142-148.
THE PLEDGE
Arnold, Armin. Friedrich Dürrenmatt. New York: Frederick Ungar, 1972. pp. 55-57.

Leah, Gordon N. "Dürrenmatt's Detective Stories." ML 48:66-69. June 1967.

Ramsey, Roger. "Parody and Mystery in Dürrenmatt's THE PLEDGE." MFS 17:525-532. Winter 1971-1972.

Tiusanen, Timo. Dürrenmatt: A Study in Plays, Prose, Theory. Princeton: Princeton University Press, 1977. pp. 165-174.
THE QUARRY
Arnold, Armin. Friedrich Dürrenmatt. New York: Frederick Ungar, 1972. pp. 51-55.

Elkhadem, Saad. "Dürrenmatt's DER VERDACHT: A Defective Mystery Story or a Sophisticated Novel?" IFR 4:178-181. July 1977.

Tiusanen, Timo. Dürrenmatt: A Study in Plays, Prose, Theory. Princeton: Princeton University Press, 1977. pp. 134-142.

Edschmid, Kasimir
SPORT UM GAGALY
Mornin, Edward. "Taking Games Seriously: Observations on the German Sports-Novel." GR 51:284-286. November 1976.

Rothe, Wolfgang. "When Sports Conquered the Republic: A Forgotten Chapter from the 'Roaring Twenties.'" StTCL 4:16-21. Fall 1979.

Eichendorff, Joseph
AHNUNG UND GEGENWART
Blackall, Eric A. "Moonlight and Moonshine: A Disquisition on Eichendorff's Novels." Seminar 6:111-127. June 1970.

Schwartz, Egon. Joseph von Eichendorff. New York: Twayne, 1972. pp. 24-78.
DICHTER UND IHRE GESELLEN
Blackall, Eric A. "Moonlight and Moonshine: A Disquisition on Eichendorff's Novels." Seminar 6:111-127. June 1970.
FROM THE LIFE OF A GOOD-FOR-NOTHING
Nygaard, Loisa. "Eichendorff's AUS DEM LEBEN EINES TAUGENICHTS: 'Eine leise Persiflage' der Romantik." SIR 19:193-216. Summer 1980.

Pickar, Gertrud Bauer. "Eichendorff's AUS DEM LEBEN EINES TAUGENICHTS: Postures of Naïveté and Irony." LangQ 15:7-13; 16. Fall/Winter 1976.

Radner, Lawrence. Eichendorff: The Spiritual Geometer. Lafayette: Purdue University Studies, 1970. pp. 271-351.

Swales, Martin. "Nostalgia as Conciliation: A Note on Eichendorff's AUS DEM LEBEN EINES TAUGENICHTS and Heine's DER DOPPELGÄNGER." GL&L 30:36-45. October 1976.
DAS MARMORBILD
Mornin, Edward. "DER GOLDENE TOPF and DAS MARMORBILD: A Comparison." UP 11:32-38. Spring 1978.

Radner, Lawrence. Eichendorff: The Spiritual Geometer. Lafayette: Purdue University Studies, 1970. pp. 201-268.

Feuchtwanger, Lion
JEFTA UND SEINE TOCHTER

Spalek, John M. Lion Feuchtwanger. Los Angeles: Hennessey and Ingalls, 1972. pp. 245-261.
JOSEPHUS
Kahn, Lothar. Insight and Action: The Life and Work of Lion Feuchtwanger. Rutherford: Fairleigh Dickinson University Press, 1975. pp. 256-260.

Raphael, Marc Lee. "An Ancient and Modern Identity Crisis: Lion Feuchtwanger's JOSEPHUS Trilogy." Judaism 21:409-414. Fall 1972.

Spalek, John M. Lion Feuchtwanger. Los Angeles: Hennessey and Ingalls, 1972. pp. 187-199.
JUD SUSS
Boa, Elizabeth and J. H. Reid. Critical Strategies: German Fiction in the Twentieth Century. London: Edward Arnold, 1972. pp. 64-68.

Rühle, Jürgen. Literature and Revolution: A Critical Study of the Writer and Communism in the Twentieth Century. New York: Frederick A. Praeger, 1969. pp. 185-188.

Spalek, John M. Lion Feuchtwanger. Los Angeles: Hennessey and Ingalls, 1972. pp. 113-130.
DIE JUDEN VON TOLEDO
Spalek, John M. Lion Feuchtwanger. Los Angeles: Hennessey and Ingalls, 1972. pp. 231-243.
NARRENWEISHEIT ODER TOD UND VERKLÄRUNG DES JEAN-JACQUES ROUSSEAU
Spalek, John M. Lion Feuchtwanger. Los Angeles: Hennessey and Ingalls, 1972. pp. 217-229.
THE OPPERMANNS
Spalek, John M. Lion Feuchtwanger. Los Angeles: Hennessey and Ingalls, 1972. pp. 141-147.
PARIS GAZETTE
Spalek, John M. Lion Feuchtwanger. Los Angeles: Hennessey and Ingalls, 1972. pp. 147-155.
RAQUEL
Kahn, Lothar. Insight and Action: The Life and Work of Lion Feuchtwanger. Rutherford: Fairleigh Dickinson University Press, 1975. pp. 327-331.
SUCCESS
Spalek, John M. Lion Feuchtwanger. Los Angeles: Hennessey and Ingalls, 1972. pp. 131-141; 157-182.
THIS IS THE HOUR
Spalek, John M. Lion Feuchtwanger. Los Angeles: Hennessey and Ingalls, 1972. pp. 201-215.
TIS FOLLY TO BE WISE
Kahn, Lothar. Insight and Action: The Life and Work of Lion Feuchtwanger. Rutherford: Fairleigh Dickinson University Press, 1975. pp. 315-321.

Fischart, Johann
  GESCHICHTKLITTERUNG
      Knight, K. G.  "Fischart's GESCHICHTKLITTERUNG."
      GL&L 29:90-97.  October 1975.

Fontane, Theodor
  L'ADULTERA
      Garland, Henry.  The Berlin Novels of Theodor Fontane.  Oxford:  Clarendon, 1980.  pp. 45-72.
  BEFORE THE STORM
      Garland, Henry.  The Berlin Novels of Theodor Fontane.  Oxford:  Clarendon, 1980.  pp. 5-28.
  CECILE
      Garland, Henry.  The Berlin Novels of Theodor Fontane.  Oxford:  Clarendon, 1980.  pp. 73-98.
  EFFI BRIEST
      Borchardt, Edith.  "Leitmotif and Structure in Fassbinder's EFFI BRIEST."  LFQ 7:201-207.  No. 3, 1979.

      Garland, Henry.  The Berlin Novels of Theodor Fontane.  Oxford:  Clarendon, 1980.  pp. 169-208.

      Gilbert, Anna Marie.  "A New Look at EFFI BRIEST: Genesis and Interpretation."  DVLG 53:96-114.  March 1979.

      Riechel, Donald C.  "EFFI BRIEST and the Calendar of Fate."  GR 48:189-211.  May 1973.

      Swales, Erika.  "Private Mythologies and Public Unease: On Fontane's EFFI BRIEST."  MLR 75:114-123.  January 1980.

      Thum, Reinhard H.  "Symbol, Motif and Leitmotif in Fontane's EFFI BRIEST."  GR 54:115-124.  Summer 1979.
  FRAU JENNY TREIBEL
      Betz, Frederick.  "'Wo sich Herz zum Herzen find't': The Question of Authorship and Source of the Song and Sub-title in Fontane's FRAU JENNY TREIBEL."  GQ 49:312-317.  May 1976.

      Garland, Henry.  The Berlin Novels of Theodor Fontane.  Oxford:  Clarendon, 1980.  pp. 140-168.

      Subiotto, Frances M.  "Aspects of the Theatre in Fontane's Novels."  FMLS 6:161-166.  April 1970.

      Turner, David.  "Coffee or Milk?--That Is the Question: On An Incident from Fontane's FRAU JENNY TREIBEL."  GL&L 21:330-335.  July 1968.

      _____.  "Fontane's FRAU JENNY TREIBEL:  A Study in Ironic Discrepancy."  FMLS 8:132-147.  April 1972.

Fontane, Theodor

IRRUNGEN, WIRRUNGEN
Garland, Henry. The Berlin Novels of Theodor Fontane. Oxford: Clarendon, 1980. pp. 99-127.

Harrigan, Renny. "The Limits of Female Emancipation: A Study of Theodor Fontane's Lower Class Women." Monatshefte 70: 117-128. Summer 1978.
MATHILDE MOHRING
Bance, A. F. "Fontane's MATHILDE MÖHRING." MLR 69:121-133. January 1974.

Garland, Henry. The Berlin Novels of Theodor Fontane. Oxford: Clarendon, 1980. pp. 228-238.

Harrigan, Renny. "The Limits of Female Emancipation: A Study of Theodor Fontane's Lower Class Women." Monatshefte 70:117-128. Summer 1978.
DIE POGGENPUHLS
Garland, Henry. The Berlin Novels of Theodor Fontane. Oxford: Clarendon, 1980. pp. 209-227.
SCHACH VON WUTHENOW
Garland, Henry. The Berlin Novels of Theodor Fontane. Oxford: Clarendon, 1980. pp. 29-44.
DER STECHLIN
Cartland, Harry E. "The 'Old' and the 'New' in Fontane's STECHLIN." GR 54:20-28. Winter 1979.

Garland, Henry. The Berlin Novels of Theodor Fontane. Oxford: Clarendon, 1980. pp. 239-272.

George, E. F. "The Symbol of the Lake and Related Themes in Fontane's DER STECHLIN." FMLS 9:143-152. April 1973.
STINE
Garland, Henry. The Berlin Novels of Theodor Fontane. Oxford: Clarendon, 1980. pp. 128-139.

Harrigan, Renny. "The Limits of Female Emancipation: A Study of Theodor Fontane's Lower Class Women." Monatshefte 70:117-128. Summer 1978.
UNTERM BIRNBAUM
Thomas, Lionel. "Fontane's UNTERM BIRNBAUM." GL&L 23:193-205. April 1970.
UNWIEDERBRINGLICH
Subiotto, Frances M. "The Function of Letters in Fontane's UNWIEDERBRINGLICH." MLR 65:306-318. April 1970.

Frank, Bruno
DER REISEPASS
Kalma, Thomas A. "Bruno Frank's DER REISEPASS: The Exile as an Aristocrat of Humanity." Monatshefte 67:37-47. Spring 1975.

Frank, Leonhard
IM LETZTEN WAGEN
Bance, A. F. "The Intellectual and the Crisis of Weimar: Heinrich Mann's KOBES and Leonhard Frank's IM LETZTEN WAGEN." JES 8:155-170. September 1978.

Freytag, Gustave
DEBIT AND CREDIT
Carter, T. E. "Freytag's SOLL UND HABEN; A Liberal National Manifesto as a Best-seller." GL&L 21:320-329. July 1968.

Gelber, Mark. "Teaching 'Literary Anti-Semitism': Dickens' OLIVER TWIST and Freytag's SOLL UND HABEN." CLS 16:5-9. March 1979.

Sammons, Jeffrey L. "The Evaluation of Freytag's SOLL UND HABEN." GL&L 22:315-323. July 1969.

Friedel, Johann
ELEONORE
Horwath, Peter. "Richardsonian Characters and Motifs in Johann Friedel's Novel ELEONORE." FMLS 13:97-107. April 1977.

Frisch, Max
ANSWER FROM THE SILENCE
Weisstein, Ulrich. Max Frisch. New York: Twayne, 1967. pp. 37-42.
BIN ODER DIE REISE NACH PEKING
Weisstein, Ulrich. Max Frisch. New York: Twayne, 1967. pp. 43-47.
HOMO FABER
Boa, Elizabeth and J. H. Reid. Critical Strategies: German Fiction in the Twentieth Century. London: Edward Arnold, 1972. pp. 52-57.

Butler, Michael. "The Dislocated Environment: The Theme of Itinerancy in Max Frisch's HOMO FABER." NGS 4:101-118. Autumn 1976.

─────────. The Novels of Max Frisch. London: Wolff, 1976. pp. 88-120.

Latta, Alan D. "Walter Faber and the Allegorization of Life: A Reading of Max Frisch's Novel HOMO FABER." GR 54:152-159. Fall 1979.

Petersen, Carol. Max Frisch. New York: Ungar, 1972. pp. 83-88.

Waidson, H. M. "Prose Fiction: Some Outstanding German Novels." Twentieth Century German Literature.

Frisch, Max

ed. August Closs.  New York:  Barnes and Noble, 1969.
pp. 150-155.

Wailes, Stephen L.  "The Inward Journey:  HOMO FAB-
ER and HEART OF DARKNESS."  NGS 6:31-44.  Spring
1978.

Weisstein, Ulrich.  Max Frisch.  New York:  Twayne,
1967.  pp. 64-77.
JÜRG REINHART
Butler, Michael.  The Novels of Max Frisch.  London:
Wolff, 1976.  pp. 17-25.

Weisstein, Ulrich.  Max Frisch.  New York:  Twayne,
1967.  pp. 24-31.
MEIN NAME SEI GANTENBEIN
Botheroyd, Paul F.  Ich und er:  First and Third Per-
son Self-Reference and Problems of Identity in Three
Contemporary German-Language Novels.  The Hague:
Mouton, 1976.  pp. 95-122.

Butler, Michael.  The Novels of Max Frisch.  London:
Wolff, 1976.  pp. 121-150.

Weisstein, Ulrich.  Max Frisch.  New York:  Twayne,
1967.  pp. 78-89.
MONTAUK
Butler, Michael.  The Novels of Max Frisch.  London:
Wolff, 1976.  pp. 151-155.

Shipe, Timothy.  "MONTAUK:  The Invention of Max
Frisch."  Crit 22:55-70.  No. 3, 1980.
DIE SCHWIERIGEN
Butler, Michael.  The Novels of Max Frisch.  London:
Wolff, 1976.  pp. 26-53.

Weisstein, Ulrich.  Max Frisch.  New York:  Twayne,
1967.  pp. 31-37.
STILLER
Butler, Michael.  "The Ambivalence of 'Ordnung':  The
Nature of the 'Nachwort des Staatsanwaltes' in Max
Frisch's STILLER."  FMLS 12:149-155.  April 1976.

──────.  The Novels of Max Frisch.  London:  Wolff,
1976.  pp. 54-87.

Cock, Mary E.  "'Countries of the Mind':  Max Frisch's
Narrative Technique."  MLR 65:820-828.  October 1970.

Cunliffe, W. G.  "Existentialist Elements in Frisch's
Works."  Monatshefte 62:113-122.  Summer 1970.

Helmetag, Charles H.  "The Image of the Automobile in
Max Frisch's STILLER."  GR 47:118-126.  March 1972.

Manger, Philip. "Kierkegaard in Max Frisch's STILL-
ER." GL&L 20:119-131. January 1967.

Musgrave, Marian E. "The Evolution of the Black
Character in the Works of Max Frisch." Monatshefte
66:120-124. Summer 1974.

Pender, Malcolm. "The Role of Rolf the 'Staatsanwalt'
in Max Frisch's STILLER." GL&L 32:332-342. July
1979.

Petersen, Carol. Max Frisch. New York: Ungar,
1972. pp. 77-82.

Weisstein, Ulrich. Max Frisch. New York: Twayne,
1967. pp. 48-63.
A WILDERNESS OF MIRRORS
Petersen, Carol. Max Frisch. New York: Ungar,
1972. pp. 100-106.

Führmann, Franz
BOHMEN AM MEER
Hutchinson, Peter. "Franz Führmann's BOHMEN AM
MEER: A Socialist Version of THE WINTER'S TALE."
MLR 67:579-589. July 1972.
DAS JUDENAUTO
Maier, Kurt S. "Franz Führmann's JUDENAUTO: A
Study of Judeophobia." GR 47:41-49. January 1972.

Gellert, Christian
DAS LEBEN DER SCHWEDISCHEN GRÄFIN VON G * *
Van Abbé, D. M. "Some Unspoken Assumptions in Gel-
lert's SCHWEDISCHE GRÄFIN." OL 28:113-123. 1973.

Van Cleve, John. "A Countess in Name Only: Gellert's
Schwedische Gräfin." GR 55:152-154. Fall 1980.

Goering, Reinhard
JUNG SCHUK
Eben, M. C. "Reinhard Goering's JUNG SCHUK: The
Moment of Encounter." CollG 12:106-111. No. 1/2,
1979.

Goethe, Johann von
ELECTIVE AFFINITIES
Atkins, Stuart. "DIE WAHLVERWANDTSCHAFTEN:
Novel of German Classicism." GQ 53:1-45. January
1980.

Barnes, H. G. Goethe's DIE WAHLVERWANDTSCHAFTEN:
A Literary Interpretation. Oxford: Clarendon Press,
1967. 206 pp.

Blackall, Eric A. Goethe and the Novel. Ithaca: Cornell University Press, 1976. pp. 163-189.

Brown, Jane K. "DIE WAHLVERWANDTSCHAFTEN and the English Novel of Manners." CL 28:97-108. Spring 1976.

Dieckmann, Liselotte. Johann Wolfgang Goethe. New York: Twayne, 1974. pp. 131-144.

Gould, Robert. "The Critical Reception of DIE WAHLVERWANDTSCHAFTEN in the French Press: An Unknown Review of OTTILIA, OU LE POUVOIR DE LA SYMPATHIE." Seminar 9:28-35. March 1973.

Gray, Ronald. Goethe: A Critical Introduction. Cambridge: Cambridge University Press, 1967. pp. 216-225.

Hammer, Carl, Jr. Goethe and Rousseau. Lexington: University of Kentucky Press, 1973. pp. 107-121.

Hargreaves, R. "'Die Novelle in den WAHLVERWANDTSCHAFTEN': A Note on the Hamburg Edition." MLR 62:98-101. January 1967.

Huntley, H. Robert. "THE GOOD SOLDIER and DIE WAHLVERWANDTSCHAFTEN." CL 19:133-141. Spring 1967.

Leu, Paul. "Time and Transcendence in Goethe's WAHLVERWANDTSCHAFTEN." Monatshefte 60:369-378. Winter 1968.

Lillyman, W. J. "Affinity, Innocence and Tragedy: The Narrator and Ottilie in Goethe's DIE WAHLVERWANDTSCHAFTEN." GQ 53:46-63. January 1980.

Macey, Samuel L. "On the Relationship Between Eduard and Ottilie in Goethe's WAHLVERWANDTSCHAFTEN." Seminar 7:79-84. June 1971.

Milfull, John. "The Function of the Novelle DIE WUNDERLICHEN NACHBARSKINDER in Goethe's DIE WAHLVERWANDTSCHAFTEN." GL&L 25:1-5. October 1971.

_____. "The 'Idea' of Goethe's WAHLVERWANDTSCHAFTEN." GR 47:83-94. March 1972.

Muenzer, Clark S. "Eduard and Rhetoric: Characterization and Narrative Strategy in Goethe's DIE WAHLVERWANDTSCHAFTEN." MLN 94:493-509. April 1979.

Nisbet, H. B. "DIE WAHLVERWANDTSCHAFTEN: Explanation and Its Limits." DVLG 43:458-486. August 1969.

Peacock, R. "The Ethics of Goethe's DIE WAHLVERWANDTSCHAFTEN." MLR 71:330-343. April 1976.

Reiss, Hans. Goethe's Novels. London: Macmillan, 1969. pp. 145-221.

Roberts, David. "DIE WAHLVERWANDTSCHAFTEN: A Note on the Symbolism of the Seasons and the Time Structure of DIE WAHLVERWANDTSCHAFTEN with Reference to WERTHER." AUMLA 38:197-203. November 1972.

Snyder, Caroline. "The Helmsman-Rescue Motif in Goethe's DIE WAHLVERWANDTSCHAFTEN." Monatshefte 63:41-47. Spring 1971.

Stock, Irvin. "Goethe's Tragedy: A View of ELECTIVE AFFINITIES." Mosaic 7:17-27. Spring 1974.

Van Abbé, Derek. Goethe: New Perspectives on a Writer and His Times. London: Allen and Unwin, 1972. pp. 150-154.

HERMANN AND DOROTHEA

Dieckmann, Liselotte. Johann Wolfgang Goethe. New York: Twayne, 1974. pp. 148-151.

DAS MÄRCHEN

Bangerter, Lowell A. "The Serpent-Ring in Goethe's DAS MÄRCHEN." GL&L 33:111-115. January 1980.

Bartscht, Waltraud. Goethe's DAS MÄRCHEN: Translation and Analysis. Lexington: University of Kentucky Press, 1972. 107 pp.

Milfull, John. "The Symbolism of Goethe's DAS MÄRCHEN." AUMLA 29:52-59. May 1968.

NOVELLE

Balfour, Rosemary Picozzi. "The Field of View in Goethe's NOVELLE." Seminar 12:63-72. May 1976.

Brown, Jane K. "The Tyranny of the Ideal: The Dialectics of Art in Goethe's NOVELLE." SIR 19:217-231. Summer 1980.

Clouser, Robin. "Ideas of Utopia in Goethe's NOVELLE." PEGS 49:1-44. 1979.

Finger, Ellis. "Indirect Narration and Characterization in Goethe's NOVELLE and 'Klassische Walpurgisnacht.'" CollG 10:16-19. No. 1, 1976-1977.

Goethe, Johann von

Swales, Martin W. "The Threatened Society: Some Remarks on Goethe's NOVELLE." PEGS 38:43-68. 1968.

Wells, Larry D. "Organic Structure in Goethe's NOVELLE." GQ 53:418-429. November 1980.

## WERTHER

Ames, Carol. "Competition, Class, and Structure in DIE LEIDEN DES JUNGEN WERTHER." GQ 50:138-149. March 1977.

Bennett, Benjamin. "Goethe's WERTHER: Double Perspective and the Game of Life." GQ 53:64-81. January 1980.

Blackall, Eric A. Goethe and the Novel. Ithaca: Cornell University Press, 1976. pp. 44-55.

Dieckmann, Liselotte. Johann Wolfgang Goethe. New York: Twayne, 1974. pp. 111-120.

Dukas, Vytas and Richard A. Lawson. "WERTHER and DIARY OF A SUPERFLUOUS MAN." CL 21:146-154. Spring 1969.

Dye, Robert Ellis. "Man and God in Goethe's WERTHER." Symposium 29:314-329. Winter 1975.

Faber, M. D. "The Suicide of Young Werther." PsyR 60:239-276. Summer 1973.

Fetzer, John. "Schatten ohne Frau: Marginalia on a WERTHER Motif." GR 46:87-94. March 1971.

Feuerlicht, Ignace. "Werther's Suicide: Instinct, Reasons and Defense." GQ 51:476-492. November 1978.

Gish, Theodore G. "The Evolution of the Goethean Theme of the 'Wanderer' and the 'Cottage.'" Seminar 9:19-27. March 1973.

Goldsberry, Dennis. "Goethe and George Eliot's MIDDLEMARCH." LangQ 16:39-44. Spring/Summer 1978.

Graham, Ilse. Goethe and Lessing. New York: Barnes and Noble, 1973. pp. 115-136.

Hammer, Carl, Jr. Goethe and Rousseau. Lexington: University Press of Kentucky, 1973. pp. 65-70.

Hatch, Mary Gies. "'Krankheit Zum Tode': Goethe's Concept of Suicide." SAB 43:67-73. November 1978.

_____. "Werther and Student Protest." SAB 39:107-111. May 1974.

Kuhn, Reinhard. The Demon of Noontide: Ennui in Western Literature. Princeton: Princeton University Press, 1976. pp. 168-180.

Lange, Victor. "Fact in Fiction." CLS 6:257-260. September 1969.

Lukacs, Georg. Goethe and His Age. New York: Grosset and Dunlap, 1969. pp. 19-50.

Osborne, John. "Exhibitionism and Criticism: J. M. R. Lenz's 'Briefe über die Moralität der Leiden des jungen Werthers.'" Seminar 10:199-212. September 1974.

Reiss, Hans. Goethe's Novels. London: Macmillan, 1969. pp. 10-67.

Rockwood, Heidi M. "Jung's Psychological Types and Goethe's DIE LEIDEN DES JUNGEN WERTHERS." GR 55:118-123. Summer 1980.

Saine, Thomas P. "Passion and Aggression: The Meaning of Werther's Last Letter." OL 35:327-356. No. 4, 1980.

Salm, Peter. "Werther and the Sensibility of Estrangement." GQ 46:47-55. January 1973.

Skonnord, John. "Art and Artifact: Narrative Procedure in WERTHER." JEGP 78:157-177. April 1979.

Smith, Louise Z. "Sensibility and Epistolary Form in HELOISE and WERTHER." ECr 17:369-376. Winter 1977.

Spann, Meno. "WERTHER Revisited: Two Hundred Years of a Masterpiece." Mosaic 5:73-83. Spring 1972.

Steinhauer, Harry. "Goethe's WERTHER after Two Centuries." UTQ 44:1-13. Fall 1974.

Tellenbach, H. "The Suicide of the 'Young Werther' and the Consequences for the Circumstances of Suicide of Endogenic Melancholics." The Israel Annals of Psychiatry and Related Disciplines 15:16-18. March 1977.

Tobol, Carol E. W. and Ida H. Washington. "Werther's Selective Reading of Homer." MLN 92:596-601. April 1977.

von Molnar, Géza. "Confinement or Containment: Goethe's WERTHER and the Concept of Limitation." GL&L 23:226-234. April 1970.

Warrick, E. Kathleen. "Lotte's Sexuality and Her Responsibility for Werther's Death." ELWIU 5:129-135. Spring 1978.

Wilson, James D. "Goethe's WERTHER: A Keatsian Quest for Self-Annihilation." Mosaic 9:93-109. Fall 1975.

Wootton, Carol. "The Deaths of Goethe's WERTHER and de Vigny's CHATTERTON." RLC 50:295-303. July/September 1976.

WILHELM MEISTER
Bahr, Ehrhard. "Goethe's WANDERJAHRE as an Experimental Novel." Mosaic 5:61-71. Spring 1972.

Blackall, Eric A. Goethe and the Novel. Ithaca: Cornell University Press, 1976. pp. 56-83; 111-136; 224-269.

Brown, Jane K. Goethe's Cyclical Narratives. Chapel Hill: University of North Carolina Press, 1975. pp. 33-129.

Citati, Pietro. Goethe. New York: The Dial Press, 1974. pp. 3-139.

Dieckmann, Liselotte. Johann Wolfgang Goethe. New York: Twayne, 1974. pp. 120-131.

Duncan, Bruce. "The Marchese's Story in WILHELM MEISTERS LEHRJAHRE." Seminar 8:169-180. October 1972.

Dürr, Volker O. "The Humanistic Ideal and the Representative Public in Wilhelm Meister's Apprenticeship." PLL 12:36-48. Winter 1976.

Farrelly, D. J. "Iphigenie as 'schönen Seele.'" NGS 4:55-76. Summer 1976.

Fleischer, Stefan. "'Bekenntnisse einer schönen Seele': Figural Representation in WILHELM MEISTERS LEHRJAHRE." MLN 83:807-820. December 1968.

Frisch, Shelley. "The Disenchanted Image: From Goethe's WILHELM MEISTER to Wender's WRONG MOVEMENT." LFQ 7:208-214. No. 3, 1979.

Gerlach, U. Henry. "Wilhelm Meister's Observations About Hamlet." UDR 7:25-32. Spring 1971.

Gilby, William. "The Structural Significance of Mignon in WILHELM MEISTERS LEHRJAHRE." Seminar 16: 136-150. September 1980.

Gray, Ronald. Goethe: A Critical Introduction. Cambridge: Cambridge University Press, 1967. pp. 186-200.

Hammer, Carl, Jr. Goethe and Rousseau. Lexington: University Press of Kentucky, 1973. pp. 123-136.

Lange, Victor. "Goethe's Craft of Fiction." Goethe: A Collection of Critical Essays. ed. Victor Lange. Englewood Cliffs: Prentice-Hall, 1968. pp. 73-85.

Larrett, William. "Wilhelm Meister and the Amazons: The Quest for Wholeness." PEGS 39:31-56. 1969.

Lukács, Georg. Goethe and His Age. New York: Grosset and Dunlap, 1969. pp. 50-67.

―――――. "WILHELM MEISTERS LEHRJAHRE." Goethe: A Collection of Critical Essays. ed. Victor Lange. Englewood Cliffs: Prentice-Hall, 1968. pp. 86-98.

Meads, William. "Goethe's Concept of 'Entsagung.'" PCP 8:34-40. April 1973.

Reiss, Hans. Goethe's Novels. London: Macmillan, 1969. pp. 68-144; 222-268.

Roberts, David. "Wilhelm Meister and Hamlet: The Inner Structure of Book III of WILHELM MEISTERS LEHRJAHRE." PEGS 45:64-100. 1975.

Saine, Thomas P. "Wilhelm Meister's Homecoming." JEGP 69:450-469. July 1970.

Spranger, Eduard. "Goethe's WILHELM MEISTER." IndL 8:30-35. No. 1, 1965.

Steer, A. G. Goethe's Science in the Structure of the WANDERJAHRE. Athens: University of Georgia Press, 1979. 143 pp.

Stein, Jack M. "Musical Settings of the Songs from WILHELM MEISTER." CL 22:125-146. Spring 1970.

Temmer, Mark J. "Rousseau's LA NOUVELLE HELOÏSE and Goethe's WILHELM MEISTERS LEHRJAHRE." SIR 10:309-339. Fall 1971.

Van Abbé, Derek. Goethe: New Perspectives on a Writer and His Times. London: Allen and Unwin, 1972. pp. 150-162.

Wilkinson, Elizabeth M. and L. A. Willoughby. "Having and Being, or Bourgeois Versus Nobility: Notes for a Chapter on Social and Cultural History or for a Commentary on WILHELM MEISTER." GL&L 22:101-105. October 1968.

## Grass, Günter
### CAT AND MOUSE

Butler, Michael. "Joachim Mahlke and the 'Ritterkreuz': A Note on Narrative Perspective in Günter Grass." ML 59:69-73. June 1978.

Croft, Helen. "Günter Grass's KATZ UND MAUS." Seminar 9:253-264. October 1973.

Cunliffe, W. Gordon. Günter Grass. New York: Twayne, 1969. pp. 87-97.

Ezergailis, Inta M. "Günter Grass's 'Fearful Symmetry': Dialectic, Mock and Real, in KATZ UND MAUS and DIE BLECHTROMMEL." TSLL 16:221-235. Spring 1974.

Fickert, Kurt J. "The Use of Ambiguity in CAT AND MOUSE." GQ 44:372-378. May 1971.

Fulton, Edythe King. "Günter Grass's CAT AND MOUSE--Obsession and Life." Forum H 7:26-31. Spring 1969.

Gross, Ruth V. "The Narrator as Demon in Grass and Alain-Fournier." MFS 25:625-639. Winter 1979-1980.

Hanson, William. "An Aspect of Parody in Grass's 'Novelle' KATZ UND MAUS." ML 57:68-72. June 1976.

Hollington, Michael. Günter Grass: The Writer in a Pluralistic Society. London: Marion Boyars, 1980. pp. 51-66.

Leonard, Irene. Günter Grass. New York: Barnes and Noble, 1974. pp. 26-36.

Mason, Ann L. The Skeptical Muse: A Study of Günter Grass' Conception of the Artist. Bern: Lang, 1974. pp. 62-68.

Miles, Keith. Günter Grass. London: Vision Press, 1975. pp. 84-107.

Pfeiffer, John R. "KATZ UND MAUS: Grass's Debt to Augustine." PLL 7:279-292. Summer 1971.

Pickar, Gertrud Bauer. "The Aspect of Colour in Günter Grass's KATZ UND MAUS." GL&L 23:304-309. July 1970.

_____. "Intentional Ambiguity in Günter Grass' KATZ UND MAUS." OL 26:232-245. 1971.

Reddick, John. The 'Danzig Trilogy' of Günter Grass. New York: Harcourt Brace Jovanovich, 1974. pp. 89-169.

Roberts, David. "The Cult of the Hero: An Interpretation of KATZ UND MAUS." GL&L 29:307-322. April 1976.

Ryan, Judith. "Resistance and Resignation: A Re-Interpretation of Günter Grass' KATZ UND MAUS." GR 52:148-165. March 1977.

Spaethling, Robert H. "Günter Grass: CAT AND MOUSE." Monatshefte 62:141-153. Summer 1970.

Thomas, N. L. "An Analysis of Günter Grass' KATZ UND MAUS with Particular Reference to the Religious Themes." GL&L 26:227-237. April 1973.

Thomas, R. Hinton and Wilfried van der Will. The German Novel and the Affluent Society. Manchester: Manchester University Press, 1968. pp. 83-85.

Yates, Norris W. Günter Grass: A Critical Essay. London: Eerdmans, 1967. pp. 28-34.

Ziolkowski, Theodore. Fictional Transfigurations of Jesus. Princeton: Princeton University Press, 1972. pp. 238-250.

DOG YEARS

Alter, Maria P. "Günter Grass: Man as a Scarecrow." PCL 1:20-29. November 1975.

Blomster, W. V. "The Demonic in History: Thomas Mann and Günter Grass." ConL 10:75-84. Winter 1969.

_____. "The Documentation of a Novel: Otto Weininger and HUNDEJAHRE by Günter Grass." Monatshefte 61:122-138. Summer 1969.

Bosmajian, Hamida. Metaphors of Evil: Contemporary German Literature and the Shadow of Nazism. Iowa City: University of Iowa Press, 1979. pp. 82-114.

Cunliffe, W. Gordon. Günter Grass. New York:
Twayne, 1969. pp. 98-123.

Forster, Leonard. "Günter Grass." UTQ 38:9-13.
October 1968.

Ghurye, Charlotte W. The Writer and Society: Studies in the Fiction of Günter Grass and Heinrich Böll. Bern: Lang, 1976. pp. 11-20.

Hollington, Michael. Günter Grass: The Writer in a Pluralistic Society. London: Marion Boyars, 1980. pp. 67-87.

Kurz, Paul Konrad, S. J. On Modern German Literature. Vol. I. University, Ala.: The University of Alabama Press, 1967. pp. 131-148.

Leonard, Irene. Günter Grass. New York: Barnes and Noble, 1974. pp. 37-50.

Miles, Keith. Günter Grass. London: Vision Press, 1975. pp. 108-141.

Mitchell, Breon. "The Demonic Comedy: Dante and Grass's HUNDEJAHRE." PLL 9:65-77. Winter 1973.

Reddick, John. The 'Danzig Trilogy' of Günter Grass. New York: Harcourt Brace Jovanovich, 1974. pp. 173-270.

Sliažas, Rimvydas. "Elements of Old Prussian Mythology in Günter Grass' DOG YEARS." Lituanus 19:39-48. Spring 1973.

Stowell, H. Peter. "Grass's DOG YEARS: Apocalypse, the Old and the New." PCL 5:79-96. 1979.

Waidson, H. M. "Prose Fiction: Some Outstanding German Novels." Twentieth Century German Literature. ed. August Closs. New York: Barnes and Noble, 1969. pp. 158-162.

Yates, Norris W. Günter Grass: A Critical Essay. London: Eerdmans, 1967. pp. 34-42.

THE FLOUNDER
Butler, G. P. "'Übersetzt klingt alles plausibel': Some Notes on DER BUTT and THE FLOUNDER." GL&L 34: 3-9. October 1980.

Durrani, Osman. "'Here Comes Everybody': An Appraisal of Narrative Technique in Günter Grass's DER BUTT." MLR 75:810-822. October 1980.

Hollington, Michael. Günter Grass: The Writer in a Pluralistic Society. London: Marion Boyars, 1980. pp. 158-169.

Russell, Peter. "Floundering in Feminism: The Meaning of Günter Grass's DER BUTT." GL&L 33:245-256. April 1980.

Thomas, Noel L. "Günter Grass's DER BUTT: History and the Significance of the Eighth Chapter ('Vatertag')." GL&L 33:75-85. October 1979.

FROM THE DIARY OF A SNAIL

Hollington, Michael. Günter Grass: The Writer in a Pluralistic Society. London: Marion Boyars, 1980. pp. 136-157.

LOCAL ANAESTHETIC

Bruce, James C. "The Motif of Failure and the Act of Narrating in Günter Grass's ORTLICH BETAUBT." MFS 17:45-60. Spring 1971.

Friedrichsmeyer, Erhard. "The Dogmatism of Pain: LOCAL ANAESTHETIC." A Günter Grass Symposium. ed. A. Leslie Willson. Austin: University of Texas Press, 1971. pp. 32-45.

Graves, Peter J. "Günter Grass's DIE BLECHTROMMEL and ORTLICH BETAUBT: The Pain of Polarities." FMLS 9:132-142. April 1973.

Hollington, Michael. Günter Grass: The Writer in a Pluralistic Society. London: Marion Boyars, 1980. pp. 136-157.

Mason, Ann L. The Skeptical Muse: A Study of Günter Grass' Conception of the Artist. Bern: Lang, 1974. pp. 86-92; 121-128.

Pickar, Gertrud Bauer. "Günter Grass' ORTLICH BETAUBT: The Fiction of Fact and Fantasy." GR 52: 289-303. November 1977.

Reddick, John. "Action and Impotence: Günter Grass's ORTLICH BETAUBT." MLR 67:561-578. July 1972.

THE TIN DRUM

Baker, Donna. "Nazism and the Petit Bourgeois Protagonist: The Novels of Grass, Böll, and Mann." NGC 5:88-94. Spring 1975.

Bance, A. F. "The Enigma of Oskar in Grass's BLECHTROMMEL." Seminar 3:147-156. Fall 1967.

Beyersdorf, H. E. "The Narrator as Artful Deceiver: Aspects of Narrative Perspective in DIE BLECHTROMMEL." GR 55: 129-138. Fall 1980.

Blomster, Wesley V. "Oskar at the 'Zoppoter Waldoper.'" MLN 84:467-472. April 1969.

Boa, Elizabeth. "Günter Grass and the German Gremlin." GL&L 23:144-151. January 1970.

Boa, Elizabeth and J. H. Reid. Critical Strategies: German Fiction in the Twentieth Century. London: Edward Arnold, 1972. pp. 190-194.

Botheroyd, Paul F. Ich und er: First and Third Person Self-Reference and Problems of Identity in Three Contemporary German-Language Novels. The Hague: Mouton, 1976. pp. 28-61.

Caltvedt, Lester. "Oskar's Account of Himself: Narrative 'Guilt' and the Relationship of Fiction to History in DIE BLECHTROMMEL." Seminar 14:285-294. November 1978.

Crumm, David. "Skat and the Mad Midget." RLSt 6: 63-70. 1975.

Cunliffe, W. Gordon. Günter Grass. New York: Twayne, 1969. pp. 52-86.

Dimler, G. Richard. "Simplicius Simplicissimus and Oskar Matzerath as Alienated Heroes: Comparison and Contrast." A Bn G 4:113-134. 1975.

Elliott, John R., Jr. "The Cankered Muse of Günter Grass." Dimension 1:516-523. No. 3, 1968.

Ezergailis, Inta M. "Günter Grass's 'Fearful Symmetry': Dialectic, Mock and Real, in KATZ UND MAUS and DIE BLECHTROMMEL." TSLL 16:221-235. Spring 1974.

Forster, Leonard. "Günter Grass." UTQ 38:5-9. October 1968.

Freedman, Ralph. "The Poet's Dilemma: The Narrative Worlds of Günter Grass." A Günter Grass Symposium. ed. A. Leslie Willson. Austin: University of Texas Press, 1971. pp. 46-59.

Gelley, Alexander. "Art and Reality in DIE BLECHTROMMEL." FMLS 3:115-125. April 1967.

Graves, Peter J. "Günter Grass's DIE BLECHTROMMEL and ÖRTLICH BETÄUBT: The Pain of Polarities." FMLS 9:132-142. April 1973.

Hollington, Michael. Günter Grass: The Writer in a

Pluralistic Society. London: Marion Boyars, 1980. pp. 20-50.

Leonard, Irene. Günter Grass. New York: Barnes and Noble, 1974. pp. 13-25.

Mason, Ann L. "Günter Grass and the Artist in History." ConL 14:347-362. Summer 1973.

―――――. The Skeptical Muse: A Study of Günter Grass' Conception of the Artist. Bern: Lang, 1974. pp. 27-54; 77-86.

Maurer, Robert. "The End of Innocence: Günter Grass's THE TIN DRUM." BuR 16:45-65. May 1968.

Miles, Keith. Günter Grass. London: Vision, 1975. pp. 48-83.

O'Neill, Patrick. "Musical Form and the Pauline Message in a Key Chapter of Grass's BLECHTROMMEL." Seminar 10:298-307. November 1974.

Palencia-Roth, Michael. "The Anti-Faustian Ethos of DIE BLECHTROMMEL." JES 9:174-184. September 1979.

Parry, Idris. "Aspects of Günter Grass's Narrative Technique." FMLS 3:101-114. April 1967.

Pearce, Richard. Stages of the Clown: Perspectives on Modern Fiction from Dostoyevsky to Beckett. Carbondale: Southern Illinois University Press, 1970. pp. 117-128.

Reddick, John. The "Danzig Trilogy" of Günter Grass. New York: Harcourt Brace Jovanovich, 1974. pp. 1-86.

Russell, Peter. "Siegfried Lenz's DEUTSCHSTUNDE: A North German Novel." GL&L 28:409-417. July 1975.

Schow, H. Wayne. "The Functional Complexity of Grass's Oskar." Crit 19:5-19. No. 3, 1978.

Sosnoski, M. K. "Oskar's Hungry Witch." MFS 17:61-77. Spring 1971.

Steig, Michael. "The Grotesque and the Aesthetic Response in Shakespeare, Dickens, and Günter Grass." CLS 6:177-180. June 1969.

Thomas, N. L. "Oskar, the Unreliable Narrator in Günter Grass's DIE BLECHTROMMEL." NGS 3:31-47. Spring 1975.

Thomas, R. Hinton and Wilfried van der Will. The German Novel and the Affluent Society. Manchester: Manchester University Press, 1968. pp. 69-82.

Van Abbé, Derek. "Metamorphoses of 'Unbewältigte Vergangenheit' in DIE BLECHTROMMEL." GL&L 23: 152-160. January 1970.

Yates, Norris W. Günter Grass: A Critical Essay. London: Eerdmans, 1967. pp. 19-28.
DAS TREFFEN IN TELGTE
    Thomas, Noel. "Simon Dach and Günter Grass' DAS TREFFEN IN TELGTE." NGS 8:91-108. Summer 1980.

Grillparzer, Franz
DER ARME SPIELMANN
    Browning, Robert M. "Language and the Fall from Grace in Grillparzer's SPIELMANN." Seminar 12:215-235. November 1976.

    Ellis, John M. "Grillparzer's DER ARME SPIELMANN." GQ 45:662-683. November 1972. (From Narration in the German Novelle: Theory and Interpretation.)

    _____. Narration in the German Novelle: Theory and Interpretation. London: Cambridge University Press, 1974. pp. 113-135.

    Hodge, James L. "Symmetry and Tension in DER ARME SPIELMANN." GQ 47:262-264. March 1974.

    Liedke, Otto K. "Considerations on the Structure of Grillparzer's DER ARME SPIELMANN." MAL 3:7-12. Fall 1970.

    Reeve, W. C. "Proportion and Disproportion in Grillparzer's DER ARME SPIELMANN." GR 53:41-49. Spring 1978.

    Swales, M. W. "The Narrative Perspective in Grillparzer's DER ARME SPIELMANN." GL&L 20:107-116. January 1967.

    Yates, W. E. Grillparzer: A Critical Introduction. London: Cambridge University Press, 1972. pp. 76-83.
DAS KLOSTER BEI SENDOMIR
    Allen, Richard. "The Fine Art of Concealment in Grillparzer's DAS KLOSTER BEI SENDOMIR." MGS 1:181-187. Fall 1975.

    Lawson, Richard H. "The Starost's Daughter: Elga in Grillparzer's KLOSTER BEI SENDOMIR." MAL 1:31-37. Fall 1968.

Grimmelshausen
COURASCHE
Jacobson, John W. "A Defense of Grimmelshausen's Courasche." GQ 41:42-54. January 1968.
SIMPLICISSIMUS
Ashcroft, Jeffrey. "Ad Astra Volandum: Emblems and Imagery in Grimmelshausen's SIMPLICISSIMUS." MLR 68:843-862. October 1973.

Bjornson, Richard. The Picaresque Hero in European Fiction. Madison: University of Wisconsin Press, 1977. pp. 166-187.

Dimler, G. Richard. "Alienation in DON QUIXOTE and SIMPLICIUS SIMPLICISSIMUS." Thought 49:72-80. March 1974.

_____. "Simplicius Simplicissimus and Oskar Matzerath as Alienated Heroes: Comparison and Contrast." A Bn G 4:113-134. 1975.

Heckman, John. "Emblematic Structures in SIMPLICISSIMUS TEUTSCH." MLN 84:876-890. December 1969.

Hofmeister, Rudolf. "The 893 Gold Coins in Grimmelshausen's SIMPLICISSIMUS." Argenis 1:131-140. 1977.

Holzinger, Walter. "DER ABENTHEURLICHE SIMPLICISSIMUS and Sir Philip Sidney's ARCADIA." CollG 3: 184-198. No. 2, 1969.

Mandel, Siegfried. "From the Mummelsee to the Moon: Refractions of Science in Seventeenth-Century Literature." CLS 9:411-413. December 1972.

McQueen, Marian. "Narrative Structure and Reader Response in SIMPLICISSIMUS and DON QUIXOTE: A Contrastive Study." Argenis 1:229-256. 1977.

Morewedge, Rosmarie T. "The Circle and the Labyrinth in Grimmelshausen's SIMPLICISSIMUS." Argenis 1:373-409. 1977.

Negus, Kenneth. Grimmelshausen. New York: Twayne, 1974. pp. 47-143.

Over, Paul. "Some VO and OV Patterns in the Language of SIMPLICISSIMUS (Bk. I)." Neophil 60:534-540. October 1976.

Sheppard, Richard. "The Narrative Structure of Grimmelshausen's SIMPLICISSIMUS." FMLS 8:15-26. January 1972.

Spahr, Blake Lee. "Grimmelshausen's SIMPLICISSI-
MUS: Astrological Structure?" Argenis 1:7-29. 1977.

Grosse, Karl
DER GENIUS
Wright, Elizabeth. E. T. A. Hoffmann and the Rhetoric
of Terror: Aspects of Language Used for the Evocation
of Fear. Leeds: Maney, 1978. pp. 14-49.

Gutzkow, Karl
WALLY DIE ZWEIFLERIN
Flavell, M. Kay. "Women and Individualism: A Reexamination of Schlegel's LUCINDE and Gutzkow's
WALLY DIE ZWEIFLERIN." MLR 70:561-566. July
1975.

Handke, Peter
THE GOALIE'S ANXIETY AT THE PENALTY KICK
Schlueter, June. "Handke's 'Kafkaesque' Novel: Semiotic Processes in DIE ANGST DES TORMANNS BEIM
ELFMETER." StTCL 4:75-87. Fall 1979.
WUNSCHLOSES UNGLÜCK
Zorach, Cecile Cazort. "Freedom and Remembrance:
The Language of Biography in Peter Handke's WUNSCH-
LOSES UNGLÜCK." GQ 52:486-502. November 1979.

Hauptmann, Gerhart
BAHNWÄRTER THIEL
Clouser, Robin A. "The Spiritual Malaise of a Modern
Hercules, Hauptmann's BAHNWÄRTER THIEL." GR 55:
98-108. Summer 1980.

Driver, Beverly and Walter K. Francke. "The Symbolism of Deer and Squirrel in Hauptmann's BAHNWÄRTER
THIEL." SAB 37: 47-51. May 1972.

Ellis, John M. Narration in the German Novelle: Theory and Interpretation. London: Cambridge University
Press, 1974. pp. 169-187.

Hodge, James L. "The Dramaturgy of BAHNWÄRTER
THIEL." Mosaic 9: 97-116. Spring 1976.
FASCHING
Carr, G. J. "Gerhart Hauptmann's FASCHING: The
Grandmother." NGS 5: 59-61. Spring 1977.

Hammer, A. E. "A Note on the Dénouement of Gerhart
Hauptmann's FASCHING." NGS 4: 87-89. Summer
1976.

Turner, David. "Setting the Record Straight on Hauptmann's FASCHING." NGS 4: 157-159. Autumn 1976.

Washington, Ida H. "The Symbolism of Contrast in Gerhart Hauptmann's FASCHING." GQ 52: 248-251. March 1979.

DER NARR IN CHRISTO EMANUEL QUINT
Riley, Graham A. "An Examination of the Autobiographical Elements in Gerhart Hauptmann's Novel: DER NARR IN CHRISTO EMANUEL QUINT." FMLS 6: 169-172. April 1970.

Ziolkowski, Theodore. Fictional Transfigurations of Jesus. Princeton: Princeton University Press, 1972. pp. 110-122.

Heine, Heinrich
AUS DEN MEMOIREN DES HERRN VON SCHNABELEWOPSKI
Thomas, Barry G. "The van der Pissen Scene in Heinrich Heine's SCHNABELEWOPSKI: A Suggestion." GQ 51: 39-46. January 1978.

DAS BUCH LE GRAND
Veit, Philipp F. "Heine and His Cousins: A Reconsideration." GR 47: 24-29. January 1972.

*Weigand, Hermann J. "The Double Love-Tragedy in Heine's BUCH LE GRAND." GR 13: 121-126. April 1938.

Heinse, Wilhelm
ARDINGHELLO UND DIE GLÜCKSEELIGEN INSELN
Klinger, Uwe R. "Wilhelm Heinse's ARDINGHELLO: A Re-Appraisal." LY 7: 28-52. 1975.

Hesse, Hermann
BENEATH THE WHEEL
Boulby, Mark. Hermann Hesse: His Mind and Art. Ithaca: Cornell University Press, 1967. pp. 39-69.

Field, George Wallis. Hermann Hesse. New York: Twayne, 1970. pp. 25-31.

BERTHOLD
Taylor, Harley U. "Hermann Hesse's BERTHOLD: Probable Source of NARZISS UND GOLDMUND." WVUPP 20: 43-46. September 1973.

DEMIAN
Baron, Frank. "Who Was Demian?" GQ 49: 45-49. January 1976.

Boulby, Mark. Hermann Hesse: His Mind and Art. Ithaca: Cornell University Press, 1967. pp. 81-120.

Brink, A.W. "Hermann Hesse and the Oedipal Quest." L&P 24: 67-70. No. 2, 1974.

Butler, Colin. "Literary Malpractice in Some Works of Hermann Hesse." UTQ 40: 168-171. Winter 1971.

Fickert, Kurt J. Hermann Hesse's Quest: The Evolution of the "Dichter" Figure in His Work. Fredericton: York Press, 1978. pp. 60-72.

Field, George Wallis. Hermann Hesse. New York: Twayne, 1970. pp. 43-61.

Horowitz, Renee B. "Cain and Abel as Existentialist Symbols for Unamuno and Hesse." PLL 16: 174-183. Spring 1980.

Mann, Thomas. "Introduction to DEMIAN." Hesse: A Collection of Critical Essays. ed. Theodore Ziolkowski. Englewood Cliffs: Prentice-Hall, 1973. pp. 15-20.

Mileck, Joseph. Hermann Hesse: Life and Art. Berkeley: University of California Press, 1978. pp. 89-99.

Reichert, Herbert W. The Impact of Nietzsche on Hermann Hesse. Mount Pleasant: Enigma Press, 1972. pp. 40-50.

Sokel, Walter H. "The Problem of Dualism in Hesse's DEMIAN and Musil's TÖRLESS." MAL 9: 35-42. No. 3/4, 1976.

Ziolkowski, Theodore. Fictional Transfigurations of Jesus. Princeton: Princeton University Press, 1972. pp. 154-161.

\_\_\_\_\_. "The Quest for the Grail in Hesse's DEMIAN." GR 49: 44-59. January 1974. Reprinted in Hesse: A Collection of Critical Essays. ed. Theodore Ziolkowski. Englewood Cliffs: Prentice-Hall, 1973. pp. 134-152.

GLASS BEAD GAME

Bandy, Stephen C. "Hermann Hesse's DAS GLASPERLENSPIEL: In Search of Josef Knecht." MLQ 33: 299-311. September 1972.

Boa, Elizabeth and J. H. Reid. Critical Strategies: German Fiction in the Twentieth Century. London: Edward Arnold, 1972. pp. 28-34.

Boulby, Mark. Hermann Hesse: His Mind and Art. Ithaca: Cornell University Press, 1967. pp. 261-321.

Butler, Colin. "Literary Malpractice in Some Works of Hermann Hesse." UTQ 40: 177-180. Winter 1971.

Casebeer, Edwin F. Hermann Hesse. New York: Crowell, 1972. pp. 141-189.

Fickert, Kurt J.  Hermann Hesse's Quest: The Evolution of the "Dichter" Figure in His Work.  Fredericton: York Press, 1978.  pp. 121-139.

Field, G. W.  "Goethe and DAS GLASPERLENSPIEL: Reflections on 'Alterswerke.'"  GL&L 23: 93-101.  October 1969.

_____.  Hermann Hesse.  New York: Twayne, 1970.  pp. 142-172.

_____.  "Hermann Hesse:  Polarities and Symbols of Synthesis."  QQ 81: 96-100.  Spring 1974.

_____.  "Music and Morality in Thomas Mann and Hermann Hesse."  Hesse: A Collection of Critical Essays.  ed. Theodore Ziolkowski.  Englewood Cliffs: Prentice-Hall, 1973.  pp. 94-111.

_____.  "On the Genesis of the GLASPERLENSPIEL."  GQ 41: 673-688.  November 1968.

Friedrichsmeyer, Erhard.  "The Bertram Episode in Hesse's GLASS BEAD GAME."  GR 49: 284-297.  November 1974.

Goldgar, Harry.  "Hesse's GLASPERLENSPIEL and the Game of Go."  GL&L 20: 132-137.  January 1967.

Götz, Ignacio L.  "Platonic Parallels in Hesses's [sic] DAS GLASPERLENSPIEL."  GQ 51: 511-519.  November 1978.

Koester, Rudolf.  "Hesse's Music Master: In Search of a Prototype."  FMLS 3: 135-141.  April 1967.

Mileck, Joseph.  "DAS GLASPERLENSPIEL."  Hesse Companion.  ed. Anna Otten.  Frankfurt: Suhrkamp, 1970.  pp. 189-221.

_____.  "DAS GLASPERLENSPIEL: Genesis, Manuscripts, and History of Publication."  GQ 43: 55-83.  January 1970.

_____.  Hermann Hesse: Life and Art.  Berkeley: University of California Press, 1978.  pp. 255-283.

Norton, Roger C.  "Hermann Hesse's Criticism of Technology."  GR 43: 267-273.  November 1968.

_____.  "Variant Endings of Hesse's GLASPERLENSPIEL."  Monatshefte 60: 141-146.  Summer 1968.

Pavlyshyn, Marko. "Music in Hermann Hesse's DER STEPPENWOLF and DAS GLASPERLENSPIEL." Seminar 15: 39-55. February 1979.

Reichert, Herbert W. The Impact of Nietzsche on Hermann Hesse. Mt. Pleasant: Enigma Press, 1972. pp. 76-86.

Schneider, Christian J. "Hermann Hesse's GLASPERLENSPIEL." Hesse Companion. ed. Anna Otten. Frankfurt: Suhrkamp, 1970. pp. 222-259.

Stern, J. P. "A Game of Utopia." GL&L 34: 94-107. October 1980.

Waidson, H. M. "Prose Fiction: Some Outstanding German Novels." Twentieth Century German Literature. ed. August Closs. New York: Barnes and Noble, 1969. pp. 118-122.

Wood, Carl. "Hesse's Literary Glass Bead Game: The Unity of DAS GLASPERLENSPIEL." FWF 1: 95-108. February 1974.

Zeller, Bernhard. Portrait of Hesse: An Illustrated Biography. New York: Herder and Herder, 1971. pp. 134-157.

Ziolkowski, Theodore. "Hermann Hesse: 'Der Vierte Lebenslauf.'" GR 42: 124-143. March 1967.

## JOURNEY TO THE EAST

Antosik, Stanley J. "The Confession of a Cultural Elitist: Hesse's Homecoming in DIE MORGENLANDFAHRT." GR 53: 63-68. Spring 1978.

Boulby, Mark. Hermann Hesse: His Mind and Art. Ithaca: Cornell University Press, 1967. pp. 245-261.

Crenshaw, Karen O. and Richard H. Lawson. "Technique and Function of Time in Hesse's MORGENLANDFAHRT: A Culmination." Mosaic 5:53-59. Spring 1972.

Derrenberger, John. "Who Is Leo? Astrology in Hermann Hesse's DIE MORGENLANDFAHRT." Monatshefte 67: 167-172. Summer 1975.

Fickert, Kurt J. Hermann Hesse's Quest: The Evolution of the "Dichter" Figure in His Work. Fredericton: York Press, 1978. pp. 121-139.

Freedman, Ralph. Hermann Hesse: Pilgrim of Crisis. New York: Pantheon, 1978. pp. 268-275.

Gide, André. "Preface to THE JOURNEY TO THE EAST." Hesse: A Collection of Critical Essays. ed. Theodore Ziolkowski. Englewood Cliffs: Prentice-Hall, 1973. pp. 21-24.

*Hallamore, Joyce. "Paul Klee, H. H. and DIE MORGENLANDFAHRT." Seminar 1: 17-24. Spring 1965.

Middleton, J.C. "Hermann Hesse's MORGENLANDFAHRT." Hesse Companion. ed. Anna Otten. Frankfurt: Suhrkamp, 1970. pp. 170-188.

KLEIN UND WAGNER
Fickert, Kurt J. "The Portrait of the Artist in Hesse's KLEIN UND WAGNER." HSL 6: 180-186. No. 2, 1974.

KURGAST
Maurer, Warren R. "Some Aspects of the Jean Paul-Hermann Hesse Relationship with Special Reference to KATZENBERGER and KURGAST." Seminar 4: 113-128. Fall 1968.

NARZISS UND GOLDMUND
Becker, Gustave H. "A Note on Creative Vitality in Hermann Hesse's NARZISS UND GOLDMUND and Alberto Moravia's TWO: A PHALLIC NOVEL." FurmS 21: 49-54. June 1974.

Boulby, Mark. Hermann Hesse: His Mind and Art. Ithaca: Cornell University Press, 1967. pp. 207-243.

Casebeer, Edwin F. Hermann Hesse. New York: Crowell, 1972. pp. 100-140.

Fickert, Kurt J. Hermann Hesse's Quest: The Evolution of the "Dichter" Figure in His Work. Fredericton: York Press, 1978. pp. 101-111.

Field, George Wallis. Hermann Hesse. New York: Twayne, 1970. pp. 109-120.

Freedman, Ralph. Hermann Hesse: Pilgrim of Crisis. New York: Pantheon, 1978. pp. 314-318.

Koch, Stephen. "Prophet of Youth: Hermann Hesse's NARCISSUS AND GOLDMUND." Hermann Hesse: A Collection of Criticism. ed. Judith Liebmann. New York: McGraw-Hill, 1977. pp. 85-89.

Neuswanger, Russell. "Names as Glass Beads in Hesse's NARZISS UND GOLDMUND." Monatshefte 67: 48-58. Spring 1975.

Rose, Ernst. "The Fulness of Art." Hesse Companion. ed. Anna Otten. Frankfurt: Suhrkamp, 1970. pp. 158-169.

Taylor, Harley U. "Hermann Hesse's BERTHOLD: Probable Source of NARZISS UND GOLDMUND." WVUPP 20: 43-46. September 1973.
PETER CAMENZIND
Boulby, Mark. Hermann Hesse: His Mind and Art. Ithaca: Cornell University Press, 1967. pp. 1-38.

Freedman, Ralph. Hermann Hesse: Pilgrim of Crisis. New York: Pantheon, 1978. pp. 107-117.
SIDDHARTHA
Boulby, Mark. Hermann Hesse: His Mind and Art. Ithaca: Cornell University Press, 1967. pp. 121-158.

Brown, Madison. "Toward a Perspective for the Indian Element in Hermann Hesse's SIDDHARTHA." GQ 49: 191-202. March 1976.

Butler, Colin. "Hermann Hesse's SIDDHARTHA: Some Critical Objections." Monatshefte 63: 117-124. Summer 1971.

_____. "Literary Malpractice in Some Works of Hermann Hesse." UTQ 40: 171-174. Winter 1971.

Casebeer, Edwin F. Hermann Hesse. New York: Crowell, 1972. pp. 23-54.

Conard, Robert C. "Hermann Hesse's SIDDHARTHA, EINE INDISCHE DICHTUNG, as a Western Archetype." GQ 48: 358-369. May 1975.

Fickert, Kurt J. Hermann Hesse's Quest: The Evolution of the "Dichter" Figure in His Work. Fredericton: York Press, 1978. pp. 79-86.

Field, George Wallis. Hermann Hesse. New York: Twayne, 1970. pp. 71-85.

Freedman, Ralph. Hermann Hesse: Pilgrim of Crisis. New York: Pantheon, 1978. pp. 230-237.

Hughes, Kenneth. "Hesse's Use of GILGAMESH-Motifs in the Humanization of Siddhartha and Harry Haller." Seminar 5: 129-140. Fall 1969.

Mileck, Joseph. Hermann Hesse: Life and Art. Berkeley: University of California Press, 1978. pp. 159-172.

von Molnár, Géza. "The Ideological Framework of Hermann Hesse's SIDDHARTHA." UP 4: 82-86. Fall 1971.

Paslick, Robert H. "Dialectic and Non-Attachment:

The Structure of Hermann Hesse's SIDDHARTHA."
Symposium 27: 64-74. Spring 1973.

Schludermann, Brigitte and Rosemarie Finlay. "Mythical Reflections of the East in Hermann Hesse." Mosaic 2: 100-105. Spring 1969.

Shaw, Leroy R. "Time and the Structure of Hermann Hesse's SIDDHARTHA." Hermann Hesse: A Collection of Criticism. ed. Judith Liebmann. New York: McGraw-Hill, 1977. pp. 66-84.

Timpe, Eugene F. "Hesse's SIDDHARTHA and the BHAGAVAD GITA." CL 22: 346-357. Fall 1970.

Ziolkowski, Theodore. "SIDDHARTHA: The Landscape of the Soul." Hesse Companion. ed. Anna Otten. Frankfurt: Suhrkamp, 1970. pp. 71-100.

STEPPENWOLF

Abood, Edward. "Jung's Concept of Individuation in Hesse's STEPPENWOLF." SHR 3: 1-12. Winter 1968.

Artiss, David. "Key Symbols in Hesse's STEPPENWOLF." Seminar 7: 85-101. June 1971.

Boulby, Mark. Hermann Hesse: His Mind and Art. Ithaca: Cornell University Press, 1967. pp. 159-206.

_____. "THE STEPPENWOLF." Hesse Companion. ed. Anna Otten. Frankfurt: Suhrkamp, 1970. pp. 101-157.

Brink, A.W. "Hermann Hesse and the Oedipal Quest." L&P 24: 72-76. No. 2, 1974.

Butler, Colin. "Literary Malpractice in Some Works of Hermann Hesse." UTQ 40: 174-177. Winter 1971.

Casebeer, Edwin F. Hermann Hesse. New York: Crowell, 1972. pp. 55-99.

Cohn, Dorrit. "Narration of Consciousness in DER STEPPENWOLF." GR 44: 121-131. March 1969.

Dhority, Lynn. "Who Wrote the 'Tractat vom Steppenwolf'?" GL&L 27: 59-66. October 1973.

Fickert, Kurt J. Hermann Hesse's Quest: The Evolution of the "Dichter" Figure in His Work. Fredericton: York Press, 1978. pp. 89-99.

Field, George Wallis. Hermann Hesse. New York: Twayne, 1970. pp. 86-108.

_____. "Hermann Hesse: Polarities and Symbols of Synthesis." QQ 81: 91-94. Spring 1974.

Freedman, Ralph. Hermann Hesse: Pilgrim of Crisis. New York: Pantheon, 1978. pp. 281-295.

_____. "'Person' and 'Persona': The Magic Mirrors of STEPPENWOLF." Hesse: A Collection of Critical Essays. ed. Theodore Ziolkowski. Englewood Cliffs: Prentice-Hall, 1973. pp. 153-179.

Hertz, Peter D. "STEPPENWOLF as a Bible." GaR 25: 439-449. Winter 1971.

Hollis, Andrew. "Political Ambivalence in Hesse's STEPPENWOLF." MLR 73: 110-118. January 1978.

_____. "STEPPENWOLF--The Laughter in the Music." NGS 6: 15-30. Spring 1978.

Hughes, Kenneth. "Hesse's Use of GILGAMESH-Motifs in the Humanization of Siddhartha and Harry Haller." Seminar 5: 129-140. Fall 1969.

*Joyce, Robert E. "Toward the Resolution of Polarities in Hermann Hesse's STEPPENWOLF." ABR 17:336-341. Autumn 1966.

Merrill, Reed B. "Ivan Karamazov and Harry Haller: The Consolation of Philosophy." CLS 8:58-78. March 1971.

Mileck, Joseph. Hermann Hesse: Life and Art. Berkeley: University of California Press, 1978. pp. 174-197.

Pachmuss, Temira. "Dostoevsky and Hermann Hesse: Analogies and Congruences." OL 30:210-224. 1975.

Pavlyshyn, Marko. "Music in Hermann Hesse's DER STEPPENWOLF and DAS GLASPERLENSPIEL." Seminar 15:39-55. February 1979.

Reichert, Herbert W. The Impact of Nietzsche on Hermann Hesse. Mt. Pleasant: Enigma Press, 1972. pp. 60-70.

Stanek, Lou Willett. "Hesse and Moffett Team Teach the Theory of Discourse." EJ 61:985-993. October 1972.

Stelzig, Eugene L. "The Aesthetics of Confession: Hermann Hesse's CRISIS Poems in the Context of the

STEPPENWOLF Period." Criticism 21:49-70. Winter 1979.

*Stelzmann, Rainulf A. "Kafka's THE TRIAL and Hesse's STEPPENWOLF: Two Views of Reality and Transcendence." XUS 5:165-172. December 1966.

Webb, Eugene. "Hermine and the Problem of Harry's Failure in Hesse's STEPPENWOLF." MFS 17:115-124. Spring 1971.

Ziolkowski, Theodore. "Hermann Hesse's STEPPENWOLF: A Sonata in Prose." Hermann Hesse: A Collection of Criticism. ed. Judith Liebmann. New York: McGraw-Hill, 1977. pp. 90-109.

Heym, Georg
DER IRRE
Blunden, Allan. "Notes on Georg Heym's Novelle DER IRRE." GL&L 28:107-119. January 1975.

Heyse, Paul
ANDREA DELFIN
Ullmann, Christiane. "Form and Content of Paul Heyse's Novelle ANDREA DELFIN." Seminar 12:109-120. May 1976.

Hildesheimer, Wolfgang
TYNSET
Hoyt, Giles R. "Guilt in Absurdity: Wolfgang Hildesheimer's TYNSET." Seminar 14:133-140. May 1978.

Stanley, Patricia Haas. "The Structure of Wolfgang Hildesheimer's TYNSET." Monatshefte 71:29-39. Spring 1979.

_____. "Verbal Music in Theory and Practice." GR 52:217-225. May 1977.

Hoffmann, E. T. A.
DIE ABENTEUER DER SILVESTER-NACHT
Holbeche, Yvonne Jill Kathleen. Optical Motifs in the Works of E. T. A. Hoffmann. Göppingen: Kümmerle, 1975. pp. 74-87.
THE DEVIL'S ELIXIRS
Daemmrich, Horst S. "THE DEVIL'S ELIXIRS: Precursor of the Modern Psychological Novel." PLL 6:374-386. Fall 1970.

_____. The Shattered Self: E. T. A. Hoffmann's Tragic Vision. Detroit: Wayne State University Press, 1973. pp. 93-107.

McGlathery, James M. "Demon Love: E. T. A. Hoffmann's ELIXIERE DES TEUFELS." Coll G 12:61-74. No. 1/2, 1979.

Passage, Charles E. "E. T. A. Hoffmann's THE DEVIL'S ELIXIRS: A Flawed Masterpiece." JEGP 75:531-545. October 1976.

Romero, Christiane Zehl. "M. G. Lewis' THE MONK and E. T. A. Hoffmann's DIE ELIXIERE DES TEUFELS-- Two Versions of the Gothic." Neophil 63:574-581. October 1979.

Wright, Elizabeth. E. T. A. Hoffmann and the Rhetoric of Terror: Aspects of Language Used for the Evocation of Fear. Leeds: Maney, 1978. pp. 14-49; 146-234.
DON JUAN
Swales, Martin. "Narrative Sleight-of-Hand: Some Notes on Two German Romantic Tales." NGS 6:4-12. Spring 1978.
DAS FRÄULEIN VON SCUDERI
Ellis, J. M. "E. T. A. Hoffmann's DAS FRÄULEIN VON SCUDERI." MLR 64:340-350. April 1969.

Holbeche, Yvonne. "The Relationship of the Artist to Power: E. T. A. Hoffmann's DAS FRÄULEIN VON SCUDERI." Seminar 16:1-11. February 1980.

Weiss, Hermann F. "'The Labyrinth of Crime.' A Reinterpretation of E. T. A. Hoffmann's DAS FRÄULEIN VON SCUDERI." GR 51:181-189. May 1976.
DAS GELÜBDE
Wright, Elizabeth. E. T. A. Hoffmann and the Rhetoric of Terror: Aspects of Language Used for the Evocation of Fear. Leeds: Maney, 1978. pp. 116-145.
THE GOLDEN POT
Daemmrich, Horst S. The Shattered Self: E. T. A. Hoffmann's Tragic Vision. Detroit: Wayne State University Press, 1973. pp. 28-32.

Holbeche, Yvonne Jill Kathleen. Optical Motifs in the Works of E. T. A. Hoffmann. Göppingen: Kümmerle, 1975. pp. 55-74.

McGlathery, James M. "'Bald dein Fall ins-Ehebett'? A New Reading of E. T. A. Hoffmann's GOLDNER [sic] TOPF." GR 53:106-114. Summer 1978.

Reddick, John. "E. T. A. Hoffmann's DER GOLDNE TOPF and Its 'durchgehaltene Ironie.'" MLR 71:577-594. July 1976.

Tatar, Maria M. "Mesmerism, Madness, and Death in

E. T. A. Hoffmann's DER GOLDNE TOPF." SIR 14:365-389. Fall 1975.
KLEIN ZACHES GENANNT ZINNOBER
Elardo, Ronald J. "E. T. A. Hoffmann's Klein Zaches, the Trickster." Seminar 16:151-169. September 1980.
KREISLERIANA
Findlay, Charles. "The Opera and Operatic Elements in the Fragmentary Biography of Johannes Kreisler." GL&L 27:22-34. October 1973.

Kolb, Jocelyne. "E. T. A. Hoffmann's KREISLERIANA: A la Recherche d'une Forme Perdue?" Monatshefte 69: 34-44. Spring 1977.
DIE MARQUISE DE LA PIVARDIERE
Wright, Elizabeth. E. T. A. Hoffmann and the Rhetoric of Terror: Aspects of Language Used for the Evocation of Fear. Leeds: Maney, 1978. pp. 276-296.
THE MINES OF FALUN
Holbeche, Yvonne Jill Kathleen. Optical Motifs in the Works of E. T. A. Hoffmann. Göppingen: Kümmerle, 1975. pp. 125-138.

Wright, Elizabeth. E. T. A. Hoffmann and the Rhetoric of Terror: Aspects of Language Used for the Evocation of Fear. Leeds: Maney, 1978. pp. 50-74.
NUTCRACKER AND MOUSE KING
Daemmrich, Horst S. The Shattered Self: E. T. A. Hoffmann's Tragic Vision. Detroit: Wayne State University Press, 1973. pp. 55-62.

Elardo, Ronald J. "E. T. A. Hoffmann's NUSSKNACKER UND MAUSEKÖNIG: The Mouse-Queen in the Tragedy of the Hero." GR 55:1-8. Winter 1980.
PRINZESSIN BRAMBILLA
Dunn, Hough-Lewis. "The Circle of Love in Hoffmann and Shakespeare." SIR 11:113-137. Spring 1972.

Holbeche, Yvonne Jill Kathleen. Optical Motifs in the Works of E. T. A. Hoffmann. Göppingen: Kümmerle, 1975. pp. 155-188.

Slessarev, Helga. "E. T. A. Hoffmann's PRINZESSIN BRAMBILLA: A Romanticist's Contribution to the Aesthetic Education of Man." SIR 9:147-160. Summer 1970.
RAT KRESPEL
Ellis, John M. Narration in the German Novelle: Theory and Interpretation. London: Cambridge University Press, 1974. pp. 94-112.

Haberland, Paul M. "Number Symbolism: The Father-Daughter Relationship in E. T. A. Hoffmann's RAT KRESPEL." LangQ 13:39-42. Spring/Summer 1975.

Hoffmann, E. T. A. 331

Rippley, La Vern J. "The House as Metaphor in E. T. A. Hoffmann's RAT KRESPEL." PLL 7:52-60. Winter 1971.
RITTER GLUCK
Fetzer, John. "Ritter Gluck's 'Unglück': The Crisis of Creativity in the Age of the Epigone." GQ 44:317-330. May 1971.

Struc, Roman S. "Madness as Existence: An Essay on a Literary Theme." RS 38:77-80. June 1970.
THE SANDMAN
Holbeche, Yvonne Jill Kathleen. Optical Motifs in the Works of E. T. A. Hoffmann. Göppingen: Kümmerle, 1975. pp. 88-105.

Mahlendorf, Ursula. "E. T. A. Hoffmann's THE SANDMAN: The Fictional Psycho-Biography of a Romantic Poet." AI 32:217-239. Fall 1975.

Wright, Elizabeth. E. T. A. Hoffmann and the Rhetoric of Terror: Aspects of Language Used for the Evocation of Fear. Leeds: Maney, 1978. pp. 75-115.
TOMCAT MURR
Daemmrich, Horst S. The Shattered Self: E. T. A. Hoffmann's Tragic Vision. Detroit: Wayne State University Press, 1973. pp. 39-46.

Frye, Lawrence O. "The Language of Romantic High Feeling. A Case of Dialogue Technique in Hoffmann's KATER MURR and Novalis' HEINRICH VON OFTERDINGEN." DVLG 49:520-545. September 1975.

Graves, Peter J. "E. T. A. Hoffmann's Johannes Kreisler: 'Verruckter Musikus'?" MLQ 30:222-233. June 1969.

Jones, Michael T. "Hoffmann and the Problem of Social Reality: A Study of KATER MURR." Monatshefte 69: 45-57. Spring 1977.

Scher, Steven Paul. "Hoffmann and Sterne: Unmediated Parallels in Narrative Method." CL 28:309-325. Fall 1976.

Wright, Elizabeth. E. T. A. Hoffmann and the Rhetoric of Terror: Aspects of Language Used for the Evocation of Fear. Leeds: Maney, 1978. pp. 235-275.

Hofmannsthal, Hugo von
ANDREAS
Bangerter, Lowell A. Hugo von Hofmannsthal. New York: Ungar, 1977. pp. 40-47.

Frink, Helen. "The Hunting Motif in Hofmannsthal's Works." MLN 95:687-690. April 1980.

Miles, David H. Hofmannsthal's Novel, ANDREAS: Memory and Self. Princeton: Princeton University Press, 1972. 210 pp.

DAS MÄRCHEN DER 672. NACHT
Barker, Andrew W. "The Triumph of Life in Hofmannsthal's DAS MÄRCHEN DER 672. NACHT." MLR 74: 341-348. April 1979.

Cohn, Dorrit. "'Als Traum erzählt': The Case for a Freudian Reading of Hofmannsthal's MÄRCHEN DER 672. NACHT." DVLG 54:284-305. No. 2, 1980.

RAOUL RICHTER, 1896
Dierick, Augustinus. "Epiphany Shared: An Interpretation of Hofmannsthal's RAOUL RICHTER, 1896." MLR 74:349-360. April 1979.

REITERGESCHICHTE
Donop, William R. "Archetypal Vision in Hofmannsthal's REITERGESCHICHTE." GL&L 22:126-134. January 1969.

Hansen, Carl V. "The Death of First Sergeant Anton Lerch in Hofmannsthal's REITERGESCHICHTE: A Military Analysis." MAL 13:17-26. No. 2, 1980.

Lakin, Michael. "Hofmannsthal's REITERGESCHICHTE and Kafka's EIN LANDARZT." MAL 3:39-48. Spring 1970.

Robertson, Ritchie. "The Dual Structure of Hofmannsthal's REITERGESCHICHTE." FMLS 14:316-331. October 1978.

SOMMERREISE
Wellbery, David E. "Narrative Theory and Textual Interpretation: Hofmannsthal's SOMMERREISE as Test Case." DVLG 54:306-333. No. 2, 1980.

Hölderlin, Friedrich
HYPERION
Brown, Marshall. "The Eccentric Path." JEGP 77:104-112. January 1978.

Frye, Lawrence O. "Seasonal and Psychic Time in the Structuring of Hölderlin's HYPERION." Friedrich Hölderlin: An Early Modern. ed. Emery E. George. Ann Arbor: University of Michigan Press, 1972. pp. 148-179.

Harrison, R. B. Hölderlin and Greek Literature. Oxford: Clarendon Press, 1975. pp. 43-83.

Hölderlin, Friedrich

> Ryan, Lawrence. "Hölderlin's HYPERION: A Romantic Novel?" Friedrich Hölderlin: An Early Modern. ed. Emery E. George. Ann Arbor: University of Michigan Press, 1972. pp. 180-191.
>
> Silz, Walter. Hölderlin's HYPERION: A Critical Reading. Philadelphia: University of Pennsylvania Press, 1969. 129 pp.

Jahnn, Hans Henny
FLUSS OHNE UFER
> Brown, Russell E. "On Classifying the Setting of the Novel." Neophil 51:395-401. October 1967.

THE MEMOIRS OF GUSTAV ANIAS HORN
> Detsch, Richard. "The Theme of the Black Race in the Works of Hans Henny Jahnn." Mosaic 7:181-186. Winter 1974.
>
> Heck, Francis S. "Hans Henny Jahnn, Disciple of André Gide." RS 42:36-43. March 1974.
>
> Jenkinson, D. E. "The Rôle of Vitalism in the Novels of Hans Henny Jahnn." GL&L 25:362-368. July 1972.

PERRUDJA
> Freeman, Thomas. "The Lotus and the Tigress: Symbols of Mediation in Hans Henny Jahnn's PERRUDJA." Genre 7:91-107. March 1974.
>
> Mitchell, Breon. "Hans Henny Jahnn and James Joyce: The Birth of the Inner Monologue in the German Novel." Arcadia 6:44-71. 1971.

Johnson, Uwe
JAHRESTAGE
> Boulby, Mark. "Surmises on Love and Family Life in the Work of Uwe Johnson." Seminar 10:131-141. May 1974.
>
> Miller, Leslie L. "Uwe Johnson's JAHRESTAGE: The Choice of Alternatives." Seminar 10:50-70. February 1974.

SPECULATIONS ABOUT JACOB
> Boulby, Mark. Uwe Johnson. New York: Ungar, 1974. pp. 7-36.
>
> Cock, Mary E. "Uwe Johnson: An Interpretation of Two Novels." MLR 69:348-353. April 1974.
>
> Friedrichsmeyer, Erhard. "Quest by Supposition: Johnson's MUTMASSUNGEN ÜBER JAKOB." GR 42:215-226. May 1967.
>
> Good, Colin H. "Uwe Johnson's Treatment of the Nar-

rative in MUTMASSUNGEN ÜBER JAKOB." GL&L 24: 358-370. July 1971.

Jackiw, Sharon Edwards. "The Manifold Difficulties of Uwe Johnson's MUTMASSUNGEN ÜBER JAKOB." Monatshefte 65:126-143. Summer 1973.

Thomas, R. Hinton and Wilfried van der Will. The German Novel and the Affluent Society. Manchester: Manchester University Press, 1968. pp. 112-116.

THE THIRD BOOK ABOUT ACHIM
Botheroyd, Paul F. Ich und er: First and Third Person Self-Reference and Problems of Identity in Three Contemporary German-Language Novels. The Hague: Mouton, 1976. pp. 62-94.

Boulby, Mark. Uwe Johnson. New York: Ungar, 1974. pp. 37-65.

Cock, Mary E. "Uwe Johnson: An Interpretation of Two Novels." MLR 69:353-358. April 1974.

Diller, Edward. "Uwe Johnson's Karsch: Language as a Reflection of the Two Germanies." Monatshefte 60:35-39. Spring 1968.

Fletcher, John. "The Themes of Alienation and Mutual Incomprehension in the Novels of Uwe Johnson." IFR 1:84-87. July 1974.

Mornin, Edward. "Taking Games Seriously: Observations on the German Sports-Novel." GR 51:292-294. November 1976.

Thomas, R. Hinton and Wilfried van der Will. The German Novel and the Affluent Society. Manchester: Manchester University Press, 1968. pp. 116-126.

Van Abbé, Derek. "From Proust to Johnson: Some Notes After DAS DRITTE BUCH ÜBER ACHIM." ML 55:73-79. June 1974.

Watt, Roderick H. "Uwe Johnson's Use of Documentary Material and Style in DAS DRITTE BUCH ÜBER ACHIM." FMLS 13:240-252. July 1977.

Jünger, Ernst
THE GLASS BEES
Loose, Gerhard. Ernst Jünger. New York: Twayne, 1974. pp. 98-106.
HELIOPOLIS
Loose, Gerhard. Ernst Jünger. New York: Twayne, 1974. pp. 80-89.

Jünger, Ernst
IN STAHLGEWITTERN
Stern, J. P. "The Embattled Style: Ernst Jünger, IN STAHLGEWITTERN." The First World War in Fiction: A Collection of Critical Essays. ed. Holger Klein. London: Macmillan, 1976. pp. 112-125.
ON THE MARBLE CLIFFS
Loose, Gerhard. Ernst Jünger. New York: Twayne, 1974. pp. 57-69.

McQueen, Marian. "Ernst Jünger's AUF DEN MARMORKLIPPEN and Northrop Frye's Theory of Romance." CGP 6:37-56. 1978.
THE SLINGSHOT
Loose, Gerhard. Ernst Jünger. New York: Twayne, 1974. pp. 125-131.

Kafka, Franz
AMERIKA
Bridgwater, Patrick. Kafka and Nietzsche. Bonn: Grundmann, 1974. pp. 62-66.

Burwell, Michael L. "Kafka's AMERIKA as a Novel of Social Criticism." Ger SR 2:193-209. May 1979.

Durrani, Osman. "Partners in Isolation. An Inquiry into Some Correspondences Between Kafka's DER VERSCHOLLENE and Pintner's THE CARETAKER." FMLS 16:308-317. October 1980.

Emrich, Wilhelm. Franz Kafka: A Critical Study of His Writings. New York: Ungar, 1968. pp. 276-315.

Gray, Ronald D. Franz Kafka. Cambridge [Eng.]: Cambridge University Press, 1973. pp. 67-82.

*Greenberg, Martin. The Terror of Art: Kafka and Modern Literature. New York: Basic Books, 1965. pp. 92-103.

Hall, Calvin S. and Richard E. Lind. Dreams, Life, and Literature: A Study of Franz Kafka. Chapel Hill: University of North Carolina Press, 1970. pp. 63-70.

Hibberd, John. Kafka in Context. London: Studio Vista, 1975. pp. 50-58.

Kuna, Franz. Kafka: Literature as Corrective Punishment. London: Paul Elek, 1974. pp. 64-98.

Livermore, Ann Lapraik. "Kafka and Stendhal's DE L'AMOUR." RLC 43:205-218. April/June 1969.

Malmsheimer, Richard R. "Kafka's 'Nature Theatre of

Oklahoma': The End of Karl Rossman's Journey to Maturity." MFS 13:493-501. Winter 1967-1968.

Mann, Klaus. "Preface to AMERIKA." Franz Kafka: A Collection of Criticism. New York: McGraw-Hill, 1975. pp. 133-139.

Osborne, Charles. Kafka. New York: Barnes and Noble, 1967. pp. 56-73.

Schlant, Ernestine. "Kafka's AMERIKA: The Trial of Karl Rossmann." Criticism 12:213-225. Summer 1970.

Spann, Meno. Franz Kafka. Boston: Twayne, 1976. pp. 74-89.

Tauber, Herbert. Franz Kafka: An Interpretation of His Works. New York: Haskell House, 1967. pp. 27-57.

Weinberg, Helen. The New Novel in America: The Kafkan Mode in Contemporary Fiction. Ithaca: Cornell University Press, 1970. pp. 1-13.

THE BURROW

Bangerter, Lowell A. "DER BAU: Franz Kafka's Final Punishment Tragedy." RS 42:11-19. March 1974.

Bridgwater, Patrick. Kafka and Nietzsche. Bonn: Grundmann, 1974. pp. 139-142.

Emrich, Wilhelm. Franz Kafka: A Critical Study of His Writings. New York: Ungar, 1968. pp. 206-224.

Goodden, Christian. "Two Quests for Surety--A Comparative Interpretation of Stifter's ABDIAS and Kafka's DER BAU." JES 5:341-361. December 1975.

Sussman, Henry. "The All-Embracing Metaphor: Reflections on Kafka's THE BURROW." Glyph 1:100-131. 1977.

Thorlby, Anthony. Kafka: A Study. Totowa: Rowman and Littlefield, 1972. pp. 47-51.

Weigand, Hermann J. "Franz Kafka's THE BURROW (DER BAU): An Analytical Essay." PMLA 87:152-166. March 1972. Reprinted in Franz Kafka: A Collection of Criticism. ed. Leo Hamalian. New York: McGraw-Hill, 1975. pp. 85-108.

THE CASTLE

Alter, Maria Pospischil. "The Over-Certified Castle: Or Look Who Is Talking." PCL 3:5-11. November 1977.

Arneson, Richard J. "Power and Authority in THE CASTLE." Mosaic 12:99-113. Summer 1979.

Boa, Elizabeth and J. H. Reid. Critical Strategies: German Fiction in the Twentieth Century. London: Edward Arnold, 1972. pp. 159-168.

Bridgmann, Patrick. Kafka and Nietzsche. Bonn: Grundmann, 1974. pp. 90-103.

Church, Margaret. "The Isolated Community: Kafka's Village and Thomas Mann's Davos." UDR 13:105-112. Spring 1979.

Cohn, Dorrit. "K. Enters THE CASTLE: On the Change of Person in Kafka's Manuscript." Euphorion 62:28-45. 1968.

Emrich, Wilhelm. Franz Kafka: A Critical Study of His Writings. New York: Ungar, 1968. pp. 365-507.

Fickert, Kurt J. "Kafka's 'Assistants' from the Castle." IFR 3:3-6. January 1976.

Friederich, Reinhard H. "K.'s 'bitteres Kraut' and EXODUS." GQ 48:355-357. May 1975.

_____. "Kafka and Hamsum's MYSTERIES." CL 28:38-49. Winter 1976.

Gray, Ronald D. Franz Kafka. Cambridge: Cambridge University Press, 1973. pp. 140-172.

*Greenberg, Martin. The Terror of Art: Kafka and Modern Literature. New York: Basic Books, 1965. pp. 154-200.

Grimes, Margaret. "Kafka's Use of Cue-Names: Its Importance for an Interpretation of THE CASTLE." CentR 18:221-230. Summer 1974.

Hall, Calvin S. and Richard E. Lind. Dreams, Life, and Literature: A Study of Franz Kafka. Chapel Hill: University of North Carolina Press, 1970. pp. 57-62.

Heller, Erich. Franz Kafka. New York: Viking, 1974. pp. 98-130.

_____. Kafka. Glasgow: Collins, 1974. pp. 110-138.

Hibberd, John. Kafka in Context. London: Studio Vista, 1975. pp. 120-129.

Kartiganer, Donald M. "'A Ceremony of the Usual Thing': Notes on Kafka's Development." Criticism 20: 58-64. Winter 1978.

Koelb, Clayton. "The Deletions from Kafka's Novels." Monatshefte 68:365-372. Winter 1976.

Kröller, Eva-Marie. "Kafka's CASTLE as Inverted Romance." Neohelicon 4:283-294. No. 3/4, 1976.

Kudszus, Winfried. "Between Past and Future: Kafka's Later Novels." Mosaic 3:107-118. Summer 1970.

Kuna, Franz. Kafka: Literature as Corrective Punishment. London: Paul Elek, 1974. pp. 136-182.

Livermore, Ann Lapraik. "Kafka and Stendhal's DE L'AMOUR." RLC 43:173-195. April/June 1969.

Mykyta, Larysa. "Woman as the Obstacle and the Way." MLN 95:627-640. April 1980.

Osborne, Charles. Kafka. New York: Barnes & Noble, 1967. pp. 92-104.

Perry, Ruth. "Madness in Euripides, Shakespeare, and Kafka: An Examination of THE BACCHAE, HAMLET, KING LEAR, and THE CASTLE." PsyR 65:270-275. Summer 1978.

*Peters, F. G. "Kafka and Kleist: A Literary Relationship." OGS 1:133-148. 1966.

Politzer, Heinz. "The Alienated Self--A Key to Franz Kafka's CASTLE?" MQR 14:398-412. Fall 1975.

Robert, Marthe. The Old and the New: From Don Quixote to Kafka. Berkeley: University of California Press, 1977. pp. 171-322.

Rolleston, James. Kafka's Narrative Theater. University Park: Pennsylvania State University Press, 1974. pp. 112-129.

Sandbank, S. "Action as Self-Mirror: On Kafka's Plots." MFS 17:23-29. Spring 1971.

_____. "Structures of Paradox in Kafka." MLQ 28: 462-472. December 1967.

Sebald, W. G. "The Law of Ignominy: Authority, Messianism and Exile in THE CASTLE." On Kafka: Semi-Centenary Perspectives. ed. Franz Kuna. London: Paul Elek, 1976. pp. 42-58.

Kafka, Franz

_____. "The Undiscover'd Country: The Death Motif in Kafka's CASTLE." JES 2:22-34. March 1972.

Spann, Meno. Franz Kafka. Boston: Twayne, 1976. pp. 140-163.

Steinberg, Erwin R. "K. of THE CASTLE: Ostensible Land-Surveyor." Franz Kafka: A Collection of Criticism. ed. Leo Hamalian. New York: McGraw-Hill, 1975. pp. 126-132.

Szanto, George H. Narrative Consciousness: Structure and Perception in the Fiction of Kafka, Beckett, and Robbe-Grillet. Austin: University of Texas Press, 1972. pp. 28-35.

Tate, Eleanor. "Kafka's THE CASTLE: Another Dickens Novel?" SoRA 7:157-168. No. 2, 1974.

Tauber, Herbert. Franz Kafka: An Interpretation of His Works. New York: Haskell House, 1967. pp. 131-185.

Thorlby, Anthony. Kafka: A Study. Totowa: Rowman and Littlefield, 1972. pp. 68-83.

Wagenbach, Klaus. "Kafka's Castle?" The World of Franz Kafka. ed. J.P. Stern. New York: Holt, Rinehart and Winston, 1980. pp. 79-84.

Waidson, H.M. "Prose Fiction: Some Outstanding German Novels." Twentieth Century German Literature. ed. August Closs. New York: Barnes and Noble, 1969. pp. 123-128.

Winkelman, John. "An Interpretation of Kafka's DAS SCHLOSS." Monatshefte 64:115-131. Summer 1972.

A COUNTRY DOCTOR

Birch, Joan. "What Happens to the Doctor in Kafka's EIN LANDARZT?" MAL 9:13-25. No. 1, 1976.

Brancato, John J. "Kafka's A COUNTRY DOCTOR: A Tale for Our Time." SSF 15:173-176. Spring 1978.

Bridgwater, Patrick. Kafka and Nietzsche. Bonn: Grundmann, 1974. pp. 111-115.

Cohn, Dorrit. "Kafka's Eternal Present: Narrative Tense in EIN LANDARZT and Other First-Person Stories." PMLA 83:144-150. March 1968.

Emrich, Wilhelm. Franz Kafka: A Critical Study of His Writings. New York: Ungar, 1968. pp. 151-161.

Fickert, Kurt J. "Fatal Knowledge: Kafka's EIN
LANDARZT." Monatshefte 66:381-386. Winter 1974.

Friederich, Reinhard H. "The Dream-Transference in
Kafka's EIN LANDARZT." PLL 9:28-34. Winter 1973.

Goldstein, Bluma. "Franz Kafka's EIN LANDARZT: A
Study in Failure." DVLG 42:745-759. November 1968.

Gray, Ronald D. Franz Kafka. Cambridge: Cambridge
University Press, 1973. pp. 126-139.

Hanlin, Todd C. "Franz Kafka's LANDARZT: 'Und
heilt er nicht....'" MAL 11:333-344. No. 3/4, 1978.

Harroff, Stephen. "The Structure of EIN LANDARZT:
Rethinking Mythopoesis in Kafka." Symposium 34:42-55.
Spring 1980.

Kurz, Paul Konrad. On Modern German Literature.
University: University of Alabama Press, 1967. pp.
149-172.

Lakin, Michael. "Hofmannsthal's REITERGESCHICHTE
and Kafka's EIN LANDARZT." MAL 3:39-48. Spring
1970.

Loewen, Harry. "Human Involvement in Turgenev's and
Kafka's Country Doctors." G Slav 1:47-53. Spring 1974.

Sokel, Walter H. "On THE COUNTRY DOCTOR."
Franz Kafka: A Collection of Criticism. ed. Leo
Hamalian. New York: McGraw-Hill, 1975. pp. 81-84.

Spann, Meno. Franz Kafka. Boston: Twayne, 1976.
pp. 125-130.

Stockholder, Katherine. "A COUNTRY DOCTOR: The
Narrator as Dreamer." AI 35:331-346. Winter 1978.

DESCRIPTION OF A STRUGGLE
Sandbank, S. "The Unity of Kafka's BESCHREIBUNG
EINES KAMPFES." Archiv 210:1-21. June 1973.

THE GREAT WALL OF CHINA
Emrich, Wilhelm. Franz Kafka: A Critical Study of
His Writings. New York: Ungar, 1968. pp. 225-249.

Goodden, Christian. "THE GREAT WALL OF CHINA:
The Elaboration of an Intellectual Dilemma." On Kafka:
Semi-Centenary Perspectives. ed. Franz Kuna. London: Paul Elek, 1976. pp. 128-145.

Tauber, Herbert. Franz Kafka: An Interpretation of
His Works. New York: Haskell House, 1967. pp. 123-130.

Kafka, Franz

A HUNGER ARTIST
Bridgwater, Patrick. Kafka and Nietzsche. Bonn: Grundmann, 1974. pp. 132-139.

Hibberd, John. Kafka in Context. London: Studio Vista, 1975. pp. 113-116.

Mahony, Patrick. "A HUNGER ARTIST: Content and Form." AI 35:357-374. Winter 1978.

Neumarkt, Paul. "Kafka's A HUNGER ARTIST: The Ego in Isolation." AI 27:109-120. Summer 1970.

Norris, Margot. "Sadism and Masochism in Two Kafka Stories: IN DER STRAFKOLONIE and EIN HUNGERKÜNSTLER." MLN 93:430-447. April 1978.

Satz, Martha and Zsuzsanna Ozsvath. "A HUNGER ARTIST and IN THE PENAL COLONY in the Light of Schopenhauerian Metaphysics." Ger SR 1:200-210. May 1978.

Sheppard, Richard W. "Kafka's EIN HUNGERKÜNSTLER: A Reconsideration." GQ 46:219-233. March 1973.

Waldeck, Peter B. "Kafka's DIE VERWANDLUNG and EIN HUNGERKÜNSTLER as Influenced by Leopold von Sacher-Masoch." Monatshefte 64:147-152. Summer 1972.

IN THE PENAL COLONY
Beck, Evelyn Torton. Kafka and the Yiddish Theater: Its Impact on His Work. Madison: University of Wisconsin Press, 1971. pp. 146-154.

Bridgwater, Patrick. Kafka and Nietzsche. Bonn: Grundmann, 1974. pp. 104-111.

Dodd, William J. "Kafka and Freud: A Note on IN DER STRAFKOLONIE." Monatshefte 70:129-137. Summer 1978.

Emrich, Wilhelm. Franz Kafka: A Critical Study of His Writings. New York: Ungar, 1968. pp. 268-275.

Fickert, Kurt J. "A Literal Interpretation of IN THE PENAL COLONY." MFS 17:31-36. Spring 1971.

Fowler, Doreen F. "IN THE PENAL COLONY: Kafka's Unorthodox Theology." Coll L 6:113-119. Spring 1979.

Gray, Ronald D. Franz Kafka. Cambridge: Cambridge University Press, 1973. pp. 93-102.

Hadomi, Leah. "The Utopian Dimension of Kafka's IN THE PENAL COLONY." OL 35:235-249. No. 3, 1980.

Kramer, Dale. "The Aesthetics of Theme: Kafka's IN THE PENAL COLONY." SSF 5:362-367. Summer 1968.

Mendelsohn, Leonard R. "Kafka's IN THE PENAL COLONY and the Paradox of Enforced Freedom." SSF 8:309-316. Spring 1971.

Neumeyer, Peter. "Do Not Teach Kafka's IN THE PENAL COLONY." Coll L 6:103-111. Spring 1979.

Norris, Margot. "Sadism and Masochism in Two Kafka Stories: IN DER STRAFKOLONIE and EIN HUNGERKÜNSTLER." MLN 93:430-447. April 1978.

Pascal, Roy. "Kafka's IN DER STRAFKOLONIE: Narrative Structure and Interpretation." OGS 11:123-145. 1980.

Politzer, Heinz. "Parable and Paradox: IN THE PENAL COLONY." Franz Kafka: A Collection of Criticism. ed. Leo Hamalian. New York: McGraw-Hill, 1975. pp. 65-80.

Rolleston, James. Kafka's Narrative Theater. University Park: Pennsylvania State University Press, 1974. pp. 88-100.

Sacharoff, Mark. "Pathological, Comic, and Tragic Elements in Kafka's IN THE PENAL COLONY." Genre 4:392-409. December 1971.

Satz, Martha and Zsuzsanna Ozsvath. "A HUNGER ARTIST and IN THE PENAL COLONY in the Light of Schopenhauerian Metaphysics." Ger SR 1:200-210. May 1978.

Spann, Meno. Franz Kafka. Boston: Twayne, 1976. pp. 108-119.

Steinberg, Erwin R. "The Judgment in Kafka's IN THE PENAL COLONY." JML 5:492-514. September 1976.

Street, James B. "Kafka Through Freud: Totems and Taboos in IN DER STRAFKOLONIE." MAL 6:93-104. No. 3/4, 1973.

Tauber, Herbert. Franz Kafka: An Interpretation of His Works. New York: Haskell, 1967. pp. 58-64.

Kafka, Franz    343

Thorlby, Anthony. Kafka: A Study. Totowa: Rowman and Littlefield, 1972. pp. 40-47.
INVESTIGATIONS OF A DOG
Emrich, Wilhelm. Franz Kafka: A Critical Study of His Writings. New York: Ungar, 1968. pp. 180-200.

Tauber, Herbert. Franz Kafka: An Interpretation of His Works. New York: Haskell, 1967. pp. 201-211.

Tiefenbrun, Ruth. Moment of Torment: An Interpretation of Franz Kafka's Short Stories. Carbondale: Southern Illinois University Press, 1973. pp. 62-78.
JOSEPHINE
Bridgwater, Patrick. Kafka and Nietzsche. Bonn: Grundmann, 1974. pp. 142-149.

Emrich, Wilhelm. Franz Kafka: A Critical Study of His Writings. New York: Ungar, 1968. pp. 200-206.

Mahlendorf, Ursula R. "Kafka's JOSEPHINE THE SINGER OR THE MOUSEFOLK: Art at the Edge of Nothingness." MAL 11:199-242. No. 3/4, 1978.

Rolleston, James. Kafka's Narrative Theater. University Park: Pennsylvania State University Press, 1974. pp. 130-139.

Sattler, Emil E. "Kafka's Artist in a Society of Mice." GN 9:49-53. No. 4, 1978.

Tauber, Herbert. Franz Kafka: An Interpretation of His Works. New York: Haskell, 1967. pp. 193-198.

Wiley, Marion E. "Kafka's Piping Mice as Spokesmen for Communication." MFS 25:253-258. Summer 1979.
METAMORPHOSIS
Beck, Evelyn Torton. Kafka and the Yiddish Theater: Its Impact on His Work. Madison: University of Wisconsin Press, 1971. pp. 142-146.

Cantrell, Carol Helmstetter. "THE METAMORPHOSIS: Kafka's Study of a Family." MFS 23:578-586. Winter 1977-1978.

Corngold, Stanley. The Commentator's Despair: The Interpretation of Kafka's METAMORPHOSIS. Port Washington: Kennikat, 1973. 255 pp.

_____. "Kafka's DIE VERWANDLUNG: Metamorphosis of the Metaphor." Mosaic 3:91-106. Summer 1970.

D'Haen, Theo. "The Liberation of the Samsas." Neophil 62:262-278. April 1978.

Eggenschwiler, David. "DIE VERWANDLUNG, Freud, and the Chains of Odysseus." MLQ 39:363-385. December 1978.

Emrich, Wilhelm. Franz Kafka: A Critical Study of His Writings. New York: Ungar, 1968. pp. 136-148.

Friedman, Norman. "The Struggle of Vermin: Parasitism and Family Love in Kafka's METAMORPHOSIS." BSUF 9:23-32. Winter 1968.

Gilman, Sander L. "A View of Kafka's Treatment of Actuality in DIE VERWANDLUNG." GN 2:26-30. No. 4, 1971.

Gray, Ronald D. Franz Kafka. Cambridge: Cambridge University Press, 1973. pp. 83-92.

Greenberg, Martin. "Gregor Samsa and Modern Spirituality." Franz Kafka: A Collection of Criticism. ed. Leo Hamalian. New York: McGraw-Hill, 1975. pp. 50-64.

\*_____. The Terror of Art: Kafka and Modern Literature. New York: Basic Books, 1965. pp. 69-91.

Jofen, Jean. "METAMORPHOSIS." AI 35:347-355. Winter 1978.

Kuna, Franz. Kafka: Literature as Corrective Punishment. London: Paul Elek, 1974. pp. 49-63.

MacAndrew, M. Elizabeth. "A Splacknuck and a Dung-Beetle: Realism and Probability in Swift and Kafka." CE 31:385-391. January 1970.

Moss, Leonard. "A Key to the Door Image in THE METAMORPHOSIS." MFS 17:37-42. Spring 1971.

Pearce, Richard. Stages of the Clown: Perspectives on Modern Fiction from Dostoyevsky to Beckett. Carbondale: Southern Illinois University Press, 1970. pp. 6-25.

\*Peters, F. G. "Kafka and Kleist: A Literary Relationship." OGS 1:124-133. 1966.

Rhein, Philip H. "Two Fantastic Visions: Franz Kafka and Alfred Kubin." SAB 42:61-65. May 1977.

Rolleston, James. Kafka's Narrative Theater. University Park: Pennsylvania State University Press, 1974. pp. 52-68.

Spann, Meno. Franz Kafka. Boston: Twayne, 1976. pp. 63-74.

Sparks, Kimberly. "Kafka's METAMORPHOSIS: On Banishing the Lodgers." JES 3:230-240. September 1973.

Tauber, Herbert. Franz Kafka: An Interpretation of His Works. New York: Haskell, 1967. pp. 18-26.

Thiher, Allen. "Kafka's Legacy." MFS 26:551-557. Winter 1980-1981.

Thorlby, Anthony. Kafka: A Study. Totowa: Rowman and Littlefield, 1972. pp. 34-40.

Tiefenbrun, Ruth. Moment of Torment: An Interpretation of Franz Kafka's Short Stories. Carbondale: Southern Illinois University Press, 1973. pp. 111-135.

Waldeck, Peter B. "Kafka's DIE VERWANDLUNG and EIN HUNGERKÜNSTLER as Influenced by Leopold von Sacher-Masoch." Monatshefte 64:147-152. Summer 1972.

Witt, Mary Ann. "Confinement in DIE VERWANDLUNG and LES SEQUESTRES D'ALTONA." CL 23:32-44. Winter 1971.

Wolkenfeld, Suzanne. "Christian Symbolism in Kafka's THE METAMORPHOSIS." SSF 10:205-207. Spring 1973.

THE TRIAL
Beck, Evelyn Torton. Kafka and the Yiddish Theater: Its Impact on His Work. Madison: University of Wisconsin Press, 1971. pp. 154-171.

Bridgwater, Patrick. Kafka and Nietzsche. Bonn: Grundmann, 1974. pp. 67-90.

Bryant, Jerry H. "The Delusion of Hope: Franz Kafka's THE TRIAL." Symposium 23:116-128. Summer 1969.

Church, Margaret. "Dostoevsky's CRIME AND PUNISHMENT and Kafka's THE TRIAL." L&P 19:47-55. No. 3/4, 1969.

Cohen, Cynthia B. "The Trials of Socrates and Joseph K." Philosophy and Literature 4:212-228. Fall 1980.

Corngold, Stanley. "The Question of the Law, the Question of Writing." Twentieth Century Interpretations of THE TRIAL: A Collection of Critical Essays. ed.

James Rolleston. Englewood Cliffs: Prentice-Hall, 1976. pp. 100-104.

Diller, Edward. "'Heteronomy' Versus 'Autonomy': A Retrial of THE TRIAL by Franz Kafka." CLAJ 12:214-222. March 1969.

_____. "'Theonomous' Homiletics 'Vor dem Gesetz': Franz Kafka and Paul Tillich." RLV 36:289-294. No. 3, 1970.

Emrich, Wilhelm. Franz Kafka: A Critical Study of His Writings. New York: Ungar, 1968. pp. 316-364.

_____. "The Role of Women." Twentieth Century Interpretations of THE TRIAL: A Collection of Critical Essays. ed. James Rolleston. Englewood Cliffs: Prentice-Hall, 1976. pp. 36-39.

Feuerlicht, Ignace. "Kafka's Josef K. --A Man with Qualities." Seminar 3:103-116. Fall 1967.

_____. "Omissions and Contradictions in Kafka's TRIAL." GQ 40:339-350. May 1967.

Friedman, Maurice. "The Problematic of Guilt and the Dialogue with the Absurd: Images of the Irrational in Kafka's TRIAL." Review of Existential Psychology & Psychiatry 14:11-25. No. 1, 1975-1976.

Gray, Ronald D. Franz Kafka. Cambridge: Cambridge University Press, 1973. pp. 103-125.

*Greenberg, Martin. The Terror of Art: Kafka and Modern Literature. New York: Basic Books, 1965. pp. 116-151.

Grossvogel, David I. Limits of the Novel: Evolutions of a Form from Chaucer to Robbe-Grillet. Ithaca: Cornell University Press, 1968. pp. 160-188.

Handler, Gary. "A Note on the Structure of Kafka's DER PROZESS." MLN 84:798-799. October 1969.

_____. "A Textual Omission in the English Translation of DER PROZESS." MLN 83:454-456. April 1968.

Heller, Erich. Franz Kafka. New York: Viking, 1974. pp. 71-97.

_____. Kafka. Glasgow: Collins, 1974. pp. 80-106.

## Kafka, Franz

———. "Man Guilty." Twentieth Century Interpretations of THE TRIAL: A Collection of Critical Essays. ed. James Rolleston. Englewood Cliffs: Prentice-Hall, 1976. pp. 94-99.

*Heller, Peter. Dialectics and Nihilism: Essays on Lessing, Nietzsche, Mann, and Kafka. Amherst: University of Massachusetts Press, 1966. pp. 259-263.

Henel, Ingeborg. "The Legend of the Doorkeeper and Its Significance for Kafka's Trial." Twentieth Century Interpretations of THE TRIAL: A Collection of Critical Essays. ed. James Rolleston. Englewood Cliffs: Prentice-Hall, 1976. pp. 40-55.

Hibberd, John. Kafka in Context. London: Studio Vista, 1975. pp. 65-73.

Hobson, Irmgard. "The Kafka Problem Compounded: TRIAL and JUDGMENT in English." MFS 23:511-529. Winter 1977-1978.

Jaffe, Adrian. The Process of Kafka's TRIAL. Detroit: Michigan State University Press, 1967. 146 pp.

Kartiganer, Donald M. "'A Ceremony of the Usual Thing': Notes on Kafka's Development." Criticism 20:53-58. Winter 1978.

Kavanagh, Thomas M. "Kafka's THE TRIAL: The Semiotics of the Absurd." Novel 5:242-253. Spring 1972. Reprinted in Twentieth Century Interpretations of THE TRIAL: A Collection of Critical Essays. ed. James Rolleston. Englewood Cliffs: Prentice-Hall, 1976. pp. 86-93.

Koelb, Clayton. "The Deletions from Kafka's Novels." Monatshefte 68:365-372. Winter 1976.

Kontje, Todd. "The Reader as Josef K." GR 54:62-66. Spring 1979.

Kudszus, Winfried. "Between Past and Future: Kafka's Later Novels." Mosaic 3:107-118. Summer 1970.

Kuepper, Karl J. "Gesture and Posture as Elemental Symbolism in Kafka's THE TRIAL." Mosaic 3:143-152. Summer 1970. Reprinted in Twentieth Century Interpretations of THE TRIAL: A Collection of Critical Essays. ed. James Rolleston. Englewood Cliffs: Prentice-Hall, 1976. pp. 60-69.

Kuna, Franz. Kafka: Literature as Corrective Punishment. London: Paul Elek, 1974. pp. 99-135.

Livermore, Ann Lapraik. "Kafka and Stendhal's DE L'AMOUR." RLC 43:195-205. April/June 1969.

Loewen, Harry. "Solzhenitsyn's Kafkaesque Narrative Art in THE GULAG ARCHIPELAGO." G Slav 3:5-13. Spring 1979.

*Marson, Eric. "Justice and the Obsessed Character in MICHAEL KOHLHAAS, DER PROZESS and L'ETRANGER." Seminar 2:21-33. Fall 1966.

McGowan, John P. "THE TRIAL: Terminable/Interminable." TCL 26:1-14. Spring 1980.

Mellen, Joan. "Joseph K. and the Law." TSLL 12:295-302. Summer 1970.

Mykyta, Larysa. "Woman as the Obstacle and the Way." MLN 95:627-640. April 1980.

Osborne, Charles. Kafka. New York: Barnes and Noble, 1967. pp. 74-91.

Pasley, Malcolm. "Two Literary Sources of Kafka's DER PROZESS." FMLS 3:142-147. April 1967.

Pearce, Richard. Stages of the Clown: Perspectives on Modern Fiction from Dostoyevsky to Beckett. Carbondale: Southern Illinois University Press, 1970. pp. 26-46.

Pickar, Gertrud Bauer. "Kafka's 'Vor dem Gesetz': The Case for an Integrated Approach." UP 8:28-34. Spring 1975.

Pondrom, Cyrena Norman. "Kafka and Phenomenology: Josef K.'s Search for Information." WSCL 8:78-95. Winter 1967. Reprinted in Twentieth Century Interpretations of THE TRIAL: A Collection of Critical Essays. ed. James Rolleston. Englewood Cliffs: Prentice-Hall, 1976. pp. 70-85.

Purdy, Strother B. "Religion and Death in Kafka's DER PROZESS." PLL 5:170-182. Spring 1969.

_____. "A Talmudic Analogy to Kafka's Parable 'Vor dem Gesetz.'" PLL 4:420-427. Fall 1968.

Roazen, Deborah Heller. "A Peculiar Attraction: BLEAK HOUSE, DER PROZESS, and the Law." ELWIU 5:251-266. Fall 1978.

Rolleston, James. Kafka's Narrative Theater. University Park: Pennsylvania State University Press, 1974. pp. 69-87.

Siefken, Hinrich. "Man's Inhumanity to Man--Crime and Punishment: Kafka's Novel DER PROZESS and Novels by Tolstoy, Dostoyevsky and Solzhenitsyn." Trivium 7:33-39. May 1972.

Sokel, Walter H. "The Opaqueness of THE TRIAL." Twentieth Century Interpretations of THE TRIAL: A Collection of Critical Essays. ed. James Rolleston. Englewood Cliffs: Prentice-Hall, 1976. pp. 56-59.

_____. "The Programme of K.'s Court: Oedipal and Existential Meanings of THE TRIAL." On Kafka: Semi-Centenary Perspectives. ed. Franz Kuna. London: Paul Elek, 1976. pp. 1-21.

Spiro, Solomon J. "Verdict--Guilty! A Study of THE TRIAL." TCL 17:169-178. July 1971.

*Stelzmann, Rainulf A. "Kafka's THE TRIAL and Hesse's STEPPENWOLF: Two Views of Reality and Transcendence." XUS 5:165-172. December 1966.

Stern, J. P. "The Law of THE TRIAL." On Kafka: Semi-Centenary Perspectives. ed. Franz Kuna. London: Paul Elek, 1976. pp. 22-41.

Struc, Roman S. "'Negative Capability' and Kafka's Protagonists." MAL 11:88-94. No. 3/4, 1978.

Sussman, Henry. "The Court as Text: Inversion, Supplanting, and Derangement in Kafka's DER PROZESS." PMLA 92:41-55. January 1977.

Szanto, George H. Narrative Consciousness: Structure and Perception in the Fiction of Kafka, Beckett, and Robbe-Grillet. Austin: University of Texas, 1972. pp. 20-39.

Tauber, Herbert. Franz Kafka: An Interpretation of His Works. New York: Haskell, 1967. pp. 77-120.

Thorlby, Anthony. Kafka: A Study. Totowa: Rowman and Littlefield, 1972. pp. 53-68.

Vallette, Rebecca M. "DER PROZESS and LE PROCES: A Study in Dramatic Adaptation." MD 10:87-94. May 1967.

Walser, Martin. "Description of a Form." Twentieth Century Interpretations of THE TRIAL: A Collection of

Critical Essays. ed. James Rolleston. Englewood
Cliffs: Prentice-Hall, 1976. pp. 21-35.

Weinberg, Helen. The New Novel in America: The
Kafkan Mode in Contemporary Fiction. Ithaca: Cornell
University Press, 1970. pp. 1-13.

Wildman, Eugene. "The Signal in the Flames: Ordeal
as Game." Tri Q 11:145-162. Winter 1968.

Wirth-Nesher, Hana. "The Modern Jewish Novel and
the City: Franz Kafka, Henry Roth, and Amos Oz."
MFS 24:105-108. Spring 1978.

Wright, Elizabeth. E. T. A. Hoffmann and the Rhetoric
of Terror: Aspects of Language Used for the Evocation
of Fear. Leeds: Maney, 1978. pp. 146-234.

Ziolkowski, Theodore. Dimensions of the Modern Novel:
German Texts and European Contexts. Princeton:
Princeton University Press, 1969. pp. 37-67.

Kant, Hermann
DIE AULA
Andrews, R. C. "The Novel of Social Consciousness:
Hermann Kant's DIE AULA." NGS 1:28-39. Spring
1973.

Gerber, Margy. "Confrontations with Reality in Hermann Kant's DIE AULA." Monatshefte 67:173-184.
Summer 1975.

Langenbruch, Theodor. Dialectical Humor in Hermann
Kant's Novel DIE AULA: A Study in Contemporary East
German Literature. Bonn: Grundmann, 1975. 115 pp.

Van Abbé, Derek. "Autobiography of an Extrovert Generation." GL&L 26:50-58. October 1972.

Kasack, Hermann
FALSCHUNGEN
Reinhardt, George W. "The Ordeal of Art: Hermann
Kasack's FALSCHUNGEN." SSF 9:365-372. Fall 1972.
DAS GROSSE NETZ
Schütz, Herbert. Hermann Kasack: The Role of the
Critical Intellect in the Creative Writer's Work. Bern:
Lang, 1972. pp. 13-111.
DIE STADT HINTER DEM STROM
Gutmann, Helmut. "A Clash of Symbols: Historical and
Universal Dimensions in DIE STADT HINTER DEM
STROM." GR 46:182-197. May 1971.

Schueler, H. J. "Initiatory Patterns and Symbols in Alfred Döblin's MANAS and Hermann Kasack's DIE STADT HINTER DEM STROM." GL&L 24:182-192. January 1971.

Schütz, Herbert. Hermann Kasack: The Role of the Critical Intellect in the Creative Writer's Work. Bern: Lang, 1972. pp. 11-114.

Keller, Gottfried
DIE DREI GERECHTEN KAMMACHER
Ellis, John M. Narration in the German Novelle: Theory and Interpretation. London: Cambridge University Press, 1974. pp. 136-154.
DER GRÜNE HEINRICH
Karcic, Lucie. Light and Darkness in Gottfried Keller's DER GRÜNE HEINRICH. Bonn: Grundmann, 1976. 131 pp.

Lee, Meredith. "The Flute Miracle as a Turning-Point in Keller's DER GRÜNE HEINRICH." Seminar 16:181-192. September 1980.

Lindsay, J. M. Gottfried Keller: Life and Works. London: Dufour, 1969. pp. 109-143.

Temmer, Mark J. "Jean-Jacques Rousseau's CONFESSIONS and Gottfried Keller's DER GRÜNE HEINRICH." RLC 44:155-182. April/June 1970.
KLEIDER MACHEN LEUTE
Shaw, Michael. "The Mirror and Its Uses: A Study of a Pattern in Gottfried Keller's Prose." Symposium 22: 363-368. Winter 1968.
DER LANDVOGT VON GREIFENSEE
Shaw, Michael. "The Mirror and Its Uses: A Study of a Pattern in Gottfried Keller's Prose." Symposium 22: 372-375. Winter 1968.
DIE LEUTE VON SELDWYLA
Lindsay, J. M. Gottfried Keller: Life and Works. London: Dufour, 1969. pp. 144-173.
MARTIN SALANDER
Lindsay, J. M. Gottfried Keller: Life and Works. London: Dufour, 1969. pp. 229-239.
PANKRAZ, DER SCHMOLLER
Jackson, David. "PANKRAZ, DER SCHMOLLER and Gottfried Keller's Sentimental Education." GL&L 30:52-63. October 1976.

Shaw, Michael. "The Mirror and Its Uses: A Study of a Pattern in Gottfried Keller's Prose." Symposium 22: 358-363. Winter 1968.
ROMEO AND JULIA
Clouser, Robin. "ROMEO UND JULIA AUF DEM DORFE: Keller's Variations upon Shakespeare." JEGP 77:161-182. April 1978.

Cooke, A. T. "Gottfried Keller's ROMEO UND JULIA
AUF DEM DORFE." GL&L 24:235-243. April 1971.

Dickerson, Harold D., Jr. "The Music of This Sphere
in Keller's ROMEO UND JULIA AUF DEM DORFE."
GQ 51:47-59. January 1978.

Lindsay, J. M. Gottfried Keller: Life and Works.
London: Dufour, 1969. pp. 148-151.

Puknat, E. M. and S. B. "Edith Wharton and Gottfried
Keller." CL 21:245-254. Summer 1969.

Tucker, Harry, Jr. "Post-Traumatic Psychosis in
ROMEO UND JULIA AUF DEM DORFE." GL&L 25:247-
251. April 1972.
DAS SINNGEDICHT
Lindsay, J. M. Gottfried Keller: Life and Works.
London: Dufour, 1969. pp. 211-228.

Kinkel, Johanna
HANS IBELES IN LONDON
Joeres, Ruth-Ellen Boetcher. "The Triumph of the
Woman: Johanna Kinkel's HANS IBELES IN LONDON
(1860)." Euphorion 70:187-197. 1976.

Kleist, Heinrich von
THE EARTHQUAKE IN CHILE
Aldridge, Alfred Owen. "The Background of Kleist's
DAS ERDBEBEN IN CHILI." Arcadia 3:173-180. 1968.

Dyer, Denys. The Stories of Kleist: A Critical Study.
London: Duckworth, 1977. pp. 13-30.

Ellis, John M. Heinrich von Kleist: Studies in the
Character and Meaning of His Writings. Chapel Hill:
University of North Carolina Press, 1979. pp. 36-53.

_____. Narration in the German Novelle: Theory
and Interpretation. London: Cambridge University
Press, 1974. pp. 46-76.

Gearey, John. Heinrich von Kleist: A Study in Tragedy
and Anxiety. Philadelphia: University of Pennsylvania
Press, 1968. pp. 43-48.

Graham, Ilse. Heinrich von Kleist: Word into Flesh;
A Poet's Quest for the Symbol. Berlin: Gruyter, 1977.
pp. 159-167.

Helbling, Robert E. The Major Works of Heinrich von
Kleist. New York: New Directions, 1975. pp. 106-
113.

Johnson, Richard L. "Kleist's ERDBEBEN IN CHILI." Seminar 11:33-45. February 1975.

Lucas, R. S. "Studies in Kleist." DVLG 44:145-170. January 1970.

Ossar, Michael. "Kleist's DAS ERDBEBEN IN CHILI and DIE MARQUISE VON O...." RLV 34:151-169. No. 2, 1968.

Thayer, Terence. "Kleist's Don Fernando and DAS ERDBEBEN IN CHILI." Coll G 11:263-288. No. 3/4, 1978.

## THE FOUNDLING

Dyer, Denys. The Stories of Kleist: A Critical Study. London: Duckworth, 1977. pp. 48-59.

Ellis, John M. Heinrich von Kleist: Studies in the Character and Meaning of His Writings. Chapel Hill: University of North Carolina Press, 1979. pp. 1-20.

Parkes, Ford B. "Shifting Narrative Perspectives in Kleist's FINDLING." JEGP 76:165-176. April 1977.

*Peters, F. G. "Kafka and Kleist: A Literary Relationship." OGS 1:117-124. 1966.

Reinhardt, George W. "Turbulence and Enigma in Kleist's DER FINDLING." ELWIU 4:265-274. Fall 1977.

Ryder, Frank G. "Kleist's FINDLING: Oedipus 'manque'?" MLN 92:509-524. April 1977.

Wright, Elizabeth. E. T. A. Hoffmann and the Rhetoric of Terror: Aspects of Language Used for the Evocation of Fear. Leeds: Maney, 1978. pp. 116-145.

## DIE HEILIGE CÄCILIE ODER DIE GEWALT DER MUSIK

Graham, Ilse. Heinrich von Kleist: Word into Flesh; A Poet's Quest for the Symbol. Berlin: Gruyter, 1977. pp. 195-201.

Heine, Thomas. "Kleist's ST. CECILIA and the Power of Politics." Seminar 16:71-82. May 1980.

## DIE MARQUISE VON O...

Blume, Bernhard. "The Marquise of O...'s Knitting: A New Look at Kleist's Novella." BUJ 26:45-49. No. 2, 1978.

Cohn, Dorrit. "Kleist's MARQUISE VON O...: The Problem of Knowledge." Monatshefte 67:129-144. Summer 1975.

Crosby, Donald H. "Psychological Realism in the Works of Kleist: PENTHESILEA and DIE MARQUISE VON O...." L&P 19:9-15. No. 1, 1969.

Dünnhaupt, Gerhard. "Kleist's MARQUISE VON O... and Its Literary Debt to Cervantes." Arcadia 10:147-157. No. 2, 1975.

Dyer, Denys. The Stories of Kleist: A Critical Study. London: Duckworth, 1977. pp. 60-79.

Ellis, John M. Heinrich von Kleist: Studies in the Character and Meaning of His Writings. Chapel Hill: University of North Carolina Press, 1979. pp. 21-35.

Fries, Thomas. "The Impossible Object: The Feminine, the Narrative (Laclos' LIAISONS DANGEREUSES and Kleist's MARQUISE VON O...)." MLN 91:1316-1326. December 1976.

Gearey, John. Heinrich von Kleist: A Study in Tragedy and Anxiety. Philadelphia: University of Pennsylvania Press, 1968. pp. 60-70.

Gelus, Marjorie. "Laughter and Joking in the Works of Heinrich von Kleist." GQ 50:453-458. November 1977.

Ossar, Michael. "Kleist's DAS ERDBEBEN IN CHILI and DIE MARQUISE VON O...." RLV 34:151-169. No. 2, 1968.

*Peters, F. G. "Kafka and Kleist: A Literary Relationship." OGS 1:124-133. 1966.

Sokel, Walter H. "Kleist's Marquise of O., Kierkegaard's Abraham, and Musil's Tonka: Three Stages of the Absurd as the Touchstone of Faith." WSCL 8:505-516. Autumn 1967.

Swales, Erika. "The Beleaguered Citadel: A Study of Kleist's DIE MARQUISE VON O...." DVLG 51:129-147. March 1977.

Weiss, Hermann F. "Precarious Idylls. The Relationship Between Father and Daughter in Heinrich von Kleist's DIE MARQUISE VON O...." MLN 91:538-542. April 1976.

MICHAEL KOHLHAAS

Cary, John R. "A Reading of Kleist's MICHAEL KOHLHAAS." PMLA 85:212-218. March 1970.

Dyer, Denys. The Stories of Kleist: A Critical Study. London: Duckworth, 1977. pp. 107-150.

Ellis, John M. Heinrich von Kleist: Studies in the Character and Meaning of His Writings. Chapel Hill: University of North Carolina Press, 1979. pp. 67-88.

———. "'Der Herr lasst regnen uber Gerechte und Ungerechte': Kleist's MICHAEL KOHLHASS." Monatshefte 59:35-40. Spring 1967.

Gearey, John. Heinrich von Kleist: A Study in Tragedy and Anxiety. Philadelphia: University of Pennsylvania Press, 1968. pp. 102-119.

Graham, Ilse. Heinrich von Kleist: Word into Flesh: A Poet's Quest for the Symbol. Berlin: Walter de Gruyter, 1977. pp. 213-223.

Helbling, Robert E. The Major Works of Heinrich von Kleist. New York: New Directions, 1975. pp. 193-209.

Lucas, R. S. "Studies in Kleist." DVLG 44:120-145. January 1970.

*Marson, Eric. "Justice and the Obsessed Character in MICHAEL KOHLHAAS, DER PROZESS and L'ETRANGER." Seminar 2:21-33. Fall 1966.

Paulin, Harry W. "Kohlhaas and Family." GR 52:171-182. May 1977.

*Peters, F. G. "Kafka and Kleist: A Literary Relationship." OGS 1:133-148. 1966.

### DIE VERLOBUNG IN ST. DOMINGO

Angress, R. K. "Kleist's Treatment of Imperialism: DIE HERMANNSSCHLACHT and DIE VERLOBUNG." Monatshefte 69:17-33. Spring 1977.

Dyer, Denys. The Stories of Kleist: A Critical Study. London: Duckworth, 1977. pp. 31-47.

Gearey, John. Heinrich von Kleist: A Study in Tragedy and Anxiety. Philadelphia: University of Pennsylvania Press, 1968. pp. 70-76.

Gilman, Sander L. "The Aesthetics of Blackness in Heinrich von Kleist's DIE VERLOBUNG IN ST. DOMINGO." MLN 90:661-672. October 1975.

### DER ZWEIKAMPF

Dyer, Denys. The Stories of Kleist: A Critical Study. London: Duckworth, 1977. pp. 170-194.

Ellis, John M. Heinrich von Kleist: Studies in the Character and Meaning of His Writings. Chapel Hill: University of North Carolina Press, 1979. pp. 54-66.

Gearey, John. Heinrich von Kleist: A Study in Tragedy and Anxiety. Philadelphia: University of Pennsylvania Press, 1968. pp. 48-56.

Koeppen, Wolfgang
DER TOD IN ROM
Bance, A. F. "DER TOD IN ROM and DIE ROTE: Two Italian Episodes." FMLS 3:126-134. April 1967.

Koestler, Arthur
AGE OF LONGING
Pearson, Sidney A., Jr. Arthur Koestler. Boston: Twayne, 1978. pp. 85-101.
ARRIVAL AND DEPARTURE
Calder, Jenni. Chronicles of Conscience: A Study of George Orwell and Arthur Koestler. Pittsburgh: University of Pittsburgh Press, 1968. pp. 155-160.

Pearson, Sidney A., Jr. Arthur Koestler. Boston: Twayne, 1978. pp. 68-84.
THE CALL GIRLS
Pearson, Sidney A., Jr. Arthur Koestler. Boston: Twayne, 1978. pp. 119-135.
DARKNESS AT NOON
Rees, Goronwy. "DARKNESS AT NOON and the 'Grammatical Fiction.'" Astride the Two Cultures: Arthur Koestler at 70. ed. Harold Harris. New York: Random House, 1976. pp. 102-122.

Ziolkowski, Theodore. Fictional Transfigurations of Jesus. Princeton: Princeton University Press, 1972. pp. 206-214.
THE GLADIATORS
Pearson, Sidney A., Jr. Arthur Koestler. Boston: Twayne, 1978. pp. 34-50.
THIEVES IN THE NIGHT
Calder, Jenni. Chronicles of Conscience: A Study of George Orwell and Arthur Koestler. Pittsburgh: University of Pittsburgh Press, 1968. pp. 212-220.

Kubin, Alfred
THE OTHER SIDE
Roditi, Edouard. "Allegory and Alienation." A Soc 6:237-242. 1969.

Schroeder, Richard. "From 'Traumreich' to 'surréalite': Surrealism and Alfred Kubin's DIE ANDERE SEITE." Symposium 30:213-235. Fall 1976.

Langgässer, Elisabeth
THE INDELIBLE SEAL
Angress, R. K. "The Christian Surrealism of Elisabeth Langgässer." The Vision Obscured: Perceptions of

Langgässer, Elisabeth
- Some Twentieth-Century Catholic Novelists. ed. Melvin J. Friedman. New York: Fordham University Press, 1970. pp. 189-195.
  Riley, Anthony W. "Elisabeth Langgässer and Juan Donoso Cortés: A Source of the 'Turm-Kapitel' in DAS UNAUSLÖSCHLICHE SIEGEL." PMLA 83:357-367. May 1968.
- THE QUEST
  Angress, R. K. "The Christian Surrealism of Elisabeth Langgässer." The Vision Obscured: Perceptions of Some Twentieth-Century Catholic Novelists. ed. Melvin J. Friedman. New York: Fordham University Press, 1970. pp. 195-199.

Lasswitz, Kurd
- ON TWO PLANETS
  Rottensteiner, Franz. "Kurd Lasswitz: A German Pioneer of Science Fiction." RQ 4:4-7. August 1969.

Le Fort, Gertrud von
- DIE LETZTE AM SCHAFOTT
  Falk, Eugene H. "The Leap to Faith: Two Paths to the Scaffold." Symposium 21:241-250. Fall 1967.

Lehmann, Wilhelm
- MICHAEL LIPPSTOCK
  Scrase, David. "Wilhelm Lehmann's MICHAEL LIPPSTOCK: A Reassessment of an Erstwhile 'Poeta Pittore' and His Repudiated Work." NGS 8:109-128. Summer 1980.

Lenz, J. M. R.
- DER LANDPREDIGER
  Osborne, John. "The Postponed Idyll: Two Moral Tales by J. M. R. Lenz." Neophil 59:68-81. January 1975.
- ZERBIN ODER DIE NEUERE PHILOSOPHIE
  Osborne, John. "The Postponed Idyll: Two Moral Tales by J. M. R. Lenz." Neophil 59:68-81. January 1975.

Lenz, Siegfried
- BROT UND SPIELE
  Mornin, Edward. "Taking Games Seriously: Observations on the German Sports-Novel." GR 51:289-292. November 1976.

  Murdoch, Brian and Malcolm Read. Siegfried Lenz. London: Oswald Wolff, 1978. pp. 35-39.
- DUEL WITH THE SHADOW
  Murdoch, Brian and Malcolm Read. Siegfried Lenz. London: Oswald Wolff, 1978. pp. 27-35.
- AN EXEMPLARY LIFE
  Murdoch, Brian and Malcolm Read. Siegfried Lenz. London: Oswald Wolff, 1978. pp. 75-88.

THE GERMAN LESSON
 Gohlman, Susan A. "Making Words Do for Paint: 'Seeing' and Self-Mastery in Siegfried Lenz's THE GERMAN LESSON." MLS 9:80-88. Spring 1979.

 Kontje, Todd. "Captive Creator in Siegfried Lenz's DEUTSCHSTUNDE: Writer, Reader, and Response." GQ 53:458-465. November 1980.

 Murdock, Brian and Malcolm Read. Siegfried Lenz. London: Oswald Wolff, 1978. pp. 55-74.

 Paslick, Robert H. "Narrowing the Distance: Siegfried Lenz's DEUTSCHSTUNDE." GQ 46:210-218. March 1973.

 Russell, Peter. "The 'Lesson' in Siegfried Lenz's DEUTSCHSTUNDE." Seminar 13:42-54. February 1977.

 ———. "Siegfried Lenz's DEUTSCHSTUNDE: A North German Novel." GL&L 28:405-417. July 1975.

HEIMATMUSEUM
 Butler, G. P. "Zygmunt's Follies? On Siegfried Lenz's HEIMATMUSEUM." GL&L 33:172-178. January 1980.

TOPIC OF CONVERSATION
 Murdoch, Brian and Malcolm Read. Siegfried Lenz. London: Oswald Wolff, 1978. pp. 40-54.

DER WALDBRUDER
 Furst, Lilian R. "The Dual Face of the Grotesque in Sterne's TRISTRAM SHANDY and Lenz's DER WALDBRUDER." CLS 13:15-21. March 1976.

 Heine, Thomas. "Lenz's WALDBRUDER: Inauthentic Narration as Social Criticism." GL&L 33:183-189. April 1980.

Ludwig, Otto
 AUS DEM REGEN IN DIE TRAUFE
  Turner, David. Roles and Relationships in Otto Ludwig's Narrative Fiction. Mansfield: Linneys, 1975. pp. 40-47.
 DIE HEITERETEI
  Thomas, Lionel. "Otto Ludwig's DIE HEITERETEI UND IHR WIDERSPIEL." FMLS 6:226-230. July 1970.

  Turner, David. Roles and Relationships in Otto Ludwig's Narrative Fiction. Mansfield: Linneys, 1975. pp. 29-39.
 MARIA
  Turner, David. Roles and Relationships in Otto Ludwig's Narrative Fiction. Mansfield: Linneys, 1975. pp. 15-28.

Washington, Ida H. "Religious Symbolism in Otto Ludwig's MARIA." MLN 85:385-391. April 1970.

ZWISCHEN HIMMEL UND ERDE
Dickson, Keith A. "'Die Moral von der Geschicht': Art and Artifice in ZWISCHEN HIMMEL UND ERDE." MLR 68:115-128. January 1973.

Lillyman, W. J. "The Interior Monologue in James Joyce and Otto Ludwig." CL 23:51-54. Winter 1971.

Turner, David. Roles and Relationships in Otto Ludwig's Narrative Fiction. Mansfield: Linneys, 1975. pp. 48-64.

## Mackay, John Henry
DER SCHWIMMER
Mornin, Edward. "Taking Games Seriously: Observations on the German Sports-Novel." GR 51:279-284. November 1976.

## Mann, Heinrich
DIE ARMEN
Winter, Lorenz. Heinrich Mann and His Public. Coral Gables: University of Miami Press, 1970. pp. 72-78.

DER ATEM
Linn, Rolf N. Heinrich Mann. New York: Twayne, 1967. pp. 119-124.

Winter, Lorenz. Heinrich Mann and His Public. Coral Gables: University of Miami Press, 1970. pp. 112-117.

DIE BRANZILLA
Linn, Rolf N. Heinrich Mann. New York: Twayne, 1967. pp. 53-58.

DIE GOTTINNEN
Linn, Rolf N. Heinrich Mann. New York: Twayne, 1967. pp. 24-35.

THE HEAD
Winter, Lorenz. Heinrich Mann and His Public. Coral Gables: University of Miami Press, 1970. pp. 78-89.

HENRI QUATRE
Gross, David. The Writer and Society: Heinrich Mann and Literary Politics in Germany, 1890-1940. Atlantic Highlands: Humanities Press, 1980. pp. 256-262.

Linn, Rolf N. Heinrich Mann. New York: Twayne, 1967. pp. 105-112.

Roberts, David. Artistic Consciousness and Political Conscience: The Novels of Heinrich Mann 1900-1938. Berne: Lang, 1971. pp. 190-242.

Waidson, H. M. "Prose Fiction: Some Outstanding Ger-

man Novels." Twentieth Century German Literature.
ed. August Closs. New York: Barnes and Noble, 1969.
pp. 113-117.
IM SCHLARAFFENLAND
    Mackinnon, E. "Heinrich Mann's IM SCHLARAFFEN-
LAND: The Aesthetic Rejection of the 'Bürger.'"
NGS 4:119-127. Autumn 1976.
DIE KLEINE STADT
    Linn, Rolf N. Heinrich Mann. New York: Twayne,
1967. pp. 58-65.

    Roberts, David. Artistic Consciousness and Political
Conscience: The Novels of Heinrich Mann 1900-1938.
Berne: Lang, 1971. pp. 52-83.
KOBES
    Bance, A. F. "The Intellectual and the Crisis of Weimar: Heinrich Mann's KOBES and Leonhard Frank's IM LETZTEN WAGEN." JES 8:155-170. September 1978.
PROFESSOR UNRAT
    Allison, J. E. "An Analysis of the Nietschean 'Wille zur Macht' as Portrayed in Heinrich Mann's PROFESSOR UNRAT." NGS 7:189-203. Autumn 1979.

    Linn, Rolf N. Heinrich Mann. New York: Twayne,
1967. pp. 40-46.

    Shchurowsky, G. Roman and Pierre R. Hart. "A Somber Madness: Dionysian Excess in THE PETTY DEMON and PROFESSOR UNRAT." GSlav 3:33-43. Spring 1979.
ROYAL WOMEN
    Linn, Rolf N. Heinrich Mann. New York: Twayne,
1967. pp. 89-93.

    Winter, Lorenz. Heinrich Mann and His Public. Coral Gables: University of Miami Press, 1970. pp. 102-108.
DER UNTERTAN
    Boa, Elizabeth and J. H. Reid. Critical Strategies: German Fiction in the Twentieth Century. London: Edward Arnold, 1972. pp. 109-114.

    Linn, Rolf N. Heinrich Mann. New York: Twayne,
1967. pp. 67-73.

    Roberts, David. Artistic Consciousness and Political
Conscience: The Novels of Heinrich Mann 1900-1938.
Berne: Lang, 1971. pp. 84-124.

    Siefken, Hinrich. "Emperor William II and His Loyal Subject--Montage and Historical Allusions in Heinrich Mann's Satirical Novel DER UNTERTAN." Trivium 8: 69-81. May 1973.

Mann, Thomas
THE BELOVED RETURNS
Albright, Daniel. Personality and Impersonality: Lawrence, Woolf, and Mann. Chicago: University of Chicago Press, 1978. pp. 270-283.

Apter, T. E. Thomas Mann: The Devil's Advocate. London: Macmillan, 1978. pp. 115-120.

Berendsohn, Walter E. Thomas Mann, Artist and Partisan in Troubled Times. University: University of Alabama Press, 1973. pp. 114-124.

Feuerlicht, Ignace. Thomas Mann. New York: Twayne, 1968. pp. 59-66.

Hatfield, Henry. From THE MAGIC MOUNTAIN: Mann's Later Masterpieces. Ithaca: Cornell University Press, 1979. pp. 94-107.

Hollingdale, R. J. Thomas Mann: A Critical Study. London: Rupert Hart-Davis, 1971. pp. 117-124.

Reed, T. J. Thomas Mann: The Uses of Tradition. Oxford: Clarendon, 1974. pp. 350-359.

Schmidt, Willa. "The 'Wiedersehen' Motif in the Works of Thomas Mann." Monatshefte 65:149-153. Summer 1973.

Siefken, Hinrich. "The Goethe Centenary of 1932 and Thomas Mann's LOTTE IN WEIMAR." PEGS 49:84-101. 1979.

──────. "LOTTE IN WEIMAR--'Contactnahme' and Thomas Mann's Novel About Goethe." Trivium 13:38-51. May 1978.

──────. "Thomas Mann's Novel LOTTE IN WEIMAR --a 'Lustspiel'?" OGS 11:103-122. 1980.
BUDDENBROOKS
Albright, Daniel. Personality and Impersonality: Lawrence, Woolf, and Mann. Chicago: University of Chicago Press, 1978. pp. 214-219.

Apter, T. E. Thomas Mann: The Devil's Advocate. London: Macmillan, 1978. pp. 15-31.

Bauer, Arnold. Thomas Mann. New York: Ungar, 1971. pp. 5-13.

Berendsohn, Walter E. Thomas Mann, Artist and Partisan in Troubled Times. University: University of Alabama Press, 1973. pp. 23-30.

Beston, John B. "Three Conclusions: BUDDEN-
BROOKS, THE AUNT'S STORY and VOSS." LHY 20:
134-140. January 1979.

Feuerlicht, Ignace. Thomas Mann. New York: Twayne,
1968. pp. 13-21.

Hamilton, Nigel. The Brothers Mann: The Lives of
Heinrich and Thomas Mann. London: Secker and Warburg, 1978. pp. 54-69.

Hollingdale, R. J. Thomas Mann: A Critical Study.
London: Rupert Hart-Davis, 1971. pp. 56-62.

Jolles, Charlotte. "Sesemi Weichbrodt: Observations
on a Minor Character of Thomas Mann's Fictional
World." GL&L 22:32-38. October 1968.

Koester, Rudolf. "Is Infallibility Necessary? A Note
on the Chronology of BUDDENBROOKS." CLAJ 11:163-
166. December 1967.

Nachman, Larry David and Albert S. Braverman, M. D.
"Thomas Mann's BUDDENBROOKS: Bourgeois Society
and the Inner Life." GR 45:201-225. May 1970.

Oeser, Hans-Christian. "The Problematical Nature of
Decline in Thomas Mann's Novel BUDDENBROOKS."
Univ 22:119-124. No. 2, 1980.

Reed, T. J. Thomas Mann: The Uses of Tradition.
Oxford: Clarendon, 1974. pp. 37-85.

Ridley, Hugh. "Nature and Society in BUDDENBROOKS."
OL 28:138-147. 1973.

Swales, Martin. Thomas Mann: A Study. London:
Heinemann, 1980. pp. 15-29.

DEATH IN VENICE
Albright, Daniel. Personality and Impersonality: Lawrence, Woolf, and Mann. Chicago: University of Chicago Press, 1978. pp. 226-237.

Apter, T. E. Thomas Mann: The Devil's Advocate.
London: Macmillan, 1978. pp. 50-57.

Bance, A. F. "DER TOD IN VENEDIG and the Triadic
Structure." FMLS 8:148-161. April 1972.

Baron, Frank. "Sensuality and Morality in Thomas
Mann's TOD IN VENEDIG." GR 45:115-125. March
1970.

Berendsohn, Walter E. Thomas Mann, Artist and Partisan in Troubled Times. University: University of Alabama Press, 1973. pp. 34-40.

Braverman, Albert and Larry David Nachman. "The Dialectic of Decadence: An Analysis of Thomas Mann's DEATH IN VENICE." GR 45:289-298. November 1970.

Cadieux, André. "The Jungle of Dionysus: The Self in Mann and Nietzsche." Philosophy and Literature 3:53-63. Spring 1979.

Consigny, Scott. "Aschenbach's 'Page and a Half of Choicest Prose': Mann's Rhetoric of Irony." SSF 14: 359-367. Fall 1977.

Cox, Catherine. "Pater's 'Apollo in Picardy' and Mann's DEATH IN VENICE." Anglia 86:143-154. No. 1/2, 1968.

Davidson, Leah. "Mid-Life Crisis in Thomas Mann's DEATH IN VENICE." Journal of the American Academy of Psychoanalysis 4:203-213. April 1976.

Dyson, A. E. "The Stranger God: DEATH IN VENICE." CritQ 13:5-20. Spring 1971.

Egri, Peter. "The Function of Dreams and Visions in A PORTRAIT and DEATH IN VENICE." JJQ 5:96-101. Winter 1968.

Ezergailis, Inta Miske. Male and Female: An Approach to Thomas Mann's Dialectic. The Hague: Nijhoff, 1975. pp. 47-71.

Farrelly, D. J. "Apollo and Dionysus Interpreted in Thomas Mann's DER TOD IN VENEDIG." NGS 3:1-15. Spring 1975.

Feuerlicht, Ignace. Thomas Mann. New York: Twayne, 1968. pp. 117-126.

Good, Graham. "The Death of Language in DEATH IN VENICE." Mosaic 5:43-52. Spring 1972.

von Gronicka, André. Thomas Mann: Profile and Perspectives. New York: Random House, 1970. pp. 6-12; 106-112.

Hanson, W. P. "The Achievement of Chandos and Aschenbach." NGS 7:41-57. Spring 1979.

Hollingdale, R. J. Thomas Mann: A Critical Study. London: Rupert Hart-Davis, 1971. pp. 90-94.

Jonas, Ilsedore B. Thomas Mann and Italy. University: University of Alabama Press, 1979. pp. 34-41.

Kelley, Alice van Buren. "Von Aschenbach's 'Phaedrus': Platonic Allusions in DER TOD IN VENEDIG." JEGP 75:228-240. January/April 1976.

Leppmann, Wolfgang. "Time and Place in DEATH IN VENICE." GQ 48:66-75. January 1975.

Mazzella, Anthony J. "DEATH IN VENICE: Fiction and Film." CollL 5:183-194. Fall 1978.

McIntyre, Allan J. "Psychology and Symbol: Correspondence Between HEART OF DARKNESS and DEATH IN VENICE." HSL 7:216-232. No. 3, 1975.

McWilliams, J. R. "The Failure of a Repression: Thomas Mann's TOD IN VENEDIG." GL&L 20:233-241. April 1967.

Northcote-Bade, James. "DER TOD IN VENEDIG and FELIX KRULL: The Effect of the Interruption in the Composition of Thomas Mann's FELIX KRULL Caused by DER TOD IN VENEDIG." DVLG 52:271-278. June 1978.

Phillips, Kathy J. "Conversion to Text, Initiation to Symbolism, in Mann's DER TOD IN VENEDIG and James' THE AMBASSADORS." CRCL 6:376-388. Fall 1979.

Reed, T. J. Thomas Mann: The Uses of Tradition. Oxford: Clarendon Press, 1974. pp. 144-178.

Slochower, Harry. "Thomas Mann's DEATH IN VENICE." AI 26:99-122. Summer 1969.

Stewart, Walter K. "DER TOD IN VENEDIG: The Path to Insight." GR 53:50-55. Spring 1978.

Swales, Martin. Thomas Mann: A Study. London: Heinemann, 1980. pp. 37-45.

Tarbox, Raymond. "DEATH IN VENICE: The Aesthetic Object as Dream Guide." AI 26:123-144. Summer 1969.

Vaget, Hans Rudolf. "Film and Literature. The Case of DEATH IN VENICE: Luchino Visconti and Thomas Mann." GQ 54:159-175. March 1980.

Wolf, Ernest M. "A Case of Slightly Mistaken Identity: Gustav Mahler and Gustav Aschenbach." TCL 19:40-52. January 1973.

## DOCTOR FAUSTUS

Albright, Daniel. Personality and Impersonality: Lawrence, Woolf, and Mann. Chicago: University of Chicago Press, 1978. pp. 273-294.

Apter, T. E. Thomas Mann: The Devil's Advocate. London: Macmillan, 1978. pp. 139-157.

――――. "Thomas Mann's DOKTOR FAUSTUS: Nihilism or Humanism?" FMLS 11:59-73. January 1975.

Baker, Donna. "Nazism and the Petit Bourgeois Protagonist: The Novels of Grass, Böll, and Mann." NGC 5:80-88. Spring 1975.

Bauer, Arnold. Thomas Mann. New York: Frederick Ungar, 1971. pp. 87-91.

Berendsohn, Walter E. Thomas Mann, Artist and Partisan in Troubled Times. University: University of Alabama Press, 1973. pp. 144-164.

Bergsten, Gunilla. Thomas Mann's DOCTOR FAUSTUS: The Sources and Structure of the Novel. Chicago: University of Chicago Press, 1969. 218 pp.

Blomster, W. V. "The Demonic in History: Thomas Mann and Günter Grass." ConL 10:75-84. Winter 1969.

――――. "A Pietà in Mann's FAUSTUS?" MLN 90: 336-344. April 1975.

Boa, Elizabeth and J. H. Reid. Critical Strategies: German Fiction in the Twentieth Century. London: Edward Arnold, 1972. pp. 18-22.

Carnegy, Patrick. Faust as Musician: A Study of Thomas Mann's Novel DOCTOR FAUSTUS. New York: New Directions, 1973. 173 pp.

Daemmrich, Horst S. "Thomas Mann's Perception of Self-Insight." PLL 13:278-282. Summer 1977.

Ezergailis, Inta Miske. Male and Female: An Approach to Thomas Mann's Dialectic. The Hague: Nijhoff, 1975. pp. 72-91.

Fass, Barbara F. "The Little Mermaid and the Artist's Quest for a Soul." CLS 9:298-301. September 1972.

Fetzer, John F. "Clemens Brentano's Muse and Adrian Leuerkühn's Music: Selective Affinities in Thomas Mann's DOKTOR FAUSTUS." ELWIU 7:115-131. Spring 1980.

Feuerlicht, Ignace. Thomas Mann. New York: Twayne, 1968. pp. 67-84.

Field, G. W. "Music and Morality in Thomas Mann and Hermann Hesse." Hesse: A Collection of Critical Essays. ed. Theodore Ziolkowski. Englewood Cliffs: Prentice-Hall, 1973. pp. 94-111.

Furness, Raymond. The Twentieth Century: 1890-1945. London: Croom Helm, 1978. pp. 269-274.

Gilliam, H. S. "Mann's Other Holy Sinner: Adrian Leuerkühn as Faust and Christ." GR 52:122-147. March 1977.

Hannum, Hildegarde Drexl. "Self-Sacrifice in DOKTOR FAUSTUS: Thomas Mann's Contribution to the Faust Legend." MLQ 35:289-301. September 1974.

Hatfield, Henry. From THE MAGIC MOUNTAIN: Mann's Later Masterpieces. Ithaca: Cornell University Press, 1979. pp. 108-134.

_____. "The Magic Square: Thomas Mann's DOKTOR FAUSTUS." Euphorion 62:415-420. 1968.

Honsa, William M., Jr. "Parody and Narrator in Thomas Mann's DR. FAUSTUS and THE HOLY SINNER." OL 29:61-76. 1974.

Jonas, Ilsedore B. Thomas Mann and Italy. University: University of Alabama Press, 1979. pp. 66-74.

Kahler, Erich. The Orbit of Thomas Mann. Princeton: Princeton University Press, 1969. pp. 20-43.

Kamla, Thomas A. "'Christliche Kunst mit negativem Vorzeichen': Kierkegaard and DOKTOR FAUSTUS." Neophil 63:583-586. October 1979.

Magliola, Robert. "The Magic Square: Polar Unity in Thomas Mann's DOCTOR FAUSTUS." HSL 6:55-70. No. 1, 1974.

Meyers, Jeffrey. "Durer and Mann's DOCTOR FAUSTUS." Art Internat 17:56-60; 63. October 1973.

_____. "Shakespeare and Mann's DOCTOR FAUSTUS." MFS 19:541-545. Winter 1973.

Nixen, Liana De Bona. "The Concept of Barbarism in Thomas Mann's DOCTOR FAUSTUS." MQ 16:438-452. July 1975.

Mann, Thomas

    Oates, Joyce Carol. "'Art at the Edge of Impossibility': Mann's DR. FAUSTUS." SoR 5:375-397. April 1969.

    Puknat, S. B. and E. M. "Mann's DOCTOR FAUSTUS and Shakespeare." RS 35:148-152. June 1967.

    Reed, T. J. Thomas Mann: The Uses of Tradition. Oxford: Clarendon, 1974. pp. 360-402.

    _____. "Thomas Mann: The Writer as Historian of His Time." MLR 71:92-95. January 1976.

    Rose, Marilyn Gaddis. "More on the Musical Composition of DOKTOR FAUSTUS." MFS 17:81-89. Spring 1971.

    Scher, Steven Paul. "Thomas Mann's 'Verbal Score': Adrian Leuerkühn's Symbolic Confession." MLN 82:403-420. October 1967.

    Seidlin, Oskar. "The Open Wound: Notes on Thomas Mann's DOKTOR FAUSTUS." MGS 1:301-315. Fall 1975.

    Siefken, Hinrich. "Romanticism and Chauvinism: Reflections on the Ironic Concept of 'Durchbruch' in Thomas Mann's Novel DOKTOR FAUSTUS." Trivium 6:116-119. May 1971.

    Stern, J. P. History and Allegory in Thomas Mann's DOKTOR FAUSTUS. London: Lewis, 1975. 23 pp.

    Swales, Martin. Thomas Mann: A Study. London: Heinemann, 1980. pp. 80-97.

    Viswanathan, Jacqueline. "Point of View and Unreliability in Bronte's WUTHERING HEIGHTS, Conrad's UNDER WESTERN EYES and Mann's DOKTOR FAUSTUS." OL 29:42-60. 1974.

    Waidson, H. M. "Prose Fiction: Some Outstanding German Novels." Twentieth Century German Literature. ed. August Closs. New York: Barnes and Noble, 1969. pp. 107-113.

    Weigand, Hermann J. "An Interview on DOKTOR FAUSTUS." Thomas Mann in Context: Papers of the Clark University Centennial Colloquium. ed. Kenneth Hughes. Worcester: Clark University Press, 1978. pp. 95-126.

FELIX KRULL

    Albright, Daniel. Personality and Impersonality: Lawrence, Woolf, and Mann. Chicago: University of Chicago Press, 1978. pp. 301-307.

Apter, T. E. Thomas Mann: The Devil's Advocate. London: Macmillan, 1978. pp. 121-134.

Berendsohn, Walter E. Thomas Mann, Artist and Partisan in Troubled Times. University: University of Alabama Press, 1973. pp. 173-192.

Ezergailis, Inta Miske. Male and Female: An Approach to Thomas Mann's Dialectic. The Hague: Nijhoff, 1975. pp. 116-126.

Feuerlicht, Ignace. Thomas Mann. New York: Twayne, 1968. pp. 92-107.

Gurewitsch, M. Anatole. "Counterpoint in Thomas Mann's FELIX KRULL." MFS 22:525-541. Winter 1976-1977.

Hatfield, Henry. From THE MAGIC MOUNTAIN: Mann's Later Masterpieces. Ithaca: Cornell University Press, 1979. pp. 144-157.

Kearful, Frank J. "The Role of Hermes in THE CONFESSIONS OF FELIX KRULL." MFS 17:91-108. Spring 1971.

Nelson, Donald F. "Felix Krull or: 'All the World's a Stage.'" GR 45:41-51. January 1970.

Northcote-Bade, James. "DER TOD IN VENEDIG and FELIX KRULL: The Effect of the Interruption in the Composition of Thomas Mann's FELIX KRULL Caused by DER TOD IN VENEDIG." DVLG 52:271-278. June 1978.

Swales, Martin. Thomas Mann: A Study. London: Heinemann, 1980. pp. 100-109.

Wilson, Eric. "The Private Games of Thomas Mann." GQ 47:1-12. January 1974.

GEFALLEN
Lindsay, J. M. "Thomas Mann's First Story, GEFALLEN." GL&L 28:297-307. April 1975.

DIE GESCHICHTEN JAAKOBS
Hughes, Kenneth. "Theme and Structure in Thomas Mann's DIE GESCHICHTEN JAAKOBS." Monatshefte 62: 24-36. Spring 1970.

GLADIUS DEI
Hoffmann, Ernst Fedor. "Thomas Mann's GLADIUS DEI." PMLA 83:1353-1361. October 1968.

THE HOLY SINNER
Berendsohn, Walter E. Thomas Mann, Artist and Partisan in Troubled Times. University: University of Alabama Press, 1973. pp. 143-152.

Hatfield, Henry. From THE MAGIC MOUNTAIN:
Mann's Later Masterpieces. Ithaca: Cornell University
Press, 1979. pp. 135-144.

Honsa, William M., Jr. "Parody and Narrator in
Thomas Mann's DR. FAUSTUS and THE HOLY SINNER."
OL 29:61-76. 1974.

Jonas, Ilsedore B. Thomas Mann and Italy. University:
University of Alabama Press, 1979. pp. 77-81.

Zeiss, Cecelia. "A Comment on Thomas Mann's THE
HOLY SINNER." UES 15:33-36. April 1977.

JOSEPH Novels

Albright, Daniel. Personality and Impersonality: Lawrence, Woolf, and Mann. Chicago: University of Chicago Press, 1978. pp. 252-270.

Bauer, Arnold. Thomas Mann. New York: Frederick
Ungar, 1971. pp. 68-73.

Berendsohn, Walter E. Thomas Mann, Artist and Partisan in Troubled Times. University: University of Alabama Press, 1973. pp. 86-114.

Daemmrich, Horst S. "Fertility-Sterility: A Sequence
of Motifs in Thomas Mann's JOSEPH Novels." MLQ
31:461-473. December 1970.

———. "Thomas Mann's Perception of Self-Insight."
PLL 13:275-278. Summer 1977.

Dassin, Joan. "The Dialectics of Recurrence: The Relation of the Individual to Myth and Legend in Thomas
Mann's JOSEPH AND HIS BROTHERS." CentR 15:362-390. Fall 1971.

Feuerlicht, Ignace. Thomas Mann. New York: Twayne,
1968. pp. 43-58.

Hatfield, Henry. From THE MAGIC MOUNTAIN: Mann's
Later Masterpieces. Ithaca: Cornell University Press,
1979. pp. 68-94.

*Heller, Peter. Dialectics and Nihilism: Essays on
Lessing, Nietzsche, Mann, and Kafka. Amherst: University of Massachusetts Press, 1966. pp. 151-226.

Heltay, Hilary. "Der Mann auf dem Felde: Virtuosity
in Thomas Mann's Later Narrative Technique." GL&L
24:192-204. January 1971.

Hollingdale, R.J. Thomas Mann: A Critical Study.
London: Rupert Hart-Davis, 1971. pp. 113-117.

Hughes, Kenneth. "The Sources and Function of Serach's Song in Thomas Mann's JOSEPH, DER ERNAHRER." GR 45:126-133. March 1970.

King, J. Robin. "Thomas Mann's JOSEPH AND HIS BROTHERS: Religious Themes and Modern Humanism." Thought 53:416-432. December 1978.

Koelb, Clayton. "Mann's Use of Hebrew in the JOSEPH Novel." Monatshefte 70:138-150. Summer 1978.

_____. "Thomas Mann's 'Coat of Many Colors.'" GQ 49:472-484. November 1976.

Koelb, Clayton and Reena Spicehandler. "The Influence of Flaubert's SALAMMBÔ on Mann's JOSEPH UND SEINE BRÜDER." CLS 13:315-322. December 1976.

Murdaugh, Elaine. Salvation in the Secular: The Moral Law in Thomas Mann's JOSEPH UND SEINE BRUDER. Bern: Lang, 1976. 112 pp.

_____. "Thomas Mann and the Bitch Goddess: Rejection and Reconstruction of the Primal Mother in JOSEPH AND HIS BROTHERS." RLV 44:395-407. No. 5, 1978.

Reed, T. J. Thomas Mann: The Uses of Tradition. Oxford: Clarendon, 1974. pp. 341-350.

Schmidt, Willa. "The 'Wiedersehen' Motif in the Works of Thomas Mann." Monatshefte 65:153-159. Summer 1973.

Slade, Joseph W. "The Functions of Eternal Recurrence in Thomas Mann's JOSEPH AND HIS BROTHERS." Symposium 25:180-197. Summer 1971.

Spininger, Dennis J. "The 'Thamar' Section of Mann's JOSEPH UND SEINE BRÜDER: A Formal Analysis." Monatshefte 61:157-172. Summer 1969.

Swales, Martin. Thomas Mann: A Study. London: Heinemann, 1980. pp. 68-76.
KÖNIGLICHE HOHEIT
Siefken, Hinrich. "Thomas Mann and the Concept of 'Repräsentation': KÖNIGLICHE HOHEIT." MLR 73:337-350. April 1978.
LITTLE HERR FRIEDEMANN
Garrison, Joseph M. "LITTLE HERR FRIEDEMANN: Thomas Mann's First Critique of Perfection." SSF 11: 277-282. Summer 1974.

MAGIC MOUNTAIN
Abbott, Scott H. "DER ZAUBERBERG and the German Romantic Novel." GR 55:139-144. Fall 1980.

Albright, Daniel. Personality and Impersonality: Lawrence, Woolf, and Mann. Chicago: University of Chicago Press, 1978. pp. 243-252.

Apter, T. E. Thomas Mann: The Devil's Advocate. London: Macmillan, 1978. pp. 58-77.

Basilius, Harold A. "Mann's Naphta-Settembrini and the Battle of the Books." MFS 14:415-421. Winter 1968-1969.

Bauer, Arnold. Thomas Mann. New York: Ungar, 1971. pp. 42-49.

Berendsohn, Walter E. Thomas Mann, Artist and Partisan in Troubled Times. University: University of Alabama Press, 1973. pp. 71-83.

Blomster, Wes. "A Bridge Not Built: Mann and Hesse on Germany and Russia." GSlav 3:45-63. Spring 1979.

Boa, Elizabeth and J. H. Reid. Critical Strategies: German Fiction in the Twentieth Century. London: Edward Arnold, 1972. pp. 176-188.

Braverman, Albert S. and Larry Nachman. "Nature and the Moral Order in THE MAGIC MOUNTAIN." GR 53:1-12. January 1978.

Brennan, Joseph Gerard. "Heard and Unheard Speech in THE MAGIC MOUNTAIN." Novel 3:129-138. Winter 1970.

_____. "Three Novels of 'Dépaysement.'" CL 22: 223-236. Summer 1970.

Bulhof, Francis. "ZAUBERBERG, MAGIC MOUNTAIN, TOVERBERG." Babel 21:173-179. No. 4, 1975.

Campbell, Joseph. "Erotic Irony and Mythic Forms in the Art of Thomas Mann." BUJ 24:16-23. No. 1, 1976.

Church, Margaret. "The Isolated Community: Kafka's Village and Thomas Mann's Davos." UDR 13:105-112. Spring 1979.

Cunliffe, W. Gordon. "Cousin Joachim's Steel Helmet: DER ZAUBERBERG and the War." Monatshefte 68:409-417. Winter 1976.

Daemmrich, Horst S. "Thomas Mann's Perception of Self-Insight." PLL 13:272-275. Summer 1977.

Elstun, Esther N. "Two Views of the Mountain: Thomas Mann's ZAUBERBERG and Konstantin Fedin's SANATORIUM ARKTUR." GSlav 3:55-71. Spring 1974.

Ezergailis, Inta Miske. Male and Female: An Approach to Thomas Mann's Dialectic. The Hague: Nijhoff, 1975. pp. 21-46; 135-154.

Feuerlicht, Ignace. Thomas Mann. New York: Twayne, 1968. pp. 28-42.

Firchow, Peter. "Mental Music: Huxley's POINT COUNTERPOINT and Mann's MAGIC MOUNTAIN as Novels of Ideas." SNNTS 9:518-535. Winter 1977.

Furst, Lilian R. "Italo Svevo's LA COSCIENZA DI ZENO and Thomas Mann's DER ZAUBERBERG." ConL 9:492-506. Autumn 1968.

von Gronicka, André. Thomas Mann: Profile and Perspectives. New York: Random House, 1970. pp. 159-164.

Hatfield, Henry. From THE MAGIC MOUNTAIN: Mann's Later Masterpieces. Ithaca: Cornell University Press, 1979. pp. 34-67.

──────. "The Journey and the Mountain." MLN 90: 363-370. April 1975.

Holesovsky, Hanne Weill. "Hint and Incantation: The Preface to Thomas Mann's ZAUBERBERG." Symposium 34:217-232. Fall 1980.

Hollingdale, R. J. Thomas Mann: A Critical Study. London: Rupert Hart-Davis, 1971. pp. 28-40.

Hunt, Joel A. "Thomas Mann and André Spire: The 'Walpurgisnacht' Chapter." MLN 87:502-505. April 1972.

Jonas, Ilsedore B. Thomas Mann and Italy. University: University of Alabama Press, 1979. pp. 43-59.

Kuhn, Reinhard. The Demon of Noontide: Ennui in Western Literature. Princeton: Princeton University Press, 1976. pp. 346-355.

Latta, Alan D. "The Mystery of Life: A Theme in DER ZAUBERBERG." Monatshefte 66:19-32. Spring 1974.

_____. "Symbolic Structure: Toward an Understanding of the Structure of Thomas Mann's ZAUBERBERG." GR 50:34-54. January 1975.

Loose, Gerhard. "Ludovico Settembrini und 'Soziologie der Leiden': Notes on Thomas Mann's ZAUBERBERG." MLN 83:420-429. April 1968.

Mueller, William R. "Thomas Mann's THE MAGIC MOUNTAIN." Thought 49:419-435. December 1974.

Myers, David. "Sexual Love and 'Caritas' in Thomas Mann." JEGP 68:593-604. October 1969.

Newsom, Jon. "Hans Pfitzner, Thomas Mann and THE MAGIC MOUNTAIN." M&L 55:136-150. April 1974.

Prusok, Rudi. "Science in Mann's ZAUBERBERG: The Concept of Space." PMLA 88:52-61. January 1973.

Reed, T. J. Thomas Mann: The Uses of Tradition. Oxford: Clarendon, 1974. pp. 226-274.

_____. "Thomas Mann: The Writer as Historian of His Time." MLR 71:85-91. January 1976.

Schuster, Ingrid. "Taoism and DER ZAUBERBERG." CRCL 4:81-88. Winter 1977.

Seidlin, Oskar. "The Lofty Game of Numbers: The Mynheer Peeperkorn Episode in Thomas Mann's DER ZAUBERBERG." PMLA 86:924-939. October 1970.

Struc, Roman S. "THE MAGIC MOUNTAIN: Time and Timelessness." RS 39:83-95. June 1971.

Swales, Martin. "The Story and the Hero: A Study of Thomas Mann's DER ZAUBERBERG." DVLG 46:359-376. March 1976.

_____. Thomas Mann: A Study. London: Heinemann, 1980. pp. 52-62.

Tate, Lucile C. "Death, the Cradle of Life." BYUS 8:303-306. Spring 1968.

Thayer, Terence K. "Hans Castorp's Hermetic Adventures." GR 46:299-312. November 1971.

Tobin, Frank J. "Final Irony in DER ZAUBERBERG." GL&L 30:72-76. October 1976.

Wesche, Ulrich. "Beyond 'Bourgeois Realism': The

Grotesque and the Sublime in Thomas Mann's MAGIC
MOUNTAIN." UDQ 13:81-91. Summer 1978.

White, I. A. and J. J. "The Importance of F. C. Müller-
Lyer's Ideas for DER ZAUBERBERG." MLR 75:333-348.
April 1980.

Williams, C. E. "Not an Inn, but an Hospital. THE
MAGIC MOUNTAIN and CANCER WARD." FMLS 9:311-
332. October 1973.

Wolfe, Susan Smith. "Thomas Mann's DER ZAUBER-
BERG: The 'Snow-Spiral.'" Seminar 13:270-277. November 1977.

Ziolkowski, Theodore. Dimensions of the Modern Novel:
German Texts and European Contexts. Princeton:
Princeton University Press, 1969. pp. 68-98.

MARIO AND THE MAGICIAN

Garrin, Stephen H. "Thomas Mann's MARIO UND DER
ZAUBERER: Artistic Means and Didactic Ends." JEGP
77:92-103. January 1978.

Hollingdale, R. J. Thomas Mann: A Critical Study.
London: Rupert Hart-Davis, 1971. pp. 40-44.

Jonas, Ilsedore B. Thomas Mann and Italy. University:
University of Alabama Press, 1979. pp. 59-66.

Mandel, Siegfried. "Mann's MARIO AND THE MAGI-
CIAN, or Who Is Silvestra?" MFS 25:593-611. Winter
1979-1980.

McIntyre, Allan J. "Determinism in MARIO AND THE
MAGICIAN." GR 52:205-216. May 1977.

Schwarz, Egon. "Fascism and Society: Remarks on
Thomas Mann's Novella MARIO AND THE MAGICIAN."
MGS 2:47-67. Spring 1976.

Wagener, Hans. "Mann's Cipolla and Early Prototypes
of the Magician." MLN 84:800-802. October 1969.

ROYAL HIGHNESS

Berendsohn, Walter E. Thomas Mann, Artist and Partisan in Troubled Times. University: University of Alabama Press, 1973. pp. 46-51.

Feuerlicht, Ignace. Thomas Mann. New York: Twayne,
1968. pp. 22-27.

Siefken, Hinrich. "Thomas Mann and the Concept of
'Repräsentation': KÖNIGLICHE HOHEIT." MLR 73:337-
350. April 1978.

## SCHWERE STUNDE
Daemmrich, Horst S. "Thomas Mann's SCHWERE STUNDE Reconsidered." PLL 3:34-41. Winter 1967.
## TONIO KRÖGER
Bennett, Benjamin. "Casting Out Nines: Structure, Parody and Myth in TONIO KRÖGER." RLV 42:126-146. No. 2, 1976.

Feuerlicht, Ignace. Thomas Mann. New York: Twayne, 1968. pp. 109-114.

von Gronicka, André. Thomas Mann: Profile and Perspectives. New York: Random House, 1970. pp. 113-122.

Hoile, Christopher. "Lambert Strether and the Boaters --Tonio Kröger and the Dancers: Confrontation and Self-Acceptance." CRCL 2:243-261. Fall 1975.

Kirchberger, Lida. "Popularity as a Technique: Notes on TONIO KRÖGER." Monatshefte 63:321-334. Winter 1971.

O'Neill, Patrick. "Dance and Counterdance: A Note on TONIO KRÖGER." GL&L 29:291-295. April 1976.

Schmidt, Willa. "The 'Wiedersehen' Motif in the Works of Thomas Mann." Monatshefte 65:147-149. Summer 1973.

Swales, M. W. "Punctuation and the Narrative Mode: Some Remarks on TONIO KRÖGER." FMLS 6:235-242. July 1970.

──────. Thomas Mann: A Study. London: Heinemann, 1980. pp. 29-34.

Wetzel, Heinz. "The Seer in the Spring: On TONIO KRÖGER and THE WASTE LAND." RLC 44:322-332. July/September 1970.

Witthoft, Brucia. "TONIO KRÖGER and Muybridge's ANIMALS IN MOTION." MLR 62:459-461. July 1967.
## TRISTAN
Albright, Daniel. Personality and Impersonality: Lawrence, Woolf, and Mann. Chicago: University of Chicago Press, 1978. pp. 220-224.

Ezergailis, Inta. "Spinell's Letter: An Approach to Thomas Mann's TRISTAN." GL&L 25:377-382. July 1972.

Northcote-Bade, James. "Thomas Mann's Use of Wagner's 'Sehnsuchtsmotiv' in TRISTAN." Seminar 8:55-60. March 1972.

Schnitman, Sophia. "Musical Motives in Thomas Mann's TRISTAN." MLN 86:399-414. April 1971.
WÄLSUNGENBLUT
Sjögren, Christine Oertel. "The Variant Ending as a Clue to the Interpretation of Thomas Mann's WÄLSUNGENBLUT." Seminar 14:97-104. May 1978.

──────. "Wendelin and the Theme of Transformation in Thomas Mann's WÄLSUNGENBLUT." CLS 14:346-359. December 1977.

Meyer, Conrad Ferdinand
DAS AMULETT
Burkhard, Marianne. Conrad Ferdinand Meyer. Boston: Twayne, 1978. pp. 69-74.

Jackson, D. A. "Schadau, the Satirized Narrator, in C. F. Meyer's DAS AMULETT." Trivium 7:61-68. May 1972.

McCort, Dennis. "Historical Consciousness Versus Action in C. F. Meyer's DAS AMULETT." Symposium 32: 114-132. Summer 1978.

Reinhardt, George W. "The Political Views of the Young Conrad Ferdinand Meyer. With a Note on DAS AMULETT." GQ 45:282-285. March 1972.

Schimmelpfennig, Paul. "C. F. Meyer's Religion of the Heart: A Reevaluation of DAS AMULETT." GR 47:181-202. May 1972.
DER HEILIGE
Burkhard, Marianne. Conrad Ferdinand Meyer. Boston: Twayne, 1978. pp. 86-94.

Jacobson, Manfred R. "The Motif of the Hunt in C. F. Meyer's DER HEILIGE." FMLS 16:46-52. January 1980.

──────. "The Narrator's Allusions to Art and Ambiguity: A Note on C. F. Meyer's DER HEILIGE." Seminar 10:265-273. November 1974.

Walker, Colin. "Unbelief and Martyrdom in C. F. Meyer's DER HEILIGE." GL&L 21:111-121. January 1968.
DIE HOCHZEIT DES MÖNCHS
Burkhard, Marianne. Conrad Ferdinand Meyer. Boston: Twayne, 1978. pp. 129-136.

Jackson, D. A. "Dante the Dupe in C. F. Meyer's DIE

HOCHZEIT DES MÖNCHS." GL&L 25:5-15. October 1971.

Plater, Edward M. V. "The Figure of Dante in DIE HOCHZEIT DES MÖNCHS." MLN 90:678-686. October 1975.

Reinhardt, George W. "Two Romance Wordplays in C. F. Meyer's 'Novellen.'" GR 46:44-51. January 1971.
JURG JENATSCH
Burkhard, Marianne. Conrad Ferdinand Meyer. Boston: Twayne, 1978. pp. 74-83.
DAS LEIDEN EINES KNABEN
Jacobson, Manfred R. "The King and the Court Jester: A Reading of C. F. Meyer's DAS LEIDEN EINES KNABEN." Seminar 15:27-38. February 1979.

Reinhardt, George W. "Two Romance Wordplays in C. F. Meyer's 'Novellen.'" GR 46:51-62. January 1971.

Thompson, Bruce. "The Relevance of the Text. A Report on the Teaching of Conrad Ferdinand Meyer's DAS LEIDEN EINES KNABEN." NGS 5:63-74. Summer 1977.
DIE RICHTERIN
Burkhard, Marianne. Conrad Ferdinand Meyer. Boston: Twayne, 1978. pp. 137-141.

Jackson, David. "C. F. Meyer's DIE RICHTERIN. A Tussle with Tolstoy?" Trivium 9:39-49. 1974.

Plater, Edward M. V. "Alcuin's 'Harmlose Fabel' in C. F. Meyer's DIE RICHTERIN." GL&L 32:318-326. July 1979.
DER SCHUSS VON DER KANZEL
Jennings, Lee B. "The Ambiguous Explosion: C. F. Meyer's DER SCHUSS VON DER KANZEL." GQ 43:210-222. March 1970.
DIE VERSUCHUNG DES PESCARA
Burkhard, Marianne. Conrad Ferdinand Meyer. Boston: Twayne, 1978. pp. 141-147.

Plater, Edward M. V. "The Banquet of Life: Conrad Ferdinand Meyer's DIE VERSUCHUNG DES PESCARA." Seminar 8:88-98. June 1972.

Mörike, Eduard
MOZART AUF DER REISE NACH PRAG
Benn, M. B. "Comments of an 'Advocatus Diaboli' on Mörike's MOZART AUF DER REISE NACH PRAG." GL&L 25:368-376. July 1972.

Field, G. Wallis. "Silver and Oranges: Notes on

Mörike's Mozart-Novelle." Seminar 14:243-254. November 1978.

Woods, Jean M. "Memory and Inspiration in Mörike's MOZART AUF DER REISE NACH PRAG." RLV 41:6-14. No. 1, 1975.

PAINTER NOLTEN
Immerwahr, Raymond. "The Loves of Maler Nolten." RUS 57:73-85. Fall 1971.

*Mare, Margaret. Eduard Mörike: The Man and the Poet. London: Methuen, 1957. pp. 81-98.

Slessarev, Helga. Eduard Mörike. New York: Twayne, 1970. pp. 91-110.

Moritz, Karl Philipp
ANTON REISER
Boulby, Mark. "ANTON REISER and the Concept of the Novel." LY 4:183-194. 1972.

──────. "The Gates of Brunswick: Some Aspects of Symbol, Structure and Theme in Karl Philipp Moritz's ANTON REISER." MLR 68:105-114. January 1973.

──────. Karl Philipp Moritz: At the Fringe of Genius. Toronto: University of Toronto Press, 1979. pp. 3-50.

Durden, William G. "Parallel Designs: Space, Time and Being in Karl Philipp Moritz's ANTON REISER." GR 54:67-71. Spring 1979.

Musil, Robert
GRIGIA
Appignanesi, Lisa. Femininity & the Creative Imagination: A Study of Henry James, Robert Musil & Marcel Proust. New York: Barnes & Noble, 1973. pp. 105-109.

Bedwell, Carol B. "Musil's GRIGIA: An Analysis of Cultural Dissolution." Seminar 3:117-126. Fall 1967.

Boa, Elizabeth J. "Austrian Ironies in Musil's DREI FRAUEN." MLR 63:119-123. January 1968.

Peters, Frederick G. Robert Musil, Master of the Hovering Life: A Study of the Major Fiction. New York: Columbia University Press, 1978. pp. 107-126.

THE LADY FROM PORTUGAL
Appignanesi, Lisa. Femininity & the Creative Imagination: A Study of Henry James, Robert Musil & Marcel Proust. New York: Barnes & Noble, 1973. pp. 109-112.

Boa, Elizabeth J. "Austrian Ironies in Musil's DREI
FRAUEN." MLR 63:123-126. January 1968.

Paulson, Ronald M. "A Re-examination and Re-interpretation of Some of the Symbols in Robert Musil's DIE
PORTUGIESIN." MAL 13:111-119. No. 2, 1980.

Peters, Frederick G. Robert Musil, Master of the Hovering Life: A Study of the Major Fiction. New York:
Columbia University Press, 1978. pp. 126-145.

Titche, Leon L., Jr. "Robert Musil's DIE PORTU-
GIESIN: The Psychology of the Modern Fairy Tale."
UDR 14:71-76. Spring 1980.

THE MAN WITHOUT QUALITIES

Appignanesi, Lisa. Femininity & the Creative Imagination: A Study of Henry James, Robert Musil & Marcel
Proust. New York: Barnes & Noble, 1973. pp. 124-156.

Charney, Hanna. "Monsieur Teste and der Mann ohne
Eigenschaften: 'Homo Possibilis' in Fiction." CL 27:
1-7. Winter 1975.

Furness, Raymond. The Twentieth Century: 1890-1945.
London: Croom Helm, 1978. pp. 227-234.

Hartzell, Richard E. "The Three Approaches to the
'Other' State in Musil's MANN OHNE EIGENSCHAFTEN."
CollG 10:204-217. No. 3, 1976-1977.

Heald, David. "'All the World's a Stage'--A Central
Motif in Musil's MANN OHNE EIGENSCHAFTEN."
GL&L 27:51-59. October 1973.

Luft, David S. Robert Musil and the Crisis of European
Culture 1880-1942. Berkeley: University of California
Press, 1980. pp. 214-268.

Noble, C. A. M. "Musil's Novel Without Qualities."
RLV 39:28-38. No. 1, 1973.

Pachter, Henry M. "Walter Rathenau: Musil's Arnheim
or Mann's Naphta?" BUJ 25:17-28. No. 3, 1978.

Payne, Philip. "Moosbrugger and the Question of Free
Will." NGS 3:139-154. Autumn 1975.

_____. "On Reading Robert Musil's DER MANN OHNE
EIGENSCHAFTEN." Sprachkunst 9:88-100. 1978.

_____. "Robert Musil's Reality--A Study of Some Aspects of 'Wirklichkeit' in DIE MANN OHNE EIGEN-
SCHAFTEN." FMLS 12:314-328. October 1976.

Peters, Frederick G. Robert Musil, Master of the Hovering Life: A Study of the Major Fiction. New York: Columbia University Press, 1978. pp. 188-242.

Prawer, S. S. "Robert Musil and the 'Uncanny.'" OGS 3:163-182. 1968.

Strelka, Joseph. "The Afterglow of Imperial Austria: Robert Musil." GR 54:49-53. Spring 1979.

Titche, Leon L., Jr. "The Concept of the Hermaphrodite: Agathe and Ulrich in Musil's Novel DER MANN OHNE EIGENSCHAFTEN." GL&L 23:160-168. January 1970.

_____. "Into the Millennium: The Theme of the Hermaphrodite in Robert Musil's DER MANN OHNE EIGENSCHAFTEN." OGS 7:143-160. 1973.

Waidson, H. M. "Prose Fiction: Some Outstanding German Novels." Twentieth Century German Literature. ed. August Closs. New York: Barnes and Noble, 1969. pp. 136-141.

Wilkins, Eithne. "DER MANN OHNE EIGENSCHAFTEN and Musil's 'Steinbaukastenzeit.'" OGS 3:183-205. 1968.

_____. "The Musil Manuscripts and a Project for a Musil Society." MLR 62:451-458. July 1967.

_____. "Musil's 'Affair of the Major's Wife' with an Unpublished Text." MLR 63:74-93. January 1968.
THE PERFECTING OF A LOVE
Appignanesi, Lisa. Femininity & the Creative Imagination: A Study of Henry James, Robert Musil & Marcel Proust. New York: Barnes & Noble, 1973. pp. 88-98.

Peters, Frederick G. Robert Musil, Master of the Hovering Life: A Study of the Major Fiction. New York: Columbia University Press, 1978. pp. 59-70.
THE TEMPTATION OF SILENT VERONIKA
Appignanesi, Lisa. Femininity & the Creative Imagination: A Study of Henry James, Robert Musil & Marcel Proust. New York: Barnes & Noble, 1973. pp. 98-105.

Langman, F. H. and E. A. "A Tale of Robert Musil's." CR 11:91-100. 1968.

Peters, Frederick G. Robert Musil, Master of the Hovering Life: A Study of the Major Fiction. New York: Columbia University Press, 1978. pp. 70-104.
TONKA

Musil, Robert

Appignanesi, Lisa. Femininity & the Creative Imagination: A Study of Henry James, Robert Musil & Marcel Proust. New York: Barnes & Noble, 1973. pp. 112-115.

Boa, Elizabeth J. "Austrian Ironies in Musil's DREI FRAUEN." MLR 63:126-128. January 1968.

Peters, Frederick G. Robert Musil, Master of the Hovering Life: A Study of the Major Fiction. New York: Columbia University Press, 1978. pp. 145-187.

Sjögren, Christine Oertel. "The Enigma of Musil's TONKA." MAL 9:100-113. No. 3/4, 1976.

————. "An Inquiry into the Psychological Condition of the Narrator in Musil's TONKA." Monatshefte 64: 153-161. Summer 1972.

Sokel, Walter H. "Kleist's Marquise of O., Kierkegaard's Abraham, and Musil's Tonka: Three Stages of the Absurd as the Touchstone of Faith." WSCL 8:505-516. Autumn 1967.

Stelzmann, Rainulf A. "Kantian Faith in Musil's TONKA." GR 50:294-304. November 1975.

YOUNG TÖRLESS
Luft, David S. Robert Musil and the Crisis of European Culture 1880-1942. Berkeley: University of California Press, 1980. pp. 52-62.

Peters, Frederick G. Robert Musil, Master of the Hovering Life: A Study of the Major Fiction. New York: Columbia University Press, 1978. pp. 28-57.

Rose, Marilyn Gaddis. "Musil's Use of Simile in Törless." SSF 8:295-300. Spring 1971.

Sokel, Walter H. "The Problem of Dualism in Hesse's DEMIAN and Musil's TÖRLESS." MAL 9:35-42. No. 3/4, 1976.

Stopp, Elisabeth. "Musil's TÖRLESS: Content and Form." MLR 63:94-118. January 1968.

Turner, David. "The Evasions of the Aesthete Törless." FMLS 10:19-44. January 1974.

Neutsch, Erik
    SPUR DER STEINE
        Parkes, K. S. "Criticism of East German Society in Some Incidents in Erik Neutsch's Novel SPUR DER STEINE." GL&L 25:261-269. April 1972.

Novalis (Friedrich von Hardenberg)
   ATLANTIS
      Birrell, Gordon. The Boundless Present: Space and Time in the Literary Fairy Tales of Novalis and Tieck. Chapel Hill: University of North Carolina Press, 1979. pp. 22-25; 71-78.
   EROS UND FABEL
      Birrell, Gordon. The Boundless Present: Space and Time in the Literary Fairy Tales of Novalis and Tieck. Chapel Hill: University of North Carolina Press, 1979. pp. 25-38; 78-89.
   HEINRICH VON OFTERDINGEN
      Frye, Lawrence O. "The Language of Romantic High Feeling. A Case of Dialogue Technique in Hoffmann's KATER MURR and Novalis' HEINRICH VON OFTERDINGEN." DVLG 49:520-545. September 1975.

      Furst, Lilian R. "The Structure of Romantic Agony." CLS 10:127-137. June 1973.

      Kahn, Robert L. "Tieck's FRANZ STERNBALDS WANDERUNGEN and Novalis' HEINRICH VON OFTERDINGEN." SIR 7:40-64. Autumn 1967.

      Neubauer, John. Novalis. Boston: Twayne, 1980. pp. 126-152.

      O'Brien, William Arctander. "Twilight in Atlantis." MLN 95:1294-1326. December 1980.

      Rogers, Elwin E. "Novalis' 'Atlantis-Erzählung': Goethe Surpassed?" GQ 50:130-137. March 1977.

      Scrase, David A. "The Movable Feast: The Role and Relevance of the 'Fest' Motif in Novalis' HEINRICH VON OFTERDINGEN." NGS 7:23-36. Spring 1979.

      Stopp, Elisabeth. "'Übergang vom Roman zur Mythologie': Formal Aspects of the Opening Chapter of Hardenberg's HEINRICH VON OFTERDINGEN, Part II." DVLG 48:318-341. No. 2, 1974.
   HYAZINTH UND ROSENBLÜTE
      Birrell, Gordon. The Boundless Present: Space and Time in the Literary Fairy Tales of Novalis and Tieck. Chapel Hill: University of North Carolina Press, 1979. pp. 9-20; 63-70.
   DIE LEHRLINGE ZU SAIS
      Neubauer, John. Bifocal Vision: Novalis' Philosophy of Nature and Disease. Chapel Hill: University of North Carolina Press, 1971. pp. 113-127.

Paul, Jean (Richter)
   HESPERUS

Berger, Dorothea. Jean Paul Friedrich Richter. New York: Twayne, 1972. pp. 49-54.
THE INVISIBLE LODGE
Berger, Dorothea. Jean Paul Friedrich Richter. New York: Twayne, 1972. pp. 38-49.

Rowson, P. D. "The Opening Scene of Jean Paul's DIE UNSICHTBARE LOGE." GL&L 31:221-226. April 1978.

_____. "The Role of the Practical Joke in Jean Paul's DIE UNSICHTBARE LOGE." Neophil 60:412-419. July 1976.
KATZENBERGER
Maurer, Warren R. "Some Aspects of the Jean Paul-Hermann Hesse Relationship with Special Reference to KATZENBERGER and KURGAST." Seminar 4:113-128. Fall 1968.
SIEBENKAS
Berger, Dorothea. Jean Paul Friedrich Richter. New York: Twayne, 1972. pp. 83-95.
TITAN
Berger, Dorothea. Jean Paul Friedrich Richter. New York: Twayne, 1972. pp. 55-82.

Swediuk-Cheyne, Helen. "'Einkräftigkeit,' Jean Paul's Term for Self-Destruction." GL&L 26:136-142. January 1973.
THE TWINS
Berger, Dorothea. Jean Paul Friedrich Richter. New York: Twayne, 1972. pp. 96-125.
WUTZ
Blake, Kathleen. "What the Narrator Learns in Jean Paul's WUTZ." GQ 48:52-65. January 1975.

Pausewang, Gudrun
DER WEG NACH TONGAY
Glenn, Jerry. "Gudrun Pausewang and DER WEG NACH TONGAY: A New Voice in German Literature." SSF 7:556-563. Fall 1970.

Plenzdorf, Ulrich
DIE NEUEN LEIDEN DES JUNGEN W.
Hoegl, Juergen K. "Language, Metaphor, and Strategy of Composition in Ulrich Plenzdorf's Novel DIE NEUEN LEIDEN DES JUNGEN W." UDR 13:37-47. Winter 1978.

Langenbruch, Theodor. "Goethe and Salinger as Models for Ulrich Plenzdorf's Novel DIE NEUEN LEIDEN DES JUNGEN W." PCL 2:60-68. November 1976.

Pickar, Gertrud Bauer. "Plenzdorf's DIE NEUEN LEIDEN DES JUNGEN W.: The Interaction of Portrayal and Social Criticism." MFS 24:542-549. Winter 1978-1979.

Thomas, N. L. "WERTHER in a New Guise: Ulrich Plenzdorf's DIE NEUEN LEIDEN DES JUNGEN W." ML 57:178-182. December 1976.

Plievier, Theodor
STALINGRAD
Nahrgang, W. Lee. "What Is the Most Significant German Novel of World War II?" UDR 13:72-77. Spring 1979.

Purdy, Strother. "STALINGRAD and My Lai: A Literary-Political Speculation." CritI 5:651-661. Summer 1979.

Raabe, Wilhelm
DIE AKTEN DES VOGELSANGS
Bullivant, Keith. "Wilhelm Raabe and the European Novel." OL 31:277-280. 1976.
ALTE NESTER
Webster, W. T. "Hesitation and Decision: Wilhelm Raabe's Road to Reality." FMLS 15:70-76. January 1979.
ALTERSHAUSEN
Webster, W. T. "Hesitation and Decision: Wilhelm Raabe's Road to Reality." FMLS 15:76-81. January 1979.
DIE CHRONIK DER SPERLINGSGASSE
Bullivant, Keith. "Wilhelm Raabe and the European Novel." OL 31:271-272. 1976.
ELSE VON DER TANNE
King, Janet K. "Raabe's ELSE VON DER TANNE." GQ 40:653-663. November 1967.

Radcliffe, Stanley. "Wilhelm Raabe, the Thirty Years War and the Novelle." GL&L 22:220-229. April 1969.
IM ALTEN EISEN
Lensing, Leo A. "The Caricatured Reader in IM ALTEN EISEN: Raabe, Marlitt and the 'Familienblattroman.'" GL&L 31:318-327. July 1978.

_____. Narrative Structure and the Reader in Wilhelm Raabe's IM ALTEN EISEN. Berne: Lang, 1977. 107 pp.
PFISTERS MÜHLE
Bullivant, Keith. "Wilhelm Raabe and the European Novel." OL 31:272-274. 1976.
STOPFKUCHEN
Bullivant, Keith. "Wilhelm Raabe and the European Novel." OL 31:274-277. 1976.

Reimann, Brigitte
FRANZISKA LINKERHAND
McPherson, Karin. "FRANZISKA LINKERHAND--Introduction and Analysis of the Last (Unfinished) Work by the Late GDR Novelist Brigitte Reimann." UDR 13:13-24. Winter 1978.

Remarque, Erich
ALL QUIET ON THE WESTERN FRONT
Bance, A. F. "IM WESTEN NICHTS NEUES: A Bestseller in Context." MLR 72:359-373. April 1977.

Liedloff, Helmut. "Two War Novels: A Critical Comparison." RLC 42:390-406. July/September 1968.

Olstad, Charles. "Sender's IMAN and Remarque's ALL QUIET ON THE WESTERN FRONT." REH 11:133-140. January 1977.

Rowley, Brian A. "Journalism into Fiction: IM WESTEN NICHTS NEUES." The First World War in Fiction: A Collection of Critical Essays. ed. Holger Klein. London: Macmillan, 1976. pp. 101-111.
DIE TRAUMBUDE
Firda, Richard Arthur. "Young Erich Maria Remarque: DIE TRAUMBUDE." Monatshefte 71:49-55. Spring 1979.

Reuter, Gabriele
AUS GUTER FAMILIE
Johnson, Richard L. "Men's Power Over Women in Gabriele Reuter's AUS GUTER FAMILIE." ABnG 10: 235-253. 1980.

Pickle, Linda Schelbitzki. "Woman as the Outsider: Implications for the Development of Literary and Social Attitudes as Seen in AUS GUTER FAMILIE and NACHDENKEN ÜBER CHRISTA T." UDR 14:101-105. Spring 1980.

Rilke, Rainer Maria
THE NOTEBOOKS OF MALTE LAURIDS BRIGGE
Bauer, Arnold. Rainer Maria Rilke. New York: Ungar, 1972. pp. 67-74.

Garber, Frederick. "Time and the City in Rilke's MALTE LAURIDS BRIGGE." ConL 11:324-339. Summer 1970.

Hayman, David. "The Broken Cranium--Headwounds in Zola, Rilke, Céline: A Study in Contrasting Modes." CLS 9:215-221. June 1972.

Herd, E. W. "An Interpretation of DIE AUFZEICH-
NUNGEN DES MALTE LAURIDS BRIGGE Based on an
Analysis of the Structure." Seminar 9:208-228. October 1973.

Jephcott, E. F. N. Proust and Rilke: The Literature of
Expanded Consciousness. London: Chatto and Windus,
1972. pp. 155-175.

Klieneberger, H. R. "Romanticism and Modernism in
Rilke's DIE AUFZEICHNUNGEN DES MALTE LAURIDS
BRIGGE." MLR 74:361-367. April 1979.

Lyon, Laurence Gill. "Related Images in MALTE
LAURIDS BRIGGE and LA NAUSEE." CL 30:53-71.
Winter 1978.

Pachmuss, Temira. "Dostoevskii and Rainer Maria
Rilke: The Alienated Man." CASS 12:392-401. Fall
1978.

Ruppert, Peter. "The Aesthetic Solution in NAUSEA
and MALTE LAURIDS BRIGGE." CL 29:17-34. Winter
1977.

St. Aubyn, F. C. "Rilke, Sartre, and Sarraute: The
Role of the Third." RLC 41:275-284. April/June 1967.

Sokel, Walter H. "The Devolution of the Self in THE
NOTEBOOKS OF MALTE LAURIDS BRIGGE." Rilke:
The Alchemy of Alienation. ed. Frank Baron, Ernst S.
Dick and Warren R. Maurer. Lawrence: Regents,
1968. pp. 171-188.

Ziolkowski, Theodore. Dimensions of the Modern Novel:
German Texts and European Contexts. Princeton:
Princeton University Press, 1969. pp. 3-36.

Rosegger, Peter
    ERDSEGEN
        Dow, James R. and James P. Sandrock. "Peter Rosegger's ERDSEGEN: The Function of Folklore in the
        Work of an Austrian 'Heimatdichter.'" JFI 13:227-239.
        No. 3, 1976.

Roth, Joseph
    DIE HUNDERT TAGE
        Broerman, Bruce M. "Joseph Roth's DIE HUNDERT
        TAGE: A New Perspective." MAL 11:35-48. No. 2,
        1978.
    DER LEVIATHAN
        Bell, Robert F. "The Jewish Experience as Portrayed
        in Three German Exile 'Novellen.'" SAB 42:3-12.
        November 1977.

Saar, Ferdinand von
    SCHLOSS KOSTENITZ
        von Nardroff, Ernest H. "Ferdinand von Saar's
        SCHLOSS KOSTENITZ: A Prelude to Schnitzler?" MAL
        4:21-33. Winter 1971.

Schallück, Paul
    ENGELBERT REINEKE
        Andrews, R. C. "The German School-Story: Some Observations on Paul Schallück and Thomas Valentin."
        GL&L 23:103-112. January 1970.
    WENN MAN AUFHOREN KONNTE ZU LUGEN
        Keele, Alan Frank. "Ethics in Embryo: Abortion and
        the Problem of Morality in Post-War German Literature." GR 51:231-233. May 1976.

Scherr, Johannes
    EINE DEUTSCH GESCHICHTE
        McBryde, M. J. "Georg Weerth, Johannes Scherr and
        Robert Prutz: Three Novelists of 1848 and Their Attitudes Towards the Fourth Estate." GL&L 29:355-358.
        July 1976.

Schlegel, Dorothea
    FLORENTIN
        Hibberd, J. "Dorothea Schlegel's FLORENTIN and the
        Precarious Idyll." GL&L 30:198-207. April 1977.

Schlegel, Friedrich
    LUCINDE
        Flavell, M. Kay. "Women and Individualism: A Reexamination of Schlegel's LUCINDE and Gutzkow's
        WALLY DIE ZWEIFLERIN." MLR 70:556-560. July
        1975.

        Littlejohns, Richard. "The 'Bekenntnisse eines Ungeschickten': A Re-examination of Emancipatory Ideas
        in Friedrich Schlegel's LUCINDE." MLR 72:605-614.
        July 1977.

Schnabel, Johann Gottfried
    INSEL FELSENBURG
        *Lamport, F. J. "Utopia and 'Robinsonade': Schnabel's
        INSEL FELSENBURG and Bachstrom's LAND DER INQUIRANER." OGS 1:10-30. 1966.

Schneider, Rolf
    JOURNEY TO JAROSLAV
        Mohr, Heinrich. "Vacation from Reality: Rolf Schneider's Novel DIE REISE NACH JAROSLAW." NGC 9:113-122. Fall 1976.

Schnitzler, Arthur
    ANDREAS THAMEYERS LETZTER BRIEF

Swales, Martin. Arthur Schnitzler: A Critical Study.
Oxford: Clarendon, 1971. pp. 93-97.
DER BLINDE GERONIMO UND SEIN BRUDER
Cook, William K. "Arthur Schnitzler's DER BLINDE
GERONIMO UND SEIN BRUDER: A Critical Discussion."
MAL 5:120-135. No. 3/4, 1972.
BLUMEN
Russell, Peter. "Schnitzler's BLUMEN: The Treatment
of a Neurosis." FMLS 13:289-302. October 1977.
DOKTOR GRASLER, BADEARZT
von Nardroff, Ernest H. "DOKTOR GRASLER, BAD-
EARZT: Weather as an Aspect of Schnitzler's Symbolism." GR 43:109-119. March 1968.
FLUCHT IN DIE FINSTERNIS
Swales, Martin. Arthur Schnitzler: A Critical Study.
Oxford: Clarendon, 1971. pp. 127-133.
FRAU BERTA GARLAN
Driver, Beverley R. "Arthur Schnitzler's FRAU BERTA
GARLAN: A Study in Form." GR 46:285-298. November 1971.
DIE FRAU DES RICHTERS
Dickerson, Harold D., Jr. "Arthur Schnitzler's DIE
FRAU DES RICHTERS: A Statement of Futility." GQ
43:223-236. March 1970.
FRÄULEIN ELSE
Alexander, Theodor W. and Beatrice W. "Maupassant's
YVETTE and Schnitzler's FRÄULEIN ELSE." MAL 4:44-
53. Fall 1971.

Bareikis, Robert. "Arthur Schnitzler's FRÄULEIN ELSE:
A Freudian Novella?" L&P 19:19-32. No. 1, 1969.

Beharriell, Frederick J. "Schnitzler's FRÄULEIN
ELSE: 'Reality' and Invention." MAL 10:247-264. No.
3/4, 1977.
DER GANG ZUM WEIHER
Dickerson, Harold D., Jr. "Water and Vision as Mystical Elements in Schnitzler's DER GANG ZUM WEIHER."
MAL 4:24-34. Fall 1971.
DIE GRIECHISCHE TÄNZERIN
Swales, Martin. Arthur Schnitzler: A Critical Study.
Oxford: Clarendon, 1971. pp. 81-86.
DIE HIRTENFLÖTE
Reid, Maja D. "DIE HIRTENFLÖTE." MAL 4:18-27.
Summer 1971.
DER LETZTE BRIEF EINES LITERATEN
Swales, Martin. Arthur Schnitzler: A Critical Study.
Oxford: Clarendon, 1971. pp. 86-91.
LEUTNANT GUSTL
Alexander, Theodor W. and Beatrice W. "Schnitzler's
LEUTNANT GUSTL and Dujardin's LES LAURIERS SONT
COUPES." MAL 2:7-15. Summer 1969.

Swales, Martin. Arthur Schnitzler: A Critical Study. Oxford: Clarendon, 1971. pp. 103-114.
THE MURDERER
Sherman, Murray H. "Reik, Schnitzler, Freud, and THE MURDERER: The Limits of Insight in Psychoanalysis." MAL 10:195-212. No. 3/4, 1977. Reprinted in PsyR 65:68-90. Spring 1978.
SPIEL IM MORGENGRAUEN
Ekfelt, Nils. "Arthur Schnitzler's SPIEL IM MORGENGRAUEN: Free Will, Fate, and Chaos." GQ 51:170-181. March 1978.
STERBEN
Berlin, Jeffrey B. "The Element of 'Hope' in Arthur Schnitzler's STERBEN." Seminar 10:38-49. February 1974.

Conner, Maurice W. "Schnitzler's STERBEN and Dürrenmatt's DER METEOR: Two Responses to the Prospect of Death." GN 11:36-38. No. 3, 1980.
DIE TOTEN SCHWEIGEN
Cook, William K. "Isolation, Flight, and Resolution in Arthur Schnitzler's DIE TOTEN SCHWEIGEN." GR 50: 213-226. May 1975.
TRAUMNOVELLE
Segar, Kenneth. "Determinism and Character: Arthur Schnitzler's TRAUMNOVELLE and His Unpublished Critique of Psychoanalysis." OGS 8:114-127. 1973.

Swales, Martin. Arthur Schnitzler: A Critical Study. Oxford: Clarendon, 1971. pp. 138-149.
DER WEG INS FREIE
Allen, Richard H. "Schnitzler's DER WEG INS FREIE: Structure or Structures?" JIASRA 6:4-15. Fall 1967.

Swales, Martin. Arthur Schnitzler: A Critical Study. Oxford: Clarendon, 1971. pp. 29-52.

_____. "Nürnberger's Novel: A Study of Arthur Schnitzler's DER WEG INS FREIE." MLR 70:567-575. July 1975.

Sealsfield, Charles
DER VIREY UND DIE ARISTOKRATEN, ODER MEXIKO IM JAHRE 1812
Friesen, Gerhard. "Charles Sealsfield and the German Panoramic Novel of the 19th Century." MLN 84:738-763. October 1969.

Seghers, Anna
POST INS GELOBTE LAND
Bell, Robert F. "The Jewish Experience as Portrayed in Three German Exile 'Novellen.'" SAB 42:3-12. November 1977.

TRANSIT
    Szepe, Helena. "The Problem of Identity in Anna Seghers' TRANSIT." OL 27:145-152. 1972.
ÜBERFAHRT
    Thomaneck, Jürgen. "The Iceberg in Anna Seghers's Novel ÜBERFAHRT." GL&L 28:36-45. October 1974.

## Shallück, Paul
DON QUICHOTTE IN KÖLN
    Keele, Alan Frank. Paul Shallück and the Post-War German Don Quixote: A Case-History Prolegomenon to the Literature of the Federal Republic. Bern: Lang, 1976. pp. 45-64.
ENGELBERT REINEKE
    Keele, Alan Frank. Paul Shallück and the Post-War German Don Quixote: A Case-History Prolegomenon to the Literature of the Federal Republic. Bern: Lang, 1976. pp. 34-42; 88-93.

## Spitteler, Carl
IMAGO
    McHaffie, Margaret. "Prometheus and Viktor: Carl Spitteler's IMAGO." GL&L 31:67-76. October 1977.

## Stifter, Adalbert
ABDIAS
    George, E. F. "The Place of ABDIAS in Stifter's Thought and Work." FMLS 3:148-156. April 1967.

    Goodden, Christian. "Two Quests for Surety--A Comparative Interpretation of Stifter's ABDIAS and Kafka's DER BAU." JES 5:341-361. December 1975.

    Klieneberger, H.R. "Stifter's ABDIAS and Its Interpreters." FMLS 14:332-344. October 1978.
BERGKRISTALL
    Whiton, John. "Symbols of Social Renewal in Stifter's BERGKRISTALL." GR 47:259-280. November 1972.
BRIGITTA
    Branscombe, Peter. "The Use of Leitmotifs in Stifter's BRIGITTA." FMLS 13:145-154. April 1977.
DER HOCHWALD
    Sjögren, Christine Oertel. "'Tuch' as a Symbol for Art in Stifter's DER HOCHWALD." JEGP 73:375-387. July 1974.
THE INSCRIBED FIR TREE
    Stern, J.P. "Stifter's Fiction: 'Erhebung' Without Motion." Novel 1:244-249. Spring 1968.
DER NACHSOMMER
    Browning, Barton W. "Stifter's NACHSOMMER and the Fourth Commandment." CollG 7:301-315. No. 4, 1973.

    Gump, Margaret. Adalbert Stifter. New York: Twayne, 1974. pp. 92-117.

Latimer, Renate. "On Translating Stifter's NACHSOMMER." MAL 12:67-79. No. 2, 1979.

Sjögren, Christine Oertel. "The 'Cereus Peruvianus' in Stifter's NACHSOMMER: Illustration of a 'Gestalt.'" GQ 40:664-672. November 1967.

──────. "The Configuration of Ideal Love in Stifter's DER NACHSOMMER." MAL 8:190-196. No. 3/4, 1975.

──────. "The Equivocal Light of the 'Marmorsaal': Traces of Mysticism in Stifter's Novel, DER NACHSOMMER." JEGP 69:108-117. January 1970.

──────. "The Human 'Gestalten' and the Fools in Adalbert Stifter's DER NACHSOMMER." JEGP 70:86-101. January 1971.

──────. The Marble Statue as Idea: Collected Essays on Adalbert Stifter's DER NACHSOMMER. Chapel Hill: University of North Carolina Press, 1972. 96 pp.

──────. "The Monstrous Painting in Stifter's DER NACHSOMMER." JEGP 68:92-99. January 1969.

──────. "Stifter's Affirmation of Formlessness in NACHSOMMER." MLQ 29:407-414. December 1968.

Stowell, J.D. "Some Archetypes in Stifter's DER NACHSOMMER: An Attempt at Restoring Fictional Interest." Seminar 6:31-47. March 1970.

PROKOPUS
Zwiebel, William L. "Time and the Temporal in Stifter's PROKOPUS." GQ 53:432-442. November 1980.

TURMALIN
Mason, Eve. "Stifter's TURMALIN: A Reconsideration." MLR 72:348-358. April 1977.

WITIKO
Gump, Margaret. Adalbert Stifter. New York: Twayne, 1974. pp. 118-131.

Storm, Theodor
AQUIS SUBMERSUS
Alt, A. Tilo. Theodor Storm. New York: Twayne, 1973. pp. 82-90.

Duroche, Leonard L. "Like and Look Alike: Symmetry and Irony in Theodor Storm's AQUIS SUBMERSUS." Seminar 7:1-13. March 1971.

A DOPPELGÄNGER
Alt, A. Tilo. Theodor Storm. New York: Twayne, 1973. pp. 115-121.

DRAUSZEN IM HEIDEDORF

Barrick, Raymond E. "Ambivalence in Character Portrayal in Theodore Storm's Novelle DRAUSZEN IM HEIDEDORF." LangQ 11:29-34; 56. Fall/Winter 1972.
EKENHOF
 Alt, A. Tilo. Theodor Storm. New York: Twayne, 1973. pp. 90-102.
IMMENSEE
 Alt, A. Tilo. Theodor Storm. New York: Twayne, 1973. pp. 75-81.
DER SCHIMMELREITER
 Alt, A. Tilo. Theodor Storm. New York: Twayne, 1973. pp. 121-131.

 Artiss, David S. "Bird Motif and Myth in Theodor Storm's SCHIMMELREITER." Seminar 4:1-16. Spring 1968.

 Ellis, John M. Narration in the German Novelle: Theory and Interpretation. London: Cambridge University Press, 1974. pp. 155-168.

 ———. "Narration in Storm's DER SCHIMMELREITER." GR 44:21-30. January 1969.

 Findlay, Ian. "Myth and Redemption in Theodor Storm's DER SCHIMMELREITER." PLL 11:397-403. Fall 1975.

Tieck, Ludwig
 ABDALLAH
  Corkhill, Alan. The Motif of "Fate" in the Works of Ludwig Tieck. Stuttgart: Heinz, 1978. pp. 29-55.
 DER BLONDE ECKBERT
  Birrell, Gordon. The Boundless Present: Space and Time in the Literary Fairy Tales of Novalis and Tieck. Chapel Hill: University of North Carolina Press, 1979. pp. 39-52; 90-102.

  Corkhill, Alan. The Motif of "Fate" in the Works of Ludwig Tieck. Stuttgart: Heinz, 1978. pp. 147-164.

  Ellis, John M. Narration in the German Novelle: Theory and Interpretation. London: Cambridge University Press, 1974. pp. 77-93.

  Ewton, Ralph W., Jr. "Childhood Without End: Tieck's DER BLONDE ECKBERT." GQ 46:410-427. May 1973.

  Kimpel, Richard W. "Nature, Quest, and Reality in Tieck's DER BLONDE ECKBERT and DER RUNENBERG." SIR 9:176-192. Summer 1970.

  Lillyman, W. J. "The Enigma of DER BLONDE ECKBERT: The Significance of the End." Seminar 7:144-155. June 1971.

Tieck, Ludwig

_____. Reality's Dark Dream: The Narrative Fiction of Ludwig Tieck. Berlin: de Gruyter, 1979. pp. 79-92.

Rippere, Victoria L. "Ludwig Tieck's DER BLONDE ECKBERT: A Psychological Reading." PMLA 85:473-486. May 1970.

Sellner, Timothy F. "Jungian Psychology and the Romantic Fairy Tale: A New Look at Tieck's DER BLONDE ECKBERT." GR 55:89-97. Summer 1980.

Swales, Martin. "Reading One's Life: An Analysis of Tieck's DER BLONDE ECKBERT." GL&L 29:165-175. October 1975.

Wells, Larry D. "Sacred and Profane: A Spatial Archetype in the Early Tales of Ludwig Tieck." Monatshefte 70:31-36. Spring 1978.

DIE ELFEN

Lillyman, William J. Reality's Dark Dream: The Narrative Fiction of Ludwig Tieck. Berlin: de Gruyter, 1979. pp. 107-114.

FRANZ STERNBALDS WANDERUNGEN

Hibberd, J. L. "The Idylls in Tieck's STERNBALD." FMLS 12:236-249. July 1976.

Kahn, Robert L. "Tieck's FRANZ STERNBALDS WANDERUNGEN and Novalis' HEINRICH VON OFTERDINGEN." SIR 7:40-64. Autumn 1967.

Lillyman, William J. Reality's Dark Dream: The Narrative Fiction of Ludwig Tieck. Berlin: de Gruyter, 1979. pp. 61-76.

Mornin, Edward. "Art and Alienation in Tieck's FRANZ STERNBALDS WANDERUNGEN." MLN 94:510-523. April 1979.

_____. "Tieck's Revision of FRANZ STERNBALDS WANDERUNGEN." Seminar 15:79-96. May 1979.

DES LEBENS ÜBERFLUSS

Lillyman, W. J. "Ludwig Tieck's DES LEBENS ÜBERFLUSS: The Crisis of a Conservative." GQ 46:393-409. May 1973.

_____. Reality's Dark Dream: The Narrative Fiction of Ludwig Tieck. Berlin: de Gruyter, 1979. pp. 116-130.

LIEBESZAUBER

Wright, Elizabeth. E. T. A. Hoffmann and the Rhetoric of Terror: Aspects of Language Used for the Evocation of Fear. Leeds: Maney, 1978. pp. 75-115.

DER RUNENBERG
Birrell, Gordon. The Boundless Present: Space and Time in the Literary Fairy Tales of Novalis and Tieck. Chapel Hill: University of North Carolina Press, 1979. pp. 52-62; 103-115.

Ewton, Ralph W., Jr. "Life and Death of the Body in Tieck's DER RUNENBERG." GR 50:19-33. January 1975.

Frye, Lawrence O. "Irretrievable Time and the Poems in Tieck's DER RUNENBERG." LJGG 18:147-171. 1977.

Kimpel, Richard W. "Nature, Quest, and Reality in Tieck's DER BLONDE ECKBERT and DER RUNENBERG." SIR 9:176-192. Summer 1970.

Lillyman, W. J. "Ludwig Tieck's DER RUNENBERG: The Dimensions of Reality." Monatshefte 62:231-244. Fall 1970.

_____. Reality's Dark Dream: The Narrative Fiction of Ludwig Tieck. Berlin: de Gruyter, 1979. pp. 92-107.

Tatar, Maria M. "Deracination and Alienation in Ludwig Tieck's DER RUNENBERG." GQ 51:285-304. May 1978.

Wells, Larry D. "Sacred and Profane: A Spatial Archetype in the Early Tales of Ludwig Tieck." Monatshefte 70:36-40. Spring 1978.

Wright, Elizabeth. E. T. A. Hoffmann and the Rhetoric of Terror: Aspects of Language Used for the Evocation of Fear. Leeds: Maney, 1978. pp. 50-74.

VITTORIA ACCOROMBONA
Lillyman, W. J. "Ludwig Tieck's VITTORIA ACCOROMBONA." JEGP 70:468-487. July 1971.

_____. Reality's Dark Dream: The Narrative Fiction of Ludwig Tieck. Berlin: de Gruyter, 1979. pp. 131-154.

WILLIAM LOVELL
Corkhill, Alan. The Motif of "Fate" in the Works of Ludwig Tieck. Stuttgart: Heinz, 1978. pp. 87-139.

Lillyman, William J. Reality's Dark Dream: The Narrative Fiction of Ludwig Tieck. Berlin: de Gruyter, 1979. pp. 21-41.

Proskauer, Paul F. "Ludwig Tieck's WILLIAM LOVELL and Young Hugo von Hofmannsthal." MAL 3:36-40. Fall 1970.

Tieck, Ludwig

>Trainer, James. "WILLIAM LOVELL: Tieck's World of Chaos." EG 23:191-201. April/June 1968.

Torberg, Friedrich
DIE MANNSCHAFT
> Mornin, Edward. "Taking Games Seriously: Observations on the German Sports-Novel." GR 51:286-289. November 1976.

DER 94. PSALM
> Bell, Robert F. "The Jewish Experience as Portrayed in Three German Exile 'Novellen.'" SAB 42:3-12. November 1977.

Valentin, Thomas
DIE UNBERATENEN
> Andrews, R. C. "The German School-Story: Some Observations on Paul Schallück and Thomas Valentin." GL&L 23:103-112. January 1970.

Vischer, Friedrich Theodor
AUCH EINER
> Bruford, W. H. "The Idea of 'Bildung' in Friedrich Theodor Vischer's AUCH EINER." Essays in German Language, Culture and Society. ed. Siegbert S. Prawer et al. London: Maney, 1969. pp. 7-17.

Von Suttner, Bertha
DIE WAFFEN NIEDER!
> Wiener, P. B. "Bertha von Suttner and the Political Novel." Essays in German Language, Culture and Society. ed. Siegbert S. Prawer et al. London: Maney, 1969. pp. 163-174.

Walser, Martin
DIE EHEN IN PHILIPPSBURG
> Keele, Alan Frank. "Ethics in Embryo: Abortion and the Problem of Morality in Post-War German Literature." GR 51:233-237. May 1976.

> Nelson, Donald F. "The Depersonalized World of Martin Walser." GQ 42:204-211. March 1969.

> Pickar, Gertrud Bauer. "Narrative Perspective in the Novels of Martin Walser." GQ 44:48-57. January 1971.

DAS EINHORN
> Pickar, Gertrud Bauer. "Narrative Perspective in the Novels of Martin Walser." GQ 44:48-57. January 1971.

> Thomas, R. Hinton and Wilfried van der Will. The German Novel and the Affluent Society. Manchester: Manchester University Press, 1968. pp. 104-111.

EIN FLIEHENDES PFERD
> Thomas, Noel L. "Martin Walser Rides Again: EIN

FLIEHENDES PFERD." ML 60:168-171. September 1979.
HALBZEIT
Andrews, R. C. "Comedy and Satire in Martin Walser's HALBZEIT." ML 50:6-10. March 1969.

Nelson, Donald F. "The Depersonalized World of Martin Walser." GQ 42:211-215. March 1969.

Parkes, K. S. "An All-German Dilemma: Some Notes on the Presentation of the Theme of the Individual and Society in Martin Walser's HALBZEIT and Christa Wolf's NACHDENKEN ÜBER CHRISTA T." GL&L 28: 58-64. October 1974.

Pickar, Gertrud Bauer. "Narrative Perspective in the Novels of Martin Walser." GQ 44:48-57. January 1971.

Thomas, R. Hinton and Wilfried van der Will. The German Novel and the Affluent Society. Manchester: Manchester University Press, 1968. pp. 90-103.

Walser, Robert
DER GEHÜLFE
Avery, George C. Inquiry and Testament: A Study of the Novels and Short Prose of Robert Walser. Philadelphia: University of Pennsylvania Press, 1968. pp. 61-82; 130-138.
GESCHWISTER TANNER
Avery, George C. Inquiry and Testament: A Study of the Novels and Short Prose of Robert Walser. Philadelphia: University of Pennsylvania Press, 1968. pp. 36-60; 124-130.
JAKOB VON GUNTEN
Avery, George C. Inquiry and Testament: A Study of the Novels and Short Prose of Robert Walser. Philadelphia: University of Pennsylvania Press, 1968. pp. 84-120; 138-145.

Parry, Idris. "A Study in Servitude: Robert Walser's JAKOB VON GUNTEN." GL&L 30:283-293. July 1977.

Walter, Otto F.
HERR TOUREL
Waidson, H. M. "Otto F. Walter. Roads to Desolation." Trivium 10:77-82. May 1975.

Weber, Carl Maria von
TONKÜNSTLERS LEBEN, EINE ARABESKE
Scher, Steven Paul. "Carl Maria von Weber's TONKÜNSTLERS LEBEN: The Composer as Novelist?" CLS 15:30-42. March 1978.

## Weerth, Georg
FRAGMENT EINES ROMANS

McBryde, M. J. "Georg Weerth, Johannes Scherr and Robert Prutz: Three Novelists of 1848 and Their Attitudes Towards the Fourth Estate." GL&L 29:351-354. July 1976.

Ridley, Hugh. "A Note on Georg Weerth's Unfinished Novel." GL&L 26:275-278. July 1973.

## Weiss, Peter
DER SCHATTEN DES KÖRPERS DES KUTSCHERS

Cunliffe, W. G. "'The Would-be Novelist': An Interpretation of Peter Weiss' DER SCHATTEN DES KÖRPERS DES KUTSCHERS." MLN 86:414-419. April 1971.

Perry, R. C. "Weiss's DER SCHATTEN DES KÖRPERS DES KUTSCHERS: A Forerunner of the Nouveau Roman?" GR 47:203-219. May 1972.

## Wiechert, Ernst
JEDERMANN

Klein, Holger. "Projections of Everyman: The Common Soldier in Franconi, Wiechert and Williamson." The First World War in Fiction: A Collection of Critical Essays. ed. Holger Klein. London: Macmillan, 1976. pp. 84-100.

## Wieland, Christoph
AGATHODÄMON

McCarthy, John. Fantasy and Reality: An Epistemological Approach to Wieland. Bern: Lang, 1974. pp. 141-149.

AGATHON

Swales, Martin. "An Unreadable Novel? Some Observations on Wieland's AGATHON and the 'Bildungsroman' Tradition." PEGS 45:101-130. 1975.

ARISTIPP UND EINIGE SEINER ZEITGENOSSEN

Phelan, Tony. "Ironic Lovers: Wieland's ARISTIPP UND EINIGE SEINER ZEITGENOSSEN." GL&L 29:97-108. October 1975.

DIE DIALOGEN DES DIOGENES

McCarthy, John A. Christoph Martin Wieland. Boston: Twayne, 1979. pp. 91-95.

DON SYLVIO OF ROSALVA

Kurth-Voigt, Lieselotte E. Perspectives and Points of View: The Early Works of Wieland and Their Background. Baltimore: Johns Hopkins University Press, 1974. pp. 115-135.

McCarthy, John A. Christoph Martin Wieland. Boston: Twayne, 1979. pp. 58-69.

_____. Fantasy and Reality: An Epistemological Approach to Wieland. Bern: Lang, 1974. pp. 43-66.

  Van Abbé, Derek. "Wieland and the 'Stately Homes' of Faëry: The Rococo Substructure of DON SYLVIO DE ROSALVA." PEGS 47:28-46. 1977.
PEREGRINUS PROTEUS
  McCarthy, John. Fantasy and Reality: An Epistemological Approach to Wieland. Bern: Lang, 1974. pp. 107-134.

Wolf, Christa
 DER GETEILTE HIMMEL
  Cirker, Willkie K. "The Socialist Education of Rita Seidel: The Dialectics of Humanism and Authoritarianism in Christa Wolf's DER GETEILTE HIMMEL." UDR 13:105-111. Winter 1978.
 KINDHEITSMUSTER
  Kane, B. M. "In Search of the Past: Christa Wolf's KINDHEITSMUSTER." ML 59:19-23. March 1978.
 THE QUEST FOR CHRISTA T.
  Love, Myra. "Christa Wolf and Feminism: Breaking the Patriarchal Connection." NGC 16:31-53. Winter 1979.

  McGauran, Fergus. "'Gebrochene Generationen': Christa Wolf and Theodor Storm." GL&L 31:328-333. July 1978.

  Parkes, K. S. "An All-German Dilemma: Some Notes on the Presentation of the Theme of the Individual and Society in Martin Walser's HALBZEIT and Christa Wolf's NACHDENKEN ÜBER CHRISTA T." GL&L 28:58-64. October 1974.

  Pickle, Linda Schelbitzki. "Woman as the Outsider: Implications for the Development of Literary and Social Attitudes as Seen in AUS GUTER FAMILIE and NACHDENKEN ÜBER CHRISTA T." UDR 14:105-110. Spring 1980.

  Probst, Gerhard F. "Thematization of Alterity in Christa Wolf's NACHDENKEN ÜBER CHRISTA T." UDR 13:25-35. Winter 1978.

Zweig, Arnold
 DAS BEIL VON WANDSHEK
  Salamon, George. Arnold Zweig. Boston: Twayne, 1975. pp. 147-158.
 THE CASE OF SERGEANT GRISCHA
  Salamon, George. Arnold Zweig. Boston: Twayne, 1975. pp. 79-96.

Zweig, Arnold

Sebald, W. G. "Humanitarianism and Law: Arnold Zweig, DER STREIT UM DEN SERGEANTEN GRISCHA." The First World War in Fiction: A Collection of Critical Essays. ed. Holger Klein. London: Macmillan, 1976. pp. 126-135.

EINSETZUNG EINES KONIGS
Salamon, George. Arnold Zweig. Boston: Twayne, 1975. pp. 117-123.

ERZIEHUNG VOR VERDUN
Salamon, George. Arnold Zweig. Boston: Twayne, 1975. pp. 106-117; 163-171.

DIE FEUERPAUSE
Salamon, George. Arnold Zweig. Boston: Twayne, 1975. pp. 163-171.

JUNGE FRAU VON 1914
Salamon, George. Arnold Zweig. Boston: Twayne, 1975. pp. 94-106.

Schroeder-Krassnow, Sabine. "The Changing View of Abortion: A Study of Friedrich Wolf's CYANKALI and Arnold Zweig's JUNGE FRAU VON 1914." StTCL 4:38-46. Fall 1979.

DIE NOVELLEN UM CLAUDIA
Salamon, George. Arnold Zweig. Boston: Twayne, 1975. pp. 25-29.

VERSUNKENE TAGE
Salamon, George. Arnold Zweig. Boston: Twayne, 1975. pp. 141-145.

Zweig, Stefan

BUCH MENDEL
Turner, David. "Memory and the Humanitarian Ideal: An Interpretation of Stefan Zweig's BUCH MENDEL." MAL 12:43-60. No. 1, 1979.

SCHACHNOVELLE
Daviau, Donald G. and Harvey I. Dunkle. "Stefan Zweig's SCHACHNOVELLE." Monatshefte 65:370-384. Winter 1973.

Douglas, D. B. "The Humanist Gambit: A Study of Stefan Zweig's SCHACHNOVELLE." AUMLA 53:17-23. May 1980.

THE SCANDINAVIAN NOVEL

Ahlin, Lars
    BARK AND LEAVES
        Lundell, Torborg. <u>Lars Ahlin</u>. Boston: Twayne, 1977. pp. 134-139.
    CINNAMON GIRL
        Lundell, Torborg. <u>Lars Ahlin</u>. Boston: Twayne, 1977. pp. 68-73.
    THE GREAT AMNESIA
        Lundell, Torborg. <u>Lars Ahlin</u>. Boston: Twayne, 1977. pp. 94-108.
    IF, ABOUT, AROUND
        Lundell, Torborg. <u>Lars Ahlin</u>. Boston: Twayne, 1977. pp. 74-89.
    MY DEATH IS MY OWN
        Lundell, Torborg. <u>Lars Ahlin</u>. Boston: Twayne, 1977. pp. 45-55.
    NIGHT IN THE MARKET TENT
        Lundell, Torborg. <u>Lars Ahlin</u>. Boston: Twayne, 1977. pp. 117-129.
    NORMAL COURSE
        Lundell, Torborg. <u>Lars Ahlin</u>. Boston: Twayne, 1977. pp. 129-134.
    PIOUS MURDERS
        Lundell, Torborg. <u>Lars Ahlin</u>. Boston: Twayne, 1977. pp. 56-93.
    A STOVE OF ONE'S OWN
        Lundell, Torborg. <u>Lars Ahlin</u>. Boston: Twayne, 1977. pp. 89-93.
    TABB WITH THE MANIFESTO
        Lundell, Torborg. <u>Lars Ahlin</u>. Boston: Twayne, 1977. pp. 30-42.

Almqvist, Carl Jonas Love
    THE QUEEN'S JEWELPIECE
        Blackwell, Marilyn J. "Friedrich Schlegel and C. J. L. Almqvist: Romantic Irony and Textual Artifice." <u>SS</u> 52:127-141. Spring 1980.

        Johns, Marilyn E. "Almqvist's Novel THE QUEEN'S JEWELPIECE and Friedrich Schlegel's Concept of the Novel." <u>Monatshefte</u> 72:135-148. Summer 1980.

Andersen, Tryggve
  MOT KVAELD
    Schiff, Timothy H. "Tryggve Andersen's Novel MOT KVAELD and Its Motto." SS 48:146-155. Spring 1976.

Bjorneboe, Jens
  UNDER EN HARDERE HIMMEL
    Hoberman, John M. "The Political Imagination of Jens Bjorneboe: A Study of UNDER EN HARDERE HIMMEL." SS 48:52-70. Winter 1976.

Bjørnson, B.
  ARNE
    Sehmsdorf, Henning K. "The Self in Isolation: A New Reading of Bjørnson's ARNE." SS 45:310-323. Autumn 1973.

Borgen, Johan
  BLUE PEAK
    Birn, Randi. Johan Borgen. New York: Twayne, 1974. pp. 97-112.
  JEG
    Birn, Randi. Johan Borgen. New York: Twayne, 1974. pp. 84-96.
  LITTLE LORD
    Birn, Randi. Johan Borgen. New York: Twayne, 1974. pp. 63-83.
  MY ARM, MY INTESTINE
    Birn, Randi. Johan Borgen. New York: Twayne, 1974. pp. 133-154.
  THE RED MIST
    Birn, Randi. Johan Borgen. New York: Twayne, 1974. pp. 112-129.

Branner, H. C.
  ANGUISH
    Markey, T. L. H. C. Branner. New York: Twayne, 1973. pp. 94-99.
  THE CHILD PLAYS ON THE BEACH
    Markey, T. L. H. C. Branner. New York: Twayne, 1973. pp. 35-50.
  THE DREAM ABOUT A WOMAN
    Markey, T. L. H. C. Branner. New York: Twayne, 1973. pp. 50-63.
  THE MOUNTAINS
    Markey, T. L. H. C. Branner. New York: Twayne, 1973. pp. 122-129.
  NO MAN KNOWS THE NIGHT
    Markey, T. L. H. C. Branner. New York: Twayne, 1973. pp. 131-142.
  THE RIDING MASTER
    Markey, T. L. H. C. Branner. New York: Twayne, 1973. pp. 99-112.

TOYS
    Markey, T. L. H. C. Branner. New York: Twayne, 1973. pp. 28-34.

Dinesen, Isak
  THE POET
    Billy, Ted. "Werther Avenged: Isak Dinesen's THE POET." WVUPP 24:62-67. November 1977.

Duun, Olav
  MENNESKE OG MAKTENE
    Voss, James. "Olav Duun's MENNESKE OG MAKTENE: Form, Vision, Contemporary Significance." SS 52:361-380. Autumn 1980.

Enquist, Olov
  SEKONDEN
    Shideler, Ross. "Putting Together the Puzzle in Per Olov Enquist's SEKONDEN." SS 49:311-329. Summer 1977.

Grieg, Nordahl
  THE SHIP SAILS ON
    Dahlie, Hallvard. "On Nordahl Grieg's THE SHIP SAILS ON." IFR 2:49-53. January 1975.

Gyllensten, Lars
  THE BLUE SHIP
    Isaksson, Hans. Lars Gyllensten. Boston: Twayne, 1978. pp. 51-59.
  CAIN'S MEMOIRS
    Isaksson, Hans. Lars Gyllensten. Boston: Twayne, 1978. pp. 109-116.
  THE CAVE IN THE DESERT
    Isaksson, Hans. Lars Gyllensten. Boston: Twayne, 1978. pp. 154-165.
  THE DEATH OF SOCRATES
    Isaksson, Hans. Lars Gyllensten. Boston: Twayne, 1978. pp. 93-101.
  DIARIUM SPIRITUALE
    Isaksson, Hans. Lars Gyllensten. Boston: Twayne, 1978. pp. 133-142.
  IN THE SHADOW OF DON JUAN
    Isaksson, Hans. Lars Gyllensten. Boston: Twayne, 1978. pp. 166-171.
  INFANTILIA
    Isaksson, Hans. Lars Gyllensten. Boston: Twayne, 1978. pp. 59-68.
  JUVENILIA
    Isaksson, Hans. Lars Gyllensten. Boston: Twayne, 1978. pp. 116-125.
  LOTUS IN HADES
    Isaksson, Hans. Lars Gyllensten. Boston: Twayne, 1978. pp. 125-130.

Gyllensten, Lars

 PALACE IN THE PARK
  Isaksson, Hans. Lars Gyllensten. Boston: Twayne, 1978. pp. 141-150.
 THE SENATOR
  Isaksson, Hans. Lars Gyllensten. Boston: Twayne, 1978. pp. 85-93.
 SENILIA
  Isaksson, Hans. Lars Gyllensten. Boston: Twayne, 1978. pp. 74-85.

Hamsun, Knut
 AUGUST
  Naess, Harald. "Knut Hamsun and America." SS 39: 321-324. November 1967.
 GROWTH OF THE SOIL
  Naess, Harald. "Knut Hamsun and America." SS 39: 316-320. November 1967.

  Simpson, Allen. "Hamsun and Camus: Consciousness in MARKENS GRODE and 'The Myth of Sisyphus.'" SS 48:272-283. Summer 1976.
 HUNGER
  Bolckmans, Alex. "Henry Miller's TROPIC OF CANCER and Knut Hamsun's SULT." Scan 14:115-126. November 1975.

  Mishler, William. "Ignorance, Knowledge and Resistance to Knowledge in Hamsun's SULT." Edda 74:161-177. No. 3, 1974.
 MYSTERIES
  Friederich, Reinhard H. "Kafka and Hamsun's MYSTERIES." CL 28:34-50. Winter 1976.
 PAN
  Sehmsdorf, Henning K. "Knut Hamsun's PAN. Myth and Symbol." Edda 74:345-393. No. 6, 1974.
 THE RING IS CLOSED
  Naess, Harald. "Knut Hamsun and America." SS 39: 324-327. November 1967.
 SISTE KAPITEL
  van Marken, Amy. "One of Knut Hamsun's Female Main Characters, Julie d'Espard." Scan 13:107-115. November 1974.
 VICTORIA
  Eddy, Beverley D. "Hamsun's VICTORIA and Munch's 'Livsfrisen': Variations on a Theme." SS 48:156-168. Spring 1976.

Hansen, Martin A.
 JONATAN'S JOURNEY
  Ingwersen, Faith and Niels. Martin A. Hansen. Boston: Twayne, 1976. pp. 45-58.
 THE LIAR
  Ingwersen, Faith and Niels. Martin A. Hansen. Boston: Twayne, 1976. pp. 111-129.

Schow, H. Wayne. "Kierkegaardian Perspectives in Martin A. Hansen's THE LIAR." Crit 15:53-64. No. 3, 1974.
### LUCKY KRISTOFFER
Ingwersen, Faith and Niels. Martin A. Hansen. Boston: Twayne, 1976. pp. 59-72.

## Heinesen, William
### THE BLACK POT
Brønner, Hedin. Three Faroese Novelists. New York: Twayne, 1973. pp. 53-58.

Jones, W. Glyn. William Heinesen. New York: Twayne, 1974. pp. 84-102.
### THE GOOD HOPE
Brønner, Hedin. Three Faroese Novelists. New York: Twayne, 1973. pp. 72-78.

Jones, W. Glyn. William Heinesen. New York: Twayne, 1974. pp. 140-161.
### THE LOST MUSICIANS
Brønner, Hedin. Three Faroese Novelists. New York: Twayne, 1973. pp. 58-64.

Jones, W. Glyn. William Heinesen. New York: Twayne, 1974. pp. 103-124.
### MOTHER PLEIADES
Jones, W. Glyn. William Heinesen. New York: Twayne, 1974. pp. 125-139.
### NOATUN
Brønner, Hedin. Three Faroese Novelists. New York: Twayne, 1973. pp. 48-53.

Jones, W. Glyn. "NOATUN and the Collective Novel." SS 41:217-230. August 1969.

_____. William Heinesen. New York: Twayne, 1974. pp. 68-83.
### STORMY DAYBREAK
Brønner, Hedin. Three Faroese Novelists. New York: Twayne, 1973. pp. 42-48.

Jones, W. Glyn. William Heinesen. New York: Twayne, 1974. pp. 48-67.
### TARNET VED VERDENS ENDE
Jones, W. Glyn. "William Heinesen's TARNET VED VERDENS ENDE: A Restatement and an Extension." SS 50:19-30. Winter 1978.

## Jacobsen, Hans Jacob
### FAIR PLAY
Brønner, Hedin. Three Faroese Novelists. New York: Twayne, 1973. pp. 97-101.

Jacobsen, Hans Jacob

FATHER-AND-SON JOURNEY
Brønner, Hedin. Three Faroese Novelists. New York: Twayne, 1973. pp. 101-108.
A FIRM GRIP ON LIFE
Brønner, Hedin. Three Faroese Novelists. New York: Twayne, 1973. pp. 91-97.
MIRAGE
Brønner, Hedin. Three Faroese Novelists. New York: Twayne, 1973. pp. 85-91.

Jacobsen, Jens Peter
MARIE GRUBBE
Ingwersen, Niels. "Problematic Protagonists: Marie Grubbe and Niels Lyhne." The Hero in Scandinavian Literature from Peer Gynt to the Present. ed. John M. Weinstock and Robert T. Rovinsky. Austin: University of Texas Press, 1975. pp. 41-60.
NIELS LYHNE
Ingwersen, Niels. "Problematic Protagonists: Marie Grubbe and Niels Lyhne." The Hero in Scandinavian Literature from Peer Gynt to the Present. ed. John M. Weinstock and Robert T. Rovinsky. Austin: University of Texas Press, 1975. pp. 41-60.

Macainsh, Noel. "The Nordic Mirror--Some Notes on Henry Handel Richardson and the Reception of NIELS LYHNE." LiNQ 5:12-18. No. 2, 1976.

_____. "The Shock of Recognition--Henry Handel Richardson and J. P. Jacobsen's NIELS LYHNE." Southerly 36:99-111. No. 1, 1976.

Jacobsen, Jørgen-Frantz
BARBARA
Brønner, Hedin. Three Faroese Novelists. New York: Twayne, 1973. pp. 25-37.

Jaeger, Frank
DEN UNGE JAEGERS LIDELSER
Hugus, Frank. "The Dilemma of the Artist in Selected Prose Works of Frank Jaeger." SS 47:52-65. Winter 1975.

Johnson, Eyvind
BOBINACK
Orton, Gavin. Eyvind Johnson. New York: Twayne, 1972. pp. 40-44.
THE CLOUDS OVER METAPONTION
Orton, Gavin. Eyvind Johnson. New York: Twayne, 1972. pp. 97-107.
COMMENTARY ON A FALLING STAR
Orton, Gavin. Eyvind Johnson. New York: Twayne, 1972. pp. 28-32.

THE DAYS OF HIS GRACE
    Orton, Gavin. Eyvind Johnson. New York: Twayne, 1972. pp. 115-124.
DREAMS OF ROSES AND FIRE
    Orton, Gavin. Eyvind Johnson. New York: Twayne, 1972. pp. 108-115.
KRILON
    Orton, Gavin. Eyvind Johnson. New York: Twayne, 1972. pp. 69-82.
LIFE'S LONG DAY
    Orton, Gavin. Eyvind Johnson. New York: Twayne, 1972. pp. 125-132.
NÅGRA STEG MOT TYSTNADEN
    Warme, Lars G. "Eyvind Johnson's NÅGRA STEG MOT TYSTNADEN: An Apologia." SS 49:452-463. Autumn 1977.
NIGHT MANEUVERS
    Orton, Gavin. Eyvind Johnson. New York: Twayne, 1972. pp. 48-52.
THE NOVEL ABOUT OLAF
    Orton, Gavin. Eyvind Johnson. New York: Twayne, 1972. pp. 55-65.
PUT AWAY THE SUN
    Orton, Gavin. Eyvind Johnson. New York: Twayne, 1972. pp. 133-138.
RAIN AT DAWN
    Orton, Gavin. Eyvind Johnson. New York: Twayne, 1972. pp. 44-47.
THE SWELL ON THE BEACHES
    Orton, Gavin. Eyvind Johnson. New York: Twayne, 1972. pp. 84-97; 143-147.
TOWN IN DARKNESS
    Orton, Gavin. Eyvind Johnson. New York: Twayne, 1972. pp. 23-27.

Jörgensen, Johannes
    OUR LADY OF DENMARK
        Jones, W. Glyn. Johannes Jörgensen. New York: Twayne, 1969. pp. 54-58.
    SPRING LEGEND
        Jones, W. Glyn. Johannes Jörgensen. New York: Twayne, 1969. pp. 31-35.
    A STRANGER
        Jones, W. Glyn. Johannes Jörgensen. New York: Twayne, 1969. pp. 36-39.
    SUMMER
        Jones, W. Glyn. Johannes Jörgensen. New York: Twayne, 1969. pp. 39-45.
    THE TREE OF LIFE
        Jones, W. Glyn. Johannes Jörgensen. New York: Twayne, 1969. pp. 45-48.

Kristensen, Tom
    HAERVAERK

Byram, M. S. "The Reality of Tom Kristensen's HAERVAERK." Scan 15:29-36. May 1976.

LIVETS ARABESK

Byram, Michael. "Tom Kristensen's LIVETS ARABESK Seen as a Political Gesture." Scan 16:109-118. November 1977.

# Lagerkvist, Pär
BARABBAS

Sjöberg, Leif. Pär Lagerkvist. New York: Columbia University Press, 1976. pp. 29-33.

Spector, Robert Donald. Pär Lagerkvist. New York: Twayne, 1973. pp. 64-81.

THE DEATH OF AHASUERUS

Spector, Robert Donald. Pär Lagerkvist. New York: Twayne, 1973. pp. 100-112.

THE DWARF

Ramsey, Roger. "Pär Vagerkvist [sic]: THE DWARF and Dogma." Mosaic 5:97-106. Spring 1972.

Sjöberg, Leif. Pär Lagerkvist. New York: Columbia University Press, 1976. pp. 25-29.

Spector, Robert Donald. Pär Lagerkvist. New York: Twayne, 1973. pp. 45-63.

Swanson, Roy Arthur. "Lagerkvist's Dwarf and the Redemption of Evil." Discourse 13:192-209. Spring 1970.

THE ETERNAL SMILE

Sjöberg, Leif. Pär Lagerkvist. New York: Columbia University Press, 1976. pp. 14-18.

Spector, Robert Donald. Pär Lagerkvist. New York: Twayne, 1973. pp. 37-39.

THE HANGMAN

Ellestad, Everett M. "Lagerkvist and Cubism: A Study of Theory and Practice." SS 45:41-45. Winter 1973.

Sjöberg, Leif. Pär Lagerkvist. New York: Columbia University Press, 1976. pp. 21-25.

Spector, Robert Donald. Pär Lagerkvist. New York: Twayne, 1973. pp. 41-44.

THE HOLY LAND

Spector, Robert Donald. Pär Lagerkvist. New York: Twayne, 1973. pp. 118-126.

MARIAMNE

Scobbie, Irene. "An Interpretation of Lagerkvist's MARIAMNE." SS 45:128-134. Spring 1973.

Spector, Robert Donald. Pär Lagerkvist. New York: Twayne, 1973. pp. 127-136.

THE PILGRIM
　　Ellestad, Everett M. "Lagerkvist and Cubism: A
　　Study of Theory and Practice." SS 45:47-52. Winter
　　1973.

　　　　Spector, Robert Donald. Pär Lagerkvist. New York:
　　　　Twayne, 1973. pp. 99-126.
　　THE SIBYL
　　　　Spector, Robert Donald. Pär Lagerkvist. New York:
　　　　Twayne, 1973. pp. 82-98.

Lagerlöf, Selma
　　THE STORY OF GOSTA BERLING
　　　　Danielson, Larry W. "The Uses of Demonic Folk Tradition in Selma Lagerlöf's GÖSTA BERLINGS SAGA."
　　　　WF 34:187-199. July 1975.

Laxness, Halldór Kiljan
　　THE ATOM STATION
　　　　Hallberg, Peter. Halldór Laxness. New York: Twayne,
　　　　1971. pp. 156-164.
　　THE BEAUTY OF THE SKIES
　　　　Hallberg, Peter. Halldór Laxness. New York: Twayne,
　　　　1971. pp. 122-131.
　　THE BELL OF ICELAND
　　　　Hallberg, Peter. "The Dialogue in ISLANDSKLUKKAN."
　　　　Scan 11:33-44. May 1972.

　　　　_____. Halldór Laxness. New York: Twayne, 1971.
　　　　pp. 144-155.
　　THE HAPPY WARRIORS
　　　　Hallberg, Peter. Halldór Laxness. New York: Twayne,
　　　　1971. pp. 165-179.

　　　　McTurk, R.W. "Swift, Laxness, and the Eskimos."
　　　　Scan 10:45-62. Supplement 1972.
　　THE HOUSE OF THE POET
　　　　Hallberg, Peter. Halldór Laxness. New York: Twayne,
　　　　1971. pp. 120-131.
　　INDEPENDENT PEOPLE
　　　　Hallberg, Peter. Halldór Laxness. New York: Twayne,
　　　　1971. pp. 93-116.
　　THE LIGHT OF THE WORLD
　　　　Hallberg, Peter. Halldór Laxness. New York: Twayne,
　　　　1971. pp. 124-131.

　　　　Nedelyaeva-Steponavichiene, Svetlana. "On the Style of
　　　　Laxness' Tetralogy: WORLD LIGHT." Scan 10:71-87.
　　　　Supplement 1972.
　　A LOCAL CHRONICLE
　　　　Sørensen, Preben Meulengracht. "Being Faithful to
　　　　Oneself." Scan 10:89-100. Supplement 1972.
　　THE PALACE OF THE SUMMERLAND

Hallberg, Peter. Halldór Laxness. New York: Twayne, 1971. pp. 124-131.
SALKA VALKA
Hallberg, Peter. Halldór Laxness. New York: Twayne, 1971. pp. 68-92.

Markey, T. L. "SALKA VALKA: A Study in Social Realism." Scan 10:63-69. Supplement 1972.

Lidman, Sara
BARA MISTEL
Borland, Harold H. "Sara Lidman's Progress: A Critical Survey of Six Novels." SS 39:105-107. May 1967.
HJORTRONLANDET
Borland, Harold H. "Sara Lidman's Progress: A Critical Survey of Six Novels." SS 39:101-102. May 1967.
JAG OCH MIN SON
Borland, Harold H. "Sara Lidman's Progress: A Critical Survey of Six Novels." SS 39:107-111. May 1967.
MED FEM DIAMANTER
Borland, Harold H. "Sara Lidman's Progress: A Critical Survey of Six Novels." SS 39:111-114. May 1967.
REGNSPIRAN
Borland, Harold H. "Sara Lidman's Progress: A Critical Survey of Six Novels." SS 39:102-105. May 1967.
TJARDALEN
Borland, Harold H. "Sara Lidman's Progress: A Critical Survey of Six Novels." SS 39:97-100. May 1967.

Lie, Jonas
ADAM SCHRADER
Lyngstad, Sverre. Jonas Lie. Boston: Twayne, 1977. pp. 50-55.
THE BARQUE "FUTURE"
Lyngstad, Sverre. Jonas Lie. Boston: Twayne, 1977. pp. 36-40.
THE COMMODORE'S DAUGHTERS
Lyngstad, Sverre. Jonas Lie. Boston: Twayne, 1977. pp. 88-94.
DYRE REIN
Lyngstad, Sverre. Jonas Lie. Boston: Twayne, 1977. pp. 140-149.
EAST OF THE SUN, WEST OF THE MOON, AND BEHIND THE TOWER OF BABEL
Lyngstad, Sverre. Jonas Lie. Boston: Twayne, 1977. pp. 167-173.
EVIL POWERS

Lyngstad, Sverre. Jonas Lie. Boston: Twayne, 1977.
pp. 104-111.
THE FAMILY AT GILJE
Lyngstad, Sverre. Jonas Lie. Boston: Twayne, 1977.
pp. 72-84.
FASTE FORLAND
Lyngstad, Sverre. Jonas Lie. Boston: Twayne, 1977.
pp. 149-153.
GO ONWARD
Lyngstad, Sverre. Jonas Lie. Boston: Twayne, 1977.
pp. 60-65.
MAELSTROM
Lyngstad, Sverre. Jonas Lie. Boston: Twayne, 1977.
pp. 83-88.
MAISA JONS
Lyngstad, Sverre. Jonas Lie. Boston: Twayne, 1977.
pp. 100-103.
A MARRIAGE
Lyngstad, Sverre. Jonas Lie. Boston: Twayne, 1977.
pp. 94-99.
NIOBE
Lyngstad, Sverre. Jonas Lie. Boston: Twayne, 1977.
pp. 125-134.
THE PILOT AND HIS WIFE
Lyngstad, Sverre. Jonas Lie. Boston: Twayne, 1977.
pp. 40-45.
RUTLAND
Lyngstad, Sverre. Jonas Lie. Boston: Twayne, 1977.
pp. 56-60.
THE SLAVE OF LIFE
Lyngstad, Sverre. Jonas Lie. Boston: Twayne, 1977.
pp. 67-72.
THOMAS ROSS
Lyngstad, Sverre. Jonas Lie. Boston: Twayne, 1977.
pp. 46-50.
THE ULFVUNGS
Lyngstad, Sverre. Jonas Lie. Boston: Twayne, 1977.
pp. 162-167.
THE VISIONARY
Lyngstad, Sverre. Jonas Lie. Boston: Twayne, 1977.
pp. 24-34.
WHEN THE IRON CURTAIN FALLS
Lyngstad, Sverre. Jonas Lie. Boston: Twayne, 1977.
pp. 154-161.
WHEN THE SUN SETS
Lyngstad, Sverre. Jonas Lie. Boston: Twayne, 1977.
pp. 135-140.

Lind, Jakov
   SOUL OF WOOD
      Karpowitz, Stephen. "Conscience and Cannibals: An Essay on Two Exemplary Tales--SOUL OF WOOD and THE PAWNBROKER." PsyR 64:46-51. Spring 1977.

Moberg, Vilhelm
SOLDAT MED BRUTET GEVAR
Orton, Gavin and Philip Holmes. "Memoirs of an Idealist: Vilhelm Moberg's SOLDAT MED BRUTET GEVAR." SS 48:29-51. Winter 1976.

Olsson, Hagar
CHITAMBO
Schoolfield, George C. "Hagar Olsson's CHITAMBO: Anniversary Thoughts on Names and Structure." SS 45:223-262. Summer 1973.

Pontoppidan, Henrik
THE KINGDOM OF THE DEAD
Mitchell, P. M. Henrik Pontoppidan. Boston: Twayne, 1979. pp. 115-123.

Ober, Kenneth H. "The Incomplete Self in Pontoppidan's DE DODES RIGE." SS 50:396-402. Autumn 1978.
LUCKY PETER
Bredsdorff, Elias. "Georg Brandes as a Fictional Character in Some Danish Novels and Plays." SS 45:18-26. Winter 1973.

Mitchell, P. M. Henrik Pontoppidan. Boston: Twayne, 1979. pp. 83-111.
MAN'S HEAVEN
Mitchell, P. M. Henrik Pontoppidan. Boston: Twayne, 1979. pp. 125-127.
THE PROMISED LAND
Mitchell, P. M. Henrik Pontoppidan. Boston: Twayne, 1979. pp. 61-74.
SANDINGE PARISH
Mitchell, P. M. Henrik Pontoppidan. Boston: Twayne, 1979. pp. 29-34.

Schack, Hans Egede
PHANTASTERNE
Jorgensen, Aage. "Hans Egede Schack's PHANTASTERNE." FMLS 6:173-176. April 1970.

Söderberg, Hjalmar
DOCTOR GLAS
Merrill, Reed. "Ethical Murder and DOCTOR GLAS." Mosaic 12:47-59. Summer 1979.

Strindberg, August
ALONE
Johannesson, Eric O. The Novels of August Strindberg: A Study in Theme and Structure. Berkeley: University of California Press, 1968. pp. 210-226.

Johnson, Walter. August Strindberg. Boston: Twayne, 1976. pp. 55-57.

BLACK BANNERS
    Johannesson, Eric O. The Novels of August Strindberg: A Study in Theme and Structure. Berkeley: University of California Press, 1968. pp. 227-245.

    Johnson, Walter. August Strindberg. Boston: Twayne, 1976. pp. 119-122.

    Steene, Birgitta. The Greatest Fire: A Study of August Strindberg. Carbondale: Southern Illinois University Press, 1973. pp. 147-150.

BY THE OPEN SEA
    Johannesson, Eric O. The Novels of August Strindberg: A Study in Theme and Structure. Berkeley: University of California Press, 1968. pp. 146-171.

    Johnson, Walter. August Strindberg. Boston: Twayne, 1976. pp. 114-116.

    Steene, Birgitta. The Greatest Fire: A Study of August Strindberg. Carbondale: Southern Illinois University Press, 1973. pp. 38-40.

INFERNO
    Johannesson, Eric O. The Novels of August Strindberg: A Study in Theme and Structure. Berkeley: University of California Press, 1968. pp. 172-209.

    Johnson, Walter. August Strindberg. Boston: Twayne, 1976. pp. 47-51.

    Steene, Birgitta. The Greatest Fire: A Study of August Strindberg. Carbondale: Southern Illinois University Press, 1973. pp. 76-78.

A MADMAN'S DEFENSE
    Johannesson, Eric O. The Novels of August Strindberg: A Study in Theme and Structure. Berkeley: University of California Press, 1968. pp. 91-108.

    Johnson, Walter. August Strindberg. Boston: Twayne, 1976. pp. 44-47.

    Steene, Birgitta. The Greatest Fire: A Study of August Strindberg. Carbondale: Southern Illinois University Press, 1973. pp. 31-33.

THE PEOPLE OF HEMSO
    Johannesson, Eric O. The Novels of August Strindberg: A Study in Theme and Structure. Berkeley: University of California Press, 1968. pp. 82-90.

    Johnson, Walter. August Strindberg. Boston: Twayne, 1976. pp. 110-112.

    Steene, Birgitta. The Greatest Fire: A Study of Au-

gust Strindberg. Carbondale: Southern Illinois University Press, 1973. pp. 33-37.
PROGRESS
Johannesson, Eric O. The Novels of August Strindberg: A Study in Theme and Structure. Berkeley: University of California Press, 1968. pp. 46-54.
THE RED ROOM
Johannesson, Eric O. The Novels of August Strindberg: A Study in Theme and Structure. Berkeley: University of California Press, 1968. pp. 25-45.

Johnson, Walter. August Strindberg. Boston: Twayne, 1976. pp. 100-102.

Steene, Birgitta. The Greatest Fire: A Study of August Strindberg. Carbondale: Southern Illinois University Press, 1973. pp. 16-22.
THE ROMANTIC ORGANIST ON RANO
Carlson, Harry G. "Ambiguity and Archetypes in Strindberg's ROMANTIC ORGANIST." SS 48:256-271. Summer 1976.

Johannesson, Eric O. The Novels of August Strindberg: A Study in Theme and Structure. Berkeley: University of California Press, 1968. pp. 109-120.
THE ROOFING FEAST
Johannesson, Eric O. The Novels of August Strindberg: A Study in Theme and Structure. Berkeley: University of California Press, 1968. pp. 246-266.

Johnson, Walter. August Strindberg. Boston: Twayne, 1976. pp. 122-124.
THE SCAPEGOAT
Johannesson, Eric O. The Novels of August Strindberg: A Study in Theme and Structure. Berkeley: University of California Press, 1968. pp. 267-294.

Johnson, Walter. August Strindberg. Boston: Twayne, 1976. pp. 124-126.

Steene, Birgitta. The Greatest Fire: A Study of August Strindberg. Carbondale: Southern Illinois University Press, 1973. pp. 153-155.
THE SON OF A SERVANT
Johannesson, Eric O. The Novels of August Strindberg: A Study in Theme and Structure. Berkeley: University of California Press, 1968. pp. 55-81.

Johnson, Walter. August Strindberg. Boston: Twayne, 1976. pp. 36-42.

Steene, Birgitta. The Greatest Fire: A Study of August Strindberg. Carbondale: Southern Illinois University Press, 1973. pp. 27-31.

TSCHANDALA
> Johannesson, Eric O. The Novels of August Strindberg: A Study in Theme and Structure. Berkeley: University of California Press, 1968. pp. 121-133.

A WITCH
> Johannesson, Eric O. The Novels of August Strindberg: A Study in Theme and Structure. Berkeley: University of California Press, 1968. pp. 134-145.

Undset, Sigrid

THE BRIDAL WREATH
> Bayerschmidt, Carl F. Sigrid Undset. New York: Twayne, 1970. pp. 91-96.

THE BURNING BUSH
> Bayerschmidt, Carl F. Sigrid Undset. New York: Twayne, 1970. pp. 128-137.

THE CROSS
> Bayerschmidt, Carl F. Sigrid Undset. New York: Twayne, 1970. pp. 99-104.

THE FAITHFUL WIFE
> Bayerschmidt, Carl F. Sigrid Undset. New York: Twayne, 1970. pp. 143-147.

IDA ELISABETH
> Bayerschmidt, Carl F. Sigrid Undset. New York: Twayne, 1970. pp. 137-143.

JENNY
> Bayerschmidt, Carl F. Sigrid Undset. New York: Twayne, 1970. pp. 68-74.

KRISTIN LAVRANSDATTER
> Bayerschmidt, Carl F. Sigrid Undset. New York: Twayne, 1970. pp. 91-111.

MADAME DOROTHEA
> Bayerschmidt, Carl F. Sigrid Undset. New York: Twayne, 1970. pp. 147-153.

THE MASTER OF HESTVIKEN
> Dunn, Margaret Mary. "THE MASTER OF HESTVIKEN: A New Reading, II." SS 40:210-224. August 1968.

THE MISTRESS OF HUSABY
> Bayerschmidt, Carl F. Sigrid Undset. New York: Twayne, 1970. pp. 96-99.

MRS. MARTA OULIE
> Bayerschmidt, Carl F. Sigrid Undset. New York: Twayne, 1970. pp. 55-58.

SPRING
> Bayerschmidt, Carl F. Sigrid Undset. New York: Twayne, 1970. pp. 77-81.

THE WILD ORCHID
> Bayerschmidt, Carl F. Sigrid Undset. New York: Twayne, 1970. pp. 128-137.

## THE RUSSIAN AND EAST EUROPEAN NOVEL

Andreyev, Leonid
    JUDAS ISCARIOT
        Woodward, James B. Leonid Andreyev: A Study. Oxford: Clarendon, 1969. pp. 168-178.
    THE RED LAUGH
        Davis, Ruth. The Great Books of Russia. Norman: University of Oklahoma Press, 1968. pp. 351-354.

        Woodward, James B. Leonid Andreyev: A Study. Oxford: Clarendon, 1969. pp. 98-107.
    THE STORY OF SEVEN WHO WERE HANGED
        Woodward, James B. Leonid Andreyev: A Study. Oxford: Clarendon, 1969. pp. 190-199.

Andrić, Ivo
    BRIDGE ON THE DRINA
        Matejic, Mateja. "Elements of Folklore in Andrić's NA DRINI CUPRIJA." CSP 20:348-357. September 1978.

        Moravcevich, Nicholas. "Ivo Andrić and the Quintessence of Time." SEEJ 16:313-318. Fall 1972.
    DEVIL'S YARD
        Coote, Mary P. "Narrative and Narrative Structure in Ivo Andrić's DEVIL'S YARD." SEEJ 21:56-63. Spring 1977.
    TRAVNIK CHRONICLE
        Ferguson, Alan. "Public and Private Worlds in TRAVNIK CHRONICLE." MLR 70:830-838. October 1975.

Andrzejewski, Jerzy
    ASHES AND DIAMOND
        Krzyżanowski, Jerzy R. "On the History of ASHES AND DIAMOND." SEEJ 15:324-331. Fall 1971.

Babel, Izaak
    RED CAVALRY
        Davies, Norman. "Izaak Babel's KONARMIYA Stories, and the Polish-Soviet War." MLR 67:845-857. October 1972.

        Falchikov, Michael. "Conflict and Contrast in Isaak

Babel's KONARMIYA." MLR 72:125-133. January 1977.

Hallett, Richard. Isaac Babel. New York: Ungar, 1973. pp. 32-43.

Iribarne, Louis. "Babel's RED CAVALRY as a Baroque Novel." ConL 14:58-77. Winter 1973.

Klotz, Martin B. "Poetry of the Present: Isaak Babel's RED CAVALRY." SEEJ 18:160-169. Summer 1974.

Lee, Alice. "Epiphany in Babel's RED CAVALRY." RLT 2:249-260. May 1972.

Luplow, Carol. "Paradox and the Search for Value in Babel's RED CAVALRY." SEEJ 23:216-232. Summer 1979.

Mathewson, Rufus W., Jr. The Positive Hero in Russian Literature. Stanford: Stanford University Press, 1975. pp. 201-204.

Thomson, Boris. Lot's Wife & the Venus of Milo: Conflicting Attitudes to the Cultural Heritage in Modern Russia. Cambridge: Cambridge University Press, 1978. pp. 109-113.

Voronskij, Aleksandr. "Isaac Babel." Twentieth-Century Russian Literary Criticism. ed. Victor Erlich. New Haven: Yale University Press, 1975. pp. 189-196.

Williams, Gareth. "Two Leitmotifs in Babel's KONARMIJA." WSl 17:308-317. No. 2, 1972.

Belyj, Andrej
    FOUR SYMPHONIES

Cioran, Samuel D. The Apocalyptic Symbolism of Andrej Belyj. The Hague: Mouton, 1973. pp. 70-91.

Janecek, Gerald. "Literature as Music: Symphonic Form in Andrei Belyi's FOURTH SYMPHONY." CASS 8:501-512. Winter 1974.

Kovac, Anton. "Belyj's Symphony No. 3." NZSJ 12:27-68. Summer 1973.

    KOTIK LETAEV

Anschuetz, Carol. "Recollection as Metaphor in KOTIK LETAEV." RusL 4:345-354. October 1976.

Cioran, Samuel D. The Apocalyptic Symbolism of Andrej Belyj. The Hague: Mouton, 1973. pp. 160-179.

_____. "The Eternal Return: Andrej Belyj's KOTIK LETAEV." SEEJ 15:22-37. Spring 1971.

Hart, Pierre. "Psychological Primitivism in KOTIK LETAEV." RLT 4:319-330. 1972.

Janecek, Gerald. "An Acoustico-Semantic Complex in Belyj's KOTIK LETAEV." SEEJ 18:153-159. Summer 1974.

_____. "Anthroposophy in KOTIK LETAEV." OL 29:245-267. 1974.

_____. "The Spiral as Image and Structural Principle in Andrej Belyj's KOTIK LETAEV." RusL 4:357-363. October 1976.

MASKI
Steinberg, Ada. "Colour and the Embodiment of Theme in Bely's 'Urbanistic' Novels." SEER 57:208-213. April 1979.

MOSCOW
Elsworth, John D. "Bely's MOSCOW Novels." Andrey Bely: A Critical Review. ed. Gerald Janecek. Lexington: University Press of Kentucky, 1978. pp. 128-134.

Steinberg, Ada. "Colour and the Embodiment of Theme in Bely's 'Urbanistic' Novels." SEER 57:201-208. April 1979.

PETERSBURG
Berberova, Nina. "A Memoir and a Comment: The 'Circle' of PETERSBURG." Andrey Bely: A Critical Review. ed. Gerald Janecek. Lexington: University Press of Kentucky, 1978. pp. 115-120.

Cioran, Samuel D. The Apocalyptic Symbolism of Andrej Belyj. The Hague: Mouton, 1973. pp. 137-159.

Doležel, Lubomír. "The Visible and the Invisible Petersburg." RusL 7:465-489. September 1979.

Hartmann-Flyer, Helene. "The Time Bomb." Andrey Bely: A Critical Review. ed. Gerald Janecek. Lexington: University Press of Kentucky, 1978. pp. 121-126.

Kellman, Steven G. "Circles, Squares, and the Mind's Ear in ST. PETERSBURG." PLL 14:464-469. Fall 1978.

Lottridge, Stephen S. "Andrej Belyj's PETERBURG: The City and the Family." RusL 6:175-196. April 1978.

Mochulsky, Konstantin. Andrei Bely: His Life and Works. Ann Arbor: Ardis, 1977. pp. 147-172.

Steinberg, Ada. "Colour and the Embodiment of Theme in Bely's 'Urbanistic' Novels." SEER 57:195-201. April 1979.

_____. "Fragmentary 'Prototypes' in Andrey Bely's Novel PETERBURG." SEER 56:522-545. October 1978.

_____. "On the Structure of Parody in Andrej Belyj's PETERBURG." Slavica Hierosolymitana 1:132-157. 1977.

Woronzoff, Alexander. "Andrej Belyj's PETERBURG, James Joyce's ULYSSES, and the Stream-of-Consciousness Method." RLJ 30:101-106. Fall 1976.

THE SILVER DOVE
Beyer, Thomas R., Jr. "Andrej Belyj's 'The Magic of Words' and THE SILVER DOVE." SEEJ 22:464-472. Winter 1978.

_____. "Belyj's SEREBRJANYJ GOLUB': Gogol' in Gugolevo." RLJ 30:79-86. Fall 1976.

Cioran, Samuel D. The Apocalyptic Symbolism of Andrej Belyj. The Hague: Mouton, 1973. pp. 112-136.

Elsworth, J.D. "THE SILVER DOVE: An Analysis." RusL 4:365-391. October 1976.

Mochulsky, Konstantin. Andrei Bely: His Life and Works. Ann Arbor: Ardis, 1977. pp. 137-146.

ZAPISKI CHUDAKA
Cioran, Samuel D. The Apocalyptic Symbolism of Andrej Belyj. The Hague: Mouton, 1973. pp. 180-195.

_____. "In the Imitation of Christ: A Study of Andrei Belyi's ZAPISKI CHUDAKA." CSS 4:74-92. Spring 1970.

Bogdanov, A.A.
RED STAR
Lewis, Kathleen and Harry Weber. "Zamyatin's WE, the Proletarian Poets, and Bogdanov's RED STAR." RLT 12:266-276. 1975.

Bondarev, Yuri
THE SHORE
Kuznetsov, Felix. "Yuri Bondarev's Latest Novel." SovL 4:145-148. 1976.

Shneidman, N.N. Soviet Literature in the 1970's: Artistic Diversity and Ideological Conformity. Toronto: University of Toronto Press, 1979. pp. 57-59.

Borshchagovsky, Alexander
WHERE THE BLACKSMITH SETTLES

"Discussion of the Novel, WHERE THE BLACKSMITH SETTLES." SovL 1:161-165. 1977.

Bulgakov, Mixail
THE FATAL EGGS
McLaughlin, Sigrid. "Structure and Meaning in Bulgakov's THE FATAL EGGS." RLT 15:263-278. 1978.

Wright, A. Colin. Mikhail Bulgakov: Life and Interpretations. Toronto: University of Toronto Press, 1978. pp. 54-57.

THE HEART OF A DOG
Burgin, Diana L. "Bulgakov's Early Tragedy of the Scientist-Creator: An Interpretation of THE HEART OF A DOG." SEEJ 22:494-508. Winter 1978.

Goscilo, Helena. "Point of View in Bulgakov's HEART OF A DOG." RLT 15:281-290. 1978.

THE MASTER AND MARGARITA
Bagby, Lewis. "Eternal Themes in Mixail Bulgakov's THE MASTER AND MARGARITA." IFR 1:27-31. January 1974.

Beatie, Bruce A. and Phyllis Powell. "Story and Symbol: Notes Toward a Structural Analysis of Bulgakov's THE MASTER AND MARGARITA." RLT 15:219-251. 1978.

Beaujour, Elizabeth Klosty. "The Use of Witches in Fedin and Bulgakov." SlavR 33:695-705. December 1974.

Bolen, Val. "Theme and Coherence in Bulgakov's THE MASTER AND MARGARITA." SEEJ 16:427-437. Winter 1972.

Chudakova, M. "THE MASTER AND MARGARITA: The Development of a Novel." RLT 15:177-207. 1978.

Delaney, Joan. "THE MASTER AND MARGARITA: The Reach Exceeds the Grasp." SlavR 31:89-100. March 1972.

Haber, Edythe C. "The Mythic Structure of Bulgakov's THE MASTER AND MARGARITA." RusR 34:382-409. October 1975.

Hart, Pierre R. "THE MASTER AND MARGARITA as Creative Process." MFS 19:169-178. Summer 1973.

Ilgner, Richard. "Goethe's 'Geist, der stets verneint,' and Its Emergence in the Faust Works of Odoevsky, Lunacharsky, and Bulgakov." GSlav 2:178-180. Spring 1977.

Kejna-Sharratt, Barbara. "Narrative Techniques in THE MASTER AND MARGARITA." CSP 16:1-12. Spring 1974.

Lakshin, Vladimir. "Mikhail Bulgakov's THE MASTER AND MARGARITA." Twentieth-Century Russian Literary Criticism. ed. Victor Erlich. New Haven: Yale University Press, 1975. pp. 247-283.

Leatherbarrow, W. J. "The Devil and the Creative Visionary in Bulgakov's MASTER I MARGARITA." NZSJ 1: 29-43. 1975.

Lowe, David. "Bulgakov and Dostoevsky: A Tale of Two Ivans." RLT 15:253-262. 1978.

Mahlow, Elena N. Bulgakov's THE MASTER AND MARGARITA: The Text as a Cipher. New York: Vantage, 1975. 187 pp.

Pearce, C. E. "A Closer Look at Narrative Structure in Bulgakov's THE MASTER AND MARGARITA." CSP 22:358-371. September 1980.

Piper, D. G. B. "An Approach to Bulgakov's THE MASTER AND MARGARITA." FMLS 7:134-157. April 1971.

Pope, Richard W. F. "Ambiguity and Meaning in THE MASTER AND MARGARITA: The Role of Afranius." SlavR 36:1-24. March 1977.

Prizel, Yuri. "M. Bulgakov's MASTER I MARGARITA: The True Absolute." RLJ 30:109-117. Fall 1976.

Proffer, Ellendea. "On THE MASTER AND MARGARITA." RLT 6:533-564. 1973.

Rzhevsky, L. "Pilate's Sin: Cryptography in Bulgakov's Novel, THE MASTER AND MARGARITA." CSP 13:1-19. Spring 1971.

Stenbock-Fermor, Elisabeth. "Bulgakov's THE MASTER AND MARGARITA and Goethe's FAUST." SEEJ 13:309-325. Fall 1969.

Wright, A. C. "Satan in Moscow: An Approach to Bulgakov's THE MASTER AND MARGARITA." PMLA 88: 1162-1172. October 1973.

Zigelis, Andrew. "Bulgakov's MASTER I MARGARITA: Three Types of Reductive Ambiguity." RLJ 30:119-128. Fall 1976.

ROKOVYE IAITSA

Doyle, Peter. "Bulgakov's Satirical View of Revolution in ROKOVYE and SOBACH'E SERDTSE." CSP 20:468-475. December 1978.
### SOBACH'E SERDTSE
Doyle, Peter. "Bulgakov's Satirical View of Revolution in ROKOVYE and SOBACH'E SERDTSE." CSP 20:475-481. December 1978.

Graham, Sheelagh Duffin. "Bulgakov's SOBACH'E SERDTSE: A Polemical 'Povest'.'" JRS 33:27-31. 1977.
### TEATRAL'NYY ROMAN
Doyle, Peter. "Bulgakov's Revenge on Stanislavsky: TEATRAL'NYY ROMAN." NZSJ 1:61-86. No. 1, 1976.
### THE WHITE GUARD
Pertsov, Victor. "Two Novels About Nineteen-Eighteen --Alexei Tolstoy and Mikhail Bulgakov." SovL 1:158-162. 1968.

Schultze, Sydney. "The Epigraphs in WHITE GUARD." RLT 15:213-217. 1978.

Wright, A. Colin. Mikhail Bulgakov: Life and Interpretations. Toronto: University of Toronto Press, 1978. pp. 65-80.

## Bulgarin, Faddei
### IVAN VYZHIGIN
Alkire, Gilman H. "Gogol and Bulgarin's IVAN VYZHIGIN." SlavR 28:289-296. June 1969.

## Bunin, Ivan
### THE BROTHERS
Woodward, James B. Ivan Bunin: A Study of His Fiction. Chapel Hill: University of North Carolina Press, 1980. pp. 107-120.
### DARK ALLEYS
Kryzytski, Serge. The Works of Ivan Bunin. The Hague: Mouton, 1971. pp. 204-214.
### DEREVNJA
Marullo, Thomas Gaiton. "Ivan Bunin's DEREVNJA: The Demythologization of the Peasant." RLJ 31:79-96. Spring 1977.
### DRY VALLEY
Kryzytski, Serge. The Works of Ivan Bunin. The Hague: Mouton, 1971. pp. 99-102.

Marullo, Thomas Gaiton. "Bunin's DRY VALLEY: The Russian Novel in Transition from Realism to Modernism." FMLS 14:193-205. July 1978.

Woodward, James B. Ivan Bunin: A Study of His Fiction. Chapel Hill: University of North Carolina Press, 1980. pp. 62-67.

THE GENTLEMAN FROM SAN FRANCISCO
    Woodward, James B.  Ivan Bunin: A Study of His Fiction.  Chapel Hill: University of North Carolina Press, 1980.  pp. 126-134.

THE LIFE OF ARSENYEV
    Woodward, James B.  Ivan Bunin: A Study of His Fiction.  Chapel Hill: University of North Carolina Press, 1980.  pp. 174-181.

MITYA'S LOVE
    Kryzytski, Serge.  The Works of Ivan Bunin.  The Hague: Mouton, 1971.  pp. 169-178.

    Woodward, James B.  Ivan Bunin: A Study of His Fiction.  Chapel Hill: University of North Carolina Press, 1980.  pp. 187-195.

THE VILLAGE
    Kryzytski, Serge.  The Works of Ivan Bunin.  The Hague: Mouton, 1971.  pp. 66-84.

    Woodward, James B.  Ivan Bunin: A Study of His Fiction.  Chapel Hill: University of North Carolina Press, 1980.  pp. 48-62; 79-95.

Chekhov, Anton
    THE BISHOP
        Nilsson, Nils Åke.  Studies in Cechov's Narrative Technique: THE STEPPE and THE BISHOP.  Stockholm: Almqvist & Wiksell, 1968.  pp. 62-109.

    THE BLACK MONK
        *Winner, Thomas.  Chekhov and His Prose.  New York: Holt, Rinehart & Winston, 1966.  pp. 113-122.

    A DREARY STORY
        Hahn, Beverly.  Chekhov: A Study of the Major Stories and Plays.  London: Cambridge University Press, 1977.  pp. 156-177.

        Kramer, Karl D.  The Chameleon and the Dream: The Image of Reality in Cexov's Stories.  The Hague: Mouton, 1970.  pp. 106-113.

        Rayfield, Donald.  Chekhov: The Evolution of His Art.  London: Elek, 1975.  pp. 87-92.

        *Winner, Thomas.  Chekhov and His Prose.  New York: Holt, Rinehart & Winston, 1966.  pp. 91-97.

    THE DUEL
        Hahn, Beverly.  Chekhov: A Study of the Major Stories and Plays.  London: Cambridge University Press, 1977.  pp. 178-200.

        Rayfield, Donald.  Chekhov: The Evolution of His Art.  London: Elek, 1975.  pp. 119-124.

*Winner, Thomas. Chekhov and His Prose. New York: Holt, Rinehart & Winston, 1966. pp. 100-107.
THE HOUSE WITH THE MEZZANINE
Rayfield, Donald. Chekhov: The Evolution of His Art. London: Elek, 1975. pp. 156-162.
IN THE RAVINE
Rayfield, Donald. Chekhov: The Evolution of His Art. London: Elek, 1975. pp. 181-185.

*Winner, Thomas. Chekhov and His Prose. New York: Holt, Rinehart & Winston, 1966. pp. 155-161.
THE LADY WITH THE DOG
Smith, Virginia Llewellyn. Anton Chekhov and the Lady with the Dog. London: Oxford University Press, 1973. pp. 212-218.
MURDER
Rayfield, Donald. Chekhov: The Evolution of His Art. London: Elek, 1975. pp. 171-177.
MY LIFE
Rayfield, Donald. Chekhov: The Evolution of His Art. London: Elek, 1975. pp. 162-170.

*Winner, Thomas. Chekhov and His Prose. New York: Holt, Rinehart & Winston, 1966. pp. 142-150.
PEASANTS
Rayfield, Donald. Chekhov: The Evolution of His Art. London: Elek, 1975. pp. 177-181.

Speirs, Logan. Tolstoy and Chekhov. Cambridge: The University Press, 1971. pp. 162-166.

*Winner, Thomas. Chekhov and His Prose. New York: Holt, Rinehart & Winston, 1966. pp. 150-154.
THE STEPPE
Hahn, Beverly. Chekhov: A Study of the Major Stories and Plays. London: Cambridge University Press, 1977. pp. 97-102.

Katsell, Jerome H. "Cexov's THE STEPPE Revisited." SEEJ 22:313-323. Fall 1978.

Kramer, Karl D. The Chameleon and the Dream: The Image of Reality in Cexov's Stories. The Hague: Mouton, 1970. pp. 86-93.

Nilsson, Nils Åke. Studies in Cechov's Narrative Technique: THE STEPPE and THE BISHOP. Stockholm: Almqvist & Wiksell, 1968. pp. 5-48.

Rayfield, Donald. Chekhov: The Evolution of His Art. London: Elek, 1975. pp. 64-77.

Sklovskij, Viktor. "A. P. Cexov." Anton Cexov as a

Master of Story-Writing: Essays in Modern Soviet Literary Criticism. ed. Leo Hulanicki and David Savignac. The Hague: Mouton, 1976. pp. 78-83.

*Winner, Thomas. Chekhov and His Prose. New York: Holt, Rinehart and Winston, 1966. pp. 45-56.
### THREE YEARS
Speirs, Logan. Tolstoy and Chekhov. Cambridge: The University Press, 1971. pp. 169-182.

*Winner, Thomas. Chekhov and His Prose. New York: Holt, Rinehart and Winston, 1966. pp. 126-134.
### WARD NO. 6
Hahn, Beverly. Chekhov: A Study of the Major Stories and Plays. London: Cambridge University Press, 1977. pp. 148-152.

Kramer, Karl D. The Chameleon and the Dream: The Image of Reality in Cexov's Stories. The Hague: Mouton, 1970. pp. 129-133.

Rayfield, Donald. Chekhov: The Evolution of His Art. London: Elek, 1975. pp. 125-132.

*Winner, Thomas. Chekhov and His Prose. New York: Holt, Rinehart and Winston, 1966. pp. 106-113.

## Chernyshevsky, N. G.
### WHAT IS TO BE DONE?
Barstow, Jane. "Dostoevsky's NOTES FROM UNDERGROUND Versus Chernyshevsky's WHAT IS TO BE DONE?" Coll L 5:24-33. Winter 1978.

Frank, Joseph. "N. G. Chernyshevsky: A Russian Utopia." SoR 3:68-84. January 1967.

Mathewson, Rufus W., Jr. The Positive Hero in Russian Literature. Stanford: Stanford University Press, 1975. pp. 74-83.

Randall, Francis B. N. G. Chernyshevskii. New York: Twayne, 1967. pp. 104-130.

## Chulkov, Mikhail
### THE COMELY COOK
Garrard, J. G. Mixail Culkov: An Introduction to His Prose and Verse. The Hague: Mouton, 1970. pp. 117-143.

_____. "Narrative Technique in Chulkov's PRIGOZHAIA POVARIKHA." SlavR 27:554-563. December 1968.
### THE MOCKER

Chulkov, Mikhail

  Garrard, J. G. Mixail Culkov: An Introduction to His Prose and Verse. The Hague: Mouton, 1970. pp. 43-62; 92-116.

Crnjanski, Miloš
 MIGRATIONS
  Moravcevich, Nicholas. "The Theme of the Irreversible Fall in Miloš Crnjanski's MIGRATIONS." CSP 20:369-379. September 1978.

Dabrowska, Maria
 NIGHTS AND DAYS
  Folejewski, Zbigniew. Maria Dabrowska. New York: Twayne, 1967. pp. 37-78.

Daniel, Yuli
 ATONEMENT
  Chapple, Richard L. "The Theme of Atonement in Yuli Daniel's ATONEMENT." SAB 40:53-60. November 1975.

  Dalton, Margaret. Andrei Siniavskii and Julii Daniel': Two Soviet "Heretical" Writers. Würzburg: Verlagsanstalt, 1973. pp. 160-169.
 THE MAN FROM MINAP
  Dalton, Margaret. Andrei Siniavskii and Julii Daniel': Two Soviet "Heretical" Writers. Würzburg: Verlagsanstalt, 1973. pp. 154-160.
 THIS IS MOSCOW SPEAKING
  Dalton, Margaret. Andrei Siniavskii and Julii Daniel': Two Soviet "Heretical" Writers. Würzburg: Verlagsanstalt, 1973. pp. 144-154.

Déry, Tibor
 MR. G. A. IN X
  Varnai, Paul. "Tibor Déry and His MR. G. A. IN X." CSP 10:100-108. Spring 1968.

Dombrovskij, Jurij
 THE KEEPER OF ANTIQUITIES
  Hassanoff, Olga. "Dombrovskij's THE KEEPER OF ANTIQUITIES." MelbSS 5/6:194-202. 1971.

Dostoevsky, Feodor
 THE BROTHERS KARAMAZOV
  Anderson, Roger B. "The Meaning of Carnival in THE BROTHERS KARAMAZOV." SEEJ 23:458-478. Winter 1979.

  Bakhtin, Mikhail. Problems of Dostoevsky's Poetics. Ann Arbor: Ardis, 1973. pp. 209-220.

  Barksdale, E. C. "Dostoevsky and Euripides: A New

Humanism in Christian Tragedy." RBPH 52:626-635. No. 3, 1974.

Belknap, Robert L. "The Rhetoric of an Ideological Novel." Literature and Society in Imperial Russia, 1800-1914. ed. William Mills Todd III. Stanford: Stanford University Press, 1978. pp. 173-201.

──────. The Structure of THE BROTHERS KARAMAZOV. The Hague: Mouton, 1967. 112 pp.

Berdyaev, Nicholas. "The Grand Inquisitor: Christ and Antichrist." THE GRAND INQUISITOR. ed. Jerry Wasserman. Columbus: Merrill, 1970. pp. 68-76.

Braun, Maximilian. "THE BROTHERS KARAMAZOV as an Expository Novel." CASS 6:199-208. Summer 1972.

Camus, Albert. "Ivan and Rebellion Against God." THE BROTHERS KARAMAZOV and the Critics. ed. Edward Wasiolek. Belmont: Wadsworth, 1967. pp. 73-78.

Chaitin, Gilbert D. "Religion as Defense: The Structure of THE BROTHERS KARAMAZOV." L&P 22:69-87. No. 2, 1972.

Cox, Roger L. "Dostoevsky's Grand Inquisitor." Cross Currents 17:427-444. Fall 1967. Reprinted in THE GRAND INQUISITOR. ed. Jerry Wasserman. Columbus: Merrill, 1970. pp. 77-92.

Crone, Anna Lisa. "Unamuno and Dostoevsky: Some Thoughts on Atheistic Humanitarianism." Hispano 64:43-59. 1978.

Danow, David K. "Semiotics of Gesture in Dostoevskian Dialogue." RusL 8:69-72. January 1980.

Davis, Ruth. The Great Books of Russia. Norman: University of Oklahoma Press, 1968. pp. 216-233.

Dolenc, Ivan. Dostoevsky and Christ: A Study of Dostoevsky's Rebellion Against Belinsky. Toronto: York, 1978. pp. 105-113.

Der Eng, Jan van and Jan M. Meyer. THE BROTHERS KARAMAZOV by F. M. Dostoevsky. The Hague: Mouton, 1971. 162 pp.

Freud, Sigmund. "Dostoevsky and Parricide." THE BROTHERS KARAMAZOV and the Critics. ed. Edward Wasiolek. Belmont: Wadsworth, 1967. pp. 41-55.

Gibson, A. Boyce. The Religion of Dostoevsky. London: SCM Press, 1973. pp. 169-208.

——. "The Riddle of the Grand Inquisitor." MelbSS 4:46-56. 1970.

Goldstein, Martin. "The Debate in THE BROTHERS KARAMAZOV." SEEJ 14:326-340. Fall 1970.

Guardini, Romano. "The Christianity of the Legend." THE GRAND INQUISITOR. ed. Jerry S. Wasserman. Columbus: Merrill, 1970. pp. 104-110.

Guerard, Albert J. The Triumph of the Novel: Dickens, Dostoevsky, Faulkner. New York: Oxford University Press, 1976. pp. 94-103.

Hesse, Hermann. "The Brothers Karamazov, or The Decline of Europe: Thoughts on Reading Dostoevsky." My Belief: Essays on Life and Art. New York: Farrar, Straus and Giroux, 1974. pp. 70-85.

Hingley, Ronald. Dostoevsky: His Life and Work. London: Paul Elek, 1978. pp. 187-196.

Holquist, Michael. Dostoevsky and the Novel. Princeton: Princeton University Press, 1977. pp. 165-191.

Idinopulos, Thomas A. "Dostoevsky's Criminal Heroes: The Ethics of Russian Atheism." Cross Currents 25: 137-145. Summer 1975.

Ivanits, Linda J. "Hagiography in BRAT'JA KARAMAZOVY: Zosima, Ferapont, and the Russian Monastic Saint." RLJ 34:109-126. Winter 1980.

*Jackson, Robert Louis. "Chateaubriand and Dostoevsky: A Posing of the Problem." SSl 12:28-37. 1966.

Jones, Malcolm V. Dostoyevsky: The Novel of Discord. London: Paul Elek, 1976. pp. 166-193.

Kabat, Geoffrey C. Ideology and Imagination: The Image of Society in Dostoevsky. New York: Columbia University Press, 1978. pp. 142-162.

Kanzer, Mark. "A Psychological View of Alyosha's Reaction to Father Zossima's Death." THE BROTHERS KARAMAZOV and the Critics. ed. Edward Wasiolek. Belmont: Wadsworth, 1967. pp. 103-107.

Kellogg, Jean. Dark Prophets of Hope. Chicago: Loyola University Press, 1975. pp. 33-53.

Kent, Leonard J.  The Subconscious in Gogol' and Dostoevskij and Its Antecedents.  The Hague:  Mouton, 1969.  pp. 148-157.

Koprince, Ralph.  "Background Characters and THE BROTHERS KARAMAZOV."  RLT 10:343-350.  1974.

*Krag, Erik.  Dostoevsky:  The Literary Artist.  New York:  Humanities Press, 1962.  pp. 247-291.

Lary, N. M.  Dostoevsky and Dickens:  A Study of Literary Influence.  London:  Routledge and Kegan Paul, 1973.  pp. 139-148.

Lawrence, D. H.  "The Grand Inquisitor."  THE BROTHERS KARAMAZOV and the Critics.  ed. Edward Wasiolek.  Belmont:  Wadsworth, 1967.  pp. 78-85.

_____.  "Preface to THE GRAND INQUISITOR."  THE GRAND INQUISITOR.  ed. Jerry S. Wasserman.  Columbus:  Merrill, 1970.  pp. 96-103.

Lebowitz, Naomi.  Humanism and the Absurd in the Modern Novel.  Evanston:  Northwestern University Press, 1971.  pp. 85-102.

Lord, Robert.  Dostoevsky:  Essays and Perspectives.  Berkeley:  University of California Press, 1970.  pp. 144-174.

Lowe, David.  "Bulgakov and Dostoevsky:  A Tale of Two Ivans."  RLT 15:253-262.  1978.

Matlaw, Ralph.  "Myth and Symbol in THE BROTHERS KARAMAZOV."  THE BROTHERS KARAMAZOV and the Critics.  ed. Edward Wasiolek.  Belmont:  Wadsworth, 1967.  pp. 108-118.

Mermall, Thomas.  "Unamuno and Dostoevsky's Grand Inquisitor."  Hispania 61:851-858.  December 1978.

Merrill, Reed B.  "Ivan Karamazov and Harry Haller:  The Consolation of Philosophy."  CLS 8:58-78.  March 1971.

Mochulsky, Konstantin.  Dostoevsky:  His Life and Work.  Princeton:  Princeton University Press, 1967.  pp. 565-636.

Oates, Joyce Carol.  "The Double Vision of THE BROTHERS KARAMAZOV."  JAAC 27:203-213.  Winter 1968.

Pachmuss, Temira. "The Metaphysics of Evil." THE GRAND INQUISITOR. ed. Jerry S. Wasserman. Columbus: Merrill, 1970. pp. 119-127.

──────. "Prometheus and Job Reincarnated: Melville and Dostoevskij." SEEJ 23:30-36. Spring 1979.

Panichas, George A. The Burden of Vision: Dostoevsky's Spiritual Art. Grand Rapids: Eerdmans, 1977. pp. 152-189.

Peace, Richard. Dostoyevsky: An Examination of the Major Novels. Cambridge [Eng.] University Press, 1971. pp. 218-296.

Perring, Ronald Edward. "The Grand Inquisition." StHum 7:52-56. September 1979.

Porter, Laurence M. "The Devil as Double in Nineteenth-Century Literature: Goethe, Dostoevsky, and Flaubert." CLS 15:329-333. September 1978.

Rabinowitz, Peter J. "The Click of the Spring: The Detective Story as Parallel Structure in Dostoyevsky and Faulkner." MP 76:361-365. May 1979.

Rahv, Philip. "The Legend of the Grand Inquisitor." THE GRAND INQUISITOR. ed. Jerry S. Wasserman. Columbus: Merrill, 1970. pp. 36-55.

*──────. The Myth and the Powerhouse. New York: Farrar, Straus and Giroux, 1965. pp. 144-174.

──────. "The Sources and Significance of THE LEGEND OF THE GRAND INQUISITOR." THE BROTHERS KARAMAZOV and the Critics. ed. Edward Wasiolek. Belmont: Wadsworth, 1967. pp. 85-103.

Rosen, Nathan. "Style and Structure in THE BROTHERS KARAMAZOV (The Grand Inquisitor and the Russian Monk)." RLT 1:352-365. 1971.

──────. "Why Dmitrii Karamazov Did Not Kill His Father." CASS 6:209-224. Summer 1972.

Ross, Rochelle H. "Who Is Ivan Karamazov?" ForumH 8:39-43. Summer 1970.

Rowe, William W. "CRIME AND PUNISHMENT and THE BROTHERS KARAMAZOV: Some Comparative Observations." RLT 10:331-342. 1974.

──────. Dostoevsky: Child and Man in His Works.

New York: New York University Press, 1968. pp. 50-59.

_____. Nabokov and Others: Patterns in Russian Literature. Ann Arbor: Ardis, 1977. pp. 73-84.

Rudicina, Alexandra F. "Crime and Myth: The Archetypal Pattern of Rebirth in Three Novels of Dostoevsky." PMLA 87:1069-1072. October 1972.

Shein, Louis J. "An Examination of the Kantian Antinomies in THE BROTHERS KARAMAZOV." GSlav 1:49-59. Fall 1973.

Simmons, Ernest. "A Historical and Analytic Introduction to THE BROTHERS KARAMAZOV." THE BROTHERS KARAMAZOV and the Critics. ed. Edward Wasiolek. Belmont: Wadsworth, 1967. pp. 27-41.

Simons, John D. "The Grand Inquisitor in Schiller, Dostoevsky and Huxley." NZSJ 8:20-30. Summer 1971.

Steiner, George. "Tolstoy and THE GRAND INQUISITOR." THE GRAND INQUISITOR. ed. Jerry S. Wasserman. Columbus: Merrill, 1970. pp. 56-67.

Strauss, G. "The Prophet: Dostoevsky's 'Grand Inquisitor' and Gide's 'El Hadj.'" AJFS 14:88-104. January/April 1977.

Terras, Victor. "Turgenev and the Devil in THE BROTHERS KARAMAZOV." CASS 6:265-271. Summer 1972.

Vivas, Eliseo. "Dostoyevsky, 'Poet' in Spite of Himself." SoR 10:307-328. April 1974.

_____. "The Two Dimensions of Reality in THE BROTHERS KARAMAZOV." THE BROTHERS KARAMAZOV and the Critics. ed. Edward Wasiolek. Belmont: Wadsworth, 1967. pp. 55-72.

Wasiolek, Edward. "THE BROTHERS KARAMAZOV: Idea and Technique." THE BROTHERS KARAMAZOV and the Critics. ed. Edward Wasiolek. Belmont: Wadsworth, 1967. pp. 118-144.

_____. "THE GRAND INQUISITOR and the Critics." THE GRAND INQUISITOR. ed. Jerry S. Wasserman. Columbus: Merrill, 1970. pp. 113-118.

Weisgerber, Jean. Faulkner and Dostoevsky. Athens: Ohio University Press, 1974. pp. 251-321.

Westbrook, Perry D. The Greatness of Man: An Essay on Dostoyevsky and Whitman. Rutherford: Fairleigh Dickinson University Press, 1973. pp. 33-80.

Wharton, Robert V. "Evil in an Earthly Paradise: Ivan Karamazov's 'Dialectic' Against God and Zossima's 'Euclidean' Response." Thomist 41:567-584. October 1977.

Yarmolinsky, Avrahm. Dostoevsky: Works and Days. New York: Funk and Wagnalls, 1971. pp. 284-410.

CRIME AND PUNISHMENT

Adams, Barbara Block. "Sisters Under Their Skins: The Women in the Lives of Raskolnikov and Razumov." Conradiana 6:113-124. No. 2, 1974.

Alm, Brian R. "The Four Horsemen and the Lamb: Structure and Balance in CRIME AND PUNISHMENT." McNR 21:72-79. 1974-1975.

Anderson, Roger B. "CRIME AND PUNISHMENT: Psycho-Myth and the Making of a Hero." CASS 11:523-538. Winter 1977.

──────. "Raskol'nikov and the Myth Experience." SEEJ 20:1-17. Spring 1976.

Bakhtin, Mikhail. Problems of Dostoevsky's Poetics. Ann Arbor: Ardis, 1973. pp. 71-75; 138-143.

Brody, Ervin C. "Meaning and Symbolism in the Names of Dostoevsky's CRIME AND PUNISHMENT and THE IDIOT." Names 27:121-128. June 1979.

Brown, Edward J. "Pisarev and the Transformation of Two Russian Novels." Literature and Society in Imperial Russia, 1800-1914. ed. William Mills Todd III. Stanford: Stanford University Press, 1978. pp. 166-170.

Busch, Robert L. "Humor in Dostoevskii's CRIME AND PUNISHMENT." CASS 9:54-68. Spring 1975.

Chapple, Richard L. "Character Parallels in CRIME AND PUNISHMENT and SANCTUARY." GSlav 2:5-13. 1976.

Church, Margaret. "Dostoevsky's CRIME AND PUNISHMENT and Kafka's THE TRIAL." L&P 19:47-55. No. 3/4, 1969.

Curtis, James M. "Spatial Form as the Intrinsic Genre of Dostoevsky's Novels." MFS 18:140-153. Summer 1972.

Danow, David K. "Semiotics of Gesture in Dostoevskian Dialogue." RusL 8:62-69. January 1980.

Davis, Ruth. The Great Books of Russia. Norman: University of Oklahoma Press, 1968. pp. 166-180.

Davison, Ray. "Clamence and Marmeladov: A Parallel." RomN 14:226-229. Winter 1972.

Dilman, Ilham. "Socrates and Dostoyevsky on Punishment." Philosophy and Literature 1:66-78. Fall 1976.

Fiderer, Gerald. "Raskolnikov's Confession." L&P 30:62-71. No. 2, 1980.

Freeborn, Richard. The Rise of the Russian Novel: Studies in the Russian Novel from EUGENE ONEGIN to WAR AND PEACE. London: Cambridge University Press, 1973. pp. 183-207.

Gibson, A. Boyce. The Religion of Dostoevsky. London: SCM Press, 1973. pp. 88-103.

Greenway, John L. "Kierkegaardian Doubles in CRIME AND PUNISHMENT." OL 33:45-60. 1978.

Grossman, Leonid. Balzac and Dostoevsky. Ann Arbor: Ardis, 1973. pp. 31-49.

_____. Dostoevsky: A Biography. Indianapolis: Bobbs-Merrill, 1975. pp. 342-356.

Guerard, Albert J. The Triumph of the Novel: Dickens, Dostoevsky, Faulkner. New York: Oxford University Press, 1976. pp. 175-181.

Hackel, Sergei. "Raskolnikov Through the Looking-Glass: Dostoevsky and Camus's L'ETRANGER." ConL 9:189-209. Spring 1968.

Hanan, David. "CRIME AND PUNISHMENT: The Idea of the Crime." CR 12:15-28. 1969.

Hart, Pierre R. "Looking Over Raskol'nikov's Shoulder: The Narrator in CRIME AND PUNISHMENT." Criticism 13:166-179. Spring 1971.

Hingley, Ronald. Dostoevsky: His Life and Work. London: Paul Elek, 1978. pp. 107-112; 120-124.

Holquist, Michael. Dostoevsky and the Novel. Princeton: Princeton University Press, 1977. pp. 75-101.

Horsman, Dorothea. "CRIME AND PUNISHMENT: A Study in Technique." NZSJ 6:34-52. Summer 1970.

Jones, Malcolm V. Dostoyevsky: The Novel of Discord. London: Paul Elek, 1976. pp. 67-89.

──────. "Raskol'nikov's Humanitarianism." CASS 8: 370-380. Fall 1974.

Kabat, Geoffrey C. Ideology and Imagination: The Image of Society in Dostoevsky. New York: Columbia University Press, 1978. pp. 120-131.

Kent, Leonard J. The Subconscious in Gogol' and Dostoevskij and Its Antecedents. The Hague: Mouton, 1969. pp. 112-121.

King, Henry Hall. Dostoevsky and Andreyev: Gazers Upon the Abyss. New York: Kraus, 1972. pp. 8-15.

Kiremidjian, David. "CRIME AND PUNISHMENT: Matricide and the Woman Question." AI 33:403-433. Winter 1976.

*Krag, Erik. Dostoevsky: The Literary Artist. New York: Humanities Press, 1962. pp. 115-135.

Kuhn, Alfred. "A Note on Raskol'nikov's Hats." SEEJ 15:425-432. Winter 1971.

Leatherbarrow, W.J. "The Aesthetic Louse: Ethics and Aesthetics in Dostoevsky's PRESTUPLENIYE I NAKAZANIYE." MLR 71:857-866. October 1976.

──────. "Raskolnikov and the 'Enigma of His Personality.'" FMLS 9:153-165. April 1973.

Leighton, Lauren G. "The Crime and Punishment of Monstrous Coincidence." Mosaic 12:93-106. Autumn 1978.

Lindenmeyr, Adele. "Raskolnikov's City and the Napoleonic Plan." SlavR 35:37-47. March 1976.

Matual, David. "Fate in CRIME AND PUNISHMENT." IFR 3:120-125. July 1976.

──────. "The Number 'Four' in Dostoevskij's PRESTUPLENIE I NAKAZANIE and Jung's Theory of the Quaternity." RLJ 33:54-61. Spring 1979.

Merrill, Reed B. "Brain Fever in the Novels of Dostoevsky." TQ 19:33-38. Autumn 1976.

Milosz, Czeslaw. "Dostoevsky and Swedenborg." SlavR 34:306-311. June 1975.

Naumann, Marina Turkevich. "Raskol'nikov's Shadow: Porfirij Petrovič." SEEJ 16:42-54. Spring 1972.

Nilsson, Nils Åke. "Dostoevskij and the Language of Suspense." SSl 16:35-44. 1970.

Pachmuss, Temira. "Dostoyevsky's Porfiry Petrovich: A New Socrates." NZSJ 1:17-23. 1980.

Panichas, George A. The Burden of Vision: Dostoevsky's Spiritual Art. Grand Rapids: Eerdmans, 1977. pp. 23-46.

Peace, Richard. Dostoyevsky: An Examination of the Major Novels. Cambridge [Eng.] University Press, 1971. pp. 19-58.

*Rahv, Philip. The Myth and the Powerhouse. New York: Farrar, Straus and Giroux, 1965. pp. 106-143.

Rosenshield, Gary. "First- versus Third-Person Narration in CRIME AND PUNISHMENT." SEEJ 17:399-407. Winter 1973.

Rowe, W. W. Nabokov and Others: Patterns in Russian Literature. Ann Arbor: Ardis, 1977. pp. 61-84.

Rowe, W. Woodin. "Dostoevskian Patterned Antinomy and Its Function in CRIME AND PUNISHMENT." SEEJ 16:287-296. Fall 1972.

Rowe, William W. "CRIME AND PUNISHMENT and THE BROTHERS KARAMAZOV: Some Comparative Observations." RLT 10:331-342. 1974.

Rubinstein, S. Leonard. "Dostoyevsky: The Identity of Crime and Punishment." JGE 26:139-146. Summer 1974.

Rudicina, Alexandra F. "Crime and Myth: The Archetypal Pattern of Rebirth in Three Novels of Dostoevsky." PMLA 87:1065-1067. October 1972.

Santangelo, Gennaro. "The Five Motives of Raskolnikov." DR 54: 710-719. Winter 1974-1975.

Seeley, Frank Friedeberg. "The Two Faces of Svidrigailov." CASS 12:413-417. Fall 1978.

Shaw, J. Thomas. "Raskol'nikov's Dreams." SEEJ 17: 131-145. Summer 1973.

*Smith, Raymond. "A Note on Dostoyevsky's Dr. Zossimov." CLAJ 10:162-164. December 1966.

Stanton, Robert. "Outrageous Fiction: CRIME AND PUNISHMENT, THE ASSISTANT, and NATIVE SON." PCP 4:52-57. April 1969.

Sutherland, Stewart R. "Language and Interpretation in CRIME AND PUNISHMENT." Philosophy and Literature 2:223-236. Fall 1978.

Toporov, V. N. "On Dostoevsky's Poetics and Archaic Patterns of Mythological Thought." NLH 9:335-347. Winter 1978.

Vladiv, Slobodanka. "The Use of Circumstantial Evidence in Dostoevskii's Works." CASS 12:359-370. Fall 1978.

Wasiolek, Edward. "Dostoevsky's Notebooks for CRIME AND PUNISHMENT." PsyR 55:349-359. No. 3, 1968.

―――. "Raskolnikov's Motives: Love and Murder." AI 31:252-269. Fall 1974.

Weisgerber, Jean. "Faulkner's Monomaniacs: Their Indebtedness to Raskolnikov." CLS 5:181-191. June 1968.

Welch, Lois M. "Luzhin's Crime and the Advantages of Melodrama in Dostoevsky's CRIME AND PUNISHMENT." TSLL 18:135-145. Spring 1976.

Werge, Thomas. "The Word as Deed in CRIME AND PUNISHMENT." Renascence 27:207-218. Summer 1975.

Willett, Maurita. "The 'Ending' of CRIME AND PUNISHMENT." OL 25:244-258. 1970.

Wilson, Raymond J. III. "Raskolnikov's Dream in CRIME AND PUNISHMENT." L&P 26:159-165. No. 4, 1976.

Yarmolinsky, Avrahm. Dostoevsky: Works and Days. New York: Funk and Wagnalls, 1971. pp. 210-222.

Zdanys, Jonas. "Raskolnikov and Frankenstein: The Deadly Search for a Rational Paradise." Cithara 16:57-62. November 1976.

THE DEVILS
Bakhtin, Mikhail. Problems of Dostoevsky's Poetics. Ann Arbor: Ardis, 1973. pp. 204-208.

Baumgarten, Murray. "The Extraordinary Events of THE DEVILS." WHR 22:23-33. Winter 1968.

Brody, E. C. "The Liberal Intellectual in THE POSSESSED." GSlav 2:253-271. Fall 1977.

_____. "The Mask and the Substance: The Kirilov Theme in Dostoevsky's THE POSSESSED and Camus's LES POSSEDES." Neohelicon 3:121-170. No. 3/4, 1975.

Cerny, Vaclav. Dostoevsky and His Devils. Ann Arbor: Ardis, 1975. 77 pp.

Danow, David K. "Semiotics of Gesture in Dostoevskian Dialogue." RusL 8:50-55. January 1980.

Davis, Ruth. The Great Books of Russia. Norman: University of Oklahoma Press, 1968. pp. 189-207.

Davison, R. M. "Dostoyevsky's THE DEVILS: The Role of Stepan Trofimovich Verkhovensky." FMLS 16: 109-119. April 1980.

Dolenc, Ivan. Dostoevsky and Christ: A Study of Dostoevsky's Rebellion Against Belinsky. Toronto: York, 1978. pp. 76-92.

Frank, Joseph. "The Masks of Stavrogin." SR 77:660-691. Autumn 1969.

Gibson, A. Boyce. The Religion of Dostoevsky. London: SCM Press, 1973. pp. 125-153.

Gregory, Serge V. "Dostoevsky's THE DEVILS and the Antinihilist Novel." SlavR 38:444-455. December 1979.

Guerard, Albert J. The Triumph of the Novel: Dickens, Dostoevsky, Faulkner. New York: Oxford University Press, 1976. pp. 41-47.

Hingley, Ronald. Dostoevsky: His Life and Work. London: Paul Elek, 1978. pp. 149-155.

Holquist, Michael. Dostoevsky and the Novel. Princeton: Princeton University Press, 1977. pp. 124-147.

Ivanits, Linda J. "Dostoevskij's Mar'ja Lebjadkina." SEEJ 22:127-140. Summer 1978.

Jones, Malcolm V. Dostoyevsky: The Novel of Discord. London: Paul Elek, 1976. pp. 128-153.

Kabat, Geoffrey C. Ideology and Imagination: The Image of Society in Dostoevsky. New York: Columbia University Press, 1978. pp. 131-142.

Kent, Leonard J. The Subconscious in Gogol' and Dostoevskij and Its Antecedents. The Hague: Mouton, 1969. pp. 137-143.

King, Henry Hall. Dostoevsky and Andreyev: Gazers Upon the Abyss. New York: Kraus, 1972. pp. 18-22.

*Krag, Erik. Dostoevsky: The Literary Artist. New York: Humanities Press, 1962. pp. 172-211.

Lary, N. M. Dostoevsky and Dickens: A Study of Literary Influence. London: Routledge and Kegan Paul, 1973. pp. 106-137.

Linner, Sven. "Bishop Tichon in THE POSSESSED." RusL 4:273-284. July 1976.

Lord, Robert. Dostoevsky: Essays and Perspectives. Berkeley: University of California Press, 1970. pp. 102-107; 212-217.

Merrill, Reed B. "Brain Fever in the Novels of Dostoevsky." TQ 19:42-45. Autumn 1976.

Oates, Joyce Carol. "The Tragic Vision of THE POSSESSED." GaR 32:868-893. Winter 1978.

Panichas, George A. The Burden of Vision: Dostoevsky's Spiritual Art. Grand Rapids: Eerdmans, 1977. pp. 89-112.

Peace, Richard. Dostoyevsky: An Examination of the Major Novels. Cambridge [Eng.] University Press, 1971. pp. 140-217.

Peterson, Dale E. "Dostoevsky's Mock Apocalypse." CentR 18:76-90. Winter 1974.

Reid, Stephen. "Dostoevski's Kirilov and Freedom of the Will." HSL 3:197-207. No. 3, 1971.

Rudicina, Alexandra F. "Crime and Myth: The Archetypal Pattern of Rebirth in Three Novels of Dostoevsky." PMLA 87:1067-1069. October 1972.

Rysten, Felix S. A. False Prophets in the Fiction of Camus, Dostoevsky, Melville, and Others. Coral Gables: University of Miami Press, 1972. pp. 71-91.

Rzhevsky, Leonid. "Dostoevskij's BESY: Its Language and the Author's Image." RLJ 34:101-108. Winter 1980.

Vladiv, Slobodanka B. Narrative Principles in Dostoevskij's BESY: A Structural Analysis. Berne: Lang, 1979. 173 pp.

Yarmolinsky, Avrahm. Dostoevsky: Works and Days. New York: Funk and Wagnalls, 1971. pp. 294-312.

THE DOUBLE

Anderson, Roger B. "Dostoevsky's Hero in THE DOUBLE: A Re-examination of the Divided Self." Symposium 26:101-113. Summer 1972.

Bakhtin, Mikhail. "The Hero's Monologic Discourse and Narrational Discourse in Dostoevsky's Early Novels." Dostoevsky and Gogol: Texts and Criticism. ed. Priscilla Meyer and Stephen Rudy. Ann Arbor: Ardis, 1979. pp. 255-271.

_____. Problems of Dostoevsky's Poetics. Ann Arbor: Ardis, 1973. pp. 175-190.

Bem, A. L. "'The Nose' and THE DOUBLE." Dostoevsky and Gogol: Texts and Criticism. ed. Priscilla Meyer and Stephen Rudy. Ann Arbor: Ardis, 1979. pp. 229-248.

Hoffmeister, Charles C. "'William Wilson' and THE DOUBLE: A Freudian Insight." Coranto 9:24-27. No. 2, 1974.

Leatherbarrow, W. J. "The Rag with Ambition: The Problem of Self-Will in Dostoevsky's BEDNYYE LYUDI and DVOYNIK." MLR 68:610-618. July 1973.

Sherry, Charles. "Folie à Deux: Gogol and Dostoevsky." TSLL 17:258-267. Sp. Issue, 1975.

Struc, Roman S. "Madness as Existence: An Essay on a Literary Theme." RS 38:84-87. June 1970.

Terras, Victor. The Young Dostoevsky (1846-1849): A Critical Study. The Hague: Mouton, 1969. pp. 128-134; 168-184.

Vinogradov, V. V. "Towards a Morphology of the 'Naturalist' Style." Dostoevsky and Gogol: Texts and Criticism. ed. Priscilla Meyer and Stephen Rudy. Ann Arbor: Ardis, 1979. pp. 217-228.

THE DREAM OF A RIDICULOUS MAN

Bakhtin, Mikhail. Problems of Dostoevsky's Poetics. Ann Arbor: Ardis, 1973. pp. 122-128.

Gibson, A. Boyce. The Religion of Dostoevsky. London: SCM Press, 1973. pp. 161-168.

Holquist, Michael. Dostoevsky and the Novel. Princeton: Princeton University Press, 1977. pp. 155-164.

Phillips, Roger W. "Dostoevsky's DREAM OF A RIDICULOUS MAN: A Study in Ambiguity." Criticism 17:355-363. Fall 1975.

THE GAMBLER

Debreczeny, Paul. "Dostoevskij's Use of MANON LESCAUT in THE GAMBLER." CL 28:1-18. Winter 1976.

Geha, Richard, Jr. "Dostoevsky and THE GAMBLER: A Contribution to the Psychogenesis of Gambling, Part I." PsyR 57:95-123. No. 1, 1970. Part II, PsyR 57:289-301. No. 2, 1970.

*Krag, Erik. Dostoevsky: The Literary Artist. New York: Humanities Press, 1962. pp. 105-114.

Vinograde, Ann C. "THE GAMBLER: Prokof'ev's Libretto and Dostoevskij's Novel." SEEJ 16:414-418. Winter 1972.

THE IDIOT

Brody, Ervin C. "Meaning and Symbolism in the Names of Dostoevsky's CRIME AND PUNISHMENT and THE IDIOT." Names 27:128-137. June 1979.

Dalton, Elizabeth. "Myshkin's Epilepsy." PR 45:595-610. No. 4, 1978.

_____. Unconscious Structure in THE IDIOT. Princeton: Princeton University Press, 1979. 208 pp.

Danow, David K. "Semiotics of Gesture in Dostoevskian Dialogue." RusL 8:55-62. January 1980.

Davis, Ruth. The Great Books of Russia. Norman: University of Oklahoma Press, 1968. pp. 180-188.

Dolenc, Ivan. Dostoevsky and Christ: A Study of Dostoevsky's Rebellion Against Belinsky. Toronto: York, 1978. pp. 67-73.

Farakos, Mary. "The Narrator in THE IDIOT." NZSJ 11:123-132. Winter 1973.

Fiene, Donald M. "Pushkin's 'Poor Knight': The Key to Perceiving Dostoevsky's IDIOT as Allegory." IDSB 8:10-21. November 1978.

Frank, Joseph. "A Reading of THE IDIOT." SoR 5:303-331. April 1969.

Gibson, A. Boyce. The Religion of Dostoevsky. London: SCM Press, 1973. pp. 104-124.

Grossvogel, David I. Limits of the Novel: Evolutions of a Form from Chaucer to Robbe-Grillet. Ithaca: Cornell University Press, 1968. pp. 310-319.

Guerard, Albert J. "On the Composition of Dostoevsky's THE IDIOT." Mosaic 8:201-215. Fall 1974.

_____. The Triumph of the Novel: Dickens, Dostoevsky, Faulkner. New York: Oxford University Press, 1976. pp. 193-203.

Hardesty, William H. III. "The 'Femme Fatale' in THE IDIOT and THE ARROW OF GOLD." RS 44:175-181. September 1976.

Hesse, Hermann. "Thoughts on THE IDIOT by Dostoevsky." My Belief: Essays on Life and Art. New York: Farrar, Straus and Giroux, 1974. pp. 86-92.

Hollander, Robert. "The Apocalyptic Framework of Dostoevsky's THE IDIOT." Mosaic 7:123-139. Winter 1974.

Holquist, Michael. Dostoevsky and the Novel. Princeton: Princeton University Press, 1977. pp. 102-123.

Jones, Malcolm V. Dostoyevsky: The Novel of Discord. London: Paul Elek, 1976. pp. 90-127.

Kent, Leonard J. The Subconscious in Gogol' and Dostoevskij and Its Antecedents. The Hague: Mouton, 1969. pp. 122-131.

Kirk, Irina. "Buddhistic Elements in THE IDIOT." NZSJ 8:10-17. Summer 1971.

_____. "Buddhistic Elements in THE IDIOT." SSASH 18:77-84. 1972.

*Krag, Erik. Dostoevsky: The Literary Artist. New York: Humanities Press, 1962. pp. 136-162.

Lary, N. M. Dostoevsky and Dickens: A Study of Literary Influence. London: Routledge and Kegan Paul, 1973. pp. 51-104.

Lesser, Simon O. "Saint and Sinner--Dostoevsky's IDIOT--1958." MFS 21:387-401. Autumn 1975.

Lord, Robert. Dostoevsky: Essays and Perspectives.

Berkeley: University of California Press, 1970. pp. 81-101.

──────. "A Reconsideration of Dostoyevsky's Novel, THE IDIOT." SEER 45:30-45. January 1967.

Louria, Yvette. "Dostoevskii and Goncharov." MLN 88:1325-1328. December 1973.

Magretta, Joan. "Radical Disunities: Models of Mind and Madness in PIERRE and THE IDIOT." SNNTS 10: 234-250. Summer 1978.

Merrill, Reed B. "Brain Fever in the Novels of Dostoevsky." TQ 19:38-42. Autumn 1976.

Miller, Robin Feuer. "The Role of the Reader in THE IDIOT." SEEJ 23:190-202. Summer 1979.

Panichas, George A. The Burden of Vision: Dostoevsky's Spiritual Art. Grand Rapids: Eerdmans, 1977. pp. 47-88.

Peace, Richard. Dostoyevsky: An Examination of the Major Novels. Cambridge [Eng.] University Press, 1971. pp. 59-139.

Pearce, Richard. Stages of the Clown: Perspectives on Modern Fiction from Dostoyevsky to Beckett. Carbondale: Southern Illinois University Press, 1970. pp. 6-25.

Rowe, William Woodin. Dostoevsky: Child and Man in His Works. New York: New York University Press, 1968. pp. 178-184.

Seeley, Frank Friedeberg. "Aglaja Epančina." SEEJ 18:1-10. Spring 1974.

*Selig, Karl-Ludwig. "Cervantes and Dostoyevsky: Some Observations on THE IDIOT." Arcadia 1:312-318. 1966.

Sellin, Eric. "Meursault and Myshkin on Executions: A Parallel." RomN 10:11-14. Autumn 1968.

Slattery, Dennis P. "The Frame Tale: Temporality, Fantasy and Innocence in THE IDIOT." IDSB 9:6-22. November 1979.

Yarmolinsky, Avrahm. Dostoevsky: Works and Days. New York: Funk and Wagnalls, 1971. pp. 260-269.

THE INSULTED AND INJURED

Frank, Joseph. "Dostoevsky's Discovery of 'Fantastic Realism.'" RusR 27:291-295. July 1968.

Guerard, Albert J. The Triumph of the Novel: Dickens, Dostoevsky, Faulkner. New York: Oxford University Press, 1976. pp. 96-108.

*Krag, Erik. Dostoevsky: The Literary Artist. New York: Humanities Press, 1962. pp. 84-93.

THE LANDLADY

Leatherbarrow, W.J. "Dostoevsky's Treatment of the Theme of Romantic Dreaming in KHOZYAYKA and BELYYE NOCHI." MLR 69:586-592. July 1974.

Neuhauser, R. "THE LANDLADY: A New Interpretation." CSP 10:42-67. Spring 1968.

A LITTLE HERO

Bell, Gerda. "'The Child Is Father to the Man': A Brief Study on Dostoevsky's Knowledge of Children, Exemplified by His Story A LITTLE HERO." NZSJ 8:32-47. Summer 1971.

Koehler, Ludmila. "THE LITTLE HERO of a Great Writer." IDSB 8:22-29. November 1978.

NETOCHKA NEZVANOVA

Jones, Malcolm V. "An Aspect of Romanticism in Dostoyevsky: NETOCHKA NEZVANOVA and Eugène Sue's MATHILDE." RMS 17:38-61. 1973.

*Krag, Erik. Dostoevsky: The Literary Artist. New York: Humanities Press, 1962. pp. 52-61.

NOTES FROM UNDERGROUND

Annas, Julia. "Action and Character in Dostoyevsky's NOTES FROM UNDERGROUND." Philosophy and Literature 1:257-275. Fall 1977.

Bakhtin, Mikhail. Problems of Dostoevsky's Poetics. Ann Arbor: Ardis, 1973. pp. 190-199.

Barstow, Jane. "Dostoevsky's NOTES FROM UNDERGROUND Versus Chernyshevsky's WHAT IS TO BE DONE?" CollL 5:24-33. Winter 1978.

Cardaci, Paul F. "Dostoevsky's Underground as Allusion and Symbol." Symposium 28:248-258. Fall 1974.

Cash, Earl A. "The Narrators in INVISIBLE MAN and NOTES FROM UNDERGROUND: Brothers in the Spirit." CLAJ 16:505-507. June 1973.

Consigny, Scott. "The Paradox of Textuality: Writing as Entrapment and Deliverance in NOTES FROM UNDERGROUND." CASS 12:341-352. Fall 1978.

Doody, Terrence. "The Underground Man's Confession and His Audience." RUS 61:27-37. Winter 1975.

Fortin, Rene E. "Responsive Form: Dostoyevsky's NOTES FROM UNDERGROUND and the Confessional Tradition." ELWIU 7:225-243. Fall 1980.

Freeborn, Richard. The Rise of the Russian Novel: Studies in the Russian Novel from EUGENE ONEGIN to WAR AND PEACE. London: Cambridge University Press, 1973. pp. 179-183.

Furst, Lilian R. "Dostoyevsky's NOTES FROM UNDERGROUND and Salinger's THE CATCHER IN THE RYE." CRCL 5:72-85. Winter 1978.

Gibson, A. Boyce. The Religion of Dostoevsky. London: SCM Press, 1973. pp. 78-87.

Gregg, Richard. "Apollo Underground: His Master's Still, Small Voice." RusR 32:64-71. January 1973.

Haltresht, Michael. "Symbolism of Rats and Mice in Dostoevsky's NOTES FROM UNDERGROUND." SAB 39:60-62. November 1974.

Holquist, James M. "Plot and Counter-Plot in NOTES FROM UNDERGROUND." CASS 6:225-238. Summer 1972.

Holquist, Michael. Dostoevsky and the Novel. Princeton: Princeton University Press, 1977. pp. 54-74.

Holzapfel, Tamara. "Dostoevsky's NOTES FROM THE UNDERGROUND and Sabato's EL TUNEL." Hispania 51:440-445. September 1968.

Jones, Malcolm V. Dostoyevsky: The Novel of Discord. London: Paul Elek, 1976. pp. 55-66.

Kavanagh, Thomas M. "Dostoyevsky's NOTES FROM UNDERGROUND: The Form of the Fiction." TSLL 14:491-507. Fall 1972.

Kirk, Irina. Dostoevskij and Camus: The Themes of Consciousness, Isolation, Freedom and Love. München: Fink, 1974. 144 pp.

_____. "Dramatization of Consciousness in Camus and Dostoevsky." BuR 16:96-104. March 1968.

_____. "Polemics and Art in Dostoevsky and Camus." NZSJ 8:49-62. Summer 1971.

*Krag, Erik. Dostoevsky: The Literary Artist. New York: Humanities Press, 1962. pp. 94-104.

Lord, Robert. Dostoevsky: Essays and Perspectives. Berkeley: University of California Press, 1970. pp. 35-47.

McKinney, David M. "NOTES FROM UNDERGROUND: A 'Dostoevskean' Faust." CASS 12:189-229. Summer 1978.

Merrill, Reed. "The Mistaken Endeavor: Dostoevsky's NOTES FROM UNDERGROUND." MFS 18:505-516. Winter 1972-1973.

Mikhailovsky, Nikolai K. Dostoevsky: A Cruel Talent. Ann Arbor: Ardis, 1978. pp. 13-19.

Neuhäuser, Rudolph. "Observations on the Structure of NOTES FROM UNDERGROUND with Reference to the Main Themes of Part II." CASS 6:239-255. Summer 1972.

_____. "Romanticism in the Post-Romantic Age: A Typological Study of Antecedents of Dostoevskii's Man from Underground." CASS 8:333-358. Fall 1974.

Nisly, Paul W. "A Modernist Impulse: NOTES FROM UNDERGROUND as Model." CollL 4:152-157. Spring 1977.

Paris, Bernard J. "NOTES FROM UNDERGROUND: A Horneyan Analysis." PMLA 88:511-522. May 1973.

_____. A Psychological Approach to Fiction: Studies in Thackeray, Stendhal, George Eliot, Dostoevsky, and Conrad. Bloomington: Indiana University Press, 1974. pp. 190-214.

Peace, Richard. Dostoyevsky: An Examination of the Major Novels. Cambridge [Eng.] University Press, 1971. pp. 1-18.

Pondrom, Cyrena Norman. "Two Demonic Figures: Kierkegaard's Merman and Dostoevsky's Underground Man." OL 23:161-177. 1968.

Pribić, Rado. "Alienation in NACHTWACHEN by Bonaventura and Dostoevskij's NOTES FROM THE UNDERGROUND." GSlav 5:19-27. Spring 1975.

_____. Bonaventura's NACHTWACHEN and Dostoevsky's NOTES FROM THE UNDERGROUND: A Comparison in Nihilism. München: Verlag Otto Sagner, 1974. 149 pp.

Rice, Martin P. "Dostoevskii's NOTES FROM UNDERGROUND and Hegel's 'Master and Slave.'" CASS 8:359-369. Fall 1974.

Smalley, Barbara. "The Compulsive Patterns of Dostoyevsky's Underground Man." SSF 10:389-396. Fall 1973.

Sperber, Michael A. "Symptoms and Structure of Borderline Personality Organization: Camus' THE FALL and Dostoevsky's NOTES FROM UNDERGROUND." L&P 23:108-112. No. 3, 1973.

Struc, Roman S. "Dostoevsky's 'Confessions' as Critique of Literature." RS 46:84-89. June 1978.

Traschen, Isadore. "Existential Ambiguities in NOTES FROM UNDERGROUND." SAQ 73:363-376. Summer 1974.

Warrick, Patricia. "The Sources of Zamyatin's WE in Dostoevsky's NOTES FROM UNDERGROUND." Extrapolation 17:63-76. December 1975.

Weisberg, Richard. "An Example Not to Follow: 'Ressentiment' and the Underground Man." MFS 21:553-563. Winter 1975-1976.

Winfield, William. "Reflection/Negation/Reality: Dostoyevsky and Hegel." CLS 17:399-408. December 1980.

Yarmolinsky, Avrahm. Dostoevsky: Works and Days. New York: Funk and Wagnalls, 1971. pp. 190-197.

## POOR FOLK

Bakhtin, Mikhail. "The Hero's Monologic Discourse and Narrational Discourse in Dostoevsky's Early Novels." Dostoevsky and Gogol: Texts and Criticism. ed. Priscilla Meyer and Stephen Rudy. Ann Arbor: Ardis, 1979. pp. 249-255.

_____. Problems of Dostoevsky's Poetics. Ann Arbor: Ardis, 1973. pp. 169-175.

Frank, Joseph. Dostoevsky: The Seeds of Revolt. Princeton: Princeton University Press, 1976. pp. 137-155.

*Krag, Erik. Dostoevsky: The Literary Artist. New York: Humanities Press, 1962. pp. 15-22.

Lary, N. M. Dostoevsky and Dickens: A Study of Literary Influence. London: Routledge and Kegan Paul, 1973. pp. 21-34.

Leatherbarrow, W. J. "The Rag with Ambition: The Problem of Self-Will in Dostoevsky's BEDNYYE LYUDI and DVOYNIK." MLR 68:607-610. July 1973.

Terras, Victor. The Young Dostoevsky (1846-1849): A Critical Study. The Hague: Mouton, 1969. pp. 15-19; 160-168.

Vinogradov, Viktor. "The School of Sentimental Naturalism." Dostoevsky and Gogol: Texts and Criticism. ed. Priscilla Meyer and Stephen Rudy. Ann Arbor: Ardis, 1979. pp. 186-215.

## A RAW YOUTH

Jones, Malcolm V. Dostoyevsky: The Novel of Discord. London: Paul Elek, 1976. pp. 154-165.

*Krag, Erik. Dostoevsky: The Literary Artist. New York: Humanities Press, 1962. pp. 212-235.

Panichas, George A. The Burden of Vision: Dostoevsky's Spiritual Art. Grand Rapids: Eerdmans, 1977. pp. 113-151.

## VECHNYI MUZH

Woodward, James B. "'Transferred Speech' in Dostoevskii's VECHNYI MUZH." CASS 8:398-407. Fall 1974.

————. "'Transferred Speech' in Dostoevskij's VECNYJ MUZ." SSASH 21:167-177. 1975.

## THE VILLAGE OF STEPANCHIKOVA

*Krag, Erik. Dostoevsky: The Literary Artist. New York: Humanities Press, 1962. pp. 77-83.

Mikhailovsky, Nikolai K. Dostoevsky: A Cruel Talent. Ann Arbor: Ardis, 1978. pp. 20-28.

Monter, Barbara Heldt. "The Quality of Dostoevskij's Humor: THE VILLAGE OF STEPANCIKOVO." SEEJ 17:33-41. Spring 1973.

Pervushin, N. V. "Dostoevsky's Foma Opiskin and Gogol'." CSP 14:87-90. Spring 1972.

Tynjanov, Jurij. "Dostoevsky and Gogol." Twentieth-Century Russian Literary Criticism. ed. Victor Erlich. New Haven: Yale University Press, 1975. pp. 102-116.

Van Holk, A. G. F. "Verbal Aggression and Offended Honour in Dostoevskij's SELO STEPANCIKOVO I EGO OBITATELI: A Text-Grammatical Approach." RusL 4:67-107. January 1976.

Erenburg, Il'ja
    XULIO XURENITO

Erenburg, Il'ja

> Avins, Carol. "Revolution as Carnival: Il'ja Erenburg's XULIO XURENITO." RLJ 34:127-132. Winter 1980.

Fadeyev, Alexander
> THE ROUT
>> Rzhevsky, Nicolaes. "Idea and Heritage in Soviet Literature." CLS 6:422-433. December 1969.

Fedin, Konstantin
> CITIES AND YEARS
>> Beaujour, Elizabeth Klosty. "Some Problems of Construction in Fedin's CITIES AND YEARS." SEEJ 16:1-18. Spring 1972.
>>
>> _____. "The Use of Witches in Fedin and Bulgakov." SlavR 33:695-707. December 1974.
>>
>> Blum, Julius M. Konstantin Fedin: A Descriptive and Analytic Study. The Hague: Mouton, 1967. pp. 41-63.
>
> SANATORIUM ARKTUR
>> Elstun, Esther N. "Two Views of the Mountain: Thomas Mann's ZAUBERBERG and Konstantin Fedin's SANATORIUM ARKTUR." GSlav 1:55-71. Spring 1974.
>>
>> Struc, Roman S. "SANATORIUM ARKTUR: Fedin's Polemic Against Thomas Mann's MAGIC MOUNTAIN." RS 35:301-307. December 1967.

Gladkov, F. V.
> CEMENT
>> Busch, Robert L. "Gladkov's CEMENT: The Making of a Soviet Classic." SEEJ 22:348-361. Fall 1978.
>>
>> Stephan, Halina. "CEMENT: From Gladkov's Monumental Epos to Müller's Avant-garde Drama." GSlav 3:85-103. Fall 1979.

Gogol, Nikolai
> DEAD SOULS
>> Annenskij, Innokentij. "The Aesthetics of Gogol's DEAD SOULS and Its Legacy." Twentieth-Century Russian Literary Criticism. ed. Victor Erlich. New Haven: Yale University Press, 1975. pp. 51-60.
>>
>> Davis, Ruth. The Great Books of Russia. Norman: University of Oklahoma Press, 1968. pp. 37-46.
>>
>> Erlich, Victor. Gogol. New Haven: Yale University Press, 1969. pp. 120-143; 172-182.
>>
>> Fanger, Donald. The Creation of Nikolai Gogol. Cambridge: Harvard University Press, 1979. pp. 164-191.

────────. "DEAD SOULS: The Mirror and the Road." NCF 33:24-47. June 1978.

Freeborn, Richard. "DEAD SOULS: A Study." SEER 49:18-44. January 1971.

────────. The Rise of the Russian Novel: Studies in the Russian Novel from EUGENE ONEGIN to WAR AND PEACE. London: Cambridge University Press, 1973. pp. 74-114.

Glass, Elliot S. "DEAD SOULS and the Hispanic Picaresque Novel." REH 11:77-90. January 1977.

Hemmings, F. W. J. et al. The Age of Realism. Baltimore: Penguin Books, 1974. pp. 87-92.

Karlinsky, Simon. "Portrait of Gogol as a Word Glutton." Cal SS 5:170-184. 1970.

────────. The Sexual Labyrinth of Nikolai Gogol. Cambridge: Harvard University Press, 1976. pp. 225-247.

Lindstrom, Thais S. Nikolay Gogol. New York: Twayne, 1974. pp. 135-178; 188-194.

Merezhkovsky, Dmitry. "Gogol and the Devil." Gogol from the Twentieth Century: Eleven Essays. ed. Robert A. Maguire. Princeton: Princeton University Press, 1974. pp. 76-94.

Proffer, Carl. The Simile and Gogol's DEAD SOULS. The Hague: Mouton, 1967. 200 pp.

Rowe, W. W. Nabokov and Others: Patterns in Russian Literature. Ann Arbor: Ardis, 1977. pp. 37-46.

Seeley, Frank Friedeberg. "Gogol's DEAD SOULS." FMLS 4:33-44. January 1968.

Snyder, Harry C. "Airborne Imagery in Gogol's DEAD SOULS." SEEJ 23:173-189. Summer 1979.

Timmer, Charles B. "DEAD SOULS Speaking." SEER 45:273-291. July 1967.

Troyat, Henri. Divided Soul: The Life of Gogol. Garden City: Doubleday, 1973. pp. 245-292. 1973.

Vroon, Ronald. "Gogol in Oblomovka." RLT 3:282-295. 1972.

Wolterstorff, Nicholas. "Characters and Their Names." Poetics 8:101-127. April 1979.

Woodward, James B. Gogol's DEAD SOULS. Princeton: Princeton University Press, 1978. 255 pp.

Zeldin, Jesse. Nikolai Gogol's Quest for Beauty: An Exploration into His Works. Lawrence: The Regents Press of Kansas, 1978. pp. 87-149.

## DIARY OF A MADMAN

Erlich, Victor. Gogol. New Haven: Yale University Press, 1969. pp. 90-97.

Karlinsky, Simon. The Sexual Labyrinth of Nikolai Gogol. Cambridge: Harvard University Press, 1976. pp. 117-122.

Lindstrom, Thais S. Nikolay Gogol. New York: Twayne, 1974. pp. 77-83.

Zeldin, Jesse. Nikolai Gogol's Quest for Beauty: An Exploration into His Works. Lawrence: The Regents Press of Kansas, 1978. pp. 43-48.

Zolotussky, Igor. "DIARY OF A MADMAN and the 'Severnaya Pchela.'" SovL 10:38-52. 1975.

## EVENINGS ON A FARM NEAR DIKANKA

Karlinsky, Simon. The Sexual Labyrinth of Nikolai Gogol. Cambridge: Harvard University Press, 1976. pp. 30-48.

Troyat, Henri. Divided Soul: The Life of Gogol. Garden City: Doubleday, 1973. pp. 77-83.

## MIRGOROD

Erlich, Victor. Gogol. New Haven: Yale University Press, 1967. pp. 52-74.

Karlinsky, Simon. The Sexual Labyrinth of Nikolai Gogol. Cambridge: Harvard University Press, 1976. pp. 58-96.

## THE OLD WORLD LANDOWNERS

Peace, R.A. "Gogol"s OLD WORLD LANDOWNERS." SEER 53:504-520. October 1975.

Woodward, James B. "Allegory and Symbol in Gogol's Second Idyll." MLR 73:351-367. April 1978.

## ST. PETERSBURG Cycle

Karlinsky, Simon. The Sexual Labyrinth of Nikolai Gogol. Cambridge: Harvard University Press, 1976. pp. 108-144.

## TARAS BULBA

Karlinsky, Simon. The Sexual Labyrinth of Nikolai Gogol. Cambridge: Harvard University Press, 1976. pp. 77-86.

Sirskyj, Wasyl. "Ideological Overtones in Gogol's

TARAS BULBA." Ukrainian Quarterly 35:279-287. Autumn 1979.

Stromecky, O. The How of Gogol: A Study of the Methods and Sources of Gogol. Huntsville: UAH Press, 1975. pp. 21-68.

――――. "Ukrainian Elements in Mykola Hohol's TARAS BULBA." UQ 25:350-360. Winter 1969.

VIJ
Karlinsky, Simon. The Sexual Labyrinth of Nikolai Gogol. Cambridge: Harvard University Press, 1976. pp. 86-103.

Rancour-Laferriere, Daniel. "The Identity of Gogol's VIJ." HUS 2:211-233. June 1978.

ZAPISKI SUMASSHEDSHEGO
Peace, R. A. "The Logic of Madness: Gogol''s ZAPISKI SUMASSHEDSHEGO." OSP 9:28-45. 1976.

Gołubiew, Antoni
  BOLESŁAW THE BRAVE
    Gasiorowska, Xenia. "BOLESŁAW THE BRAVE by A. Gołubiew: A Modern Polish Epic." CalSS 4:119-144. 1967.

Gombrowicz, Witold
  COSMOS
    Merivale, Patricia. "The Esthetics of Perversion: Gothic Artifice in Henry James and Witold Gombrowicz." PMLA 93:992-1002. October 1978.

    Thompson, Ewa M. Witold Gombrowicz. Boston: Twayne, 1979. pp. 63-70; 95-100.
  FERDYDURKE
    Atchity, Kenneth John. "Vision and Perspective in Witold Gombrowicz." RS 37:17-26. March 1969.

    Jelenski, K. A. "Witold Gombrowicz." TriQ 9:37-41. Spring 1967.

    Thompson, Ewa M. Witold Gombrowicz. Boston: Twayne, 1979. pp. 63-79.
  PORNOGRAFIA
    Atchity, Kenneth John. "Vision and Perspective in Witold Gombrowicz." RS 37:17-26. March 1969.

    Merivale, Patricia. "The Esthetics of Perversion: Gothic Artifice in Henry James and Witold Gombrowicz." PMLA 93:992-1002. October 1978.

    Petro, Peter. "The Pyrotechnics of an Infernal Machine: Fictional Reality in Gombrowicz's PORNOGRAFIA." IFR 6:55-61. Winter 1979.

Thompson, Ewa M. Witold Gombrowicz. Boston: Twayne, 1979. pp. 63-70; 89-95.
TRANS-ATLANTIC
Thompson, Ewa M. Witold Gombrowicz. Boston: Twayne, 1979. pp. 79-89.

Goncharov, Ivan
THE JOURNEY OF THE FRIGATE PALLAS
Ehre, Milton. Oblomov and His Creator: The Life and Art of Ivan Goncharov. Princeton: Princeton University Press, 1973. pp. 142-153.
OBLOMOV
Davis, Ruth. The Great Books of Russia. Norman: University of Oklahoma Press, 1968. pp. 51-64.

Ehre, Milton. Oblomov and His Creator: The Life and Art of Ivan Goncharov. Princeton: Princeton University Press, 1973. pp. 154-232.

Freeborn, Richard. The Rise of the Russian Novel: Studies in the Russian Novel from EUGENE ONEGIN to WAR AND PEACE. London: Cambridge University Press, 1973. pp. 145-155.

Hadfield, Claire H. G. "What Is Oblomovism?: A Sociological Approach." NZSJ 10:106-113. Summer 1972.

Hainsworth, J. D. "DON QUIXOTE, HAMLET and 'Negative Capability': Aspects of Goncharov's OBLOMOV." AUMLA 53:42-53. May 1980.

Harjan, George. "Dobroliubov's 'What Is Oblomovism?': An Interpretation." CSP 18:284-292. September 1976.

Kuhn, Alfred. "Dobroliubov's Critique of OBLOMOV: Polemics and Psychology." SlavR 30:93-109. March 1971.

Louria, Yvette and Morton I. Seiden. "Ivan Goncharov's OBLOMOV: The Anti-Faust as Christian Hero." CSS 3:39-68. Spring 1969.

Lyngstad, Alexandra and Sverre Lyngstad. Ivan Goncharov. New York: Twayne, 1971. pp. 72-114.

Mays, Milton A. "Oblomov as Anti-Faust." WHR 21:141-152. Spring 1967.

Seeley, Frank Friedeberg. "OBLOMOV." SEER 54:335-354. July 1976.

Setchkarev, Vsevolod. Ivan Goncharov: His Life and His Works. Würzburg: Liebing, 1974. pp. 127-161.

Vroon, Ronald. "Gogol in Oblomovka." RLT 3:282-295. 1972.
### AN ORDINARY STORY
Ehre, Milton. Oblomov and His Creator: The Life and Art of Ivan Goncharov. Princeton: Princeton University Press, 1973. pp. 114-141.

Freeborn, Richard. The Rise of the Russian Novel: Studies in the Russian Novel from EUGENE ONEGIN to WAR AND PEACE. London: Cambridge University Press, 1973. pp. 140-145.

Lyngstad, Alexandra and Sverre Lyngstad. Ivan Goncharov. New York: Twayne, 1971. pp. 41-71.

Setchkarev, Vsevolod. Ivan Goncharov: His Life and His Works. Würzburg: Liebing, 1974. pp. 41-72.
### THE PRECIPICE
Lyngstad, Alexandra and Sverre Lyngstad. Ivan Goncharov. New York: Twayne, 1971. pp. 115-148.

Setchkarev, Vsevolod. Ivan Goncharov: His Life and His Works. Würzburg: Liebing, 1974. pp. 203-239.
### THE RAVINE
Ehre, Milton. Oblomov and His Creator: The Life and Art of Ivan Goncharov. Princeton: Princeton University Press, 1973. pp. 233-263.

## Gorky, Maxim
### THE LIFE OF KLIM SAMGIN
Byalik, Boris. "A Great Epopee." SovL 3:147-152. 1968.
### MOTHER
Mathewson, Rufus W., Jr. The Positive Hero in Russian Literature. Stanford: Stanford University Press, 1975. pp. 165-176.

## Grigorovich, D.V.
### THE VILLAGE
Pursglove, M. "D.V. Grigorovich (1822-1899): DEREVNYA and ANTON-GOREMYKA." SEER 51:505-516. October 1973.

Strong, Robert L., Jr. "Grigorovič's THE VILLAGE: An Etude in Sentimental Naturalism." SEEJ 12:169-175. Summer 1968.

## Grin, Alexander
### THE GOLDEN CHAIN
Luker, N.J.L. Alexander Grin. Letchworth: Bradda Books, 1973. pp. 96-100.
### JESSY AND MORGIANA
Luker, Nicholas. "Alexander Grin's JESSY AND MOR-

GIANA: Literary Lapse or New Departure?" JRS 35: 16-20. 1978.
THE ROAD TO NOWHERE
   Luker, Nicholas J. L. "Alexander Grin's Last Novel THE ROAD TO NOWHERE." NZSJ 11:51-71. Winter 1973.
SCARLET SAILS
   Luker, N. J. L. Alexander Grin. Letchworth: Bradda Books, 1973. pp. 73-80.
SHE WHO RUNS ON THE WAVES
   Luker, N. J. L. Alexander Grin. Letchworth: Bradda Books, 1973. pp. 103-106.
THE SHINING WORLD
   Luker, N. J. L. Alexander Grin. Letchworth: Bradda Books, 1973. pp. 87-93.

Hašek, Jaroslav
   THE GOOD SOLDIER SCHWEIK
      *Frynta, Emanuel. Hašek the Creator of Schweik. Czechoslovakia: Brno, 1965. 145 pp.

      Stern, J. P. "War and the Comic Muse: THE GOOD SOLDIER SCHWEIK and CATCH-22." CL 20:193-216. Summer 1968.

Herzen, Alexander
   WHO IS TO BLAME?
      Partridge, Monica. "Herzen's Changing Concept of Reality and Its Reflection in His Literary Works." SEER 46:414-418. July 1968.

Horia, Vintila
   GOD WAS BORN IN EXILE
      Gruzinska, Aleksandra. "Ovid in Exile in Vintila Horia's DIEU EST NE EN EXIL." Miorita 6:65-74. July 1979.

Hronský, Jozef
   THE WORLD ON A QUAGMIRE
      Rydlo, Joseph M. "THE WORLD ON A QUAGMIRE: The Last Literary Work of Jozef Cíger Hronský." Slovak Stud 15:117-142. 1975.

Irzykowski, Karol
   PAŁUBA
      Sen, Colleen Taylor. "Karol Irzykowski's PAŁUBA: A Guidebook to the Future." SEEJ 17:288-300. Fall 1973.

Iskander, Fazil
   THE GOATIBEX CONSTELLATION
      Burlingame, Helen P. "The Prose of Fazil Iskander." RLT 14:138-143. 1977.
   SANDRO FROM CHEGEM
      Burlingame, Helen P. "The Prose of Fazil Iskander." RLT 14:154-159. 1977.

Kalve, Aivars
    TUMBLEWEED
        Melngaile, Valda. "Portrait of a Stranger in Aivars Kalve's VĒJA KANEPES." JBalS 5:198-204. Fall 1974.

Katayev, Valentin
    THE GRASS OF OBLIVION
        Talmy, Vladimir, trans. "Discussion of Valentin Katayev's Two Latest Works." SovL 7:142-151. 1968.
    THE SACRED WELL
        Reilly, Alayne P. America in Contemporary Soviet Literature. New York: New York University Press, 1971. pp. 117-171.

        Talmy, Vladimir, trans. "Discussion of Valentin Katayev's Two Latest Works. SovL 7:142-151. 1968.

Kaverin, Valentin
    BEFORE THE MIRROR
        Beaujour, Elizabeth Klosty. "Kaverin's BEFORE THE MIRROR." SEEJ 24:233-244. Fall 1980.
    FULFILLMENT OF DESIRES
        Oulanoff, Hongor. "V. Kaverin's Novels of Development and Adventure." CSS 2:464-485. Winter 1968.
    THE OPEN BOOK
        Oulanoff, Hongor. "V. Kaverin's Novels of Development and Adventure." CSS 2:464-485. Winter 1968.
    SKANDALIST
        Piper, D. G. B. V. A. Kaverin: A Soviet Writer's Response to the Problem of Commitment. Pittsburgh: Duquesne University Press, 1970. pp. 63-109.
    TWO CAPTAINS
        Oulanoff, Hongor. "V. Kaverin's Novels of Development and Adventure." CSS 2:464-485. Winter 1968.
    THE UNKNOWN ARTIST
        Beaujour, Elizabeth Klosty. The Invisible Land: A Study of the Artistic Imagination of Iurii Olesha. New York: Columbia University Press, 1970. pp. 148-154.

        Piper, D. G. B. V. A. Kaverin: A Soviet Writer's Response to the Problem of Commitment. Pittsburgh: Duquesne University Press, 1970. pp. 111-165.

        Struve, Gleb. Russian Literature Under Lenin and Stalin, 1917-1953. Norman: University of Oklahoma Press, 1971. pp. 114-118.

Kharms, Daniil
    THE OLD WOMAN
        Nakhimovsky, Alice Stone. "The Ordinary, the Sacred,

and the Grotesque in Daniil Kharms's THE OLD WOMAN." SlavR 37:203-216. June 1978.

Kiik, Heino
TONDIÖÖMAJA
Lehiste, Ilse. "Where Hobgoblins Spend the Night." JBalS 4:321-326. Winter 1973.

Kolokolov, Nikolay
HONEY AND BLOOD
Freeborn, Richard. "Nikolay Kolokolov." SEER 56:24-31. January 1978.

Komarov, Matvej
VAN'KA KAIN
Titunik, I. R. "Matvej Komarov's VAN'KA KAIN and Eighteenth-Century Russian Prose Fiction." SEEJ 18:351-366. Winter 1974.

Krestovskii, V. V.
PANURGE'S HERD
Gregory, Serge V. "Dostoevsky's THE DEVILS and the Antinihilist Novel." SlavR 38:448-453. December 1979.
PETERBURSKIE TRUSHCHOBY
Sobkowska-Ashcroft, Irina. "PETERBURSKIE TRUSHCHOBY: A Russian Version of LES MYSTERES DE PARIS." RLC 53:163-175. April/June 1979.

Krleža, Miroslav
THE RETURN OF PHILIP LATINOVICZ
Engelsfeld, Mladen. "Time as a Structural Unit in Krleža's THE RETURN OF PHILIP LATINOVICZ." SEEJ 22:362-371. Fall 1978.

Ktorova, Alla
THE FACE OF FIREBIRD
Hughes, Olga. "Alla Ktorova: A New Face." TriQ 28:509-520. Fall 1973.

Kuncewicz, Maria
THE STRANGER
Smith, Mary C. "THE STRANGER: A Study and Note About Maria Kuncewicz." PolR 17:77-86. Winter 1972.

Kundera, Milan
THE JOKE
Heim, Michael. "Moravian Folk Music: A Czechoslovak Novelist's View." JFI 9:45-53. No. 1, 1972.

Porter, Robert. "Milan Kundera and His Novel THE JOKE." Trivium 8:1-10. May 1973.

Kuprin, Alexander
THE DUEL

Luker, Nicholas. *Alexander Kuprin*. Boston: Twayne, 1978. pp. 73-109.
THE PIT
    Luker, Nicholas. *Alexander Kuprin*. Boston: Twayne, 1978. pp. 133-153.
SULAMIF'
    Gamburg, Haim. "Kuprin's SULAMIF': A Case of Biblical Stylization or an Independent Artistic Work." *RLJ* 32:57-65. Fall 1978.

Kuvayev, Oleg
    THE TERRITORY
        Anjaparidze, Georgi. "Very Far from Moscow." *SovL* 8:165-172. 1977.

Kuzmin, Mikhail
    WINGS
        Gillis, Donald C. "The Platonic Theme in Kuzmin's WINGS." *SEEJ* 22:336-347. Fall 1978.

        Granoien, Neil. "WINGS and 'The World of Art.'" *RLT* 11:393-404. 1975.

Lem, Stanislaw
    THE INVESTIGATION
        Fogel, Stanley. "THE INVESTIGATION: Stanislaw Lem's Pynchonesque Novel." *RQ* 6:286-289. December 1977.
    SOLARIS
        Ketterer, David. "SOLARIS and the Illegitimate Suns of Science Fiction." *Extrapolation* 14:73-88. December 1972.

Leonov, Leonid
    THE BADGERS
        Harjan, George. *Leonid Leonov: A Critical Study*. Toronto: Arowhena, 1979. pp. 29-38.

        Plank, D. L. "Unconscious Motifs in Leonid Leonov's THE BADGERS." *SEEJ* 16:19-35. Spring 1972.
    ROAD TO THE OCEAN
        Harjan, George. *Leonid Leonov: A Critical Study*. Toronto: Arowhena, 1979. pp. 106-130.
    THE RUSSIAN FOREST
        Harjan, George. *Leonid Leonov: A Critical Study*. Toronto: Arowhena, 1979. pp. 163-180.
    SKUTAREVSKY
        Harjan, George. *Leonid Leonov: A Critical Study*. Toronto: Arowhena, 1979. pp. 85-101.
    SOVIET RIVER
        Harjan, George. *Leonid Leonov: A Critical Study*. Toronto: Arowhena, 1979. pp. 63-74.
    THE THIEF

Harjan, George. Leonid Leonov: A Critical Study. Toronto: Arowhena, 1979. pp. 42-59; 181-187.

Lermontov, Mikhail
GEROY NASHEGO VREMENI
Peace, R.A. "The Role of Taman' in Lermontov's GEROY NASHEGO VREMENI." SEER 45:12-29. January 1967.

A HERO OF OUR TIME
Angeloff, A. and Pr. Klingenburg. "Lermontov's Uses of Nature in the Novel HERO OF OUR TIME." RLJ 24:3-11. July 1970.

Arian, I. "Some Aspects of Lermontov's A HERO OF OUR TIME." FMLS 4:22-32. January 1968.

Bagby, Lewis. "Narrative Double-Voicing in Lermontov's A HERO OF OUR TIME." SEEJ 22:265-286. Fall 1978.

Eagle, Herbert. "Lermontov's 'Play' with Romantic Genre Expectations in A HERO OF OUR TIME." RLT 10:299-315. 1974.

Faletti, Heidi E. "Elements of the Demonic in the Character of Pechorin in Lermontov's HERO OF OUR TIME." FMLS 14:365-377. October 1978.

Freeborn, Richard. The Rise of the Russian Novel: Studies in the Russian Novel from EUGENE ONEGIN to WAR AND PEACE. London: Cambridge University Press, 1973. pp. 38-73.

Kelly, Laurence. Lermontov: Tragedy in the Caucasus. London: Constable, 1977. pp. 95-101.

Reid, Robert. "Eavesdropping in A HERO OF OUR TIME." NZSJ 1:13-20. 1977.

Ripp, Victor. "A HERO OF OUR TIME and the Historicism of the 1830's: The Problem of the Whole and the Parts." MLN 92:969-986. December 1977.

Rowe, W.W. Nabokov and Others: Patterns in Russian Literature. Ann Arbor: Ardis, 1977. pp. 27-36.

Turner, C.J.G. "The System of Narrators in Part I of A HERO OF OUR TIME." CSP 17:617-628. Winter 1975.

Leskov, Nikolay
AT KNIVES POINT
McLean, Hugh. Nikolai Leskov: The Man and His Art.

CATHEDRAL FOLK
 Cambridge: Harvard University Press, 1977. pp. 217-222.

CATHEDRAL FOLK
 Lantz, K. A. Nikolay Leskov. Boston: Twayne, 1979. pp. 65-69.

 McLean, Hugh. Nikolai Leskov: The Man and His Art. Cambridge: Harvard University Press, 1977. pp. 173-208.

THE DEVIL'S PUPPETS
 McLean, Hugh. Nikolai Leskov: The Man and His Art. Cambridge: Harvard University Press, 1977. pp. 503-512.

LADY MACBETH OF MTSENSK
 McLean, Hugh. Nikolai Leskov: The Man and His Art. Cambridge: Harvard University Press, 1977. pp. 145-151.

LEVSHA
 Keenan, William. "Leskov's Left-Handed Craftsman and Zamyatin's Flea: Irony into Allegory." FMLS 16:66-78. January 1980.

NIGHT OWLS
 McLean, Hugh. Nikolai Leskov: The Man and His Art. Cambridge: Harvard University Press, 1977. pp. 598-609.

NO WAY OUT
 McLean, Hugh. Nikolai Leskov: The Man and His Art. Cambridge: Harvard University Press, 1977. pp. 72-77; 123-138.

WHITE EAGLE
 O'Connor, Katherine Tiernan. "The Specter of Political Corruption: Leskov's WHITE EAGLE." RLT 8:393-405. 1974.

Mel'nikov-Pechersky, Pavel
 GRANDMA'S YARNS
  Hoisington, Thomas H. "Romance--A Congenial Form: Mel'nikov-Pecherskii's GRANDMA'S YARNS and OLDEN TIMES." RusR 36:463-476. October 1977.
 IN THE FORESTS
  Hoisington, Thomas H. "Mel'nikov-Pechersky: Romancer of Provincial and Old Believer Life." SlavR 33:688-694. December 1974.
 THE KRASIL'NIKOVS
  Hoisington, Thomas H. "Dark Romance in a Provincial Setting: Mel'nikov-Pečerskij's THE KRASIL'NIKOVS." SEEJ 22:15-25. Spring 1978.
 OLDEN TIMES
  Hoisington, Thomas H. "Romance--A Congenial Form: Mel'nikov-Pecherskii's GRANDMA'S YARNS and OLDEN TIMES." RusR 36:463-476. October 1977.
 ON THE HILLS
  Hoisington, Thomas H. "Mel'nikov-Pechersky: Romancer

**Mel'nikov-Pechersky, Pavel**

of Provincial and Old Believer Life." SlavR 33:688-694. December 1974.

**Meras, Icchokas**
STRIPTEASE, OR PARIS-ROME-PARIS
Willeke, Audrone B. "The Cyclical Experience of Time in Recent Soviet Lithuanian Prose." SEEJ 23:96-102. Spring 1979.

**Nekrasov, N. A.**
ZIZN' I POXOZDENIJA TIXONA TROSTNIKOVA
Marullo, Thomas Gaiton. "ZIZN' I POXOZDENIJA TIXONA TROSTNIKOVA: Nekrasov's Portrait of the Artist as a Young Man." RLJ 33:63-70. Winter 1979.

**Odoevsky, V. F.**
RUSSIAN NIGHTS
Ilgner, Richard. "Goethe's 'Geist, der stets verneint,' and Its Emergence in the Faust Works of Odoevsky, Lunacharsky, and Bulgakov." GSlav 2:174-176. Spring 1977.

**Okudžava, Bulat**
PUTESESTVIE DILETANTOV
Corten, Irina H. "Okudžava's PUTESESTVIE DILETANTOV: Its Literary Sources and the Image of Its Hero." RLJ 34:153-162. Winter 1980.

**Olesha, Yury**
ENVY
Avins, Carol. "Eliot and Oleša: Versions of the Anti-Hero." CRCL 6:64-74. Winter 1979.

Beaujour, Elizabeth Klosty. The Invisible Land: A Study of the Artistic Imagination of Iurii Olesha. New York: Columbia University Press, 1970. pp. 38-58.

Belinkov, Arkady V. "The Soviet Intelligentsia and the Socialist Revolution: On Yury Olesha's ENVY." Part I. RusR 30:356-368. October 1971; Part II. RusR 31:25-37. January 1972.

Berczynski, T. S. "Kavalerov's Monologue in ENVY: A Baroque Soliloquy." RLT 1:375-384. 1971.

Piper, D. G. B. "Yuriy Olesha's ZAVIST': An Interpretation." SEER 48:27-43. January 1970.

Slonin, Marc. Soviet Russian Literature: Writers and Problems 1917-1977. New York: Oxford University Press, 1977. pp. 122-127.

Struve, Gleb. Russian Literature Under Lenin and

Stalin, 1917-1953. Norman: University of Oklahoma Press, 1971. pp. 105-112.

Wilson, Wayne P. "The Objective of Jurij Oleša's ENVY." SEEJ 18:31-40. Spring 1974.

LIOMPA

Barratt, Andrew. "Yury Olesha's Three Ages of Man: A Close Reading of LIOMPA." MLR 75:597-614. July 1980.

Pasternak, Boris

DOCTOR ZHIVAGO

Angeloff, Alexander. "Water Imagery in the Novel DOCTOR ZHIVAGO." RLJ 22:6-13. February/June 1968.

Anning, N. J. "Pasternak." Russian Literary Attitudes from Pushkin to Solzhenitsyn. ed. Richard Freeborn. London: Macmillan, 1976. pp. 114-119.

Barksdale, E. C. and Daniel Popp. "Hamsun and Pasternak: The Development of Dionysian Tragedy." Edda 76:343-350. No. 6, 1976.

Barnes, Christopher J. "Boris Pasternak's Revolutionary Year." FMLS 11:334-348. October 1975.

Bodin, Per Arne. Nine Poems from DOKTOR ZIVAGO: A Study of Christian Motifs in Boris Pasternak's Poetry. Stockholm: Almqvist & Wiksell, 1976. 136 pp.

Costello, D. P. "ZHIVAGO Reconsidered." FMLS 4:70-80. January 1968.

Dyck, J. W. Boris Pasternak. New York: Twayne, 1972. pp. 108-139.

Dyck, Sarah. "In Search of a Poet: Buckler and Pasternak." G Slav 2:325-335. Spring 1978.

Erlich, Victor. "A Testimony and a Challenge--Pasternak's DOCTOR ZHIVAGO." Pasternak: A Collection of Critical Essays. ed. Victor Erlich. Englewood Cliffs: Prentice-Hall, 1978. pp. 131-136.

Fortin, René E. "Home and the Uses of Creative Nostalgia in DOCTOR ZHIVAGO." MFS 20:203-209. Summer 1974.

Gifford, Henry. Pasternak: A Critical Study. Cambridge: Cambridge University Press, 1977. pp. 176-244.

Griffiths, F. T. and S. J. Rabinowitz. "DOCTOR ZHIVAGO and the Tradition of National Epic." CL 32:63-79. Winter 1980.

Hampshire, Stuart. "DOCTOR ZHIVAGO: As from a Lost Culture." Pasternak: A Collection of Critical Essays. ed. Victor Erlich. Englewood Cliffs: Prentice-Hall, 1978. pp. 126-130.

Hughes, Olga R. The Poetic World of Boris Pasternak. Princeton: Princeton University Press, 1974. pp. 74-104.

Ignatieff, Leonid. "A Philosopher Who Lived His Philosophy: Yuri Zhivago." QQ 75:703-717. Winter 1968.

Jackson, Robert Louis. "DOCTOR ZHIVAGO: 'Liebestod' of the Russian Intelligentsia." Pasternak: A Collection of Critical Essays. ed. Victor Erlich. Englewood Cliffs: Prentice-Hall, 1978. pp. 137-150.

Kayden, Eugene M. "On Re-reading the Poems of Doctor Zhivago." ColQ 23:396-400. Winter 1975.

Lamont, Rosette C. "Yuri Zhivago's 'Fairy Tale': A Dream Poem." WLT 51:517-521. Autumn 1977.

Livingstone, Angela. "Allegory and Christianity in DOCTOR ZHIVAGO." MelbSS 1:24-33. 1967.

de Mallac, Guy. "Pasternak and Religion." RusR 32:360-375. October 1973.

Masing-Delic, Irene. "Some Allusions to BESY in DOKTOR ZIVAGO." IDSB 8:31-41. November 1978.

_____. "Some Alternating Opposites in the Zhivago Poems." RusR 36:438-462. October 1977.

Mihajlov, Mihajlo. Russian Themes. New York: Farrar, Straus and Giroux, 1968. pp. 250-263.

Obolensky, Dimitri. "The Poems of DOCTOR ZHIVAGO." Pasternak: A Collection of Critical Essays. ed. Victor Erlich. Englewood Cliffs: Prentice-Hall, 1978. pp. 151-165.

Perelmuter, Joanna. "Reflection of Urban Speech in the Language of DOKTOR ZIVAGO." RLJ 32:13-20. Fall 1978.

Rogers, Thomas F. "The Implications of Christ's Passion in DOKTOR ZIVAGO." SEEJ 18:384-391. Winter 1974.

Rühle, Jürgen. Literature and Revolution: A Critical Study of the Writer and Communism in the Twentieth Century. New York: Frederick A. Praeger, 1969. pp. 117-129.

Silbajoris, Rimvydas. "Pasternak and Tolstoj: Some Comparisons." SEEJ 11:23-34. Spring 1967.

Slonin, Marc. Soviet Russian Literature: Writers and Problems 1917-1977. New York: Oxford University Press, 1977. pp. 230-235.

Stepun, Fyodor. "Boris Pasternak." Pasternak: A Collection of Critical Essays. ed. Victor Erlich. Englewood Cliffs: Prentice-Hall, 1978. pp. 118-125.

Wain, John. "The Meaning of DR. ZHIVAGO." CritQ 10:113-137. Spring/Summer 1968.

Yashaschandra, Sitansu. "Boris Pasternak: Persuasion to Rejoice." Quest 95:31-39. May/June 1975.

Zaslove, Jerald. "DR. ZHIVAGO and the Obliterated Man: The Novel and Literary Criticism." JAAC 26:65-79. Fall 1967.

Pavlova, Karolina
    A DOUBLE LIFE
        Monter, Barbara Heldt. "From an Introduction to Pavlova's A DOUBLE LIFE." RLT 9:346-352. 1974.

Pil'nyak, Boris
    KRASNOYE DEREVO
        Falchikov, Michael. "Rerouting the Train of Time--Boris Pil'nyak's KRASNOYE DEREVO." MLR 75:138-147. January 1980.
    MACHINES AND WOLVES
        Browning, Gary L. "Civilization and Nature in Boris Pil'njak's MACHINES AND WOLVES." SEEJ 20:155-166. Summer 1976.

        Tulloch, A. R. "The 'Man vs. Machine' Theme in Pil'nyak's MACHINES AND WOLVES." RLT 8:329-339i. 1974.
    MAHOGANY
        Reck, Vera T. Boris Pil'niak: A Soviet Writer in Conflict with the State. Montreal: McGill-Queen's University Press, 1975. pp. 61-93.
    MOTHER EARTH
        Mills, Judith M. "Narrative Technique in Pil'nyak's MOTHER EARTH." JRS 28:13-20. 1974.
    THE NAKED YEAR
        Brostrom, Kenneth. "Pilnyak's NAKED YEAR: The Problem of Faith." RLT 16:114-153. 1979.

Browning, Gary L. "Polyphony and the Accretive Refrain in Boris Pilnyak's NAKED YEAR." RLT 16:154-170. 1979.

SOLJANOJ AMBAR
Browning, Gary L. "Pil'njak's SOLJANOJ AMBAR: A Commentary on Its Unpublished Part." RLJ 32:89-100. Spring 1978.

THE VOLGA FALLS TO THE CASPIAN SEA
Brostrom, Kenneth N. "The Enigma of Pil'njak's THE VOLGA FALLS TO THE CASPIAN SEA." SEEJ 18:271-298. Fall 1974.

Prus, Boleslaw
THE OUTPOST
Nagurski, Irene. "Prus's THE OUTPOST: Peasants and Positivism." RusR 23:3-29. No. 1, 1978.

Pushkin, Alexander
THE BLACKAMOOR OF PETER THE GREAT
Debreczeny, Paul. "THE BLACKAMOOR OF PETER THE GREAT: Puškin's Experiment with a Detached Mode of Narration." SEEJ 18:119-131. Summer 1974.

THE CAPTAIN'S DAUGHTER
Anderson, Roger B. "A Study of Pëtr Grinëv as the Hero of Pushkin's CAPTAIN'S DAUGHTER." CSS 5:477-486. Winter 1971.

Bayley, John. Pushkin: A Comparative Commentary. Cambridge [Eng.] University Press, 1971. pp. 331-354.

Grossman, Leonid. "A Story of the Peasant War." SovL 7:145-151. 1969.

Mikkelson, Gerald E. "The Mythopoetic Element in Pushkin's Historical Novel THE CAPTAIN'S DAUGHTER." CASS 7:296-313. Fall 1973.

Troyat, Henri. Pushkin. Garden City: Doubleday, 1970. pp. 510-515.

DUBROVSKII
Debreczeny, Paul. "The Three Styles of DUBROVSKII." CASS 10:264-278. Summer 1976.

THE QUEEN OF SPADES
Bayley, John. Pushkin: A Comparative Commentary. Cambridge [Eng.] University Press, 1971. pp. 316-322.

Bocharov, S. G. "THE QUEEN OF SPADES." NLH 9:315-332. Winter 1978.

Clayton, J. Douglas. "SPADAR DAME, PIQUE-DAME, and PIKOVAIA DAMA: A German Source for Pushkin?" GSlav 1:5-10. Fall 1974.

Debreczeny, Paul. "Poetry and Prose in THE QUEEN OF SPADES." CASS 11:91-113. Spring 1977.

Faletti, Heidi E. "Remarks on Style as Manifestation of Narrative Technique in THE QUEEN OF SPADES." CASS 11:114-133. Spring 1977.

Kodjak, Andrej. "THE QUEEN OF SPADES in the Context of the Faust Legend." Alexander Puškin: A Symposium on the 175th Anniversary of His Birth. ed. Andrej Kodjak and Kiril Taranovsky. New York: New York University Press, 1976. pp. 87-116.

Leighton, Lauren G. "Gematria in THE QUEEN OF SPADES: A Decembrist Puzzle." SEEJ 21:455-469. Winter 1977.

_____. "Numbers and Numerology in THE QUEEN OF SPADES." CSP 19:417-443. December 1977.

Roberts, Carolyn. "Puškin's PIKOVAJA DAMA and the Opera Libretto." CRCL 6:9-26. Winter 1979.

Rosen, Nathan. "The Magic Cards in THE QUEEN OF SPADES." SEEJ 19:255-275. Fall 1975.

Schwartz, Murray M. and Albert Schwartz. "THE QUEEN OF SPADES: A Psychoanalytic Interpretation." TSLL 17:275-288. Sp. Issue, 1975.

Troyat, Henri. Pushkin. Garden City: Doubleday, 1970. pp. 467-472.

Rasputin, Valentin
   UPSTREAM, DOWNSTREAM
      Bagby, Lewis. "A Concurrence of Psychological and Narrative Structures: Anamnesis in Valentin Rasputin's UPSTREAM, DOWNSTREAM." CSP 22:388-399. September 1980.

Rebreanu, Liviu
   ION
      Manolescu, Nicolae. "Liviu Rebreanu or the Tragic Novel." RoR 33:111-123. No. 9, 1979.

Remizov, Aleksej
   PJATAJA JAZVA
      Bialy, Renate S. "Parody in Remizov's PJATAJA JAZVA." SEEJ 19:403-410. Winter 1975.
   PRUD
      Shane, Alex M. "Remizov's PRUD: From Symbolism to Neo-Realism." CalSS 6:71-82. 1971.

Reymont, Wladyslaw
  THE COMEDIENNE
    Krzyzanowski, Jerzy R. Wladyslaw Stanislaw Reymont.
    New York: Twayne, 1972. pp. 27-39.
  THE FERMENTS
    Krzyzanowski, Jerzy R. Wladyslaw Stanislaw Reymont.
    New York: Twayne, 1972. pp. 31-39.
  THE INSURRECTION
    Krzyzanowski, Jerzy R. Wladyslaw Stanislaw Reymont.
    New York: Twayne, 1972. pp. 113-118.
  THE LAST DIET
    Krzyzanowski, Jerzy R. Wladyslaw Stanislaw Reymont.
    New York: Twayne, 1972. pp. 96-107.
  NIL DESPERANDUM
    Krzyzanowski, Jerzy R. Wladyslaw Stanislaw Reymont.
    New York: Twayne, 1972. pp. 107-114.
  THE PEASANTS
    Krzyzanowski, Jerzy R. Wladyslaw Stanislaw Reymont.
    New York: Twayne, 1972. pp. 73-93.
  THE PROMISED LAND
    Krzyzanowski, Jerzy R. Wladyslaw Stanislaw Reymont.
    New York: Twayne, 1972. pp. 44-62.

Sadoveanu, Mihail
  THE HATCHET
    Simms, Norman. "From Stasis to Freedom in Mihail Sadoveanu's THE HATCHET." Mosaic 7:45-56. Winter 1974.

Saltykov-Shchedrin, Mikhail
  THE GOLOVLYOVS
    Ehre, Milton. "A Classic of Russian Realism: Form and Meaning in THE GOLOVLYOVS." SNNTS 9:3-15. Spring 1977.

    Foote, I. P. "M. E. Saltykov-Shchedrin: THE GOLOVLYOV FAMILY." FMLS 4:53-63. January 1968.

    Kramer, Karl D. "Satiric Form in Saltykov's GOSPODA GOLOVLEVY." SEEJ 14:453-464. Winter 1970.

    Todd, William Mills III. "The Anti-Hero with a Thousand Faces: Saltykov-Shchedrin's Porfiry Golovlev." SLitI 9:87-105. Spring 1976.
  THE HISTORY OF A TOWN
    Foote, I. P. "Reaction or Revolution? The Ending of Saltykov's THE HISTORY OF A TOWN." OSP 1:105-125. 1968.

Schulz, Bruno
  THE STREET OF CROCODILES
    Lukashevich, Olga. "Bruno Schulz's THE STREET OF

CROCODILES: A Study in Creativity and Neurosis."
<u>PolR</u> 13:63-79. Spring 1968.

Selimović, Meŝa
    THE DERVISH AND DEATH
        Butler, Thomas J. "Literary Style and Poetic Function in Meŝa Selimović's THE DERVISH AND DEATH."
<u>SEER</u> 52:533-547. October 1974.

Serafimovich, A. S.
    CITY IN THE STEPPE
        Lafferty, Vera. "A. S. Serafimovich's Forgotten Novel, CITY IN THE STEPPE (1912)." <u>CSP</u> 16:202-219. Summer 1974.

Shevtsov, Ivan
    PLANT LOUSE
        Sinyavsky, Andrei. <u>For Freedom of Imagination</u>. New York: Holt, Rinehart and Winston, 1971. pp. 78-91.

Shklovsky, Viktor
    THIRD FACTORY
        Erlich, Victor. "On Being Fair to Viktor Shklovsky or the Act of Hedged Surrender." <u>SlavR</u> 35:111-118. March 1976.

        Sheldon, Richard. "Reply to Victor Erlich." <u>SlavR</u> 35:119-121. March 1976.

        _____. "Viktor Shklovsky and the Device of Ostensible Surrender." <u>SlavR</u> 34:86-106. March 1975.
    ZOO
        Sheldon, Richard. "Shklovsky's ZOO and Russian Berlin." <u>RusR</u> 29:262-274. July 1970.

Sholokhov, Mikhail
    DESTINY OF A MAN
        Waddington, Patrick. "'Attack or Defend....'--Sholokhov Examined." <u>Survey</u> 69:99-106. October 1968.

        Yakimenko, L. <u>Sholokhov: A Critical Appreciation</u>. Moscow: Progress Publishers, 1973. pp. 345-360.
    PODNJATAJA CELINA
        Schaarschmidt, Gunter. "Interior Monologue in Soloxov's PODNJATAJA CELINA." <u>SEEJ</u> 11:257-265. Fall 1967.
    QUIET FLOWS THE DON
        Daglish, Robert. "Making a New English Translation of TIKHIY DON." <u>SovL</u> 5:114-118. 1980.

        Dangulov, Savva. "The Artist: Sketches for a Portrait." <u>SovL</u> 5:119-138. 1980.

        Ermolaev, Herman. "Riddles of THE QUIET DON: A Review Article." <u>SEEJ</u> 18:299-310. Fall 1974.

──────. "The Role of Nature in THE QUIET DON." CalSS 6:97-111. 1971.

──────. "Who Wrote THE QUIET DON?: A Review Article." SEEJ 20:293-307. Fall 1976.

Gura, Victor. "The World of Great Feelings and Strong Passions." SovL 5:139-147. 1980.

Hallett, Richard. "Soviet Criticism of TIKHIY DON 1928-1940." SEER 46:60-74. January 1968.

Kjetsaa, Geir. "Storms on the Quiet Don. A Pilot Study." SSl 22:5-24. 1976.

Klimenko, Michael. The World of Young Sholokhov: Vision of Violence. North Quincy: Christopher, 1972. 283 pp.

Medvedev, Roy A. Problems in the Literary Biography of Mikhail Sholokhov. Cambridge: Cambridge University Press, 1977. pp. 1-188.

──────. "The Riddles Grow: 'A Propos' Two Review Articles." SEEJ 21:104-116. Spring 1977.

Murphy, A. B. "The Changing Face of TIKHIY DON." JRS 34:3-11. 1977.

Murphy, A. B., ed. "An Introduction and Commentary to Sholokhov's TIKHIY DON." NZSJ 1:47-56. 1975. Continued in NZSJ 2:33-60. 1975; 1:35-59. 1976; 2:55-84. 1976; 1:77-97. 1977; 2:43-63. 1977.

Palievsky, Pyotr. "Mikhail Sholokhov's QUIET FLOWS THE DON." SovL 5:150-156. 1980.

Price, Robert F. "Tragic Features in the Character of Grigorij Melexov." SEEJ 23:63-71. Spring 1979.

Stewart, D. H. Mikhail Sholokhov: A Critical Introduction. Ann Arbor: University of Michigan Press, 1967. pp. 43-131.

Yakimenko, L. Sholokov: A Critical Appreciation. Moscow: Progress Publishers, 1973. pp. 25-214.
SEEDS OF TOMORROW
    Mihajlov, Mihajlo. Russian Themes. New York: Farrar, Straus and Giroux, 1968. pp. 191-249.
THEY FOUGHT FOR THEIR COUNTRY
    Medvedev, Roy A. Problems in the Literary Biography of Mikhail Sholokhov. Cambridge: Cambridge University Press, 1977. pp. 161-166.

Yakimenko, L. Sholokhov: A Critical Appreciation. Moscow: Progress Publishers, 1973. pp. 337-345.
VIRGIN SOIL UPTURNED
Medvedev, Roy A. Problems in the Literary Biography of Mikhail Sholokhov. Cambridge: Cambridge University Press, 1977. pp. 144-160.

Stewart, D. H. Mikhail Sholokhov: A Critical Introduction. Ann Arbor: University of Michigan Press, 1967. pp. 132-162.

Yakimenko, L. Sholokov: A Critical Appreciation. Moscow: Progress Publishers, 1973. pp. 217-332.

Slepcov, Vasilij
HARD TIMES
Brumfield, William C. "Bazarov and Rjazanov: The Romantic Archetype in Russian Nihilism." SEEJ 21:495-505. Winter 1977.

Sokolov, Sasha
A SCHOOL FOR FOOLS
Karriker, Alexandra H. "Double Vision: Sasha Sokolov's SCHOOL FOR FOOLS." WLT 53:610-613. Autumn 1979.

Moody, Fred. "Madness and the Pattern of Freedom in Sasha Sokolov's A SCHOOL FOR FOOLS." RLT 16:7-32. 1979.

Sologub, Fyodor
BAD DREAMS
Smith, Vassar. "On BAD DREAMS." RLT 16:86-91. 1979.
THE PETTY DEMON
Masing-Delic, Irene. "'Peredonov's Little Tear'--Why Is It Shed? (The Sufferings of a Tormentor)." SS1 24:107-124. 1978.

Rabinowitz, Stanley J. "Fedor Sologub's Literary Children: The Special Case of MELKII BES." CSP 21:503-519. December 1979.

Shchurowsky, G. Roman and Pierre R. Hart. "A Somber Madness: Dionysian Excess in THE PETTY DEMON and PROFESSOR UNRAT." GSlav 3:33-43. Spring 1979.

Thurston, G. J. "Sologub's MELKIY BES." SEER 55:30-44. January 1977.
TVORIMAJA LEGENDA
Dienes, L. "Creative Imagination in Fedor Sologub's TVORIMAJA LEGENDA." WS1 23:176-186. No. 1, 1978.

Ronen, Omry. "Toponyms of Fedor Sologub's TVORIMAJA LEGENDA." WS1 13:307-316. No. 3, 1968.

Solzhenitsyn, Alexander
AUGUST 1914

Allaback, Steven. Alexander Solzhenitsyn. New York: Toplinger, 1978. pp. 175-205.

Atkinson, Dorothy. "AUGUST 1914: Historical Novel or Novel History." Aleksandr Solzhenitsyn: Critical Essays and Documentary Materials. ed. John B. Dunlop, Richard Haugh, and Alexis Klimoff. New York: Collier, 1975. pp. 408-429.

Atkinson, Dorothy and Nicholas S. Pashin. "AUGUST 1914: Art and History." RusR 31:1-10. January 1972.

Barker, Francis. Solzhenitsyn: Politics and Form. New York: Barnes and Noble, 1977. pp. 67-80.

Blake, Patricia. "Solzhenitsyn and the Theme of War." Solzhenitsyn: A Collection of Critical Essays. ed. Kathryn Feuer. Englewood Cliffs: Prentice-Hall, 1976. pp. 84-89.

Bolen, Val G. "Language and Style in Solženicyn's AUGUST 1914." SEEJ 21:344-353. Fall 1977.

Burg, David and George Feifer. Solzhenitsyn. New York: Stein and Day, 1972. pp. 332-340.

Christesen, Nina. "AUGUST 1914. Alexander Solzhenitsyn." AUMLA 36:153-156. November 1971.

Clardy, Jesse V. and Betty S. Clardy. The Superfluous Man in Russian Letters. Washington: University Press of America, 1980. pp. 117-143.

Dowler, Wayne. "Echoes of 'Pochvennichestvo' in Solzenitsyn's AUGUST 1914." SlavR 34:109-122. March 1975.

Ehre, Milton. "On AUGUST 1914." Aleksandr Solzhenitsyn: Critical Essays and Documentary Materials. ed. John B. Dunlop, Richard Haugh, and Alexis Klimoff. New York: Collier, 1975. pp. 365-371.

Ericson, Edward E., Jr. Solzhenitsyn: The Moral Vision. Grand Rapids: Eerdmans, 1980. pp. 115-136.

Feuer, Kathryn B. "AUGUST 1914: Solzhenitsyn and Tolstoy." Aleksandr Solzhenitsyn: Critical Essays and Documentary Materials. ed. John B. Dunlop, Richard Haugh, and Alexis Klimoff. New York: Collier, 1975. pp. 372-381.

Glenny, Michael. "A New Russian Epic: Solzhenitsyn's AUGUST 1914." Survey 18:112-122. Spring 1972.

Kohan, John. "The Writer as Cameraman: Pictorial Narrative in AUGUST 1914." MFS 23:73-83. Spring 1977.

Krasnov, Vladislav. Solzhenitsyn and Dostoevsky: A Study in the Polyphonic Novel. Athens: University of Georgia Press, 1980. pp. 173-197.

Mathewson, Rufus W., Jr. The Positive Hero in Russian Literature. Stanford: Stanford University Press, 1975. pp. 328-340.

McCarthy, Mary. "The Tolstoy Connection." Aleksandr Solzhenitsyn: Critical Essays and Documentary Materials. ed. John B. Dunlop, Richard Haugh, and Alexis Klimoff. New York: Collier, 1975. pp. 332-350.

Medvedev, Zhores A. Ten Years After IVAN DENISOVICH. New York: Alfred A. Knopf, 1973. pp. 154-160.

Moody, Christopher. Solzhenitsyn. New York: Barnes and Noble, 1973. pp. 168-185.

Rahv, Philip. "In Dubious Battle." Aleksandr Solzhenitsyn: Critical Essays and Documentary Materials. ed. John B. Dunlop, Richard Haugh, and Alexis Klimoff. New York: Collier, 1975. pp. 356-364.

Rickwood, T.M. "Themes and Style in Solzhenitsyn's AUGUST 1914." ESl 17:20-37. 1972.

Rzhevsky, Leonid. Solzhenitsyn: Creator and Heroic Deed. University: University of Alabama Press, 1972. pp. 86-97.

Schmemann, Alexander. "A Lucid Love." Aleksandr Solzhenitsyn: Critical Essays and Documentary Materials. ed. John B. Dunlop, Richard Haugh, and Alexis Klimoff. New York: Collier, 1975. pp. 382-392.

Struve, Gleb. "Behind the Front Lines: On Some Neglected Chapters in AUGUST 1914." Aleksandr Solzhenitsyn: Critical Essays and Documentary Materials. ed. John B. Dunlop, Richard Haugh, and Alexis Klimoff. New York: Collier, 1975. pp. 430-446.

Struve, Nikita. "The Debate over AUGUST 1914." Aleksandr Solzhenitsyn: Critical Essays and Documentary Materials. ed. John B. Dunlop, Richard Haugh, and Alexis Klimoff. New York: Collier, 1975. pp. 393-407. Reprinted in Solzhenitsyn: A Collection of Critical Essays. ed. Kathryn Feuer. Englewood Cliffs: Prentice-Hall, 1976. pp. 71-83.

Watt, Donald. "'The Harmony of the World': Polyphonic Structure in Solzhenitsyn's Longer Fiction." MFS 23:106-111. Spring 1977.

Windle, Kevin. "The Theme of Fate in Solzhenitsyn's AUGUST 1914." SlavR 31:399-411. June 1972.

## THE CANCER WARD

Allaback, Steven. Alexander Solzhenitsyn. New York: Taplinger, 1978. pp. 119-174.

Anning, N. J. "Solzhenitsyn." Russian Literary Attitudes from Pushkin to Solzhenitsyn. ed. Richard Freeborn. London: Macmillan, 1976. pp. 135-138.

Atkinson, Dorothy and Nicholas S. Paskin. "AUGUST 1914: Art and History." RusR 31:1-10. January 1972.

"A. V. Belinkov's Defense of Solzhenitsyn's THE CANCER WARD at a Special Meeting of the Writers' Union, November 17, 1966." RusR 28:453-458. October 1969.

Bradley, Thompson. "Aleksandr Solzhenitsyn's CANCER WARD: The Failure of Defiant Stoicism." Aleksandr Solzhenitsyn: Critical Essays and Documentary Materials. ed. John B. Dunlop, Richard Haugh, and Alexis Klimoff. New York: Collier, 1975. pp. 295-302.

Brown, Deming. "CANCER WARD and THE FIRST CIRCLE." SlavR 28:304-313. June 1969.

_____. Soviet Russian Literature Since Stalin. Cambridge: Cambridge University Press, 1978. pp. 310-327.

Brown, Edward J. "Solženicyn's Cast of Characters." SEEJ 15:153-166. Summer 1971.

Burg, David and George Feifer. Solzhenitsyn. New York: Stein and Day, 1972. pp. 227-234.

Ericson, Edward E., Jr. Solzhenitsyn: The Moral Vision. Grand Rapids: Eerdmans, 1980. pp. 87-114.

Esam, Irene. "The Imagery of Solzhenitsyn." NZSJ 3: 83-98. Winter 1969.

Harari, Manya. "Solzhenitsyn's CANCER WARD--Part II." Survey 69:145-149. October 1968.

Jordin, Martin. "One Step Forward, Two Steps Back: The Logic of CANCER WARD." NZSJ 2:85-96. 1976.

Kern, Gary. "The Case of Kostoglotov." RLT 11:407-434. 1975.

Kodjak, Andrej. Alexander Solzhenitsyn. Boston: Twayne, 1978. pp. 48-74.

Koehler, Ludmila. "Eternal Themes in Solzhenitsyn's THE CANCER WARD." RusR 28:53-65. January 1969.

Korg, Jacob. "Solzhenitsyn's Metaphors." CentR 17:80-87. Winter 1973.

Krasnov, Vladislav. Solzhenitsyn and Dostoevsky: A Study in the Polyphonic Novel. Athens: University of Georgia Press, 1980. pp. 143-172.

Lucid, Luellen. "Solzhenitsyn's Rhetorical Revolution." TCL 23:507-511. December 1977.

Mathewson, Rufus W., Jr. The Positive Hero in Russian Literature. Stanford: Stanford University Press, 1975. pp. 310-327.

Moody, Christopher. Solzhenitsyn. New York: Barnes and Noble, 1973. pp. 141-167.

Muchnic, Helen. "CANCER WARD: Of Fate and Guilt." Aleksandr Solzhenitsyn: Critical Essays and Documentary Materials. ed. John B. Dunlop, Richard Haugh, and Alexis Klimoff. New York: Collier, 1975. pp. 277-294.

Nielsen, Niels C., Jr. Solzhenitsyn's Religion. Nashville: Thomas Nelson, 1975. pp. 72-79.

Porter, R.C. "Irony and Morality in Solzhenitsyn's CANCER WARD." NZSJ 1:59-73. 1978.

————. "Lyrical Episodes in Solzhenitsyn's CANCER WARD." JRS 29:3-9. 1975.

Rothberg, Abraham. Aleksandr Solzhenitsyn: The Major Novels. Ithaca: Cornell University Press, 1971. pp. 134-190.

Rzhevsky, Leonid. Solzhenitsyn: Creator and Heroic Deed. University: University of Alabama Press, 1972. pp. 70-85.

Siegel, Paul N. "CANCER WARD: A Stage in Solzhenitsyn's Political Evolution." MFS 23:31-45. Spring 1977.

Watt, Donald. "'The Harmony of the World': Polyphonic Structure in Solzhenitsyn's Longer Fiction." MFS 23:103-106. Spring 1977.

Weissbort, Daniel. "Solzhenitsyn's CANCER WARD." Survey 68:179-185. July 1968.

Williams, C. E. "Not an Inn, But an Hospital. THE MAGIC MOUNTAIN and CANCER WARD." FMLS 9:311-332. October 1973.

Williams, Raymond. "On Solzhenitsyn." TriQ 23/24: 326-331. Winter/Spring 1972.

Windle, Kevin. "Symbolism and Analogy in Solzhenitsyn's CANCER WARD." CSP 13:193-206. Summer/Fall 1971.

THE FIRST CIRCLE

Allaback, Steven. Alexander Solzhenitsyn. New York: Taplinger, 1978. pp. 62-118.

Anning, N. J. "Solzhenitsyn." Russian Literary Attitudes from Pushkin to Solzhenitsyn. ed. Richard Freeborn. London: Macmillan, 1976. pp. 131-135.

Atkinson, Dorothy G. "Solzhenitsyn's Heroes as Russian Historical Types." RusR 30:1-16. January 1971.

Awsienko, Nina. "An Islet of Beauty Outside the 'First Circle.'" Interpretations 10:56-63. No. 1, 1978.

Böll, Heinrich. "The Imprisoned World of Solzhenitsyn's THE FIRST CIRCLE." Aleksandr Solzhenitsyn: Critical Essays and Documentary Materials. ed. John B. Dunlop, Richard Haugh, and Alexis Klimoff. New York: Collier, 1975. pp. 219-230.

Brown, Deming. "CANCER WARD and THE FIRST CIRCLE." SlavR 28:304-313. June 1969.

_____. Soviet Russian Literature Since Stalin. Cambridge: Cambridge University Press, 1978. pp. 310-327.

Brown, Edward J. "Solženicyn's Cast of Characters." SEEJ 15:153-166. Summer 1971.

Dunlop, John B. "The Odyssey of a Skeptic: Gleb Nerzhin." Aleksandr Solzhenitsyn: Critical Essays and

Documentary Materials. ed. John B. Dunlop, Richard Haugh, and Alexis Klimoff. New York: Collier, 1975. pp. 24-259.

Eagle, Herbert. "Existentialism and Ideology in THE FIRST CIRCLE." MFS 23:47-61. Spring 1977.

Ericson, Edward E., Jr. Solzhenitsyn: The Moral Vision. Grand Rapids: Eerdmans, 1980. pp. 55-86.

Haase, Kathleen. "Solženicyn's V KRUGE PERVOM: The Significance of the Holy Grail Allusion." RLJ 30: 90-97. Winter 1976.

Halperin, David M. "The Role of the Lie in THE FIRST CIRCLE." Aleksandr Solzhenitsyn: Critical Essays and Documentary Materials. ed. John B. Dunlop, Richard Haugh, and Alexis Klimoff. New York: Collier, 1975. pp. 260-276.

Kern, Gary. "Solzhenitsyn's Portrait of Stalin." SlavR 33:1-22. March 1974.

Kisseleff, Natalia. "Literary Allusions and Themes in THE FIRST CIRCLE." CSP 13:219-232. Summer/Fall 1971.

Kodjak, Andrej. Alexander Solzhenitsyn. Boston: Twayne, 1978. pp. 75-103.

Korg, Jacob. "Solzhenitsyn's Metaphors." CentR 17: 70-80. Winter 1973.

Krasnov, Vladislav. Solzhenitsyn and Dostoevsky: A Study in the Polyphonic Novel. Athens: University of Georgia Press, 1980. pp. 24-142.

Layton, Susan. "The Mind of the Tyrant: Tolstoj's Nicholas and Solženicyn's Stalin." SEEJ 23:479-490. Winter 1979.

Liapunov, Vadim. "Limbo and Sharashka." Aleksandr Solzhenitsyn: Critical Essays and Documentary Materials. ed. John B. Dunlop, Richard Haugh, and Alexis Klimoff. New York: Collier, 1975. pp. 231-240.

Mathewson, Rufus W., Jr. The Positive Hero in Russian Literature. Stanford: Stanford University Press, 1975. pp. 280-309.

Medvedev, Zhores A. Ten Years After IVAN DENISOVICH. New York: Alfred A. Knopf, 1973. pp. 30-47.

Moody, Christopher. Solzhenitsyn. New York: Barnes and Noble, 1973. pp. 104-140.

Muchnic, Helen. "Solzhenitsyn's THE FIRST CIRCLE." RusR 29:154-166. April 1970.

Nielsen, Niels C., Jr. Solzhenitsyn's Religion. Nashville: Thomas Nelson, 1975. pp. 39-53.

Orth, Samuel F. "Solženicyn's Portrait of the 'Establishment' Writer: Galaxov in V KRUGE PERVOM." RLJ 30:153-158. Spring 1976.

Porter, Robert. "The Form of Solzhenitsyn's THE FIRST CIRCLE." Trivium 10:19-32. May 1975.

Rea, Natalie. "Nerzhin: A Sartrean Existential Man." CSP 13:209-216. Summer/Fall 1971.

Rothberg, Abraham. Aleksandr Solzhenitsyn: The Major Novels. Ithaca: Cornell University Press, 1971. pp. 60-133.

Rzhevsky, Leonid. Solzhenitsyn: Creator and Heroic Deed. University: University of Alabama Press, 1972. pp. 49-69.

Schillinger, John. "The Function of Love in Solzhenitsyn's THE FIRST CIRCLE." StTCL 1:183-198. Spring 1977.

Schillinger, John A. "Irony and the Influence of the Potemkin Facade in V KRUGE PERVOM." RLJ 32:149-162. Spring 1978.

Theimer, Catharine S. "The Function and Representation of Time in THE FIRST CIRCLE." MFS 23:63-72. Spring 1977.

Watt, Donald. "'The Harmony of the World': Polyphonic Structure in Solzhenitsyn's Longer Fiction." MFS 23:111-117. Spring 1977.

Weisberg, Richard. "Solzhenitsyn's View of Soviet Law in THE FIRST CIRCLE." HSL 9:110-133. No. 2/3, 1977.

THE GULAG ARCHIPELAGO
Carpovich, Vera. "THE GULAG ARCHIPELAGO, Volume One: Notes on Its Lexical Peculiarities." Aleksandr Solzhenitsyn: Critical Essays and Documentary Materials. ed. John B. Dunlop, Richard Haugh, and Alexis Klimoff. New York: Collier, 1975. pp. 527-533.

Carter, Stephen. The Politics of Solzhenitsyn. New York: Holmes & Meier, 1977. pp. 24-47.

Christesen, Nina. "The Power of Unarmed Truth: Solzhenitsyn's Plea for Human Values." Meanjin 33:93-99. March 1974.

Conquest, Robert. "Evolution of an Exile: GULAG ARCHIPELAGO." Solzhenitsyn: A Collection of Critical Essays. ed. Kathryn Feuer. Englewood Cliffs: Prentice-Hall, 1976. pp. 90-95.

Ericson, Edward E., Jr. Solzhenitsyn: The Moral Vision. Grand Rapids: Eerdmans, 1980. pp. 146-176.

Erlich, Victor. "On Reading THE GULAG ARCHIPELIGO [sic]." Solzhenitsyn: A Collection of Critical Essays. ed. Kathryn Feuer. Englewood Cliffs: Prentice-Hall, 1976. pp. 120-129.

Gibian, George. "How Solzhenitsyn Returned His Ticket." Solzhenitsyn: A Collection of Critical Essays. ed. Kathryn Feuer. Englewood Cliffs: Prentice-Hall, 1976. pp. 112-119.

Goldfarb, Clare R. "Solzhenitsyn's Literary Experiment." SAQ 75:173-181. Spring 1976.

Heller, Michael. "The Gulag Archipelago and Its Inhabitants." Survey 20:211-227. Spring/Summer 1974.

_____. "THE GULAG ARCHIPELAGO, Volume 2: Life and Death in the Camps." Survey 20:152-166. Autumn 1974.

_____. "THE GULAG ARCHIPELAGO, Vol. 3: Outlines of the Future." Survey 22:165-176. Winter 1976.

Keller, Howard H. "Art in Mixed Media: Solženicyn's ARXIPELAG GULAG and Rivers's THE RUSSIAN REVOLUTION." RLJ 33:108-113. Winter 1979.

Kennan, George F. "Between Earth and Hell." Aleksandr Solzhenitsyn: Critical Essays and Documentary Materials. ed. John B. Dunlop, Richard Haugh, and Alexis Klimoff. New York: Collier, 1975. pp. 501-511.

Loewen, Harry. "Solzhenitsyn's Kafkaesque Narrative Art in THE GULAG ARCHIPELAGO." GSlav 3:5-13. Spring 1979.

Malia, Martin. "A War on Two Fronts: Solzhenitsyn

and THE GULAG ARCHIPELAGO." RusR 36:46-63. January 1977.

Medvedev, Roy. "On Solzhenitsyn's GULAG ARCHIPELAGO." Solzhenitsyn: A Collection of Critical Essays. ed. Kathryn Feuer. Englewood Cliffs: Prentice-Hall, 1976. pp. 96-111.

_____. "On Solzhenitsyn's THE GULAG ARCHIPELAGO." Aleksandr Solzhenitsyn: Critical Essays and Documentary Materials. ed. John B. Dunlop, Richard Haugh, and Alexis Klimoff. New York: Collier, 1975. pp. 460-476.

Moody, Christopher. Solzhenitsyn. New York: Barnes and Noble, 1973. pp. 186-202.

Nicholson, Michael. "THE GULAG ARCHIPELAGO: A Survey of Soviet Responses." Aleksandr Solzhenitsyn: Critical Essays and Documentary Materials. ed. John B. Dunlop, Richard Haugh, and Alexis Klimoff. New York: Collier, 1975. pp. 477-500.

Nielsen, Niels C., Jr. Solzhenitsyn's Religion. Nashville: Thomas Nelson, 1975. pp. 109-121.

Rigby, T.H. "The Last Circle: Solzhenitsyn on the Dwellers in Gulag." Meanjin 34:92-95. Autumn 1975.

Rosefielde, Steven. "The First 'Great Leap Forward' Reconsidered: Lessons of Solzhenitsyn's GULAG ARCHIPELAGO." SlavR 39:559-587. December 1980.

Rothberg, Abraham. "Prison of Peoples." SWR 60:73-80. Winter 1975.

Schmemann, Alexander. "Reflections on THE GULAG ARCHIPELAGO." Aleksandr Solzhenitsyn: Critical Essays and Documentary Materials. ed. John B. Dunlop, Richard Haugh, and Alexis Klimoff. New York: Collier, 1975. pp. 515-526.

## LENIN IN ZURICH

Carter, Stephen. The Politics of Solzhenitsyn. New York: Holmes & Meier, 1977. pp. 109-120.

Elwood, R.C. "Scoundrel or Saviour?: Solzhenitsyn's View of Roman Malinovskii." CSP 19:161-166. June 1977.

Ericson, Edward E., Jr. Solzhenitsyn: The Moral Vision. Grand Rapids: Eerdmans, 1980. pp. 136-145.

Friedberg, Maurice. "Solzhenitsyn's and Other Literary Lenins." CSP 19:129-137. June 1977.

Heller, Michael. "Lenin, Parvus and Solzhenitsyn." Survey 21:188-194. Autumn 1975.

Meyer, Alfred G. "On the Tracks of the Arch-Fiend." CSP 19:140-152. June 1977.

Senn, Alfred Erich. "Solzhenitsyn and the Historical Lenin." CSP 19:153-160. June 1977.

MATRYONA'S HOME
Jackson, Robert Louis. "MATRYONA'S HOME: The Making of a Russian Icon." Solzhenitsyn: A Collection of Critical Essays. ed. Kathryn Feuer. Englewood Cliffs: Prentice-Hall, 1976. pp. 60-70.

Lottridge, Stephen S. "Solzhenitsyn and Leskov." RLT 6:478-488. 1973.

Rossbacher, Peter. "Solzhenitsyn's MATRENA'S HOME." ESl 12:114-120. Summer/Fall 1967.

Spitz, Sheryl A. "The Impact of Structure in Solzhenitsyn's MATRYONA'S HOME." RusR 36:167-183. April 1977.

ONE DAY IN THE LIFE OF IVAN DENISOVICH
Allaback, Steven. Alexander Solzhenitsyn. New York: Taplinger, 1978. pp. 18-61.

Atkinson, Dorothy and Nicholas S. Paskin. "AUGUST 1914: Art and History." RusR 31:1-10. January 1972.

Burg, David and George Feifer. Solzhenitsyn. New York: Stein and Day, 1972. pp. 161-170.

Ericson, Edward E., Jr. Solzhenitsyn: The Moral Vision. Grand Rapids: Eerdmans, 1980. pp. 34-44.

Kern, Gary. "Ivan the Worker." MFS 23:5-30. Spring 1977.

_____. "Solženicyn's Self-Censorship: The Canonical Text of ODIN DEN' IVANA DENISOVICA." SEEJ 20:421-436. Winter 1976.

Kodjak, Andrej. Alexander Solzhenitsyn. Boston: Twayne, 1978. pp. 26-47.

Leighton, Lauren G. "On Translation: ONE DAY IN THE LIFE OF IVAN DENISOVIC." RLJ 32:117-127. Winter 1978.

Lukács, Georg. Solzhenitsyn. Cambridge: M.I.T. Press, 1969. pp. 7-32.

Luplow, Richard. "Narrative Style and Structure in ONE DAY IN THE LIFE OF IVAN DENISOVICH." RLT 1:399-412. 1971.

Matthews, Irene J. "The Struggle for Survival in A. Solženicyn's ODIN DEN' IVANA DENISOVICA." RLJ 28: 32-38. Spring 1974.

Medvedev, Zhores A. Ten Years After IVAN DENISOVICH. New York: Alfred A. Knopf, 1973. pp. 13-21.

Mihajlov, Mihajlo. Russian Themes. New York: Farrar, Straus and Giroux, 1968. pp. 78-118.

Moody, Christopher. Solzhenitsyn. New York: Barnes and Noble, 1973. pp. 34-55.

Nielsen, Niels C., Jr. Solzhenitsyn's Religion. Nashville: Thomas Nelson, 1975. pp. 17-26.

Perelmuter, Joanna. "Syntactic Aspects of Solženicyn's ODIN DEN' IVANA DENISOVICA." RLJ 30:8-22. Winter 1976.

Ros, Vladimir J. "ONE DAY IN THE LIFE OF IVAN DENISOVICH: A Point of View Analysis." CSP 13:165-178. Summer/Fall 1971.

Rothberg, Abraham. Aleksandr Solzhenitsyn: The Major Novels. Ithaca: Cornell University Press, 1971. pp. 19-59.

_____. "One Day--Four Decades: Solzhenitsyn's Hold on Reality." SWR 56:109-125. Spring 1971.

Ruttner, Eckhard. "The Names in Solzhenitsyn's Short Novel: ONE DAY IN THE LIFE OF IVAN DENISOVICH." Names 23:103-111. June 1975.

Rzhevsky, Leonid. Solzhenitsyn: Creator and Heroic Deed. University: University of Alabama Press, 1972. pp. 33-48.

Vrolyk, John. "ONE DAY IN THE LIFE OF IVAN DENISOVICH and PAPILLON (A Comparative Study)." NZSJ 9:3-17. Winter 1972.

Tertz (Andrei Sinyavsky)
    AT THE CIRCUS

Dalton, Margaret. Andrei Siniavskii and Julii Daniel': Two Soviet "Heretical" Writers. Würzburg: Verlagsanstalt, 1973. pp. 50-56.

GRAPHOMANIACS
   Dalton, Margaret. Andrei Siniavskii and Julii Daniel':
   Two Soviet "Heretical" Writers. Würzburg: Verlagsanstalt, 1973. pp. 56-64.
THE ICICLE
   Dalton, Margaret. Andrei Siniavskii and Julii Daniel':
   Two Soviet "Heretical" Writers. Würzburg: Verlagsanstalt, 1973. pp. 77-92.

   Pevear, Richard. "Sinyavsky in Two Worlds." HudR 25:392-397. Autumn 1972.
LIUBIMOV
   Dalton, Margaret. Andrei Siniavskii and Julii Daniel':
   Two Soviet "Heretical" Writers. Würzburg: Verlagsanstalt, 1973. pp. 98-128.
PKHENTS
   Dalton, Margaret. Andrei Siniavskii and Julii Daniel':
   Two Soviet "Heretical" Writers. Würzburg: Verlagsanstalt, 1973. pp. 92-98.
THE TENANTS
   Dalton, Margaret. Andrei Siniavskii and Julii Daniel':
   Two Soviet "Heretical" Writers. Würzburg: Verlagsanstalt, 1973. pp. 64-70.
THE TRIAL BEGINS
   Brown, Deming. "The Art of Andrei Siniavsky." SlavR 29:667-679. December 1970.

   _____. Soviet Russian Literature Since Stalin. Cambridge: Cambridge University Press, 1978. pp. 339-347.

   Chapple, Richard L. "The Bible and the Zoo in Andrey Sinyavsky's THE TRIAL BEGINS." OL 33:349-358. 1978.

   Dalton, Margaret. 'Andrei Siniavskii and Julii Daniel':
   Two Soviet "Heretical" Writers. Würzburg: Verlagsanstalt, 1973. pp. 33-49.

   Leatherbarrow, W.J. "The Sense of Purpose and Socialist Realism in Tertz's THE TRIAL BEGINS." FMLS 11:268-279. July 1975.

   Lourie, Richard. Letters to the Future. Ithaca: Cornell University Press, 1975. pp. 75-96.
YOU AND I
   Dalton, Margaret. Andrei Siniavskii and Julii Daniel':
   Two Soviet "Heretical" Writers. Würzburg: Verlagsanstalt, 1973. pp. 70-77.

Tolstoy, Alexei
   1918
      Pertsov, Victor. "Two Novels About Nineteen-Eighteen

--Alexei Tolstoy and Mikhail Bulgakov." SovL 1:158-162. 1968.
THE ROAD OF TORMENTS
Wrassky, H. "A. N. Tolstoy and His Trilogy THE ROAD OF TORMENTS." NZSJ 3:77-82. Winter 1969.

Tolstoy, Leo
ANNA KARENINA
Armstrong, Judith. The Novel of Adultery. London: Macmillan, 1976. pp. 105-117.

Benson, Ruth Crego. Women in Tolstoy: The Ideal and the Erotic. Urbana: University of Illinois Press, 1973. pp. 75-110.

Blackmur, R. P. "The Dialectic of Incarnation: Tolstoy's ANNA KARENINA." Tolstoy: A Collection of Critical Essays. ed. Ralph E. Matlaw. Englewood Cliffs: Prentice-Hall, 1967. pp. 127-145.

Blumberg, Edwina Jannie. "Tolstoy and the English Novel: A Note on MIDDLEMARCH and ANNA KARENINA." SlavR 30:561-569. September 1971.

Cain, T. G. S. Tolstoy. London: Paul Elek, 1977. pp. 95-123.

Call, Paul. "Anna Karenina's Crime and Punishment: The Impact of Historical Theory Upon the Russian Novel." Mosaic 1:94-102. October 1967.

Christian, R. F. "The Passage of Time in ANNA KARENINA." SEER 45:207-210. January 1967.

_____. "The Problem of Tendentiousness in ANNA KARENINA." CSP 21:276-288. September 1979.

_____. Tolstoy: A Critical Introduction. [London]: Cambridge University Press, 1969. pp. 165-213.

Cook, Albert. "The Moral Vision: Tolstoy." Tolstoy: A Collection of Critical Essays. ed. Ralph E. Matlaw. Englewood Cliffs: Prentice-Hall, 1967. pp. 122-126.

Crankshaw, Edward. Tolstoy: The Making of a Novelist. New York: Viking, 1974. pp. 239-252.

Futrell, Michael. "Levin, the Land and the Peasants." CSP 21:314-323. September 1979.

Greene, Gayle. "Women, Character, and Society in Tolstoy's ANNA KARENINA." Frontiers 2:106-125. Spring 1977.

Greenwood, E. B. Tolstoy: The Comprehensive Vision. London: Dent, 1975. pp. 103-118.

Grossman, Joan Delaney. "Tolstoy's Portrait of Anna: Keystone in the Arch." Criticism 18:1-14. Winter 1976.

Gunn, Elizabeth. A Daring Coiffeur: Reflections on WAR AND PEACE and ANNA KARENINA. Totowa: Rowman and Littlefield, 1971. pp. 91-146.

Harvey, J.R. "Tolstoy in England." CQ 5:123-132. Autumn 1970.

Howell, Robert. "Fictional Objects: How They Are and How They Aren't." Poetics 8:129-176. April 1979.

Johnson, Doris V. "The Autobiographical Heroine in ANNA KARENINA." HSL 11:111-120. No. 2, 1979.

Jones, Malcolm V. "Problems of Communication in ANNA KARENINA." New Essays on Tolstoy. ed. Malcolm Jones. Cambridge: Cambridge University Press, 1978. pp. 85-107.

Jones, Peter. "Action and Passion in ANNA KARENINA." FMLS 7:1-27. January 1971.

Jones, T. Robert. "ANNA KARENINA and the Tragic Genre." MelbSS 4:57-66. 1970.

Knowles, A.V. "Russian Views of ANNA KARENINA, 1875-1878." SEEJ 22:301-312. Fall 1978.

Lampert, E. "Tolstoy." Nineteenth-Century Russian Literature: Studies of Ten Russian Writers. ed. John Fennell. Berkeley: University of California Press, 1973. pp. 286-290.

*Leavis, F.R. "ANNA KARENINA: Thought and Significance in a Great Creative Work." CQ 1:5-27. Winter 1965-1966.

Ledkovsky, Marina. "Dolly Oblonskaia as a Structural Device in ANNA KARENINA." CASS 12:543-548. Winter 1978.

McLaughlin, Sigrid. "Some Aspects of Tolstoy's Intellectual Development: Tolstoy and Schopenhauer." CalSS 5:207-219. 1970.

Mooney, Harry J. Tolstoy's Epic Vision: A Study of WAR AND PEACE and ANNA KARENINA. Tulsa: University of Tulsa, 1968. 88 pp.

Pursglove, Michael. "The Smiles of ANNA KARENINA." SEEJ 17:42-48. Spring 1973.

Reichbart, Richard. "Psi Phenomena and Tolstoy." Journal of the American Society for Psychical Research 70:249-264. July 1976.

Rowe, W. W. Nabokov and Others: Patterns in Russian Literature. Ann Arbor: Ardis, 1977. pp. 47-57.

Schultze, Sydney. "The Chapter in ANNA KARENINA." RLT 10:351-358. 1974.

⎯⎯⎯⎯. "Notes on Imagery and Motifs in ANNA KARENINA." RLT 1:366-373. 1971.

Simmons, Ernest J. Tolstoy. London: Routledge and Kegan Paul, 1973. pp. 94-103.

Sorokin, Boris. "Dostoevsky on Tolstoy: The Immoral Message of ANNA KARENINA." ConnR 6:25-33. April 1973.

⎯⎯⎯⎯. Tolstoy in Prerevolutionary Russian Criticism. [Columbus]: Ohio State University Press, 1979. pp. 114-123.

Speirs, Logan. Tolstoy and Chekhov. Cambridge: The University Press, 1971. pp. 84-123.

Stevens, Martin. "A Source for Frou-Frou in ANNA KARENINA." CL 24:63-71. Winter 1972.

Troyat, Henri. Tolstoy. New York: Harmony Books, 1967. pp. 376-390.

Walsh, Harry Hill. "A Buddhistic Leitmotif in ANNA KARENINA." CASS 11:561-567. Winter 1977.

Wasiolek, Edward. Tolstoy's Major Fiction. Chicago: University of Chicago Press, 1978. pp. 129-164.

Zweers, A. F. "Is There Only One Anna Karenina?" CSP 11:272-281. Summer 1969.

CHILDHOOD, BOYHOOD AND YOUTH

Cain, T. G. S. Tolstoy. London: Paul Elek, 1977. pp. 19-41.

Christian, R. F. Tolstoy: A Critical Introduction. [London]: Cambridge University Press, 1969. pp. 20-38.

Eikhenbaum, Boris. The Young Tolstoi. Ann Arbor: Ardis, 1972. pp. 48-74.

Greenwood, E. B. Tolstoy: The Comprehensive Vision. London: Dent, 1975. pp. 22-28.

Jones, W. Gareth. "The Nature of the Communication Between Author and Reader in Tolstoy's CHILDHOOD." SEER 55:506-516. October 1977.

Ketchian, Sonia. "Linguostylistic Devices in the Temporal Structure of Lev Tolstoy's CHILDHOOD, BOYHOOD and YOUTH." WSl 23:140-152. No. 1, 1978.

Troyat, Henri. Tolstoy. New York: Harmony Books, 1967. pp. 97-102.

Wasiolek, Edward. Tolstoy's Major Fiction. Chicago: University of Chicago Press, 1978. pp. 18-29.

THE COSSACKS

Bondanella, Peter F. "Rousseau, the Pastoral Genre, and Tolstoy's THE COSSACKS." SHR 3:288-292. Summer 1969.

Cain, T. G. S. Tolstoy. London: Paul Elek, 1977. pp. 46-55.

Christian, R. F. Tolstoy: A Critical Introduction. [London]: Cambridge University Press, 1969. pp. 67-77.

Clardy, Jesse V. and Betty S. Clardy. The Superfluous Man in Russian Letters. Washington, D. C.: University Press of America, 1980. pp. 53-65.

Gustafson, Richard F. "The Three Stages of Man." CASS 12:488-492. Winter 1978.

Hagan, John. "Ambivalence in Tolstoy's THE COSSACKS." Novel 3:28-47. Fall 1969.

Jepsen, Laura. "To Kill Like a Cossack." SAB 43:86-94. January 1978.

Turner, C. J. G. "Tolstoy's THE COSSACKS: The Question of Genre." MLR 73:562-572. July 1978.

Wasiolek, Edward. Tolstoy's Major Fiction. Chicago: University of Chicago Press, 1978. pp. 51-64.

THE DEATH OF IVAN ILYCH

Bartell, James. "The Trauma of Birth in THE DEATH OF IVAN ILYCH: A Therapeutic Reading." Psycul R 2:97-117. Spring 1978.

Cain, T. G. S. Tolstoy. London: Paul Elek, 1977. pp. 159-164.

Cate, Hollis L. "ON DEATH AND DYING in Tolstoy's THE DEATH OF IVAN ILYCH." HSL 7:195-204. No. 3, 1975.

Dayananda, Y. J. "THE DEATH OF IVAN ILYCH: A Psychological Study on Death and Dying." L&P 22:191-198. No. 4, 1972.

Eng, Jan van der. "THE DEATH OF IVAN IL'IC: The Construction of the Theme; Some Aspects of Language and Time." RusL 7:159-189. March 1979.

Olney, James. "Experience, Metaphor, and Meaning: THE DEATH OF IVAN ILYCH." JAAC 31:101-113. Fall 1972.

Schaarschmidt, Gunter. "Time and Discourse Structure in THE DEATH OF IVAN IL'ICH." CSP 21:356-366. September 1979.

Sorokin, Boris. "Ivan Il'ich as Jonah: A Cruel Joke." CSS 5:487-507. Winter 1971.

Turner, C. J. G. "The Language of Fiction: Word-Clusters in Tolstoy's THE DEATH OF IVAN ILYICH." MLR 65:116-121. January 1970.

Wasiolek, Edward. Tolstoy's Major Fiction. Chicago: University of Chicago Press, 1978. pp. 165-179.

_____. "Tolstoy's THE DEATH OF IVAN ILYTCH and Jamesian Fictional Imperatives." Tolstoy: A Collection of Critical Essays. ed. Ralph E. Matlaw. Englewood Cliffs: Prentice-Hall, 1967. pp. 146-156.

Zimmerman, Eugenia N. "Death and Transfiguration in Proust and Tolstoy." Mosaic 6:161-172. Winter 1973.

## FAMILY HAPPINESS

Benson, Ruth Crego. Women in Tolstoy: The Ideal and the Erotic. Urbana: University of Illinois Press, 1973. pp. 23-44.

Cain, T. G. S. Tolstoy. London: Paul Elek, 1977. pp. 57-61.

Kisseleff, Natalia. "Idyll and Ideal: Aspects of Sentimentalism in Tolstoy's FAMILY HAPPINESS." CSP 21: 336-346. September 1979.

Wasiolek, Edward. Tolstoy's Major Fiction. Chicago: University of Chicago Press, 1978. pp. 39-50.

## GOD SEES THE TRUTH, BUT WAITS

Jahn, Gary R. "A Structural Analysis of Leo Tolstoy's

GOD SEES THE TRUTH, BUT WAITS." SSF 12:261-269. Summer 1975.

HADJI MURAT

Briggs, A. D. P. "HADJI MURAT: The Power of Understatement." New Essays on Tolstoy. ed. Malcolm Jones. Cambridge: Cambridge University Press, 1978. pp. 109-126.

Cain, T. G. S. Tolstoy. London: Paul Elek, 1977. pp. 185-200.

Christian, R. F. Tolstoy: A Critical Introduction. [London]: Cambridge University Press, 1969. pp. 240-246.

Dworsky, Nancy. "HADJI MURAD: A Summary and a Vision." Novel 8:138-146. Winter 1975.

Fanger, Donald. "Nazarov's Mother: On the Poetics of Tolstoi's Late Epic." CASS 12:571-582. Winter 1978.

Heier, Edmund. "HADJI MURAT in the Light of Tolstoy's Moral and Aesthetic Theories." CSP 21:324-335. September 1979.

Layton, Susan. "The Mind of the Tyrant: Tolstoj's Nicholas and Solženicyn's Stalin." SEEJ 23:479-490. Winter 1979.

Woodward, James B. "Tolstoy's HADJI MURAT: The Evolution of Its Theme and Structure." MLR 68:870-882. October 1973.

THE KREUTZER SONATA

Baehr, Stephen. "Art and THE KREUTZER SONATA: A Tolstoian Approach." CASS 10:39-46. Spring 1976.

Benson, Ruth Crego. Women in Tolstoy: The Ideal and the Erotic. Urbana: University of Illinois Press, 1973. pp. 112-138.

Cain, T. G. S. Tolstoy. London: Paul Elek, 1977. pp. 148-154.

Ellis, Keith. "Ambiguity and Point of View in Some Novelistic Representations of Jealousy." MLN 86:892-899. December 1971.

Green, Dorothy. "THE KREUTZER SONATA: Tolstoy and Beethoven." MelbSS 1:11-23. 1967.

Greenwood, E. B. Tolstoy: The Comprehensive Vision. London: Dent, 1975. pp. 138-142.

McLaughlin, Sigrid. "Some Aspects of Tolstoy's Intellectual Development: Tolstoy and Schopenhauer." CalSS 5:233-238. 1970.

## MASTER AND MAN

Cain, T. G. S. Tolstoy. London: Paul Elek, 1977. pp. 154-159.

Hagan, John. "Detail and Meaning in Tolstoy's MASTER AND MAN." Criticism 11:31-58. Winter 1969.

Shestov, Leo. "The Last Judgment: Tolstoy's Last Works." Tolstoy: A Collection of Critical Essays. ed. Ralph E. Matlaw. Englewood Cliffs: Prentice-Hall, 1967. pp. 163-172.

## RESURRECTION

Cain, T. G. S. Tolstoy. London: Paul Elek, 1977. pp. 165-184.

Christian, R. F. Tolstoy: A Critical Introduction. [London]: Cambridge University Press, 1969. pp. 218-229.

Davis, Ruth. The Great Books of Russia. Norman: University of Oklahoma Press, 1968. pp. 297-307.

Greenwood, E. B. Tolstoy: The Comprehensive Vision. London: Dent, 1975. pp. 142-146.

Holquist, James M. "Resurrection and Remembering: The Metaphor of Literacy in Late Tolstoi." CASS 12: 549-570. Winter 1978.

Simmons, Ernest J. Tolstoy. London: Routledge & Kegan Paul, 1973. pp. 191-200.

Sorokin, Boris. Tolstoy in Prerevolutionary Russian Criticism. [Columbus]: Ohio State University Press, 1979. pp. 191-199.

Wasiolek, Edward. Tolstoy's Major Fiction. Chicago: University of Chicago Press, 1978. pp. 191-200.

## VOJNA I MIR

de Haard, E. A. "On Narration in VOJNA I MIR." RusL 7:95-119. March 1979.

Woronzoff, Alexander. "Tolstoj's VOJNA I MIR and the Historical Novel." RLJ 33:63-72. Spring 1979.

## WAR AND PEACE

Benson, Ruth Crego. Women in Tolstoy: The Ideal and the Erotic. Urbana: University of Illinois Press, 1973. pp. 45-74.

Bier, Jesse. "A Century of WAR AND PEACE--Gone, Gone with the Wind." Genre 4:107-141. June 1971.

Cain, T. G. S.  Tolstoy.  London:  Paul Elek, 1977.
pp. 62-94.

_____. "Tolstoy's Use of DAVID COPPERFIELD."
CritQ 15:237-246.  Autumn 1973.

Carden, Patricia.  "The Expressive Self in WAR AND
PEACE."  CASS 12:519-534.  Winter 1978.

Chapple, Richard L.  "The Role and Function of Nature
in L. N. Tolstoy's WAR AND PEACE."  NZSJ 11:86-101.
Winter 1973.

Christian, R. F.  "Style in WAR AND PEACE."  Tolstoy:
A Collection of Critical Essays.  ed. Ralph E. Matlaw.
Englewood Cliffs:  Prentice-Hall, 1967.  pp. 102-110.

_____. Tolstoy:  A Critical Introduction.  [London]:
Cambridge University Press, 1969.  pp. 97-164.

Cook, Albert.  "The Moral Vision: Tolstoy."  Tolstoy:
A Collection of Critical Essays.  ed. Ralph E. Matlaw.
Englewood Cliffs:  Prentice-Hall, 1967.  pp. 111-122.

Crankshaw, Edward.  Tolstoy: The Making of a Novelist.
New York:  Viking, 1974.  pp. 199-234.

Curtis, James M.  "The Function of Imagery in WAR
AND PEACE."  SlavR 29:460-480.  September 1970.

Davis, Ruth.  The Great Books of Russia.  Norman:
University of Oklahoma Press, 1968.  pp. 259-275.

Debreczeny, Paul.  "Freedom and Necessity: A Reconsideration of WAR AND PEACE."  PLL 7:185-198.
Spring 1971.

Dukas, Vytas and Glenn A. Sandstrom.  "Taoistic Patterns in WAR AND PEACE."  SEEJ 14:182-193.  Summer 1970.

Feuer, Kathryn B.  "Alexis de Tocqueville and the Genesis of WAR AND PEACE."  CalSS 4:92-118.  1967.

Freeborn, Richard.  The Rise of the Russian Novel:
Studies in the Russian Novel from EUGENE ONEGIN to
WAR AND PEACE.  London:  Cambridge University
Press, 1973.  pp. 223-266.

_____. "Tolstoy."  Russian Literary Attitudes from
Pushkin to Solzhenitsyn.  ed. Richard Freeborn.  London:  Macmillan, 1976.  pp. 68-71.

Greenwood, E. B. Tolstoy: The Comprehensive Vision. London: Dent, 1975. pp. 57-92.

_____. "Tolstoy's Poetic Realism in WAR AND PEACE." CritQ 11:219-233. Autumn 1969.

Gunn, Elizabeth. A Daring Coiffeur: Reflections on WAR AND PEACE and ANNA KARENINA. Totowa: Rowman and Littlefield, 1971. pp. 3-87.

Gustafson, Richard F. "The Three Stages of Man." CASS 12:492-509. Winter 1978.

Hagan, John. "A Pattern of Character Development in Tolstoj's WAR AND PEACE: P'er Bezuxov." TSLL 11:985-1010. Summer 1969.

_____. "A Pattern of Character Development in WAR AND PEACE: Prince Andrej." SEEJ 13:164-190. Summer 1969.

_____. "Patterns of Character Development in Tolstoy's WAR AND PEACE: Nicholas, Natasha, and Mary." PMLA 84:235-244. March 1969.

Harkins, William E. "A Note on the Use of Narrative and Dialogue in WAR AND PEACE." SlavR 29:86-92. March 1970.

Harvey, J. R. "Tolstoy in England." CQ 5:119-123. Autumn 1970.

Holdheim, W. Wolfgang. "Speranski's Dinner and the Duality of WAR AND PEACE." ConnR 9:40-51. May 1976.

Jackson, Robert Louis. "The Second Birth of Pierre Bezukhov." CASS 12:535-542. Winter 1978.

Jepsen, Laura. "Prince Andrey as Epic Hero in Tolstoy's WAR AND PEACE." SAB 34:5-7. November 1969.

_____. "Two Immodest Proposals in Tolstoy's WAR AND PEACE." SAB 41:68-70. May 1976.

Jones, W. Gareth. "A Man Speaking to Men: The Narratives of WAR AND PEACE." New Essays on Tolstoy. ed. Malcolm Jones. Cambridge: Cambridge University Press, 1978. pp. 63-83.

Knowles, A. V. "War over WAR AND PEACE: Prince Andrey Bolkonsky and Critical Literature of the 1860s and Early 1870s." New Essays on Tolstoy. ed. Malcolm Jones. Cambridge: Cambridge University Press, 1978. pp. 39-62.

Kuk, Zenon M. "Depiction of Fictional Characters in WAR AND PEACE and ASHES." PolR 25:3-13. No. 2, 1980.

_____. "The Napoleonic Era in Tolstoy's WAR AND PEACE and Zeromski's ASHES: Realities and Legends." HSL 11:94-101. No. 2, 1979.

Lampert, E. "Tolstoy." Nineteenth-Century Russian Literature: Studies of Ten Russian Writers. ed. John Fennell. Berkeley: University of California Press, 1973. pp. 268-286.

Lehrman, Edgar H. A Guide to the Russian Text of Tolstoy's WAR AND PEACE. Ann Arbor: Ardis, 1980. 225 pp.

Lengyel, József. "Marginal Notes on Tolstoy's WAR AND PEACE." Mosaic 6:85-102. Winter 1973.

Lyngstad, Alexandra H. "Tolstoj's Use of Parentheses in WAR AND PEACE." SEEJ 16:403-413. Winter 1972.

McLaughlin, Sigrid. "Some Aspects of Tolstoy's Intellectual Development: Tolstoy and Schopenhauer." CalSS 5:189-200. 1970.

Mooney, Harry J. Tolstoy's Epic Vision: A Study of WAR AND PEACE and ANNA KARENINA. Tulsa: University of Tulsa, 1968. 88 pp.

Raleigh, John Henry. "Tolstoy and the Ways of History." Novel 2:55-68. Fall 1968.

Rzhevsky, Nicholas. "The Shapes of Chaos: Herzen and WAR AND PEACE." RusR 34:367-381. October 1975.

Sherman, David J. "Philosophical Dialogue and Tolstoj's WAR AND PEACE." SEEJ 24:14-24. Spring 1980.

Simmons, Ernest J. Tolstoy. London: Routledge and Kegan Paul, 1973. pp. 81-93.

Simonov, Konstantin. "On Reading Tolstoy: An Essay on the Centenary of the First Edition of WAR AND PEACE." PR 38:208-216. No. 2, 1971.

Sorokin, Boris. "Moral Regeneration: N. N. Straxov's 'Organic' Critiques of WAR AND PEACE." SEEJ 20:130-147. Summer 1976.

Tolstoy, Leo

>___. *Tolstoy in Prerevolutionary Russian Criticism.* [Columbus]: Ohio State University Press, 1979. pp. 58-65; 95-111.

>Speirs, Logan. *Tolstoy and Chekhov.* Cambridge: The University Press, 1971. pp. 16-83.

>Spurdle, Sonia. "Tolstoy and Martin Du Gard's LES THIBAULT." CL 23:325-345. Fall 1971.

>Walsh, Harry Hill. "Schopenhauer's ON THE FREEDOM OF THE WILL and the Epilogue to WAR AND PEACE." SEER 57:572-575. October 1979.

>Wasiolek, Edward. "The Theory of History in WAR AND PEACE." Midway 9:117-135. Autumn 1968.

>___. *Tolstoy's Major Fiction.* Chicago: University of Chicago Press, 1978. pp. 65-128.

>Wilson, Edmund. "The Original of Tolstoy's Natasha." *Tolstoy: A Collection of Critical Essays.* ed. Ralph E. Matlaw. Englewood Cliffs: Prentice-Hall, 1967. pp. 95-101.

Trifonov, Iurii
>UTOLENIE ZHAZHDY
>>Hughes, Anne C. "Bol'shoi mir' or 'zamknutyi mirok': Departure from Literary Convention in Iurii Trifonov's Recent Fiction." CSP 22:470-480. December 1980.

Turgenev, Ivan
>COUNTRY DOCTOR
>>Loewen, Harry. "Human Involvement in Turgenev's and Kafka's Country Doctors." GSlav 1:47-53. Spring 1974.
>
>DIARY OF A SUPERFLUOUS MAN
>>Dukas, Vytas and Richard H. Lawson. "WERTHER and DIARY OF A SUPERFLUOUS MAN." CL 21:146-154. Spring 1969.
>
>DVORJANSKOE GNEZDO
>>Frost, Edgar L. "The Function of Music in DVORJANSKOE GNEZDO." RLJ 28:8-17. Spring 1974.
>
>FATHERS AND SONS
>>Bachman, Charles R. "Tragedy and Self-deception in Turgenev's FATHERS AND SONS." RLV 34:269-276. No. 3, 1968.
>>
>>Blair, Joel. "The Architecture of Turgenev's FATHERS AND SONS." MFS 19:555-563. Winter 1973.
>>
>>Brown, Edward J. "Pisarev and the Transformation of Two Russian Novels." *Literature and Society in Im-*

perial Russia, 1800-1914. ed. William Mills Todd III. Stanford: Stanford University Press, 1978. pp. 156-166.

Brumfield, William C. "Bazarov and Rjazanov: The Romantic Archetype in Russian Nihilism." SEEJ 21:495-505. Winter 1977.

Burns, Virginia M. "The Structure of the Plot in OTCY I DETI." RusL 6:33-53. 1974.

Chamberlin, Vernon A. and Jack Weiner. "Galdos' DOÑA PERFECTA and Turgenev's FATHERS AND SONS: Two Interpretations of the Conflict Between Generations." PMLA 86:19-24. January 1971.

Davis, Ruth. The Great Books of Russia. Norman: University of Oklahoma Press, 1968. pp. 82-89.

Fischler, Alexander. "The Garden Motif and the Structure of Turgenev's FATHERS AND SONS." Novel 9:243-255. Spring 1976.

Gifford, H. "Turgenev." Nineteenth-Century Russian Literature: Studies of Ten Russian Writers. ed. John Fennell. Berkeley: University of California Press, 1973. pp. 154-158.

Hart, Pierre. "Nature as the Norm in OTCY I DETI." RLJ 31:55-62. Fall 1977.

Jahn, Gary R. "Character and Theme in FATHERS AND SONS." CollL 4:80-91. Winter 1977.

Lowe, David A. "Comedy and Tragedy in FATHERS AND SONS: A Structural Analysis." CASS 13:283-294. Fall 1979.

Pritchett, V. S. The Gentle Barbarian: The Life and Work of Turgenev. New York: Random House, 1977. pp. 144-155.

Schapiro, Leonard. Turgenev: His Life and Times. Oxford: Oxford University Press, 1978. pp. 176-190.
FIRST LOVE
Chernov, Nikolai. "Ivan Turgenev's Story FIRST LOVE and Its Actual Sources." SovL 10:61-72. 1975.
NEST OF GENTLEFOLK
Mlikotin, Anthony M. Genre of the "International Novel" in the Works of Turgenev and Henry James: A Critical Study. Los Angeles: University of Southern California Press, 1971. pp. 36-48.

Pritchett, V. S. The Gentle Barbarian: The Life and Work of Turgenev. New York: Random House, 1977. pp. 118-126.

ON THE EVE

Chamberlain, Lesley. "The Opening Chapter of NAKANUNE: Some Thoughts on Possible German Origins." JES 8:93-105. June 1978.

Mlikotin, Anthony M. Genre of the "International Novel" in the Works of Turgenev and Henry James: A Critical Study. Los Angeles: University of Southern California Press, 1971. pp. 48-61.

Schapiro, Leonard. Turgenev: His Life and Times. Oxford: Oxford University Press, 1978. pp. 153-157.

RUDIN

McLean, Hugh. "Eugene Rudin." Literature and Society in Imperial Russia, 1800-1914. ed. William Mills Todd III. Stanford: Stanford University Press, 1978. pp. 259-266.

Ripp, Victor. "Turgenev as a Social Novelist: The Problem of the Part and the Whole." Literature and Society in Imperial Russia, 1800-1914. ed. William Mills Todd III. Stanford: Stanford University Press, 1978. pp. 244-253.

SMOKE

Mlikotin, Anthony M. Genre of the "International Novel" in the Works of Turgenev and Henry James: A Critical Study. Los Angeles: University of Southern California Press, 1971. pp. 61-71.

Pritchett, V. S. The Gentle Barbarian: The Life and Work of Turgenev. New York: Random House, 1977. pp. 168-176.

Schapiro, Leonard. Turgenev: His Life and Times. Oxford: Oxford University Press, 1978. pp. 209-216.

SPORTSMAN'S SKETCHES

Pritchett, V. S. The Gentle Barbarian: The Life and Work of Turgenev. New York: Random House, 1977. pp. 54-63.

Ripp, Victor. "Ideology in Turgenev's NOTES OF A HUNTER: The First Three Sketches." SlavR 38:75-88. March 1979.

SPRING TORRENTS

Schapiro, Leonard. Turgenev: His Life and Times. Oxford: Oxford University Press, 1978. pp. 232-262.

VIRGIN SOIL

Briggs, Anthony D. "Someone Else's Sledge: Further Notes on Turgenev's VIRGIN SOIL and Henry James's THE PRINCESS CASAMASSIMA." OSP 5:52-60. 1972.

Pritchett, V. S. The Gentle Barbarian: The Life and Work of Turgenev. New York: Random House, 1977. pp. 215-225.

Schapiro, Leonard. Turgenev: His Life and Times. Oxford: Oxford University Press, 1978. pp. 257-271.

Vežinov, Pavel
  WITH THE WHITE HORSES AT NIGHT
    Matejić, Mateja. "Artistic Intracacy [sic] in Vežinov's WITH THE WHITE HORSES AT NIGHT." SEEJ 22:175-191. Summer 1978.

Voinovich, Vladimir
  THE LIFE AND EXTRAORDINARY ADVENTURES OF PRIVATE IVAN CHONKIN
    Lecomte, Serge. "Scatological Details in Vojnovič's ZIZN' I NEOBYCAJNYE PRIKLJUCENIJA SOLDATA IVANA CONKINA." RLJ 34:145-151. Winter 1980.

    Lewis, Barry E. "Vladimir Voinovich's Anecdotal Satire: THE LIFE AND EXTRAORDINARY ADVENTURES OF PRIVATE IVAN CHONKIN." WLT 52:544-549. Autumn 1978.

    Porter, R. C. "Vladimir Voinovich and the Comedy of Innocence." FMLS 16:97-108. April 1980.

    Szporluk, Mary Ann. "Vladimir Voinovich: The Development of a New Satirical Voice." RLT 14:112-116. 1977.

Witkiewicz, Stanislaw I.
  INSATIABILITY
    Galassi, Frank. "The Catastrophic Society: S. I. Witkiewicz's INSATIABILITY." PolR 25:34-48. No. 1, 1980.

Zamyatin, Eugeny
  SEVER
    Connolly, Julian W. "A Modernist's Palette: Color in the Fiction of Evgenij Zamjatin." RLJ 33:86-92. Spring 1979.
  UEZDNOE
    Connolly, Julian W. "A Modernist's Palette: Color in the Fiction of Evgenij Zamjatin." RLJ 33:83-86. Spring 1979.
  WE
    Angeloff, Alexander. "The Relationship of Literary Means and Alienation in Zamiatin's WE." RLJ 23:3-9. June 1969.

    Barker, Murl G. "Onomastics and Zamiatin's WE." CASS 11:551-560. Winter 1977.

Beauchamp, Gorman. "Of Man's Last Disobedience: Zamiatin's WE and Orwell's 1984." CLS 10:289-293. December 1973.

Brown, E. J. BRAVE NEW WORLD, 1984, and WE: An Essay on Anti-Utopia. Ann Arbor: Ardis, 1976. 52 pp.

Browning, Gordon. "Toward a Set of Standards for Everlasting [Evaluating] Anti-Utopian Fiction." Cithara 10: 18-31. December 1970.

———. "Zamiatin's WE: An Anti-Utopian Classic." Cithara 7:13-19. May 1968.

Connors, James. "Zamyatin's WE and the Genesis of 1984." MFS 21:107-124. Spring 1975.

Lewis, Kathleen and Harry Weber. "Zamyatin's WE, the Proletarian Poets, and Bogdanov's RED STAR." RLT 12:253-276. 1975.

McClintock, James I. "United State Revisited: Pynchon and Zamiatin." ConL 18:475-490. Autumn 1977.

Moody, C. "Zamyatin's WE and English Antiutopian Fiction." UES 14:24-33. April 1976.

Parrott, Ray. "The Eye in WE." RLT 16:59-71. 1979.

Rhodes, Carolyn H. "Frederick Winslow Taylor's System of Scientific Management in Zamiatin's WE." JGE 28:31-42. Spring 1976.

*Richards, D. J. Zamyatin: A Soviet Heretic. London: Bowes & Bowes, 1962. pp. 54-69.

Rosenshield, Gary. "The Imagination and the 'I' in Zamjatin's WE." SEEJ 23:51-62. Spring 1979.

Russell, Robert. "Literature and Revolution in Zamyatin's MY." SEER 51:36-46. January 1973.

Stenbock-Fermor, Elizabeth. "A Neglected Source of Zamiatin's Novel WE." RusR 32:187-188. April 1973.

Thomson, Boris. The Premature Revolution: Russian Literature and Society. London: Weidenfeld & Nicolson, 1972. pp. 16-20.

Ulph, Owen. "I-330: Reconsiderations on the Sex of Satan." RLT 9:262-274. 1974.

Warrick, Patricia. "The Sources of Zamyatin's WE in Dostoevsky's NOTES FROM UNDERGROUND." Extrapolation 17:63-76. December 1975.

Zeromski, Stefan
   ASHES
      Kuk, Zenon M. "Depiction of Fictional Characters in WAR AND PEACE and ASHES." PolR 25:3-13. No. 2, 1980.

      _____. "The Napoleonic Era in Tolstoy's WAR AND PEACE and Zeromski's ASHES: Realities and Legends." HSL 11:101-108. No. 2, 1979.

Zoshchenko, Mikhail
   BEFORE SUNRISE
      Brown, Edward J. Major Soviet Writers: Essays in Criticism. London: Oxford University Press, 1973. pp. 310-320.

      Masing-Delic, Irene. "Biology, Reason and Literature in Zoščenko's PERED VOSCHODOM SOLNCA." RusL 8:77-101. January 1980.

      Von Wiren-Garczyński, Vera. "Zoščenko's Psychological Interests." SEEJ 11:12-17. Spring 1967.
   YOUTH RESTORED
      Von Wiren-Garczyński, Vera. "Zoščenko's Psychological Interests." SEEJ 11:8-12. Spring 1967.